MW00814115

Venture Capital

Venture Capital

LAW, BUSINESS STRATEGIES, AND INVESTMENT PLANNING

Joseph W. Bartlett
Gaston & Snow
New York, New York

John Wiley & Sons
New York • Chichester • Brisbane • Toronto • Singapore

This publication is designed to provide accurate and authoritative information in regard to the subject matter covered. It is sold with the understanding that the publisher is not engaged in rendering legal, accounting, or other professional service. If legal advice or other expert assistance is required, the services of a competent professional person should be sought. *From a Declaration of Principles jointly adopted by a Committee of the American Bar Association and a Committee of Publishers.*

Library of Congress Cataloging in Publication Data:

Bartlett, Joseph W., 1933-
Venture capital: law, business strategies, investment planning / Joseph W. Bartlett.
p. cm.
Bibliography: p.
ISBN 0-471-85076-4
1. Venture capital—Law and legislation—United States. 2. Small business—Finance—Law and legislation—United States. 3. Securities—United States. 4. Venture capital—United States. 5. Small business—United States—Finance. I. Title.

KF1366.B37 1988
346.73'0652—dc19
[347.306652] 87-30352

Printed in the United States of America
10 9 8 7 6 5 4 3 2 1

Preface

To date there exists no single volume (or set of volumes) on venture capital which attempts to deal with the subject as a coherent entity. To be sure, there are ample publications of various genres which deal with a given aspect or aspects of venture capital; there are a number of popular books giving anecdotal evidence on the methods used by a variety of founders to make their fortunes; there are legal, tax, and accounting volumes on very specific issues: "How to implement an initial public offering" . . . "How to account for software development costs" . . . "How to structure a leveraged buyout." There are treatises on areas ultimately involved in venture finance (such as full-blown, multivolume commentaries on trademark, copyright, and patent law and extended works on the law of the computer), as well as glossaries of available sources of financing for development stage companies. These works are usually written for a specific audience—lawyers, investors, budding entrepreneurs. A principal objective of this material, therefore, is to fill a gap. The text attempts to cover the significant issues of interest to anyone involved, about to be involved, or hoping to become involved in one aspect or another of venture capital. This treatment, while dealing with technical issues, is designed to be read and understood by all interested parties. For those who want to go beyond the discussion in the text—a lawyer, for instance, wishing to research a particular problem involving employment agreements—the footnote discussions take the issues further into the realm of the specialist and reference as many source materials on the issue as are deemed pertinent.

The object, in short, is to provide a resource which can be used at several different levels, which can be read not only by attorneys and accountants but by venture capitalists, entrepreneurs, financial and other business consultants, and anyone else interested in becoming involved with venture capital. In such an ambitious undertaking, there are bound to be compromises. Thus, for an entrepreneur solely interested in how to raise capital, some of the discussion may appear overly technical.

The hope is that such readers will be selective and able to at least skim those portions which are not of immediate concern (and will, in fact, skim the technical discussions since a nodding acquaintance may come in handy). Moreover, there are necessary gaps if a work of this sort is to be held to manageable length. For example, the emphasis throughout is on early stage financings; there is only one chapter on leveraged buyouts, a couple of sections on problems peculiar to late round financings and only a few legal forms have been included. Again, the hope is that the text and footnotes contain sufficient trailblazers to point the reader interested in going further in the right direction.

A number of people have reviewed portions of the book and offered helpful suggestions. Among partners (and former partners) in my law firm I include Edward H. Fleischman, Robert Kohl, Robert Mendelson, Thomas Vitale, Thomas Motley, Jeremiah Bresnahan, John Chambliss, J. Thomas Franklin, Karl Fryzel, David E. Place, Cameron Read (with an assist from Will Rogers and Richard Hoehn), Jason Mirabito, Frederick Herberich. Outside comments have come from a number of sources, notably Paul Wythes, William Elfers, and Walter Channing. The use of the New York University Law School Library, courtesy of Professor John Slain, is much appreciated. Invaluable research assistance has been provided by Anita Schneider, Robert Deyling, Matthew Marino, and Frank Oinon. Last, but not least, editing and typing from the desks of Joan Taylor and Renee Williams has been first-class.

JOSEPH W. BARTLETT

New York, New York
February 1988

Contents Summary

TABLES

Contents

15 Licensing Agreements 293

16 Intellectual Property 318

Venture Capital

One

Introduction

This chapter reviews various definitions of venture capital, identifies some of the specialized terminology venture capitalists use, outlines certain business areas which lie outside the scope of the material, provides some notations on the topics to be discussed subsequently and concludes with brief remarks on the significance of venture capital in today's economy.

§1.1 WHAT IS "VENTURE CAPITAL"?

The Text (referred to throughout as the Text) will discuss the legal and business aspects of a phenomenon arising in the postwar United States known as "venture capital." The composer of the phrase is unknown[1] and there is no standard, fixed-in-concrete definition. It is, however, generally agreed that the venture capital era began in earnest in 1946, when General Georges Doriot,[2] Ralph Flanders, Carl Compton, Merrill Griswold and others organized American Research & Development, the first (and, after it went public, for many years the only) public corporation specializing in investing in illiquid securities of early-stage issuers.

[1]Benno Schmidt attributes the phrase to John H. Whitney. Wilson, *The New Venturers: Inside the High Stakes World of Venture Capital* 17 (1985). Schmidt is the managing partner of J. H. Whitney & Co. and one of the early pioneers in the venture capital business. The earliest firms, other than AR&D, were those organized to invest on behalf of a particular family; the Whitney, Phipps (Bessemer Securities), and Rockefeller family offices (Venrock) were early and major players.

[2]The complete biography of General Doriot, who died in early 1987, has not as yet been written. For a partial history, *see* Dominguez, *Venture Capital* 15 (1974).

One way to define "venture capital," therefore, is to repeat General Doriot's rules of investing, the thought being that an investment process entailing Doriot's rules is, by definition, a venture capital process. According to Doriot,[3] investments considered by AR&D (as American Research & Development is commonly known) involved: (1) new technology, new marketing concepts, and new product application possibilities; (2) a significant, although not necessarily controlling participation by the investors in the company's management; (3) investment in ventures staffed by people of outstanding competence and integrity (herein the rule often referred to in venture capital as "bet the jockey, not the horse"); (4) products or processes which have passed at least through the early prototype stage and are adequately protected by patents, copyrights, or trade secret agreements (the latter rule often referred to as investing in situations where the information is "proprietary"); (5) situations which show promise to mature within a few years to the point of an initial public offering or a sale of the entire company (commonly referred to as the "exit strategy"); (6) opportunities in which the venture capitalist can make a contribution beyond the capital dollars invested (often referred to as the "value-added strategy").

General Doriot's boundary conditions are to be treated with great deference because it is commonly agreed that Doriot is the single most significant figure in postwar venture capital. Not only did he provide AR&D with its primary guidance (until it was acquired by Textron), but he also introduced a significant percentage of today's venture capitalists to the business through the courses he taught at Harvard Business School. And, he showed the world how a venture capital investment strategy could produce enormous rewards when AR&D's modest investment in Digital Equipment Corporation (DEC) ballooned into investor values in the billions.[4]

Parenthetically, in the eyes of the public of his day, Doriot's record at AR&D included only a few "home runs," DEC in particular, and a bunch of losers, leading inexperienced observers to conclude that a well-managed venture portfolio should concentrate on the long ball, so to speak—the one investment that will return two or three hundred times one's money and justify a drab performance by the rest of the portfolio. This fallacious conclusion fostered the 1960s notion that an ultra-high-risk strategy is characteristic of venture capital investing, the managers plunging exclusively into new and untried schemes with the hope of

[3]Merrill, *Investing in the Scientific Revolution: A Serious Search for Growth Stocks in Advanced Technology* 168 (1962).

[4]Kozmetsky, Gill, & Smilor, *Financing and Managing Fast Growth Companies: The Venture Capital Process* xii, xiii (1985).

"winning big" every now and then.[5] In fact, the AR&D strategy was never tied to the solo home run.[6] Moreover, venture strategies have become highly varied. Some venture pools focus in whole or in part on late-round investments, infusions of cash shortly before the company is planning to go public, for example. On the opposite end of the spectrum, other funds focus on the earliest stages of a company's existence, the so-called "preseed" stage, when applied research is still going on. Leveraged buyouts involving mature firms (dealt with in Chapter 19) are a popular venture strategy, as are so-called "turnarounds," investments in troubled companies, including some actually in bankruptcy. And, some funds are hybrids, sharing more than one strategy, even including a portion of the assets invested in public securities. The point is that a venture manager balances risk against reward; a "preseed" investment should forecast sensational returns, while a late-round purchase of convertible debt will promise a more modest payoff.[7]

The term "venture capital" is grammatically multifaceted. General Doriot's exegesis specifies a certain type of investment as characteristic of the venture universe. He assumes, a priori, the proposition that venture capital involves a *process*,[8] the making and managing (and ulti-

[5]Besides DEC and High Voltage Engineering, AR&D enjoyed significant profits in, among others, Cooper Laboratories, Teledyne, and Optical Scanning Corp. Merrill, *supra* n. 3, at 160. *See also* Silver, *Entrepreneurial Megabucks: The 100 Greatest Entrepreneurs of the Last Twenty Five Years* 337 (1985).

[6]The "bet a million, make a million" aura of venture capital has been fostered by a number of entertaining and provocatively titled monographs, *see, e.g.,* Wilson, *The New Venturers: Inside the High Stakes World of Venture Capital* (1985). Wilson cites Joseph Schumpeter and his theory of entrepreneurs presiding over the process of "creative destruction." *Id.* at 203. Wilson also discusses some of the big winners: Venrock in Apple Computer, *Id.* at 80; Kleiner Perkins in Genentech, *Id.* at 96; Arthur Rock and "Tommy" Davis of Mayfield Associates in Scientific Data Systems, *Id.* at 36, 80, 96. *See also,* Silver, *supra* n. 5, at 175, 219, and 401, citing Greylock & Co.'s highly successful investment in Teradyne, Arthur Rock's in Intel Corp. and, along with Davis, in Teledyne.

[7]Venture capital returns have been handsome in recent years. *Pratt's Guide to Venture Capital Sources* 8–9 (11th ed. 1986) (Pratt's Guide). *See also,* the remarks of one of the premier venture investors: "Over the years I have not found a single instance in which an experienced staff has decimated the venture capital pool provided by its investors." Bigler, *Venture Capital: A Perspective* (forword) (1983).

[8]Since the 1950s and 1960s, when General Doriot was most active, the types of opportunities venture managers invest in has become increasingly all-inclusive. The current notion of venture capital as an *activity,* in this case the activity of managing venture investments, is aptly described by the editors of one of the best known industry chronicles:

> What delineates venture capital from traditional investment is not what a venture capitalist invests in but how the investments are managed, i.e., the skills and strategies employed once the investment is made . . . the three key characteristics of venture investing utilized by professionals [are] 1) equity participation, 2) long-term investment orientation and 3) ongoing active involvement in the company.

"What is Venture Capital: Something Old, Something New," *Venture Cap. J.* (Mar. 1987) at 10.

mately selling) investments. In addition, the phrase is sometimes used as an adjective applied to players in the game, that is, "venture-backed companies," meaning the portfolio opportunities in which the venture capital partnerships or "funds" invest. The phrase becomes a noun when it describes the capital provided by individuals, families, and firms, which entities, along with the partnership managers, are called venture capitalists.

In terms of the people involved, venture capital is an intense business. The symbiotic relationship between the venture capitalist and his investment (assuming he is the "lead investor," meaning the investor most closely identified with the opportunity) is such that each professional can carry a portfolio of no more than a handful of companies. The investors are usually experienced professionals with formal academic training in business and finance and on-the-job training as apprentices at a venture fund or financial institution. Their universe is still relatively small; they and their advisers tend to be on a first-name basis, veterans of a deal or two together. And the work is hard, particularly since on-site visits impose an enormous travel burden.

In fixing venture capital chronologically, one must pay attention to the famous remark of Stanley Pratt, the recording secretary of the venture capital business,[9] who likes to refer to Queen Isabella[10] as the first venture capitalist, inasmuch as she staked Columbus to an adventure into unknown territory, the voyage entailing high risks and commensurate rewards. Pratt is remarking that the venture capital process, before it was so labeled, has existed for centuries; antedating American Research & Development, it is as old as commercial society itself. In this century, for example, Vanderbilt interests financed Juan Trippe[11] in the organization of Pan American Airways, Henry Ford was financed by Alexander Malcolmson, and Captain Eddie Rickenbacker was able to organize Eastern Airlines in the 1930s with backing from the Rockefellers.[12] However, the era of professionally managed venture capital—pools of money contributed by unrelated investors and organized into separate legal entities, managed by experts according to stated objectives, set forth in a contract between managers and investors, describing a structured activity, an activity that conforms to definite (albeit changing) patterns and rules—is a process that dates from the organization of AR&D.

[9]Pratt's firm publishes, among others, a leading periodical, *Venture Capital Journal* and the annual *Pratt's Guide to Venture Capital Sources. See supra* n. 7.
[10]*See* Pratt's Guide, *supra.* n. 7, at 7.
[11]Wilson, *supra* n. 1, at 15.
[12]*Id.*

In sum, the term venture capital can be applied in a number of ways: to investments, people, or activities. With full appreciation for the multiple uses of the term, the thrust and emphasis of the Text (although by no means exclusively) is on venture capital of the type which is compatible with the Doriot rules. First, venture capital is an *activity* involving the investment of funds. It ordinarily involves investments in illiquid securities[13] which carry higher degrees of risk (and commensurately higher possibilities of reward) than so-called traditional investments in the publicly traded securities of mature firms. The venture capital investor ordinarily expects that his participation in the investment (or the participation of one of the investors in the group which he has joined, designated usually as the "lead investor") will add value, meaning that the investors will be able to provide advice and counsel designed to improve the chances of the investment's ultimate success. The investment is made with an extended time horizon, required by the fact that the securities are illiquid. (In this connection, most independent venture funds are partnerships scheduled to liquidate 10 to 12 years from inception, in turn suggesting that a venture capital investment is expected to become liquid somewhere around four to six years from initial investment).

Since the most celebrated rewards in the past have generally accrued to investments involving advances in science and technology to exploit new markets, venture capital investment is often thought of as synonomous with high tech start-ups. However, as stated earlier, that is not an accurate outer boundary, even in the start-up phase. For example, the technology of one of the great venture capital winners—Federal Express—is as old as the Pony Express and it would take a great stretch of the imagination to perceive of fast food chains such as McDonald's as involving additions to our store of scientific learning. But, whether high or low tech, the venture capitalist thrives when the companies in which he invests have an advantage over potential competition in a defined segment of the market, often referred to as a "niche." The product or service is as differentiated as possible, not a "commodity." Exploitation of scientific and technological breakdowns has, historically, been a principal way (but not the only way) for emerging companies to differentiate themselves from their more mature and better financed competitors.

[13]The Securities Act of 1933 ('33 Act), contains a broad definition of the term "security." *See* the leading case of *SEC v. Howey* Co., 328 U.S. 293 (1946), for the most celebrated discussion of the concept. As the *Howey* opinion states, a security is a relatively passive investment, evidence of an interest in an enterprise managed by people other than the investor. *See id.*, at 297. Thus, limited partnership interests in a venture fund are "securities," as are the shares which the fund purchases in portfolio companies. Indeed, the right to purchase a security is itself a security.

§1.2 GLOSSARY OF TERMS: VENTURE CAPITAL JARGON OR "BUZZ WORDS"

The discussion in the Text will make use of terminology commonly used in the venture world. First, the entities into which capital sources are aggregated for purposes of making investments are usually referred to as "funds," "venture companies," or "venture partnerships." They resemble mutual funds in a sense but are not, with rare exceptions (AR&D was one), registered under the Investment Company Act of 1940 because they are not publicly held and do not offer to redeem their shares frequently or at all.[14] The paradigmatic venture fund is an outgrowth of the Greylock model,[15] a partnership with a limited group of investors, or limited partners, and an even more limited group of managers who act as general partners, the managers enjoying a so-called "carried interest," entitling them to a share in the profits of the partnership in ratios disproportionate to their capital contributions. Venture funds include federally assisted Small Business Investment Companies (which can be either corporations or partnerships) and, on occasion, a publicly held corporation along the AR&D model, styled since 1980 as "business development corporations."[16] The Text, following common usage, will refer to any managed pool of capital as a "fund" or "partnership."

Once a fund makes an investment in an operating entity, the fund or group of funds doing the investing are the "investors." A company newly organized to exploit an idea is usually called a "start-up," founded by an individual sometimes referred to as the "entrepreneur" or the "founder."[17] Any newly organized company, particularly in the context of a

[14]Under § 3(c)(1) of the Investment Company Act, an entity is not subject to the Act if its outstanding voting securities are owned by not more than 100 persons. Venture funds usually are owned by a handful of investors; the definition can, however, be a problem in certain instances. *See* Ch. 20, § 20.25.

[15]One of the first private funds managed on behalf of more than one family, Greylock & Co., was founded in 1965 by General Doriot's chief lieutenant, William Elfers, with the author cutting his teeth as one of the draftsmen of the partnership agreement. As is customary with the leading firms, Greylock is now into its sixth partnership.

[16]The institution of the Business Development Company is discussed extensively in Halloran, "Investment Company Act and Investment Advisers Act: Considerations for Private and Public Venture Capital Funds—The Small Business Investment Incentive Act of 1980," in Halloran, Benton, & Lovejoy, *Venture Capital and Public Offering Negotiation* 159 (1984) (Halloran). The most important requirement is that a Business Development Company maintain 70% of its assets in private companies which it controls or influences. 15 U.S.C. § 80a–2(2)(48). *See* Ch. 20, § 20.23(b)

[17]The three powerful motives of the entrepreneur, according to Joseph Schumpeter, are (1) "the dream to found a private kingdom in the world, usually, though not necessarily, also a dynasty"; (2) "the world to conquer: the impulse to fight . . . to succeed for the sake, not of the fruits of success, but of success itself"; (3) "the joy of creating, getting things done, or of simply exercising one's energy and ingenuity." Schumpeter, *Capitalism, Socialism and Democracy* 132 (1980).

leveraged buyout (LBO) is routinely labeled "Newco." The stock issued by a founder to himself (and his key associates) is usually sold for nominal consideration and those shares are labeled "founders stock." (The use of the male gender is used throughout for ease of reference only.) The founder, as he pushes his concept, attracts professional management, usually known as the "key employees." If his concept holds particular promise, he may seek from others (vs. providing himself) the capital required to prove the concept works—that is, the capital invested prior to the production of a working model or prototype. This is called "seed investment" and the tranche is called the "seed round." Each financing in the venture process is referred to as a "round" and given a name or number: "seed" round, "first venture" round, "second" round, "mezzanine" round, and so forth.

Once the prototype has been proven in the lab, the next task ordinarily is to place it in the hands of a customer for testing—called the "Beta Test" (the test coming after the lab, or "Alpha," test). At a Beta Test site(s), the machine or process will be installed free and customers will use and debug it over a period of several weeks or months. While the product is being Beta tested, capital is often raised to develop and implement a sales and marketing strategy, the financing required at this stage being, as indicated above, "the first round."[18]

The next (and occasionally the last) round is a financing calculated to bring the company to cash breakeven. Whenever a robust market exists for initial public offerings—for example, the late 1960s, 1983, 1986—this round is often financed by investors willing to pay a relatively high price for the security on the theory that their investment will soon be followed by a sale of the entire company in an initial public offering. Hence, this round is often called the "mezzanine round." A caution at this juncture: The term mezzanine has at least two meanings in venture capital phraseology. It also appears as a label for junior debt in leveraged buyouts. In either event, it means something right next to or immediately anterior to something else. As used in venture finance, the financing is next to the occasion on which the founder and investors become liquid—an initial public offering (IPO) or sale of the entire

[18]The nomenclature used to describe the several rounds of financing is varied. *See* for example, Bigler, *Venture Capital: A Perspective* (1983). Bigler talks about that round referred to in the Text as the "seed" round as the "start-up" round—i.e., money for product development; in his lexicon, first-stage financing is for initiating manufacturing, the second stage sustains the operation while the product is shipped, the third stage is expansion capital for a profitable company, the fourth stage, or "mezzanine," carries the company through an "IPO," which is stage five. *Id.* at 3. Stanley Pratt likes to list the rounds as: seed; start-up; first stage; second stage; third stage or mezzanine, and bridge. *See,* Pratt's Guide, *supra* n. 7, at 2–3; Lipper, *Venture's Guide to Investing In Private Companies: A Financing Manual for the Entrepreneurial Investor* 101 (1984) lists: seed, start-up, development or second stage, and "profitable but private."

company. As earlier indicated, the measures taken to get liquid are categorized as the "exit strategies."

One of the critical elements in venture investing is the rate at which a firm incurs expenses, since most financings occur at a time when the business has insufficient income to cover expenses. The monthly expense burden indicates how long the company can exist until the next financing and that figure is colorfully known as the "burn rate." (Other common terms are defined as they appear in the Text.)

§1.3 SCOPE

Next, a word about the scope and schematic of the Text:

(a) SMALL BUSINESS OUTSIDE THE "VENTURE CAPITAL" UMBRELLA

Every start-up does not dance to the venture capital tune. Hundreds of thousands of new enterprises[19] are originated every year for reasons having nothing to do with a venture play—that is, grocery stores, filling stations, suburban construction companies, truck farms—conventional businesses organized by an entrepreneur who feels that his skill and experience can be employed more profitably on his own. The object of such business organizations is to provide an income for the organizer(s), and perhaps members of his or their families; if the business takes hold, it can be a legacy for the founders' children. Usually the founder has been in the particular line of business for enough years to gather the requisite experience and is striking out on his own on the basis of his repressed energy and his reservoir of experience. There is no "exit strategy," no expectation of a dynamic multiple of earnings being paid for the business five years down the road, no equity investors other than the founder (and his equity is often "sweat" equity), no sources of cash capital other than the local bank. This category of endeavor has acquired the somewhat pejorative label (because it is often family oriented) of the "mom and pop" business. With apologies to a number of experienced, rich, successful, and satisfied entrepreneurs, that label will be continued in the Text. In periods when venture capital is much in the news, the proprietors of mom and pop businesses will occasionally draft a business plan and circulate it among venture partnerships. This is

[19]Less than 2% of new business incorporations annually are financed by professionally managed venture capital pools. Lipper, *supra* n. 18, at 30.

usually a waste of time because venture firms can rarely, if ever, be interested in businesses with modest objectives and local markets.

(b) FRANCHISES

A cousin of the mom and pop business is the franchise opportunity. Franchises can be hugely successful, of course; some, such as soft drink-bottling franchises, are major public companies in their own right. In recent years, fast food franchises have been veritable gold mines for the operators; indeed, the franchise for distributing lottery tickets has made the owners of some lucky newsstands wealthy. Franchising is an art unto itself and there are a number of helpful books on the subject.[20] However, the franchisee's end of the transaction has not been ordinarily financed by venture capitalists; the business is often heavily dependent on one individual and the unique, on-site services he provides.[21] The entrepreneur whom the venture capitalist would prefer to finance is the owner of the idea, Ray Kroc at McDonald's, for example, rather than the franchisee.[22]

A word of caution at this point. Franchising has become increasingly regulated in recent years in an effort to curb sharp and unfair practices by muscular franchisors. Many agreements customarily used by emerging companies—for example, licensing and distribution contracts—may qualify as franchise agreements under state or federal law, requiring compliance with quite detailed statutes.[23] Failure to recognize the issue often carries severe and unintended consequences. Moreover, some franchise agreements are considered to be "securities," requiring registration under federal and (particularly) state law.[24]

[20]Metz, *Franchising: How to Select A Business of Your Own* (1969); Brown, *Franchising: Realities and Remedies* (rev. ed. 1982); Vaughn, *Franchising: Its Nature, Scope, Advantages and Development* (1974).

[21]In actuality, many franchisors provide their franchisees with financing. In those cases where the franchisee must come up with his own money, he usually does so through personal funds or bank loans, not equity financing from outside investors. Vaughn, *supra* n. 20, at 149.

[22]One element common to both the franchising format and venture capital will be featured—the licensing process. Licensing technology is a legitimate and necessary element in the venture capital world. *See* Ch. 15 *infra.*

[23]*See, e.g.,* Cal. Corp. Code § 31000–31516. (West 1987 & Supp. 1987). Agreements which one would ordinarily categorize as distributorship or licensing agreements may be deemed franchises subject to both procedural—i.e., disclosure, filing—and substantive—i.e., limitations on rights to terminate—constraints. *See, e.g.,* Fern, "The Overbroad Scope of Franchise Regulations: A Definitional Dilemma," 34 *Bus. Law.* 1387 (Apr. 1979).

[24]Sowards & Hinsch, *Business Organizations: Blue Sky Regulation* § 2.05 (1977); *SEC v. Glenn W. Turner Enterprises, Inc.,* 348 F. Supp. 766 (D. Or. 1972), *aff'd,* 474 F.2d 476 (9th Cir. 1973).

§1.4 SOME REMARKS ON SOURCE MATERIALS

To date there is no single volume on venture capital which attempts to deal with the subject as a coherent entity. To be sure, there are ample publications of various genres which deal with a given aspect or aspects;[25] there are a number of popular books giving anecdotal evidence on the methods used by founders to make their fortunes; there are legal, tax, and accounting volumes on specific issues: "How to implement an initial public offering"; "How to account for software development costs"; "How to structure a leveraged buyout;" there are treatises on areas ultimately involved in venture finance (such as full blown, multivolume commentaries on trademark, copyright and patent law, extended works on the law of the computer); as well as glossaries of available sources of financing for development-stage companies. These works are usually written for a specific audience, for example, lawyers, investors, budding entrepreneurs. A principal objective of this material, therefore, is to fill a gap. The Text attempts to cover the significant issues of interest to someone involved, about to be involved, or hoping to become involved in some aspect of venture capital. This treatment, while dealing with technical issues, is designed to be read and understood by all interested parties. For those who want to go beyond the discussion in the Text (e.g., a lawyer wishing to research a particular problem involving, say, employment agreements[26]) the footnote discussions take the issues further into the realm of the specialist, with references to pertinent source materials.

The object, in short, is to provide a resource which can be used at several different levels, which can be read not only by attorneys and accountants but by venture capitalists, entrepreneurs, financial and other business consultants, and anyone else interested in becoming involved with venture capital. In such an ambitious undertaking, there are bound to be compromises. Thus, for an entrepreneur solely interested in how to raise capital, some of the discussion may appear overly technical;

[25]Helpful works of general application include Pratt's Guide, *supra* n. 7; Halloran, *supra* n. 16; Harroch, *Start-Up Companies: Planning, Financing and Operating the Successful Business* (1986) (Harroch).

[26]*See* Ch. 10 § 3 *et seq.* The footnotes contain frequent reference to course handbooks of the Practicing Law Institute (PLI), paperbound outlines of course materials used in the seminars the institute sponsors each year. Although PLI materials are not usually cited in works of this type, the author offers no apologies. The lecturers at such seminars are, by and large, the most experienced practitioners in their field. And, the emphasis in the Text is on practical knowledge, information that can be put to use by people who make a living in venture capital.

the hope is that such readers will be selective and able to at least skim those portions which are not of immediate concern (and will, in fact, skim the technical discussions since a nodding acquaintance may come in handy). Moreover, there are necessary gaps if a work of this sort is to be held to manageable length. For example, the emphasis throughout is on early-stage financings; there is only one chapter on leveraged buy-outs, a couple of sections on problems peculiar to late-round financings, and only a few legal forms have been included. Again, the hope is that the Text and footnotes contain sufficient trailblazers to point the interested reader in the right direction.

§1.5 WHY VENTURE CAPITAL? ECONOMIC IMPACT OF VENTURE FINANCE

Lastly, a brief word about the significance of venture capital. In our trillion dollar economy, why are we wasting so much time and lung power on a process which occupies, at any one point in time, a very small percentage of the gross national product?

In the late 1970s, David Birch, impressed with the enormous ability of the American economy over the last several years to create new jobs (25 million net new positions in 10 years), interrogated the data base and found that 70% of the job creation in the U. S. economy occurred in small business firms, those with fewer than a hundred employees.[27] Of the 2 million incorporated businesses in the United States, fewer than one half of 1% are publicly owned.[28] Indeed, the most striking economic statistic in this country in recent periods has been the creation of new firms—small by definition. Some 600,000 new incorporations were launched in 1983, a continuation of the steady upsurge in corporate formation that saw new ventures jump from 234,000 a year just 15 years earlier. "Business" in the United States means, in large part, "small

[27]"The Job Generation Process," Cambridge, MA: MIT program on Neighborhood and Regional Change, 1979, Report submitted to the Economic Development Administration, U.S. Dept. of Commerce. *See* the discussion of Birch's findings in Gilder, *The Spirit of Enterprise* 248 (1984). The comparable figure for Europe during this period is zero. Gumpert, *Growing Concerns: Building and Managing the Smaller Business* 3 (1984). *See also* Solomon, *Small Business USA: The Role of Small Companies in Sparking America's Economic Transformation* (1986).

[28]Lipper, *supra* n. 18, at 171.

business."[29] Moreover, small business has a major impact on innovation in the American economy; more than one half of the major innovations which drive our economy occur in small firms.[30]

The fact that the U. S. is hospitable to small business is not intrinsically good news. The lesser developed countries specialize in small business, to the exclusion of any other kind. The economic wallop in the U. S. comes from the expansion of small firms into large firms. It doesn't happen that often but, when it does, the economic effects are enormously salubrious. If just 1% of the small companies in existence today were to reach mid-size—$25 million in sales—the American economy could more than double. Venture capital, if it is about anything at all, is about the process of small business growing into big business. It is the one technique our competitors in other industrial countries have yet to master. Venture capital is, in this context, vital to success in the so-called postindustrial era.

[29]For some of the many discussions of this issue, including multitudinous legislative hearings, *see,* "The Role of Small Business Enterprise in Economic Development," a study prepared for the use of the Joint Economic Committee, Congress of the U.S., May 14, 1981; Garn, *The Role of Small Business Enterprise in Economic Development* (1981); Legler, Frank, & Hoy, *Building a Comprehensive Data Base on the Role of Small Business in the U.S. Economy, and Its Policy Implication Questions. Small Business and Job Creation,* "Hearings Before the Subcommittee On Antitrust, Consumers and Employment of the Committee on Small Business, House of Representatives," Washington, 1979; *Small Business Access to Equity and Venture Capital,* "Hearings Before the Subcommittee on Capital, Investment and Business Opportunities of the Committee on Small Business, House of Representatives, Washington, 1977; *Economic Growth,* "Hearings Before the Select Committee on Small Business, United States Senate," Washington, 1980; *Capital Formation,* "Hearing Before the Select Committee on Small Business, United States Senate," Washington, 1978; *Future of Small Business in America, Part 1,* "Hearings Before the Subcommittee on Antitrust, Consumers and Employment of the Committee on Small Business, House of Representatives," Washington, 1978.

[30]*Small, High Technology Firms and Innovation,* Report prepared by Subcommittee on Investigations and Oversight, House of Representatives, Washington, 1980. Many studies and discussions have focused on the engines of innovation, *see, e.g., Innovation Revisited,* "Hearing Before the Committee on Small Business, House of Representatives," Washington 1982; Brock & Evans, *The Economics of Small Businesses: Their Role and Regulation in the U.S. Economy* (1986).

Two

Formulating the Business Plan

Advice on drafting a business plan ranges from the obvious—"be brief and specific"—to the quite detailed, involving certain legal incidents of the document. Each plan being tailored to the business at hand, it is risky to draft according to a preconceived formula. However, certain elements are more important than others, in the eyes of most potential investors at least, and the discussion focuses on those highlights. The material is oriented around techniques for organizing business plans which will attract investors, and give them required information.

§2.1 INTRODUCTION

The starting point for every founder is, of course, the strategy he fixes upon as he puts his enterprise in motion. There are a series of key questions he has to ask himself as he is mulling over the decision whether or not to invest an enormous amount of his own time and energy, perhaps his life savings and those of his friends and relatives, in a new venture.

> Is my new idea practical? Will it work? If it does work, will someone buy the product from me? If so, will they pay enough to allow me to make a

profit commensurate with my risk? Can my idea be protected against competition, at least during the phase when my business operations are most fragile? Can I hope to raise enough money to get the business to a break-even point? Can I find associates, directors and/or employees who will fill in the gaps in my knowledge and experience?

Ordinarily, the proposed answers to these questions are drafted by the founder (with the help of any experts he may retain) in a document called a "business plan." The plan contains a description of the product or service the company is being organized to exploit, a summary of marketing strategy to be employed, the curricula vitae of the key managers and directors and, last but not least, financial projections.

There is a copious amount of material instructing founders in detail on how to draft business plans that will attract interest in the investment community.[1] Of course, every business is different. The organization of a plan that makes good sense for one enterprise may be wholly inappropriate for another. However, there is a consensus on the key elements that should be discussed if the plan is to compete with others in the capital markets. And, one way to understand those key elements is to examine the table of contents of someone else's plan or, better, a composite of a number of plans. The Appendix to this chapter sets out such a composite, prepared by one of the most experienced lawyers in the venture capital business, a useful guide against which to check one's own efforts, if only to see what is being left out. The following discussion will not attempt to comment on each item set forth in the composite table; the several authorities cited in the footnotes are devoted to carrying out that function in detail. Rather, areas of unusual interest which deserve special attention are highlighted in the following discussion.

§2.2 THE THRESHOLD DECISION FOR ENTREPRENEURS—SHOULD I GO THIS ROUTE AT ALL?

Prior to preparation of a business plan, the entrepreneur should ask some hard questions. Hundreds of thousands of new businesses are organized in the United States each year; unhappily, most of them fail within the first year or so. Since the great majority of start-ups are

[1]*See* Haslett & Smollen, "Preparing A Business Plan," in Pratt's Guide, *supra* Ch. 1, n. 7, at 22–32. Mancuso, *How to Write a Winning Business Plan* (1985); Mancuso, *How to Prepare and Present a Business Plan* (1983); Kravitt, *How to Raise Capital: Preparing and Presenting a Business Plan* (1984); White, *The Entrepreneur's Manual: Business Start-Ups, Spin-Offs, and Innovative Management* (1977); Siegel, Schultz, Ford, & Carney, *The Arthur Young Business Plan Guide* (1987).

financed out of the pockets of their founders,[2] the high failure rate should be a sobering statistic for would-be entrepreneurs. It may be fortunate for the economy as a whole that so few are daunted by the sober statistics but it is hard on the individuals who do not make it. Nonetheless, available literature on the business aspects of organizing one's own firm rarely inquires into this threshold issue—whether one should set out on one's own in the first instance.[3]

(a) DON'T BE BEGUILED BY SUCCESS STORIES—THE ODDS ARE STEEP

Much of the popular material on venture capital is potentially misleading in its ebullient optimism. It can be hard to keep one's head in the face of popular literature extolling the giant winners in the game—Jobs, Wozniak, Wang, and their peers, creators of new technologies which dominate the market and return hundreds of times the initial investment. The giants are an integral part of the mystique of venture capital but an Apple Computer or Wang Laboratories comes along once in a lifetime. The odds against hitting that big are astronomical. Accordingly, books which record the anecdotal history of how Ken Olson organized Digital Equipment, how Ed DeCastro put together Data General, make fine reading but the home run expectations they promote can be dangerously intoxicating. A founder faced with the "go, no go" decision—whether or not to invest his entire savings in a new enterprise—is fooling himself if he stacks the reward side of the equation with the possibility of making hundreds of millions of dollars. It sometimes happens, of course, and someone has to win the lottery, but the vision of those sugarplums is not a sound basis for an intelligent investment decision. To be sure, it remains realistic for many founders to think of big rewards—perhaps even millions of dollars, albeit after a period of enormously hard work and great risk. Nonetheless, it is important to understand that, in the vast majority of the cases—indeed, for the majority of the survivors—the returns on the founder's investment (and that investment must be calculated to include opportunity costs and sweat equity) are modest. Many founders find that, at the end of the game, they have either lost money or been working for a peon's wages.

[2]Dean Kelly of the Boston College School of Business has estimated that fewer than one percent of the founders seeking financing are ultimately successful in the venture capital community. Dominguez, *supra* Ch. 1, n. 2, at xv.

[3]The question of failure is seldom mentioned in business school curricula. Simpson, "Business Schools—and Students—Want to Talk Only About Success," *Wall St. J.*, Dec. 15, 1986, § 2, at 2.

There is a saying, attributed to Lord Palmerston, that many foolish wars have been started because political leaders got to reading small maps. Many businesses have been imprudently started because of the founder's inability to understand how difficult it is to achieve a double digit compounded rate of return. Venture investments have, in fact, outperformed the stock market in the postwar years and, in many cases, quite handsomely. There have been periods when 25% compounded rates of return have been available to the investors—indeed, substantially higher rates have been achieved by many venture funds, and over long periods of time. But, it is a mathematical impossibility to compound any substantial sum of money at a 25% rate of return indefinitely unless the investors are entitled to believe they will own all the assets in the world within one man's lifetime. It has been remarked that the greatest individual fortune assembled in this country in recent years is that of J. Paul Getty, who started with a modest stake as a young man and wound up with a personal fortune in excess of $3 billion. It is a wildly successful story, but sobering when one considers that Getty's annual compounded rate of return on his initial few thousand dollars has been calculated at about 14%. In short, in reading the success stories reprinted in the popular books,[4] the part to focus on is the hard work and risk involved. Enormous returns are contingent and should not be the foundation of the analytical planning process.

(b) "YOU CAN MAKE IT . . . O.K. . . . WILL SOMEONE BUY IT?"

Another major source of error is a love affair between a founder and the technology he has developed in the lab. The number of new and interesting ideas brought into being every year is astonishing. A field trip to any respectable college or university will reveal a fascinating array of projects in the laboratories, many of which, if brought to fruition, will certainly improve the state of the art. However, a critical error of founders considering whether to commit capital to a project is to assume that the novelty and utility of a new technology is both necessary *and* sufficient for the success of a start-up. Novelty may be enough to secure a patent but it is only one part of the venture capital equation. No one can make any money unless there is a market for the product, unless people are willing to buy it at a price that returns a profit to the

[4]The life-styles of the rich and famous in venture capital are outlined in a number of books, *e.g.*, Silver, *Entrepreneurial Megabucks: The 100 Greatest Entrepreneurs of the Last Twenty-Five Years* (1985); Lipper, *Venture's Guide to Investing in Private Companies* (1984); Perez, *Inside Venture Capital: Past, Present and Future* (1986); Wilson, *The New Venturers: Inside the High-Stakes World of Venture Capital* (1985).

manufacturer. This simple, banal truth is overlooked time and again by fledgling entrepreneurs. Assuming the idea is any good, is there a market for it? Is there a market which can be penetrated at a reasonable cost? The classic example is the pen that writes under water—interesting technically but, as it turned out, no one wanted to buy one. Thus, the single most commonly cited reason for failure of a start-up is the inability to implement a well-thought-out marketing plan. Selling is a matter of airplanes, hotel rooms, and shoe leather; as Willie Loman put it, on the road with a smile and a shoe shine.[5] Marketing, on the other hand, has to do with understanding the demand for the product, pricing strategy, evaluating channels of distribution, and maximizing dollars spent on sales.[6] Moreover, the market has to be large enough to support an interesting company. The enterprise with less than $10 million in sales and nowhere to go is usually not a suitable target for venture capital financiers. Companies of that size are known as the "walking dead" in a venture portfolio—too small to go public and too large to abandon.[7]

[5]The instinct of many entrepreneurs is to assume that sales and marketing are essentially the same. They tend to let the salespeople operate on their own, without marketing guidance, assuming the lure of commission income will motivate the salespeople in the field to maximize their outcomes by investing their time, and the company's expenses, intelligently. The cost of a bad salesperson, even one not on salary, is seldom understood. The cost of mismanaging a sales force, compensating them in such a way that, for example, they concentrate on the lower rather than the higher profit items, is lost sight of by the neophyte. Business plans often come accompanied with a consultant's report on the technical feasibility of the core product. It is rare to find a document setting out an expertised marketing strategy.

[6]The classics on marketing strategy include Heskoff, *Marketing* (1976); Hansen, *Marketing: Text and Cases* (4th ed. 1977); Downing, *Basic Marketing: A Strategic Systems Approach* (1971); Andrews, *Creative Product Development: A Marketing Approach to New Product Innovation and Revitalisation* (1975); Winkler, *Marketing for the Developing Company* (1969); Cohen & Reddick, *Successful Marketing for Small Business* (1981).

[7]One prominent analyst has suggested that the following conditions be within the four corners of the forecasted market if one is to take the plunge in earnest:

Over $50 million in total size (annual sales volume).

Growing at a rate significantly greater than the real GNP.

Sufficiently fragmented or noncompetitive to allow an aggressive new entry to grow to $25 million or more in sales within five years.

Amenable to profit making by a new entry at a rate of at last 5 to 10% (after tax) on sales within 2 to 3 years after start-up.

Socially and politically acceptable to the business world in general so that:

a. Traditional forms of financing, such as bank loans, are available to the company once it is established.
b. Sale of stock to the public or a larger corporation at a fair price is possible at a later point in time.

Brandt, *Entrepreneuring: The 10 Commandments for Building a Growth Company* (1982).

§2.3 BUSINESS PLAN AS AN "OFFER"

First, a business plan has considerable legal significance. If the plan contains any reference to the terms of the financing the founder is considering, the plan itself may be to be deemed an "offer"[8] of a "security," as those terms are used in the Securities Act of 1933. If a business plan containing an offer is transmitted to a third party, the '33 Act requires that the offer be registered under federal law unless an appropriate exemption from registration can be found.[9] The point is that a founder, by flaunting his business plan without following the procedures which keep the securities laws at bay, may be making illegal "offers" without the foggiest idea that a violation is occurring. In 99 cases out of 100, no permanent damage is done. Absent the existence of a fraudulent scheme to bilk the public, prosecutions for offering unregistered securities are rare. The existence however, of illegal offers has mischief-making capacity in that the illegal offer may contaminate subsequent, carefully drafted and otherwise legal plans to sell stock. There is no definitive precedent to provide guidance on this issue. In the author's view the issuer is most likely to be tagged with an offer in the '33 Act sense if either, (i) the document or conversation describe some or all of the features of the offer (price and terms of the security, aggregate amount of financing sought, prospective returns on the investment); or, (ii) the document or conversation are so contemporaneous that either can be deemed to constitute "conditioning the market," that is, an issuer involved in multiple financings running an ad in the paper describing a closed deal when a similar deal is "on the street."[10] A business plan unaccompanied by offering documents and in the hands of persons other than those whose only link is as potential investors should not be considered an offer.

[8]Section 2(3) of the '33 Act provides in part:

> the term "offer to sell," "offer for sale," or "offer," shall include every attempt or offer to dispose of, or solicitation of an offer to buy a security or interest in a security, for value. . . .

Most practitioners, in the author's judgment at least, subscribe as a practical matter to the view that an "offer" does not ordinarily occur until at least some terms of the deal are described—the price of the security to be sold, for example.

It remains to be seen whether that view would prevail over the SEC's oft-stated notion that attempts to "condition the market" for an offer, *see* Ch. 7, § 7.4, are themselves an offer.

[9]A discussion of exemptions from registration under federal and state securities laws is contained in Ch. 7.

[10]*See* Ch. 7, § 7.4.

§2.4 DISCLOSURE IN THE BUSINESS PLAN

Beyond constituting an ambulatory offer, the plan is legally significant since it often forms the heart of the disclosure document ordinarily required in connection with a sale of securities. The point is that, whether or not the sale enjoys an exemption from federal (or state) registration requirements, almost all sales (and purchases) of a security are subject to the antifraud provisions of the pertinent federal and state statutes;[11] and, the thrust of the antifraud statutes, in addition to impacting on schemes deliberately designed to swindle investors, is oriented on disclosure. If the business plan is (as it often is) the only paperwork purporting to disclose the business of the issuer, accuracy and completeness is more than of literary importance—all material facts are to be included. The operative word is "material"; under tests laid down by the Supreme Court,[12] any fact is material if there is a substantial likelihood a reasonable investor would want the fact disclosed, a broad test since investors can be counted on to claim, if only reflexively, they want *all* the facts.

Thus, it is only good practice to give the business plan the full treatment—all the facts, warts and all. The various audiences studying the business plan include, (whether the founder likes it or not) potential plaintiffs and plaintiffs' lawyers interested in the unlawful circulation of the document and/or errors or omissions occurring in the text of the plan. It is incumbent, accordingly, on the founder and his advisers, from the first draft forward, to monitor the plan's habitats and include all pertinent information.

§2.5 BUSINESS PLAN AS A SALES AND MANAGEMENT DOCUMENT

Looking at the document from a 180-degree different angle, the plan is a sales presentation, indeed an element in a very difficult sale. Venture

[11]The principal federal statutes are §§ 11, 12(2), and 17(a) of the '33 Act and § 10, including particularly Rule 10b–5, of the Securities and Exchange Act of 1934 ('34 Act). State securities laws tend to contain language patterned after the federal antifraud proscriptions and, in particular, Rule 10b–5, which provides:

> It shall be unlawful for any person .... 1) to employ any device, scheme, or artifice to defraud, 2) to make any untrue statement of a material fact or to omit to state a material fact necessary in order to make the statements made, in the light of the circumstances under which they were made, not misleading, or 3) to engage in any act, practice, or course of business which operates or would operate as a fraud or deceit upon any person, in connection with the purchase or sale of any security.

[12]The landmark case is *TSC Indus., Inc. v. Northway, Inc.*, 426 U.S. 438 (1976).

capitalists may, as they often do, decry the lack of good deals but the fact is that every venture capital firm of any note is literally inundated with business plans from hopeful founders. In a particularly busy period, as many as a thousand business plans a year may come to a given venture firm "over the transom." Unless the plan is accompanied by an introduction from someone who carries great weight, the odds against acceptance of a humdrum document are about equivalent to the odds against Mrs. Onassis responding to an unsolicited dinner invitation. Accordingly, the draftsmen must incorporate unique and unusual features, particularly if the company's financial results are entirely projected, to get the plan to rise up out of the pile on its own motion.

To be sure, the business plan cannot be too optimistic because it sets out the agreed goals of the firm and the methods to be employed in getting there. To that extent, it is analogous to the forecasts and goal statements developed periodically by any organization for use by the managers. If the targets are too lofty, the managers are setting themselves up for later, unpleasant sessions with investors.

§2.6 THE SINGLE MOST IMPORTANT SECTION: THE MARKETING SECTION

As earlier indicated, the marketing section is the most troublesome for many founders to write convincingly and should, in view of the significance venture investors pay to the issue, be the most carefully drafted. It is relatively easy to obtain industry statistics and divide by some number, for example:

> the overall market for product X is $1.5 billion per year and we plan to capture, "conservatively," 10%, which means we project $150 million in annual sales. Our strategy is to pursue the following niches. . . .

All the words are appealing and familiar; venture capitalists are expected to applaud a niche strategy, meaning that the approach to the market is focused on an area where competition will be minimal and a substantial market share ripe for the plucking. The term "conservative" is also routinely joined to an entrepreneur's forecast. However, a well-done plan does not stop there—a number of questions remain to be answered. For example, what determines the niche. Price? (Few successful venture strategies are driven by the idea of being the lowest cost producer.) Quality? Performance? Geography? Service? Proprietary information? Is the market growing? How will competitors (presumably larger and better financed) be kept at bay? How will the market be penetrated? Will the issuer train its own sales force, use manufacturers' representatives, joint venture with another supplier or vendor? Will it advertise? What are the promotional plans (direct mail? trade shows?) What service and warranty policies will be followed?

One critical feature for many sophisticated investors is evidence that the marketing section has been drafted and then subjected to multiple revisions, that the plan has been gone over a number of times by persons bringing varying backgrounds and experience to the issue. Many a venture capitalist will be delighted to find a candid confession that the overall business strategy actually changed after an in-the-field investigation of market potential.

Indeed, the more specificity the better. Thus, a sophisticated marketing plan will designate the magazines and other media outlets in which the firm plans to advertise, and identify the trade shows, the territories a sales office can be expected to cover, perhaps even provide proposed ratios, such as the expected ratio of successful sales per salesman's call.

The coda to the marketing section, either made a part of it or placed in the immediate vicinity, is the section on competition. One experienced investor representative starts each discussion with a founder by asking for a discourse on competition; if the founder has not thought the issue through, the interview is rapidly brought to a close. Investors are generally unwilling to believe that, even with the most impregnable protection for proprietary information, competition can be kept at bay for very long. It is essential, therefore, to zero in on the existing (and likely future) competition and indicate as specifically as possible why and how the new entrant will be able to steal a march on the other firms, what legal and economic obstacles can be strewn in their path, how long the monopoly will last, and so forth.

§2.7 BUSINESS STRATEGY AND THE SINGLE-PRODUCT PROBLEM

Many start-up companies, organized around what the founder believes is an earth-shaking item of "science,"[13] are puzzled and upset when venture investors turn the cold shoulder. Often, the problem is that the investors perceive the company as lacking a long-range strategy, incapable of producing more than the single product then on the drawing

[13]In venture jargon, the term "science" has been reified, becoming a label not for a discipline but for a particular item, a product of scientific research, as in "So and so is doing some interesting science these days."

board or in production; that capability is generally viewed as too limited by the professional investment community. A successful business plan, at least for a technologically oriented start-up, should admit that high tech companies cannot survive solely by selling their current products, no matter how advanced and revolutionary. They must sell as well an intangible—the belief that they will be able to offer future sophisticated and reliable products so that the customer will be assured of a stable and reliable vendor who will always provide state-of-the-art products at competitive prices. The "value" purchased by investors and customers alike is, in large part, the capacity of the company to follow today's "great products" with unlimited future "great products."[14] The business plan should, accordingly, explore at some length how the company is going to grow into long pants, the strategies for expanding markets and product lines once the initial products have been successfully marketed.

§2.8 MANAGEMENT

(a) PRINCIPAL OFFICERS

Of vast importance is the quality of management, the venture investor's rubric being to "bet the jockey, not the horse." In addition to describing current team members, the business plan should discuss how and when new members will be added, how the management team will be compensated and how the team members will be motivated to perform to maximize the objectives of the business as laid out in the plan.[15] It is not easy to recruit experienced quality people for a new venture; romance or no romance, school tuitions are a source of concern. If the management team is skeletal, investors may be cynical, recalling the old saw that recruitment takes 1 month for each $10,000 in salary—that is, it takes nine months to recruit a $90,000-a-year marketing manager.

(b) BOARD OF DIRECTORS

Locating useful directors for a start-up company is difficult but often vital. While the founder, his wife and his lawyer comprise the paradig-

[14]The thoughts expressed were originally those of the author's partner, J. Thomas Franklin, at the time serving as general counsel to Encore Computer Corporation.
[15]Rich & Gumpert, *Business Plans that Win $$$: Lessons from the MIT Enterprise Forum* 124, 125 (1985).

matic start-up board, perceptive organizers try to fill gaps in their business expertise by adding experienced directors. Start-ups backed by professionally managed venture firms are lucky—the investors' representative ordinarily make an enormous contribution. Many emerging companies do not enjoy professional backing in the first round. Accordingly, with no money to pay for full-or part-time experts, a founder is often well advised to dangle directorships, coupled with cheap stock, in front of experienced individual businessmen. In today's corporate world, as multinationals change ownership in staccato fashion and fashion dictates that white collar staffs be pared to the bone, a large cohort of relatively young, dynamic, and highly competent businessmen have been released into the workforce. Many are loath to return to the large corporate environment—they are disgusted and enraged at the big company culture—and they have "parachutes" which relieve them of the necessity of working full time. Thus they are prime candidates to help nurture an emerging business to maturity. Accordingly, it is becoming increasingly an integral part of an advanced venture strategy to harness the energy of early retirees, inducing them to join start-up boards and fill in the experience gap.

There are subtle issues to be resolved in pursuing this strategy, however. To be sure, the engagement of an experienced businessman to sit in a key board seat may, indeed, provide a greater degree of "hands-on" oversight than can be expected from a harassed, overworked young partner in a venture capital pool; often the fledgling venture manager's advice can grate on the founder's ears, particularly if the board member's prior experience is limited to attending classes at the Harvard Business School. However, it may be equally troublesome for the founder to take advice from someone other than the man who put up the money, particularly a refugee from a big company culture. A venture manager may lose vital impact and feel for a portfolio company if his advice is filtered through a retiree whose stake in the company is limited to the upside on his options. When a partner in the investment firm takes a position, his hide is on the line. He made the investment, and the founder may be more inclined to view him as entitled to lay down the law.

§2.9 OTHER ISSUES

The plan should, of course, articulate the exit strategy, explaining how the venture proposes to get to the point where it can cash out the investors.[16] A carefully prepared business plan will usually contain third-

[16]One articulation of the various exit strategies is as follows: "Go public, become a giant, be acquired, be a niche company, be a cash cow, become a partner in a joint venture, become a licensing company, acquire other companies." Rich & Gumpert, *supra* n. 15, at 51–57.

party endorsements, ranging in letters from satisfied customers to studies by independent consultants to a "cold comfort"[17] or "negative assurance" letter from public accountants concerning the projections.

The writer should organize his topics, particularly the executive summary, with the understanding that investors are extraordinarily busy and will skim the document. Brevity is thus critical.[18] Indeed, one expert suggests the plan be prepared assuming the reader will only devote five minutes to it, attempting in that period to accomplish the following:

Determine the characteristics of the company and the industry;
Determine the terms of the deal;
Read the latest balance sheet;
Determine the caliber of the people in the deal;
Determine what is different about this deal;
Give the plan a once-over lightly.[19]

In terms of quick "turn-ons," additional attractions to investors include: Hard evidence the managers plan to "focus," another way of saying that a target market has been thoroughly researched and identified; testimonials (if possible) from actual or potential customers, validating in checkable form the marketing assumptions; and a documented story on proprietary protection of intellectual property, including not just a reference to, but a discussion of existing or pending patents and the trade secret protection program.[20]

§2.10 PROJECTIONS

(a) THE "BULLS EYE"[21] THEORY OF FORECASTING—"SHOOT HIGH"

The art of preparing forecasts in a business plan—and it is an art, not a science—involves the founder in a delicate balancing process. On the one hand, a forecast is a representation of a fact—the founder's state of

[17]"Cold comfort" technically refers to the term used for the accountants' letter respecting the financial statements rendered on the eve of a public offering, cold comfort meaning the accountants will not stand behind their opinion as if it were certified, but bringing the statements down to the effective date. Negative assurance—that is, "nothing has come to our attention"—is the more appropriate term for the comments accountants are accustomed to make on the projections.
[18]One of the reasons for excess prolixity is, ironically, a venture capital success story, the Lotus 1-2-3 spreadsheet software, which allows the drafter to include an enormous number of spreadsheet pages. Larson "The Best Laid Plans," *Inc.* (Feb. 1987) 27, 60, 64.
[19]Mancuso, *How to Write a Winning Business Plan, supra* n. 1, at 14.
[20]*See,* Rich & Gumpert, *supra* n. 15, at 16–21 (1985).
[21]Under the "bulls eye" theory, one shoots the arrow first and then paints the bulls eye around the arrow wherever it happens to land.

mind—and an intellectually honest founder will represent his state of mind accurately. Indeed, careless, let alone dishonest, preparations may involve liability.[22] On the other hand, the forecast is a critical element in the negotiation process. Thus, as one prominent source on business plan preparation has noted:

> The entrepreneur should be careful to avoid negotiating in the business plan. For example, the entrepreneur who indicates he or she will sell 20 percent of the company for $200,000 has just established the upper end of the negotiating range. Sophisticated reviewers will realize that at worst they can acquire 20 percent of the venture for $200,000, and that they might be able to negotiate a better price.[23]

The problem is that the forecast is an "indication" of price and value since it drives valuation, even though the business plan says nothing about "20% for $200,000." The standard language of venture capital valuation (outlined in Chapter 13) will be decoded by potential investors, reading the forecast as an offer by the founder to value his company at a given number. Consequently, it would be ingenuous to prepare a forecast without at least knowing how it will be read by the investment community. To be sure, if the founder does nothing more than work backwards in the forecasting process, targeting the valuations he wishes to achieve and then filling in the forecast behind that number, he may have made less than a bona fide effort to be candid. Nonetheless, ignorance of how the audience will react to a forecast is not bliss in the venture universe.

The answer, then, is that the forecast should be prepared with two considerations in mind. It should represent the founder's best thinking as to likely future events. But, at the same time, the founder should not close his eyes to what the consequences of his forecast will be; accordingly, he should at least understand how venture capitalists approach the forecasts in the context of the valuation process.

Thus, most venture capitalists contemplate a five-year time horizon, on the theory an exit strategy is feasible at the end of five years. Therefore, the founder's forecast should go out as far as the investors are looking.[24] Depending upon the maturity of the company and the ability

[22]The preparer's liability for faulty forecasts in a business plan has not been the subject of much reported litigation. In the public venue, the case of *Beecher v. Able* 374 F. Supp. 341 (S.D.N.Y. 1974) suggests that the forecast must be based on facts which would lead one to conclude the results are "highly probable." *Id.* at 348. The overall atmosphere has changed since that case was decided, spurred by the SEC's more tolerant attitude toward forecasts. *See* Ch. 14, § 914.6.

[23]Siegel et al., *supra* n. 1, at 129.

[24]*See generally* Morris, "The Pricing of a Venture Capital Investment," in Pratt's Guide, *supra* Ch. 1, n. 7, at 55; Ch. 12, § 12.3.

of its product to excite, an informed founder can usually estimate what kind of compounded rates of return the venture capitalists are looking at over a five-year period. If, to reverse the example used in Chapter 13, the founder "guesstimates" that the venture capitalist will be looking for a 38% compounded rate of return, a quick calculation shows the venture capitalist will be anticipating its investment will quintuple in five years. If the founder is planning to raise $250,000 from the venture capitalists, then the founder knows a forecast which shows anything less than $1 million in net after tax earnings in year five will mean he has to surrender more than 12.5% of the company. To illustrate, the venture captalist can then be counted on to multiply 1 million times a price/earnings multiple (and that usually is somewhere around 10 because, among other reasons, that number appears often in the marketplace and is easy to work with); once the venture capitalist comes up with a $10 million valuation, he will then calculate that his $250,000 should be worth $1.25 million in year five and find himself agreeing to take 12.5% of the company for $250,000 in year one if and only if he sees (and believes) forecast earnings of $1 million or more in year five.

A final word on this point. Borrowing from the speech of Kenneth Olson to the 1987 M.I.T. graduating class,[25] the forecast is both a prediction and a target. If you don't shoot high, the Law of Self-fulfilling Prophecies dictates that you won't reach high. Exuberance in preparing one's forecast, if intellectually honest, is an integral part of a founder's mental terrain.

(b) THE PROMISSORY NATURE OF THE FORECAST—"SHOOT LOW"

Lest one get the impression that the previous section baldly suggests the forecast should come out exactly where the founder wants it to, it should be remembered that professional venture capital investors are not stupid. They will test the forecast and explore thoroughly the assumptions used, smoking out numbers that are intellectually dishonest or, to put it in the vernacular, do not pass the "red face" test. A very steep climb in earnings in some remote period, for example, will be suspect. It being easier to kibitz a forecast in the early years, a spike upward in year five, when anybody's guess is as good as anybody else's, will reveal itself as result-oriented. Moreover, an intellectually dishonest set of projections may provoke a negative reaction—outright rejection without further investigation. And, many investors view the forecast as a quasi-promise[26] by the founder, a representation that he proposes

[25] Olson, "Learning the Dangers of Success: The Education of an Entrepreneur," N.Y. *Times* July 19, 1987.
[26] *See* White, *supra* n. 1, at 147–148.

(albeit not legally bound) to make the forecast come true. The forecast is not so much a prediction of the future—five years is too long a time frame for precise predictions[27]—but an undertaking by the party in control to accomplish a given objective. Indeed, a confident forecast of summary results may become a critical issue in the financing negotiations. Experienced investors are accustomed to confront the founder with his rosy forecast, agree to a valuation based thereupon, and then insist that a system of penalties be institutionalized, taking equity away from the founder if and to the extent he fails to achieve the projections he authored. As elsewhere noted, most venture financings entail multiple rounds and, accordingly, are of the benchmark variety even if not explicitly so provided in the Purchase Agreement. The second-round investors, generally the same parties who invested in the first round, will be influenced in their pricing decision (in turn driving the founder's dilution) by the founder's record measured by the forecast. On occasion, the inability to meet an overly optimistic forecast may be the trigger for a control "flip," ousting the founder from office.

APPENDIX[28]

COMPOSITE TABLE OF CONTENTS OF BUSINESS PLAN

1. Introduction (or Executive Summary)
   Short description of:
      Business objectives
      Principal products or services
      Technology and development program
      Market and customers
      Management team
      Financing requirements
2. Company description
      History and status
      Background and industry
      Company's objectives
      Company's strategies
      What makes the company different from others

[27]In Regulation S–K, Item 10(b), the SEC, while "encouraging" forecasts in public disclosure statements, appears to endorse the conventional view that long-term forecasts are misleading. The Commission is correct, of course, but that view is not apposite in a venture placement. The investors know the forecast will not come true unless the founder somehow makes them come true.

[28]The Appendix was prepared by Paul Brountas of Hale & Dorr for an informal panel discussion in which the author participated in 1985.

3. Products
 Product description and comparisons
 Innovative features (patent coverage)
 Applications
 Technology
 Product development and R&D effort
 Product introduction schedule and major milestones
 Future products (product evolution)

4. Market
 Market summary and industry overview
 Market analysis and forecasts
 Industry trends
 Initial product(s)

5. Competition

6. Marketing program
 Objectives
 Marketing strategy
 Sales and distribution channels
 Customers
 Staffing

7. Manufacturing

8. Service and field engineering

9. Facilities

10. Management and ownership
 Founders—Key employees
 Stock ownership
 Organization and personnel
 Future key employees and staffing
 Incentives (stock option and stock purchase plans)

11. Capital required and use of proceeds

12. Financial data and financial forecasts
 Assumption used
 3-year plan
 5-year plan

13. Appendixes
 Detailed management profiles
 References
 Product descriptions, sketches, photos
 Recent literature on product, market, etc.[29]

[29] Haslett & Smollen, "Preparing A Business Plan," in Pratt's Guide, *supra* Ch. 1, n. 7, at 29.

One of the sections not specifically set out above, which may be appropriate in the context of a given plan, is a "milestones" section, the forecasted major events in the life cycle of the enterprise and a timetable for their achievement.

Three

Selecting the Form of Organization

The choice of the vehicle in which to start or continue a business can have significant tax and economic consequences. The discussion in this chapter is largely technical but nonlawyers are urged at least to skim the discussion, particularly § 3.6, outlining the principal distinctions between corporations and partnerships. In the final analysis, the judgment will be a business judgment, one for the organizers to make based on the best "fit" for the opportunity they plan to pursue.

§3.1 BACKGROUND

When a business plan is developed, consideration must be given to the form in which the business is to be conducted. The several possibilities start with a general business corporation, sometimes referred to as a "C Corporation" for that subchapter of the Internal Revenue Code (Subchapter C), which governs the tax attributes of corporations generally. The C Corporation is the residual norm, elected after the other alternatives have been eliminated, the old reliable to which planners turn after exotic formats have been considered and rejected. Before the Text focuses on the corporate form in detail, discussion of the alternatives is in order.

§3.2 S CORPORATIONS

A special subtype of the incorporated entity is named the "S Corporation" (formerly "Subchapter S" Corporation),[1] again the name taken from the location of the governing provisions in the Code.[2] For most purposes, S Corporations are garden variety corporations under state law, the distinguishing factor being that, if they configure themselves to meet special rules of the Internal Revenue Code, no corporate tax is assessed, thereby passing through corporate income and losses directly to the shareholders. Under the Tax Reform Act of 1986, S Corporations will be increasingly popular because, for the first time since 1916, personal tax rates are lower than the corporate tax rates, thereby putting a premium on the ability of a business entity to pass through its income to its shareholders without the imposition of tax. Moreover, while losses from passive activities may not be set off against income other than from passive activity under the Tax Reform Act of 1986, losses garnered by an S Corporation and allocable to a shareholder who materially participates—as an officer, for example—in the S Corporation's business may elude the "passive activity" trap and, thus, be more widely useful.[3] Such losses are, however, limited generally to the shareholder's tax basis in his stock and any loans he has made to the corporation.[4]

The constraints on the structure of S Corporations are relatively rigid. Congress contemplated a limited exemption to the obligation to pay corporate tax, benefiting uncomplicated, modestly capitalized businesses. Thus, only one class of stock is allowed to an S Corporation, a constraint that bites hard on venture-backed firms, since start-up organizers like to use preferred stock for a variety of reasons, including alleviation of the tax problems facing employees receiving "cheap" stock.

[1]The history of S Corporations, beginning in 1939 with special tax privileges for personal service corporations and culminating in 1958, when substantially the current provisions were added by the Technical Amendments Act of that year, is set out in Crumbley & Davis, *Organizing, Operating and Terminating Subchapter S Corporations* Ch. 2 (rev. ed. 1980).

[2]Some state statutes separately distinguish professional corporations. *See* Harroch, *supra* Ch. 1, n. 25, at § 1.09. Professional corporations are established to allow individuals to practice a regulated profession—law, accounting, dentistry—in corporate form, a privilege sought because of the favorable tax treatment of certain fringe benefits for corporate employees. The principal distinction in the law between a C Corporation and a professional corporation ("P.C.s" as they are called) is that the shareholders of a P.C. must be licensed practitioners. Some states explicitly acknowledge the existence of closely held or "close" corporations, allowing the shareholders to act as if they were partners; *e.g.*, no formal board of directors is required. *See, e.g.*, Del. Code Ann. tit. 8, §§ 341–356 (1983 & Supp. 1986). *See* Ch. 4, § 4.7.

[3]The test is whether the taxpayer "materially participate[s]" in the activity, I.R.C. § 469(c), meaning "regular . . . continuous . . . and substantial participation." I.R.C. § 469(h)(1).

[4]I.R.C. § 1366(d)(1).

Common stock divided into series with varying voting rights is permissible[5] (a result that could also be achieved through contractual arrangements)[6] but the inability to issue preference stock puts out of reach the "eat 'em all up" fiction which has blessed the tax-free issuance of cheap stock for services.[7]

Only individual U.S. citizens, certain estates and certain kinds of trusts can be shareholders,[8] excluding quite prominently corporations and partnerships, which means that a corporation (or partnership) can hold an equity interest in an S Corporation only by taking convertible debentures or debentures with warrants attached, conversion or warrant exercise occurring once the corporation has elected to terminate its S Corporation status. (This gambit must be approached with caution since "debt" may be reclassified as equity by the I.R.S., thereby terminating the election in years in which it was thought to be effective.)[9] In light of the foregoing, it is obviously critical that the organizers of an S Corporation impose strict limitations on the transfer of shares. While an S Corporation is not subject to dollar-size limitations, in keeping with the notion that the exemption is designed for small, uncomplicated businesses, an S Corporation can have no more than 35 shareholders and cannot be a member of an affiliated group, meaning (among other things) it cannot own 80% or more of the equity or voting power of any other entity.[10] The S Corporation can, however, be used as a general partner of a limited partnership. If the S Corporation has adequate net worth—roughly 10% of the amount of the financing being raised by the limited partnership—it can serve as the sole general partner, meaning that total "pass through" treatment has been achieved and yet no individual's liability is unlimited.[11]

One point on which an S Corporation is inferior to a partnership involves the distribution of appreciated property, generally a tax-free event for partnerships but the occasion of a tax at the corporate level in the case of an S Corporation.[12] An S Corporation succeeding to the business of a C Corporation may forfeit its status if more than 25% of its gross receipts for the three years preceding the election was "passive"

[5]I.R.C. § 1361(c)(4).

[6]Prior to 1982, the issue whether an agreement among shareholders dividing up the voting rights constituted two classes of stock (thus, breaking S Corporation status) was often litigated; *see, e.g., Paige v. United States*, 580 F.2d 960 (9th Cir. 1978).

[7]*See* Ch. 5, § 5.1(c).

[8]I.R.C. § 1361(b)(1)(B).

[9]*See generally* Haynsworth, *Organizing a Small Business Entity* § 3.02(d) (1986), on the question whether convertible debt will be construed as a second class of stock. The author concludes that it probably will not.

[10]I.R.C. §§ 1361(b)(1)(A) and (b)(2)(A).

[11]For the required net worth of a sole corporate general partner of a limited partnership under I.R.S. guidelines, *see* Ch. 20, § 20.5(a).

[12]I.R.C. § 1363(d); *see* Haynsworth, *supra* n. 9, at § 303(b).

and the corporation had earnings and profits accumulated at the end of each such year.[13] However, S Corporations, unlike C Corporations, will not be required (by the necessity of calculating alternative minimum tax under I.R.C. § 56) to keep two sets of books for tax purposes; the 1986 amendments greatly increase the likelihood that C Corporations will be subject to alternative minimum tax.[14]

Consideration of the question whether to elect S Corporation status should not stop at the federal tax level. The treatment of S Corporations for local tax purposes can complicate the issue substantially since some states refuse to recognize S Corporations as "flow-through" entities.[15] Moreover, a large element of any individual or corporate tax strategy has to do with the treatment of fringe benefits. A person owning 2% or more of the voting stock of an S Corporation is a "partner" for certain fringe benefit purposes[16]—for example, group term life insurance and medical insurance—and a partner still fares less well in the fringe benefit area than a stockholder/employee of a C Corporation.

The good news is that S Corporation status is relatively easy to achieve and, when the circumstances warrant,[17] to surrender—a timely election approved by the shareholders filed with the I.R.S. is all that is required. There are constraints, as one would expect, in attempting to manipulate S Corporation status—that is, if a C Corporation builds up unrealized appreciation in its assets and then switches to S status prior to a sale of those assets in order to avoid double tax, the I.R.S. has statutory weapons.[18] However, it appears that the S Corporation device can be a useful technique to escape an "excess of accumulated earnings" problem.[19]

[13]I.R.C. § 1362(d)(3).

[14]Tax Reform Act of 1986 § 701(a).

[15]*See* Leegstra & McArthur, "State Tax Considerations in Structuring a Business Venture as a Joint Venture/Partnership, C Corporation or S Corporation," 2 *N.Y.U. Inst. on St. & Loc. Tax'n. & Conf. on Prop. Tax'n.* Ch. 13 (1984). *See* Austin, "Getting Started: Tax Considerations in Organizing the High Tech New Venture," *70th Forum, Federal Tax Inst. of New Eng.* 1,2 (1984). (Forum).

[16]I.R.C. § 1372. Since the enactment of the Tax Equity and Fiscal Responsibility Act of 1982, many of the special disadvantages of S Corporations in the area of retirement plans have disappeared.

[17]The election to adopt S Corporation status must be filed with the I.R.S. within two and a half months of incorporation and the issuance of shares or the acquisition of assets or the beginning of business, whichever is first. I.R.C. § 1362(b). The planning point is that the S Corporation election should be filed with the incorporation papers.

[18]*See* § 632(a) of the Tax Reform Act of 1986, amending I.R.C. § 1374. Short-term assets held by the predecessor C Corporation—inventory and receivables—may give rise to a tax on what is called "built-in gain," being the amount by which the fair market value of the assets exceeds the aggregate adjusted basis of such assets on the day S Corporation status is effective. I.R.C. §§ 1374(a), 1374(d)(1). This gain will be twice taxed if the company or asset is sold or liquidated in the next 10 years.

[19]I.R.C. § 531.

An S Corporation should not be confused with the world of tax shelter; tax shelter vehicles were (and are, to the extent any still are) routinely organized as partnerships because, as earlier indicated, a shareholder in an S Corporation cannot generally deduct losses in excess of the basis in his stock. (The same is true ostensibly in partnerships but partners can, in effect, "borrow" basis by appropriating a share of the partnership's debt as to which they are liable or, in certain cases, no one is liable).[20] Thus, in a start-up, S Corporation status means that the cash investors can take advantage of the early losses but the founders, with their low basis "cheap" stock, ordinarily cannot—their share of the losses is not immediately usable. Moreover, by the time the start-up has achieved profitable status, chances are that more than 35 shareholders will be involved, a corporation has acquired some shares, the start-up has organized a subsidiary—fully active business operations and S Corporation status are often incompatible. Another small item of disadvantage to an S Corporation *vis-à-vis* a partnership should be mentioned; when a partnership interest changes hands or is redeemed, the partnership is ordinarily able to step up the basis of its assets under § 754 of the Code in the amount of the gain; not so in an S Corporation.

A final word. Many small, closely held corporations need not (and/or should not) bother with filing for S Corporation status; to avoid double tax, the management may simply pay out all the profits each year in year-end bonuses. If the company needs to retain earnings, the key managers can make loans back to the company, the company paying (and deducting) interest at the "federal rate" (the rate a loan must carry to avoid taxes on assumed interest).[21] In fact, a company owned solely by shareholder/employees can wind up paying more tax if it elects S over C status.[22] However, there are problems in pursuing the task of distributing all earnings in a venture context. If the founder is trying to bail out some day at a multiple of historical earnings, the "clean out the store" approach leaves a slim trail of earnings to which a high multiple can attach. When such businesses are bought and sold, the income statement can be re-created pro forma, but the very fact an explanation is required may put the founder at a disadvantage in negotiating price.

[20]*See* Mullaney & Blau, "An Analytic Comparison of Partnerships and S Corporations as Vehicles for Leveraged Investments," 59 *J. Tax'n* 142 (Sept. 1 1983).

[21]I.R.C. § 7872(f)(2).

[22]*See* Kramer, "Take a Hard Look Before Electing S Corporation Status," *Tax Times* 14 (Dec. 1986).

§3.3 MULTIPLE CORPORATIONS

Since the tax on incorporated businesses is graduated, it is occasionally tempting to split different profit centers into discrete corporate entities, a technique popular in the early 1960s, before the 1969 amendments to the Code extended the "controlled group" concept and brought the practice more or less to a halt.[23] There still may be reasons, however, to use more than one corporate entity, namely: (i) limiting liability; and (ii) isolating into separate pools the recipients of stock options and other performance-related compensation plans and/or the beneficiaries of employee benefit plans.[24] The inconvenience and expense of operating in this mode has largely discouraged the use of multiple corporate entities by venture capitalists, with the possible exception of leveraged buyouts, where multiple corporations may be used for the convenience of differentiated secured lenders—that is, one lending on real estate, the second on machinery and equipment, the third on rolling stock.

§3.4 UNINCORPORATED BUSINESS

(a) SOLE PROPRIETORSHIPS

The most popular form of small business organization is the sole proprietorship, an individual conducting business for his own account and under his own or an assumed name, but without any legal, documented entity imposed between himself and the people with whom he does business. For tax purposes, the individual is deemed to be self-employed.

Lacking a shell, the proprietor's liability is unlimited except to the extent he contains his exposure through insurance and/or limits his contractual obligations by specifying in each instrument he is not personally liable. The business dies with him. No statute governs the activity as such; ordinarily the only legal paper required is a publicly filed fictitious name certificate[25]—"Joe's Garage" . . . "Ray's Pizza"—which declares the ownership behind the name of the business as displayed to the public. Curiously, transferring one's interest in a sole proprietorship can be complicated. Each asset owned by the proprietor must be separately listed on the bill of sale and some assets—for example, a

[23]I.R.C. § 1561. *See* Cavitch, *Business Organizations* 74.02[5][b] (1986).

[24]The antidiscrimination provisions of ERISA cannot be defeated if the corporations are all members of a controlled group. *Id.* at 74.02[4].

[25]Fictitious name certificates are required to be filed under state law by unincorporated businesses "doing business" under a name other than that of the proprietors or members. Del. Code Ann. tit. 6, § 3101 (1975).

real estate lease—may require recordation and third-party consents prior to vesting ownership in a new party. By way of contrast, the exchange of a single piece of paper—that is, the one certificate representing all the outstanding stock—vests title to a corporation's entire assets in a new owner.

(b) GENERAL PARTNERSHIPS

As a rule, unincorporated businesses comprising two or more principals are (often unwittingly) general partnerships; the definitional sections in the Uniform Partnership Act (UPA), in effect in one form or another in almost all states, include any group of two or more individuals or entities carrying on a business for profit, whether or not the players deem themselves operating in partnership form.[26]

Whether formed by design or not, general partnerships are creatures of statute, the local version of the UPA. As with a sole proprietorship, the public filing requirements are minimal—only a fictitious name certificate—but it is always advisable to draw up a formal agreement setting out the terms of the partnership. Otherwise the terms are imposed by the provisions of the Act, with which none of the partners may be familiar. For some purposes the partnership is a legal entity—holding title to the property—and for others (paying taxes) it is viewed solely as an aggregation of individual partners.[27]

A general partnership is an awkward vehicle for managing capital contributed by diverse parties previously unknown to each other. The structure is egalitarian and necessarily founded on mutual trust and confidence of the most personal nature. Thus, unless a party dealing with the partnership has knowledge of provisions in the agreement to the contrary, the act of one partner within the scope of his apparent authority as a partner binds the partnership.[28] The management of a general partnership, again unless the agreement provides otherwise, is democratic; the partners are deemed co-owners of the business with an equal right to share in its management.[29] (On occasion, a similar result has been reached by courts when considering the intent of the parties establishing closely held corporations.)[30] The word "partner" carries with it, unless the agreement otherwise provides, the notion of financial equality as well. If the allocation of the respective profits interests is not set out in the partnership agreement, it is presumed that the profits

[26]Section 6(1) of the UPA defines a partnership as "an association of two or more persons to carry on as co-owners of a business for profit." U.P.A. § 6(1).

[27]*See infra*, n. 35.

[28]U.P.A. § 9(1).

[29]U.P.A. § 18(e).

[30]*See, e.g., Donahue v. Rodd Electrotype Co. of New England, Inc.* 367 Mass. 578 (1975).

interests are equal.[31] A general partnership can continue after the death of a partner—technically, an event of dissolution[32]—but provisions in the agreement must be inserted to that end.[33] General partnership interests are not freely transferable[34]; partners have the right to vote on the admission of new partners. General partnerships, in short, entail the elements one most often thinks of as envisioned by the term "partnership"—mutual trust, collegiality, and equality.

(c) LIMITED PARTNERSHIPS

Like general partnerships, limited partnerships are creatures of state law and governed by local versions of a uniform law, in this case the Uniform Limited Partnership Act or its 1976 successor, the Revised Uniform Limited Partnership Act.

A limited partnership is a hybrid. Conceptually, it is akin to a general partnership; in practice, however, it can be made to look and act like a corporation. Indeed, as earlier mentioned, a partnership is legally schizophrenic, treated in the law for some purposes as a single legal person and for others as a collection of the individual partners, the so-called "entity" and "aggregate" theories.[35] A limited partnership can, for example, hold title to property in its own name—that is, as an entity—but it vanishes when federal income taxes are owed, that obligation descending upon the shoulders of the individual partners in accordance with their profits interests. An analogy in the physical sciences is to the properties of light, which can either be viewed as a stream of particles or a wave.

This Janus-like power means that planners are often faced with muddy and complex choices when considering whether to elect the limited partnership form. A first cut at the issue might persuade a founder that the corporate form was superior because it promised limited liability, perpetual existence, continuity of management, and free transferability of interests. The difficulty with that view is that, while those elements are viewed as peculiarly the property of a corporation, a skillful planner can, as discussed more fully in § 3.6, structure a limited partnership so that it meets, to a greater or lesser extent, all the criteria.

[31] U.P.A. § 18(a).
[32] U.P.A. § 29.
[33] U.P.A. § 31.
[34] U.P.A. § 27(1).
[35] *See generally* Jensen, "Is Partnership under the Uniform Partnership Act an Aggregate or an Entity?," 16 *Vand. L. Rev.* 377 (1963). As an entity, a partnership may, among other things, hold and convey property, sue and be sued, and declare bankruptcy.

§3.5 BUSINESS TRUSTS AND OTHER ARRANGEMENTS

There are variations on the foregoing themes, created in most instances by contract rather than statute—the so-called Massachusetts Business Trust, for example, an entity organized under the principles of the law of trusts but designed to look, in most important respects, like a corporation, including (principally) transferable shares.[36] The "business trust" form of organization was devised in response to perceived, and now extinct, advantages under tax laws of certain states; the genre is still popular among organizers of certain types of public companies, real estate investment trusts (REIT) and investment companies for example, because the organic document governing a business trust, a creature of the draftsman's imagination and not generally subject to the rigidities of a general corporation law, does not require formalities such as annual meetings of shareholders.[37] A Massachusetts Business Trust is treated for federal tax purposes as if it were a corporation;[38] special "pass through" tax treatment is provided by the Code for qualifying REITs[39] and investment companies,[40] but that treatment is available whether they are organized as trusts or corporations.

Another nonstatutory animal is the joint venture, a contractual arrangement, usually for a determinate period of time, tied to a specific project and involving a few, often no fewer than two, parties. A joint venture is usually a general partnership under state law although the relationship may shade over into that of principal and agent if one "venturer" is calling all the shots (and, indeed, some arrangements styled as "joint ventures" are incorporated).[41] The distinction, if there

[36]Massachusetts Business Trusts are creatures of statute in some states, *e.g.*, Mass. Gen. Laws Ann. Ch. 182 (West 1987), acknowledged by custom in others and in danger of being treated as partnerships in a few. It is important to recall that artificial entities are legal fictions and, therefore, do not exist unless some statute or legal doctrine says they do. Most such trusts are in fact organized under Massachusetts law because it is clear that the trust will be treated in most material respects like a corporation rather than a private trust.

[37]The shares of open end mutual funds are not listed on NASDAQ and, accordingly, not affected by the amendments to '34 Act Rule 11Aa–2 and Schedule D to the NASD's bylaws requiring, in effect, that all the issuers of all listed securities and all securities for which real-time quotes are available obey certain rules of corporate governance, including the holding of annual meetings. *See* Sec. Act Rel. No. 34–24633 (June 23, 1987).

[38]Treas. Reg. § 301.7701–1(c).

[39]I.R.C. § 856, *et seq.*

[40]I.R.C. § 851, *et seq.*

[41]*See, e.g.*, materials collected in Stevens & Henn, *Law of Corporations* 120 (1965). Certain states admit the existence of an archaic entity, an unincorporated corporation called a "joint stock" company or association. *E.g.*, Cal. Corp. Code § 22000-22003 (West 1977 & Supp. 1987) And, depending on local law, there are any number of variations and hybrids—i.e., cooperatives, mutual benefit corporations, societies and associations, municipal corporations, and so forth.

is one, between joint venture and partnership is that a joint venture usually implies limited life and a single business purpose.[42] As a planning point, it is important for a joint venture to pick its form consciously; otherwise unexpected tax surprises may result.[43]

Finally, there are a variety of entities which are not "owned" by partners or shareholders as such and operate according to special legal provisions—nonprofit corporations[44] and mutual thrift and life insurance associations are prime examples.

§3.6 CORPORATION VERSUS LIMITED PARTNERSHIP

In the final analysis, the choice of entity usually comes down to an election between a corporation and a limited partnership. In a real sense, there need be no practical distinction. Limited partners enjoy the same limitation on liability as corporate shareholders; management continuity may be assured by introducing a corporate general partner or other immortal entity; previously onerous public disclosure requirements on limited partnerships (including particularly, a requirement to file publicly the names of the limited partners) have been moderated in several states with the enactment of the Revised Uniform Limited Partnership Act,[45] and the Revised Act gives limited partners in large part the powers of corporate shareholders to influence the business, including the power to expel individual general partners, without sacrificing limited liability.[46]

Nonetheless, significant distinctions do exist at the margin, pulling now one way and now the other.[47] In this sense, the "corporation versus

[42]*See* Ch. 17, § 17.10. *See generally* Henn & Alexander, *Law of Corporations* § 49 (3d ed. 1983).

[43]*See* Haynsworth, *Selecting the Form of a Small Business Entity* (1985) § 1.05(b).

[44]Cal. Corp. Code §§ 5000 *et seq.* (West 1977 & Supp. 1987).

[45]Revised Uniform Limited Partnership Act (R.U.L.P.A.) § 202(b). Although the law of the state in which the certificate is filed controls on most issues, R.U.L.P.A. § 901, foreign limited partnerships may be required to file a more extensive certificate in a state in which they do business than in the state of domicile. Thus, as per the R.U.L.P.A., Delaware no longer requires that the certificate be amended each time a limited partner is admitted or withdraws. *See* Basile, "The 1985 Delaware Revised Uniform Limited Partnership Act," 41 *Bus. Law.* 571, 573 (Feb. 1986). Nonetheless, the organizers of a limited partnership headquartered in New York may have no reason, at least on this account, to domicile the partnership in Delaware, since New York law appears to require such amendments for both domestic and foreign partnerships. The issue is not free from doubt in New York, however. The New York statute governing foreign partnerships may be read to provide only that the *initial* filing disclose the names of the limited partners, in which case only the name of the "dummy" used to make the first filing would be on the record. N.Y. Partnership Law § 120–b&c (McKinney 1948 & Supp. 1987).

[46]R.U.L.P.A. § 303(b)(6)(v).

[47]For useful commentaries, *see* Henn & Alexander, *supra* n. 42, at §§ 16–77; Painter, *Corporate and Tax Aspects of Closely Held Corporations* §§ 1–1.5 (2d ed. 1981).

limited partnership" election is a classic legal conundrum—"on one hand . . . on the other hand"—reminding cynical laymen of the desirability of finding a one-armed lawyer.

To understand the specific issues, some introductory remarks on general principles are in order. The underlying thesis is that it is equitable to afford partners the quintessential corporate attribute—limited liability[48]—if and only if creditors and others dealing with the partnership are on notice that the individual pocketbooks of the limited partners do not stand behind the obligations of the partnership. Thus, an entity aspiring to be a limited partnership must cause to be filed a document called the Certificate of Limited Partnership, a public document which announces that liability is limited and gives other information deemed salient. Further, the name of the entity must contain reference to the fact that it is a *limited* partnership—"XYZ Associates, *L.P.*," for example[49]—and a limited partner's shield against liability is compromised if his surname appears in the partnership name (thereby, again theoretically, leading creditors to believe he is a general partner.)[50] Once an entity is announced as a limited partnership, the issue comes down to the practical consequences that label entails. As Humpty Dumpty said, should not the words mean what we want them to mean, in which case the speaker, not the word, is master? More importantly, whatever the phrase "limited partnership" means, how is it a different animal from a corporation?

(a) LIQUIDITY

Public trading in shares of corporate stock is perceived by most practitioners as easier—that is, more efficiently accomplished—than trading in limited partnership interests. Corporate shares were designed to be liquid; not so limited partnership interests, particularly in those states in which the certificate is to be amended each time a limited partner

[48]Limited partners enjoy the same immunity from liability (beyond their contributions, which they have knowingly put at risk) as corporate shareholders. In each case, liability over and above the capital committed to the enterprise extends to a requirement that distributions made to proprietors while the entity is insolvent be returned, R.U.L.P.A. § 107. For instances in which limited partners have been held liable because they crossed over the line into positions of control, *see* the materials collected in Crane & Bromberg, *Partnerships* § 26(c) (1968).

[49]The R.U.L.P.A. requires that the name contain the words "limited partnership" without abbreviation. R.U.L.P.A. § 102(2).

[50]R.U.L.P.A. § 303(d).

assigns his interest.[51] To be sure, through use of the master limited partnership (MLP) device, (freely transferable undivided interests in a single, limited partnership interest), units essentially equivalent to limited partnership interests may trade actively. Some MLPs are listed on the New York Stock Exchange, the charm of the device lying in the fact that, because double taxation is avoided, the market has been known to apply the appropriate price/earnings multiple to pretax, versus after-tax, earnings (despite the fact that distributions must be made to enable the partners to pay their tax). However, each holder of a master limited partnership certificate must report for federal tax purposes the profits and losses of the underlying business, whether he has received any distributions or not, and attach the partnership's information return, known as a K–1, to his tax return. The discussion of the tax issues entailed in a public master limited partnership runs 20 pages or more in the typical prospectus. Moreover, accounting for each partner's capital account means the bookkeeping is "very complex."[52] Accordingly, the world may eventually tire of that instrument (apart from its tax advantages) as investors are faced with the preparation of their personal tax returns festooned with attached partnership information returns and burdened with the attendant calculations.[53] In short, the liquidity issue inherently favors the corporate form even though partnership interests can be brought to a stage of respectable liquidity.

(b) FEES AND EXPENSES

Each state exacts a one-time filing fee and an annual franchise tax in consideration of its grant of limited liability to corporations domesticated in that state. These expenses may appear trivial to someone intent on organizing a multimillion-dollar enterprise but a few hundred dollars is no joke to many start-ups. While a limited partnership does require a central filing with the state secretary and the payment of a fee, the

[51] *See supra* n. 45. The several sources which deal with the corporation versus partnership issue, *see, e.g.*, Crumbley & Davis, *supra* n. 1, at 339, often suggest that it is easier to split income among family members by distributing stock certificates versus interests in a partnership. Such is certainly the case if the partnership is general; distribution of limited partnership interests can be structured, however, to be tantamount to the distribution of stock. *See generally* Slater, "Publicly Traded Limited Partnerships: An Emerging Financial Alternative to the Public Corporation," 39 *Bus. Law.* 709 (Feb. 1984).

[52] Murray & Langley, "Taxing Matters: Relatively New Form of Business Structure Is Causing Controversy," *Wall St. J.* June 30, 1987 at 1.

[53] The master limited partnership not only requires that limited partners report their share of the partnership's income or loss on their federal return, the unit holder may have to file state tax returns in the jurisdictions in which the partnership does business. Nonetheless, the popularity of the MLP device continues. *See* Monroe, "Master Limited Partnerships Are Defying Death Notices," *Wall St. J.* Mar. 30, 1987 at 6. As the text went to press, the Revenue Act of 1987 imposes corporate tax treatment on partnerships with "readily tradable" interests.

fees are more modest than those charged for the limited liability afforded to those operating in the corporate form.

(c) FLEXIBILITY VERSUS FORMALITY

Except to the extent the general corporation law of a given state provides relief,[54] corporate existence entails a higher degree of formality (and therefore, expense) than life under a partnership. Corporations require a formally elected board of directors, statutory officers, stockholders meetings, class votes on certain issues, records of meetings. These formalities are often neglected but at some peril; if there is no evidence of formal directors' meetings, plaintiffs can contend the board was ipso facto negligent in carrying out its "fiduciary" duties to the stockholders because one of the functions of a board is to hold formal meetings.

(d) FAMILIARITY

Corporate law has been more thoroughly developed than partnership law in the litigated cases. There is more predictability, accordingly, from a legal standpoint. Counsel can forecast with a higher degree of confidence what the leading oracles on corporate law—the Chancery and Supreme Courts in Delaware—will do on a given state of facts. Indeed, for every case construing the Uniform Partnership Act or Uniform Limited Partnership Act, there are hundreds construing the general corporation laws. The schizophrenic nature of a partnership—now an entity, now just a see-through label for an aggregate of individual partners—makes for potential confusion. And, there exists a more or less constant threat by the Internal Revenue Service to treat large limited partnerships—35 members or more—as corporations.[55] If large partnerships are to survive and prosper, there will be a long period in which state legislatures play "catch up" with the general corporation laws; for example, most state laws deal primitively, if at all, with the processes by which one partnership may be empowered to merge with another.[56]

[54]*E.g.,* Del. Code Ann. tit. 8, § 351 (1983 & Supp. 1986), authorizing less formality for certain closely held corporations. *See* Ch. 4, § 4.7.
[55]*See* Murray & Langley, *supra* n. 52. That threat has been realized in the Revenue Act of 1987 as this text went to press. A partnership whose interests are readily tradable on an exchange or on a secondary market (or the substantial equivalent thereof) will be taxed as a corporation unless 90% of its income is passive, including real estate and oil and gas.
[56]*See* Basile, *supra* n. 45, at 578.

§3.7 TAX ISSUES INFLUENCING THE CHOICE[57]

Now that the distinction in rates of tax between capital gains and ordinary income is on its way to the boneyard (at least until the federal tax law changes again), corporate tax issues will revolve principally around the fact that earnings by a business operated in corporate form generate federal and state income tax on the corporate level;[58] when those earnings are distributed (if they are) by way of dividends (or in liquidation), they ordinarily generate additional tax again, this time levied upon the shareholders, and such dividends are not deductible corporate expenses. Avoidance of "double taxation" will drive the preference of planners toward the partnership format. There are, to be sure, ways to avoid double taxation[59] but the gate is substantially narrower than it was pre-Jan. 1, 1987.

The tax issues are extremely complicated and no attempt will be made to set them out in detail.[60] Much depends on facts and circumstances in a given case interacting with special rules, such as the exclusion from taxable income of a large portion (80%, down from 85%) of corporate dividends paid to corporate shareholders.[61] This discussion will outline only *general* principles, to be used as guides in analyzing particular cases. To get into the subject in detail, a number of Code provisions must be analyzed carefully—for example, the new rules re-

[57]As indicated in the Text, some of the learning on the taxation of small business has been rendered moot by the passage of the Tax Reform Act of 1986; however, the old rules are generally intact. For two first-class discussions which antedate the 1986 Act, *see* Forum, *supra* n. 15, and Deloitte, Haskins, & Sells, *Tax Aspects of High Technology Operations* (1985).

[58]In 1988, corporate tax rates are to be 15% of annual taxable income up to $50,000, 25% of the next $25,000 and 34% of all additional income. I.R.C. § 11. An additional tax on income between $100,000 and $335,000 means that corporations with income of at least $335,000 will pay at a flat 34% rate.

[59]Double taxation is not a foregone conclusion. Dividends are taxable to the recipient only to the extent a corporation has accumulated or concurrently enjoys "earnings and profits." I.R.C. § 316(a). If the loss corporation is legally empowered under state law to declare and pay dividends, they constitute a return of capital, nontaxable to the extent the recipient has basis. And, as indicated in the Text, 80% (formerly 85%) of the dividends paid to a corporate shareholder are excluded from taxable income. I.R.C. § 243(a).

[60]The discussion in the Text contrasts the varying tax impacts entailed in operating as a partnership versus a C (or fully taxable) Corporation. Obviously, (*see supra* § 3.2) doing business as an S Corporation allows generally the same "pass through" or conduit treatment of income and loss as a partnership.

[61]I.R.C. § 243(a)(1).

stricting the ability of corporations to carry forward net operating losses[62] and the application of alternative minimum tax to corporations, including a provision that the half of a corporation's book income over taxable income is now a tax preference item.[63]

Starting one's business in noncorporate form will prove to be popular for yet another reason. The first-ever favorable spread between individual and corporate rates means that cash can reach the hands of the proprietors not only at the cost of only a single tax but that, even if profits are not distributed by the corporation, the government still gets less tax revenue than if a partnership holds the assets. It is true that partners pay tax on revenue whether it is distributed or not and it may be necessary to retain earnings in the entity to expand the business. That is not, however, a major problem in most instances. The partnership simply distributes enough cash to the partners to pay tax at an assumed rate (28 to 34%, plus something for state taxes) and retains the rest, the danger being that the partnership will have taxable income but no cash, in a year of large principal payments on debt, for example.

The combination of low personal rates and elimination of favorable capital gains taxation is a twofold reason against sequestering earnings in a corporation[64] with hope of later "capitalizing" those earnings by selling stock or liquidating at an advantaged rate. "Capitalizing" earnings—postponing their enjoyment, in other words—is of less utility (but not of *no*[65] utility) if the tax is all the same; to the extent the firm does not need to retain them, the shareholders may wish use the earnings now. (Parenthetically, it should be noted that the Tax Reform Act of 1986 has eliminated the different *levels* of tax on income and gains but

[62]*See* Ch. 19, § 19.13(a). It should be noted that the tax treatment of partnership items shall be made at the partnership level, I.R.S. § 6221, and the partners are bound thereby, I.R.C. § 6222(a). The rights of various partners to receive notice of, and participate in, such determinations as coordinated by the "tax matters partners" is set out in Gideon, "Partnership Audit," Fourth Annual Structuring Partnership Agreements (Halloran & Nathan Chm. 1987).

[63]I.R.C. § 56(f)(1).

[64]*See generally* Freidrich, "The Unincorporation of America?," 64 *J. Tax'n* 3, 4 (1987).

[65]The elimination of the income/gains distinction should not be overplayed. In an important sense, capital gains are now (and always have been) taxed at a zero rate; a shareholder has a present and perpetual claim on the appreciation in his shares (he can, for example, borrow against that gain) without paying any tax. On the other hand, a dividend or other distribution, once passed, is gone forever. The very notion of a dividend implies a tax.

not the *distinction,* a distinction which can be significant for various purposes, including using capital gains to offset capital losses of more than $3,000.)

Migration from one form of organization to another is a one-way street: A partnership can organize a corporation and transfer its assets thereto without tax, assuming that the partners contributing cash and/or property hold 80% or more of the resultant voting stock and the liabilities of the partnership do not exceed the fair value of its assets;[66] if a corporation wants to organize itself as a partnership, however, there is a double tax under the new tax law; appreciated assets are taxed at the corporate level and the shareholders taxed on the liquidation distributions. This can be a key issue. The Treasury and some members of Congress have on occasion advocated that widely held limited partnerships (35 partners or more is the most often mentioned number) be taxed as corporations.[67] If such a proposal goes through, it will be critical that those partnerships seriously impacted be able to convert to corporate form, tax-free.

Further, election of the partnership structure allows somewhat greater flexibility in allocating items of income and loss among the partners.[68] The dream of the organizers of a business is to be able to strike a deal between the suppliers of capital and the managers in a tax-neutral

[66]I.R.C. § 351. For tax and other purposes, there are three ways in which a partnership can incorporate: the partnership transfers its assets to Newco, takes back stock and distributes the same; the partnership liquidates and the partners transfer assets to Newco; or the partners transfer their partnership interests to Newco. There are tax differences dependent on which form is used. For example, in format 1, Newco will have in the year of transfer a partnership as a shareholder, meaning S Corporation status cannot be elected for that year. The transformation of a partnership to a corporation, like any legal process, is not simple. There is always the possibility that certain prior deductions—i.e., investment tax credit or R&E deductions under I.R.C. § 174—may be recaptured. See Austin, "Getting Started—Tax Considerations in Organizing the High Tech or New Venture," in Forum, *supra* n. 15 at 21. Parenthetically, the fact that the organization has been a partnership at one time may influence a court more readily to construe the relationship of the shareholders as one of the quasipartnership. *See* O'Neal, *Oppression of Minority Shareholders* § 7.14 (1975).

[67]As this text went to press, the Treasury's proposal has in effect been adopted in the Revenue Act of 1987, imposing corporate tax on partnerships with readily tradable interests. Partnerships existing as of December 17, 1987, are "grandfathered" until December 31, 1997. A partnership caught in the trap will be treated as having converted to corporate form under I.R.C. §§ 351, 731 and 732.

[68]Starr, "The S Corporation: Is It The Right Choice?" 43 *N.Y.U. Inst. on Fed. Tax'n* Ch. 5, § 5.06 (1985). S Corporation shareholders share in income and loss strictly on a per day, per share basis. I.R.C. § 1377(a)(1).

setting. The founder and the investors want to be able to arrange the split between them of calls on the company's future income (in the person of shares of capital stock or interests in partnership profits) without worrying about the consequences of that allocation as a taxable event to either party. In a partnership, interests in profits can be allocated and reallocated more or less as the parties agree, without regard to the respective contributions of capital. The allocation must have "substantial economic effect," which means not much more than that a scheme directly keyed to the tax status of the partners is questionable.[69] A corporation can distribute stock disproportionate to paid in capital but only within certain limits.[70]

On the other hand, the Tax Reform Act of 1986 diminishes what had heretofore been a principal motivation for electing partnership status. As members of partnerships or sole proprietorships, providers of capital were able to set the initial losses against their income from other sources, in turn meaning that the federal government was subsidizing up to half the cost of the entity's initial capitalization. The Tax Reform Act of 1986 effectively establishes four categories of income (and loss)—(i) compensatory;[71] (ii) portfolio income,[72] including interest and dividends;[73] (iii) gains; and, (iv) passive income.[74] The 1986 Act provides that, for individual taxpayers, (as well as "personal service" corporations and corporations subject to the personal holding company stock ownership rules), losses from "passive activity" cannot be set against income from other than "passive activity"—like to like—meaning that losses allowable to limited partners will not offset portfolio or compensation income.[75] Moreover, even if a taxpayer has passive income he can shelter, the relaxation of marginal rates depreciates the utility of losses. A taxpayer in the 70% bracket (the maximum rate on unearned income not so long ago) will pay a lot for losses; in the 28% bracket, the investment

[69]I.R.C. § 704(b)(2).

[70]*See* Ch. 5 on the methods used to split claims to corporate profits between the cash investors and those providing services. *See also* the discussion of I.R.C. § 305 in Ch. 13, § 13.9. A partnership distributes appreciated property free of tax at the partnership or partner level unless the cash distributed exceeds the partner's basis. I.R.C. § 731.

[71]I.R.C. § 469(e)(3).

[72]I.R.C. § 469(e)(1)(A)(i)

[73]I.R.C. § 469(e)(1)(A)(i)(I)

[74]I.R.C. § 469(a).

[75]Loss allocable to a limited partnership interest is, by definition, a passive activity loss. I.R.C. § 469(h)(2).

may not be worth the transaction costs, again diminishing the attraction of those vehicles—for example, partnerships—traditionally used to pass along losses. If early losses are expected, in fact, an affirmative case can be made for the election of corporate form since corporations can carry forward losses and offset them against taxable income in subsequent periods. Losses from the operations of a partnership cannot be "carried forward" in that sense since a partnership is not a tax-paying entity. If limited partners cannot use the losses against passive income currently, the usefulness of the loss is postponed until such income is realized or the interests are sold.[76] The time-value-of-money effect, accordingly, may suggest the corporate form to the extent the losses will become useful earlier in time. Indeed, certain types of losses passed through to the partners are dangerous—R&E deductions, for example—because they can create alternative minimum tax problems.[77]

Moreover, partnerships are not eligible to participate in tax-postponed reorganizations under § 368. Because a partnership can be incorporated without tax, that problem may not be insuperable, but attempts to incorporate a partnership on the eve of a statutory merger could run afoul of the "step transaction" test.[78]

The complexity of the analysis, corporation versus partnership, is multiplied by the fact that there are issues other than federal income tax to take into account, including the impact of Social Security taxes. Until 1990, when full parity has been designed into the system, the Social Security contribution by a corporation in a loss position is greater than would otherwise be the case if the business were conducted as a partnership because the corporation's contribution is currently structured on the theory that there is a tax deduction, equal to the payment, available to the corporation.[79]

There are, in the final analysis, two ways in which to illuminate and decide the most intelligent election between the corporate and the partnership form. The first is easy: Certain investors—for example, venture funds with offshore investors or endowment funds—may (for reasons

[76]Oil and gas drilling funds are organizing themselves as general partnerships to avoid the "passive activity" loss rules, to the extent individuals with the appropriate appetite for risk can be found.

[77]*See* Ch. 5, § 5.4

[78]Rev. Rul. 70–140, 1970–1 C.B. 73. Austin, "Getting Started—Tax Considerations in Organizing the High-Tech or New Venture," Forum, *supra* n. 15, at 19.

[79]*Id.* at 3. A modest additional advantage of the partnership form stems from the fact that owner/managers, but not partners, are employees of a corporation, S or C, for unemployment and worker's compensation purposes. *Ibid.*

discussed later)[80] want each investment in which they are directly or indirectly interested to be a corporation and, if so, that is what they will get. The second method requires some work: Take the business forecast and run two scenarios: limited partnership versus corporation. Compare the after-tax wealth of the shareholders assuming, say, a sale of their shares in year five at a multiple of 10 times earnings. Look at the difference and decide.[81]

[80]*See* Ch. 20, § 20.24.

[81]One chart, reproduced in, "Growing Companies: Tax and Business Planning for the '80s," *ALI–ABA Course of Study* (cosponsored by Mass. CLE, 1984), lists some 25 factors to be considered in selecting the form of organization, *viz.* Ease of initial formation; acquisition of ownership interest; ease of transfer of ownership; splitting income among family members; taxable year; taxation of income; tax rates; compensation (tax treatment); Social Security taxes; unemployment taxes; workmens compensation coverage; health and accident insurance; group term life; charitable contributions; taxability of dividends; withholding of dividends and interest; accumulated earnings tax; capital gains; retirement plans; net operating loss carry forwards; passive income consequences; tax on liquidation; sale of the business; withdrawal of cash.

Four

The Incorporation Process

The process of organizing a corporation is usually deemed the exclusive province of the lawyers, and a low-level chore at that. However, certain important elections, sometimes difficult to reverse, are made at the initial incorporation stage. Nonlawyers, particularly by reading §§ 4.9–11 and § 4.17, should become generally familiar with the incorporation process and some of the legal and business decisions to be made.

§4.1 WHAT IS A "CORPORATION"?

A corporation is an artificial legal entity chartered by one of the 50 states[1] and endowed by the legislature with certain valuable privileges; it follows that its powers are limited to those expressly or impliedly set out by statute. With exceptions not generally significant,[2] a corporation is managed by its directors.[3]

[1]The federal government has the power to, and in fact does, create corporations, the most common being national banks. 12 U.S.C. § 21. The great majority of business corporations are, however, chartered by the states. Start-up corporations are often referred to as "closely held" or "close" corporations (versus publicly held), meaning that the shares are held by a limited group of individuals. The most prominent handbook on closely held corporations is O'Neal, *Close Corporations* (1986).
[2]See *infra* § 4.7
[3]The significance of a board made up of people able to contribute to the program is outlined *supra* Ch.2, § 2.8(b).

The general corporation laws in each state vary in detail but they follow a generally similar pattern. The Model Revised Business Corporation Act, drafted by a select committee of the American Bar Association, is a composite of the most advanced thinking.[4]

§4.2 CORPORATE CHARTER

A corporation is created by the preparation and filing of a document entitled the "certificate of incorporation" or "charter." This is the fundamental, organic document governing the relationships between the various interests—the officers, directors, shareholders, and creditors. Since the charter predates the existence of directors or stockholders, it is signed by individuals known as incorporators—often personnel in the incorporating lawyer's office. A number of significant issues, detailed in the following sections, are encountered at an early stage, that is, when the charter is drafted.

§4.3 NAME

By statute and under the common-law principles of unfair competition, the corporation may not adopt a name which is deceptively similar to the name of an existing corporation either incorporated under the laws of, or duly qualified to do business in, a given state.[5] Further, most statutes require that the corporation signify its incorporated status by including in its name words such as "Corporation," "Corp.," "Ltd." or "Inc."[6] The state secretary's office maintains a list of all domestic corporations and all foreign corporations registered to do business in the state. By perusing the list, a founder or his counsel can see whether a given name has already been taken. If a multistate operation is contemplated, certain agents—for example, the CT Corporation System—will search the rosters of the important commercial states to see if a given name is available. It is usually possible to reserve a name in most states for up to 90 days. The exclusive use of the name is then nailed down by formally going through the process of qualifying to do business as a foreign corporation in that state. The name of the corporation (versus the trade name) is not always critical; if the name Biodynamics has

[4]Model Revised Business Corporation Act Annotated (1984). The Act was most recently revised in 1984 by the ABA Committee on Corporate Law (Section of Corporation, Banking and Business Law). (Revised Model Act.).

[5]Del. Code Ann. tit. 8, § 102(a)(1) (1983 & Supp. 1986).

[6]*Ibid.*

already been taken, for example, the state secretary will usually accept the name of, say, "Biodynamics Informatics." Hence, a right to reserve a corporate name by qualifying to business in a number of states is not usually a justified (in view of the expense) strategy for a start-up. If, however, the corporate name is to be used as the distinctive name under which goods are to be sold to consumers, a search and registration procedure qualifying the name as part of a distinctive trademark or trade name should be conducted under the federal trademark law, known as the Lanham Act.[7]

§4.4 PAR VALUE OF STOCK

The charter denominates the par value of each share of common and preferred stock, the number of shares of each class of stock authorized and the various rights and privileges of each class of stock.[8] The original purpose of a stated par value was to protect the creditors of the corporation by requiring that the consideration for the shares issued equal at least their aggregate par value and that the capital equivalent of the number of shares issued times the par value of each share be permanent capital of the corporation, not subject to decrease by voluntary acts of the directors in favor of the stockholders, such as dividends or repurchases of shares. While creditors no longer rely, if they ever did, on the stated capital of a corporation,[9] it remains customary to assign each share a nominal par value (versus no par stock) and allocate the remaining consideration paid for the issuance of shares to a "paid-in" surplus account generally available for dividends and redemptions. Although no par value shares are legally possible, it is often advisable to

[7] 15 U.S.C. § 1051 *et seq. See generally* Miller & Davis, *Intellectual Property: Patents, Trademarks and Copyright* 143 (1983).

[8] The founder faces a choice at this point. Stock can be divided into either classes or series—i.e., either Class A preferred and Class B preferred or Class A preferred, Series 1 and Series 2. The purpose of either division is to treat different groups of investors differently. The legal significance of the choice is that there are certain matters on which (unless the charter otherwise provides and in some cases the charter is powerless otherwise to provide) the stockholders vote by class. Hence, the owner of the Class A preferred (and the Class B preferred and the common) will have a veto over certain corporate activities by reason of a statutory requirement that such action be authorized by a favorable vote of each *class* of stock. If the preferred is divided only into series, the owners of a given series of preferred have no special voting power.

[9]
> The question of what amount of assets must be paid in to an enterprise by its shareholders before it will be permitted to enter the market place has never been candidly addressed in American corporation law . . . the creditor has received little or no direct protection through legislative or regulatory prescriptions requiring an incorporated enterprise to have a minimum amount of assets at its inception.

Manning, *Legal Capital* 17 (1980).

issue shares at some par value—say 1 cent—versus no par value, because the franchise tax and annual license fees in many states are tied to the number of outstanding shares valued at their par value and no par shares may be assigned a par value of as much as $1.[10]

§4.5 PAYMENT FOR STOCK

An atavistic desire to protect creditors explains why state statutes continue to regulate the types of consideration for which corporate stock can be issued—cash and property is eligible but promissory notes are questionable ("no" in Massachusetts,[11] "yes" in Delaware)[12] and stock rarely may be issued for future services. The trick, of course, is to designate some form of eligible consideration in the minutes—intellectual "property" instead of services, for example.[13] Alternatively, if stock is to be paid for in installments and a promissory note is not eligible consideration under state law, it may be possible to work with the concept of assessable stock, stock issued under the provisions of state law which authorize partly paid stock to be issued, subject to calls for further payments.[14]

§4.6 PURPOSES

The charter requires a statement of the purpose(s) for which the corporation is organized, a section into which the draftsmen were once accustomed to pour a good deal of care. Recent usage, however, supports the practice of making brief mention of the principal purpose of the corporation and then tagging on a line authorizing the corporation to engage in any business in which a corporation organized in the state may lawfully engage. Such "basket" language is now thought adequate to overcome any objection that a particular corporate activity is *ultra vires* (beyond the power of the corporation) because no specific mention thereof has been made in the charter. When investors or creditors wish to restrain a corporation from roaming far afield, negative covenants in a loan or stock purchase agreement are deemed more flexible than charter provisions.[15]

[10]Haynsworth, *supra* Ch. 3, n. 9, at § 505(d)(4), n. 490.
[11]Mass. Gen. Laws Ann. Ch. 156, § 15 (West 1970 & Supp. 1987).
[12]Del. Code Ann., tit. 8, § 152. (1983 & Supp. 1986).
[13]*See* Ch. 5, § 5.1(b), for a discussion of the distinction under the Internal Revenue Code.
[14]*See* Del. Code Ann. tit. 8, § 156. (1983 & Supp. 1986).
[15]*See* Ch. 10, § 10.1(h).

§4.7 STATUTORILY DEFINED "CLOSE" CORPORATIONS

To alleviate the exigencies facing small business, a number of states have created by statute an entity called a "close corporation." Under Delaware law, the stock of a close corporation may not be held by more than 30 persons; additional requirements are that the close corporation's stock will be subject to restrictions on transfer and that such corporation will make no public offering of its stock.[16]

The provisions governing close corporations[17] are designed to reduce or eliminate the expense and inconvenience required to maintain the corporate entity while retaining the corporate characteristic of limited liability. Generally, the statutes provide that shareholder agreements can install any system of management and control desired by the shareholders. If the shareholders wish, they need not have formal meetings of the board of directors, and voting rights may be tied up in ways that would be otherwise impermissible. However, the law applicable to these entities is not fully developed, entailing uncertainty; the shareholders may be exposing themselves to liability if they exercise directorial control; and, drafting a comprehensive agreement can be expensive since the typical law office has not developed the customery "boilerplate"—provisions refined by multiple draftings at the hands of several lawyers. Accordingly, the option extended by the legislature has not been widely utilized.

§4.8 MISCELLANEOUS CHARTER PROVISIONS

The charter lists the principal place of business and the names and addresses of the initial officers and directors of the corporation. It does not require that the stockholders be identified.[18] If the corporation is organized by a law firm, it is customary to file the papers using "dummy" officers and directors, the "dummies" being employees of the law office involved, and make the necessary changes at the initial shareholders' and directors' meetings. Some states insist that each corporation have at least three directors and that the charter name at least three officers:

[16]Del. Code Ann. tit. 8, §§ 341–356 (1983 & Supp. 1986).

[17]*See* O'Neal, "Close Corporation Legislation: A Survey and an Evaluation," 1972 *Duke L.J.* 867; Jordan, "The Close Corporation Provisions of the New California General Corporation Law," 23 *UCLA L. Rev.* 1094 (1976); Rohrlich, *Organizing Corporate and Other Business Enterprises* § 2A (rev. ed. 1986).

[18]The issue whether one stockholder can insist on learning the identity of his fellow stockholders is often litigated whenever a contest for corporate control is in progress. In Delaware, the rule is established by statute. Del. Code Ann. tit. 8, § 220 (1983 & Supp. 1986).

i.e., president, treasurer, and clerk or secretary.[19] The more modern statutes now allow a corporation to exist with as few as one director (in some states, close corporations may operate with none)[20] and the founder can hold all the offices: the sole director, president, treasurer, clerk or secretary. There are, on occasion, curious local requirements, such as that the clerk be a resident of the state in which the corporation is domiciled; again, modern statutes omit such anachronisms.[21]

The charter is deemed to be a contract[22] between the state and the incorporators, a public document available to inspection by all. Therefore, its provisions can, by virtue of one of the many handy fictions through which the law operates, be deemed binding on all the world, including everybody who takes an interest in the corporation subsequent to the publication of the charter. There is no other instrument with this all-encompassing effect and, therefore, a careful drafter will load up the charter with those provisions meant to be universally effective. Such provisions are known as "optional" provisions since they are in addition to the material the corporation must provide if the charter documents are to be accepted for filing. They are, however, optional in name only; if no mention is made in the charter, the law may either insert a given provision automatically or deny its right to

[19]*See* Haynsworth, *supra* Ch. 3, n. 9, at § 5.05(d)(7). *See generally* Henn & Alexander, *Law of Corporations* § 130 (3d ed. 1983).

[20]Del. Code Ann., tit. 8, § 351 (1983 & Supp. 1986); *see also* O'Neal, *supra* n. 1, at § 3.60.

[21]A cost conscious founder would do well to purchase at the local legal stationery store the forms necessary to incorporate a corporation and pay a visit to the local office of the State Secretary to discuss incorporation formalities with the staff. The first crack at drafting the incorporation papers can then be accomplished by the founder. Alternatively, most lawyers have a standard version of the so called "boilerplate" that goes into incorporation papers. Many will be happy to furnish a blank draft without charge. The object is to combine the founder's ideas and the boilerplate into as complete a document as possible *before* the lawyer's time clock starts running, saving time and legal fees. The founder can handle some of the administrative chores himself, carrying the papers to the State Secretary's office, paying the filing fee and, in the process, getting an education on what it means to be incorporated. The founder should not, however, try to go it alone or attempt to incorporate without advice; the thrust of this chapter is that significant issues are involved in incorporation. The narrow planning point is that precious cash can be conserved if the founder takes the first crack.

[22]The question whether the charter is a contract which cannot be constitutionally altered by the state was one of the thorniest constitutional law questions in the pre-Franklin Roosevelt era. In *Trustees of Dartmouth College v. Woodward* 17 U.S. 518 (1819), the Supreme Court held that a corporate charter constituted such a contract, meaning that amendments of the statute could not affect existing charters. Taking their cue from Justice Story's concurring opinion, states exercise such control over corporations today by reserving a power to amend, alter, or repeal charters either in state constitutions or in corporation laws. *See* Del. Code Ann., tit. 8, § 394 (1983 & Supp. 1986) (the corporation law "and all amendments thereof, shall be a part of the charter or certificate of incorporation of every corporation . . .").

exist outside the charter. As indicated below, the competent planner makes sure he understands the difference.

§4.9 RESTRICTIONS ON TRANSFER

In some states, agreements respecting the corporation's power to restrict the transfer of its shares, once issued, are not deemed to be effective unless they are set out in the charter (and, like all restrictions, "legended" upon the face of the share certificates themselves); moreover, any agreement purporting to bind shareholders not signatories to the agreement may only be legally effective if set out in the charter.[23] The typical restriction, in the nature of a first refusal option,[24] is a significant element of governance in closely held corporations, important to ensure that stock not fall into the hands of strangers without an opportunity in the company (or the remaining shareholders) to buy back some or all of the shares. In small companies, the shareholders feel the need to relate to each other as partners and a maverick shareholder can be disruptive. Moreover, certain valuable privileges, for example, S Corporation status, can be forfeited by the wrong transfer.

Well-drafted charter provisions set out a first option on all proposed transfers, whether voluntary or involuntary and including insolvency, divorce, incompetence, and death. The list should be specific and comprehensive since courts may construe any restrictions on alienability narrowly. The provisions usually contemplate a repurchase by the company (if the company so elects) at either a price fixed in advance, at a price varying according to a formula (i.e., book value or an earnings multiple), at a price that matches the price offered by a third party or at "fair value." There are a number of drafting points to keep in mind; for example, whether the first option applies to pledges (when stock is technically transferred, albeit only as collateral); how "fair value" is established in the case of disputes (by arbitrators picked at the time of

[23]Unless the provision is in the charter, it is not clear that a transferee of unlegended certificates who does not consent or have actual notice of the restriction will be bound. Haynsworth, *supra* Ch. 3, n. 9, at § 5.04(b)(2). *See also* Rohrlich, *Organizing Corporate and Other Business Enterprises* § 2A.07–.09 (5th ed. 1986).

[24]There is some authority for the proposition that an absolute prohibition on transfers may be enforceable, if the issuer's consent to a request for transfer cannot be "unreasonably withheld." Del. Code Ann. tit. 8, § 202(c) (1983 & Supp. 1986); Haysnworth, *supra* Ch. 3 n. 9, at § 504(b). Needless to say, absolute restrictions, particularly those restricting transfers to anyone in the world, are not favored. The Revised Model Act permits consent restrictions that are "not manifestly unreasonable." § 6.27. Obviously, a restriction limited to avoiding the loss of favorable tax status or an exemption under the securities laws so qualifies. One must keep in mind that a first option restriction which gives the optionee a lengthy period in which to make up its mind constitutes an absolute restraint absent the existence of an unusually patient third-party buyer.

the disagreement, by named experts such as the company's accountants); whether the party seeking the transfer, if also a director, may vote in favor or against the company's election to exercise its option;[25] and what sanctions (loss of dividends and voting rights) may be imposed and enforced if the shares are mistakenly transferred against the restriction.[26] Often there are permitted groups—for example, family members[27] and trusts, related corporations—among which shares can be transferred without triggering the option, assuming the transferee independently accepts the restriction.

First option restrictions should collapse by their own terms upon the pendency of an initial public offering, since the underwriters and the purchasing public will brook no such encumbrance on the liquidity of the public shares. Restrictions of this nature are to be differentiated from so-called "investment letter" restrictions,[28] which evidence the illiquidity of unregistered shares and "buy–sell" restrictions designed to recapture stock when an employee terminates.[29] Charter provisions respecting first refusal restraints should be compared with similar provisions found in the Stockholders Agreement relating to the rights of other shareholders to a preview of any proposed sales.[30] Sometimes first option restrictions are exercisable by the corporation and, if it elects to pass, the restrictions segue to the stockholders.

Finally, it should be noted that the discussion of transfer restrictions in the venture capital context deals with restrictions to which the stockholders have agreed, at least constructively, when they bought stock in corporations with such restrictions in place. An entirely different set of considerations is involved in attempts by management of besieged public companies to impose ex post facto restrictions on publicly held shares so as to disenfranchise intruders.[31]

[25]For a case upholding interested party voting, *see Kentucky Package Store Inc. v. Checani* 331 Mass. 125, 117 N.E. 2d 139 (1954).

[26]*See* 1 Balotti & Finkelstein, *The Delaware Law of Corporations and Business Organizations* § 6.10 (1986).

[27]The question of who is a family member can be difficult. The Internal Revenue Code defines the issue variously. *Compare* I.R.C. § 267(c)(4) with § 318(a)(1).

[28]*See* Ch. 8, § 8.11.

[29]*See* Ch. 10, § 10.3(k).

[30]*See* Ch. 10, § 10.2.

[31]*See, e.g., Joseph E. Seagram & Sons Inc. v. Conoco, Inc.* 519 F.Supp 506 (D. Del. 1981), striking down restrictions imposed ex post facto on outstanding shares. Some of the state antitakeover statutes, post the Supreme Court's decision in the *Mite* case, *Edgar v. Mite Corp.*, 457 U.S. 624 (1982), are of this flavor, so-called "control share" statues which insist on a disinterested shareholder vote in the face of an impending change of control. The court has recently upheld the Indiana "control share" scheme. *C.T.S. Corp. v. Dynamics Corp. of Am.* 55 U.S.L.W. 4478 (April 21, 1987). For issuers contemplating an IPO, there may be merit in electing incorporation in a state which has a "control share" system similar to Indiana's since it appears that the Indiana system will chill, albeit not absolutely prevent, unwanted takeovers.

§4.10 PREFERRED STOCK PROVISIONS

The typical statute requires that the rights and privileges of each class of stock be set out in the charter,[32] meaning and including the preferred stock agreement, *unless* authority is delegated to the board of directors to fix the terms of the preferred stock on such basis as the board shall deem appropriate at the time of issuance, thereby creating so-called "blank check preferred." Practitioners have generally elected to leave the details of the preferred stock to the directors, the exact drafting to take place when the occasion arises to issue the stock.[33] Blank check preferred has acquired a pejorative gloss recently since it has become significant in the public corporation arena as an antitakeover (or "shark repellant") provision.[34] Nonetheless, it remains convenient for most start-ups to pursue the less cumbersome course: let the directors fix the terms. If the investors want a say in fixing the terms of the preferred stock to be issued in the future, the thought is that they should so provide by agreement.[35]

§4.11 CUMULATIVE VOTING AND PRE-EMPTIVE RIGHTS

Cumulative voting[36] is a method of preserving minority representation on the board by allowing any shareholder to accumulate the votes that he would otherwise have to cast for a panel of directors and "bullet" them for a fewer number of directors—one, for example—in order to ensure the presence of his nominee(s) on the board. Thus, if a company has 1,000 shares outstanding and minority shareholder Smith owns 100 shares, Smith can take advantage of cumulative voting provisions in the charter to ensure his own election to the board, assuming that a panel of 10 or more directors is standing for election. Smith has the option of casting his 100 shares for each of the 10 nominees or casting 1,000 votes (his shares times the number of directors to be elected) for

[32]Del. Code Ann. tit. 8, § 102(a)(4) (1983 & Supp. 1986).

[33]There are dissenters from that view, lawyers who feel, for example, that a given state statute, while authorizing the directors to create the preferred in the first instance, is less than specific on the directors' power to amend the preferred stock agreement once in place. *See* Ch. 13, § 13.4.

[34]Because of the statutory requirement that certain major corporate events, such as mergers, be acted on by a separate vote of each class, "blank check preferred" has been seized on by ingenious counsel as a way of intercepting a hostile raider's ability to merge or sell assets once the raid is complete. An entire class of preferred can be issued to one individual, for example, who would then, theoretically, retain a veto power over any merger.

[35]The substantive provisions of the preferred stock agreement are discussed in Ch. 13, § 13.4,5, and 6.

[36]*See* Del. Code Ann. tit. 8, § 214 (1983 & Supp. 1986); N.Y. Bus. Corp. Law § 618 (McKinney 1986); Cal. Corp. Code § 708 (West 1977 & Supp. 1987).

one nominee—that is, himself. The opposition will have 9,000 votes to split up as they see fit among 10 directors, but, with Smith having 1,000 votes, it is obvious that he cannot be knocked off a 10-person slate.[37] Cumulative voting is a clumsy way of ensuring board representation because it depends on the accidental fallout of numbers of shares, which can change over time, versus the number of directors standing for election, a number which can also be changed by the parties in control; it is not, accordingly, a popular charter provision,[38] the better practice being to organize the allocation of board seats in a contract among the shareholders, that is, the Stock Purchase Agreement.

Similarly, pre-emptive rights as such are designated by the statute as proper charter provisions since they are part of the "rights and privileges" of a given class of stock. Such rights mean what the name implies—that the existing shareholders of the company have a right to subscribe to any new issuance of shares in such proportions as will maintain their equity position in the company before shares may be offered outside of the existing shareholder group. Again, rights in the nature of pre-emptive rights are often bargained for by investors but usually not as a charter provision.[39] Once inserted in the charter, they can only be eliminated, as they must when an initial public offering occurs, by a vote of the shareholders—indeed, by a vote of each class of shareholders affected. The investors bargaining for pre-emptive rights usually want to be able to trigger or waive those rights on their own, so that the Stock Purchase Agreement is the more likely home for provisions of this nature. Planners should be careful to inspect the corpo-

[37]There are various methods for calculating how one maximizes one's outcome in a cumulative voting situation. Mills, "Mathematics of Cumulative Voting," 1968 *Duke L.J.* 28; *See* Skinner, "Understanding Cumulative Voting," 25 *Prac. Law.* 79 (Mar. 1979). The usual formula is as follows:

$X = s$ number of shares needed to elect a given number of directors
$Y = s$ total number of shares outstanding
$N' = s$ number of directors one desires to elect
$N = s$ number of directors to be elected

The formula is:

$$X = \frac{Y \times N' \text{ plus } 1}{N \text{ plus } 1}$$

This formula is taken from a research study prepared at the Harvard Business School. Williams, *Cumulative Voting for Directors* (1951).

[38]Cumulative voting is required in the charters of national banks. 12 U.S.C. § 61. Organizers of small banks can attest to the fact that some real screwballs have been able, using cumulative voting, to find their way onto the board of a national bank. The solution is to form a holding company, since cumulative voting is not required by the Bank Holding Company Act.

[39]Some studies indicate that the removal of pre-emptive rights from the charter, on average, decreases shareholder wealth. Bhagat, "The Effect of Pre-Emptive Right Amendments on Shareholder Wealth," 12 *J. of Fin. Economics* 289, 308 (1983).

ration law of the domicile to ascertain whether the statute is of the "opt in"[40] or "opt out" variety; whether, if the charter is silent (i.e., the organizers do not make a conscious election), cumulative voting or preemptive rights are [are not] in effect. Silence is a choice; the trick is to make sure it is a conscious choice.[41]

§4.12 WHO ISSUES THE STOCK?

Usually, but not always, the board is empowered in the charter to issue all authorized but unissued common stock in its discretion; unless so expressly delegated, this power will be retained by the stockholders. A hold back of the power to issue stock is commonly specified by investors interested in residual controls but, again, the locus of the language is, more often than not, the Stock Purchase Agreement versus the charter, since the Agreement is easier to amend or cancel.

§4.13 INDEMNIFICATION

The Revised Model Act provides perhaps the most extensive and best considered provisions on indemnification by the corporation of directors and officers to be found in any codification.[42] Indemnification provisions may be drafted either in the charter or bylaws but one school of thought, to which this author subscribes, will place them in the charter so as to provide maximum dignity to often controversial provisions.[43] The ultimate "belt and suspenders" approach includes the practice of executing a contract between the corporation and each director, providing that the director has a specific contractual right to be indemnified.

The issues involved in drafting indemnification provisions are complex and significant, particularly since the ability of start-ups to attract first-class directors is inhibited by the universal unavailability of liability insurance at affordable prices. Indeed, the indemnification provisions in a significant sense set the statutory standard of conduct to

[40]The Revised Model Act provides that both pre-emptive rights (§ 6.30) and cumulative voting (§ 7.28) are out unless opted in.

[41]Under Delaware law, pre-emptive rights are of the "opt in" variety. Del. Code Ann. tit. 8, § 102(b)(3) (1983 & Supp. 1986).

[42]Revised Model Act §§ 8.50–8.58. *See generally* Bishop, *The Law of Corporate Officers and Directors—Indemnification and Insurance* (1981).

[43]The strongest possible route is to put the provisions in the charter *after* the corporation has outside shareholders so the directors can make the argument that independent shareholders (versus incorporators) have blessed the arrangement. *See* Brown & Davis, "Indemnification of Directors and Officers and Limitations on Director Liability," 18 *Ann. Inst. on Sec. Reg.* Vol. 2, 117, 139 (P.L.I. Course Handbook Series No. 544, 1986).

which directors are to be held, assuming the corporation is solvent; if a director is to be indemnified in every action he takes or omits unless he is ultimately adjudged "grossly negligent," then the standard has been established for directors: "Do what you want as long as your conduct is not grossly negligent (or worse)."

Few difficulties are presented if a director is sued and ultimately wins, that is, exonerated. Under any conjugation of the law of indemnification, that director is entitled to be made whole by the corporation for his reasonable expenses. The Revised Model Act[44] and the Delaware statute[45] provide for mandatory indemnification in such cases; unless the charter otherwise provides, the directors must be indemnified. However, most suits, particularly so-called "strike" suits (actions brought for purposes of badgering the corporation into paying legal fees), are settled prior to judgment; the company pays some modest amount on behalf of its directors but no admission or determination is made—other than the implicit force of a settlement[46]—that anyone has done anything wrong.

A further problem arises when the strike suit is brought in the name of the corporation, that is, a derivative action.[47] The theory of the derivative action is that the directors have violated their duties to the corporation—looted it, in the strongest case—and recovery should go

[44]Revised Model Act § 8.52.

[45]Del. Code Ann. tit. 8, § 145(c) (1983 & Supp. 1986). Two recent developments in the area of D&O (directors and officers) liability insurance are worthy of note. First, a number of large companies are setting up captive insurance entities to self-insure against liability. *See* Yeager, "Getting In On the Self-Insurance Trend," *Am. Lawyer* 14 (May, 1987). Secondly, when insurance does exist, coverage questions crop up when the suit is brought under the civil provisions of the increasingly popular RICO statute (Racketeer Influenced and Corrupt Organizations Act, 18 U.S.C. §§ 1961 *et seq.*) A RICO claim raises issues under policies which exclude coverage for "fraudulent" and "criminal" acts. *See generally, Directors' and Officers' Liability 1986: A Review of the Business Judgment Rule* at 349–56, 655–71 (P.L.I. Course Handbook Series No. 525, 1986) ("Directors' and Officers' Liability 1986").

[46]In order to obtain judicial approval of a settlement and payment of legal fees in a class action or derivative claim, it is often necessary for plaintiff's counsel to show that they have negotiated some benefit on behalf of the party—the corporation—footing the bill; hence, one finds a pro forma undertaking by the defendant directors not to do something for a brief period in the future (i.e., freeze out the minority), an act the directors do not plan to pursue anyway. *See* Haudek, "The Settlement and Dismissal of Stockholders' Action—Part II: The Settlement," 23 *SW. L.J.* 765, 783–785 (1969).

[47]On derivative actions against directors generally, *see* Block, Barton, & Radin, "The Business Judgment Rule: Application, Limitations and the Burden Of Proof," in *Directors' and Officers' Liability 1986 supra* n. 45 at 94. The authors discuss the power of the board of directors, acting through the device of a special litigation committee (a committee of disinterested directors), to dismiss derivative actions. *See also, Wolf v. Blair* 348 F.2d 994 (2d Cir.), *cert. denied,* 382 U.S. 941 (1965); Manning, "Reflections and Practical Tips on Life in the Boardroom After Van Gorkom," 41 *Bus. Law.* 1 (Nov. 1985): *Auerbach v. Bennett,* 47 N.Y.2d 619, 393 N.E. 2d 994, 419 N.Y.S. 2d 920 (1979); *Smith v. Van Gorkom* 488 A.2d 958 (Del. 1985).

to the corporation. (Strike suit counsel usually bring their complaints as either derivative or class actions, or both, so that the damages claimed—for the benefit of the corporation or all the shareholders as a class—are large enough to get someone's attention. Were counsel limited to claiming damages only on behalf of the shareholders they have recruited as plaintiffs, the damages would be trivial.) If a settlement is reached, the cash paid, over and above attorney's fees, goes to the corporate treasury; if the corporation pays that money out as indemnification, the process is circular.

Moreover, when a suit is filed and the directors scramble for counsel, fees mount rapidly; arguably, since there is always the possibility the directors will lose in a big way (judged liable for actual fraud, for instance), the company should hold off paying out any money until the outcome is known. On the other hand, good defense lawyers do not work for free; indeed, their fees could impoverish some directors and blackmail them into settling.

The SEC has further confused matters by expressing the view[48] that any indemnification of a director for expenses in settling a claim that the securities laws have been violated (an almost universally encountered claim in the pleadings, if only because it gets counsel into federal court where the activist judges lurk) is against public policy.

Outside the mandatory case—that is, the defendants win—the issues are touchy, particularly since those directors who authorize indemnification payments (usually those not initially sued) are naturally concerned about getting sued themselves by reason of that action.

The modern statutes (e.g., the Revised Model Act[49] and Delaware Statute[50]) take some of the heat off by dealing expressly with many of the problems. Thus, directors can advance to their defendant colleagues or themselves payments of legal fees and expenses against an undertaking to restore the same if found ultimately liable.[51] In a derivative action, directors can be reimbursed for amounts paid as expenses (i.e., plaintiff's counsel fees) but not for any cash paid to the corporation,[52] meaning that derivative actions (unless a policy of insurance is in force) are rarely settled for amounts in excess of counsel fees.

Since a settlement leaves the issue of culpability hanging in the air,

[48]*Globus v. Law Research Service Inc.*, 418 F.2d 1276 (2d Cir. 1969), *cert. denied* 397 U.S. 913 (1970) *Globus* involved a suit against an underwriter under § 11 of the '33 Act. *See generally* Block & Barton, "Securities Litigation: Contribution and Indemnification Under the Federal Securities Laws," 11 *Sec. Reg. L.J.* 351, 352–353 (Winter 1984). Indemnification of individuals adjudged liable under certain statutes, *e.g.*, the Foreign Corrupt Practices Act, is specifically outlawed. 15 U.S.C. §§ 78ff(c)(4), 78 dd–2(b)(4).

[49]Revised Model Bus. Act § 8.50 *et seq.*

[50]*See* Del. Code Ann. tit. 8, § 145 (1983 & Supp. 1986).

[51]Del. Code Ann. tit. 8, § 145(e) (1983 & Supp. 1986).

[52]*Id.* at § 145(b).

the statute sets out the test to be applied: a director's "good faith" and a "reasonable belief" that his actions were in, or not opposed to, the best interests of the corporation.[53] If the director is deemed to pass this test, then he may be indemnified; indeed, even if he does not settle and a court or jury holds him liable on some sort of negligence theory which does not undercut his good faith or the reasonableness of his belief.[54] If the director is found to have improperly received a personal benefit at the expense of the corporation, good faith is conclusively negated.[55]

The standard of conduct—for that is what it amounts to—has been significantly alleviated in Delaware by the legislature, presumably in an attempt to reverse the quixotic holding in the recent *Van Gorkom* case,[56] a Delaware Supreme Court opinion so harsh and unreasonable on the directors concerned that it threatened to end Delaware's near-monopoly as the state of preferred incorporation.[57] The basic amendment allows shareholders to limit director exposure by approving a specific clause in the articles of incorporation eliminating liability for breaches of fiduciary duty excepting only

> A breach of the duty of loyalty, for acts or omissions not in good faith or which involve intentional misconduct or a knowing violation of law, for an unlawful payment of dividends or unlawful stock purchases or redemptions, or for any transaction from which the director derived an improper personal benefit.[58]

Additional substantive changes made by the Delaware Legislature include: (1) deleting the requirement that the advancement of litigation expenses must be "as authorized by the board of directors in the specific case," thus permitting such authorization by a provision in the certif-

[53]*Id.* § 145(a).
[54]*Id.* at § 145(a).
[55]Compare new § 102(b)(7) of the Delaware Code, discussed *infra.*
[56]*Smith v. Van Gorkom, supra* n. 47.
[57]The Legislature did not expressly refer to the *Van Gorkom* decision. As expressed on the record, the Delaware amendments represent a

> legislative response to recent changes in the market for directors' liability insurance. Recent changes in that market . . . have threatened the quality and stability of the governance of Delaware corporations because directors have become unwilling, in many instances, to serve without the protection which such insurance provides and, in other instances, may be deterred by the unavailability of insurance from making entrepreneurial decisions.

Synopsis of Ch. 289, Laws of 1986 (Delaware). The Delaware amendments will, it can be predicted, result in plaintiff's counsel changing the pleadings to focus on violations of the duty of loyalty; it remains to be seen how successful that ploy will be. Brown & Davis, *supra* n. 43, at 151.
[58]Sen. Bill No. 533, amending Del. Code. Ann. tit. 8, § 145 (1983 & Supp. 1986).

icate of incorporation or bylaws and thereby taking the heat off the individual directors at the time; (2) providing that directors and officers are not obligated to repay an advancement of expenses unless there is a specific determination made that the director or officer is not entitled to indemnification; and (3) clarifying that the advancement of expenses may be provided for in a manner other than that provided for by the statute.[59]

For the planner, the issue is clear: insert into the articles or bylaws either a provision that goes at least as far as the statute, repeating and/or paraphrasing the statutory language, or an authorization of indemnification "to the fullest extent allowable by law." Since the statute in many states[60] does not by its terms exhaust the comfort which the charter or bylaws can provide, it may be advisable to conjure up additional instances where indemnification is authorized; on the other hand, it is hard to imagine many instances where the directors voting on the issue would want to go far beyond the statute.[61] In that connection, the procedure for voting indemnification is stylized: Independent directors (if there are any) vote on the advice of outside counsel[62] paid to deliver an opinion that (with the usual caveats protecting counsel) the payment is authorized.[63]

[59]Del. Code Ann. tit. 8, §§ 145(b)(e),(f), and (j) (1985 and 1966 Amendments).
[60]*E.g.*, Del. Code Ann. tit. 8, § 145(b)(e),(f), and (j) (1985 and 1966 Amendments). Presumably there is a limit beyond which a corporation cannot go, even in those states where the remedy is nonexclusive. *See* Sebring, "Recent Legislative Changes in the Law of Indemnification of Directors, Officers and Others," 23 *Bus. Law.* 95, 105 (Nov. 1967). Some state statutes provide that the statutory formulation is exclusive. Cal. Corp. Code § 317(g) (West 1977 & Supp. 1987). The New York statute requires notice be given to the shareholders when payment is made other than by court order or shareholder action. N.Y. Bus. Corp. Law § 726(c) (McKinney 1986).
[61]Possibilities, which would not appear to leave the directors voting for indemnification out on a limb, include: upgrading the "may indemnify" language in the statute to "must indemnify;" extending coverage to heirs and personal representatives and former directors and officers; express provision for partial indemnification (i.e., of expenses) where full indemnification (a judgment rendered in a derivative action) is not allowed; extending coverage to exotic types of expenses—i.e., counsel representing directors before a special investigating committee of the board; covering the costs of enforcing the indemnification rights themselves; and authorizing the corporation to secure its obligation with a letter of credit.
[62]The question whether counsel qualifies as "independent" for this purpose is discussed in Johnston, "Corporate Indemnification and Liability Insurance for Directors and Officers," 33 *Bus. Law.* 1993, 1998–99 (Apr. 1978).
[63]On the issues generally, *see* Block, Barton, & Radin, "Indemnification and Insurance of Corporate Officials," 13 *Sec. Reg. L.J.* 239 (Fall 1985); Knepper, *Liability of Corporate Officers and Directors* (2d. ed. 1973); Schaeftler, *The Liabilities of Office: Indemnification and Insurance of Officers and Directors* (1976).

§4.14 INTERESTED DIRECTORS

The question whether and when a director may become a party to transaction between himself and the corporation can be significant in a start-up; often the directors or their affiliates are the only customers the start-up may have for a particular good or service and directors are traditionally the first (sometimes exclusive) source of equity and debt capital. Transactions between directors and the corporation involve examination of the statute, which ordinarily provides (or purports to provide) a safe harbor; that is to say, such transactions are not "voidable" solely on conflict of interest grounds if certain requisites are met—in Delaware, if all the facts are disclosed *and* a disinterested majority of directors or stockholders approve *or* the transaction is "fair."[64] The problems raised by this language go well beyond the scope of the Text; the statute must be read in light of dozens of influential cases considering director liability in the context of the so-called "business judgment rule," fairness, fiduciary duties of directors, a director's duty of loyalty and other pregnant conceptions of equal generality.[65] For the planner, there is little reason to draft an overlap to the statutory language in jurisdictions such as Delaware, where the statute is explicit; if state law is silent, the charter should contain provisions—presumably modeled after Delaware's—which specifically authorize the start-up, if it so wishes, to do business with its insiders.

§4.15 BYLAWS

The typical corporation statute authorizes the directors or the stockholders (or the incorporators prior to the date stock is issued) to adopt bylaws.[66] These are usually canned documents which rephrase, and fill gaps in, the statutory rules of governance. They are equivalent, in a sense, to Roberts Rules of Order; they specify how meetings of directors and stockholders are called, what constitutes a quorum, what votes are necessary to adopt a motion. They set out such matters as the corporation's fiscal year, the time and place of the annual meeting, standing committees of the board and their powers, the duties of principal executive officers and, of course, how the bylaws are to be amended. In some closely held companies the scope of each executive's duties and powers may be the subject of intense negotiations; the bylaw provisions should be drafted to reflect the organizers' intent, consistent with the substantive provisions on this point in the Stockholders Agreement and/or

[64]Del. Code Ann. tit. 8, § 144(2)(1) & (3) (1983 & Supp. 1986).
[65]*See generally* the discussion in *Directors' and Officers' Liability 1986, supra* n. 45.
[66]Del. Code Ann. tit. 8, § 109 (1983 & Supp. 1986).

each officer's employment contract. It is embarrassing to find one description of the president's duties in that agreement, drafted after elaborate negotiations, and another in a boilerplate paragraph in the bylaws.

In the author's view, with which some practitioners differ, the bylaws are not, as a matter of good practice, the place in which important substantive matters are to be placed;[67] that privilege belongs to the charter or to agreements among the company and specific shareholders. The bylaws contain the nuts and bolts, procedural regulations which smooth the way for the company to operate. They are largely repetitive of the statute and can be amended by the directors without shareholder consent. The bylaws are not on the public record.

§4.16 OTHER ORGANIZATIONAL DOCUMENTS

(a) MINUTES OF FIRST MEETING

The minutes of the first meeting of directors are a significant organizational document. At that meeting a number of administrative details are taken care of: The forms of stock certificate and corporate seal are adopted; the initial stock issuances are authorized; bank resolutions are passed; special committees of the board, if any, are constituted and directors appointed to the same; and additional officers—that is, vice presidents, assistant treasurers—are appointed.

(b) STOCK BOOK

Of cardinal importance is the stock record book, since it tracks critical information: who owns what number of shares. Under Article 8 of the Uniform Commercial Code (UCC), in effect in all important commercial states, the issuance and transfer of shares is monitored by an institution known as a transfer agent.[68] For large, publicly held companies, the transfer agent is usually a bank or trust company, computerized and staffed to record millions of transactions a day. Start-up companies, dealing with a limited number of stockholders, act as their own transfer agents; they (or their counsel) maintain the stock record book themselves.

[67]To be sure, the bylaws may contain any provision "not inconsistent" with the charter relating to the corporation's "rights or powers" or the "rights or powers of its stockholders, directors, officers or employees." Del. Code Ann. tit. 8, § 109(b) (1983 & Supp. 1986). Nonetheless, the charter is the contract (albeit constructive) between and among the proprietors and other interested parties of the firm—the founding document, the Ark of the Covenant, as it were, and common sense indicates its provisions will carry more weight.

[68]U.C.C. § 8–401.

For some reason, the stock book is often the least carefully maintained of the important legal records, a troublesome slip since stock certificates, the counterpart record of outstanding shares, are often misplaced by the recipients, despite the fact that the Code requires a bond (usually in an amount equal to twice market value) to indemnify the company against damage in the event a stock certificate is lost. (In its discretion, the issuer may waive a corporate surety and accept the issuer's individual indemnity,[69] the usual practice in closely held companies.) More importantly, when the need comes for counsel's opinion concerning the number of shares outstanding—as in connection with the sale of the company, a merger or an initial public offering—an enormous amount of reconstructive attention often has to be paid to the stock record book.

§4.17 STATE OF CORPORATE DOMICILE—DELAWARE OR SOMEWHERE ELSE?

If the corporate form is selected, the next issue is where the beast should be domiciled. Ordinarily one would minimize expense by incorporating the business in the state in which the business is to be conducted, thereby saving the cost of appointing an agent in, say, Delaware, the most popular state for those seeking a flag of convenience.[70] (There is rarely an income tax advantage to domiciling a business outside of its principal place of operations; the income of a business operated in Massachusetts will generally be subjected to the same Massachusetts income tax whether it is technically a Massachusetts or a Delaware corporation.)[71] Engaging a firm of professional representatives such as the Corporation Trust Company to act as resident agent in Delaware entails a modest, but not so trivial, fee each year. On the other hand, the Delaware corporate statute is well drafted and contains few of the anomalies one finds, on occasion, in the general corporation laws of certain other states. Moreover, the Delaware state secretary's office is well staffed and Delaware bureaucrats process papers at a high rate of speed.[72] It is often frus-

[69]UCC § 8–405(2)(b) (1978). *See generally* Israels & Guttman, *Modern Securities Transfers* § 13.09 (1967).

[70]There is a technical reason for incorporating in one's home state. Rule 147 of the '33 Act, fleshing out the so-called "intrastate exemption," allows the exemption for shares issued to the residents of one state if all the purchasers *and the issuer* are residents of that state. The issuer is a resident of the state in which it is incorporated. Rule 147(4)(c)(1)(i). *See* Ch. 7, § 7.14.

[71]*See generally,* Hellerstein, *State and Local Taxation* (4th ed. 1978); Belford, *State and Local Taxation and Finance in a Nutshell* (1985).

[72]Nearly 60% of the companies on the NYSE are incorporated in Delaware. Delaware gives same-day incorporation service on payment of a $100 fee. "Business Bulletin," *Wall St. J.*, Dec. 1986, at 1.

trating to attempt to merge two New York corporations because the personnel in the secretary of state's office get around to clearing the paperwork only in their own sweet time. Further, Delaware maintains a separate court system—the Court of Chancery[73]—to adjudicate (without the nuisance, for corporate practitioners anyway, of jury trials) issues involving the structure and governance of domestic corporations. Moreover, a modern statute such as Delaware's is generally permissive, the glitches which can frustrate counsel attempting to close on a financing having been ironed out.[74] For example:

(i) The Delaware statute expressly acknowledges the validity of agreements among stockholders, signed by less than all the stockholders, pursuant to which voting arrangements superseding the statutory scheme—one share, one vote—are explicitly authorized.[75] In some jurisdictions, such agreements are suspect, in which event it is necessary to go to the trouble of creating a voting trust, segregating stock into special classes or wrestling with the murky principles of a proxy "coupled with an interest."

(ii) Delaware law expressly contemplates the merger of Delaware corporations into corporations organized under the law of other jurisdictions, a curious omission for many years in some states, for example, Massachusetts.[76]

(iii) Delaware permits shareholder action without the necessity of a meeting upon the execution of signed consents by a majority of the shares outstanding.[77]

(iv) The Delaware statute expressly sets out the criteria for validating transactions when a majority of the board of directors are "interested,"[78] a common occurrence when an early-stage company does business with its own shareholders and directors.

(v) Responding to the explosion in so-called "strike suits" brought only for the purpose of rewarding plaintiff's counsel, Delaware

[73]Unlike its namesake in *Bleak House*, the Court of Chancery acts with dispatch, hearing cases without a jury. *See generally* Arsht, "How and Why of Incorporation in Delaware," 3 *Del. J. Corp. L.* 163 (Winter 1978); Balotti & Finkelstein, *The Delaware Law of Corporations and Business Organizations* (1986).

[74]The special provisions of Delaware law applicable solely to companies specifically organized as close corporations, Del. Code Ann. tit. 8, §§ 341–356 (1983 & Supp. 1986), are set out in § 4.7 *supra*.

[75]Del. Code Ann. tit. 8, § 218(2) (1983 & Supp. 1986).

[76]Del. Code Ann. tit. 8, § 252 (1983 & Supp. 1986).

[77]Del. Code Ann. tit. 8, § 228 (1983 & Supp. 1986). This section can have dramatic effect in contests for corporate control. Instead of publicly soliciting proxies for votes to be cast at a shareholder's meeting, an insurgent group can simply inform the board that a majority of the shareholders have signed consents and the directors are ousted.

[78]Del. Code Ann. tit. 8, § 144 (1983 & Supp. 1986). *See supra* § 4.14.

has, as discussed in § 4.13, recently adopted a state-of-the-art provision immunizing directors from liability unless some egregious breach of duty, principally involving personal profit, is proven.

(vi) Law firms around the country are willing to give opinions on matters involving Delaware law because of the general familiarity of the corporate bar with the Delaware statute and the cases interpreting it. The ability of counsel to opine on an issue is no trivial matter. Without the requisite opinion of counsel, no public stock offering or merger will go forward. Loan agreements routinely require comfort from the company's counsel in the form of opinions. Incorporating in Delaware gives the founder assurances that counsel will be able to render and/or appraise the necessary opinions to underwriters, lenders, merger partners, and others to enable business aims to be accomplished.

(vii) Delaware allows a corporation to stagger the terms of its directors (only one-third standing for election in any year)[79] and impose supermajorities, a routine antitakeover measure which some states, California for example, do not countenance.[80] In this connection, however, it remains to be seen whether Delaware will adopt the ultimate in antitakeover provisions, a "control share" statute along the lines of the Indiana statute recently upheld by the United States Supreme Court.[81] If Delaware does not follow suit, it may be that issuers sensitive to the ultimate possibility of hostile takeovers will prefer an alternative domicile.

The foregoing is not designed as an uncritical hymn of praise in favor of Delaware incorporation. Other states are conforming to advanced notions of corporate practice and some—for example, Maryland in the area of franchise taxes—are actually to be preferred on some issues. However, Delaware is the rod against which other possibilities should be measured.

[79]Del. Code Ann. tit. 8, § 141(d) (1983 & Supp. 1986).

[80]California has created a special category of corporation labeled "pseudoforeign," subjected by § 2115 of the California Corporation Code to a variety of provisions of domestic law, among the more important of which are those relating to the election and removal of directors, cumulative voting, prohibition of classified boards of directors, standards of liability and indemnification of directors, distributions, dividends and repurchases of shares, shareholder meetings, approval of certain corporate transactions, dissenters' and appraisal rights and inspection of corporate records.

A foreign corporation is subject to § 2115 if the average of its property "factor," payroll "factor," and sales "factor" (as such terms are defined in the California Revenue and Taxation Code) is more than 50% during its last full income year and if more than one-half of its outstanding voting securities are held of record by persons having addresses in California.

[81]*C.T.S. Corp. v. Dynamics Corp. of Am., supra* n. 31. As the text goes to print, it appears Delaware will adopt such a statute.

Five

Selected Tax Issues Involved in Organizing the Corporation

Even more critical than the corporate law elections outlined in Chapters 3 and 4, tax considerations play a crucial part in the elections made upon the commencement of a start-up business. Tax concerns are ubiquitous in any financial environment but mistakes made upon initial organization often cannot be remedied adequately; the opportunities are forever lost. This chapter is oriented toward tax planners: lawyers and accountants. However, §§ 5.1(a) and (b) and § 5.2 should be of particular interest to all parties.

§5.1 ORGANIZATIONAL ISSUES

For purposes of this discussion, it is assumed that the corporate form has been elected. To understand fully the intricacies of those provisions of the Internal Revenue Code impacting various aspects of corporate organization, one must appreciate that the federal government does not impose a wealth tax on individuals' intangible assets. State and local jurisdictions tax property—real and personal—on an annual basis and both the federal and state government levy an ad valorem (measured by the value of the asset) tax on the estates of well-off decedents. However, at the federal level and in most states, paper wealth—cash and securities—is not subject to an annual tax on dormant value and increases in an individual's wealth, without more, are not subject to a transaction tax while he is alive. Governments are not, however, sleepy. They want to take a portion of the individuals' increases in wealth—to share in their good fortune so to speak—but the governments have generally restricted themselves to assessing tax only upon the occurrence of certain events. It is thought easier to establish the amount of the increase, and therefore tax it, by focusing on transfers—the passage of assets from one hand, or form, to another. In organizing a corporation, therefore, the first rule is to circumvent taxable events: transfers which the Code (and state law)[1] recognize as an occasion for asserting a tax. If a taxable event is unavoidable, the second rule is to eliminate or avoid gain or, if the circumstances so warrant, to establish a loss.

Incorporation involves several transfers which might occasion tax. Thus, the organizing corporation typically issues stock in exchange for cash, property, or in some cases, expressly for services.[2] The issuance of equity securities does not create income to the corporation. On the other hand, the recipient of the stock is, potentially at least, taxable on any gain resulting from the exchange. However, the recipient usually avoids tax, for a variety of reasons. Thus, payment for shares in cash, and only in cash, does not trigger a tax because no gain is realized when one pays cash; the taxpayer's "basis" for tax purposes in cash is always equal to the cash paid. Similarly, the receipt of stock worth $100 for property with a tax "basis" ("basis" being a term of art with a structured meaning in the tax law) of $100 does not involve gain or loss. The possibility of exposure occurs, therefore, upon the issuance of stock: (i) in exchange for appreciated property; and/or, (ii) in payment for past or future services (in those states where such services are eligible consideration for stock issuance), including occasions upon which the IRS recharacterizes a stock-for-"property" transaction as in fact stock-for-services.[3]

(a) SECTION 1244

Section 1244 of the Code, which allows stockholders to deduct losses from the sale of stock in "small business corporations" as ordinary

[1] *See generally* the "Basis Rules of General Application," I.R.C. §§ 1011–1 24.

[2] In many States, it is not legal to issue stock expressly in consideration of services to be rendered. Cal. Corp. Code § 409(a)(1) (West 1977 & Supp. 1987).

[3] *See infra* § 5.1(b).

(versus capital) losses, remains on the books. Indeed, the importance of § 1244 continues despite the elimination of the distinction in rates of tax between capital gains and ordinary income, the reason being that § 1244 losses are not losses from "passive activity" and, therefore, can be set against portfolio income.[4]

Generally, § 1244 applies to common stock acquired in an early round (the first $1 million in financing) by an individual or individual partner in a partnership directly from the issuer (including an S Corporation) for cash or property. The maximum amount which can be claimed as an ordinary loss (versus a capital loss) is $50,000, or $100,000 in the case of a husband and wife filing jointly.[5] The most interesting issue for planners of a start-up corporation (an often overlooked question because of the amounts involved) is who gets the benefit of the deduction. The statute no longer requires an affirmative election by the issuer—if the shoe fits, the loss is deductible—but the issuer is only a small business corporation as long as the cash or property paid for its stock does not exceed $1 million.[6] What happens in a $2 million financing? Which shareholders get § 1244 treatment? A careful planner will negotiate this issue explicitly, providing in the Stock Purchase Agreement how the deduction is to be allocated by specifying which shares were bought while the financing was still less than $1 million.

(b) STOCK FOR APPRECIATED PROPERTY—SECTION 351

This section postpones gain or loss on the contribution of appreciated property to a corporation[7] in exchange for stock or securities,[8] assuming certain rules are followed. Note that, although § 351 is thought of principally in connection with organization of unseasoned start-ups, in fact

[4]I.R.C. § 469(e)(1).

[5]I.R.C. § 1244(b)(1) & (2).

[6]I.R.C. § 1244(c)(3)(A).

[7]I.R.C. § 351(a). All corporations are "corporations" for this purpose except, it appears, "personal service corporations" within the meaning of § 269A of the Code; at least the I.R.S. will not rule on transactions involving such entities. Rev. Proc. 83–59, 1983—2 C.B. 575.

[8]"Stock" eligible for § 351 treatment can be voting or nonvoting, common or preferred but warrants are not considered stock. Treas. Regs. § 1.351–1(a)(1). "Securities" are generally considered by the Service to include long-term debt instruments—at least five years and preferably 10 years maturity. The receipt of "securities" tax-free in § 351 transactions is "ripe for legislative change." *Id.* at 30. The problem is that § 351 is designed to govern contributions to capital; it is not meant to sanitize a disguised *sale* of appreciated property, as when John Smith cooks up a scheme with Jim Brown whereby Smith contributes appreciated property to Newco for a little stock and a large short-term note, Brown puts up cash for a lot of stock in Newco, Newco pays the note and Smith has in effect sold the property to Brown tax-free.

the issuer can be newly organized or pre-existing when the stock issuance occurs; it can be any size, have an unlimited number of shareholders pre- and postfinancing and issue as many classes of stock as the situation warrants. The principle of postponing tax is not dependent on the resultant corporation being small or uncomplicated. The rule of § 351 is that, immediately after the financing, the investors who contribute property and/or cash in exchange for stock or securities are in control[9]; that is, they own at least 80% of the issuer's combined voting power (all classes of voting stock) and 80% of each class of nonvoting stock. If such is the case (and the property is not subject to liabilities in excess of its basis)[10], no gain will be recognized on any appreciated property so transferred. And, according to the usual rules governing tax-postponed transactions, the tax basis of that property in the hands of the corporation will be "carried over" from the basis of the contributor.[11]

Note some of the things § 351 *does not* do. It does not solve the "cheap stock" problem: when a founder, employee, consultant, et al., is receiving stock in exchange for past or future services and wants to avoid tax.[12] In fact, if one of the stock buyers is paying in services (past or future)[13] and getting back more than 20% of the issuer's voting power, the entire transaction will be disqualified, much to the distress of the individual(s) in the buying syndicate putting up appreciated property.

If A and B have already organized Newco and Founder X wants subsequently to exchange his secret process for stock, the requirement is either that Founder X get 80% or that A and B join with Founder X in the second round and the three of them own over 80%. This last transaction is tricky since the I.R.S. is sensitive to pre-existing shareholders

[9]The definition of "control" is borrowed from I.R.C. § 368(c).

[10]*See* I.R.C. § 357(c)(1), providing that the excess of liabilities assumed over basis will be recognized as gain.

[11]I.R.C. § 362(a). If a going business is being incorporated, there may be special tax problems. Under the doctrine of *Lucas, Comm'r v. Earl,* 281 U.S. 111 (1930), receivables may provoke tax if the transferor was a cash basis taxpayer and the receivables were created for services. *See* Bittker & Eustice, *Federal Income Taxation of Corporations and Shareholders* ¶ 3.17 (4th ed. 1979). Rev. Proc. 83–59, 1983–2 C.B. 575, an elaborate checklist which must be followed in requesting a § 351 ruling, requires a representation regarding "unreported income," such as accounts receivable or commissions due. In effect, the representation must state that the transferor did not accumulate receivables or make an extraordinary payment of payables in anticipation of the transaction and that the transferee will report the items which but for the transfer would have resulted in income to the transferor as ordinary income. Thus there is no blanket prohibition against the transfer of receivables. Some practitioners recommend that the existing business pay down as many liabilities as possible prior to incorporation if there is any risk the transferor corporation cannot deduct the payments when made. *See* Painter, *Business Planning: Problems and Materials* § 1.4 (2d ed. 1984); *101–4th T.M. Corporations—Pre-Organization Planning* (1984) (101–4th T.M.)

[12]Treas. Regs. § 1.351–1(a)(1)(i).

[13]I.R.C. § 351(d)(1).

coming into the syndicate only as "accommodation" investors, for purposes of meeting the § 351 test.[14] The problem is not beyond solution, however. As stated, the founder with the secret process is the classic first-round investor; later rounds are usually sold for cash—there will be no need for § 351. Moreover, if A and B want to acquire an interest in Founder X's process in exchange for stock in their existing corporation, they can contribute their shares in that firm, along with Founder X contributing his process, to "New Newco," New Newco becoming the owner of the process plus 100% of the outstanding shares of the existing firm. The risk, of course, is that the I.R.S. may unbundle and rebundle the transaction under either the "step transaction"[15] or "sham transaction"[16] doctrines.

The more significant question is implicit in the foregoing discussion. When is the founder's secret process "property" for purposes of § 351 and when is it "services," occasioning tax to the founder and perhaps to other contributors of property relying on § 351 to shield their gain? The distinction is, again, a little bit like the opposing nature of light—both a particle and a wave at the same time; a secret process is "property"—it has an owner and can be sold, *and* it is a reflection, a result, of past services, capitalized labor. As Shakespeare has suggested, nomenclature is significant. Leaving literature in favor of the mundane provisions of the Code, Revenue Procedure 69–19[17] sets out the basic guidelines. Summarizing that complex document, the information should be legally protectible (i.e., at least a trade secret) and in fact adequate safeguards taken to guard the secret, "original, unique, and novel" (though not necessarily patentable) and not "developed especially [sic]" for the transferee. The information should not represent mere knowledge or efficiency resulting from skill or experience.[18] It is helpful in this regard if any future services to be rendered by the transferee to the issuer respecting the process are bought and paid for under a separate contract "negotiated at arm's length."[19]

[14]Treas. Regs. § 1.351–1(a)(1)(ii); ALI–ABA; *Corporate Tax Planning in the 80's* 33 (1986).
[15]*American Bantam Car Co. v. Comm'r* 11 T. C. 397 (1948). *aff'd per curiam* 177 F.2d 513 (3d Cir. 1949), *cert. denied* 399 U.S. 920 (1950). Other ways to meet this problem, with due regard to the "step transaction" issue, are collected in Painter, *Business Planning: Cases and Materials* 122 (1984).
[16]The leading case is *Gregory v. Helvering* 293 U.S. 465 (1935). The Code sections most often employed are § 482 (transactions between related corporations) and § 269 (corporate acquisitions).
[17]Rev. Proc. 69–19, 1969–2 C.B. 301. *See also* Rev. Proc. 74–36, 1974–2 C.B. 491. *See generally* Banoff, "Conversions of Services into Property Interests: Choice of Form of Business," 61 *Taxes* 844 (Dec. 1983).
[18]*See* Rev. Rul. 71–564, 1971–2 C.B. 179; Rev. Rul. 64–56, 1964–1 C.B. 1933; Treas. Regs. § 1.351–1(a)(2), Example 1.
[19]Rev. Proc. 69–19, 1969–2 C.B. 301, § 3.01.

(c) CHEAP STOCK TO EMPLOYEES AND PROMOTERS—THE "EAT 'EM ALL UP" PREFERRED STOCK APPROACH

Again to state a fundamental proposition, there is no available cash in an early-stage financing with which to pay federal and/or state income taxes. Consequently, anything that smacks of a taxable event is verboten. The norm, however, is that the founders will obtain their interests in the new entity in consideration of past services and/or the capitalized value of the founders' talents and services to be rendered; the promoters, if different from the founders, are obtaining stock for their organizational efforts. The omnipresent danger is that the I.R.S. will successfully assert the position that all or a portion of the stock issued to the founders has been, for tax purposes, issued for services and a current tax is payable. Since that position reflects the economic reality, it is dangerous.[20]

There are, however, three principal weapons on the side of the taxpayer.[21] First, as indicated, § 351 of the Code provides for nonrecognition of gain or loss upon the exchange of property for shares if the shareholders contributing cash or property are in "control" (meaning ownership of 80% of the stock) of the corporation after the transaction. The trick, within the bounds of reasonableness and good faith, is to argue that the founder's contribution is not "services" but intangible property—that is, a secret process or other proprietary information—because secret processes can be "property" under the Code."[22] The second, the "passage of time" approach, is described in the next succeeding section.

Thirdly, if the consideration paid by the founder cannot in good conscience be labeled "property," and the investors all come in together, then the inquiry turns to the value of the stock being issued. Assume the founder pays, as he always can, some small amount of cash: Is that cash sufficient to equal the "value" of the stock received so that no gain is recognizable? At first blush, if the founder pays 10¢ per share and the investors contemporaneously pay $1 per share, it looks as if the founder has made a bargain purchase and an element of taxable compensation has changed hands. However, the Internal Revenue Service has never challenged successfully the view that the issuance of shares with a liquidation preference—ordinarily labeled preferred stock—can "eat up" value in an amount equal to the preference, thereby reducing the com-

[20]The entire question of tax minimization for persons arguably providing services to corporations and partnerships in the process of organization is discussed in a helpful article, Banoff, "Conversions of Services into Property Interests: Choice of Form of Business," *Taxes* Dec. 1983, 844.

[21]The Treasury has, in turn, formidable weapons, i.e., § 61 (gross income includes income "from whatever source derived"), § 83 discussed *infra*, the "assignment of income" doctrine and § 482 (I.R.S. has power to reapportion income to reflect clearly the facts).

[22]*See supra* n. 17.

mon stock (the "cheap stock") to marginal value. Put another way, if the liquidation preference of the preferred is equal to the cash contributions of the parties contributing cash capital, then a balance sheet test immediately after organization suggests that the common is "worth" only the nominal consideration the founders have paid, thereby excluding any element that can be attributed to past or future services. A hypothetical balance sheet follows:

Assets	*Liabilities*	
Cash $10,100	....	–0–
	Shareholders' Equity	
	Preferred Stock (1,000 shares outstanding, $10 par, convertible into 1,000 shares of common stock)	$10,000
	Common Stock (1,000 shares outstanding, 10¢ par)	100
$10,000		$10,100

An uncritical examination of the balance sheet might suggest that 10¢ a share paid by the common would compare equitably—that is, no bargain purchases—with the $10 paid by the preferred, since the preferred appears superior to the common on the balance sheet in the full amount of the cash paid. Certainly, if the issuer were liquidated immediately after it was formed—that is, on the date the taxable event, if any, occurred—the common shareholders would get back just what they put in: 10¢ per share. Of course, since no one intends to liquidate the corporation either right away or, for that matter, ever (and, indeed, if it is liquidated, it is unlikely that either the common or the preferred will get anything), the liquidation value test is dependent on a contrary-to-fact convention, but nonetheless a convention that has stood the test of time in view of what appears to be the silent acquiescence of the Internal Revenue Service.

The power of the preferred to "eat up" value for tax purposes is enhanced to the extent the preferred shareholder owns additional superior rights, that is, senior as to dividends (of which there are usually none), special voting rights, registration rights, and the like. These rights are often significant to the cash investors in the early going and are helpful on the tax issue; from the founder's point of view, the fact that they fade away upon the exit date—the IPO for example—means he can be relatively indifferent. It could, of course, be argued that one must weight the common's value upwards because all the "upside" belongs to the common; however, making the preferred convertible, albeit at a price of $10 per share, means that the preferred has a chance to share in the "upside" as well. In short, ordinarily the cash investors take convertible preferred shares and the founder common (a choice which, parenthetically, excludes an election of S Corporation status).

The principal caveat has to do with excess. In the example quoted, the cash investor's payment per share is 100 times the amount of the founder's payment. Some practitioners, are uncomfortable with a spread that great. Others tend to take a more aggressive view.[23] The belt and suspenders technique is to combine the "eat 'em all up" preferred approach with the "passage of time," or *Bruce Berckmans's,* approach discussed in the next section.[24]

As indicated, it can be important to contributing shareholders other than the founder that the "eat 'em all up" approach work. To be sure, the biggest risk is to the taxpayer held to have received stock for services. However, any shareholder contributing appreciated property may be required to pay tax if the taxpayer deemed to have contributed services gets more than 20% of the resultant stock since, as stated, § 351 only works if the contributors of cash and property, not services, get 80% or more of the stock.

(d) STOCK FOR SERVICES—THE "PASSAGE OF TIME" APPROACH

The complementary device for allocating the founder his cheap stock tax-free involves organizing the start-up entity as soon as the founder starts to consider a maiden voyage. To the extent the founder receives his shares well prior to the first-round financing, the founder/taxpayer can argue that the passage of time and events accounts for the increase in value—10¢ for his stock versus $10 for the investors' shares.[25] The risk is that the I.R.S. will successfully argue "step transaction." However, that argument is vitiated if the financing was only a contingency when the founders' stock was issued, the moral of the story being that

[23]One experienced venture capital lawyer has suggested a 1:10 ratio is acceptable, although "higher risk start-ups may justify greater discounts." Aufmuth, "Selected Tax and Accounting Issues in Early and Mezzanine Financings, and Venture Capital Partnerships," *Venture Capital After The Tax Reform Act of 1986* 55, 84, (P.L.I. Course Handbook Series No. 422, 1987); *compare* Treas. Regs. § 1.83–5(c), Example 4, where the I.R.S. takes the view that book value, which is "ordinarily determinate," does not control where the parties expressly agree the common stock is issued for services.

[24]This issue should be viewed alongside the so-called *Sol Diamond* question—when a partnership issues a "carried" interest in profits to a manager—discussed in Ch. 20, § 20.10.

[25]This approach is sometimes labeled the "Bruce Berckmans" approach, after *Berckmans v. Comm'r,* 20 T.C.M. 458 (1961). One commentator makes the point that the failure to pay "reasonable" salaries to founder/employees weakens their case that stock was not awarded for services. Martin, "Raising Capital for a Closely Held Company," 43 *N.Y.U. Inst. Fed. Tax'n* § 8.06 [2](b) (1985).

it usually does not cost anything to organize the start-up as early as possible and may provide substantial tax comfort.

The lesson, in sum, signaled by the discussion in this and the previous section is that the early bird catches the worm. Once the first-round financing has occurred, the dimension of the "cheap stock" issue changes. It is considerably dicier to contend that the preferred "eats up" value when common shares have traded in the interim or otherwise been priced in arms-length transactions. The planning process must shift to the arena of executive compensation, that is, stock equivalents, stock options, restricted stock bought with borrowed company funds, and so forth. (The importance of the question whether the employee shares are issued at less than fair market value is not confined to the tax arena. Bargain stock will create compensation expense on the company's books, impacting earnings as the discussion in Chapter 11 points out in greater detail.)

§5.2 SECTION 83 AND STOCK SUBJECT TO "VESTING"

Section 83(a) of the Internal Revenue Code[26] states that if "property" is issued "in connection with the performance of services,"[27] the difference between the "fair value" of, and the amount paid by the recipient for, the property—usually stock—is taxable to the recipient (and deductible by the corporation) as additional compensation as of the first date forfeiture restraints (if any) lapse, value being calculated without regard to restrictions other than those which by their terms never lapse.[28] If an employee is buying stock at a bargain and there are no "substantial" forfeiture risks (other than those which will never lapse) attached, then the impact of § 83 is relatively simple—he pays tax on the bargain element upon receipt.

Section 83 becomes of cardinal importance in venture financings in which employees are acquiring "restricted" stock, meaning stock sub-

[26]At first blush, section 83(a)(1) appears to say that tax is postponed in an instance where a restraint on alienation *not* accompanied by a risk of forfeiture lapses. However, the import of the section (*see* § 83(c)(2)) is that both nontransferability *and* risk of forfeiture must combine if the tax is to be postponed. If there is no restraint on transferability, as a practical matter the risk of forfeiture is nugatory; it can be defeated simply by selling the stock. And if there is no risk of forfeiture, there is no reason to postpone the tax. *See, T.M. 384 Restricted Property Section 83* (1982) (T.M. 384).

[27]A recent case of great interest to practitioners held that a shareholder/employee purchasing stock at its fair value was, nonetheless, a transferee of property "in connection with" the performance of services. *Alves v. Comm'r* 79 T.C. 864 (1982), *aff'd*, 734 F.2d 478 (9th Cir. 1984).

[28]As the statutory source for imposing tax on the employee, § 83(a) overlaps with § 61 (definition of gross income). See Banoff, *supra* n. 20, at 850.

ject to contractual restraints on transferability and risks of "forfeiture." Despite the fact that "restricted" stock (in the sense of nonvested stock) can be issued at any time during a corporation's lifetime, the issue is discussed in this chapter since it routinely arises on corporate organization.[29]

The purpose of vesting restrictions is to tie footloose employees to the corporation with "golden handcuffs." Typically, an employee will be allowed to purchase at bargain prices shares of stock subject to a right in the company to buy them back at the employee's nominal cost if the employee prematurely terminates his employment for reasons other than death or disability. Thus, a 5-year "vesting" restriction will typically provide that one-fifth of the shares issued shall "vest" in each of the five years following the employee's receipt of stock; that is, they are no longer repurchasable by the corporation at cost. The vesting constraint goes hand in hand with an absolute, albeit limited in time, restraint on alienation; the employee cannot dispose of shares to anyone until they are vested. Without that constraint (unless it is clear the forfeiture restriction is binding on transferees, in which case no one would buy at any sensible price), the forfeiture restriction would have little economic bite.[30] If the employee were originally issued 1,000 shares and left of his own accord in the third year following the employee's receipt of stock, the employee would own 400 shares outright and 600 shares would be repurchasable at the employee's cost.

Under § 83(a), an employee "lucking" into the opportunity to buy restricted, nonvested stock at a bargain has a problem. He receives a piece of paper he cannot readily sell; he incurs a contingent liability to pay at some later date tax on the difference between his nominal cost and the artificial "value" of that security as at a future time. For purposes of computing the tax, such value is calculated as if, contrary to fact, the employee could sell the shares into an auction market since "investment letter" restrictions do not count in computing value.[31] Arguably, therefore, the receipt of nonvested stock is no bargain because,

[29]Nonvested stock is most common in the early stages of a firm's existence because nontaxable bargain purchases of cheap stock are most easily defended before widespread trading ends the issuer's and employee's discretion to set prices for tax purposes. If an employee is paying full value for his or her shares or paying tax out of pocket on the bargain element (which amounts to almost the same thing), naturally it is difficult for the issuer to negotiate a vesting restriction, except perhaps a restriction to resell to the company at fair market value which, under Treas. Regs. § 1.83–3(c)(1), is not a "substantial" forfeiture restriction for purposes of § 83.

[30]On restraints on transfers of stock generally, *see* Ch. 4, § 4.9.

[31]"Investment letter," restrictions are not restrictions which "by [their] terms never lapse" and, therefore, are ignored in computing § 83(a) "value." I.R.C. § 83(a)(1). Restrictions which by their terms never lapse include a permanent right of first refusal and an agreement that the stock be sold back to the company whenever employment (as it someday must) terminates, in each case at some value other than fair market value.

when the tax becomes payable (i.e., the forfeiture risk lapses), the stock may be (indeed it is expected to be) highly "valuable" and the tax burdens accordingly aggravated. The potential "Catch-22" is apparent: A owes tax on a $10 stock which he cannot sell—perhaps at any price—and has no way of realizing the cash with which to pay the tax; he pays out of other assets and holds, expecting an IPO which never materializes, and his stock eventually becomes worthless.

The answer to the predicament lies in the provisions of § 83(b). As long as value can be measured when the shares are initially issued, the tax problem is not calamitous because the employee is receiving stock at a time when its value, however calculated, is low. Thus, if the early-round cash investors are coming in at $1 per share and the employee is paying 50¢ a share, at least the amount of the tax is calculable—50¢ times the number of shares sold, times the employee's effective rate of federal tax. (Indeed, if the cash investors buy preferred stock, then the employee may claim no tax is due.)[32] And, the privilege afforded by § 83(b) is that the taxpayer may make an election; that is, he may file, within 30 days after the stock has been originally purchased, notice of his choice to pay tax on the difference between the value of the stock received at that time and the amount actually paid for the stock. Once that tax is paid, then vesting restrictions become irrelevant. The stock may go to $100 per share when the employee finally vests with respect to the last share but no taxable event will occur.

It is important to keep in mind that the § 83(b) election is available, and should be made, even though the employee purchases shares at full value.[33] It is not, in other words, the fact that the employee is purchasing *cheap* stock but that he's purchasing stock *subject to a risk of forfeiture*, which casts the taxable event out into the future; it's usually true that such stock is cheap stock—else why would anyone agree to the forfeiture restrictions—but such need not always be the case. The virtue of the § 83(b) election is that it pulls that event back to the present day, when the gap between the employee's payment and the value of the stock is presumably at its narrowest.

Section 83 also obtains when an employee acquires restricted stock pursuant to a "nonqualified" stock option, an option which does not fit the rules in the Code governing "incentive stock options."[34] The tax on shares received under a nonqualified option is measurable at option

[32] *See* § 5.1(c) *supra*.

[33] *See Alves v. Comm'r, supra* n. 27. As the Text suggests, to pay "fair value" for § 83 purposes, one must actually pay more than current value because, contrary to common sense, "section 83 fair market value" does not admit of the dampening effects of lapse restrictions. *See* Martin, *supra* n. 25, at § 8.06 [2].

[34] *See* Ch. 11, § 11.3. Incentive stock options escape the ambit of § 83. I.R.C. § 83(e)(1).

exercise[35]; that is, before the stock is or can be sold to the public (unless it is registered for sale at the time of exercise). Accordingly, it may be an advantage to the optionee, if the option shares are still subject to a risk of forfeiture, to forgo the § 83(b) election; by so doing, he avoids a tax at a time when the stock may not be able to be sold advantageously. Any method of postponing tax (i.e., by suffering forfeiture restrictions) may be preferable, particularly since an IPO may occur in the interim and, thus, liquidity become obtainable under Rule 144. On the other hand, a dramatic increase in value between option exercise and sale can render that strategy a mistake.

(a) CONDITIONS TO SECTION 83

When drafting a complex employee stock restriction, one should study § 83 with care. The gloss on the statutory provisions is important.[36]

Thus, the concept of "transfer" entails "beneficial ownership" of the stock residing in the transferee; this is taken to imply that stock which is issued subject to a restriction requiring return of the stock upon an event that is "certain to occur" may be deemed never to have been "transferred," a potentially confusing proposition when one compares the concept of restrictions which never lapse.[37] Thus, assume stock worth $1 per share is sold to an employee for 10¢, subject to recapture at cost if he leaves his employment voluntarily within 5 years and in any event resalable only to the corporation at fair market value upon leaving the company's employ. When his employment terminates (an event bound to happen sometime), the transaction can be viewed in several lights. As stated, it can be argued that there never was any "transfer"[38]; the stock only serves a security for the issuer's promise to pay fair value some day and, thus, the interim forfeiture restriction (during the first 5 years) has no tax-postponing effect. If there is deemed to have been a transfer, the permanent restriction is a nonlapse restriction; however,

[35]Section 83 deals with "transfers" of property and the option stock is not transferred until the option is exercised. Treas. Regs. § 1.83–3(a)(2). The grant of the option itself is not taxable under § 83 if, as is usually the case, it lacks a "readily ascertainable fair market value." I.R.C. § 83(e)(3).

[36]The section does not apply to "unfunded and unsecured" promises to pay money in the future since the same are not "property," meaning that the most frequently encountered category of deferred compensation is unaffected. Treas. Regs. § 1.83–3(e). Payments pursuant to such promises are taxable only on receipt. Rev. Rul. 60–31, 1960–1 C.B. 194.

[37]Treas. Regs. § 1.83–3(a)(3).

[38]A transfer probably will be found even if the forfeiture event is certain if the employee stands to lose either his or her 10¢ per share or the bargain element in the stock when it was issued (90¢). *See T.M. 384, supra* n. 26, at A–10. It can be argued that there was a transfer, and therefore, (given the proper election) a tax is payable on the difference between: (i) 10¢ and, (ii) $1.00 (diminished perhaps, by the effect, if any, of the nonlapse restriction).

it can be argued that such restriction does not impact value for § 83 purposes because the price is set at fair market value.[39] Suppose the employer and employee elect to cause the permanent restriction to be mutually rescinded? What happens then? The Service may argue that the employee has received a taxable increase in value as of that time, based on his inability to establish, in the language of § 83(d)(2)(A), that the cancellation was "not compensatory." As with most Code sections, the thought experiments can go on forever.

There are other subsidiary issues which come up frequently and deserve special mention. For example, stock which is forfeitable because a noncompetition covenant is breached is presumed not to be subject to a substantial risk of forfeiture nor are stock grants conditioned on the issuer achieving certain performance goals.[40] A source of practical problems arises by dint of the fact that the employer gets a deduction when the employee incurs tax under § 83[41] *but only* if the employer withholds[42] under the FICA, FUTA, and Wage Withholding at the Source provisions of the Code.[43] Thus, the deduction can be lost if there are no payments from which to withhold; if, for example, the employee does not make the § 83(b) election and is no longer on the payroll when the forefeiture condition lapses. Further, it is an open question how § 83 interacts with a transfer of an interest in partnership profits. A so-called "carried" partnership interest in profits is often subject to vesting; if the partner withdraws prematurely, his interest is bought back at a penalty price. However, as discussed in Chapter 20, the question whether the receipt of an interest in partnership profits is a taxable event at all is unsettled in light of what one commentator has called the "mystery" about the extent to which the Service and the courts might apply the theory of the *Sol Diamond* decision,[44] the leading (and so far only) case for the proposition that a profits interest is "property" capable of triggering tax when transferred to someone expected to render services.[45] The norm is not to make the § 83(b) election when receiving a carried interest in partnership profits on the theory that such would be backsliding from the view that a carried interest is not a "transfer" of "property" "in connection with the performance of services."

[39]As stated *supra* n. 29, the obligation to return the stock at fair market value is not a "substantial" forfeiture condition at all since fair market value negates the idea of a forfeiture. Treas. Regs. § 1.83–3(c)(1). It is not clear that any nonlapse restriction other than one involving a "formula" price clause (*see* § 83(d)(1)) will impact value. *See T.M. 384, supra* n. 26, at A–37.

[40]Treas. Regs. § 1.83–3(c)(2).

[41]Treas. Regs. § 1.83–6(a)(1).

[42]Treas. Regs. § 1.83–6(a)(2).

[43]*T.M. 384, supra* n. 26, at 67.

[44]Willis, *Partnership Taxation* 49 (Supp. 1981)

[45]*See* the discussion of *Sol Diamond* at Ch. 20, § 20.10.

§5.3 DEDUCTIBILITY OF CERTAIN EXPENSES

Since it costs money to organize and operate Newco, the trick is to get the biggest tax "bang" for the bucks spent, meaning the largest and earliest recognition of losses so as to bank those losses to shelter future income upon the first possible occasion.

(a) START-UP EXPENSES

Technically, expenses associated with the early stages of Newco's life fall into three categories for tax purposes: expenses which can be currently deducted, expenses which can be capitalized and amortized in future periods, and expenses which are considered investments in the corporate franchise and deductible, if at all, when the corporation is liquidated.

Generally, as long as revenue-generating operations have commenced—that is, some money is coming in on the income side of the business—the "ordinary and necessary" expenses incurred "in carrying on" the business are deductible currently.[46] Current deductibility is supported by the common-sense notion that matching income, however slight, is at hand. Since accounting is, a priori, a game of matching income and expense in the appropriate period, the existence of current income legitimizes the recognition of current expense; the notion is that a business already exists.

"Start-up expenses," on the other hand, are expenses paid or incurred "in connection with"[47] creating a trade or business or investigating the creation of a trade or business. These are the costs of getting *into* business; such being the case, the theory is that they relate to periods going beyond the year of organization and, therefore, should be written off gradually. Section 195 of the Code says, first, that no deduction can be made for "start-up expenditures" and then allows an election to amortize over 60 months start-up expenditures incurred "in connection with . . . investigating . . . creating . . . an active trade or business" or engaging in activity "in anticipation of such activity becoming an active trade or business." Sixty months is an arbitrary period but, in

[46]The principal Code section is § 162 ("ordinary and necessary expenses paid or incurred . . . in carrying on any trade or business"); § 162 applies to both individuals and corporations. Section 212 governs an individual's "ordinary and necessary expenses paid or incurred . . . for the production of income. . . ." There is a significant difference between the two sections in that, under the Code as amended in 1986, expenses *not* incurred in carrying on a trade or business—i.e., § 212 expenses—are only deductible by an individual to the extent the aggregate of the same, plus other itemized deductions, exceeds 2% of adjusted gross income. I.R.C. §§ 62 and 67, as amended by TRA § 132.

[47]I.R.C. § 195(c).

fact, it comports nicely with the venture rule of thumb respecting the date for an exit—5 years from inception.[48] An overlapping but separate issue is the option in § 248 (and § 709(b)(1) in the case of partnerships) to amortize organizational expenses over 60 months. These are the legal, accounting, and other costs involved in actually organizing the corporation or partnership.

Finally, expenses incurred in issuing or selling stock or partnership interests—an alliquot share of the legal fees, sales commissions, printing costs—are neither deductible nor amortizable, the thinking being that the same are an investment in the franchise. These costs will only become deductible when the entity is liquidated. Since this is the least desirable result, counsel and placement agents should be sensitive to labels—invoices to the issuer should be broken out to isolate and minimize costs (assuming reasonable support can be found) associated directly with the issuance and sale of the securities.[49]

(b) RESEARCH AND EXPERIMENTAL EXPENSES

Certain expenses may be ineligible for immediate deduction because, as stated, they antedate income production. Others cannot be currently deducted because, by their nature, they should be capitalized and amortized over the life of the asset to which they are attached.[50] The basic rule is that research expenses are, without more, not deductible currently but are to be charged to capital.[51] An exception exists under § 174 of the Code, which allows current deduction of "research and experimental"[52] expenditures. The two thresholds for treatment under § 174 of particular interest are: (i) the expenditure must qualify under Treasury Regulations as "research or experimental;" and, (ii) it must be incurred "in connection with" the taxpayer's trade or business.[53] On the first issue, the dividing line is drawn between "routine" improvements of existing products versus real innovation. (Ironically, § 174 is often referred to as encompassing R&D costs; the critical distinction is R, standing for research, *versus* D, standing for postresearch development, not R&D.) In the computer software area, the distinction has

[48]*See* Ch. 12, § 12.3.

[49]Treas. Regs. § 1.248–1(b)(3); *see* 101–4th T.M. *supra* n. 47, at A–47; Van Dorn, "Deductions for Start Up Expenditures," Forum, Ch. 3, n. 15, at 27.

[50]Section 263 states that expenditures are not currently deductible *except* in the enumerated cases, including research and development expenditures deductible under § 174. Obviously, by negative implication, research and experimental expenditures *not* deductible under § 174 are not otherwise currently deductible.

[51]Treas. Regs. § 1.174–1 and § 1.263(a)–2(a).

[52]I.R.C. § 174(a)(1). At its option, the taxpayer may amortize research and experimental expenditures over five years. I.R.C. § 174(b)(1).

[53]I.R.C. § 174(b)(1)(A).

posed all sorts of problems, because the Service's position has vacillated on the issue whether application software is R or D. Certainly § 174 includes the costs of developing software which is so experimental that there is a significant risk it cannot be written. The reluctance of the Service to go beyond this point has been criticized; and, it appears the current view that software development costs generally may be expensed under § 174.[54]

The "in connection with" requirement is looser[55] than the requirement in section § 162 governing current deductibility generally; that is, that the expense be incurred "in carrying on" a trade or business. The deductibility of R&E expense is available, therefore, to enterprises "that are upcoming and about to reach the market;" there is no requirement that revenue actually be produced contemporaneously with incurrence of the expense. In that sense, the test is similar to that posed under § 195, where the same "in connection with" language occurs. It is important again to note that R&E expenses, absent § 174, would have to be capitalized, not because they occur in the start-up period, but because they are the *kind* of expense which cannot be deducted currently but must be capitalized and depreciated over the life of the property created or taken as a loss on abandonment.[56] (The current deductibility by *individuals* of R&E expenses under § 174, a common practice by partners in the R&D partnerships discussed in the next Section, has, as therein indicated, been severely impacted by the Tax Reform Act of 1986.)

§5.4 R&D PARTNERSHIPS—(AFTER THE TAX REFORM ACT OF 1986)

Much of the learning on § 174 has accrued in connection with so-called "R&D partnerships," a device widely popular in recent years as an off-balance-sheet method of supporting research with the use of tax-sub-

[54]Rev. Proc. 69–21, 1969–2 C.B. 303, establishes the basis for current expensing, and, albeit begrudgingly, the Service is sticking with that position. GCM 38 996 (6/18/83). It appears the regulations under § 174 do not supersede Rev. Proc. 69–21. *Internal Revenue News Release* I.R. 83–71, (Apr. 19, 1983). § 231(b) of the Tax Reform Act of 1986 (P.L. 99–514) amending I.R.C. § 30(d) (now designated as § 41), sets out specific rules concerning internal use software developed by the taxpayer for use in qualified research other than research into the development of the software used.

[55]I.R.C. § 41(d)(4)(E). The leading case is *Snow v. Comm'r* 416 U.S. 500 (1974), which held that § 174 "was enacted to 'encourage expenditures and experimentation.' " *Id.* at 504.

[56]I.R.C. § 263; *see Red Star Yeast & Prods. Co. v. Comm'r* 25 T.C. 321 (1955). If an "R&E" expense occurs in the start-up period and is not amortizable under § 174, it is not amortizable under § 195 because § 195 applies only to expenditures which, if paid or incurred in connection with carrying on a trade or business, would be currently deductible. I.R.C. § 195(c)(1)(B).

sidized financing. The scenario involves the establishment of an exogenous, free-standing limited partnership, the limited partners being individuals interested, first, in tax shelter and, secondly, a possible return in the form of capital gains at the conclusion of the partnership's research efforts. The R&D partnership is structured side by side with a research-hungry company, which might be early-stage but often is mature; the corporate entity (or an affiliate) usually acts as the general partner of the partnership and directs the research the partnership performs. The partnership usually winds up paying the corporate general partner or a subsidiary thereof to do the research. The company commissioning the research, sometimes called the sponsor, will agree at the end of the process to purchase the research results if successful. If the purchase price consists of stock in the sponsor, the partnership is known as an equity partnership; if cash, a royalty partnership. Prior to the Tax Reform Act of 1986, the limited partners enjoyed ordinary losses, at least up to their cost basis, while the research was being performed and capital gains when the research was bought or licensed.[57] Accordingly, at least the theory goes, the venture investors and the founder suffered less dilution. Apart from the tax advantages, a well-constructed R&D partnership constitutes off-balance-sheet financing for the sponsor, meaning that the undertaking by the sponsor to buy the research does not appear as a liability nor impact the income statement until paid.

R&D partnerships had a number of inherent problems which caused them, well prior to the 1986 Act, to fall into disfavor. Several issuers contemplating financings, particularly IPOs, found it very messy when they attempted to work themselves out of superannuated commitments made unthinkingly and overgenerously to the limited partners of an R&D partnership.[58] The Act's limitations on the deductibility of losses from passive activities is a major threat to the future of such partnerships but the even more crippling blow occurs in new Code § 56(b)(2)(A)(ii), which states, that for purposes of alternative minimum tax calculations for individuals, R&E expenditures are not deductible currently but are to be expensed over a 10-year period.

[57]In 1984, the Service indicated it would apply the "tax benefit" rule to the sale of the technology, arguing that a subsequent sale at capital gains rates was "fundamentally inconsistent" with the earlier ordinary loss. That position was later reversed. *See* Lischner, "Previously deducted R&E expenses not subject to tax benefit recapture, says I.R.S.," 64 *J. of Tax'n* 74 (Feb. 1986).

[58]Deloitte, Haskins, & Sells, *Tax Aspects of High Technology Operations* 100 (1985). *See* the remarks of an officer of a public high tech company as reported in *Venture,* May 1987, p. 88:

> They [the Wall Street analysts] thought our science was exciting but until we did something about our R&D partnership, they weren't going to recommend us as a long term buy.

§5.5 R&D CREDIT

The Tax Reform Act of 1986 continues in modified form through 1988 the so-called R&D credit set forth in § 30 (now § 41) of the Code. The R&D credit establishes a credit (20% versus the prior 25%) against tax for incremental research expenditures, expenses by a firm in excess of a base period allowable. The credit is limited to technological research useful in a business context and involving innovation. Paralleling § 174, several categories of R&D expense are excluded; for example, debugging products while production is in process, customizing software for a specific customer, reverse engineering, costs of acquiring someone else's patent or model, market research and the like. The Conference Report requires "true experimentation in the scientific or laboratory sense,"[59] meaning research where the "means of achieving the result is uncertain at the outset."[60] An incremental 20% credit is also continued (no longer limited to 65% of the expense) for amounts paid to universities and other research institutes for "basic" research.[61] There are limitations on the amount of the R&D credit since it is now part of the general business credit, plus special rules pertaining to partnerships. Another section favoring not-for-profit institutions is I.R.C. § 170(e)(4), which allows corporations a limited deduction for scientific property used for research and donated to colleges and universities.[62]

[59]H.R. Conf. Rep. No. 99–841, 99th Cong., 2d Sess. (1986).
[60]*Id.*
[61]I.R.C. § 41(e).
[62]The general business credit in I.R.C. § 38 limits the aggregate credit for certain business related items, including the R&D credit, to $25,000 plus 75% (versus 85% pre-1987) of the excess. I.R.C. 6, 36(c)(2); *See* Black, "R & D Credit Revised by '86 Act But in Restricted Fashion," 66 *J. of Tax'n* 1, 12 (Jan. 1987).

Six

Raising the Initial Round—How to Find Capital: Strategies Useful in the Search

The sources one may interrogate in the search for capital are varied. This chapter reviews the array of possibilities, ranging from banks to high net-worth individuals. The discussion includes remarks on strategies to be employed—for example, whether to engage placement agents—and how to structure a financing so as to maximize its chances of success. Some material has been deliberately left out, principally a primer on how to raise money from a professionally managed venture firm. Several other sources, referenced in the footnotes, provide comprehensive advice on that issue. Furthermore, for a very high percentage of founders, approaching a professionally managed fund based on advice in this or any other book is a waste of time. Those funds rarely if ever favor unsolicited submissions. The material in this chapter focuses on more realistic alternatives for an unchaperoned founder.

§6.1 SOURCES OF FINANCE

Assuming a founder is content that his product is technically feasible and marketable, the chore of raising money—hiring capital—is paramount. The founder's problem is twofold: whether money can be raised at all and, if so, at a cost which leaves something in the deal for the founder. The sources of investment capital are numerous, ranging from commercial banks making fixed-rate, secured loans to individual investors willing to provide risk equity capital in hopes of a spectacular return down the road. A number of guidebooks list the types of capital sources a founder may use and others specify the name, address, and telephone number of particular firms. The discussion in this chapter will concern the potential sources, the legal constraints and some of the problems and opportunities involved in hiring capital for an emerging company.[1]

§6.2 "BACKDOOR" FINANCE—TAX DEDUCTIONS

One of the most attractive sources of financing in recent years is, post-1986, no longer promising; that is, federal assistance in the form of tax benefits accruing to investors, buying into the enterprise as limited partners and using early-stage losses to offset income from other sources. So-called "backdoor" financing has been substantially curtailed by the 1986 amendments to the Internal Revenue Code. Under the Tax Reform Act of 1986, losses from "passive" activity (subject to limited transition rules) may only be set against income from "passive" activity or utilized when the investment is sold.[2] Participation in a limited partnership does not entail, for the limited partners, "regular, continuous and substantial" participation[3] in the activity; ergo any resultant losses stem

[1]Pratt's Guide, *supra* ch. 1, n. 7, has become widely accepted as the semi-official source for identifying specific venture capital firms. For advice on how to raise capital, *see generally*, Gladstone, *Venture Capital Handbook* (1983); Rubel, *Guide to Venture Capital Sources* (4th ed. 1977); Silver, *Who's Who in Venture Capital* (2nd ed. 1986); Chase, Shields, Lambert, Baker, & Shillito, *Small Business Financing: Federal Assistance & Contracts* (1983) (Chase); Haft, *Venture Capital and Small Business Financings* (1987 ed.) (Haft); Martin, *Financing the Growing Business* (1980); Holtz, *2001 Sources of Financing for Small Business* (1983); Kravitt, *How to Raise Capital: Preparing and Presenting a Business Plan* (1984); Lindsey, *The Entrepreneur's Guide to Capital: The Techniques for Capitalizing and Refinancing New and Growing Businesses* (1986); McKeever, *Start Up Money: How to Finance Your New Small Business* (1984); Silver, *Up Front Financing: An Entrepreneur's Guide* (1982).

[2]I.R.C. § 469.

[3]*See* I.R.C. § 469(h)(2), defining "material participation." That section states that "except as provided in the regulations no interest in a limited partnership as a limited partner shall be treated as an interest with respect to which a taxpayer materially participates." Regulations have yet to be issued.

from a "passive activity." Moreover, the drop in the maximum rates means that losses are, *pro tanto,* less attractive. Accordingly, tax shelter will no longer subsidize many early-stage investments (or oil and gas drilling or real estate development, for that matter). Curiously, elimination of the spurious incentive provided by tax shelters may help venture investing in the sense that factitious opportunities will not siphon off risk-oriented dollars.

§6.3 DIRECT FEDERAL SUBSIDIES—"GREAT SOCIETY" PROGRAMS

The Reagan Revolution has curtailed several government funding programs originating in the Kennedy and Johnson administrations which politically attuned entrepreneurs had tapped. The Economic Development Administration in the Department of Commerce, for example, is largely out of the business of lending directly to private firms and Urban Development Assistance Grants (UDAG) no longer provide bounties for the support of low-cost infrastructure designed to subsidize, among other things, fledgling businesses. As discussed in the next section, there has been a pronounced shift; economic pump-priming activity is now generally the province of state and local governments. The accent is on attempts by regional authorities to emulate Northern California and Eastern Massachusetts with various forms of inducements. That is not to say that federal assistance is entirely at a standstill—such will never be the case in this country. Thus, small business "set-aside" programs[4] provide procurement leverage for small vendors selling to government agencies. And research funding remains available in several forms, the Small Business Innovation Research Program,[5] for example. The slang

[4]Many of the programs were codified at 15 U.S.C. § 644 with the passage of the Small Business Administration Act of 1953. In preparing applications for governmental assistance, the presentation in the business plan should, obviously, include material of public interest—the firm's potential impact on employment, the environment, etc. White, *The Entrepreneur's Manual* 165 (1977).

[5]Under this program, several government agencies publish annually the areas of research they will fund with grants. Eligible recipients are businesses with 500 or fewer employees. Phase I grants average $50,000 for six months of basic research and Phase II grants—financing the prototype—may provide up to $500,000 for two years of R&D. Any U.S., independently owned entity (public or private) with 500 or fewer employees can qualify. The accounting firm of Peat Marwick & Mitchell publishes a 60-page guidebook, *Small Business Innovation Research Grants: How to Obtain Them to Finance Your Ideas. See also* Lipper, *Venture's Guide to Investing in Private Companies: A Financing Manual for the Entrepreneurial Investor* 170 (1984). Similar programs include the Department of Energy's Appropriate Technology Program and the Department of Defense Small Business Technology Program. *Id.* The National Science Foundation is currently promoting a program to establish joint academic/industrial research centers. Anderson "Pushing Ivory-Tower Scientists into the High-Tech Race," N.Y. *Times,* Feb. 15, 1987, at F–6.

term "Beltway Bandits" is applied to the firms growing up along the circumferential highway around Washington, D.C., and existing in large part on the strength of research and consulting contracts given by federal agencies. However, the business of directly targeted government inducements for new industry, particularly of the high tech variety, is increasingly generated by state and local agencies.

§6.4 "SOFT" AND "HARD" STATE AND LOCAL AID

The states are trying a number of devices to incubate technologically oriented industry. The bottom line is a multitude of programs offering "hard" inducements, for example, loans and investments from a state-affiliated fund, plus "soft" dollars in the form of low-cost facilities and services and "backdoor" financing in the form of state tax deductions and credits. Such programs are usually administered in conjunction with a local college or university. A state agency will put up a modest amount of actual cash for grants and/or equity and debt investment and then sweeten the pot with such benefits as government procurement set-asides; technical assistance; state tax credits; and "incubator" space, meaning subsidized, low-cost laboratory and office space reinforced with tenant amenities, such as computer access, telephone answering, conference facilities, and word processing. The blurb for one of the oldest facilities—the Ben Franklin Partnership in Pennsylvania—gives a picture of the available array:

> In addition to the Challenge Grant Program for Technological Innovation, five other programs comprise the Ben Franklin Partnership initiative:
>
> *The Small Business Research Seed Grant Program*—provides grants of up to $35,000 for small businesses engaged in research in any of nine specific advanced technology areas.
>
> *The Small Business Incubator Loan Program*—provides loans to establish new small business incubators—facilities offering low rent, flexible space, shared business services, and an environment where emerging firms can grow.
>
> *The Seed Capital Challenge Grant Program*—establishes privately managed regional seed venture capital funds. The State will contribute up to $750,000 for each of four regional funds, matched one-to-three by private investments. In turn, these regional funds provide equity investments in small, young firms.
>
> *The Engineering School Equipment Grant Program*—awards grants to Pennsylvania's engineering colleges and universities to assure that engineering students are trained on state-of-the-art equipment.

The Economic Revitalization Tax Credit Program—makes $25 million available for qualified investment projects made between January 1, 1986 and the last day of any tax year beginning in 1988. Qualified investment projects are limited to manufacturing, processing, and research/development activities and must create or retain jobs.

In conjunction with direct assistance, several states attempt to "pump prime" by establishing focused research centers. In Pennsylvania, the campuses of various state colleges house Advanced Technology Centers, or Centers of Excellence, as their analogues are called in Massachusetts. These are established by fiat on campus, each center representing a consortium of universities, private firms, and area economic development organizations, usually organized around a specific scientific discipline.[6] Whether such centers will actually give birth to a significant quantum of research which would not otherwise have found its way into the open air remains unclear.[7]

Programs such as these are available, to varying degrees, in almost every state. As can be seen from the quoted excerpt, however, the financial impact of the programs is not of the make-or-break variety. Moreover, once having accepted government assistance, a firm is subject to conditions both special (i.e., locate in a given location, hire local residents) and general (e.g., affirmative action, union wages). If management finds it wants to move the plant to Taiwan to stay competitive, it may not be free to do so because of restrictions in loan agreements, which may survive even after the loan is repaid. Nonetheless, despite the popular joke (Q. "Name one of the three biggest lies in the world." A. "I'm from the government and I'm here to help you."), the advantages of government-sponsored assistance should not be sneezed at. Once a loan has been made, for example, the risks of a bureaucrat pulling the plug are not as formidable as in the private sector since loss ratios are not an index of great significance in a public agency. An interesting anomaly in government loan administration is that the proceeds from repayment are ordinarily credited to the general treasury rather than to the accounts of the agency concerned. Consequently, the people in

[6] Thus, the University City Science Center was founded in Philadelphia in 1964 by a group of 28 area colleges, universities and health care facilities to promote research and development and to encourage business growth in the Philadelphia region. "University City Science Center: Whaley Probes the New Role of Education for Future Managers," *Focus*, Aug. 15, 1985, at 64, 65.

[7] The mixed returns from innovation/incubator centers are outlined and summarized in Andrews, "How Much for a Security Blanket?", *Venture* (Feb. 1986) at 49. The article cites the generally unsatisfactory experience resulting from the center established in the mid-1970s at M.I.T. by the National Science Foundation.

charge are often indifferent to the issue of repayment since the money is not "theirs."[8]

§6.5 SBA LOANS

The most significant program of federal government assistance to small business is the loan, and loan guarantee, program run since 1953 by the Small Business Administration (SBA),[9] coupled in 1958 with the creation of privately owned concerns called Small Business Investment Companies (SBICs)[10], which utilize funds borrowed from the federal government at soft rates to finance small business. Both programs are administered by the SBA but have different impacts on early-stage financings.

An SBA loan (whether in the person of a direct loan from the SBA or, more commonly, a bank loan guaranteed by the SBA) is, despite the favorable terms, the equivalent of bank financing. Although interest rates can be soft,[11] a loan entails a promise of repayment within a finite period of time and an interest cost from the date the loan is made. Further, it introduces a partner to the enterprise with a lender's mentality. In the typical case—a guaranteed bank loan[12]—the fact that the SBA guarantees 90% (or less) of the loan should give no encouragement that the bank is likely to relax its attitude toward repayment. A 90% guarantee is *not* a 100% guarantee; a commercial bank that routinely loses 10% of the principal of the loans it makes would soon be out of business. The 10% exposure is taken very seriously by the administering bank and its officers can be expected to work hard to make sure it will be repaid. Moreover, the SBA ordinarily requires the founder(s) to guarantee loans personally and, on occasion, its collection efforts are rigorous. If a $150,000 loan is secured by a second mortgage on the founder's home and all of his personal assets, there is always the question

[8]Specific incubator facilities are listed in Batterson, *Raising Venture Capital and the Entrepreneur* 422 (1986).
[9]Small Business Act, 15 U.S.C. § 631–651.
[10]Small Business Investment Act, 15 U.S.C. §§ 661–697.
[11]15 U.S.C. § 636.
[12]There are several threshold requirements for SBA financial assistance. For example, the applicant must attempt to obtain financing from other nonfederal sources, including the owner's resources and private lenders. 13 C.F.R. § 122.5–1 (1987). The maturity of each loan is to be the shortest feasible term commensurate with the ability of the borrower to repay and the maximum maturity for a loan is 10 years (with some exceptions). 13 C.F.R. § 122.6–1 (1987). The limit on direct loan amounts is $350,000 by statute, $150,000 by SBA administrative ruling. 13 C.F.R. § 122.7–1 (1987). For immediate participation loans (loans the SBA purchases from financial institutions), the statutory limit is the lesser of 90% of the loan or $350,000; administratively, it is the lesser of 75% of the loan or $150,000. 13 C.F.R. § 122.7–2 (1987). *See generally* Chase, *supra* n. 1, Part II.

whether the government assistance is worth it in the first place. (Most banks are not set up to make SBA-guaranteed loans because of the red tape involved; most of the relatively small number that do have been designated by the SBA as "small business lending companies"[13] meaning that processing time has been shortened.) The principal advantage of an SBA-guaranteed loan is that the bank is likely to to go higher in the loan-to-value ratio on tangible assets and to extend maturities. Much of the financing for franchises in recent years has been arranged with the benefit of SBA guarantees.[14]

Size standards for eligible recipients of SBA loans—"small business concerns"—vary according to the classification of the firm. For manufacturing concerns, for example, the limit is generally from 500 to 1,000 employees, while retail firms are classified according to annual receipts.[15]

§6.6 SBICs

SBICs are privately organized corporations (or partnerships) licensed and regulated by the SBA.[16] They are entitled to borrow money from the SBA, up to $3 in loans at a soft interest rate for every $1 invested by the shareholders, $4 if the SBICs maintain 65% of total investment funds for "venture capital" investments.[17] SBICs which borrow funds from the SBA must pay interest, albeit at favorable rates, meaning that an interest element is usually included in the investment made in each portfolio company. (As discussed below, a special class of SBICs, organized not to borrow but to enable bank holding companies to get around certain legal restrictions, are equity investors largely indistinguishable from free-standing venture funds.) Compelled to achieve a

[13]The SBA has developed a so-called preferred lender program pursuant to which selected banks and financial institutions make the decision to loan without review by the SBA; the SBA's guarantee in such instances extends only to 75% of such loans. Such a lender was referred to as a "Subsection (b) Lender" and is presently known as a "Small Business Lending Company" or SBLC. The SBA no longer will accept applications for SBLC status but existing SBLCs continue to participate, subject to supervision and examination by the SBA. 13 C.F.R. § 120.302–1 (1987).

[14]"Financing A Franchise," *Inc.* 89, 92 (April, 1987).

[15]*See generally* Chase, *supra* n. 1, at 25.

[16]*See generally* Miller, "Small Business Investment Companies: Licensing, Tax and Securities Considerations," 36 *Bus. Law.* 1979 (July 1981); Sanders, "SBA Financing Sources," in "Financing Growth Oriented Ventures: Where The Money Is," 39 *Bus. Law.* 647 (Feb. 1984). In 1972, Minority Enterprise Small Business Investment Companies (MESBICs) were added to the program and more liberal financing terms were allowed. 15 U.S.C. § 681(d) added by Act Oct. 27, 1972, P. L. No.92–595 § 2(b).

[17]15 U.S.C. § 683 (1984).

return, SBICs are, accordingly, typical late-round investors, advancing loans coupled with equity options, often subordinated convertible debt.[18]

In recent years the SBIC program has not had a significant impact on the growth of the venture capital industry. Many of the early venture firms, however, got their start as SBICs, the organizers intrigued by their ability to obtain low-cost debt financing from the federal government at a time when commercial interest rates were in the low single digits.

An SBIC's investment program is limited to firms that qualify as small business concerns,[19] including those that qualify under the SBA standards and firms meeting net worth and income tests applicable only to SBICs. This was not an onerous requirement in the world of venture finance in the 1950s and 1960s, since the test is applied when the investment is made and few unseasoned companies enjoy 2 years of average net after-tax profit exceeding $2 million annually.[20] The constraint is confining in today's arena, however, because it can exclude SBICs from the active world of leveraged buyouts and mezzanine financings if the target company is of substantial size. The run up in interest rates in the 1970s to double digits cheapened the privilege of borrowing from the government because unseasoned companies were ill adapted to provide the SBIC with interim returns of that magnitude.[21]

§6.7 BANK-AFFILIATED SBICs

One of the more significant impelling forces in the current period behind the formation of new SBICs has not been cheap debt but the election

[18]Loans made by SBICs are subject to state usury laws. Haft, *supra* n. 1, at 2–1.

[19]As defined in 15 U.S.C. § 632 (1984), a small business concern is "deemed to be one which is independently owned and operated and which is not dominant in its field of operation." This constraint eliminates subsidiaries of large concerns; by regulation, the SBA includes the resources of "affiliates" of the firm in calculating its size. 13 C.F.R. § 107.3 (1987). The "dominance" test has not, as one might expect, proven to be troublesome. Chase, *supra* n. 1, at 168.

[20]The question whether an SBIC can participate in later rounds, when the entities have grown beyond the qualifying parameters, depends upon whether the SBA administratively determines that refinancing is necessary to protect the government's financial interest. 13 C.F.R. § 121.4(c) (1987).

[21]Sprinkled throughout the Code are various provisions favoring SBICs. Thus, the dividends-received deduction under the Code is 100% in the case of the SBICs (versus 80% for other corporations). I.R.C. § 243(a). The penalty tax on excess accumulated earnings does not apply generally to SBICs. I.R.C. § 533(b). On the other hand, the SBIC exemption from taxation as personal holding companies, I.R.C. § 542(c)(8) is no longer singular since the elimination of the capital gain/ordinary income distinction will de-emphasize the significance of the personal holding company provisions.

of many banks and bank holding companies to organize SBICs[22] so as to participate legally in a nonbank investment activity which they perceive as a profitable adjunct to the business of commercial banking, an integral part of their move away from total dependence on straight lending and into corporate finance and investment banking.

The bank pattern is to organize two subsidiaries, either of the bank[23] or bank holding company, viz., an SBIC which enables the bank to hold up to 50% of the vote in a small business concern and a so-called "5% Corporation," which can hold 5% of the voting (or 25% to 35% of the nonvoting) stock in a concern of any size.[24] To those in search of financing, a bank-affiliated SBIC is little different from a free-standing venture pool. With certain major exceptions, the tendency of the bank-affiliated pools, however, has been to focus on later-stage financings, LBOs, and investments in other venture pools (the "fund of funds" concept), versus early-round investing in emerging companies.

§6.8 BANK FINANCING

The question whether a start-up should rely on commercial bank financing (if the same is obtainable) is to be approached quite cautiously. A commercial bank can make a very poor partner for a fledgling enterprise; the lenders tend to want their money back at just the wrong moment. Often the only type of bank financing available to a start-up is a demand note secured by a floating lien on all the assets of the operation and the personal signature of the founder, a dangerous weapon in the hands of a nervous bank. Moreover, bank lending to early-stage, high tech companies is on occasion the result of a fashionable wave in banking circles, the thought being that banks should get in on the "new" game by incubating clones of Wang Laboratories through judicious extensions of credit to deserving entrepreneurs. The first problem is that only a limited number of commercial banks are staffed with loan officers with the necessary experience to discriminate among applicants in an area of lending where standard rules of thumb and guidelines are out the window. (There are, of course, significant exceptions.) Moreover, as

[22]Banks may invest an amount equal up to 5% of the bank's capital and surplus in an SBIC. 15 U.S.C. § 682(b) (1984). The previous limitation—that the bank could hold only 50% of the SBIC's stock—has been repealed. Bank holding companies can similarly invest, because § 4(c)(5) of the Bank Holding Company Act of 1956, 12 U.S.C. § 1843(c)(5), indirectly incorporates § 682.

[23]The investing entity may be organized as a subsidiary of the bank, versus the holding company, simply because the bank has more money.

[24]*See* the Bank Holding Company Act of 1956, 12 U.S.C. § 1843(c)(7). The bank or holding company may elect to organize limited partnerships, in which it (or its subsidiaries) invest as limited partners(s) and the managers act as general partners, in order to afford the managers a "carried" interest in profits. *See* Ch. 20, § 20.10.

fashions come, so fashions go. Long-time players in the venture capital game can cite a number of unfortunate instances when senior bank officers, focusing on a well-publicized disaster in the high tech business generally, have given the generic order to the lending division to "tighten the screws." The problem, of course, is that start-ups are very fragile animals; the slightest hiccup in a bank, or any, relationship can strangle the baby in its crib, so to speak. Even more tragic are instances where the bank becomes nervous about the loan in the early stages of a start-up's career, when earnings are following the well-known "hockey stick" path (i.e., trending downward for a number of periods, usually at least one full year longer than the projections suggest, followed by a sharp "ramp up" once the company breaks thorough). The bank's anxiety having been excited by the long slide downward, it springs the trap by cutting off credit and marshaling assets at the very point when the company's good news is just beginning. There are, to be sure, banks and there are banks. Some banks, particularly those located in the classic high tech areas, have become experienced in lending to early-stage companies and are less likely to panic. Indeed, some banks are willing to negotiate compensation for their added risk by accepting equity in the borrower—an equity "kicker"—or an interest rate tied to a fixed base or index plus increases depending on the fortunes of the borrower.[25]

§6.9 CAPITAL FROM OPERATIONS

The most frequent source of capital for unseasoned companies is the most obvious, right under the founder's nose; that is, saving cash by cutting the burn rate. One imperative remains constant in venture finance: survival. The death toll of venture capital start-ups is ominous; above all the founder must keep the business on the road until something good happens or until it becomes clear the cause is hopeless. And, the open road to survival is uncomplicated: at least in theory, cost control. It is a truism that costs should be controlled, true in any business. The problem is that, like Mark Twain's weather forecast, so many people talk about cost control and so few really do anything about it. Some founders, reared in a big company atmosphere, simply do not understand what cost control implies. The idea of doing without the paid services of a chief financial officer means to them that they aren't in business at all. More insidious is the siren call of the often repeated venture capital strategy, the early and pre-emptive strike. A founder in

[25]Silicon Valley Bank in San Jose and Bank of Boston are singled out as among the banks most receptive to equity "kickers" in *Venture*, Aug. 1986, at 90. One of the difficult issues posed by equity "kickers" arises if the bank calls the loan prior to the date the parties expected. Is the bank entitled to retain its entire equity position in the borrower?

command of a new technological wrinkle correctly perceives that he is a lone adventurer among titans, giants who will seize the first opportunity to steal his idea and exploit it with their unlimited resources to the point where he's unable any longer to compete. The "first strike" strategy, and it is often the right and correct strategy, can beguile the founder into thinking that he should maximize the impact of his entry by spending money, the "big bang" theory.

Whatever the problem, the fact remains that a chronic shortage of cash has two and only two (not mutually exclusive) solutions: raise some fresh cash from the outside[26] or find cash within the business. Raising cash internally involves, in turn, two methods: increase cash flow and/or cut costs; and, of these, the fastest, surest, most feasible method is to cut costs—fire people, give up space, cut R&D, reconfigure the product. Of course, it is risky to "cut out the fat." Without R&D, new product opportunities collapse; perhaps a quick death is being traded for a slow death. Nonetheless, the imperative remains: find the money necessary to survive. And that cash is often right under the founder's nose, available inside the business if and only if expenses are reduced.

§6.10 PLACEMENT AGENTS

Founders desparate for financing debate whether the faucet will turn on if they engage a placement agent, a question to be addressed in a real world context. In the first place, the great majority of first-round financings are not economically interesting to an investment banking firm. The fee for a placement is usually in the range of 2 to 5% of the amount raised;[27] assuming a $1 million first-round financing, a fee of $20,000 to $50,000 is not likely to attract many takers in the investment banking fraternity when fees for acting as financial adviser in contested merger and acquisition transactions run into eight figures. There are exceptions to this, as to any other, proposition. Encore Computer, because of the splendid reputation of its founders, attracted a high degree of interest from major bracket investment bankers in the seed round; William Poduska, on leaving Apollo Computer and organizing Stellar, was able to titillate investment banking appetites to a fever pitch. However, the traditional founder is wasting his time beating down the doors of the elite investment bankers to help him raise money in the early rounds. Smaller investment banking houses, their sights set lower than,

[26]Ceasing to pay one's bills is, of course, a temporary way to raise cash from the outside.
[27]If there is a single model for fees in private placements, it is the so-called "Lehman" formula: 5% of the first $1 million raised, 4% of the second, 3% of the third, 2% of the fourth and 1% of all sums over $4 million. That system is still a reference guide, *see* Lipper, *supra* n. 5, at 123, but the exceptions are so numerous that the rule no longer exists as a rule, if it ever did.

Morgan Stanley or Goldman Sachs, are more likely candidates but even they are not enthusiastic about hitting the pavement to arrange a first-round investment because the amount of work is enormous and the payoff is often chancey.[28]

If an agent is engaged to place securities privately, he will surely act only on a "best efforts" basis. A firm commitment in the early stages of a company's history, indeed a firm commitment on a private placement of any kind, is encountered only in special circumstances. Moreover, the founder should understand that the agent is not obligated to sell an untried security; that remains the responsibility of the founder. The agent is engaged to help prepare a private placement memorandum and to expose the opportunity to a list of prospects, to screen buyers, and to schedule meetings for the founder to do his stuff. Purchasers in early rounds are not interested in discussing the merits of the investment with a salesman. The founder, and only the founder, has that reservoir of knowledge about the technology and its potential application which potential buyers are interested to hear. Morever, the agent will look to the founder for a so-called "friends" list, that is, potential investors already known to the founder.

Since cash is at a premium, negotiations with a placement agent usually include the possibility of the fee being reinvested in the securities being offered. Indeed, since a cash fee for the first-round placement is not significant in most cases, it's likely that the placement agent will be more than happy to invest some or all of the fee.[29]

The placement fee can become a troublesome issue with the investors if a placement agent is instrumental in bringing in fewer than all of the investors. The possible sources for payment of the fee are three in number—the company (meaning in effect all the investors pro rata), the investor introduced by the agent or the founder. Investors who came across the opportunity without benefit of a broker can become rabid at the thought of their cash going to pay, indirectly, a placement fee of no benefit to them.

In the agreement between the issuer and its placement agent, the agent will expect and insist on indemnities against claims arising out of failures to disclose material information (an indemnity of dubious worth, to be sure, when dealing with an impecunious founder and a start-up company).[30] More importantly, the placement agent will usu-

[28]Much of the private placement activity is centered in the regional and/or "boutique" investment banking firms, *see* Thackray, "Investment Banking's One-Man Shops," *N.Y. Times*, Jan. 12, 1986, § 3, at 1, and the corporate finance departments of large banks and bank holding companies.

[29]The issue of "cheap" stock owned by an underwriter—whether the same is counted as part of the underwriter's compensation in an initial public offering—is discussed in Ch. 14, § 14.9(a) and 10.

[30]On the subject of underwriters' indemnities generally, *see* Lovejoy, "Underwriting Agreement," in Halloran, *supra* Ch. 1, n. 16, at 769.

ally insist on a right, in the nature of a first refusal right, to lead subsequent rounds of financing, a provision that should be approached thoughtfully. If an investment banking house known only to a few loyal adherents on Wall Street is willing to help out in a first-round financing but at a cost of controlling subsequent rounds, the founder may find that price too stiff. On the other hand, it is unrealistic to expect an investment banker to work enthusiastically on the most difficult financing—that is, the earliest—and then simply take its chances at being remembered with gratitude when subsequent, more lucrative rounds are being discussed.

One value of a placement agent at an early stage is that it will, in all likelihood, impose some important imperatives upon the founder, in some cases to his consternation. For example, experienced corporate financiers save time by introducing founders to the real world of early-stage finance and some of the "rules"—for example, all moneys raised go into the company, none of it leaks out to the founder. Often the founder has built up a debt from the company to himself for accrued and unpaid salary, money loaned, and so forth. With his own creditors knocking at his door, the founder may approach a financing with an eye to intercepting some of the money for himself, to pay his urgent bills. A placement agent will rapidly disabuse a founder of that notion.

§6.11 "HIGH NET WORTH" INDIVIDUALS

Sometimes, if the forecast returns are not attractive to professionally managed venture funds, the founder can search for those rich individuals who: (i) are anxious to invest in start-ups; (ii) are not jaded, like the "vulture capitalists"; and (iii) will accept situations the professionals are unlikely to favor. This individuals indubitably exist—indeed, he has been profiled.[31] The trick, of course, is to find him.

Businessmen and professionals with high incomes are often without organized channels for venture investment; the minimum investment required to join a private venture pool is usually quite high—in seven figures—and many of the older pools are closed to outsiders. Public

[31]According to a profile of the "informal investor," compiled under SBA sponsorship, the typical individual:

> Looks for compound annual rates of return on individual investments ranging from 50% from inventors to 20 to 25% from established firms;
>
> Looks for minimum portfolio returns of about 20%;
>
> Learns of investment opportunities primarily from friends and business associates; and
>
> Would like to look at more investment opportunities than present informal system permits.

Wetzel, "Informal Investors—When and Where to Look," in Lipper, *supra* n. 5, at 168.

vehicles for venture investing are not common—ML Partners, affiliated with Merrill Lynch, is one of the few. Accordingly, individual venture investors exist; the founder's task is to find them, through a combination of persistence and luck.

§6.12 USE YOUR PROFESSIONALS

Circulation of business plans among venture capital firms picked randomly out of a book is not likely to be particularly productive. So-called "over-the-transom" submissions to venture firms number in the hundreds each month and very few are favored. Most venture firms make their investment decision on the basis of plans they have helped develop on their own or which have been forwarded to them by sources they know and respect. The trick, therefore, is to obtain an introduction. If a placement agent is not available, one technique is to employ a law or accounting firm enjoying cordial relationships with a number of venture firms. Neither lawyers nor accountants are set up to sell securities; they ordinarily don't do it with frequent success.[32] They do, however, have access to potential investors and a sense of what will sell in the marketplace.

§6.13 VENTURE CAPITAL CLUBS AND OTHER VENUES

One often-tried gambit for raising cash is to make a presentation at a forum organized by a "venture capital club," referring to an idea first popularized by Thomas Murphy.[33] Venture capital clubs consist of an organizer and a mailing list of individuals and/or entities in a given

[32]*See* Bekey, "Don't Call Just Any Lawyer," *Venture,* Jan. 1987, at 48. The article lists the "major matchmakers" among law firms—a "Big Eight," if you will, each of which have "a perception of today's market." *See also* Rollinson, "Small Company, Big Law Firm," 63 *Harv. Bus. Rev.* 5 (Nov.–Dec. 1985) and, "The Matchmakers," *Robb Report,* July 1987, at 55.

[33]Reifsnyder, "Venture Capital Clubs," *Success* (Sept. 1986) at 60, 61. A venture capital club is sometimes called, "a dating service," "It's Like a Dating Service," *Forbes* Dec. 2, 1985, at 70; or a "venture capital kindergarten." Asinof, "Venture-Capital Clubs Become Hot Spot for Entrepreneurs Seeking to Make Deals," *Wall St. J.* Apr. 10, 1985, § 2, at 31. Venture capital clubs are not to be confused with the trade association to which most professional managers belong, the National Venture Capital Association, membership in which is limited to "venture capital organizations, corporate financiers and individual capitalists." Other professional organizations involved in representing the industry generally are NASBIC (The National Association of Small Business Investment Companies) and the AEA (the American Electronics Association).

region that have demonstrated some interest in venture capital.[34] There are about seven dozen such groups in the United States;[35] they meet monthly over breakfast or lunch.[36] They usually rely on word of mouth for attendance, as they don't ordinarily advertise.[37] The most important part of a typical meeting is the "Five Minute Forum," in which anyone can speak about his venture for a limit of one to five minutes.[38] The purported purpose of attending these meetings is for people to make "contacts," not offers.[39]

As the number of venture capital clubs has increased, so too have the number of schools and associations aimed at helping entrepreneurs in all aspects of starting and running a business.[40] Moreover, some of the venture capital conferences, such as those sponsored by the American Electronics Association and the celebrated trade shows, provide promising venues for entrepreneurs to meet investors.

At this point, some words of caution are in order. First, there are hidden legal difficulties in the venture capital club (or seminar, fair, or symposium) notion which have not been as yet adequately explored.[41] Availability of an exemption from registration of an offering under the 1933 Act can be lost because attendees at a luncheon are publicly solicited to buy securities in the companies making presentations. As far as can be ascertained, there has not yet been a suit for rescission by investors solicited at a venture club function, but some counsel view the presentation as potentially an inadvertent, and therefore illegal, public offering, posing problems for any subsequently proposed private placement or public issue of securities. Secondly, it is not clear how

[34]A similar phenomenon is the rise of regional conferences and "fairs" to test out business proposals among venture capitalists. Perez, *Inside Venture Capital: Past, Present, and Future* 109–110 (1986). *See also* "Clubs with Capital Ideas: They're Good Places to Meet People Who Might Invest in Your Business," *Changing Times*, Jan. 1986, at 77.

[35]A consulting firm, Baxter Associates, Inc., in Stamford, Conn., has organized the International Venture Capital Institute. The director of the institute lists 86 venture capital clubs in the United States. Another firm, Venture Capital Network, Inc., is marketing computerized screening systems. Logan, "Finding Your Angel," *Venture* 38, 42 (Mar. 1986). A new start-up business activity, it appears, consists in providing advice to people who want to start up businesses.

[36]"Clubs with Capital Ideas," *supra* n. 34, at 77.

[37]*Id.*, at 77–78.

[38]"It's Like a Dating Service," *Forbes* Dec. 2, 1985, at 70.

[39]"Clubs with Capital Ideas," *supra* n. 34, at 77.

[40]The Small Business Resource Guide, published by the Center for Entrepreneurial Management, lists dozens of these organizations.

[41]The mere fact that founders appear at a venture capital club and make their presence known does not, of course, mean that they have made an illegal offer. *See* Reifsnyder, "Venture Capital Clubs," *Success* Sept. 1986, at 60, 65.

effective such symposiums have been in raising money, except for the commercial sponsor of the event.[42]

§6.14 IDBs

The Tax Reform Act of 1986 suggests that industrial revenue financing will play only a limited role in future funding of development-stage issuers. The advantages of industrial development revenue bonds—IDBs or IRBs as they are known—stem from the tax-exempt feature of the interest paid on the debt. The effective interest cost can be (depending on the then-existing tax rate) as much as 200 basis points lower than would be the case were the interest fully taxable. The bonds are usually sold to finance new plant and equipment, primarily "bricks and mortar." The structure of a typical IDB is such that the ultimate credit is a lease or loan agreement executed by the user of the premises constructed with the bond proceeds and often backed by a letter of credit issued by a bank or insurance company. Regions hungry for new employment have historically organized Industrial Financing Authorities, which sponsor IDB financings for desirable private industry, including small business.[43] In some cases, venture-oriented firms have been able to take advantage of the tax-exempt interest element of IDB financing.

The tangled history of congressional attempts to close down abuses in industrial development bond financing are well beyond the scope of the Text.[44] To summarize the current state of the art, under § 103(b) of the Code, interest paid on industrial development bonds (now classified amongst the category of "private activity bonds") is taxable unless certain exceptions apply. The exception most pertinent to venture finance is contained in § 144(a)(4) for "qualified small issue bonds" no greater than $10 million for acquisition, construction, or improvement of land, plant, and equipment. With the 1986 Act, the "small issue" exemption is temporarily alive; it will expire, unless extended, on Dec. 31, 1989. The exemption is now available only for the construction and financing of "manufacturing" facilities. An annual statewide volume cap has been imposed on "private activity" bonds, including industrial development

[42]For a jaundiced view, *see* Logan, *supra* n. 35, at 40; the author remarks: "A country club's a better place to meet an angel than a venture capital club."

[43]By definition, the bonds do not involve the general obligation—the full faith and credit—of a taxing authority. The state or local agency offers expertise, prestige, and the ability to expedite the issues it sponsors, through long-standing relations with elite underwriters and the investment community.

[44]The ability to issue bonds with tax-exempt interest for industrial development was cut back with the Deficit Reduction Act of 1984. P.L. No. 98–369, 98 Stat. 494 (1984).

bonds issued pursuant to the small issue exemption. Further, certain tax advantages (on the expense side) for banks purchasing tax-exempt securities have been repealed by the 1986 Act, effectively removing banks as buyers. Until the sunset date in 1989, IBDs will continue to be issued, the market now being public investors, among whom there appears to continue an appetite for tax-exempt debt.[45]

§6.15 "CONCEPT" IPOs—HIRING THE PUBLIC'S CAPITAL BEFORE OPERATIONS COMMENCE

In some market cycles, the interest in high tech issues is so robust that so-called "concept" or "résumé" offerings are feasible. Feeding frenzies in the public market spotlight certain underwriters who are prepared, on a best efforts basis, to agree to promote a public offering of securities in a company that has no sales and earnings—only a concept and/or the impressive résumés of its officers and directors. Those underwriters come and go, the names change as some go out of business when the music stops, but a new wave seems ever ready when market conditions warrant. The prospectus of a concept offering will, to be sure, contain Draconian warnings that the offering is "speculative" and involves a "high degree of risk." In the appropriate market environment, however, those warnings often attract rather than repel investors. There are international variations on the theme. Some auction markets—the British

[45]In some states, industrial finance agencies are issuing taxable IDBs, the demand being stimulated in part, it appears, by the aura of stability and legitimacy lent by that fact that the issues are being assembled and packaged by a state agency, even though the faith and credit of the state is not involved and interest is subject to tax. The Massachusetts Industrial Finance Agency estimated it will raise between "$200 million to $300 million in taxable small business bonds" in 1987. "Life After Industrial Revenue Bonds," *Venture* (Feb. 1987) 71. In the case of taxable securities, the exemption from registration under the Securities Act of 1933 depends on a bank letter of credit—*see* § 3(a)(2) ("any security issued or guaranteed by any bank")—since the exemption for tax-exempt municipal securities contained in that section—("any security which is an industrial development bond the interest on which is" tax-exempt)—has been lost. One such authority has adopted a hybrid approach, sometimes labeled a "Delta Fund." Thus, five counties in Utah are issuing $85 million in taxable zero coupon bonds. About a third of the proceeds will be invested in local venture portfolio companies, the remainder in zero coupon Treasury securities in an amount designed to pay off the county bonds at maturity. The interest rate on the county bonds is noncompetitive (300 basis points under the market), but the investor has a chance to make up for that shortfall by a big "hit" in the venture portfolio. *See Bond Buyer*, at 279 (Mar. 26, 1987).

Unlisted,[46] the Vancouver Stock Exchange,[47] for example—will admit to trading shares of development-stage companies. Despite the occasional success stories,[48] few, if any, experienced professionals recommend the premature public offering as a desired strategy, since the burdens of public registration are so significant and the risks of failure are magnified in the public arena; there are fewer excuses and little forgiveness for red ink.

§6.16 SELF-UNDERWRITING

Self-underwriting is a process in which a private company can "go public" with an initial public offering but without using a brokerage firm as an underwriter. Instead, the company management handles the process itself.[49] The usual reason put forth in favor of self-underwriting is cost—preparing a self-underwriting can cost less, the issuers professing they are tired of "being shaken down by brokerage firms."[50] The real reason, however, is usually that the company cannot secure professional investment banking support. Certain states do not admit self-underwritten in initial public offerings[51] at all and others require an alliance with a brokerage firm.[52] Moreover, there is a hidden cost to a self-underwriting; the number of hours spent by corporate executives, who must complete all the necessary tasks (i.e., filing, registration, drafting the prospectus), can usually be done more efficiently by a brokerage

[46]Indeed, it has been suggested that the recent development of venture capital in Great Britain is linked to the rise of the Unlisted Securities Market in London. Kozmetsky, Gill & Smilor, *supra* Ch. 1, n. 4, at 73. *See also* "Entrepreneurs Come of Age on the Continent," *Bus. Wk.*, Dec. 12, 1983, at 45. Some U.S. companies have used an IPO in the U.K. as an alternative to financing options deemed unattractive in the U.S. "Adding Pounds," *Inc.*, Mar. 1985, at 140.

[47]*See* Andrews, "The Siren Song of Vancouver," *Venture*, (July 1987) 35. Vancouver will list companies with capital as low as $100,000, versus a requirement of $8 million in net worth, or $300,000 in net income, to list on NASDAQ. *NASD Manual* (CCH) ¶ 1754, (1986).

[48]Exemplifying one of the few successes, Digital Switch was originally brought public as a concept offering (by an underwriter which subsequently failed). Perez, *Inside Investment Banking* 33 (1984).

[49]"Going Public and Selling It Yourself: Self-Underwriting Picks Up in a Soft New Issues Market," *Venture*, Nov. 1984, at 182. *See* Bloomenthal, Harvey, & Wing, *1985 Going Public Handbook: Going Public, the Integrated Disclosure System and Exempt Financing* § 313 (1985). There are perfectly respectable reasons for some self-underwritten offerings; i.e., when an issuer makes an exchange offer with its own security holders.

[50]Lindsey, *The Entrepreneur's Guide to Capital: More than 40 Techniques for Capitalizing and Refinancing New and Growing Businesses* 26 (1986).

[51]*Id.* at 25.

[52]*Id.*

firm.[53] Moreover, in a self-underwritten offering, the employees doing the actual selling are faced with the question whether they must register as brokers under § 15(a)(1) of the '34 Act, in turn depending on whether they are deemed to be "engaged in the business."[54] An SEC rule provides a safe harbor if the salesperson is an employee of the issuer, no special compensation is received, no so-called "bad boy" disqualifications (previous convictions or citations for securities crimes or frauds) are involved and the employee is not affiliated with a broker/dealer.[55]

§6.17 FINANCING STRATEGIES—ISSUES TO PONDER AS THE MONEY IS BEING RAISED

(a) MULTIPLE ROUND STRATEGIES

Few, if any, start-ups survive to maturity on the basis of a single round of financing. It is in the nature of the venture capital beast that companies consume cash in their early stages at unforeseen, sometimes alarming rates. Not only must products be developed but, in the classic venture capital scenario, a new market must be penetrated and, indeed, sometimes created. Digital computers, xerography, express mail—these were not products developed to satisfy the public perception of existing demand. Rather, the existence of the product created, uncovered if one prefers, the demand; necessity was not the mother of invention. Today it is difficult to see how humanity could get along without these staples. Nonetheless, no customers' queue awaited computers until the computer was introduced and created the queue in the first instance. Accordingly, the need of a start-up for frequent and regular infusions of cash is an imperative of the business, part of the culture of venture-backed start-ups. A sensible financing strategy, accordingly, focuses not only on the round on the table but on the impact of subsequent rounds as well. Ultimate dilution of the founder will depend on the success or failure of the company in raising subsequent rounds at higher prices. In considering a given investor's offer, the founder must make a judg-

[53] *Id.*, at 34. A sample of the pertinent language in a self-underwritten prospectus:

> The sale of the 250,000 shares of Common Stock is not being underwritten. The Company is offering such shares, through solicitations by its directors, officers and employees (none of whom will receive any additional compensation therefor) in the States where such solicitation is permitted, and also through certain securities dealers who are members of the National Association of Securities Dealers, Inc. (who will be paid a commission of $.40 a share for each share sold pursuant to a subscription obtained by them). Such dealers will be under no obligation to subscribe or obtain subscriptions for any of the shares.

Sage Systems Corp. Preliminary Prospectus, Mar. 27, 1969.

[54] '34 Act § 3(a)(4).

[55] '34 Act Reg. § 240.3a–4–1, 2 (CCH) *Fed. Sec. L. Rep.* ¶ 21,152.

ment whether the investor has the staying power to support the investment in subsequent periods and will do so at fair price. Leasing money, in other words, is a longitudinal process; it extends at least until the exit strategy is implemented.

(b) MULTIPLE CLOSINGS WITHIN A SINGLE ROUND—THE "EARLY CLOSING" STRATEGY

If there is one single enemy encountered by a founder in a venture financing, it is investor indecision and delay. Founders contribute to the problem because they listen selectively, interpreting a politely worded "no" as an invitation to continue with the presentation. To induce investors to declare themselves, one strategy is to line up a lead or "bell cow" investor and hold a first closing, escrowing the proceeds of the offering until enough subscriptions are collected to round out a viable financing. The hope is to create some form of stampede among investors on the fence. At the least, an early closing will serve to freeze the terms and diminish niggling over minor points.

(c) HOW MUCH TO RAISE IN THE FIRST ROUND?

The first round is usually the most dilutive financing because, obviously, it occurs at the moment of highest risk.[56] Therefore, an intelligent founder will attempt to strike a balance in his first round between obtaining as much money as he thinks he'll need to get to the next stage of development but not so much that his equity is reduced to the borderline of triviality.

If it is assumed that later rounds will be less dilutive, then it is obvious that the first round should raise the smallest amount of money necessary to take the enterprise to the next round. On the other hand, if money is available, it could be a gross error of judgment not to take it, since the second round may (as it often is), be a good deal more difficult than anticipated, perhaps only because fashions change.

(d) THE "TOO MUCH MONEY" PROBLEM

One old saw has it that a start-up firm *never* has enough money and there are anecdotes in sufficient number to illustrate that proposition. There is, however, contrary evidence, not only to the effect that the first round can be unnecessarily dilutive but that some companies are cursed

[56]A subsequent financing may be very dilutive if the issuer has fallen on hard times and money is needed for a rescue job. Money is very dear on such occasions and these financings are referred to as "burn out" financings because they dilute, or "burn out," investors with no more money to invest.

in their early stages with too much money. For example, a dynamic manager may break away from a company he's helped found and start the process all over again. Since venture investors are no less sheeplike than the rest of us, they extrapolate the past and assume that Mr. Genius can do it again. The founder takes a pregnant idea and money falls in his lap. He's not worried about dilution in the first round because of the valuation he has been able to sell to the investment community. Forgetting the parsimonious habits of his youth, the founder then attempts to shorten the development process by doubling the number of sales and marketing people, putting on more technicians and so forth. He creates a monthly expense outlay, a "burn rate," which is out of proportion to realistic expectations of the company's development. When it comes time for a second round, the existence of a massive burn rate has inexorably postponed the date on when cash break-even will occur by a period which intimidates old and new investors. Only those who have gone through the process know how difficult it is, both logistically and in human terms, to make dramatic slashes in a burn rate. Unsympathetic landlords may refuse to take back the necessary space; firing people imposes separation costs as well as personal trauma.

In short, a higher than necessary burn rate is a bad sign, a red flag to the venture capital community. Founders consistently complain they are being starved by the investors; fed hand to mouth, they bemoan the opportunities missed for lack of capital; they cite the fact that venture capital is an early entry strategy. As General Nathan Bedford Forest said, "Get there fustest with mostest." True in some instances but the converse is equally likely, based on evidence of the past: Too much money equals potential trouble.

(e) "WHO ELSE IS IN?"—THE ART OF SELECTING INVESTORS WISELY

All other things being equal and assuming the ready availability of money, the intelligent founder will select (and sell his hardest) to those investors who are likely to add something to the offering other than, and in addition to, cash. Some investors have such prestige in the venture world that their election to invest in the first instance will attract additional capital, both in the round in which they participate in and later rounds. It is a wise issuer who carefully selects his partners—that is, investors from the pools such as Greylock, Bessemer, J. H. Whitney, Venrock, Sutter Hill, Mayfield, Brentwood, Kleiner Perkins.[57] They and

[57]The author's law firm has done work for and/or with most of the organizations named in these pages. They are identified only for purposes of illustration and not to suggest that the reputation, experience, or investment skills of the firm named are any better than any of its competitors.

others are examples of venture funds with such reputations for sagacity that their existence in the buying group almost insures the success of the offering. As any veteran of venture capital financing can testify, the first question asked by a potential investor is "who else is in?" The fact is that few venture partnerships are staffed to monitor the progress of each investment in the portfolio. Accordingly, a group of investment pools will participate in a given investment and, among themselves, designate one or two partnerships as the "lead." The lead investor will negotiate the terms of the financing and seat its representative on the board. Pursuant to informal ententes, Partnership A will lead one investment, Partnership B the second, and so forth. From the founder's standpoint, it is useful to entice a prestigious partnership in as the lead because it will bring its usual companions along. Moreover, some venture funds are set up to add technical expertise in specific areas. Market Corporation of America's venture capital affiliate, Marketcorp. Venture Associates, has the opportunity to borrow the marketing expertise of the parent; the Yankee Group's consulting prowess in computer and telecommunications is available to the investments made by its affiliate, Battery Ventures. Bain Capital, an offshoot of Bain & Company, has access to one of the world's most prestigious consulting firms;[58] a venture pool affiliated with a large bank holding company holds out the possibility of a preferred relationship with the bank, although the problems inherent in being both a lender and an investor have generally inhibited, and rightly so, the bank lending side from being intimately involved with the bank venture investing side. And, a corporate venture partner brings to the table all the possibilities entailed in the corporate partnering relationship, discussed in detail in Chapter 18.

[58]The larger firms of this type are described in "Venture Capital Consulting Firm Partnerships: A Team Approach to Venture Investing," *Venture Capital J.* 6 (Nov. 1986).

Seven

Private Placements: Critical Issues Under Regulation D and Section 4(2)

The lifeblood of the venture investment process is the private financing, the placement of debt and equity in transactions exempt from registration under the federal and state securities laws. This chapter explores the issues, most of which are legal, arising in the course of a private financing. Nonlawyers will be particularly interested in § 7.4, which discusses the problems most frequently by encountered the issuer in raising capital privately.

§7.1 BACKGROUND

The so-called § 4(2), or "private offering," exemption is the basis on which most emerging business enterprises are able to sell securities in the United States. (The term refers to that section in the '33 Act which contains the exemption.)[1] Because of a series of fundamental miscues when the legislation was first drafted, the '33 Act reads backwards. Instead of postulating a definition of exempt private offerings, or defining the offerings which must be registered, the Act suggests that *all* sales of securities are to be registered and then exempts various transactions, including ones "not including any public offering" of securities.[2] Since by far the great bulk of transactions are of the exempt variety, the tail is wagging the dog. Were the language to be interpreted literally, a crime wave could break out in this country as unsuspecting small businessmen, raising a few dollars from friends and relatives for the classic corner fruit stand, wind up invoking the civil (and, theoretically at least, criminal) sanctions for violations of § 5 of the '33 Act.

For many years, the corporate bar urged the SEC to define the entire process by which securities move from the issuer to the investing public so that transactions could go forward with certainty.[3] Until relatively recently, the Commission stoutly resisted. The SEC repeatedly denied, for example, the persistent notion that sales to 25[4] or fewer persons constituted a private offering and clung to the conceptually immacu-

[1]Section 4(2) of the Securities Act of 1933 provides: "The provisions of § 5 shall not apply to . . . . transactions by an issuer not involving any public offering." In approving § 4(2) of the Act, Congress stated: "[s]ales of stock to stockholders become subject to the Act unless the stockholders are so small in number that the sale to them does not constitute a public offering." H.R. Rep. No. 152, 73d Cong., 1st Sess. (1933). *See generally* Prifti, *Securities: Public and Private Offerings* § 4:01 (1983).

[2]The second major exemption occurs in § 4(1) of the Act for secondary transactions, those not involving an "issuer, underwriter or dealer." The problem arising when institutional consumers of privately placed securities—bank and insurance companies—elect to trade their positions in another private placement has given rise to an informal exemption known as the "4(1½) exemption." The selling institution is not an "issuer" so § 4(2) is not available and the seller, as a professional stock trader, may be viewed by an "underwriter" under § 4(1). *See generally* "The Section 4(1½) Phenomenon: Private Resales of 'Restricted' Securities," 34 *Bus. Law.* 1961 (July 1979).

[3]For an early discussion of the issue, *see In Re. Brooklyn Manhattan Transit Corp.* 1 S.E.C. 147 (1935).

[4]For many years the myth persisted among laypeople and some practitioners that a corporation could issue shares without '33 Act registration to 25 or fewer shareholders. Such was never the rule under the '33 Act; the number crept into the popular domain by accident, borrowed uncritically from references in nonpertinent statues, i.e., § 14(a)(3) of the Investment Company Act of 1940, and buttressed by an early opinion of the SEC's General Counsel, Sec. Act Rel. No. 33–1285, (CCH) 1 Fed. Sec. L. Rep. ¶ 2740 (Jan. 24, 1935). While the confusion surrounding the earlier "number of purchasers" test has been largely superseded by Reg. D's bright lines, the number of *offerees* in a proposed transaction continues to be a factor in the SEC's enforcement policy. *See, e.g., Computer Electrocardiographic Processing Servs. Inc.* SEC Ruling [1971–72 Transfer Binder] (CCH) Fed. Sec. L. Rep. ¶ 78,604 (Dec. 6, 1971); Sec. Act Rel. No. 33–5487, (CCH) 1 Fed. Sec. L. Rep. ¶ 2710 (April 23, 1974); *Colorado Life Ins. Co.* No-action letter from SEC (Feb. 2, 1977), [1977] (CCH) Fed. Sec. Microfiche 14, frame J14.; Hicks, *Exempted Transactions Under the Securities Act* §§ 11.02(1), 11.06(3) (1983).

late—but practically untidy—view that "offerees" were the key indicator,[5] a slippery criterion since the federal definition of "offer" was and is much broader than the common-sense construction of that term would indicate. Faced with a variety of devices cleverly calculated to mask disguised offers, the SEC's announcements are replete with language suggesting that the merest hint could constitute "indirect solicitation."[6]

During the period of uncertainty, practitioners worked out their own guidelines, with little help from the SEC, to determine when a placement was exempt, a body of learning that continues to be marginally pertinent since the new rules, while providing a "safe harbor" (a well-used term in the law) for certain issues, do not replace the less certain parameters of § 4(2) for offerings that cannot fit under the black letter rules of Reg. D.[7]

The Commission's first significant attempts to rationalize the private offering exemption were an outgrowth of the so-called Wheat Report,[8] which called for a general modernization of securities laws. The problems at the time were numerous. The notion of dealing with "offerees" (versus purchasers) introduced enormous uncertainties into the thought processes of counsel attempting to advise law-abiding issuers. A number of essentially factitious activities were explored in order to get out of the box. For professionals engaged in organizing placements on a more or less regular basis, an artificial convention entitled "screening" was developed, becoming quite popular in the tax-shelter syndication industry where public registration was not deemed an option.[9] The appetite of investors for tax shelter was so robust that most reputable firms were drawn into the activity, persuading themselves that screening—that is, weeding out prospects and their investment advisers by showing them something less than the terms of the deal, the private placement memoranda from closed deals, for example—was exempt from the definition of "offer." Compelled by market exigencies, the prac-

[5]The SEC's views respecting offerees were endorsed by the opinion of the Supreme Court in the leading *Ralston Purina* case. *SEC v. Ralston Purina Co.* 346 U.S. 119 (1953).

[6]Sec. Act Rel. No. 33–6455, Question 60 (CCH) 1 Fed. Sec. L. Rep ¶ 2380 (March 3, 1983).

[7]Regulation D, *Preliminary Notes* No. 3.

[8]"Disclosure to Investors—A Reappraisal of Administrative Policies Under the '33 and '34 Acts" (March, 1969), commonly referred to as the "Wheat Report" after its main author, Francis M. Wheat, then a member of the Commission. *See generally* Goldwasser, *The Practitioner's Comprehensive Guide to Rule 144* 47–50 (2d ed. 1978); *see also* Throop, "Federal Regulation of Securities Committee Comments on the Wheat Report," 25 *Bus. Law.* 39 (Nov. 1969); Chalmers, "Grist From Wheat: The New SEC Ground Rules for Venture Capital," 25 *Bus. Law.* 1001 (Apr. 1970).

[9]Screening has, by coincidence, become a legitimate technique for dealing with the ban on "general solicitation" in Regulation D. *See, e.g., E.F. Hutton & Co. Inc.* No-action letter from the SEC, [1985–86 Transfer Binder] (CCH) Fed. Sec. L. Rep. ¶ 78,135 (Sept. 26, 1985), discussed *infra* § 7.4(c).

tice was as good as the securities bar could dream up to avoid the initiation of sanctions. Heavy pressure was also put on the so-called "intrastate" exemption, sales made entirely within one state,[10] particularly in the West, where wide open spaces were thought to avoid the problems an issuer might have in the crowded Northeast in determining whether securities had "come to rest" within the borders of the state in which the issuer was located and the offering made. Since these fictions made little sense in light of the purposes of the federal securities laws, the Commission finally spoke definitively to the subject, adopting a series of rules defining the exemption under the Securities Act of 1933.[11] The principal rule was Rule 146,[12] which made significant progress by stating the exemption in terms of specific numbers of purchasers. Rule 146 was still tied, however, to fuzzy tests at the offering stage, since the SEC was not ready to let go of the notion, existing from the early days of the Commission's existence, that an offer to the wrong party could and should be fatal. A test which focuses on the sophistication of offerees may be practical for offerings solely to institutions[13]

[10]Section 3(a)(11) of the '33 Act. *See infra* § 7.14. The origin of the Intrastate Exemption was in part founded on the nervousness of Congress in the 1930s at the Supreme Court's conservative (by today's standards) notions of what constituted interstate commerce.

[11]The three rules adopted in this period were Rule 146, 240, and 242. Rule 240 entailed a limited exemption for offerings by certain closely held issuers. Sec. Act Rel. No. 5560 [1974–75 Transfer Binder] (CCH) Fed. Sec. L. Rep. ¶ 80,066. (Jan. 24, 1975). Rule 242 exempted issues up to $2 million in a six-month period if the number of buyers was limited to 35, apart from "accredited persons." Sec. Act Rel. No. 33–6180 [1979–80 Transfer Binder] (CCH) Fed. Sec. L. Rep. ¶ 82,426 (Jan. 17, 1980). The third rule, Rule 146, is discussed *infra,* n. 12. Rule 242 was enacted as a result of widespread dissatisfaction with Rule 146, expressed in a series of public hearings held by the SEC in April and May of 1978. For a discussion of the SEC's gradual changes of position, *see* Halperin, *Private Placement of Securities* 67 (1984) (Halperin); *see also* Loss, *Fundamentals of Securities Regulation* 346 (1983).

[12]Rule 146, like Reg. D but in more restricted terms, forebade general solicitation and advertising, the proscriptions focusing on seminars and mailings. Rule 146(c)(2) and (3). Prior to making an *offer,* the issuer had to believe the *offeree* was "smart" or "rich"—i.e., had enough knowledge and experience that he or she could evaluate the opportunity and enough money to bear the risk. Rule 146 (d)(i) and (ii). Prior to *purchase,* the issuer had to make an inquiry and qualify the purchaser or the representative as "smart." Rule 146(d)(2). Sec. Act. Rel. No. 33–5487 (CCH) 1 Fed. Sec. L. Rep. § 2710, at 2902 (April 23, 1974).

[13]*See generally* 1 Loss, *Securities Regulation* 689 *et seq.* (2d ed. 1961 & Supp. 1962). The institutional private placement entails a transaction negotiated face to face between representatives of the seller and selected buyers. The form of the transaction is little influenced by the securities laws; indeed, Professor Loss suggests that the form would remain substantially the same if those laws were repealed. *Id.* at 691–692. It is interesting that some issuers have recently been publicly registering transactions that would qualify as private, institutional placements. The ostensible reason is to provide liquidity but the real imperative is to foreclose negotiation—the terms are set when the registration statement is filed and, psychologically at least, it is harder for buyer's counsel to insist on their favorite "nitpicks."

or, if to individuals, then solely to insiders, persons enjoying a close nexus with the company, such as senior officers and directors. If the discussions go beyond those two cohorts, a test dependent on qualified offerees is bound to be a troublemaker. How does one know whether an offeree is qualified before the discussion starts? A chicken and egg paradox?

§7.2 REGULATION D

In 1982, after almost 40 years of tugging and hauling, the law finally came to a sensible resting place; the Commission promulgated "Reg. D,"[14] which provides a practical "safe harbor" without a host of difficult traps for issuers and their counsel.

Reg. D is not exclusive. For placements unable to fit within the black letter rules of Reg. D, § 4(2) continues to be available.[15] However, the thrill has largely gone out of this area of practice. We are dealing now with private offerings with thousands of offerees[16] and hundreds of purchasers; some such private offerings result in instant public companies, required to register (because they have more than 500 shareholders) under § 12(g) of the Securities Exchange Act of 1934. The SEC has at last come to the point one expected it would never occupy—administering a rule offering relative certainty, a rule which authorizes the issuance of billions of dollars of securities annually in major transactions without the benefit of public registration.

Reg. D breaks down into six sections.[17] Rule 501 is a definitional rule; most important is the definition of "accredited investor," which is any person within one of following categories:

[14]Sec. Act Rel. No. 33–6389, [1981–82 Transfer Binder] (CCH) Fed. Sec. L. Rep. ¶ 83,106 (Mar. 8, 1982). Reg. D was first proposed for comment in Sec. Act Rel. No. 33–6339 [Transfer Binder 1981–82] (CCH) Fed. Sec. L. Rep. ¶ 83,014 (Aug. 7, 1981). Reg. D replaced Rules 240, 242, and 146. There are, or course, areas which remain unsatisfactory even after promulgation of Reg. D. *See* Campbell, "The Plight of Small Issuers (and Others) Under Regulation D: Those Nagging Problems That Need Attention," 74 *Ky. L.J.* 127, 128–9 (1985–86). To meet some of those objections, there are currently out for comment a series of SEC proposals to amend Reg. D. Sec. Act Rel. No. 33–6683 [Transfer Binder 1986–87] (CCH) Fed. Sec. L. Rep. ¶ 84,054 (Jan. 16, 1987).

[15]Reg. D, *Preliminary Notes* No. 3.

[16]Wertheimer, "Small Issuers: Update on Regulation D; Installment Payments and Assessments as New Securities; Extension of Credit," *15th Annual Institute on Securities Regulation* 377 (P.L.I. Course Handbook Series No. 428, 1983).

[17]For commentary on Reg. D, *see, e.g.*, Warren, "A Review of Regulation D: The Present Exemption Regimen for Limited Offerings Under the Securities Act of 1933," 33 *Am. U.L. Rev.* 355 (1984).

(i) institutional investors—i.e., banks, insurance companies, investment companies, business development companies, SBICs, certain employee benefit plans,[18] and certain 501(c)(3) charitable corporations;[19]

(ii) insiders—i.e., directors, executive officers and general partners of the issuer;[20]

(iii) "big ticket" purchasers, i.e., those who buy more than $150,000 of the securities (as long as $150,000 is less than 20% of the purchaser's net worth);[21]

(iv) "rich" individuals—i.e., natural persons whose net worth exceeds $1 million or whose individual income was over $200,000 for each of the preceding two years;[22]

(v) aggregates of the above—i.e., any entity whose equity owners are entirely accredited investors under any category except "big ticket" investors.[23]

Rule 501's other key provision relates to the calculation of the number of allowable purchasers in an exempt transaction. Accredited investors are excluded from the count, meaning that there may be an unlimited number of accredited investors.[24]

Rule 502[25] sets forth the general terms and conditions to be met if Reg. D is to apply; it specifically addresses integration of contemporaneous offerings, the information to be provided investors and limitations on the "manner" of the offering and/or resale. Rule 503 adds the

[18]The plan must be managed by a bank, insurance company or registered investment advisor or have assets in excess of $5 million. Rule 501(a)(1).

[19]The assets of which must exceed $5 million. Rule 501(a)(3). The SEC has proposed amendments to Reg. D which would, among other things, expand the type of institutions qualifying as accredited investors to include, *inter alia,* (i) thrift institutions and broker/dealers and (ii) any corporation, trust, or partnership with total assets in excess of $5 million if not organized for the purpose of making the investment, and (iii) any private trust with assets in excess of $5 million, not organized for the purpose, directed by a sophisticated person and investing not more than 10% of its total assets. The proposal also makes adjustments in the income test for "rich" persons to accommodate spouses with joint incomes of more than $300,000. Sec. Act. Rel. No. 33–6683, *supra* n. 14.

[20]Rule 501(a)(4).

[21]Rule 501(a)(5).

[22]Rule 501(a)(6) and (7).

[23]Rule 501(a)(8).

[24]Rule 501(e)(1)(iv).

[25]Rule 502 contains four paragraphs that set forth the conditions applicable to offers and sales made pursuant to the exemptions in Rules 504, 505, and 506. The conditions cover:

(i) Integration (Rule 502(a));
(ii) Information requirements (Rule 502(b));
(iii) Limitations on the manner of offering (Rule 502(c)); and
(iv) Limitations on resale (Rule 502(d)).

See generally Hicks, *Limited Offering Exemptions: Regulation D* (1985 ed.).

notice requirements on Form D, to be filed by the issuer with the SEC no later than 15 days after the "first sale" of securities.[26]

The exemptions themselves are contained in § 504 (issues of $500,000 or less),[27] § 505[28] (issues of $5 million or less) and § 506[29] (all other issues).

The antifraud provisions still apply to all transactions[30] and Reg. D does not do away with the necessity for disclosure (although disclosure requirements are relaxed in some instances).[31] It is also important to note that the burden of qualifying for the exemption has not been shifted; it is still up to the issuer and its advisers to make certain that each of the requirements of Reg. D has been complied with and the SEC has (to date at least) rejected the argument that "substantial compliance" should be enough to maintain the exemption's applicability.[32]

In sum, not only is Reg. D an enormous help to issuers and their counsel but the SEC has also been forthcoming in explaining the rule. In a release published on Mar. 3, 1983,[33] the staff issued an extensive interpretation in question-and-answer format. A number of no-action letters have further fleshed out the bar's insights into the staff's views.[34]

[26]Rule 503.

[27]This number would be expanded, in a sense, to $1 million if the SEC's current proposals are adopted. Sec. Act. Rel. No. 33–6683, *supra* n. 14. The qualifier is required since the Commission's current proposal is that no more than $500,000 can be sold "without registration under a State's securities laws." It is not clear what will constitute "registration" for purposes of this Rule. In any event, many if not most venture offerings are exempted in the states and, therefore, not so "registered" under any definition of the word, so the de facto cap for § 504 would remain $500,000. The SEC's proposal is based on the view that offerings under § 504 can be either public or private offerings under existing law since the "general solicitation" and "resale" limitations do not apply to § 504 offerings registered and sold in a state which requires a disclosure document. Rule 504(b)(1). The practical utility of this provision is questionable.

[28]Rule 505. In 1980, § 4(6) was added to the '33 Act. This section largely duplicates the § 505 exemption under Reg. D—i.e., issues limited to a maximum amount of $5 million solely to accredited investors without general solicitation. The principal distinction is that certain issuers—i.e., investment companies—which cannot use § 505 are eligible for § 4(6).

[29]Rule 506.

[30]Reg. D *Preliminary Notes* No. 1. In a sense, Reg. D has increased the technical burdens on counsel, first because a notice of sale has to be filed (§ 503) and, secondly, because the precise requirements for qualifying accredited investors—keyed to the investors' income and/or net worth—mean there is no excuse for neglecting to procure an investor questionnaire accurately filled out.

[31]In general, no "specific" form of disclosure is required by Reg. D for issues under $500,000 (Rule 504) and/or issues being sold exclusively to accredited investors. *See* Rule 502(b)(1)(i).

[32]Hicks, *supra* n. 25, at 373. The SEC's proposals to loosen up Reg. D, include an invitation for comments on a "substantial or good faith compliance" test. Sec. Act. Rel. No. 33–6683, *supra* n. 14.

[33]Sec. Act Rel. No. 33–6455, *supra* n. 6.

[34]*See* Hicks, *supra* n. 25 Appendix C.

Reg. D itself is, as rules go, quite specific; it's possible, indeed, for a layman to understand the major provisions of the rule simply by reading it.

§7.3 NUMBER OF OFFEREES/PURCHASERS[35]

The rules (Reg. D is a "regulation" comprising a series of "rules")[36] ostensibly allows for the issuance and sale of securities to an unlimited number of purchasers (culled from an unlimited list of offerees) if they qualify as "accredited investors," meaning people who are "rich" or otherwise qualified in the eyes of the SEC. Contrary to all prior learning, Reg. D (with exceptions having to do with the way prospects are identified) is not *technically* offended if the placement is made available to an unlimited number of offerees, a dramatic departure from the SEC's former view. Given a pool of "rich" people and a presanitized prospect list, an issuer can make what amounts to a public offering—with perhaps as many as 1,000 or more purchasers of the security and some multiple of that number as offerees—without technically running afoul of Reg. D.[37]

[35]A specific "numbers" test is involved in offerings to both accredited and nonaccredited investors (or solely to nonaccredited investors), that is, that no more than 35 nonaccredited investors can participate in offerings over $500,000. Rule 505(b)(2)(i)&(ii). The 35-investor test is not ordinarily a matter of a great moment in start-up finance because most investors in the venture business qualify as "accredited," and those who don't (i.e., family members, friends, key employees) generally don't approach 35 in number.

[36]Under the '33 Act, the Rules run from Rule 100 to Rule 656. The Rules are grouped under Articles 1 through 6 and then Regulations A through F. Each Regulation (with one exception) denotes Rules in a single decennial series; the 500 series of Rules make up Regulation D.

[37]Venture private placements, vs. tax shelter syndications, are not typically made to purchasers numbering in the hundreds. However, counsel should be sensitive to the SEC's historical difficulty with large offerings crowded under the umbrella of private placements. Thus, Footnote 30 in Sec. Rel. Act No. 6339, proposing Reg. D, (*supra* n. 14), stated:

> The Commission is aware that, pursuant to the exclusion from counting in Rule 146 for persons who purchase $150,000 of securities, many offerings claiming the exemption provided by the Rule have been sold to hundreds of purchasers. Similarly, pursuant to the accredited investor concept in Reg. D, offerings could theoretically be made to an unlimited number of accredited investors. The Commission cautions issuers, however, that depending on the actual circumstances, offerings made to such large numbers of purchasers may involve a violation of the prohibitions against general solicitation and general advertising.

It has been viewed as significant by practitioners that statements comparable with those contained in Footnote 30 did not appear in Sec. Act Rel. No. 6389, *supra* n. 14, which adopted Reg. D. Moreover, at one of the seminar-type discussions entitled, "The SEC

§7.4 "GENERAL" SOLICITATION

A critical caution is in order at this point, however. Regardless of the number of purchasers (maybe even none) or offerees, if the placement is made on the basis of either "*general* solicitation" or "*general* advertising," then an unregistered public offering has occurred. Obviously, it's hard to get a deal in front of even a limited number of potential purchasers without participating in some kind of activity reasonably viewed as "solicitation." The problem facing a founder approaching Reg. D is how to keep from running afoul of the ban on "*general*" solicitation and yet get his business plan out widely enough so that he has a chance of raising the money.

(a) RECORD KEEPING

The first rule of thumb in this area is almost a banality, but it is one that bears constant repetition: keep careful records. An analysis of the cases in which issuers were held to have gone beyond the bounds of § 4(2) will show varying fact patterns, as one might expect but, in the author's view, one consistent theme pops up—the issuer and its agents did not keep careful records and, therefore, were unable to state with certainty when challenged in court how many people had been offered the opportunity.[38] Continuing that tradition, in a recent SEC enforcement proceeding under Reg. D involving an illegal general solicitation, the order prominently reflected the fact that the number of persons

---

Speaks," at which the SEC annually gives its informal views to the securities bar, an SEC official (speaking personally) "generally agreed" with the following statement:

> Offerings of sizeable amounts shouldn't be of so much concern to the Commission so long as the investors are accredited and so long as the manner of offering—the solicitations, the high pressure sales techniques that we all know about—are not involved in the offering.

Wolfson & Kurke, "The Offering Process Under Regulation D," in *Private Placements 1986: Current Developments in Private Financings* 55, 63–64 (P.L.I. Course Handbook Series No. 522, 1986).

To one interested in how the "law" governing important commercial transactions is sometimes made, the above gives an example of the type of "wink and nod" process which a regulatory agency sometimes uses to let the sophisticated firms know how far they can go without threat of hostile enforcement proceedings.

[38]In the 1970s, a sudden fright took hold of the securities bar as, in a brief filed in proceedings before the Fifth Circuit in the *Continental Tobacco* case, the SEC's General Counsel took an extremely narrow stand on the limits of the § 4(2) exemption and the decision appeared to be influenced by those views. *SEC v. Continental Tobacco Co.*, 463 F.2d 137 (5th Cir. 1972). The position was ultimately not pursued and the contretemps indicated the need for a rationalization of the exemption, finally winding up with Reg. D. The point is that the *Continental Tobacco* holding, although not all of its language, can be explained on the basis that the issuer lost control of the number of offerees.

solicited was not known because the issuer's records were so inadequate.[39]

(b) NO ADVERTISING

Secondly, it goes without saying that the ban on advertising, even though stated in terms of "*general* advertising," really means no advertising at all; since it is difficult to conjure up a practical scenario involving "non-general" advertising, it is an oxymoron. Thus, announcements of the offered opportunity in the newspapers, on the radio, on television, and so forth, are not in order. One would think that this constraint was clear enough—either you trumpet the investment opportunity in the media or you don't—but nothing in life is simple when the securities laws are involved. An ambiguity is likely to arise if, for example, the technology being exploited is interesting and the press wants to do an interview with a founder naturally proud to have come up with a scientific breakthrough. In theory, if the founder limits his conversation with reporters to the technology and makes no mention of the fact that he's out hustling to find funding, the media have not been used "in connection with" the sale of a security. The problem is that one hasn't control of what a reporter will actually publish; a single mention in the press of the pending offering could blow Reg. D's safe harbor inadvertently.[40] In a recent "no action" letter[41] commenting on tombstone advertising, the staff restated their view that materials designed to "condition the market"

[39]*In the matter of Kenman Corporation* [1984–1985 Transfer Binder] (CCH) Fed. Sec. L. Rep. ¶ 83,767, (Apr. 19, 1985).

[40]"Beating the gun," or "gun-jumping," usually refers to premature offers by issuers involved in public offerings of securities, as when an orchestrated story on the company's key product immediately precedes the filing. *See* 1 Loss, *Securities Regulation supra* n. 13 at 215. Private placements raise issues akin to gun-jumping. For example, one no-action request unsuccessfully sought the staff's agreement that promoting the issuer's services through radio and television at the same time it was structuring an issue under Reg. D would not constitute "general advertising." *Printing Enterprises Management Science Inc.* SEC No-action letter [1982–83 Transfer Binder] (CCH) Fed. Sec. L. Rep. ¶ 77,415 at 78,517 (Mar. 23, 1983). *See also Alma Securities Corporation,* SEC No-action letter (Aug. 2, 1982) Fed. Sec. Library, No-act file. Compare Sec. Act Rel. No. 33–5180 concerning permissible activities—i.e., normal advertisements, answering unsolicited telephone inquiries "from the press," announcing "factual business and financial developments," for a company in the midst of registering a public offering. (CCH) 1 Fed. Sec. L. Rep. ¶ 3056 (Aug. 16, 1971). The point is that a privately held company has no statutory duty to make any announcements at all.

[41]*Gerstenfeld* No-action letter (Dec. 3, 1985) (Wash. Serv. Bur. Microfiche, fiche 976, frame F 11) in which the staff opined:

> Because the primary purpose of the advertisement is to sell securities *and to condition the market for future sales,* the advertisement would constitute an offer even at a time when securities are not being sold if the syndicator expects in the near future to offer and sell securities. [Emphasis supplied.]

for the securities constituted an offer even though the tombstone did not specifically mention the transaction in question.

(c) MAILINGS

Even with the most careful records, a forbidden solicitation may still be alleged because the word "general" is not susceptible of a precise, objective test. For example, a founder may want to mail to a list, of say, all venture capital funds named in *Pratt's Guide to Venture Capital Sources,* the most common reference book in the field.[42] If a mailing does go out to 1,000 names, is that a general solicitation? The SEC has helped illuminate the issue in a series of "no-action" letters. Taken together, the letters indicate a staff view that *general* solicitation does not occur when the solicitor and his targets have a nexus—as the SEC puts it, a "substantial pre-existing" relationship.[43]

The learning comes largely from the tax shelter syndication area, where placement agents with long lists of previously screened prospects are the norm because, at least prior to 1987, tax shelter "junkies" (as they were called) tended to be repeat buyers. Thus, in a factual pattern which runs through the no-action responses most often cited as influential,[44] it is typically brokers, not the founder, who are soliciting individuals to invest in limited partnership products. In order to establish a meaningful "pre-existing business relationship" between the broker and the prospect, the brokers send out "cold" mailings well in advance of the deals—questionnaires asking individuals to fill in certain financial information and to establish a record of their "sophistication" in such transactions. Reading the requests together, the staff's view is that an offering not in existence at the time the questionnaire was mailed can be sent out widely without running afoul of the "general solicitation" constraint.[45]

This learning is only tangentially helpful in the venture context, where brokers with long mailing lists are not usually employed, generally because the business is not profitable for them. A founder doing his first, and perhaps the only, deal of his lifetime has no access to a list of prior prospects. Absent such a list, the founder is left to soliciting his friends, business acquaintances and parties with whom he can conjure up a

[42]*See supra* Ch. 1, n. 7.

[43]Based on SEC staff positions taken in a series of "no action" letters, the understanding of practitioners is that numbers will not by themselves be determinative; the question is whether the offerees have a materially substantial relationship with the offeror prior to the solicitation. *See, e.g., E.F. Hutton,* No-Action Letter, *supra* n. 9. *Bateman Eichler, Hill Richards Inc.* No-action letter from the SEC (Wash. Serv. Bur. Microfiche, fiche 976, frame E13, Dec. 3, 1985); *Woodtrails Seattle Ltd.* No-action letter from the SEC [1982–1983 Transfer Binder] (CCH) Fed. Sec. L. Rep. ¶ 77,342 (Aug. 9, 1982).

[44]*See* responses cited *supra* n. 43; *Gerstenfeld* No-action letter, *supra* n. 41.

[45]*See* the discussion in Sec. Act Rel. No. 33–6455, *supra* n. 6, at Question (60).

prior relationship of some kind. Presumably, that list can be expanded vicariously, by asking his lawyer, accountant, and/or banker to make the material available to potential purchasers with whom they are acquainted. How much further he can go is still unclear. Parenthetically, as earlier indicated, it is critical to keep careful records identifying all offerees, even though the names do not appear on a master mailing list; if an intermediary is asked to help, it is important to memorialize the intermediary's activities.

§7.5 "RICH" PEOPLE AND OTHER ACCREDITED INVESTORS

A placement under Reg. D is much smoother if the purchasers are solely "accredited investors."[46] If a single nonaccredited investor is allowed to purchase, two bad things happen. First, for offerings in excess of $500,000, specified disclosure is mandated; the issuer must prepare information as if the issuer were offering the securities publicly.[47] Secondly, in a holdover from Rule 146, nonaccredited investors in a financing in excess of $5 million must be qualified as "smart," jargon for the proposition that the purchaser (alone or together with his "purchaser representative") has sufficient "knowledge and experience in financial matters" to evaluate the merits and risks of the investment.[48] The pressure to limit placements of more than $500,000 to accredited investors only is particularly strong because the benefit of Reg. D is lost if it is not complied with to the letter.[49] That being the case, the mandatory disclosure requirement, specifying the particular items to be included, opens up a Pandora's Box of issues which must be considered; no one item of disclosure may be critical or difficult in and of itself, but the fact that the issuer and its counsel must be right in every instance on the items to be included indicates that nonaccredited investors may be more trouble than they are worth.[50]

All legal definitions are fuzzy at their margins, but "accredited investor" is less troublesome than most. The categories of persons who qualify break down along lines familiar to students of legal history in this area. First, the class includes "institutional investors," those entities which,

[46]Since there is a redundancy—§ 4(6) of the '33 Act also exempting, like Rule 505 of Reg. D, sales not in excess of $5 million solely to "accredited investors"—the term is defined not only in Reg. D but in § 2(15) of the '33 Act and Rule 215. There is no apparent logic to this happenstance.

[47]Rule 502(b)(2).

[48]Rule 506(b)(2)(ii).

[49]For the SEC's request for comments on a "substantial compliance" test, *see* Sec. Act Rel. No. 33–6683, *supra* n. 14.

[50]The issuer will not even have the benefit of the SEC staff's letter of comment to remind it of omissions or misinterpretations.

from 1933 forward, have been the paradigmatic investors eligible to participate in private offerings. Institutional investors, for Reg. D purposes, are specified as banks, insurance companies, investment companies, SBICs, and tax-exempt institutions of more than moderate size.

Next comes the buyers blessed by language in the *Ralston Purina* opinion[51]—directors and executive officers of the issuer, the classic insiders.[52] An addition not heretofore featured in the culture of private offerings—so-called "big ticket" investors—consists of persons (not limited to natural persons) who buy $150,000 or more of the securities if the purchaser's net worth is at least five times the purchase price. Penultimately, the exemption includes the new starters codified in Rule 146—that is, "rich" people, meaning individuals (*nota bene,* only natural persons) either with a net worth in excess of $1 million or an annual income for each of the last two years of at least $200,000. The last subclass is composed of entities comprised entirely of accredited investors (not including "big ticket investors).

§7.6 ENTITIES

Many of the most interesting issues arise when the investor is an entity and not accredited as an institution. For example, most corporations have no trouble qualifying as "big ticket" investors because their net worth—a minimum of $750,000 (5 × $150,000)—covers the investment handily. However, in some placements it may not be possible to get as much as $150,000 worth of stock, in which case General Motors would be nonaccredited because the alternative to "big ticket" status is "rich" status and the "rich" category ($1 million in net worth and $200,000 in annual income) is open only to natural persons.[53] If an entity qualifies as accredited only under Rule 501(a)(5)—"big ticket"—but it has been organized for "the specific purpose" of acquiring the securities offered, all the members of the entity shall, under such circumstances, be counted as purchasers and one bad apple will spoil the barrel. (A planning point. Some practitioners will approve a partnership with some nonaccredited investors organized for the purpose of investing in placement A *and* placement B—an entity organized for two purposes is not organized for the "specific purpose" or so the theory goes. It must be noted that the SEC staff has not expressly agreed with this reasoning.) The flip side of

[51]*SEC v. Ralston Purina* 346 U.S. 119 (1953).

[52]In the Court's words, qualified insiders consisted of:

> Executive personnel who because of their position have access to the same kind of information that the Act would make available in the form of a registration statement.

346 U.S. 119, 125–26 (1953).

[53]This unusual result will change if the SEC's current proposals to amend Reg. D are adopted. *See supra* n. 14.

the "single entity" question can also arise in the context of integration, discussed later. That is, if two or more entities are organized to float what amounts to a single offering of securities (the promoters' idea is that splitting the offering into two separate parts will bring each in under, say, $500,000), the separate entities may be disregarded by the SEC.[54]

Further, the final category of investors extends accredited status to an entity comprised of members, "all" of which are accredited investors other than "big ticket" investors. This looks like a handy "catch-all" provision but such is not necessarily the case. The SEC staff takes the word "all" in Rule 501(a)(8) seriously; if all but one of the shareholders of a corporation are accredited investors and the unaccredited shareholder is a director who bought one share of stock in order to comply with a state law requirement that all directors be shareholders, the corporation is not, in the staff's view, an accredited investor under Rule 501(a)(8).[55]

It is anomalous that some entities, entities common sense would deem to be eminently qualified, cannot be accredited. A single nonaccredited member keeps them out of the ambit of Rule 501(a)(8) and their only other avenue—"big ticket" status—is unavailable because the concept of net worth is not apposite. A wealthy law partnership,[56] for example, may have no need for a substantial capital account, distributing earnings as they accrue. A trust for the benefit of the minor children of a rich family may be funded in a way that does not entail "net worth" in any significant amount. Indeed, a *trust* cannot be accredited under Rule 501(a)(8) even if *all* of its beneficiaries are accredited investors;[57] the SEC staff does not interpret "equity owners" to include the beneficiaries of a conventional trust. (It has indicated that the result might be different in the case of "certain nonconventional trusts;"[58] and, if the trustee is a bank qualifying under Rule 501(a)(1), the trustee will be able to participate in a Reg. D offering as an accredited investor for the benefit of the trust.)

[54] *See* Hicks, *supra* n. 25, at 234.

[55] Sec. Act Rel. No. 6455, *supra* n. 6, Question (24).

[56] The question can hang on whether the firm has limited partners; a *general* partnership, not formed for the purpose, may qualify by aggregating the net worth of all the general partners. Sec. Act Rel. No. 6455, *supra* n. 6, Question (18). In the proposals set forth in the Jan. 16, 1987 Release, *see supra* n. 14, a partnership with total *assets* in excess of $5 million will qualify if not organized for the purpose of making the investment.

[57] Sec. Act Rel. No. 6455, *supra* n. 6, Question (30). This rule will be changed if the SEC's current proposal is adopted. *See* Sec. Act Rel. No. 33–6683, *supra* n. 14.

[58] Sec. Act Rel. No. 6455, *supra* n. 6, Question (26).

§7.7 MISCELLANEOUS

The rest of Reg. D follows generally the historical outlines of the private offering exemption. Small financings, those under $500,000, are the least heavily regulated. Purchasers need not be accredited and there is no limit on the number of buyers.[59] No specific disclosure is mandated but the antifraud rules apply.[60] Larger financings ($500,000 to $5 million, and $5 million and over) limit the number of unaccredited investors to 35 and, if any unaccredited investors participate, require specific forms of disclosure. Indeed, if any unaccredited investors participate in financings of more than $5 million, they (or their representatives) must be qualified as "smart."[61] Securities acquired in any Reg. D financing are (with an exception not frequently utilized)[62] "restricted," that is, subject to limitations on resale of the "investment letter" type. A notice of sale on Form D must be filed by the issuer in connection with each Reg. D placement.[63] As indicated earlier, the disclosure obligations in Reg. D are potentially onerous; the "same kind of information as would be required in Part 1 of Form S–18 (in the case of Rule 505 offerings up to $5,000,000) . . . [or] in part 1 of a registration statement" (in the case of offerings of more than $5 million).[64] Although the Rule provides some relief if information cannot be obtained "without unreasonable effort or expense," the problems entailed in crafting an offering document with the "same kind of information" that would go in a public prospects suggest substantial expense. The preferred solutions, wherever possible, are (i) keep the offering under $500,000; (ii) sell to no nonaccredited investors;[65] or (iii) find some other exemption, that is, the "intrastate exemption" under Rule 147.[66]

[59]The exemption in Rule 504 for offerings under $500,000 is not available to public companies. Rule 504(a).
[60]*Preliminary Notes,* No. 1.
[61]Rule 506(b)(2)(ii).
[62]The resale limitation and the ban on general solicitation or general advertising is lifted for § 504 offerings only in states which require "registration" and a "disclosure document." Rule 504(b)(1) discussed *supra* at n. 27, The tradeoff—a virtual public offering under Reg. D at a cost of state "registration"—is not frequently palatable for offerings so small.
[63]Rule 503.
[64]Rule 502(b)(2)(i)(A) and (B).
[65]Under Rule 502(b)(1), the S–18 or S–1 type of information need not be supplied in such instances, all subject, of course, to the antifraud rules.
[66]*See infra* § 7.14.

§7.8 PRACTICAL PRECAUTIONS

As a practical matter, the founder and his counsel should approach Reg. D with a sense of the historical evolution of the rule and employ selected measures so as to minimize the changes of inadvertent error.

(i) Guideline number one has been mentioned: Keep accurate records. This is an admirable goal to which all businessmen subscribe but the goal cannot be achieved by simply ordering it to happen. An individual—one and only one—should be officially appointed the "gatekeeper." All solicitation should be preapproved by that individual. The gatekeeper should maintain careful records of the destination of every item of sales literature, a record of all meetings and telephone contacts—who was present and what was said. He decides, on advice of counsel, whether a purchaser is eligible as an accredited investor, whether the investor's certification to that effect has been properly filled out, whether to go beyond and behind that certification in close cases. Purchaser questionnaires are to be sent by and returned to the gatekeeper, who makes sure Form D is filed on time. If it is necessary to qualify a purchaser as "smart" (because he is unaccredited in an over-$5 million financing), the gatekeeper issues the necessary clearance. The gatekeeper patrols the "blue sky" issue, whether it is legal to make offers into a given state under the local statute.

(ii) Next, if at all possible, restrict all offerings in excess of $500,000 to accredited investors.[67]

(iii) Third, price the shares in units, if possible, of $150,000 or more. The reason is obvious: Corporations and partnerships are eligible buyers as "big ticket" accredited investors.[68] The issuer may reserve the right to sell fractional units, but only to investors otherwise accredited. If the investors are paying in installments, restrict the final maturity to five years or less because Rule 501(a)(5) permits accreditation of an investor as a "big ticket" investor even though the investor pays his $150,000 (or more) with a note, provided the note entails an unconditional obligation to pay the balance within five years of the sale.[69]

[67]In certain instances, it may be advisable to go the other way—to characterize (and qualify) an offering of less than $500,000 as an offering exempt under Rule 506 (vs. Rule 504) because the law in a given state make it easier to qualify a Rule 506 placement.

[68]A person is an accredited investor of the "big ticket" type upon the purchase of at least $150,000 of the securities if the total purchase does not exceed 20% of the investor's net worth at the time of sale. Rule 501(a)(5). For natural persons, the joint net worth of the investor and the investor's spouse may be used in measuring the ratio of purchase to net worth.

[69]This is consistent with the theory behind Rule 501(a)(5). An installment obligation that extends for more than five years might "so reduce the present value of the purchaser's investment that he would no longer have the bargaining power to obtain desired disclosure about the securities offering from the issuer." Hicks, *supra* n. 25, at 80.

(iv) Fourth, insist that each purchaser fill out a questionnaire attesting, among other things, to his or her accredited status and keep the questionnaire in a permanent file.

(v) Fifth, specifically inform each investor the securities are restricted and obtain (a) a promise from each adequately acknowledging an undertaking to sell only in a public offering or pursuant to an exemption from registration, and (b) a series of representations (including particularly that he has read the private placement memorandum) designed to help in preserving the exemptive status of the offering and inhibit later lawsuits.[70] Rule 502(d) imposes limits on resale which are an express codification of the learning under § 4(2), meaning that the certificates should be legended.[71]

(vi) Sixth, give no press interviews during the selling period. Restrict the list of prospects to people with whom someone on the "sell" side of the transaction—the issuer and its officers and directors, placement agent, lawyers and accountants—has a "pre-existing business" relationship.[72]

(vii) Seventh, because of the possibility of the integration of two contemporaneous offerings (discussed below), raise enough money so that no financings will be necessary for six months after the date of closing.[73]

(viii) Eighth, make available to the investors all pertinent information concerning the issuer; make a record of all information furnished or accessed. Whether or not some or all of the information is assembled in a private placement memorandum, make sure each investor gets a list of the risk factors. Do not depend on the private placement memorandum as the only source of investor information—record each specific invitation to investors to meet with the founder and his key employees, to ask and receive answers to questions.[74]

(ix) Ninth, actively negotiate the terms of the offering with the lead investor (or all the investors). An offering with fixed, inflexible terms looks more like a public flotation of securities than a negotiated transaction.

[70]*See* Ch. 8, § 8.11.

[71]Rule 502(d)(3).

[72]*See supra* § 7.4.

[73]The integration principles are set out in Rule 502(a).

[74]*See* Rule 502(b)(2)(v):

> The issuer shall also make available to each purchaser at a reasonable time prior to his purchase of securities in a transaction under Rule 505 or 506, the opportunity to ask questions and receive answers concerning the terms and conditions of the offering and to obtain any additional information which the issuer possesses or can acquire without unreasonable effort or expense that is necessary to verify the accuracy of information furnished under paragraph (b)(2)(i) or (ii) of Rule 502.

§7.9 STATE REGULATION

State regulation of private placements is expensive and a nuisance. In the author's view, it is unclear that the savings to investors are justified by the expense added to each placement. State regulation theoretically complements the federal scheme since several states—the so-called "merit" states—purport to exclude offerings, regardless of the quantum of disclosure, that are deemed unworthy on the merits. State laws are routinely referred to as "blue sky" statutes, the first epiphany being the 1911 decision of the Kansas legislature to protect local citizens against fraudulent offerings.[75] The urge to regulate has resulted in the creation of large bureaucracies in many states, under the jurisdiction of a public official, usually the secretary of state, and in many instances Parkinson's Law mandates that the office find ways to keep itself busy in protecting local residents against "fraud." The occasional fraudulent offering has been blocked at the state line, but state regulation adds millions of dollars of extra transaction costs each year to the bills of small businesses attempting to raise capital.[76]

At the outset, three types of placements should be distinguished. First, some offerings exempt under Reg. D, particularly in the so-called "syndication" area, are in fact unregistered public offerings.[77] The purchasers, all accredited investors, may number in the thousands. The issue is underwritten, albeit on a best efforts basis, by a major bracket underwriter with distribution outlets around the country. The second

[75]Kansas, Ch. 133, Laws of 1911. The term "blue sky" was apparently taken from a comment of the United States Supreme Court that state securities laws were enacted to protect investors from securities transactions which had no more substance than so many feet of blue sky. *Hall v. Geiger–Jones Co.* 242 U.S. 539, 550 (1917); *see generally* Loss & Cowett, *Blue Sky Law* (1958).

[76]*See* Levine, "A Challenge to Massachusetts Merit Regulation of Securities: An Empirical Analysis," 31 *Bost. B.J.* 26 (Jan./Feb. 1987). The study indicates that the public securities offerings rejected by Massachusetts performed as well in the after market as those accepted. The record of the bureaucrats in intercepting fraud may be better *vis-à-vis* private placements but the possibility is doubtful since most placements are exempt.

[77]The term "public offering" crops up in other statutory contexts. For example, an investment pool is exempt under § 3(c)(1) of the Investment Company Act of 1940, 15 U.S.C. § 80a–3(c)(1), if it has fewer than 100 shareholders and is not making a "public offering." *See* Halloran, *supra* Ch. 1, n. 16 at 166–67. Similarly, the Federal Reserve Board does not consider staged payments in nonpublic offerings to violate Reg. T. Federal Reserve Board Release (Mar. 1972) § 5–740 (interpreting § 220.13 of Regulation T). The SEC has adopted the view that a Rule 506 transaction is not a public offering for purposes of § 3(c)(1). Sec. Act Rel. No. 6389, [1981–1982 Transfer Binder] (CCH) Fed. Sec. L. Rep. ¶ 83,106 (Mar. 8, 1982). Ironically, under the statutory scheme, the Reg. D. transaction most likely to be a de facto public offering, the over $5 million offering under Rule 506, is technically the *one* type which must be a *non*public offering since it depends for its statutory validity on § 4(2) of the '33 Act. The smaller offerings under Rules 504 and 505 are supported by the "small issue" exemption in § 3(b) of the '33 Act.

is a venture-type placement, with the securities being sold to a handful of professional venture firms by the founders; sometimes the services of a placement agent are employed, though usually not. The third is the mom and pop organization, the issuer informally offering shares to relatives and acquaintances of the founder, with no placement agent involved. (There are, of course, combinations of the above.)

Only the second and third categories are relevant in this discussion, the "venture rounds" of financing and the "founders round," as they are sometimes called. And the object of counsel in those rounds is relatively simple: Find an exemption from all "blue sky" laws even if it is necessary to change the terms of the offering or to drop the placement effort in a given state. The budget of these financings does not include money for the time-consuming and expensive process of registering such placements in any state, let alone a state that subscribes to so-called "merit" review as applied to private placements.

The hunt for exemptions requires, unfortunately, an examination of the statute and regulations in each state in which a selling effort is to be mounted.[78] Despite some attempts to coordinate the exemptive language among the states *vis-à-vis* the federal exemptive scheme,[79] the statutes are seldom exactly alike and certain states—particularly New York, California, Massachusetts, Pennsylvania, and Texas[80]—have gone largely their own way. The larger law firms house individual lawyers who specialize in "blue sky" matters and, depending on the nature of the offering, counsel will be able to set out some guidelines which will cut down the scope of the investigatory burden. Nonetheless, one negligent mistake can contaminate the entire placement; if an issue requires that purchasers in one state be offered their money back, purchasers in the remaining states will usually have a rescission claim because the issuer has warranted, expressly or impliedly, that the issue was everywhere "legal." Consequently, a state-by-state review is the only prudent course of action. One cautionary note prior to a discussion of the exemptive scheme: Despite the fact that an "exemption" from registration

[78]*See, e.g.*, MacEwan, "Blue Sky Offerings of Reg. D Offerings," 18 *Sec. & Commodity Reg.* 103 (1985), in which each state's law is analyzed.

[79]The Small Business Investment Incentive Act of 1980, which added § 4(6) to the '33 Act, also inserted § 19(c), requiring the SEC to work with state administrators toward the development of a uniform exemption from registration for small issuers. In 1982, the National Association of State Securities' Administrators (NASSA) officially adopted the Uniform Limited Offering Exemption (ULOE), designed to resonate with Reg. D. A number of states have adopted "fairly comprehensive" versions of the ULOE. Harroch, *supra* Ch. 1, n. 25, at § 504[1] listing the states. *See infra* § 7.10(b).

[80]Lipsman, "Exemptions Under the Texas Securities Act: A Logical Framework for the Practicing Attorney," 22 *Hous. L. Rev.* 725 (May 1985). *See also* Gittleman, Ponns–Townley, Wacksman, "Private Placements and the State Securities Laws," in *Private Placements 1986: Current Developments in Private Financings, supra*, n. 37 at 293, 319–341; Harroch, *supra* Ch. 1, n. 25, at § 5.05.

is open in a given state, it is critically important to appreciate that filings may still—indeed usually are—necessary. The filings may be primitive—simply a notice of the fact that a placement has occurred—but they are mandatory and time limits are imposed.

§7.10 COMMON PROVISIONS

(a) UNIFORM SECURITIES ACT[81]

The Uniform Securities Act, first adopted by the National Conference of Commissioners on State Law in 1956, is the result of Professor Louis Loss's efforts to harmonize disparate state regulations; it has been passed (with myriad local variations) in more than 35 states.[82] The Act divides into four major parts: antifraud, registration of brokers/dealers, registration of offerings, and miscellaneous (i.e., definitions, penalties, administrative matters). In terms of exemptions for private placements, the most frequently used section is § 402(b)(9), which sets out the "limited offering" exemption, an exemption for not more than 10 offers in a state in a given 12-month period if the buyer takes for investment and no selling commissions are paid.[83] Certain institutional investors are disregarded in calculating the "10 offer" boundary.[84]

Some form of this exemption is in effect in most states but a number of issues must be resolved by examining the specific state statute. Is the exemption available for nonissuer transactions? Must some sort of filing be made (i) before the first offer? (ii) before the first sale? (iii) after the closing? Is a venture limited partnership an "institutional investor?" Must noninstitutional offerees pass some "knowledge and experience" test? A "relationship with the issuer" test? Does the manner of the offering (i.e., general solicitation) make a difference? Does the statute operate extraterritorially (i.e., must the issuer count as an offer "in" state X an offer to a resident of state X made in state Y)? Do payments of expenses to officers and directors count as "selling commissions?" Does the dollar amount of the offering make a difference? Are sales pursuant to conversion and/or option or warrant exercise rights specially exempted? Must the offerees have "access" to, or be furnished with, certain types of information?

[81] *See generally* Loss & Cowett, *Blue Sky Law* 230–244 (1958).

[82] The Uniform Securities Act (U.S.A.) is found in Volume 7B, Uniform Laws Annotated, at 509–697, or at (CCH) 1 Blue Sky L. Rep. ¶ 5500.

[83] The 1985 revision of the Uniform Act shifts the emphasis to purchasers, vs. offerees, and bumps the number to 25. *See* Fass & Wittner, *Blue Sky Practice for Public and Private Limited Offerings* 9 (1987).

[84] U.S.A. § 402(b)(8).

(b) ULOE

Some 40 states have adopted versions of the Uniform Limited Offering Exemption (ULOE) promulgated by the National Association of State Securities Administrators.[85] The ULOE generally tracks Rule 505 of Reg. D (offerings of less than $5 million), and most states have extended their version to include Rule 506 offerings.[86] The major distinction between Reg. D and the ULOE has to do with the fact that most "blue sky" regulatory schemes perform double duty, regulating both broker/dealers and issuers. Reg. D is generally indifferent on the question whether the stock is placed directly or with the good offices of a placement agent. Under both the Uniform Securities Act and the ULOE, the existence of a compensated agent makes a difference. Thus, the ULOE provides that an issuer who employs a placement agent must reasonably believe that the agent is registered as a broker/dealer in the state.[87] This can be a pain because only the major wire houses maintain such a network of offices as to involve registration in all 50 states.

Indeed, under both the Uniform Securities Act and ULOE, the exemption is lost if a commission is paid, unless the purchasers are all institutional investors (or unless, as may often be the case, the state officials will grant a waiver, their disposition to do so being directly proportionate to the prestige of the broker involved).

The alternative is to use no independent placement agent and rely on the issuer's officers or partners to sell the deal.[88] For most venture placements, such is the norm, since placement agents are largely uninterested in transactions of that size.[89]

(c) MISCELLANEOUS ISSUES

Some states are particularly vexing and, unhappily, they include critical jurisdictions for venture finance (*e.g.*, Massachusetts).[90] It is occasionally

[85](CCH) NASAA Reports ¶ 6201. For the history of the ULOE, *see supra* n. 79.

[86]*Id.* at ¶ 6401. *See* Harroch, *supra* Ch. 1, n. 25, at § 5.04[2]. Rule 504 has not been widely copied in the states.

[87]"No commission, fee, or other remuneration shall be paid or given, directly or indirectly, to any person for soliciting any prospective purchaser in this State unless such person is appropriately registered in this State." ULOE Rule 1(A).

[88]Depending on the state, payments to officers of the issuer for soliciting prospects may not be viewed as a "commission" coming within the scope of Rule 1(A) of the ULOE as long as no *special* compensation is paid and nonofficer employees are not used.

[89]*See* Ch. 6, § 6.10.

[90]*See* Honig, "Massachusetts Securities Regulation: An Evolving Matrix," 27 *Boston Bar J.* 10 (Nov. 1983); Honig, "Massachusetts Securities Regulation: In Search of the Fulcrum," 13 *U. Balt. L. Rev.* 469 (1984); Gittleman, Ponns–Townley, & Wacksman, "Private Placements and the State Securities Laws," in *Private Placements 1986: Current Developments in Private Financings, supra* n. 37, at 293.

possible to structure the sale to avoid a given state; a Massachusetts-based fund might have a New York office, for example. However, this practice must be approached with caution. The fact that an offer is made outside a given state—that is, to a California resident in his summer home in Nevada—does not mean that California's legal jurisdiction is defeated.[91]

Most state exemptions, like Reg. D, close their doors in the face of general solicitation or advertising. Indeed, the mere use of sales literature accompanying the private placement memorandum may forfeit access to exemptions in a given state.[92] As with Reg. D, investment letters from purchasers[93]—indeed, "stop transfer" legends on the stock certificates—are required, as is a "notice of sale" or similar in-state filing, to obtain the exemption and/or keep it alive. The states that require a filing either shortly before (or sometimes after) a *sale* in the state pose manageable problems. The states which purport to insist on a filing before an *offer*[94] is made are inviting violations since the process of making an offer is so much more informal and harder to police than a sale.

In summary, guidelines for dealing with "blue sky" issues include the following: When in doubt, do not engage a placement agent, since the payment of commissions to outsiders is a burden on the process of squeezing within the various exemptions; limit sales (and sometimes offers) to institutions if possible; avoid contacts with certain well nigh impossible states.[95] Finally make sure that no offers or sales are made *anywhere* until the law of the state concerned has been checked. It is infinitely easier to avoid problems before they arise.

§7.11 STOCK TO EMPLOYEES

Reg. D is a workable solution for most of the problems encountered in a formal venture capital placement—sophisticated investors pumping new capital into an unseasoned company. The real world problem arises from the fact that start-ups use equity not only to attract needed capital but also to motivate employees, attract customers, make acquisitions,

[91]On this issue *see generally* Harroch, *supra* Ch. 1, n. 25, at § 5.05(3).

[92]*See* Cal. Corp. Code § 25008 (West 1977 & Supp. 1987).

[93]*See* Comment to Uniform Securities Act § 402(b)(9) "The section does not require a written representation by each buyer that he is taking for investment, but it would be prudent on the part of the seller to obtain something in writing."

[94]*E.g.*, Massachusetts, New Mexico, North Dakota, South Carolina. *See* MacEwan, "Blue Sky Regulations of Reg. D offerings," 18 *Sec. & Commodities Reg.* 103 (1985).

[95]If the issuer's place of business is in, say, Massachusetts, that avenue is, of course, closed since some of the purchasers—*e.g.*, key officers—are likely to be local residents. Some states, *e.g.*, California, have a narrow exemption for the organization of a mom and pop corporation. Cal. Corp. Code § 25102(h) (West 1977 & Supp. 1987).

hold off creditors; equity is a form of currency and, indeed, the only currency a cash-starved firm may have. The need to use equity arises ad hoc, not dictated by the rhythmic spacing of financings which provide capital; that is, the scheduled placement of securities designed to raise enough cash for, say, the next 12 months. A start-up may want to dribble stock out frequently. One month a hot scientist is available if the equity is right, the next month the mid-level employees start agitating for more generous stock option grants, shortly followed by the necessity of issuing shares to a former employee electing to exercise his previously granted stock option. As the company continues to attract employees, one of the directors advises that it should look into various other incentive programs for employees, that is, a "phantom stock" plan, an ESOP (Employee Stock Ownership Plan).[96]

The issuer is faced with a smorgasboard of exemptions from registration which overlap in unstructured ways. To be sure, some of the hunger by employees to receive shares of stock (versus cash) will be mitigated by the elimination of favorable tax treatment for capital gains. However, the company's incentive to use stock is not diminished as long as: (i) it does not have any cash; and, (ii) most forms of equity compensation do not "cost" the company anything since the numbers involved do not run through the income statement.

A simplistic hypothetical case will serve to introduce the problem. A Reg. D offering to accredited investors is flanked on one side (say, three

[96]The term "ESOP" refers generically to an employee benefit program that invests its assets primarily in the employer's stock. *See* Employee Retirement Income Security Act of 1974 (ERISA), Pub. L. No. 93–406, 88 Stat. 829 (codified as amended at 29 U.S.C. §§ 1001–1461) and parallel governing provisions under the Internal Revenue Code of 1986, as amended; *see* I.R.C. §§ 401–409 and other scattered provisions. There is a large body of literature explaining the ESOP concept and assessing its significance as an employee benefit. For discussions of the statute and implementing regulations, *see* Menke, "ESOPs New Look Under the Final Regulations," 5 *J. Pension Plan & Compliance* 213, (1979); Ludwig & Curtis, "ESOPs made substantially more attractive as a result of Economic Recovery Tax Act," 55 *J. Tax'n* 208, (1981). Under the Internal Revenue Code, an ESOP is defined as an employee stock bonus plan or a combination of a stock bonus and money purchase plan, which meets special regulatory and statutory provisions relating to its operation and holding of stock. I.R.C. §§ 409, 4975(e)(7); Treas. Reg. § 54.4975–11; T.D. 7571, 1979–1 C.B. 368. As a defined contribution plan, the ESOP credits contributions to individual employee accounts such that future benefits depend upon the return earned on the employer's stock. Osgood, *The Law of Pensions and Profit-Sharing* § 2.25 (1984); Holbrist, *Pension Reform Handbook* ¶ 181 (1984). The tax benefits opened up by an ESOP consist mainly of a deduction to the employer for stock contributed to or purchased by the plan, I.R.C. § 404(2)(9), and an exclusion of one half the interest paid to a creditor for money borrowed by the ESOP.

months before) by the creation of an incentive stock option plan (together with grants pursuant to the plan) and the institution of a stock bonus plan,[97] and on the other (three months after) by the execution of contracts with key employees which provide for the issuance of restricted stock, stock which "vests" (i.e., is no longer subject to a penalty repurchase) in installments over the period of the employee's tenure. The employees are neither key officers nor "rich" nor "big ticket" investors and, therefore, not "accredited investors" for purposes of Reg. D.

The first question is whether each offering, viewed separately, can find an exemptive home. Since the employees are not exclusively "executive officers"[98] under Reg. D, it is necessary, if the offering exceeds $500,000, to follow the elaborate disclosure provisions in Rule 502(b) with respect to the employee issuances if Reg. D is to be the operative exemption, a burdensome requirement. Fortunately, that problem is likely to be alleviated soon. On Jan. 23, 1987,[99] the Commission proposed for comment Rules 701 and 702, which would deal specifically with many of the problems as far as employee issuances are concerned. Rule 701, if adopted, will exempt stock issued by an issuer (not including the issuer's affiliates) not subject to the reporting requirements of the '34 Act "in accordance with a compensatory employee benefit plan . . . or pursuant to a written contract of employment." The shares would be restricted securities until, it appears, 90 days after the effective date of an IPO. (It is important to note that the staff views the Rules as exempting issues which do *not* involve a financing, a transaction in which the issuer uses the exemption as a device to raise cash.)

If Rules 701 and 702 do not cover the case, there are limited opportunities for arguing that a given transaction with an employee does not invoke a "sale" and/or a "security" or is otherwise exempt under provisions generally operative when qualified retirement plans are involved.[100]

[97]For this purpose, a stock bonus plan is one in which the employer "awards shares of its stock to covered employees at no direct cost to the employees." Sec. Act Rel. No. 33–6188 (Feb. 1, 1980) (CCH) 1 Fed. Sec. L. Rep. ¶ 1051.

[98]The term "executive officer" includes the president, vice-presidents in charge of "principal business units" and officers performing "policy making functions." Rule 501(f).

[99]*See* Sec. Act Rel. No. 33–6683, *supra* n. 13.

[100]The issue whether and how securities law considerations impact on interests in, and the assets of, retirement plans—pension and profit sharing—bears a complex history, generally beyond the scope of the Text. Interests in most conventional retirement plans are not considered securities by reason of (i) a limited exception from the definition of "security" in § 3(a)(2) of the '33 Act, pertaining to interests in certain multi-employer benefit plans maintained by banks or insurance companies, and (ii) the Supreme Court's decision in *International Brotherhood of Teamsters v. Daniel,* 439 U.S. 551 (1979), and the immediately following SEC releases. *e.g.,* Sec. Act Rel. No. 33–6188 *supra* n. 97; Parenthetically, one must keep in mind that a plan for the benefit of employees involves the interests in the plan—potentially a "security"—and the investments the plan makes—

Assuming each transaction is legal of and by itself, the next question has to do with "integration," a long-standing SEC notion that, when measuring an unregistered offering to see if an exemption fits, the issuer must take into account offerings that occur in the same vicinity.

§7.12 INTEGRATION

The integration doctrine was outlined by the SEC in 1962 as a "facts and circumstances" test, a doctrinal position which reflects the Commission's continuing insecurity that objective tests would open the floodgates of evasion.[101]

The 1962 release enjoins the issuer to inquire whether two or more offerings are part of a "single plan"[102] (whatever that means); involve a "single class" of security; are made at or about the same time; involve the same type of consideration; and are for the same "general purpose" (again, whatever that means).[103]

---

again a "security"—which investments (*e.g.*, stock in the employer) may be distributed out to the employee. (Interests in the plan are sometimes called "first-tier" securities and plan assets "second-tier" securities.) The questions are such as whether the securities laws apply to both (or either) "first" and/or "second tier" securities, whether such are "securities" in the first instance, whether they are "sold" within the meaning of the '33 Act when certain transfers take place and whether such securities and or sales should be subject to the registration and/or antifraud provisions of the federal securities laws. For discussion of these issues, *see generally,* Stasbury & Bedoe, "Interests in Employee Benefit Plans as Securities: *Daniel* and Beyond," 8 *Sec. Reg. L.J.* 226 (1980). The issuance of stock in connection with participation in an employee benefit plan requires attention under state as well as federal law, since the Uniform Securities Act exemption (or any other local exemption) may not cover a particular case. *Compare* Uniform Securities Act § 402(a)(11).

[101] *See* Sec. Act. Rel. No. 33–4552 (Nov. 6, 1962).

[102] For a discussion of the integration problem, *see* "Integration of Partnership Offerings: A Proposal for Identifying a Discrete Offering" 37 *Bus. Law.* 1591 (July 1982), Deaktor, "Integration of Securities Offerings," 31 *U. Fla. L. Rev.* 465 (1979). *See also,* SEC no-action letters, *Verticom Inc.* (Feb. 12, 1986); *Pacific Physician Services Inc.* (Aug. 20, 1985); *Laser Fax Inc.* (Sept. 16, 1985); *Financial Independence Investment Corporation,* (Oct. 30, 1985); *Sonnenblick, Parker, & Selvers,* (Dec. 3, 1985). *See also,* Committee on Federal Regulation of Securities, "Integration of Securities Offerings. Report of the Task Force on Integration," 41 *Bus. Law.* 595 (Feb. 1986) updating the earlier report, 37 *Bus. Law.* 1591 (July 1982).

[103] The earliest authoritative SEC expression on the issue is found in *Unity Gold Corp.,* 3 S.E.C. 618 (1938), where the Commission said:

> The determination whether securities are being offered as part of a single "issue" will depend upon a consideration of various factors concerning the methods of sale and distribution employed to effect the offerings and the disposition of the proceeds. If the offerings may be segregated into separate blocks, as evidenced by material differences in the use of the proceeds, in the manner and terms of distribution, and in similar

The integration doctrine has been both simplified and complicated since its issuance.[104] When Reg. D was enacted, the Rule provided that offerings will be integrated as per the 1962 rules[105] but that a "safe harbor" exists for a Reg. D offering if no offerings or sales of "the same or similar" class of security occur in either of the two six-month periods flanking the Reg. D offering in question. (A curiosity in drafting failed to coordinate the "integration" and the "aggregation" concepts.[106] Thus, two offerings can stand on their own two feet because they are more than six months apart for Reg. D purposes; however, because aggregation is measured by the amount *"received"* by the issuer during a 12-month period, the existence of companion offerings—say, nine months apart—could jump both of them combined over a given dollar threshold—for example, $500,000—thus, making them both different *types* of offerings for Reg. D purposes than one would have thought from examining them separately. Both could become "over $500,000" offerings even though each was for $260,000.)

Returning to the hypothetical cited in the previous section: One institutional offering; one restricted stock offering; one stock bonus plan; one stock option plan (coupled with some grants pursuant to the plan and the exercise of one or more options),[107] it is clear that three "offerings" have occurred within 12 months; and, depending on the terms of the stock bonus plan, perhaps a fourth. If one considers the entire pageant as one large offering and the offering were exempt as a whole under a single exemption—Reg. D, for example—then the problems diminish. That is unlikely, however, since each potential exemption has its peculiarities, illustrated by the following table:[108]

---

related details, each offering will be a separate "issue." In the main, of course, each case must be determined upon the basis of its own facts.

Id. at 625. One of the few court cases to consider the issue, *SEC v. Murphy* 626 F.2d 633 (9th Cir. 1980) casts a very wide net, bringing together sales of ostensibly separate issues.

[104]The SEC stopped giving no-action or interpretive advice on integration in 1979, *Cloven Financial Corp.* [1977 Transfer Binder], (CCH) Fed. Sec. L. Rep. ¶ 82,091] (Apr. 5, 1979) and then reversed its position, resuming no-action activity in 1985.

[105]Rule 502(a). The "six months" safe harbor rule also appears in Rule 147, the "intrastate" exemption. Rule 147(b)(2).

[106]*Compare* Rule 502(a), respecting integration *with* the aggregation rules set out in Rule 504(b)(2) and Rule 505(b)(2)(i).

[107]The adoption of the plan itself, absent grants to an individual, is not the issuance of a security. When granted, an option is a "security" in accordance with the explicit language of the statutory definition in the '33 Act § 2(1), but, assuming the option is not immediately exercisable, a "sale" is not involved until the option is exercised. '33 Act, § 2(3).

[108]The American Bar Association Task Force reporting on the issue of integration divides up the transactional exemptions which might be integrated as follows: § 3(a)(9) (issuer exchanging stock with its own shareholders); § 3(a)(10) (mostly used by companies in

Exemption:	Potentially lost by reason of:
1. Reg. D	• Too many nonaccredited investors. • Inadequate disclosure. • Failure to file Form D.
2. "Intrastate" Exemption	• Nonresident purchasers.
3. § 4(2)	• Too many offerees. • One or more offerees not "smart" and/or "rich."
4. Not involving the "sale" of a security	• Stock bonus plan not available to a "relatively broad class of employees."[109]

If, as suggested, Reg. D is not available for the entire offering, taken in gross, then the trick is to avoid the impact of the integration doctrine, a tall order since the integration test is slippery and full of pitfalls. As an example, in the *Laser Fax Inc.* no-action request, counsel argued that one offering was for seed capital, a second to finance accounts receivable and the third for acquisitions and R&D. Since the same class of securities were involved, the staff was unsympathetic even though, in venture terms, the offerings were not for the same "general purpose." In this connection, Reg. D gives an illusion of relief because it can be read to except from the ambit of the integration concept any contemporaneous offers and sales under "an employee benefit plan."[110] However, the language does not mean what it appears; the issuance of stock pursuant to employee plans may be integrated if the other tests are met.

---

bankruptcy); § 3(a)(11) (the "intrastate" exemption); the private offering exemption, which the Task Force construes as comprising § 4(2) and Rule 506; and the *de minimis* exception, driven by the statutory language (and dollar limits) in §§ 3(b) and 4(6) and, therefore, comprising Regulation D, Rules 504 and Rule 505. *See* "Integration of Securities Offerings: Report of the Task Force on Integration," *supra* n. 102. *See also* Harroch *supra,* Ch. 1, n. 25 at § 4.03(2)(g).

[109]Sec. Act Rel. No. 33–6188, *supra* n. 100, ¶ 5(d) n. 84. Stock given to an employee stock bonus plan is quite useful from the recipient's standpoint, tax considerations aside. The SEC's position is that unregistered stock of a reporting company distributed to plan participants who are not affiliates of the issuer may be sold immediately if the stock so distributed in any one fiscal year does not exceed 10% of the outstanding shares and trading is active. *Id.,* as amended by Sec. Act Rel. No. 33–6281, IIB, (Jan. 15, 1981) B, (CCH) 1 Fed. Sec. L. Rep. ¶ 1052.

[110]Pursuant to '33 Act, Rule 405, this net is cast wide ("purchase, savings, options, bonus . . . pension or similar plan") as long as the plan is solely for employees, directors, trustees or officers (Sept. 6, 1985).

All the language in Rule 502(a) of Reg. D means, in the SEC's view, is that such issuance will not be a bridge tying together two Reg. D transactions otherwise more than six months apart.[111]

§7.13 INTEGRATION WITH AN IPO

Assume that, within six months of an allegedly exempt offering, the issuer finds itself in the fortunate position of filing for an IPO. If the two are to be integrated, then the previous "private" offerings turn ipso facto into an illegal public[112] offering.[113] The resumption of "no action" positions by the SEC staff has provided some guidance. Thus, it appears to be the current SEC staff view that an IPO and a previous "mezzanine" offering are not part of the same offering.[114] The author's understanding is that the staff was in fact motivated by howls from issuers engaging in mezzanine financings at the implications of no-action positions, such as *Laser Fax,* discussed above.

§7.14 INTRASTATE OFFERING EXEMPTION—SECTION 3(a)(11)

Section 3(a)(11) of the Securities Act of 1933 provides an exemption for:

> Any security which is part of an issue offered and sold only to persons resident within a single State or Territory, where the issuer of such security

[111]Sec. Act Rel. No. 33–6455, 1 (CCH) Fed. Sec. L. Rep. ¶ 2380, ¶ III A, n. 41. The language of Rule 502(a) is awkward. It establishes a safe harbor for Reg. D offerings six months apart and then, in a proviso clause, scrubs the safe harbor if there are any sales of stock (pursuant to Reg. D or otherwise) during the six months except for sales under an employee benefit plan.

[112]This issue must be faced squarely upon filing the registration statement since Item 701 of Regulation S–K insists the registrant list "recent sales of unregistered securities" and identify the "facts relied upon to make the exemption available." Regulation S–K, Item 701(d).

[113]Sec. Act Rel. 33–6188, *supra* n. 109, at VI B.

[114]Compare *Laser Fax Inc.* (Sept. 16, 1985) with *Verticom Inc.* (Feb. 12, 1986). In the *Verticom* letter, the SEC staff expressly relied on Rule 152, which provides that the § 4(2) exemption applies to nonpublic offerings even though "subsequently thereto the issuer decides to make a public offering and/or files a registration statement." Reliance on Rule 152 in this context is circular because the precise issue is whether the purported private offering is indeed a private offering or part of the subsequent public offering. For an authoritative view that the two issues should not be integrated, *see* "Redefining 'Public Offering or Distribution' for Today," address of Linda C. Quinn, Director, Division of Corporation Finance to Fed'l Regulation of Securities Committee," Nov. 22, 1986, p. 5. The *Verticom* view has been followed in at least two subsequent "no-action" letters, *Vulture Petroleum Corporation* (Feb. 2, 1987) and *BBI Associates* (Dec. 29, 1986). The *Vulture Petroleum* statement of facts and staff response indicate that Rule 152 will be applied more or less routinely in the future.

is a person resident and doing business within or, if a corporation, incorporated by and doing business within, such State or Territory.[115]

This exemption applies only if the securities are both offered and sold exclusively to domiciliaries (not merely "residents")[116] of the state in which the issuer is organized *and* doing at least 80% of its business *and* if the proceeds of the offering are going to be used for local purposes in that state. The local thrust of the exemption—both as to purchase and seller—has been codified in Rule 147, adopted in 1974.

The Rule is deceptive, since it appears to open up offerings which can proceed without the trappings of a registered IPO or without the regulatory hassles concerning sophistication of offerees, and so forth. However,[117] one offer to one nondomiciliary of the state destroys the entire exemption,[118] as does a resale by an initial purchaser to a nondomiciliary within nine months of the date the offering closes (herein a quantification of the earlier "coming to rest" doctrine).[119]

Moreover, even though an offering comes to rest exclusively with domiciliaries of the relevant state, if in a related (albeit separate, as a matter of form) offering there is one nondomiciliary purchaser, or one repurchaser within nine months, the entire exemption can be lost to *both* offerings as and if the offerings are integrated;[120] indeed, integration of a private offering with an intrastate offering will almost always have a bad result because any private offering of any size not specially crafted and controlled for § 3(a)(11) is likely to have one or more nondomiciliary offerees. In part to alleviate this problem, when the Commission adopted Rule 147 it included a "safe harbor" concept, substantially identical to that later incorporated in Reg. D, that is, a § 3(a)(11) issue shall not be integrated with another issue occurring six months before or after the "intrastate" issue. Note, however, a significant distinction between the "safe harbor" in Rule 147 and in Reg. D. The safe harbor is lost if any sales occur in the safe harbor period, *including* sales to employees, meaning that a sale to an employee within six months of an intrastate sale can tie together the intrastate issue and

[115]Sec. Act Rel. 33–5450 (CCH) 1 Fed. Sec. L. Rep. ¶ 2340 (Jan. 7, 1974).

[116]"Principal residence" is the requirement. Rule 147(d)(2).

[117]For pre-Rule 147 learning on the subject, *see* Sec. Act Rel. No. 33–4434, (CCH) 1 Fed. Sec. L. Rep. ¶ 2270 (Dec. 6, 1961); *SEC v. Truckee Showboat, Inc.*, 157 F. Supp. 824 (S.D. Cal. 1957).

[118]*Armstrong, Jones & Co. v. SEC*, 421 F.2d 359 (6th Cir.), *cert. denied*, 398 U.S. 958 (1970).

[119]The staff has held that resales may not only be made to nonresidents after the nine-month period but that such later resales may be planned at the time of the initial offering, provided the number of shares involved in the plan are small and the issuer did not have an overall plan to evade the registration requirements of the '33 Act. *BSD Bancorp. Inc.*, [1982 Transfer Binder] (CCH) Fed. Sec. L. Rep. ¶ 77,219. (May 10, 1982).

[120]The § 3(a)(11) exemption is lost because of the nondomiciliary and the § 4(2) exemption because of too many offerees.

another offering if the latter is within six months of the employee sale and over six months from the intrastate sale, another example of the SEC's overall hostility to the intrastate exemption.[121]

In view of the narrow construction of the Rule, a series of planning "cautions" must be kept in mind. Thus, if an exempt "intrastate" offering involves the purchase of securities being paid for in installments—a typical device when a venture partnership is being funded—counsel must ask whether the buyer must reside in the state as of every closing or only the first.[122] The use of proceeds requirement is a potential trap; the Rule requires that the issuer "intends to use and uses at least 80% . . . in connection with the operation of a business . . . located within such state."[123] If the issuer's plant is in the state but it ships product all over the country, the fact that all the proceeds go into the plant itself may not satisfy the Rule.[124] Because of the focus on residence of the investors, the intrastate exemption is frequently looked to when the question involves issuing stock to employees. Rules 701 and 702, when enacted, should obviate this use of the Rule in most instances.

§7.15 SECTION 4(2) AFTER REGULATION D[125]

While Reg. D has proven in practice to be extremely useful in aiding venture-backed placements, not every issue can or will be sold in compliance with the exemption. Reg. D specifically provides that it is not exclusive;[126] thus, § 4(2) is (at least theoretically) available in time of need. Certainly, however, the occasion for sole reliance on § 4(2) will be infrequent. If Reg. D is lost because there has been a "general solictation," one can hardly imagine the circumstances that could encourage the issuer to turn to § 4(2).

Reliance on § 4(2) standing alone is most likely, first, in those gilt-edged placements—the classic instance of a limited placement to a small number of highly sophisticated institutional investors—when compliance with Reg. D is deemed to be a bother. The issuer does not feel it

[121] *See* Loss, *Fundamentals of Securities Regulation* 319–36 (1983 & Supp. 1986); *see also* Gadsby, "The Securities and Exchange Commission and the Financing of Small Businesses," 14 *Bus. Law.* 144 (Nov. 1958).

[122] It would appear that appropriate residence as of the first closing is sufficient. *The Diplomat Ltd.* No-action letter (avail. Jan. 13, 1984).

[123] Rule 147(c)(2)(iii).

[124] *See, e.g., SEC v. McDonald Investment Co.* 343 F. Supp. 343 (D. Minn. 1972).

[125] On § 4(2), *see generally,* 1 Loss, *Securities Regulation supra* n. 13, at 697–708 (2d. ed. 1961) and 2630–66 (Supp. 1969); Katz, "Basic Criteria for Exemptions Under Section 4(2)," 72 *N.Y.U. L.Rev.* 32 (1974); Patton, "The Private Offering: A Simplified Analysis Of The Intitial Placement," 27 *Bus. Law.* 1089 (July 1972); McDermott, "The Private Offering Exemption," 59 *Iowa L. Rev.* 525 (1974).

[126] *Preliminary Notes* No. 3.

necessary to qualify the investors as accredited or to file Form D. The second major category is after-the-fact justification, a common problem in venture finance. When Start-up, Inc. was organized, the founder was unaware of either Reg. D or § 4(2) and none of the formalities were complied with. Some years later, when Start-up, Inc. is ready for an initial public offering, it will be necessary for counsel to recreate the exemption, as it were, in aid of its opinion that the initial issue was not in violation of the securities laws.[127] Ex post facto compliance with Reg. D is not usually an option, leaving § 4(2) as the only available alternative.

The gist of § 4(2) is that it focuses on offerees. For the exemption to obtain, each person to whom the investment opportunity is exposed, each offeree, must fit within one or more of the special categories. Those categories have been developed in the case law revolving around the central notion developed in the *Ralston Purina* opinion, that the disclosure requirement entailed in a registered offering should only be relaxed if all the potential buyers were of the type that they could "fend for themselves" in the sense that each could develop "access" to the information a statutory prospectus would provide.[128]

For many years, the courts, counsel, and the SEC staff have danced around the "fend for themselves" conception without reaching a test that was, or is, entirely satisfactory. As former SEC Chairman Ray Garret has noted, the element in the equation—the "saving recipe" as he called it—has remained a moving target, a "brew" made up of a number of elements but lacking an agreed upon, objective list of ingredients.[129] There is, however, a consensus on the identity of the elements going into the brew, what facts the courts have deemed important in the past, albeit no consensus on the weight to be accorded each one.

Thus, it is clear that the offerees as a class should have one or more special abilities which give them the power and/or ability to obtain access to information about the issuer and to process that information intelligently. At one extreme, a director of the issuer, particularly one sophisticated in financial matters, is almost certainly an eligible offeree. On the other hand, the mere fact that the offerees are employees of the issuer is not (without more) sufficient to invoke the exemption; this is the holding of the *Ralston Purina* case.[130]

Over the years, the idea of the "sophisticated" investor has crept into the folklore of § 4(2), a concept now enshrined in the requirement that nonaccredited investors in Reg. D offerings of more than $500,000 have "such knowledge and experience in financial and business matters as

[127] *See* Item 701(d) of Regulation S–K.

[128] *See supra* n. 5.

[129] Federal Regulation of Securities Committee, Section of Corporation, Banking and Business Law of the American Bar Association, "Section 4(2) and Statutory Law," 31 *Bus. Law.* 485, 489 (Nov. 1975).

[130] *See supra* n. 5.

to be capable of evaluating . . . the merits and risks of the prospective investment."[131] In the strictest sense of *Ralston Purina*, a "sophisticated" or "smart" investor might have no power to obtain access to information because the issuer either did not have it[132] or would not supply it. However, the "smart" investor presumably would know how to factor in the dearth of information in making an investment decision.

Moreover, the "smartness" of the offerees is one, and only one, factor in the "recipe." Thus, the number of offerees has always been deemed important, although not determinative since an offering involving as few as one offer,[133] at least conceptually, could be outside the scope of § 4(2) if the other factors in the "brew" so militated.[134] Counsel were led to follow the suggestion of the SEC's general counsel in an early opinion that 25 or fewer offerees constituted a safe harbor[135] but no authoritative court or Commission pronouncement ever adopted that number as a rule. In the author's view, one factual thread runs through many (if not all) of the instances in which a nonfraudulent offering was deemed outside the scope of § 4(2), that is, the defendant issuer was unable to show how many offers had been made because it had failed to keep records.[136]

The number of offerees is ultimately related to an important, and obvious, factor: the manner of the offering. If an offering is made using the traditional media of public offerings—advertisements, open seminars, paid salesman, extended mailings, cold calls—it stands to reason that a public offering is in progress. The desire of issuers, particularly in the tax shelter area, to reach out to a wide number of potential purchasers has often stretched this criterion, prompting counsel to creative heights with such devices as "screening."[137] Screening involves the idea that there are allowable techniques for prequalifying potential investors, (thereby reducing the number of offerees), which do not rise to the dignity of an offer and, therefore, can be conducted more or less with impunity. One notion is to send out a private placement memorandum from a deal that has already closed and inquire of the recipient

[131]Rule 506(b)(2)(ii).

[132]In a case litigated by the author's firm, *Livens v. William D. Witter, Inc.*, 374 F. Supp. 1104 (D. Mass. 1974), the court held that the plaintiff had been adequately informed that financial statements were unavailable and nonetheless elected to proceed with the investment—at his own risk, according to the court.

[133]1 Loss, *Securities Regulation*, *supra* n. 13, at 656.

[134]In *Gilligan, Will & Co. v. SEC* 267 F.2d 461 (2d Cir. 1959), the court held that an offering involving three purchasers was not exempt under § 4(2).

[135]Sec. Act Rel. No. 33–285, *supra* n. 4.

[136]1 Loss, *Securities Regulation*, *supra* n. 13, at 664. *See, e.g., SEC v. Continental Tobacco Corp.* 463 F.2d. 137 (5th Cir. 1972). The notorious opinion of the Fifth Circuit can be explained by the fact that the issuer was unable to specify how many offers had been made. *See supra* n. 38.

[137]*See supra* § 7.4(c).

whether he would be interested in an investment resembling the "dead" deal; another is to circulate an offering only to financial advisers—lawyers, accountants, investment advisers—to induce them to disgorge names, coupled with an admonition that the deals are not to be shown to the clients until authority is given by the issuer. Since these questions are now being addressed in a series of "no action" letters construing the "general solicitation" ban in Reg. D,[138] it is likely that all subsequent learning will be developed in that venue. Reg. D being viewed generally an expansion of the ambit of § 4(2), counsel recommending that an issuer who cannot use Reg. D because of the ban on "general solicitation" may nonetheless resort to screening under § 4(2) will be taking an unusually aggressive position.

Finally, the § 4(2) exemption, like Reg. D, is conditioned on the non-existence of a subsequent public distribution. The investment letter device, coupled with a legend on the stock certificates themselves, should be employed in private placements generally.

[138]*See supra* § 7.4.

Eight

Private Placement Memorandum—Early-Stage Financing

The private placement memorandum is, obviously, the most important document in a private financing. There are significant legal issues entitled in its preparation and use. Moreover, raising the necessary capital may depend on the elegance and care with which the memorandum is drafted. This chapter describes the contents of a typical private placement memorandum and some of the issues entailed in its preparation.

§8.1(a) THRESHOLD QUESTION: IS A PRIVATE PLACEMENT MEMORANDUM MANDATORY?

The early rounds of financing entail the issuance of securities in "private placements," transactions exempt from registration under the '33 Act in accordance with one or more statutory exemptions, as discussed in the previous chapter. Most source materials suggest that the use of private placement memoranda is de rigueur in private placements.[1] The argument, properly phrased, breaks out into three major parts. A private placement memo (PPM) is required:

(i) To establish (and/or buttress) the claim for exemption from registration under the Securities Act; and,

(ii) To avoid liability for misstatements or, more importantly, omissions under the antifraud provisions of state and federal law; the memo, including the disclaimers, is a written record of what was and was not said; and,

(iii) Because state or federal law requires its use.

If the foregoing reasons are persuasive, the underlying assumption is that the private placement memorandum, (for a nonpublic company at least) will contain the same type of information that a public registration statement would provide, either on Form S–18 or Form S–1, an assumption bottomed on the observation that:

(a) The SEC is the most influential voice, next to the courts, on what Congress meant in enacting the antifraud sections (principally §§ 11, 12(2), and 17(a) of the '33 Act and 10(b) of the '34 Act) and its expertise infiltrates state proceedings as well;

(b) The SEC requires a certain quantum of information for public offerings (and a similar amount for certain private offerings); and,

(c) Prudent issuers and their counsel will follow what the SEC suggests, even if not required to do so by the letter of the law.

The counterarguments are as follows:

(i) The SEC does not *require* any specific quantum of information for the exemption to apply if the offering is only to accredited investors and otherwise fits within the four corners of Reg. D. If the Commission had wanted so to require, it knew how to say so;

(ii) The preparation of a document containing all the information required by Form S–18 and Regulation S–K is expensive. If the

[1] "Even when a private placement memorandum is not required to establish an exemption from registration, it serves to protect the issuer from antifraud violation claims under § 12(2) and 17(a) for the Securities Act of 1933, as amended, and under § 10(b) of the Securities Exchange Act of 1934 and Rule 10b–5 thereunder." Halperin, *supra* Ch. 7, n. 11, at § 7.2.

issuer is going to that expense anyway, why not register the offering publicly?[2]

(iii) The antifraud cases, taken as a whole (and there are not many outside the area of actual fraud) do not generally go off on the issue of inadequate disclosure if "smart" investors are exclusively involved; indeed, reading the *Livens, Zobrist,* and *Zissu*[3] cases as the leading precedents, one could argue that a disclosure *only* of the risk factors involved in the offering is sufficient, assuming that the issuer exercises control over the other principal points—that is, no "general" solicitation, only accredited and/or "smart" investors;

(iv) The influential *Ralston Purina* case stresses *access* to information in the hands of investors able to fend for themselves;[4]

(v) If counsel purports to follow Regulation S–K and Form S–18 and makes a mistake, it is arguable that the issuer is worse off—trapped by an undisputed omission in a document counsel concedes should have been prepared—than if counsel has simply put the unexpurgated information about the issuer in a file cabinet and shoved it in the general direction of the investors.[5] The problem is exacerbated if an initial public offering is just around the corner. The existence of a contemporaneous private memo may raise questions whether the issuer is being consistent in its presentations;[6]

(vi) In fact, millions (perhaps billions) of dollars worth of securities are placed privately without the preparation of more than a ru-

[2]Some issuers prefer, given the choice, to organize a given financing as a public offering because the terms become, in effect, nonnegotiable once the registration statement becomes effective. Usually such issuers are already public companies, entitled to use short-form registration statements on Forms S–2 and S–3.

[3]*Livens v. William D. Witter, Inc.*, 374 F. Supp. 1104 (D. Mass. 1974); *Zobrist v. Coal–X Inc.* 708 F.2d 1511 (10th Cir. 1983); *Zissu v. Bear, Stearns & Co.* 627 F. Supp. 687 (S.D.N.Y. 1986).

[4]*SEC v. Ralston Purina Co.*, 346 U.S. 119 (1953). *Ralston Purina* considered the application of the § 4(2) exemption.

[5]Conceptually, although a court might not so hold, one mistake is fatal under Reg. D, a per se violation of the '33 Act, § 5 because there is, as yet, no language in Reg. D which will sanitize a transaction in "substantial compliance" with the Rule; compare the SEC's proposals to amend Reg. D by adding a "substantial compliance" defence. *See* Ch. 7, § 7.2 n. 14. And, if Reg. D is lost and no other exemption is available, a violation has *necessarily* occurred. By way of contrast, a public offering floated on the strength of an incomplete prospectus is still a registered public offering; the defendants can argue about materiality of the omissions and, in some cases, due diligence—an open-and-shut case has not been established. The problem with complying exactly with a set of statutory precepts is fundamental. To conform to a statutory format, one must track the statute and the cases interpreting the statute with elegant care. Failing to do so to the letter is not excuseable. It should be kept in mind that the sale of unregistered securities without an exemption can be a criminal act. '33 Act, § 24.

[6]*See* Ch. 14, § 14.8, n. 92.

dimentary private placement memorandum, in many cases none at all. The classic examples of laconic disclosure are the private placement memoranda used to raise venture capital for the venture partnerships themselves.

There is no right answer to the question except in certain specific instances. Thus, if a placement in excess of $500,000 is made to one or more unaccredited investors, then a private placement memorandum is obviously in order; Reg. D does not specify that the information be assembled in one document[7] but there is no apparent reason not to do so—indeed, no reason not to follow Regulation S–K as closely as possible. If state law requires a private placement memorandum, and the state cannot be avoided, then the question answers itself as well.

However, in offerings qualified under Reg. D, solely to accredited investors and exempt in the states, the question of the quantum of disclosure is open. Counsel is bound to inform the issuer of the risks but the tradeoff—exposure versus expense—is pertinent. There can be methods of informing the investors which are cheaper, and perhaps more effective, than slavishly following the SEC form; an all-day seminar at the company's headquarters, with participants from company management, accountants, counsel, and financial consultants, for example.[8] In short, the quantum of printed disclosure can be approached on a case-by-case basis. What information do *these* investors need and what is the best and most efficient way to get it to them? And, as the question suggests, the answer will depend on the type of offering and type of investors involved.[9] The most compelling legal case for a private placement memorandum occurs when the issuer is not dealing face to face with all the investors, as in prefabricated partnerships offering interests in managed assets such as real estate and oil and gas. Caution dictates that measures should be taken to ensure that the investors farthest out in left field get all available information; the fact that the lead investor knows all is not a solid defense against a suit by another investor not formally represented by the knowledgeable party. On the other hand, if there are only a few offerees, they are sophisticated and are able to interrogate the issuer efficiently, the balance of risks obviously changes.

[7]Regulation D: Rules 502(b)(2)(i)(A) (up to $5 million) and 502(b)(2)(i)(B) (more than $5 million).

[8]For cases suggesting an issuer may satisfy its disclosure obligations by providing prospective investors with access to its own records, *see, e.g., Barrett v. Triangle Mining Corp.* [1975–76 Transfer Binder] (CCH) *Fed. Sec. Law Ref.* § 95,438 (Feb. 2, 1976); *Swenson v. Engelstad* 626 F.2d 421, 427 (5th Cir. 1980).

[9]*See* Austin & Tanner, "The Private Placement Memorandum," in Harroch, *Start-Up Companies: Planning, Financing, and Operating the Successful Business* § 10.04 (1986 ed.).

§8.2 CONTENTS OF THE PRIVATE PLACEMENT MEMORANDUM

Since the private placement memorandum is the norm in most deals, the founder should familiarize himself with the standards for memorandum preparation, having in mind that, like any legal document, there are various audiences. The audience composed of potential plaintiffs (and, theoretically at least, the SEC enforcement staff) will read the document against the requirements contained in the cases imposing liability.[10] The audience composed of investors will read the document for its substantive content: "What are the terms of the deal?". To professional investors interested enough to become potential buyers, the private placement memorandum is a handy collection of only some of the information they are interested in, plus a lot of surplus verbiage—the empty language about suitability standards, for example. To the issuer, it is a sales document, putting the best face possible on the company and its prospects. To the managers, the memorandum is a summary of the business plan—indeed, it may incorporate the business plan as an exhibit or be "wrapped around" the plan itself—a memoralization of how the business is to be conducted.

The first page of the memo,[11] the cover page, contains some of the information one might see on the front of a statutory prospectus: name of the issuer, summary description of the securities to be sold, whether the issue is primary (proceeds to the issuer) and/or secondary (proceeds to selling shareholders), the price per share, the gross and net proceeds (minus selling commissions and expenses) and a risk factor or two (that is, the offering is "highly speculative" and the securities will not be liquid). Some would argue a date is important because, legally, the document speaks as of a certain date. However, if the memo becomes substantively stale between the offer and the closing, it is critical that the issuer update and circulate it; omission of material information as of the closing is not excusable on the theory that the memo displays an earlier date. Moreover, a dated memorandum will appear just that—dated—if a few months elapse and the issue is still unsold.[12] A related issue is whether to specify a minimum amount of proceeds which must be subscribed if the offering is to go forward. If the financing is subject

[10]The disclosure requirements for a public registration statement and prospectus are set out largely in Regulation S–K. *See* Austin & Tanner, "The Private Placement Memorandum," in Harroch, *supra* n. 9, at § 10; Halperin, *supra* Ch. 7, n. 11, at § 7.1.

[11]If a private placement memorandum is printed (versus typed), the implication is that it has been widely circulated, sometimes a negative implication in venture finance.

[12]In keeping with the theory that the SEC rules for public offerings should be influential on the quantum of disclosure in placements, one writer cites Item 501(c)(10) of Regulation S–K (which requires that prospectuses be dated) as authority for the proposition that the private placement memorandum needs a date. Halperin, *supra* Ch. 7, n. 11, at § 7.27.

to a "minimum," a reference belongs on the cover page.[13] It makes common sense that there be a critical mass in most placements; however, a *stated* requirement that X dollars be raised or all subscriptions returned inhibits an early closing strategy—the ability to "close," if only in escrow, with the most eager of the issuer's potential investors. Such "closings" may not be substantively meaningful; the deal may be that the "closing" will be revisited if more money is not raised. However, a first closing can have a salubrious shock effect on the overall financing; it can bring to a halt ongoing (sometimes interminable) negotiations on the terms of the deal and create a bandwagon effect.

The cover page should be notated, a handwritten number inscribed to help record the destination of each private placement memorandum. It is also customary to reflect self-serving, exculpatory language (of varying effectiveness in protecting the issuer), that is:

(i) The offer is only an offer in jurisdictions where it can be legally made and then only to persons meeting suitability standards imposed by state and federal law (the offer is, in fact, an "offer" whenever and to whomsoever a court designates);[14]

(ii) The memorandum is not to be reproduced (about the same effectiveness as stamping Department of Defense papers "Eyes Only," a legend understood in bureaucratese to mean, "may be important .... make several copies");

(iii) No person is authorized to give out any information other than that contained in the memo (since the frequent practice is for selling agents to expand liberally on the memo's contents, it would be extraordinary if extraneous statements by an authorized agent of the issuer were not allowed in evidence against the issuer, unless

[13]Regulation S–K, Item 501, Instruction 3, requires as much of a public prospectus. Under Rule 15(e)2–4 of the '34 Act, funds received prior to achievement of a stated minimum in a public offering must be escrowed and the escrow arrangements disclosed. If the transaction is "all or none," no funds may be disbursed from the escrow until all securities are sold and fully paid for. Sec. Act Rel. No. 34–11532, [1975–1976 Transfer Binder] (CCH) Fed. Sec. L. Rep. ¶ 22,730 (July 11, 1975). If the underwriter "closes" an offering when the minimum has not been achieved, it can be disciplined by the SEC. *Rooney, Pace Inc.* Sec. Act Rel. No. 34–23,763; [1986–1987 Transfer Binder] (CCH) Fed. Sec. L. Rep. ¶ 84,048 (Oct. 31, 1986). The SEC staff has taken the position that, although the Rule uses the word "distribution," it also applies to private placements. NASD Notice to Members 84–7, Jan. 30, 1984.

[14]The SEC staff is not impressed with the notion that one can make what amounts to an offer with impunity simply by saying it is not an offer; *see generally SEC v. Murphy* 626 F.2d 633 (9th Cir. 1980); *Matter of Kenman Corporation* [1984–1985 Transfer Binder] (CCH) Fed. Sec. L. Rep. ¶ 83,767 (Apr. 19, 1985); *Gerald Gerstenfeld,* No-Action Letter from SEC (Dec. 3, 1985), Wash. Serv. Bur. Microfiche, fiche 976, frame F11. Humpty Dumpty's dictum that words should mean what one wants them to mean does not survive under the '33 Act.

perhaps they are expressly inconsistent with the language of the memo);

(iv) The private placement memorandum contains summaries of important documents (a statement of the obvious) and the summaries are "qualified by reference" to the full documentation (a materially inaccurate summary is unlikely to be excused simply because investors were cautioned to read the entire instrument);

(v) Each investor is urged to consult his own attorney and accountant. (No one knows what this means; if the legally expertised portions of the private placement memorandum are otherwise actionably false, it would take an unusually forgiving judge to decide the plaintiff should have obeyed the command and hired personal counsel.); and,

(vi) The offering has not been registered under the '33 Act and the SEC has not approved it.[15]

The foregoing is not meant as an exercise in fine legal writing and the avoidance of excess verbiage. Certain legends are mandatory as a matter of good lawyering—as indicated earlier, a summary of the "risk factors,"[16] for example; a statement that investors may ask questions and review answers and obtain additional information (an imperative of Reg. D);[17] and, of course, the language required by various state securities administrators.[18] A recitation tipping investors that they will be required in the subscription documents to make representations about their wealth and experience is generally desirable, particularly in light of cases finding against plaintiffs who falsified their representation.[19] However, in the author's opinion, a cover page loaded up with superfluous exculpations may cheapen a venture financing, signaling to readers that the deal is borderline, in a league with "double write-off" offerings in the real estate and tax shelter areas.

A well-written private placement memorandum will follow the Cover Page with a summary of the offering. This section corresponds to a Term Sheet,[20] except that the language is usually spelled out, not abbreviated. The important points are covered briefly: a description of the terms of the offering, the company's business, risk factors, additional terms (i.e., antidilution protection, registration rights, control features), expenses

[15]A redundancy, since the memorandum is entitled a private placement memorandum; the legend routinely appears because a caveat to this effect is required on the cover of public prospectuses. Regulation S–K, Item 501(c)(5).

[16]*Zissu v. Bear, Stearns & Co* and *Zobrist v. Coal–X, Inc., supra* n. 3.

[17]Regulation D, Rule 502(b)(2)(v).

[18]For examples of legends imposed by state law, *see* Austin & Tanner, "The Private Placement Memorandum," in Harroch, *supra* n. 9, at § 10.03(1).

[19]*Zissu v. Bear, Stearns & Co., supra* n. 3.

[20]*See* Ch. 9.

of the transaction[21] and (not recommended by this author)[22] summary financial information. The purpose of the summary is to make the offering easy to read and understand. As stated, suppliers of capital are inundated with business plans and private placement memoranda; the sales-conscious issuer must get all the salient facts in as conspicuous a position as possible if he hopes to have them noticed.

At this juncture, it is customary to reproduce investor suitability standards,[23] identifying and flagging the principal requirements for a Reg. D offering, that is, the definition of "accredited investor." (The content of the documents to be executed by investors in a placement, including their acknowledgment of suitability standards, is discussed in § 8.11.)

§8.3 RISK FACTORS

For maximum *caveat emptor* value, the "risk factors"[24] section should be referenced on the first page and reproduced in full in a position in the memo prior to the sections in which the attractiveness of the opportunity is trumpeted. Several recitations are standard, indeed would be conspicuous by their absence, namely:

The company is in its "development"—that is, most highly vulnerable—stage; its products haven't been proven or marketed;

Its success is highly dependent on a few key individuals, none of whom have run a company of any size before;

There are fearsome competitors on the horizon;

The company will need more than one round of financing to survive;

[21]A sensitive disclosure concerns the placement agent's compensation. *See* Ch. 14, § 14.10, for a discussion of the various guises that such compensation may assume: i.e., cheap stock, nonaccountable expenses, warrants, first refusal rights on subsequent placements, etc. In a typical private placement, legal and accounting fees should not be allowed to total more than, say, 2% of the total proceeds of an offering or the investors will, rightly, balk. As noted in § 8.1, producing memos drafted to the Queen's taste can mean the imposition of transactional costs well beyond what the market will bear.

[22]It is the author's view that any serious investor is capable of grasping unsummarized financial information at little more than a glance. Moreover, there is potential for mischief in summary financial data, leaving out critical assumptions in the projections. *Compare* Regulation S–K, Item 10(b).

[23]An expansive example is contained in Austin & Tanner, "The Private Placement Memorandum," in Harroch, *supra* n. 9, at § 10.03[3][b].

[24]The importance of the "risk factors" section is highlighted by *Zobrist v. Coal–X, Inc.*, *supra* n. 3, in which the 10th Circuit held that an experienced investor in a placement was bound by the "risk factors" section in a memo he had received but not in fact read; his reliance on inconsistent oral misrepresentations was not "justifiable reliance" within the meaning of Rule 10b–5.

The securities are illiquid;

Substantial "dilution" is involved;[25]

A few major customers form the backbone of the order bank;

The technology is not entirely (or at all) protected by patents or copyrights.

These should be fleshed out with risks specific to the issue: environmental problems, the possibility of technical obsolescence, difficulties in procuring drug licenses from the FDA, and so forth.

On occasion, the founder will argue with counsel that a given risk factor is stated too negatively. In the author's view, that argument is generally a waste of time. Few sophisticated investors are influenced by the "risk factors" section. They form their independent judgment on the issues; its utility is more prophylactic than educational.[26]

§8.4 SUBSTANTIVE TERMS

Following the "risk factors" section, the private placement memorandum should set out the terms (previously summarized) of the deal; that is, the special features of the securities being offered (preferences, voting rights, conversion privilege, dividends, etc.); the pricing terms (payable all at one time or in installments), and what the placement agent is being paid. Many private placement memoranda do not include in either the summary or the early discussion an upfront disclosure of the expenses of the transaction, particularly the legal fees. That information usually can be extruded from the pro forma financials but nondisclosure is not recommended, even though embarrassingly high placement and legal fees may mean to the experienced reader that the offering is sticky and has been "out on the street" for a while.

§8.5 USE OF PROCEEDS, PRICE JUSTIFICATION, DILUTION

At or about this point, Regulation S–K requires a public prospectus to discuss the use to which the proceeds of the offering are to be put.[27] However, unless the issuer plans to pay down debt[28] or use any such proceeds for the benefit of an insider (in which case the discussion should

[25] *See* Regulation S–K, Item 503(c); Halperin, *supra* Ch. 7, n. 11, at § 7.30. *See infra* § 8.5.

[26] For sample drafting, *see* Austin & Tanner, "The Private Placement Memorandum," in Harroch, *supra* n. 9, at § 10.05[1][b].

[27] Regulation S–K, Item 504; *see also* Item 4 of both Forms S–18 and S–1.

[28] Regulation S–K, Item 504, ¶ 4. If less than the maximum may be raised in a "maximin" offering, some attempt should be made to order the priorities.

be quite specific), the initial draft of this language is usually cryptic and stylized—"working capital" or "general corporate purposes," partly out of a desire to avoid leaking sensitive information. To be sure, once negotiations begin, the "use of proceeds" is often a heavily negotiated item. The investors often want a concrete menu, in part to meet the problem earlier discussed, when the start-up has too much money.[29] However, their policing mechanism is not necessarily a sharpened description in the private placement memorandum. The more usual provision is a promise in the Stock Purchase Agreement either tied to a specific schedule or to the effect that expenditures over, say, $25,000 are subject to an advance approval process.

State securities regulators frequently require the issuer involved in an initial public offering to explain (in effect to justify)[30] the price established for the public sale. If included in a private placement memorandum, this language is usually boilerplate. To the extent private purchasers, better able to "fend for themselves" in the language of *Ralston Purina,* have negotiated the price at arm's length,[31] a section in a private placement memorandum containing language "justifying" the price is usually superfluous.[32]

Regulation S–K also requires disclosures relating to dilution,[33] that is, when there is a substantial disparity between the public offering price and the price paid by officers, directors, promoters, and other insiders in the recent past. The SEC and state administrators are so serious about this disclosure it is not to be taken lightly. The fact is that a savvy investor can dope out the dilution without a table or narrative in the private placement memorandum leading him through the calculations. However, the SEC has stated that disclosure of dilution should not be a "jigsaw puzzle" that investors must piece together.[34] With that

[29]*See* Ch. 6, § 6.17(d).

[30]*See* Ch. 14, § 14.9(a).

[31]Of course, prices in most initial public offerings are negotiated as well. First, the underwriter fixes a price it intuitively believes will clear the market; in the "red herring" or pre-effective phase, the underwriters' salespersons call on potential buyers and sniff their appetites at various pricing levels.

[32]Austin & Tanner, "The Private Placement Memorandum," Harroch, *supra* n. 10, at § 10.05[4](b).

[33]Regulation S–K, Item 506. It is arguable that any issuance of stock entails dilution and therefore, retention of all earnings is preferable to paying out capital and then replenishing the treasury with new stock. Alternatively, one can argue that a rational management will never issue stock if the existing shareholders are to be in fact diluted. *See,* Krasker, "Stock Price Movements in Response to Stock Issues Under Asymmetric Information," 15 *J. Fin. Econ.* 93 (1986). For a summary of factors bearing on stock price changes upon announcement of a new issuance, *see* Bhagat, "The Effect of Preemptive Right Amendments on Shareholder Wealth," 12 *J. Fin. Econ.* 289, 295 (1983).

[34]*In Re Mutual Employees Trademark Inc.* Sec. Act Rel. No. 33–4478, [1963–64 Transfer Binder] (CCH) Fed. Sec. L. Rep. ¶ 76,841 (Apr. 17, 1962).

position on the record, simple prudence dictates that the dilution calculation be set out in a prominent, early place in the memo. Dilution in later rounds (or any round if the deal is "hot") can be a formidable number: stock priced at $10 per share which the founders sold to themselves and other insiders for 1¢ a share. Curiously, in a public company, dilution is usually calculated by the professional analysts by measuring the effect of the financing on earnings per share or other income statement ratios.[35] In start-ups, that calculation is seldom meaningful and book value, or net tangible book value, is the measuring stick. An investor paying $1 per share is deemed to be "diluted" if, and to the extent, book value per share after the financing is less than $1. If book value is 50¢, then the amount of the dilution is 50%. Sophisticated investors are not intimidated by dilution per se, since it is often the function of a desirable offering, but bashfulness in disclosing dilution is imprudent.[36]

§8.6 FINANCIAL DISCLOSURE

The most significant section of the private placement memorandum is the financial section: historical and projected financial results. A threshold issue, whether financial statements in the private placement memorandum should be audited,[37] often arises on the eve of the financing. Should the founder undertake to pay the accountants for a certificate if the statements have not customarily been certified?[38] If historical results have not been significant, common sense would suggest that the certificate is not worth the expense. On the other hand, all financial reporting should be done in a form which looks just like the audited version will look; audited financials will be needed sooner or later and there is no reason why one should not start out on the right foot. Public accountants can be enormously expensive if, in order for them to render a clean certificate at some later date, it is necessary to re-create the entire financial-reporting system from "day one" forward. Nonetheless, the certificate is expensive of and by itself, since it exposes the account-

[35] *See* authorities collected *supra* n. 33.

[36] For a sample of the appropriate disclosure, *see* Austin & Tanner, "The Private Placement Memorandum," in Harroch, *supra* n. 9, at § 10.05[3][b].

[37] One must not be cavalier in excluding audited financial statements. However, in many instances the proper balance of risk (from noncompliance with offering exemptions) and cost may reasonably result in the decision to fall short of the absolute technical requirements.

Austin & Tanner, "The Private Placement Memorandum," Harroch, *supra* n. 9, at § 10.08[1]; *see also* Halperin, *supra* Ch. 7, n. 11, at §§ 7.13–7.18.

[38] To be "certified," i.e., accompanied by a C.P.A.'s certificate, the financial statements must be "audited;" in common parlance, the terms are used interchangeably.

ing firm to liability. That expense may be too great a burden to bear unless operations are so significant that the issuer and other participants in the offering feel the certificate is required to protect them for liability. The question of course, is moot in those offerings in which the investors *insist* on a certificate. Moreover, if nonaccredited investors are admitted to a placement which depends on Reg. D for its exemption, there are complex requirements which insist on at least audited balance sheets in offerings in excess of $500,000.[39]

Projections are not required in public financings, and, although the SEC encourages their use in that venue, they seldom so appear. As stated in the discussion in Chapter 14 on initial public offerings, the SEC's safe harbor for "forward looking" statements—the rule stating that financial projections and management's statement of future goals will not be subject to second guessing if made on a "reasonable" basis and in "good faith"[40]—has not attracted a lot of takers in the public arena. Since the issue in court has always been one of reasonableness and good faith,[41] the SEC is adding little to the existing balance of risk.

However, forecasted goals and projections are essential in a placement. The investors will usually not bite unless they are included prominently in the presentation.[42] Well-run businesses routinely prepare forecasts and statements of objectives. The investors expect to see such material on a continuing basis and, therefore, have no reason to be shy in insisting on the information before they put up money.

The projections cannot, of course, be audited and thus, management and the issuer are responsible; the accountants cannot be the scapegoat. Moreover, by definition, projections will have been proven wrong if a serious lawsuit has been filed. On the other hand, since forecasts do not purport to represent "facts," there is no exact standard against which a plaintiff can vet the projections and expose unarguable deficiencies.[43]

[39]In a placement of more than $500,000 to nonaccredited investors under Reg. D, assuming the issuer is not a limited partnership, only a balance sheet dated within 120 days of the offering must be audited if the issuer cannot obtain audited financial statements "without unreasonable effort or expense." Rule 502(b)(2)(i)(B). *See* Sec. Act Rel. No. 6455, *supra* Ch. 7, n. 6, Question (48); Hicks, *Limited Offering Exemptions: Regulation D* 162–65 (1985).

[40]'33 Act, Rule 175 and '34 Act Rule 3b–6(a) *see* Regulation S–K, Item 10(b).

[41]*See* Ch. 14, § 14.6.

[42]On the care to be used in preparing projections in a placement, including the suggestion to involve the accountants, *see* Prifti, *Securities: Public and Private Offerings* § 1A:12.

[43]The court in *Beecher v. Able* 374 F. Supp. 341, 348 (S.D.N.Y. 1974) noted that "a high standard of care must be imposed on those who, although not required to do so, nevertheless make projections." It is questionable, however, whether Judge Motley's view remains good law in view of the SEC's *volte face* on the desirability of projections. *See also* Bloomenthal, Harvey & Wing, *Going Public Handbook, supra* Ch. 6, n. 49, at § 7.05; *R.A. Holman & Co. Inc. v. SEC* 366 F.2d 446 (2d Cir. 1966), *Dorfman v. First Boston Corp.* 62 F.R.D. 446 (E.D. Pa. 1973); *Blakely v. Lisac,* 357 F. Supp. 255 (D. Ore. 1972); Halperin, *supra* Ch. 7, n. 11, at §§ 7.89–7.93.

One sensible way to ward off trouble is to prepare the forecasts on three tracks: "best case," "worst case," and "most probable." In that way, the actual results will be closer to at least one curve on the graph—the worst case scenario—than if only one forecast had been presented.[44] This method of presentation accords, incidentally, with the way some venture investors go about their business of analyzing opportunities. They weight each alternative and then take the average of the three.[45]

§8.7 DESCRIPTION OF THE BUSINESS

The heart of the document is the description of the business. Some practitioners like to draft this section afresh, as if a prospectus were being prepared.[46] The contrary, and this author believes the better, view is that the issuer's business plan should be incorporated more or less verbatim into the private placement memorandum, by attaching it as an exhibit and/or excerpting passages into a "wrap around" or "sandwich" memo. The business plan is the meat inside the standard disclosures. The argument in favor of rewriting the business plan in legalese is that the plan may be overly optimistic and, therefore, should be sanitized before its thrust is incorporated into a disclosure document. The counterargument is that, if the case comes to trial, witnesses for the issuer may spend days on the stand under hostile cross-examination, lamely attempting to explain differences between the document that was produced for investor scrutiny and the one that management used for its own purposes.

§8.8 MANAGEMENT

One of the most widely read segments of the memo is the discussion of management, the curricula vitae of the directors and senior officers, together with an exposition of their compensation. In the start-up world, nothing is tranquil. Thus, in describing the management team, even the disclosure of names may on occasion be dicey; some senior people will agree to join the officer corps of a start-up if and only if the financing is successful. It is permissible, because there is no other solution, to denote these individuals as Doctor X and Mister Y. Disclosure of com-

[44]Projections should be accompanied by disclosure of the assumptions upon which the projections depend. *See* Regulation S–K, Item 10(b).

[45]*See* Ch. 12, § 12.3.

[46]*See* Austin & Tanner, "The Private Placement Memorandum," in Harroch, *supra* n. 9, at § 10.06[1]. The authors suggest that "if possible," the business plan should *not* be included in the private placement memorandum because it "has been prepared for other purposes." *See generally,* Halperin, *supra* Ch. 7, n. 11, at §§ 7.5–7.12.

pensation dollars can also be sensitive, but the requirements of the SEC for public offerings are sufficiently specific to indicate the Commission means business. Prudent issuers should fully set forth for all senior employees the terms of the employment agreement, any understandings concerning bonuses, the "parachutes" (i.e., the penalty paid if the employee is dismissed) and the stock arrangements.[47] The investors are likely to zero in on the agreements between the firm and its key managers; the memo should disclose how the managers have had their wagons hitched to the company with non-compete clauses and "golden handcuffs."[48]

There is a relatively high potential for embarrassment in this section for those charged with due diligence. For some perverse reason, résumés often contain easily checkable lies (X claims a doctorate in chemical engineering from Purdue when he didn't complete the course). Moreover, federal and state laws contain so-called "bad boy"[49] provisions, meaning that disclosures are required and exemptions from registration are not available if anyone connected with the issue (or the issuer) has in the recent past been convicted of crimes or subjected to administrative proceedings which are relevant to the sale of securities. An overlooked felony conviction for mail fraud (particularly if a computer search on the Nexis system would have disclosed it) can be more embarrassing than a phony degree.[50]

§8.9 CERTAIN TRANSACTIONS

The compensation issue overlaps with a section on conflicts of interest. This section, mandated by rule in public offerings[51] and by prudence in private placements, requires the disclosure of any transactions be-

[47]Disclosure requirements relating to management in public offerings are set out in Regulation S–K, Item 402 and 404; *see* Sec. Act. Rel. No. 33–6486 [1982–83 Transfer Binder] (CCH) Fed. Sec. L. Rep. ¶ 83,425 (Sept. 23, 1983); *see also* Subcommittee on Annual Review, "Annual Review of Federal Securities Regulation," 39 *Bus. Law.* 1105, 1131 (May 1984); Halperin, *supra* Ch. 7, n. 11, at §§ 7.19–7.26 Sec. Act Rel. No. 33–6441 [1982 Transfer Binder] (CCH) Fed. Sec. L. Rep. ¶ 83,281 (Dec. 2, 1982); Comment, "Golden Parachutes: A Perk That Boards Should Scrutinize Carefully," 67 *Marq. L. Rev.* 293 (1984).

[48]*See* Ch. 10, § 10.3, *et seq.*

[49]*E.g.*, ULOE Rule 1(B). *See* Sherman & Williams, "State Securities Laws Considerations of Raising Capital," in Harroch, *supra* n. 9, at § 5.04[2][b].

[50]Regulation S–K requires disclosure of certain embarrassing activities of directors and officers (i.e., bankruptcy proceedings, violations of criminal or securities laws) if disclosure is relevant to an evaluation of the person's integrity or ability to be a director or officer. *See* Regulation S–K, Item 401(f). Case law also recognizes a duty to disclose under Rule 10b–5 information regarding the integrity of management. *See, e.g., SEC v. Jos. Schlitz Brewing Co.* 452 F. Supp. 824 (E.D. Wis. 1978).

[51]*See* Regulation S–K, Item 404; Sec. Act Rel. No. 33–6441, *supra*, n. 47; "Annual Review of Federal Securities Regulation," 39 *Bus. Law.* 1105, 1129 (May 1984).

tween the issuer and its insiders, the company leasing its offices from the founder, for example. Tax implications lurk below the surface; if goods or services are exchanged with an employee at bargain prices, the bargain element may be compensation. Corporate law also imposes a gloss. Insider transactions may be avoided later as a result of a lawsuit by a disgruntled stockholder unless the transaction is approved by disinterested directors and/or shareholders or is "fair" to the corporation.[52] The institution of a financing, public or private, often is the occasion for reviewing and canceling some of those "sweetheart" deals. The disclosure requirement can be therapeutic and educational, educating the founder on what it means to have partners.

§8.10 DUE DILIGENCE AND TRADEOFFS

The level of diligence required in presenting the facts in a private placement is not as well adumbrated in the cases and authorities as in the case of a public offering. A defective disclosure document in a public offering is scrutinized against the background of § 11 of the '33 Act, where liability for misstatements can be close to absolute.[53] The prin-

[52] *E.g.*, Del. Code Ann. tit. 8, § 144(a) (1983 & Supp. 1986). Often one or more partners in the law firm acting as counsel to the issuer have an interest in the issuer; any such relationship is normally disclosed whenever reference is made to the firm's legal opinions so as to avoid actions such as that recently filed against a prestigious New York City law firm for allegedly failing to disclose relationships of one of its partners with Ivan Boesky in a private placement memorandum for a fund managed by Boesky. Glaberson "A Wall Street Firm Breaks Ranks in the Boesky Case," N.Y. *Times*, Apr. 12, 1987, § 3, at 1.

[53] A useful summary of the issue is contained in the "Report by Boston Bar Association Securities and Banking Law Committee," Nov./Dec. *Boston Bar J.* 6 (1986) where the authors state:

> The traditional private placement disclosure and information process is very different from the public offering process. Historically, investors in private placements (friends of the family, wealthy individuals, insurance companies, venture capitalists, and the other institutional and professional investors), when deciding whether to make an investment, have taken an active role in gathering financial and other information from the issuer and such other sources as they think relevant. Such investors often ignore, in whole or in part, defective or incomplete company-prepared business plans. Traditionally, most private placements have not been sold on the basis of a single written document, however denominated. Much of the information professional investors deem relevant and usually require prior to investment, such as detailed long-range projections of future sales, does not appear in public offering prospectuses.
>
> Private offerings in which a placement agent participates ordinarily utilize a written disclosure document, but the process in which that document is prepared is very different from the public offering process. The issuer and the placement agent write that document with relatively little input from counsel for the issuer or the placement agent or from the issuer's accountants (even though long-range sales and income projections are common in such documents). Few or no third-party checks are made, and the group line-by-line review of disclosure materials usual in public offerings is absent or greatly reduced.

cipal federal provision governing private placements is found in Rule 10b–5, promulgated under the '34 Act, which talks in terms of "fraud and deceit" and, thus, has been held to require proof of some form of "scienter,"[54] a legal term entailing knowing violations of the appropriate standard. The sections of the securities laws governing liability for faulty disclosure in nonregistered offerings, state and federal, vary in the standards of diligence required but the burden is less than the duty of active investigation imposed by § 11.

In the final analysis, the private placement memorandum is a compromise document, entailing a tradeoff between the durability of a bulletproof statutory prospectus versus the expense entailed in preparing such a presentation to investors. Founders and their advisers have to face this problem squarely. If the financing involves no more than, say, $750,000, there is a line which counsel cannot cross in spending time drafting the private placement memorandum. A business plan coupled with prudential caveats—for example, the risk factors—may be the best anyone can do in the circumstances.[55] The tradeoff issue should not be read to suggest the problem of antifraud liability is insignificant. Many of the built-in comforts and safeguards for the issuer in a public offering—the SEC's staff's letter of comment, the use of Regulation S—K as a guide, the existence of audited financial statements and other expertised portions of the registration statement—are not available in a private placement. Moreover, even the lawyers keep their head below the lip of the trench; most law firms take the view that issuers and placement agents are not entitled to an opinion that a private placement does not violate the antifraud provisions of the securities laws.

§8.11 SUBSCRIPTION DOCUMENTS

Prudence suggest that each purchaser be required to fill out and file with the issuer documents in aid of the issuer's ability to claim an exemption from requirement the securities be registered under federal and state law. The statements made by the purchaser also serve to estop him from claiming he was deceived in the course of the offering. The inclination of issuers—and it appears to be sound—is to load up the subscription documents with a combination of exculpatory language, concessions by the investor as to his status as a "smart" and "rich" investor (see below) and representations that he has in fact done the sort of things (i.e., read the memo, consulted his own advisers) the

[54]*Ernst & Ernst v. Hochfelder* 425 U.S. 185(1976).

[55]One interesting tradeoff has to do with inquiries of the issuer's customers by potential investors. If the issuer is posing to the trade as a solid, well-capitalized vendor, notice of the fact that the issuer is trying to raise equity may be a competitive disadvantage.

private placement memorandum urges him to do. In light of the few cases of any relevance,[56] there does not appear to be harm in going overboard, despite the fact that investors routinely sign the subscription agreement and questionnaire without reading them and the language is rarely an item for negotiation.[57]

The core minimums are, first, that the securities are being bought for investment, not resale. This protects the issuer's exemption from registration under the '33 Act and in a number of states; even though the initial sale is exempt, the issuer may be responsible for the investor reoffering his shares to the public—all part of one "distribution"—and so the issuer must demand this representation, which in turn can and should be translated, as a policing mechanism, into a legend on the stock certificates themselves.[58] Secondly, the language of Reg. D suggests[59] that every investor be specifically given to understand his investment is nonliquid, as is always the case in private placements, and the safest way to satisfy that requirement is to obtain a representation that the investor understands such to be the case. Thirdly, Reg. D requires that purchasers be given the opportunity to "ask questions and receive answers"[60] concerning the terms and conditions of the offering and to obtain additional information. Strictly speaking, this requirement—the so-called "access" rule—is not applicable to offerings under $500,000, but it only makes common sense that the procedure be followed in all placements. Thus, an investor concession that the issuer has complied with the "access rule" is routinely demanded.

Beyond these specific matters, there are several representations the issuer is well served to require, namely:

1. *"Rich"*: That the investor has the ability to bear the risk of the investment. This is the so-called "rich" test, objectified under Reg. D in specific income and net worth tests but running through the entire concept of the "private offering" exemption. Some practitioners believe it is incumbent on the issuer in close cases to obtain back-up information, that is, personal financial statements.[61]
2. *"Smart"*: That the investor has the requisite knowledge and experience to evaluate the "merits and risks" of the investment. This is the "smart" or sophistication test. It is open to cautious issuers to insist

[56]*See* cases collected *supra* n. 3.
[57]If a placement agent is employed, it may be important under federal and state law that the agent have satisfied itself as to investor suitability. See *e.g.*, ULOE Rule 1(D)(1). (Investments not exceeding 10% of the investor's net worth are "presumed" suitable.)
[58]Rule 502(d)(3).
[59]Rule 502(d)(2).
[60]Rule 502(b)(2)(v).
[61]There can be an independent reason for investigating an investor's "richness." If the investor is making installment payments, his credit is of interest to the issuer.

on back-ups—recitations of the investor's experience with venture investments and/or general business experience. The "smart" test must be passed by nonaccredited investors in offerings of more than $5 million under Reg. D[62] and both "smartness" and "richness" work to protect broker/dealers, who are subject to rules laid down by their governing body, the NASD, and various state authorities.[63]

3. "*Diligence*": That the investor has read all the offering materials, including particularly the "risk factors." This representation is designed to bind the investor to the exculpatory statements in the private placement memorandum; that is, that the investment involves a high degree of risk. Indeed, it can be used as a sword rather than a shield. A judge in the Southern District of New York recently became angered at a lawsuit brought by a disappointed investor in a tax shelter offering; the investor, a lawyer, was eminently experienced in placements. The judge approved a counterclaim in six figures based on the finding the plaintiff investor's suit was frivolous; the investor made a mistake in his testimony by brushing aside his warranty that he had read the offering materials.[64]

[62]Rule 506(b)(2)(ii).

[63]*E.g.*, ULOE Rule 1(D); NASD Rules of Fair Practice, Article III, § 2, (CCH) *NASD Securities Dealers Manual* ¶ 2152.

[64]*Zissu v. Bear, Stearns & Co., supra* n. 3. The investor, the head of a law firm, in testimony "pooh poohed" the warranties as boilerplate. The intellectual principles behind the notion that the investor's breach of the warranty "caused" the lawsuit—i.e., if he had read the materials, he would not have initiated the lawsuit—are shaky but breach of the warranty allowed an angry judge to slap down someone the judge felt to be a meretricious litigant.

Nine

Term Sheet—The Substance of the Deal Between the Founder and Investors

In the next two chapters, there is a distinction drawn between "term sheet" items and the provisions of the various full dress agreements memoralizing the deal between the founder and the investors in a venture financing. The term sheet is a curtain raiser for the plenary financing documents; the term sheet issues are each covered, and enlarged upon, in the various agreements. The discussion is bifurcated into two chapters based on the author's experience on the issues that tend to be discussed most rigorously, (i) at the term sheet stage (those in this chapter); and (ii) during the drafting of the agreements themselves (in the next chapter). Because of the overlap, the two chapters should be read together.

§9.1 BACKGROUND

It is customary to begin the negotiation of a venture investment with the circulation of a document known as a "term sheet," a summary of the terms the proposer (the issuer, the investor, or an intermediary) is prepared to accept. The term sheet is analogous to a letter of intent, a nonbinding outline of the principal points which the Stock Purchase Agreement and related agreements will cover in detail. The advantage of the abbreviated term sheet format is, first, that it expedites the process. Experienced counsel immediately know generally what is meant when the term sheet specifies "one demand registration at the issuer's expense, unlimited piggybacks at the issuer's expense, weighted average antidilution;" it saves time not to have to spell out the long-form edition of those references.[1] Second, since the term sheet does not purport to be an agreement of any sort, it is less likely that a court will find unexpected promissory content; a "letter of intent" can be a dangerous document unless it specifies very clearly, as it should, which portions are meant to be binding and which merely guide the discussion and drafting. Some portions of a term sheet can have binding effect, of course, if and to the extent an interlocutory memoralization is needed of some binding promises, that is, confidentiality of the disclosures made in the negotiation. The summary format of a term sheet, however, makes it less likely that any party will be misled into thinking that some form of enforceable agreement has been memorialized when it has not.[2]

§9.2 CONTROL ISSUES GENERALLY

To understand that cohort of issues which has to do with the control of a start-up, some background is in order. Thus, in a mature business corporation, it has been understood, at least since Berle and Means's seminal work,[3] that nonmanagement purchasers of stock in public companies are passive investors. If they don't like the way the company is being run, their remedy (absent some actionable legal wrong) is to sell their shares. Venture capital operates on an entirely different set of

[1]One should be aware that some of the typical provisions found in a term sheet, i.e., "customary representations and warranties," can constitute less than precise instructions to the draftsmen of the Stock Purchase Agreement.

[2]The fact that a writing is styled as a term sheet does not exclude the possibility the parties have contemporaneously reached an oral agreement, oral agreements being equally as binding as written contracts, given the necessary quantum of proof (and absent legal requirements of a writing for the sale of, *e.g.*, shares of stock or real estate). Williston, *Contracts* § 12 (1957 & Supp. 1986).

[3]Berle & Means, *The Modern Corporation and Private Property* (1932).

principles. When raising money from his own investors—the limited partners in his venture pool—the professional manager of a venture capital partnership holds himself out as someone with the expertise to "add value" to the investments under his control. The notion is that the typical founder is an incomplete businessman, with gaps in experience in matters such as financial management and marketing. An active board of directors, staffed by representatives of the investors, is expected to help fill these gaps. Significantly, even in successful venture-backed companies, a large percentage of the founders are fired, retired, or otherwise relieved of their duties prior to the company's achieving its maturity. It is rare to find the likes of a Ken Olson at Digital Equipment or an Ed DeCastro at Data General, executives with the necessary breadth and scope to take the company through every phase of its path toward maturity. Consequently, a term sheet will deal with a series of related control issues immediately after the question of valuation is tentatively settled.

(a) BOARD SEATS

A business corporation is, as a legal matter, run by its board of directors.[4] In point of fact, many boards elect to yield the operational management of the company's affairs to a single individual, the chief executive officer, but the residual legal responsibility is not delegable. The board remains responsible. The president is a member of the board (under the laws of some states he has to be), and certain powers are delegated to him formally, usually in the bylaws. But the president's authority is derivative; to restate this important point, a seat on the board carries with it legal power and responsibility, whether the occupant likes it or not. In negotiating the term sheet, the struggle for power concerns who sits on the board.

That question breaks down into subissues. If the investors hold a majority of the stock but elect to retain fewer than 51% of the seats, when is it appropriate for the investors, assuming that they agree together as a group, to take over control? Regardless of who holds a majority of the outstanding shares, should the founder and his management colleagues retain control of the board until something objectively goes wrong, such as a failure to meet revenue benchmarks for X quarters, for example? The term sheet often unbundles the macro-question of control and allocates the parts separately, across a spectrum of issues and across a period of time. Thus, it may provide that the investors may retain control over certain core questions—management compensation, for example—and not others. Further, the term sheet may pro-

[4] Del. Code Ann. tit. 8 § 141(a) (1983 & Supp. 1986).

vide for a control "flip," meaning that the investors are content with a minority of the board as long as everything is going well; they succeed to outright control of the board when and as the company gets in trouble, allowing them to tie a can to the founder. Control flip can occur when benchmarks are not met or for more serious reasons, such as the violation of negative covenants in a Stock Purchase Agreement.[5]

From the investors' standpoint, control is a two-edged sword, since control entails some quantum of legal responsibility. Venture capital investment is risky enough if all that has been put at risk are the dollars invested in the enterprise. If, in addition, an investor can be held liable to the creditors, and, indeed, to other investors, in an insolvent enterprise, his risk parameters are undoubtedly exceeded.[6] Further, whether or not the liability is imposed by reason of the exercise of controlling influence, any board member has an assortment of "fidiciary" duties,[7] a phrase that, once appearing in a judicial opinion, usually takes on a precise legal meaning, that is, recovery by the plaintiff.[8]

Apart from a few isolated decisions or special fact situations,[9] it has as yet not been popular to impose liability beyond the investment made on investors who are deemed to be in control of a failed corporation. Indeed, if such were to eventuate through the agency of activist judges making new law in line with their underdog sympathies, it would be a formidable problem for the venture capital industry generally. However, it is an issue that cannot be ignored, particularly in view of the fact that directors and officers' liability policies are almost never affordable at the start-up stage (if, indeed, affordable at all).[10] Various provisions can be reflected in the term sheet to deal with the problem. First, some careful investors prefer to bargain for visitation or attendance rights for their representative on the board of directors, meaning the right to attend board meetings but not to vote. Occasionally, these rights are memorialized by calling the investor representative "honorary" or "ad-

[5]*See* Ch. 10, § 10.1(h).

[6]*See* Ch. 19, § 19.9.

[7]*See* Knauss, "Corporate Governance—A Moving Target," 79 *Mich. L. Rev.* 478, 487 (1981).

[8]Bartlett, *The Law Business: A Tired Monopoly* 138 (1982).

[9]*See* Ch. 19, §§ 19.8 and 19.9. One of the most intimidating opinions, albeit from a court without particular distinction, is *State National Bank of El Paso v. Farah Manufacturing Co., Inc.,* 678 S.W.2d 661 (Tex. Ct. App. 1984). In that case, the lender assumed control of the debtor through a "management clause," installed its own people and wound up liable for damages in excess of $18 million for, among other things, "duress." *See generally,* Bartlett & Lapatin, "The Status of a Creditor as a 'Controlling Person'," 28 *Mercer L. Rev.* 639 (1977).

[10]According to a National Venture Capital Association survey, the difficulty in obtaining affordable D&O insurance has reached "crisis proportions." *Vent. Cap. J.* 2 (May 1987). *See generally* Knepper, "Officers and Directors: Indemnification and Liability Insurance—An Update," 30 *Bus. Law.* 951 (Apr. 1975).

visory" directors. These measures should be viewed in context. The real power the investor group has over a cash-poor corporation is economic, not legal; the investors are the only source of fresh funds to keep the doors open. No law requires an investor group to advance fresh money[11] (absent an agreement or except at the conclusion of a lawsuit holding it liable in damages for some form of misconduct), so the power of the purse rests with the investors. As it is sometimes phrased, the Golden Rule obtains: "He who has the gold makes the rules." The bulk of the cases to date have involved variations on the theme of the doctrine of equitable subordination,[12] whereby senior investors, those holding a debt security of some sort, have seen their priority vanish in an insolvency proceeding, the notion being that, if the creditors take control of an insolvent company and manage its affairs so as to favor themselves, it is somehow inequitable to allow them to retain their status as creditors. Because of the heavy debt structure of leveraged buyouts, the doctrine of equitable subordination is much discussed in that arena.[13] In start-ups, where the investors are not as prone to invest in debt securities, the doctrine is less intimidating.

§9.3 REGISTRATION RIGHTS

To many investors, registration rights are one of the most important issues in a financing. If an investor is in a minority position in a nonpublic company, his exit possibilities depend on decisions made by others. Thus, some founders are proud that they have turned down entreaties from investment bankers to take their companies public. They claim that public shareholders might cramp their style and interfere with their ability to run the company according to their own tastes. Well and good for the founder but not so comforting to a minority investor, locked into the founder's company. Even if the investors as a group are in control of the company, there may be differences of opinion as to when an exit strategy should be implemented; indeed, each inves-

[11]Some cases come close. In *KMC, Co., Inc. v. Irving Trust Co.*, 757 F.2d 752 (6th Cir., 1985), the creditor bank was held liable for failing to advance funds under an agreement providing for discretionary lending up to a certain amount. *See* the discussion of the case in *Emerging Theories of Lender Liability* (Davis, Chmn. ABA Div. Prof. Responsibility 1985) 39.

[12]The Seventh Circuit in *Wright v. Heizer Corporation*, 560 F.2d 236 (7th Cir. 1977), in an unhappily worded opinion, extended the doctrine of equitable subordination in a venture capital context to limits which, if pursued in subsequent decisions, may prove intimidating to investors. *See* the discussion of the case in *Bartlett, supra* n. 8, at 138.

[13]*See* Ch. 19, § 19.8.

tor may have a different sense of timing on the issue, based on facts peculiar to that investor.

The decision to sell the company as a whole is almost always dependent on at least a majority of the shareholders coming together in favor of the sale. To be sure, the shareholders could by contract agree to sell out at the election of the minority but such contracts, the tail wagging the dog so to speak, are seldom encountered in practice.[14] One primary exit strategy, however, can be implemented—in theory at least—by the shareholders singly and *seriatim.* The company can only sell its assets once, but it can have as many public offerings of its securities as the market will bear and a public offering will, at least eventually, make the investors liquid.

As has been suggested, however, the decision to go public in the first instance is often difficult; there are considerations on both sides.[15] Moreover, even if a company is already public, the election to float another offering requires thought and discussion; any offering "dilutes" existing shareholders. Some shareholders may feel the currently obtainable price accurately reflects value and some may violently disagree.

As a technical legal matter, the decision to effect an IPO is a majority decision. Even if the company is not planning itself to sell any stock, only the company can file a registration statement;[16] a minority shareholder cannot register his stock for sale without the company's consent. As the registrant,[17] the company sets the terms of the offering, including the question of how many insider shares to include. Accordingly, investors seek to bolster their position by securing that consent in advance, by insisting that there exist, as part of or allied to the Stock Purchase Agreement, an agreement called the Registration Rights Agreement. (It is important to recall that a company "going public" does not undergo an instant transformation, with all its stock ipso facto turned into liquid instruments; the only shares which become truly public—that is, are

[14]There is nothing conceptually impossible in the notion of a "sale or merger rights" clause. If all the stockholders agree in advance, the board could be bound, at the instigation of the minority, to retain an agent and authorize it to negotiate the best terms possible for a sale or merger of the entire company. There could be problems in binding the board in advance to vote for a transaction to occur well in the future—one which passes a given hurdle, for example—but, if the majority refuses the agent's recommendations, there could be other remedies: a control "flip," for example, or more stock for the minority.

[15]*See* Ch. 14, § 14.2.

[16]Section 6(a) of the '33 Act provides that the registration statement must be signed by the issuer, the CEO, the CFO, the comptroller or principal accounting officer, and a majority of the board.

[17]"[t]he term 'Registrant' means the issuer of the securities for which the registration statement is filed." Regulation C, Rule 405.

released from resale restrictions[18]—are those registered for sale[19] and sold at the time. And those shares are ordinarily issued by the company; the investors' share of the "action" in an IPO is severely limited because the market's appetite for stock in an IPO is generally confined to those transactions in which most of the money raised is going to work inside the company. Nonetheless, an IPO is the most significant step on the road to liquidity, even for those investors not selling in the offering.)

Registration rights fall into two categories: "demand" and "piggyback." Piggyback rights, as the name implies, give the shareholders a right to have their shares included in a registration the company is currently planning on behalf of itself (a "primary" offering) or other shareholders (a "secondary" offering).[20] Demand rights, as the name implies, contemplate that the company must initiate and pursue the registration of an offering including, although not necessarily limited to, the shares proffered by the requesting shareholder(s). Since demand rights are more controversial, the following discussion focuses principally (but not exclusively) on that variety. One point before leaving piggyback rights: There are various types of stock issuances, albeit registered, which should not be subject to piggyback rights by their nature, that is, issuance of shares in the course of acquiring another company or the registration of shares pursuant to an employee stock benefit plan. Moreover, the practical difference between demand and piggyback rights can be slight; the investors make a noise about demanding an IPO, the issuer (thus prodded) elects to go forward on its own and then the investors seek to piggyback on what has been, in effect, an offering they "demanded." Thus, the discussion of "haircuts," "stand asides," and "lock-ups" in § 9.3(d) applies to all types of registration rights, not just demand rights.

[18]Even publicly registered shares may not be freely resold; the privilege of investors holding nonregistered shares in a public company to "dribble" out shares pursuant to Rule 144 is limited by the provisions of that Rule and may be further limited by a "hold back" imposed by underwriters, the NASD and/or state securities administrators. *See* Ch. 14, § 14.11.

[19]Rule 415, adopted in November 1983, permits underwritten "shelf registrations," i.e., the registration of shares for later sale at the option of the holder for (i) mature public companies and (ii) for secondary issues. *See, e.g.,* Palm, "Registration Statement Preparation and Related Matters" in *Mechanics of Underwriting* (P.L.I. Course Handbook No. 547, 1987). The problem is that underwriters are reluctant to allow investors to include their shares in the registration statement for delayed sale under Rule 415 since that creates an "overhang" over the market. If the investor's stock is registered "on the shelf" under Rule 415, it must be "reasonably expected" it will be sold within two years. Rule 415(a)(2).

[20]A "reverse piggyback" right occurs when the investors exercise a demand right, compel a registration which (under the agreement) is at their expense and the company seeks the right to "piggyback" some newly issued shares on the investors' registration. *See* Frome & Max, *Raising Capital: Private Placement Forms and Techniques* 673 (1981).

(a) BACKGROUND

To comprehend adequately the various issues involved, a discussion of basic principles is in order, the first being that registration rights are seldom used in accordance with their terms and yet they are viewed by some investors and their counsel as a central element of the deal. The actual use of the demand rights, for example, could prove very awkward—a group of minority shareholders insisting on registration, the CEO agreeing only because he has to, but saying, in effect, to the minority, "Find your own underwriter, conduct your own road shows,[21] do not bother me with questions from large institutional purchasers—in a word, sell the stock yourself." Such would make for a disorderly marketing effort, to put it mildly, and the price per share would suffer.

On the other hand, as stated, registration rights are often the only exit vehicle which, as a practical matter, the minority shareholders can compel. A start-up may issue shares redeemable at the option of the holder but the instances in which that privilege has been successfully exercised are few. A company still in the development stage may not have the legal power, let alone the cash and/or the agreement of its creditors, to redeem stock. If a controlling founder is content to sit in his office, play with his high tech toys and does not need more money from his investors, the investors need leverage. There is no legal way, other than through the *threat* of enforcing the registration rights agreement, to compel the company to go public.[22] In this connection, it is important to keep in mind that liquidifying the investors' shares through a public offering can be not only a promise but also a benchmark, meaning that the remedy, if the founder refuses to cooperate, need not be a lawsuit. Reallocation of stock interests can be triggered if an IPO fails to materialize on time.[23]

The second interesting feature of the provision is that it is, in point of fact, a three-way agreement but with only two of the three parties negotiating and signing it. With a minor exception for "self-underwritten offerings,"[24] a primary or secondary offering of securities requires an issuer, selling shareholders *and* an underwriter, either on a "firm" or "best-efforts" basis. However, the underwriter is usually not in sight when the registration rights agreement is signed and the parties them-

[21]"Road shows" are meetings between the company, the underwriters and potential buyers of the company's stock held around the country after the registration statement has been filed and before it becomes effective. If a CEO wants to be obstreporous, not agreeing with the concept of an IPO, he can be less than enthusiastic about the company's near-term prospects at the road show, thereby effectively chilling the offering.

[22]The concept of a sale of the company at the demand of the minority is discussed *supra* n. 14.

[23]*See* Ch. 10, § 10.1(h).

[24]*See* Ch. 6, § 6.16.

selves have to anticipate what the underwriter will require. Following that point, underwriters as a rule do not favor secondary offerings for early-stage companies. Given a choice, the market likes to see the proceeds of the sale go into the company's treasury, to be used for productive purposes, rather than released to outsiders. Moreover, whenever stock is being sold, the underwriter wants the number of shares issued to be slightly less than its calculation of the market's appetite. An underwriting is deemed successful if the stock price moves up a bit in the after market. If the price goes down, the buyers brought in by the underwriter are unhappy; if it moves up smartly, the company is upset because the underwriter underpriced the deal. Consequently, the underwriter does not want to see new shares coming into the market shortly after the underwritten offering is sold, creating more supply than demand. These imperatives account for terms in the registration rights agreement known as the "haircut" and the "hold back," discussed below.

Finally, including one's shares in a publicly underwritten offering is not the only way shares can be sold. A holder of restricted securities can sell his shares, albeit at a discount attributable to illiquidity, in a private transaction; more importantly, he can "dribble" out the shares into the market once the company has become public, under Rule 144.[25] Registration rights for the holder of restricted shares in an already public company are, therefore, a redundancy unless the holder wants to sell before the required holding period in Rule 144 has expired or the block is so large that it cannot be "dribbled" out under the "volume" or "manner of sale" restrictions set out in that Rule.

The "points" in a registration rights negotiation (points being a slang term for contested issues)[26] are of varying degrees of intensity. Some are standard. Thus, the issuer rarely agrees to register convertible preferred stock, convertible debt or other rights to purchase common stock. The market in the hybrid securities themselves can be messy and confusing to analysts of an emerging-stage issuer's IPO; indeed, the mere existence of a class of senior security may cloud the outlook for the common stock's participation in future earnings.[27] Hence, as a rule, the

[25]*See* the discussion of Rule 144 in Ch. 14 § 14.11. *See also* the discussion of "shelf" registrations, *supra* n. 19.

[26]When negotiators want to show an increase in the fervor that they or their clients feel about a given issue, they label it a "deal point" or a "deal breaker." The way experienced negotiators respond to a litany of "deal points" issuing from the clenched lips of a red-faced, kamikaze lawyer is to create an "escrow file," meaning that the issue is left for later consideration. After a deal point sits in the escrow file for a bit, it often defuses itself. *See generally* Fisher & Ury, *Getting to Yes: Negotiating Agreements Without Giving In* (1981).

[27]Since the existence of a convertible senior security can muddy the investing public's perception of the common stock, conversion is usually mandated no later than the evening of an IPO. *See* Ch. 13, § 13.5.

holders of convertible securities must convert before they can include their stock in the offering and/or must convert in any event so as to "clean up" the balance sheet. Some "points" on the other hand, are potential battlefields. For example, a minority shareholder will want the right to threaten exercise of his rights (and thus bully the company into registration) at any time of his choosing. The company will fight to limit the permissible timing of the shareholder's election—no less than, say, five nor more than seven years after he makes his investment. The shareholder will want to be able to transfer his registration rights if he transfers his shares—they are part of the bundle of rights for which he bargained. The company will fight to keep the rights personal to the holder—a right to force registration is a formidable weapon if the timing is totally inappropriate. A disgruntled shareholder—for example, a founder recently terminated as president—may wave the rights around like a club to win some unrelated concession. Following that thought, the company needs to limit the number of fingers on the trigger, so to speak. Assume, for example, 10 investors who each hold 10% of the class of convertible preferred stock: If each investor enjoyed his personal trigger—that is, could demand registration—the company might find itself in the path of a stampede, helping neither itself nor the investors generally. Moreover, if the company agrees to pay all or a part of the cost of the registration, multiple demands could be, as indicated in the next section, expensive. It is, therefore, in the interest of the company and the major investors to vest control of the trigger in the shareholders acting in concert—at least to insist that *most* of them agree internally before the issue is brought before the company. In addition, the amount of stock they are willing to sell should also be substantial, both because of expense (a small registration is almost as expensive as a large one) and because a buoyant public market depends on "float," enough shares in circulation to interest institutional investors. From the investor's standpoint, of course, the situation is reversed. He wants the trigger to be one share less than the shares he holds.

This issue becomes more difficult when an issuer goes through multiple rounds of financing, selling off registration rights in each round. If all the shares are of the same class and series, what does one do with a 51% shareholder in round one who becomes a 35% shareholder when round two is completed? Does he "lose" his solo finger on the trigger because he did not elect to participate in the second round or the second round involved the acquisition of another company for stock in a transaction which he was not eligible to participate? Indeed, the question of inconsistent registration rights provisions occasioned by separate agreements for each round is a thorny one. If the company's norm is that the rights are not meant to mature for three years from date of investment, what is to be done with investors in earlier rounds who have held shares for almost three years? Will they have first and exclusive chance at the gateway to public securities? If series A preferred was sold last year (with a 51% trigger) and series B preferred is being sold currently, is there any way to compel the series A holders to join in with the series B (assuming the number of shares in each series is the same) to avoid a situation in which the trigger is suddenly held by 25.1% (vs. 51%) of the outstanding preferred stock? Is the language of the agreement such that investors in the earlier rounds can claim to have a first priority for including their shares in a piggyback registration?

The fact is, when the later round occurs, most practitioners attempt to induce the prior holders (who often overlap with the investors in the later round)[28] to cancel the earlier agreement and accept a new provision which affects all the existing holders, old and new, equally. Alternatively, counsel for the early-round investors may bargain for provisions which constrain the issuer in agreeing to register shares of subsequent purchasers—either an absolute prohibition without the consent of the earlier investors or a priority in their favor.

(b) EXPENSES

Responsibility for the expenses of a secondary registration is another topic for negotiation. Registration compels the company's lawyers and accountants to run up bills which are routinely in six figures; moreover, management must spend a considerable amount of time in the course of the process. The most logical argument, from the company's view at least, is to inform the selling shareholders in a demand registration, "You want it? . . . you pay for it." That is not, however, the way of the world in most financings. At least the first demand registration is usually "free," meaning that the company is responsible for all expenses except in unusual cases, that is, the demanding parties run up a big bill for professional fees and then yank the offering. As stated, these provisions are, in a sense, academic. Merely the threat to demand a registration usually prompts the company to go forward on its own and, with respect to the exercise of piggyback rights, the worst case for the holders is that they must pick up the incremental costs caused by the inclusion of their stock. It will be recalled that state securities administrators take a dim view of provisions which give selling stockholders a "free ride" in a IPO;[29] however, if the agreement dates back to the early private rounds, some states will make an exception, their fire being concentrated on

[28]Investors in the early rounds are expected to follow on with fresh capital in late rounds to show their faith in the company; however, the existing investors often insist that the founder find at least one new investor—"new blood"—to join in late rounds, if only to avoid a situation where the investors are negotiating on price and other issues with themselves.

[29]*See* Ch. 14, § 14.9(a).

investors who purchase shortly before the IPO.[30] This is a significant planning point; investors may need the agreement in writing if the issuer's obligation is to be honored.

The expense issue is significantly impacted by the ability (or inability) of the company to use year-end financials to satisfy the requirement in the '33 Act (Regulation S–X) that current (i.e., no more than 134 days old) financials be included.[31] Accordingly, the company will, as it should, argue long and hard that demand rights should be limited to a "window" following the close of the fiscal year so that the already-paid-for audited financials can alone be used. The use of unaudited stub financials also involves materially increased exposure.[32]

(c) "HAIRCUTS," "STAND ASIDES," AND "LOCK-UPS"

As stated, the underwriters are not parties to the agreement but counsel who have been through the mill understand what the underwriters want and, indeed, demand. Piggyback (and sometimes demand) provisions, accordingly, routinely provide that the underwriters can cut down—"haircut"—the amount of stock included by secondary sellers. Moreover, demand rights are not exercisable for some period (usually three to six months) before a planned primary offering or for, say, a year thereafter in order to avoid multiple offerings at the same point in time; this is often called the "stand aside" or "stand-off" provision.[33] Finally, at the request of the underwriters, all investors who are party to the registration rights agreement, or at least all significant investors, may be asked to agree to "lock up," that is, not to sell shares under Rule

[30]*See* Ch. 14, § 14.9(a).

[31]If the filing occurs more than 134 days from the end of the most recent fiscal year, the registration statement must include an unaudited balance sheet not more than 135 days old. Regulation S–X, Rule 3–01.

[32]Audited financials in a public offering are "expertised," meaning that the standard of care to be exercised by defendants in a lawsuit under § 11 of the '33 Act (other than the accountants) is ameliorated *vis-à-vis* alleged false financial statements or omissions in the matters covered thereby. '33 Act § 11(b)(3)(C). To gain some modicum of protection, unaudited financial statements in a prospectus are usually accompanied by the auditors' "cold comfort" letter. On the issue of "cold comfort" letters, *see generally* Sherman & Wong, "Cold Comfort Letters" *In Mechanics of Underwriting* (1986) (P.L.I. Course Handbook Series No. 508) at 45. The existence of a cold comfort letter respecting unaudited financial statements (usually called "stub" financials), pro forma financial information and miscellaneous financial information helps establish the "due diligence" defense under § 11(b)(3) of the '33 Act. *See also* Resnik, "Understanding Comfort Letters for Underwriters," 34 *Bus. Law.* 1725 (July 1979).

[33]The "stand-off" is, or should be, noncontroversial. If the company is planning an IPO, it is hard to envision circumstances in which investors, exercising their demand rights, would want to compete.

144, for a period from three to six months after a primary registration becomes public.

These provisions are interesting in several respects. While the parties are often inclined to argue about the exact terms *ad nauseam,* the fact is that the underwriters are in charge of most offerings. Since they (allegedly) know what will sell and what will not, what they say goes, regardless of the language in any registration rights agreement. For an early-round investor to object long and hard to the underwriter's haircut makes minimal sense because he should realize that the underwriters will, in the final analysis, *tell* him what to do.

Moreover, a "lock-up" may be very significant. There are theorists, including this author, who believe that, as a general rule in emerging company finance, a high percentage of final value is created while the company is privately held; perhaps because of lack of training, such investors do not attempt to understand or anticipate the vagaries of the public market. Once the stock is liquid, they want to sell, particularly since the market for the stock of high multiple, relatively unseasoned issuers is extremely volatile. Having worked hard to achieve the exit strategy, they want to exit, before the $10 price goes to $5. The fact that the stock may go to $15 is not as significant. The pleasure–pain index records significantly less pleasure at another $5 gain than pain at a $5 loss of what the investor already "had." Since a "lock-up" can cost the investor significant dollars,[34] there is an argument that a shrewd investor should consider staying out, if he can, of any registration rights agreement entirely if it requires agreeing in advance to a lock-up. The company is likely to go public at the first available opportunity regardless of the existence or nonexistence of a contractual compulsion to do so; the registration rights agreement does not involve a zero-sum game—everyone's interests are, ordinarily, focused in the same direction. And, if the underwriters are going to insist on a "lock-up," which they will, it is easier for them to pick out those investors who have already signed away their consent. The underwriters may not need to lock up every shareholder to achieve their results.

As indicated above, there is an alternative for investors. They may forgo a registration rights covenant as such and bargain for a promise from the issuer that, if the issuer has not publicly registered its stock and made the investors' stock liquid by a given date, the investors reap some sort of benefit, that is, more stock at the expense of the founder.

[34]Needless to say, if three separate financings have occurred and the investors in only one are subject to a potential "lock-up," the weight of the lock-up will fall disproportionately on the burdened investors since, at least technically, the issuer and the underwriter cannot get at investors in the other financings to slow them down. The remedy is a provision in the first financing that requires a lock-up (and a "haircut"—the same principle applies) for all investors in all future financings.

Such provisions can have more substantive impact than a promise to do something the issuer wants to do anyway and which cannot be performed effectively any earlier than objective circumstances dictate; moreover, it can be phrased so as to require the issuer to get the investors all the way to their goal—that is, stock they can actually sell—by the date in question.

To be sure, the underwriter's lock-up can be redundant. State securities administrators routinely insist on lock-ups of insider shares if they feel the price is at variance with the issuer's less-than-robust earnings, the theory being that, if much of the value anticipated by the market is "on the come," insiders should wait for the anticipated good things to happen like everyone else.[35] However, the "blue sky" lock-up usually extends only to recent purchasers of shares.[36]

(d) MISCELLANEOUS ITEMS

There is a miscellaneous group of largely noncontroversial provisions that fill out a registration rights agreement. The company should agree to keep the registration statement, once filed, effective by updating it for accuracy; since registration on Form S–3 (for mature companies)[37] is relatively painless, the issuer usually agrees to register shares (assuming a substantial bloc so desires) on an S–3 at any time. Finally, the agreement should terminate at some definite time in the future, if only to save administrative nuisance.

§9.4 ANTIDILUTION

In the "modern era" of venture capital—1970 and beyond—the so-called "antidilution" provisions have become increasingly important. Like so many words in the glossary of venture capital, "dilution" has multiple meanings. The core concept, however, arises from a central fact: Any new claimant to the assets and/or income of a firm reduces the percentage interests of the existing claimants. Thus, if X and Y own 50% of a firm and Z purchases newly issued securities with a claim—say, 25%—on future income, X and Y have been diluted in the sense that each necessarily owns a lesser percentage, a lesser claim. It may be, of course, that Z contributes cash or property in an amount sufficient to

[35] *See* Ch. 14, § 14.9(a).

[36] A well-drafted "lock-up" prohibits short sales and other trading strategies which amount to a sale without the shares actually being transferred.

[37] Companies which have been reporting publicly pursuant to § 12 of the '34 Act for three years are eligible to use Form S–3 in registering securities. Form S–3, *General Instructions* § 1.A.3.

enable the firm to increase its earnings by, say, 40%. In such event, it is arguable that X and Y's shares have not been diluted in the sense of watered down, because the firm enjoys surplus earning power. Nonetheless, their percentage interest, albeit in a larger pie, is smaller and some would hold to the theory that X and Y have suffered in some sense.

(a) SEVERAL MEANINGS OF "DILUTION"

The issue of dilution depends on what criteria are deemed significant in calculating value. If net earnings per share is the measure that drives stock price, then a financing which increases that result is nondilutive; if, similarly, cash flow or gross revenue per share is the critical indicator, the issue is: "Did that indicator go up or down on a per share basis?". Some firms are given an overall bill of health in terms of return on equity or on assets; a dilutive financing is one that decreases that ratio.

The same analysis can be conducted in terms of book value. If the "shareholders equity" account is $1 million and X and Y each own 50%, the appearance of Z, who contributes $100,000 for a 25% interest, dilutes X and Y. If Z contributed $400,000 for 25%, the financing is not normally considered dilutive; dilution in a balance-sheet sense is usually thought to occur only when net book value per share diminishes as a result of the financing. If Z lends the firm $1 million, it is arguable that the claim of X and Y is set back in liquidation, behind an additional layer of debt. However, since the firm has added the loan proceeds to the asset side of the ledger, dilution is not usually perceived as resulting in such instance.

The issue of dilution, however defined, arises in at least two contexts in venture finance. First, securities regulators—state and federal—are concerned that dilution be disclosed. The rules in this regard have in mind a balance-sheet test: net book value per share. The placement memo or prospectus should disclose what happens to the newly issued stock following the financing.[38] If the price paid is $10 per share and net book value immediately after the closing is $5 per share (because shares were earlier issued at 10¢), then dilution has occurred at the rate of 50%.

(b) "ANTIDILUTION" FORMULAS

The easy part of the antidilution discussion has to do with recapitalizations (changes in the number of shares outstanding in the absence of an exogenous transaction such as a third-party financing or a consolidation with another firm—that is, stock dividends, stock splits, and

[38] *See* Ch. 8, § 8.5, on private placements and Ch. 14, § 14.9(a), on IPOs.

reverse stock splits).[39] These changes are technical. A 100% stock dividend doubles the number of shares and cuts the book value of the stock in half; absent a market reaction which reflects nonfundamental factors, one $20 share of stock becomes two $10 shares of stock.[40] The more difficult issue arises when a later round of financing is at a lower price than an earlier round or rounds. Thus, assume the company sells preferred stock to investors in an early round, convertible at $1 a share, and then something changes. The issuer needs more money, as startups usually do, and so it sells more stock, perhaps common this time, at 75¢ per share. The preferred stockholders are diluted in a book value sense, but one may argue such a contingency is a business risk. There were no guarantees when they bought their preferred. The "something" may have had nothing to do with the fortunes of the company; perhaps it is developing in accordance with the plan but the investment climate changes. If the existing investors want protection against dilution, they can bargain for, and subsequently exercise, pre-emptive rights, essentially dollar averaging or averaging down to protect their percentage interest. After all, they are the people with cash to spend.

The foregoing is a plausible argument but it neglects the Golden Rule (to repeat, "He who has the gold makes the rules"). Antidilution provisions tied to the price of subsequent financings operate at the expense of one particular class—the founder and his allies, the key employees—and to the benefit of the other class, the existing cash investors. The new investors, of course, do not care; they get the percentage of equity they bargained for at the specified price. They are either indifferent on the issue or, because they overlap with the earlier cash investors, are in favor of antidilution protection. The founder has only one way to get rich, the horse he is riding, while the professional venture capitalists have a number of irons in the fire. The founder is, therefore, usually outgunned and gives up on antidilution provisions. Unfortunately, this can be a big mistake, a point to be revisited after an explanation of the way in which the provisions operate.

(c) "FULL RATCHET" AND "WEIGHTED AVERAGE"

There are two principal ways to formulate antidilution provisions, capitalizing the terms to make it clear we are talking about the ones which

[39]If antidilution adjustments result in a change in the shareholders' proportionate interests in the company, there is the possibility of a tax being imposed under I.R.C. § 305. *See* Ch. 13, § 13.6.

[40]At certain prices, albeit the price of a share is initially an artificial construct, the market changes as a result of recapitalizations. Thus, share prices of less than, say, $1, cheapen the reputation of the stock because it is in bad company—"penny stock." Similarly, 1,000 shares of stock at $10 per share are more valuable than one $10,000 share because there are more potential buyers at the lower price.

have substantive bite—the "full ratchet" and the "weighted average." Full Ratchet provisions are the real killers, at least from the founder's point of view. They provide that, if one share of stock is issued at a lower price, or one right to purchase stock is issued at a lower aggregate price (exercise price plus what is paid, if anything, for the right), then the conversion price of the existing preferred shares[41] is automatically decreased, that is, it "ratchets down," to the lower price. Depending on how many shares (or rights) are included in the subsequent issue, this can be strong medicine. A brief example will illustrate. Assume Newco, Inc. has 1 million common shares and 1 million convertible preferred shares outstanding, the founder owns all the common, and the investors own all the preferred, convertible into common at $1 per share. Newco then issues 50,000 shares of common at 50¢ per share because it desperately needs $25,000 in cash. To make the example as severe as possible, let us say the investors control the board and they make the decision to price the new round of financing at 50¢. Suddenly the preferred's conversion price is 50¢, the founder goes from 50% of the equity to under 33.3% and all the company has gained in the bargain is $25,000. Indeed, a full ratchet would drop the founder from 50% of the equity to 33.3% if the company issued *only one* share at 50¢. This is a harsh result, indeed. When a really dilutive financing occurs, say shares have to be sold at 10¢ per share, the founder drops essentially out of sight. The company takes in $5,000 and the founder goes down under 9%, never to recover because he does not have the cash to protect himself in subsequent rounds. In the jargon of venture capital, he has been "burned out" of the opportunity. There is no other provision so capable of changing the initial bargain between the parties with the dramatic effect of Full Ratchet dilution. When venture capitalists are referred to as "vulture capitalists," it is likely the wounded founders are talking about dilutive financings and a Full Ratchet provision.[42]

The more moderate position on this issue has to do with Weighted Average antidilution provisions. There are various ways of expressing the formula but it comes down to the same central idea: The investors' conversion price is reduced to a lower number but one which takes into account how many shares (or rights) are issued in the dilutive financing. If only a share or two is issued, then the conversion price does not move much; if many shares are issued—that is, there is in fact, real dilution—then the price moves accordingly.

The object is to diminish the old conversion price to a number be-

[41]For purposes of simplicity, it is assumed that the investors enjoying antidilution protection hold convertible preferred shares.

[42]Some venture capitalists argue for Full Ratchet provisions as a bargaining chip, intending to afford some relief to the founder(s) in the event of a "burnout" financing.

tween itself and the price per share in the dilutive financing, taking into account how many new shares are issued. Thus, the starting point is the total number of common shares outstanding prior to the dilutive financing. The procedure to achieve the objective is to multiply the old conversion price per share by some fraction, less than one, to arrive at a new conversion price; the latter being smaller than the former, the investors will get more shares on conversion and dilute the common shareholders (the founder) accordingly. The fraction is actually a combination of two relationships used to "weight" the computation equitably. The first relationship is between the shares outstanding before the financing versus shares outstanding after the financing (label these two numbers, A and B). This takes into account the number of shares—small or large—issued in the dilutive financing.

The second fraction takes into account the drop in price and expresses that drop in terms that can be mathematically manipulated with the first fraction to get a combined, weighted result. The relationship is between the shares which would have been issued for the price paid if the old (i.e., higher) conversion price had been used versus the shares actually issued (i.e., the shares issued at the new price.) (Call these two numbers C and D.)

The combination of these two relationships—number of shares "before and after" and price "before and after" (expressed in number of shares)—is a formula:

(A plus C) divided by (B plus D) = the fraction (or percentage) which is multiplied by the old conversion price to get the new conversion price.

It is open for theorists to argue about the fairness of that result but the above formula has the advantage of economy of expression. If one wants to use a weighted-average antidilution formula, the above is one commonly used (albeit expressed in different terms).

The calculations get more complex as rounds of financing multiply. If the investors in round one (holding series A preferred) enjoy a conversion price of \$1, *and* the price for the round two (series B) investors is \$1.50, *and* the round three (series C) preferred is convertible at \$4 *and* there then occurs a dilutive financing at 50¢, all the conversion prices are affected, but it takes a computer to figure out who is entitled to what number of shares, particularly since investors in the various rounds will tend to overlap. (In this connection, one occasionally encounters a formula which keys off accumulated dilution. Thus, in the example cited, and depending on the amount raised in each instance, only the series C preferred holders would get an adjustment in their conversion price; the earlier investors would hold fast because the weighted average price of all subsequent rounds, taken together, is above their price.)

Finally, one of the most troublesome issues in the antidilution area is the "free rider" problem. If the first-round investors own preferred stock convertible at $1 and the company gets in trouble, the existing investors will ordinarily (assuming there is hope) agree to put up more money. If the new price is 50¢, the founder will be diluted accordingly, a result he may find equitable in the case of those investors who are participating in the dilutive round. However, he is likely to view it as inequitable—as, indeed, will the investors investing fresh cash—that a first-round investor who refuses to pay "his share" of the current round, (a financing in the nature of an assessment) also gets more stock because of the automatic operation of the antidilution provisions. It has not yet become common to draft with that contingency in mind, to qualify the antidilution provisions by providing that only those investors who are in the dilutive round for a significant amount of money can enjoy an adjustment of their purchase price. Nonetheless, it is not impossible to draft; one may either exclude nonparticipating investors entirely or develop a formula which weights the antidilution adjustment by the amount each investor contributes in the current round compared with his prior percentage.[43]

§9.5 REDEMPTION OF CONVERTIBLE PREFERRED STOCK

The issuer of convertible preferred stock will ordinarily prefer to simplify its capital structure as soon as feasible. Therefore, it reserves the right to call the preferred for redemption at some date in the future. It is rarely contemplated that the convertible preferred will actually be redeemed for cash at the option of a venture-backed company,[44] entailing a return of capital to the shareholders in exchange for their shares. The object of the call is to force conversion and, accordingly, the call issues when and only when the value of the conversion stock—usually the common stock—is in excess of the conversion price. The investors will, conversely, wish to limit the issuer's right to call, desiring to leave the conversion option in their hands. Call protection is, therefore, usually agreed upon—no call for five years or until an IPO is pending, for example, and sometimes a call premium is demanded. Since a

[43]If an investor (i) owned 10% of the company prior to the dilutive offering; (ii) took only 5% of the dilutive offering; and, (iii) the effect of the antidilution provisions was to give him or her 1,000 additional conversion shares, the formula might cut that "bonus" to 500.

[44]Thus, a sinking fund is ordinarily not provided for in the Stock Purchase Agreement.

fixed-interest rate is not guaranteed, however, call protection is not as vital as in the case of a fixed-income security.

On occasions, investors with heavy leverage bargain for an additional exit door—the right to "put" their shares to the issuer for cash after the passage of time. The value of this provision as a viable exit is often questionable. Presumably, the investor will exercise if and only if the company is not prospering, meaning that its ability to come up with the cash is in question.[45]

The conversion privilege ordinarily runs from the senior security into the junior security, that is, common stock. The result is not, however, required; assuming that no holder of a senior class has the right to object, preferred can be convertible into, for example, subordinated debt. In fact, it is occasionally provided that the preferred will be mandatorily converted to debt at the option of the issuer on and after some date in the future, by which time the issuer expects profits against which interest deductions can be offset.

§9.6 SAMPLE TERM SHEETS

The Text has generally not reproduced forms of agreements, the author preferring to refer to well-prepared form books in current use. However, it is difficult to render the flavor of term sheets without exhibiting some of the various forms that they may assume. Therefore, the following discussion introduces an array of term sheets taken from actual deals, designed to illustrate varying tastes and elections. Note should be taken of certain provisions which are not separately discussed in this or the succeeding chapter. These include pre-emptive rights or rights of first refusal (*see* Ch. 4, § 4.11); reporting obligations of the issuer; rights to inspect the issuer's business and financial records and interrogate the accountants; restrictions on transfer of the founders' stock (*see* Ch. 4, § 4.9); "key man" insurance on the founder's life; and provisions to forfeit some of the founder's stock if certain events do not occur.

(a) A SHORT FORM—THE "PLAIN VANILLA" APPROACH

This term sheet reflects the style of one of the most successful venture capital funds. The investor's approach is to keep the "legalese" to a minimum and the preferred stock it acquires tends toward the "plain vanilla" variety. However, the investor in question makes a rigorous

[45]A preferred stock which must be redeemed or is redeemable at the option of the holder is not classified as an equity security for accounting purposes. FASB Statement No. 12, ¶ 7(a). *See* Ch. 13, § 13.6(b), for a discussion of the tax effect of "unreasonable" redemption premiums under I.R.C. § 305.

investigation of potential problems that may exist with respect to a company's business, viz. the ownership and protection of its assets (including intellectual property), the adequacy of and enforceability of its significant contracts, antitrust questions, employee confidentiality and noncompetition matters, regulatory compliance and tax and accounting issues.

International Technology, Inc.

	Summary of terms
1. Investor:	Limited Partnership
2. Seller: ("I.T.I.")	International Technology, Inc.
3. Amount:	$750,000
4. Security:	Convertible Preferred Stock, representing 9.375% fully diluted ownership in I.T.I., after taking account for all issued but unexercised options.
5. Registration Rights:	Unlimited piggyback rights at I.T.I.'s expense. One demand registration at I.T.I.'s expense.
6. Pre-emptive Rights:	The Investor will have the right to retain pro rate ownership in any future private financings.
7. Board Seat:	The Investor will have the right to nominate one member to the Board of Directors, subject to management's approval.
8. Financial Statements:	The Investor will have the right to receive unaudited monthly financial statements, audited annual financial statements, and annual budgets.
9. Right of Cosale:	Founder and Cofounder will agree that any time they or their families sell stock in a private sale, the Investor will have a right to sell a proportionate amount of stock to the same buyer at the same price.

10. Representations and Warranties:	I.T.I. will agree to standard financial and business representations and warranties, including a representation that all material facts relating to the business have been fully and accurately disclosed and that there has been no material adverse change in the business and its prospects prior to the closing.
11. Legal Fees:	I.T.I. will agree to bear the reasonable fees of counsel for the Investor.

(b) LONG FORM, PRO INVESTOR

Herewith a "pro-investor" term sheet[46] containing, among other provisions, a control "flip," the investors right to "put" their shares back to the company and a strong provision which provides that, if the company is merged, the preferred holders have the election of converting to common or insisting on their liquidation preference before the common shareholders take anything.

Start-up Corporation Convertible Preferred Stock

	Summary of Proposed Terms
Amount of Investment:	$930,000
Type of Security:	930,000 shares of Convertible Preferred Stock ("Preferred Stock"), at a purchase price of $1.00 per share, Convertible into Common Stock representing 53.75% of the outstanding securities of the Company on a fully diluted basis.
Purchasers:	The investment will be made by the purchasers listed below (the "Purchasers"), in the

[46]Even the most experienced venture capitalists differ on whether their ultimate outcomes can be improved by feverish negotiation on the terms of the deal. Some solidly favor tough terms—stock forfeitures, control "flips," investor rights to put stock back to the issuer, interim returns and the like. Equally experienced investors, to the author's knowledge, tend to discount those provisions, remarking that the terms of the deal rarely make a difference in the final outcome.

Summary of Proposed Terms

	respective amounts set forth opposite each of their names:

Purchaser	*Amount of Investment*
Smith	$350,000
Brown	250,000
Jones	150,000
Ryan	100,000
Cabot	30,000
O'Leary	25,000
Goldberg	25,000

	As a condition to the purchase of the Preferred Stock by the Purchasers, Messers Founder and Cofounder (the "Founders") shall contribute an aggregate of an additional $50,000 to the capital of the Company.
Conversion:	Each share of Preferred Stock will be Convertible, at any time, at the option of the holder, into shares of Common Stock, at a conversion price of $1.00 per share. Shares of Preferred Stock shall automatically be converted in the event of a firmly underwritten public offering of Common Stock of the Company at a price per share which exceeds 300% of the conversion price then in effect in which the aggregate proceeds received by the Company exceed $5 million (a "Public Offering").
Voting Rights:	On all matters submitted to a vote of holders of Common Stock generally, each share of Preferred Stock shall be entitled to exercise the number of votes equal to the number of shares of Common Stock into which it is Convertible on the appropriate record date. The board of directors shall consist of five members. Two directors shall be elected by the holders of Preferred Stock, one of whom shall be selected by Smith and one of whom shall be selected by Brown, and two directors shall be designated by management and elected by the holders of Common Stock. The fifth director shall be a person who is not employed by the Company and is mutually acceptable to the holders of Preferred Stock and management of the Company. In the event of certain events of default, the holders of Preferred Stock shall be

Start-up Corporation Convertible Preferred Stock

	Summary of Proposed Terms
	entitled to elect a majority of the members of the Board of Directors. Jones shall have the right to have an observer present at each meeting of the Board of Directors.
Dividends:	Dividends shall accrue on each share of Preferred Stock on a cumulative basis at the rate of 8% per annum. Dividends shall be payable only in the event of a redemption of shares of Preferred Stock or a liquidation, dissolution or winding up of the Company.
Redemption:	On March 16 in each of years 1990 and 1991, the Company will redeem 50% of the shares of Preferred Stock (or such lesser number then outstanding) at a price of $1.00 per share plus any accrued but unpaid dividends.
Liquidation Preference:	In the event of any liquidation, dissolution or winding up of the Company, the holders of Preferred Stock shall receive $1.00 per share of Preferred Stock plus accrued but unpaid dividends before any payments to holders of any other equity securities of the Company. The merger or consolidation of the Company into or with another corporation or the sale of substantially all of the Company's assets shall be deemed to be a liquidation, dissolution, or winding up of the Company and the holders of Preferred Stock will be entitled to receive the amount described above.
Registration Rights:	1. After March 16, 1986, two demand registrations at the company's expense upon the request of the holders of not less than 67% of the Preferred Stock then outstanding. A registration will not count for this purpose if the Company elects to sell stock pursuant to a registration at the same time. There will be no piggyback on such registrations without the consent of the participating holders of Preferred Stock. 2. Unlimited piggyback registrations, at the Company's expense, with priority over all other piggybacks. The Founders may join in piggybacks in a position subordinate to the participating holders of Preferred Stock. 3. Unlimited registrations, at the Company's expense, on Form S–3 or any similar short form.

Start-up Corporation Convertible Preferred Stock

	Summary of Proposed Terms
	4. The Company shall not grant registration rights to any other party without the consent of the holders of Preferred Stock, except for registration rights which are subordinate to those of the holders of Preferred Stock.
Covenants and Restrictions:	The Stock Purchase Agreement will contain customary covenants and restrictions and will specify certain actions which may be taken by the Company only with the consent of the holders of 67% of the Preferred Stock, including, without limitation: (1) altering, changing, or amending the preferences or rights of Preferred Stock; (2) authorizing and/or issuing any new shares of equity securities, except for up to 200,000 shares of Common Stock (or options to purchase such shares) which may be issued by the Board of Directors as incentives to key employees and consultants of the Company; (3) merging with or acquiring another entity or selling substantially all of the assets of the Company; (4) engaging in any business other than the business engaged in by the Company at the time of the closing; (5) increasing or decreasing the authorized number of directors constituting the Board of Directors; (6) paying dividends on or making other distributions with respect to any equity securities other than Preferred Stock; or (7) repurchasing or redeeming any securities, except for required redemption of Preferred Stock and repurchase under Restricted Stock Agreements with employees previously approved by the Board of Directors.
Financial Statements and Reporting:	The Company will prepare and submit to holders of Preferred Stock monthly unaudited financial statements (including income statements, summaries, balance sheets, cash flow statements, and summaries of bookings and backlogs) no later than 30 days after the close of each month, and quarterly unaudited financial statements (including income statements, summaries, balance sheets, cash flow statements, and summaries of bookings and backlogs) no later than 30 days after the end of each of the first three fiscal quarters of each year, including balance sheets and

Start-up Corporation Convertible Preferred Stock

	Summary of Proposed Terms
	statements of income and changes in financial position. Audited annual financial statements shall be provided no later than 90 days after the end of each year, together with a statement from the auditors regarding compliance by the Company with the terms of the Preferred Stock and the Stock Purchase Agreement. As soon as available, but in no event later than 30 days prior to the start of each fiscal year, the Company shall submit to the holders of Preferred Stock an annual budget and business plan prepared on a monthly basis and, promptly after preparation, any revisions thereto. All financial statements shall include comparisons to the current budget and business plan and comparisons to corresponding periods in prior years. The Company will provide other customary information and materials, including, without limitation, reports of adverse developments, copies of any management letters, communications with stockholders or directors, press releases, and registration statements.
Inspection Rights:	Smith, Brown and/or holders of at least 150,000 shares of Preferred Stock, or their designees, shall have the right to inspect the properties of the Company, examine records and make copies thereof, and discuss the Company's affairs with officers, directors, key employees, and accountants. Any holder shall be entitled to audit the Company at its own expense at any time.
Representations:	The Company will make representations and warranties in the Stock Purchase Agreement customary in transactions of this kind including, without limitation, representations regarding due incorporation, qualification and good standing, charter documents and by-laws, corporate power, subsidiaries, capitalization, authorization, due issuance, financial statements, subsequent developments, title, encumbrances, obligations, use of proceeds, assets, litigation, proprietary information, patents, contracts, and commitments.

Start-up Corporation Convertible Preferred Stock

	Summary of Proposed Terms
Key-Man Insurance:	The Company will maintain key-man life insurance in the amount of at least $1,000,000 on the life of each of the Founders.
Founders' Agreements:	The Founders shall agree not to compete with the Company during the term of their employment and for a period of two years after termination of their employment. In addition, the Founders will enter into restricted stock agreements, under which a maximum of 80% of their shares of Common Stock may be forfeited (except to the extent vested) if they are no longer employed by the Company, and which provide for the vesting of such shares in 16 equal quarterly installments beginning on April 16, 1985, and ending on April 16, 1989.
Restriction on Transfers of Stock by Founders:	The Founders shall agree not to transfer any equity securities of the Company which they own to any third party without first offering to sell such securities, on the same terms and conditions, to the holders of Preferred Stock; provided that each of the Founders may transfer up to 1% of the equity securities of the Company held by such Founder without first offering such securities to the holders of Preferred Stock pursuant to transfers approved by the Board of Directors. In the event of any such sale to a third party, the selling Founder shall provide the holders of Preferred Stock the right to sell, on the same terms and conditions, certain of their shares of their Preferred Stock to such third party. These agreements shall terminate upon the Company's Initial Public Offering.
Expenses:	All fees and expenses of special counsel to the Purchasers will be paid by the Company whether or not the financing closes.
Pre-emptive Rights:	If additional securities are sold by the Company, the holders of Preferred Stock will have the right to maintain their percentage ownership through the purchase of their pro rata share of such securities on the same terms as such securities are offered to other purchasers. This provision shall not apply to the issuance of options to purchase up to 200,000 shares of Common Stock of the Company to key employees of the Company or the issuance of

Start-up Corporation Convertible Preferred Stock

	Summary of Proposed Terms
	shares of Common Stock pursuant to such options.
Antidilution:	The Preferred Stock will have "Full Ratchet" Antidilution rights, which will reduce the conversion price of the Preferred Stock (and, correspondingly, increase the number of shares of Common Stock into which shares of Preferred Stock can be converted) upon the issuance of shares of Common Stock at a price below the conversion price then in effect or upon the happening of other specified events which customarily give rise to such adjustments. There will be no adjustment in the conversion price upon the issuance of options to purchase up to 200,000 shares of Common Stock to key employees of the Company, or the issuance of shares of Common Stock pursuant to such options.

(c) MISCELLANEOUS ADDITIONAL PROVISIONS

The following are culled from a potpourri of term sheets and illustrate representative provisions on a variety of additional subjects:

1. *Installments:* Financing will be made in two installments of $500,000 each. The first installment will be made on the closing date (on or around July 13, 1984) for Preferred Stock representing 45% of the company. The second installment will be made on November 15, 1984, for Preferred Stock representing 20% of the company such that at the conclusion of the second installment the Preferred Stock will represent 56% ownership on a fully diluted basis. The obligation to invest the second installment is contingent upon the company meeting its revenue and income projections for the period July through October 1984. If such projections are not met, the investors have the option of (a) investing $500,000 for 45% of the company, such that at the conclusion of the second installment the Preferred Stock would represent approximately 70% ownership or (b) making no further investment.
2. *Use of Proceeds:* All invested capital to be used for working capital and necessary additions to equipment, but not to reduce any out-

standing indebtedness, which indebtedness shall be converted into Common Stock at the closing.

3. *Management Addition:* It is the intention of the company and the investors to identify and hire a senior marketing executive. This executive may become the President and CEO, in which case Founder would become the Chairman, with both executives reporting to the Board. Stock options for up to 10% of the company will be available for this and other management additions, to be allocated by the Board. Any such options will dilute both the Common and Preferred holders.
4. *Exclusive Dealings:* So long as the investors are proceeding in good faith with the proposed financing, the company shall not negotiate with any other parties concerning a proposed financing.
6. *Employee Shares:* If the Company meets certain benchmarks (set forth below), the Compensation Committee of the Company's Board of Directors shall grant incentive stock options to purchase a number of shares (the "Employee Shares") of Common Stock of the Company to the Founder (the "Founder") and the Company's employees which will result in the Founder and such employees owning 39% of the Company's outstanding capital stock after the Third Round Financing (as defined below). The Founder and Cofounder shall receive shares which will result in each owning 20% and 4% of such capital stock, respectively, and will be granted options to acquire shares equal in number to 75% of such percentages at Closing. Such "early" options will only become exercisable, however, if the benchmarks set forth below are met. None of the remaining options shall be granted to the Founder, Cofounder, or other employees until closing of the Third-round Financing and will be granted at an exercise price equal to the fair market value of the Common Stock at that time. Shares acquired by the Founder and Cofounder upon their exercise of the "early" options shall vest for three years from closing of the Third-round Financing, minus the amount of time each has been employed by the Company.
7. *Benchmarks:* For the Employee Shares to become exercisable or to be granted the following benchmarks must be met:
   1. *Second-round Financing:*
      - **(a)** Price of $1.50 per share;
      - **(b)** Proceeds of $1,500,000;
      - **(c)** New investor participates;
      - **(d)** Closes within 9 months of First-round Financing; and
      - **(e)** Compensation Committee is satisfied that proceeds will support the Boston Region (8 centers) and a new Region (5 centers).

2. *Third-round Financing:*
   (a) Price of $1.75 per share;
   (b) Proceeds of $1,500,000;
   (c) New investor participates;
   (d) Closes within 12 months of Second-round Financing;
   (e) Boston Region and second Region exist; and
   (f) Compensation Committee is satisfied that proceeds will support a third Region (5 centers).

If the Company shall not satisfy the Second-round Financing benchmarks but shall satisfy the Third-round Financing benchmarks, then the number of Employee Shares issued shall be reduced from shares resulting in ownership of 39 to 34%. The Compensation Committee shall meet every six months to re-evaluate the criteria set forth above and may, in its sole discretion, alter it. However, the Committee may not change the benchmarks so that they become more difficult for the Company to meet.

8. *Compensation Committee:* The Board of Directors shall appoint a Compensation Committee consisting of the two representatives of the Purchasers and the Independent Director which shall be responsible for administering the Benchmarks, granting the Employee Shares, and compensation of all officers of the Company. Until the closing of the Second-round Financing, the Purchasers shall only have one representative serving on the Committee.
9. *Events of Default:* In the event of the occurrence of any of the "Events of Default" listed below, the Purchasers will be entitled to elect a majority of the members of the Board of Directors. "Events of Default" shall be (i) the voluntary termination of employment of the Founder, (ii) the termination of employment of the Founder for cause, or (iii) the death or complete disability of the Founder. The Purchasers' rights upon the occurrence of an Event of Default will expire on the Public Offering or the Merger.
10. *Employee Agreements:* Each employee of the Company shall execute a Proprietary Information and Assignment of Inventions Agreement and each key employee of the Company shall execute a Noncompetition Agreement.
11. *Forfeiture:*[47] Founders shares to vest as presently provided. Notwithstanding the foregoing, 50% of Founders shares (50,000 shares), pro rata among the Founders based upon their proportionate own-

[47]Any provision styled as a forfeiture or penalty raises questions as to enforceability. For a classic discussion of the general policy against restraints on alienation, *see* O'Neal, "Restrictions on Transfer of Stock in Closely Held Corporations: Planning and Drafting" 65 *Harv. L. Rev.* 773, 778 (1952).

ership interests, will be subject to forfeiture based upon second-round financing as follows: If a commitment for second-round financing is not received within 12 months from above closing date plus 60-day grace period in a total amount of $2.5 million or more, the 50,000 shares shall vest only as determined by the three outside directors (i.e., other than the two Founders who are directors) to be in the best interest of the Company, in accordance with a vesting schedule to be determined by said directors. Such vesting will be pro rata among the Founders. All shares which are not included by the directors in such a vesting schedule shall be forfeited to the Company. If commitment for second-round financing is received within twelve months from the above closing plus a 60-day grace period for a total amount of $2.5 million or more, that portion of said 50,000 shares which is equivalent to the difference between 50,000 and the number of shares being sold in the second-round financing for a total price of $2.5 million shall vest pro rata among the Founders immediately as of the closing of the second-round financing. The balance of said 50,000 shares of the Founders will be forfeited to the Company.

Ten

Key Agreements: Stock Purchase, Stockholders, Employment

This chapter surveys the principal contracts ordinarily executed in the course of a venture financing. It should be read in conjunction with Chapter 9, since the two expressly overlap. The term sheet provisions mentioned in Chapter 9 will each find their way into the agreements identified in this chapter.

§10.1 STOCK PURCHASE AGREEMENT

The Term Sheet, discussed in the preceding chapter, in time segues into a formal agreement(s). The understandings between the parties (as set out in the Term Sheet or simply oral) may be primitive: "Here's some cash, give me some stock." Nonetheless, any deal involving the sale of securities is legally complex because the law views that category of transaction in a special way; lawmakers and regulators, based on historical evidence going as far back as the South Sea Bubble,[1] entertain deep concerns that there exist unusual opportunities for fraud and over-

[1]Loss, *Securities Regulation* 4 (2d ed. 1961 & 1969 Supp.).

reaching when the commodity traded is a security. Accordingly, the simplest investment contract—"one share, one dollar"—is in reality far from simple since the agreement of the parties is complemented by rules imposed by statute and administrative regulation.

In a structured venture financing, the contract between issuer and investor is, or should be, detailed, covering a number of issues which otherwise may be the subject of future disputes and misunderstandings. The instrument recording the issues on which the parties' minds meet can bear any number of titles; it usually is called the "Stock Purchase Agreement" or "Purchase Agreement." Annotated form books are helpful in tracking the ways in which founder and investors have dealt with the issues.[2] The following discussion, consistent with the theme of the Text, is designed to illuminate not only the various deal points but also the principles underlying the negotiations—where each party is "coming from," in today's parlance, and what hangs on winning or losing a given point.

(a) DRAFTING STYLE

If artfully drafted, the Purchase Agreement, like any contract, tells a coherent story. Most legalese is rightfully condemned as "Bastard English," incomprehensible to the layman. While there are, surely, some valid reasons for using what philosophers refer to as a "meta-language" in legal agreements—"terms of art" in legal jargon—much of the mystery in legal drafting is unnecessary, the product of sloppy, lazy writers, or worshipers of archaic, out-of-date conventions.

For example, a contract, like a story, should start with an introduction, a paragraph or two which will set the stage and explain what the draftsman is trying to accomplish. Custom has it that the introduction should be segmented into a series of clauses, each introduced by the word "whereas," all of which makes the story jerky and difficult to follow. If the draftsman keeps in mind he is story telling, he can readily perceive that the easiest and most understandable way to begin a preamble is with the label "preamble," followed by a consecutive narrative of the background of the transaction and a summary description. (The preamble is not, strictly speaking, a part of the agreement but the language is significant nonetheless since, in case of a dispute, construction

[2]Massey, "Stock Purchase Agreements," in Harroch, *Start-Up Companies: Planning, Financing, and Operating the Successful Business* (1985), Ch. 20; Benton & Gunderson, "Making Portfolio Company Investments," in Halloran, Benton, & Lovejoy, *Venture Capital and Public Offering Negotiations* 247 (1985) (hereinafter Halloran.); Testa, "The Legal Process of Venture Capital Investment," in *Pratt's Guide to Venture Capital Sources* 66 (11th ed., 1987) (Pratt's Guide). Martin & Sylvester, "Key Issues in Negotiating the Venture Capital Contract," in *Private Placements, 1986: Current Developments in Private Financings* 205 (P.L.I. Course Handbook Series No. 522, 1986).

of the contested contract language will be influenced by statements in the preamble, to the extent material.) Calling a spade a spade, or in this case a preamble a preamble, is not the only aid to comprehension available. A novel has a table of contents for handy reference—the Purchase Agreement should as well.[3]

(b) BASICS

The Purchase Agreement proper should open, again for purposes of clarity, with the basics: Who is buying what and at what price and when? The "who" are the investors and they are ordinarily designated in an attached appendix, a drafting device to allow changes up to the closing at a cost of retyping a single page. Even though subscribing en masse to a single document, the investors are, technically, each entering into a separate contract to buy stock. Usually, they are not responsible for any other investor welshing on the deal; their responsibility is, in legalese, "several" and not "joint."

The "what" is the security or bundle of securities being offered. If other than common stock—that is, preferred stock, warrants, convertible debt—often the most economical way to describe what is being offered is to attach the instrument itself and incorporate it by reference. The danger in that practice, handy as it may be, is that a reader may overlook significant substantive terms by assuming that the appendix is "boilerplate"; that is, "a preferred stock is a preferred stock is a preferred stock." The fact is that many of the important points to be negotiated ("deal points" as they are called) are located in the document constituting the security, for example, the interest rate on the debentures and the conversion price. The moral of the story is to read and bargain out the appendixes; do not sign off on the Stock Purchase Agreement until the appendixes have been attached and carefully considered. Moreover, last-minute attachment of appendixes, as the parties are hurrying to close, is liable to provoke ill will as the issuer protests that counsel for the buyers is nitpicking when he (often legitimately) points out that the appendixes introduce new substantive terms.[4]

In this connection, if "units" are being sold—that is, a bundle of separate securities, debentures plus warrants, for example—it is only prudent to negotiate explicitly an agreed division of the purchase price and reflect that agreement in the Stock Purchase Agreement. This is

[3]For example, for ease of understanding, it is the author's preferred practice (not always observed) to inscribe the table of contents on the cover page of the Purchase Agreement; to collect the definitions of all specially defined terms in a central glossary, instead of sprinkling definitions throughout the text; and to number in the margin each line of the text.

[4]*See infra* § 10.1(c) for the thought that the closing date should be automatically extended at the option of the buyer if all appendixes and exhibits are not produced on time.

usually a pro-investor provision; the investors want to mitigate "original issue discount."[5] The idea of a mutually agreed allocation of the purchase price across the disparate commodities being sold is a subset of the general principle that parties to an agreement should specifically agree to take mutually consistent positions on matters of allocation—mutually agreeable filing positions on their tax returns, for example.

Describing the price is seldom a problem unless one of the investors is contributing property that requires valuation. The issuer sometimes insists the price be paid in "good funds," funds that are credited to its account the day of the closing so that "float"—that is, the loss of daily interest on the funds as they are being collected—is not the issuer's problem.[6] However, the sums involved in venture financings are usually not so large that short-term interest is crucial. Wire transfers of clearinghouse funds can be more trouble than they are worth, not a critical founder's or investors' point, in other words.

(c) CLOSING

The "when"—the closing date—is usually straightforward: the date the cash is to be paid, the securities delivered and the attendant paperwork completed. Some Purchase Agreements allow for multiple closings; indeed, this can be a significant element of the issuer's strategy on occasion. Thus, the problem, from the issuer's standpoint, in many start-up financings is delay; the investors will coo enthusiastic words in the founder's ear, exciting him to ecstasy, then sit on their hands while he edges closer and closer to the abyss. Occasionally, the tactic is deliberate; the terms may improve for the investors as the founder gets increasingly desperate. To counter investor lethargy, it is often advisable to admit the first investors as soon as they are willing to put up their money. Even if the proceeds have to be held in escrow, the fact of a closing often disciplines investors on the fence, the "train is leaving the station" effect.[7]

If the transaction is being pushed at an accelerated pace, the Purchase Agreement may be signed and delivered and the closing take place simultaneously. More often, the closing is delayed while the securities are being sold, investors subscribing *seriatim,* or the investors sign as a group but conditions to closing (federal agency approval of a license transfer, for example) must be satisfied. It is sometimes necessary, after

[5]*See* Ch. 19 § 19.13(c).

[6]Interest on collected funds is ordinarily credited by a bank daily; to qualify for a day's interest, the funds must be "in the bank," meaning credited to its account at the local Federal Reserve Bank or clearinghouse by a certain time of day, usually about 11 A.M. local time.

[7]*See* § 15(c)(3) of the'34 Act respecting the obligation of underwriters in connection with escrow accounts. *See also* Ch. 8, § 8.2.

the agreement has been executed, to change the closing date, in which event it is handy if the subscribing investors have agreed in advance to be bound, as to this and other ministerial changes, by a single signatory—their special counsel—or, at any rate, by less than all of their number.

Multiple closings can also occur if the deal is of the "milestone" or "benchmark"[8] variety, meaning that the investors parcel out the committed sums if and only if the founder is able to pass stated tests by specific dates. If the dates are missed, the founder is penalized by (i) failing to be able to call down the later installment, (ii) coughing up additional equity, or (iii) a combination of the two. "Milestone" deals are characteristic of high tech seed investments, when the viability of the entire project depends on certain technical hurdles being overcome. One milestone might be development of a prototype, the second a successful lab test, the third a successful Beta test, such as proving out and debugging the device at a customer's location.

Some founders are nervous about milestone deals since they think the deck will be stacked against them in defining the milestones. However, viewed analytically, many venture financings are in fact, if not in name, of the "milestone" variety. Most start-ups, as earlier suggested, are financed by multiple rounds: seed, first round, mezzanine, and so forth. The later rounds are, albeit not explicitly, based on milestones. If the existing investors do not think the company has made the necessary progress, they do not put up their money or do so at a reduced valuation. And, it is an article of faith in the business that no new investor will finance if the existing investors do not have enough faith to come forward as well. Therefore, in a very real sense, an explicit milestone deal favors the founder—at least he knows that, if he does what he says he is going to do, he will get some more money at a specified price. In a conventional financing, the founder has only a reasonable expectation that more cash will come in if he minds his Ps and Qs. To be sure, nothing in the foregoing discussion should lead a founder to relax in negotiating a milestone financing. It is in the nature of the beast that ambiguities can creep into even the most rigorously defined scientific test.

A final note on closings. As indicated in the succeeding sections, the structure of the "representation and warranties" section" is such that the majority of the language is in the agreement proper but the substance is in the exhibits—the problems which the issuer identifies as exceptions from the generic representations and warranties. Often the issuer will surface the all-important exhibits on the eve of the closing, accompanied by urgings that the investors' counsel not "nitpick." To

[8]Benchmark arrangements providing for penalties if the founder does not successfully implement an "exit strategy" are discussed in § 10.1(i) *infra*.

avoid this unwanted pressure, the investors are well advised to insist the closing date be the later of the scheduled date or some period, say 48 hours, after the exhibits are exposed.

(d) "REPRESENTATIONS AND WARRANTIES"

Traditionally, after the deal has been described, the Purchase Agreement plunges into the issuer's representations and warranties, one of the longest sections in the agreement. This is the section with which lawyers inexperienced in venture financings feel most comfortable and the overwriting in this section becomes almost competitive. Thus, investors' counsel from one of the major New York firms, accustomed to billion-dollar merger and acquisition transactions, will write in representations dealing with multiemployer collective bargaining agreements—for a company with two employees. The way to approach the "representations and warranties" section, accordingly, is to understand the underlying dynamics.[9]

By way of introduction, representations and warranties are not designed to serve the same purpose in venture finance as in giant merger and acquisition (commonly abbreviated as M & A) transactions between solvent buyers and sellers. If the start-up issuer misstates its balance sheet to prospective investors, the inclination of the damaged investors to seek restitution must be restrained because the guilty party, almost by definition, will be out of money. As an aid in making aggrieved investors whole from the pockets of the issuer, the representations and warranties in an early-round financing are usually a bust. Moreover, it is arguable that explicit representations and warranties are superfluous since the buyer enjoys common law remedies for the tort of deceit and statutory protection under Rule 10b–5 of the'34 Act. Why, then, bother with elaborate representations and warranties?

First of all, the section is designed, although not explicitly, as a device to draw into a lawsuit, given a misrepresentation, the perennial deep pockets in the financing: the law firm, the accountants, and the investment bankers (if any) serving as placement agents. Although the representations as to the financial statements are made by the issuer and the issuer alone, the existence of the representation makes it plain, if the question were ever in doubt, that the investors were relying on the accuracy of the statements and all the ancillary parties engaged in

[9]The use of the term "representations and warranties" is a typical legal redundancy. Whether representing or warranting, the issuer is making a statement of fact (although promises often seep into this section) which it agrees to stand behind, responding in the event of a misstatement or omission. The question is whether the issuer is liable only for a misrepresentation entailing a breach of some standard of care or is absolutely liable. The term "warranty" implies the latter and, if so, the term "representation" is superfluous.

preparing the Purchase Agreement are, or should be, aware of such reliance. Since reliance to one's detriment has historically been an element of a plaintiff's case in the tort of deceit (although not universally required in the modern cases)[10] memorialization in writing of the investors' reliance may obviate problems of proof. The issue of *scienter*[11]—a claim by the issuer that it did not know of the critical omission—is also avoided by explicit "warranties." Further, those representations that have to do with the legal facts surrounding the issuer's existence—its due organization, the number of shares outstanding—form the reference point for an opinion[12] of issuer's counsel validating those propositions which counsel are in a position to verify; again, a deep pocket if a damaging error is made. (A point of particular interest in a high tech start will often be counsel's opinion concerning the validity of the patents, copyrights or trade secrets protecting the issuer's technology.) Moreover, participation in the process of preparing the written representations—drafting the language in the case of counsel—may be enough to draw counsel into the zone of responsibility as a matter of law; the lawyers become "participants" in the entire transaction. Similarly, the founder can sometimes be induced to endorse certain of the representations personally, putting his pocketbook (for what that's worth) behind the statements made. If the founder balks, claiming he cannot be held to know certain facts absolutely, a representation can be softened to a so-called "knowledge rep"—that is, "to the best of my information and belief"—thereby catching the founder who is demonstrably lying. If the founder cannot pay in cash, the worst case is that investors can pick up some or all of his equity.

The representations also serve to motivate all hands—founder, investment bankers, lawyers, and accountants—to re-examine the facts. This is an uncontestably salubrious use of the section: to energize these parties to do their investigations carefully so as to minimize subsequent disputes. In fact, if the investors want to make (as they usually should) their own investigations—an "acquisition audit" as it is sometimes called—they may be deterred by a fear that the issuer will attempt to defend a charge of misrepresentation by claiming the buyer is estopped by its own inquiries. Unconditional written representations, perhaps accompanied by a statement that the investors may rely even in light of their own audit, serve to diminish that concern.

The representations serve an important ancillary function: as closing

[10]Prosser & Keeton, *Torts* § 108 (1984).

[11]According to the United States Supreme Court, a plaintiff seeking redress on the basis of Rule 10b–5 of the'34 Act must allege and prove the defendant's *scienter*. *Ernst & Ernst v. Hochfelder* 425 U.S. 185 (1976). The notion is that plaintiffs seeking statutory relief must show the representation to be false to the knowledge of the speaker or made with reckless disregard as to truth or falsity.

[12]*See infra* § 10.1(f).

conditions. Assuming that the Stock Purchase Agreement is not closed simultaneously with its execution, the investors will be able to withhold their investment if they discover imperfections in the period between execution and closing. In fact, one of the traditional representations is to the effect that there will be no materially adverse change in the issuer's business between signing and closing, which gives the investors an "out" even though the issuer has told the truth throughout.[13]

(e) SPECIFIC REPRESENTATIONS AND WARRANTIES

The specific representations and warranties, listed in detail in various form books,[14] deal with a series of concerns. First, the investors want basic assurance that the issuer has been validly organized and may legally issue the securities. This entails satisfying regulatory agencies, complying with the corporate charter and relevant contracts (e.g., bank loan agreements), holding the necessary meetings, avoiding prohibitions (if any) in court proceedings and so forth. Second, the investors want to know the facts about the issuer as a business concern: Is the count on the number of shares outstanding accurate? Are the financial statements complete? Are there any contingent liabilities, pending lawsuits, hidden violations of law, undisclosed encumbrances on listed assets, commissions payable to brokers, burdensome contracts, unnamed subsidiaries, infirmities in patents? Hypothetically, these representations could be covered in one paragraph, representing that the private placement memorandum is accurate and complete. However, some investors are nervous that a representation which talks in Rule 10b–5 language will inherit the 10b–5 notion that *scienter*—guilty knowledge—is required to establish recovery, or at least that as judge will not be as severe if considering only the maker's responsibility for the accuracy of a single, generic representation. Moreover, the belt and suspenders approach is customary; investors' counsel can and will insist on specific representations *and* a basket representation in 10b–5 terms. Therefore, specific representations are suggested to cover such significant matters as the existence of adequate policies of insurance, the validity of leases, the ownership of intellectual property. Sometimes, the list suggested by investors' counsel borders on the trivial, for example, compliance with ERISA requirements (laughable when the workforce totals two) and OSHA requirements (query the application to two programmers in

[13]This is sometimes called a "bring down" provision. It appears as a generic provision, bringing down all the representations so that they speak as of the closing date. It is also used specifically, bringing down the financial statements, in which case supplementary material should be filed or a statement made that the interim changes—changes which necessarily have occurred—are "in the ordinary course of business."
[14]See *supra* n. 2.

a suburban office park). It is important to keep in mind that the scheme of the entire section is to regulate by exception. Thus, a given representation in the Agreement proper will not ordinarily go into specifics. It will state, for example, there are "no leases of real property" except as listed on Exhibit X; the job of complying with representations and warranties becomes one of preparing the exhibits in sufficient detail. It is worthwhile repeating that, if the exhibits show up just before closing, a fight is likely to break out.

When the representations become agonizingly specific, the founder is entitled to nervousness at the possibility of an inadvertent violation. A representation that says *all* material contracts are listed on Exhibit X is perilous if the harried founder simply forgets about a relatively trivial agreement. Is the deal off if he is proven wrong prior to the closing? There are various palliatives. First a "basket" or minimum threshold can be established—if the amount involved is less than, say, $25,000, then nothing turns on the omission.[15] Further, the agreement may provide that the representation concerns "material" items or that items popping up "in the ordinary course of business" need not be considered. Lastly, assuming a material contract omitted from the appropriate exhibit is discovered after the closing, the issue is whether the investors are entitled to rescission under all circumstances or if (and only if) some damage results from the omission. The warranties are unconditional and rescission is the traditional equitable remedy for breach. But why, one might ask, should investors be able to rescind if the unmentioned contract is favorable or, at worst, neutral? A related question is whether the investors (if they do not elect rescission) are entitled to damages on a before-tax or after-tax basis; suppose the issuer covered up a contingent liability of $100,000 but the maximum cash "cost" of that liability to the issuer (and, therefore, to the investors) is the after-tax effect of the loss, approximately $60,000 after federal and state taxes.[16]

Certain representations deserve passing special mention because they are often overlooked. Thus, for example, in any financing following the first round, investors should look carefully at the prior registration rights[17] agreements and obtain a representation that there is no conflict between the earlier and current sets of provisions. Since there often *is* a conflict,

[15]A drafting point—a minimum threshold can either be a "go/no go" trigger and nothing else, or a deductible. Thus, if there is a $25,000 minimum and a representation is violated to the tune of $150,000, the language should make it clear whether the investors are owed $150,000 or $125,000.

[16]A recent case construing a federal statute as applied to tax shelter offerings held that the investors could recover the gross amount of their loss on the investment even though the losses had been, as advertised, useful to them. *Western Federal Corp. v. Erickson* 739 F.2d 1439 (9th Cir. 1984).

[17]*See* Ch. 9 § 9.3.

the effect of this representation is to force issuer's counsel to examine the two sets of rights and resolve the differences.

If any of the investors is an SBIC, the issuer will be required to represent it is a "small business concern" within the scope of the Small Business Act; this will be mandated routinely by counsel for the SBIC. What investors sometimes overlook is that, even if no SBIC is investing, small business status may be critical to the issuer's ability to participate in other advantageous activities: that is, small business set-aside programs authorized by the federal government.[18]

(f) OPINION OF COUNSEL

The opinion of counsel, particularly the seller's counsel, is often a rigorously negotiated document since, as mentioned, counsel may be the only deep pocket to which the investors may resort. Counsel's opinion on the status of the issuer as a "corporation," "duly organized," "in good standing," and "qualified to do business" in various jurisdictions is often viewed as boilerplate—sometimes, indeed, by the opining firm. A number of questions, some potentially serious, are overlooked when and as that attitude is adopted. For example, is counsel entitled to rely entirely (absent knowledge of facts to the contrary) on a copy of the certificate of incorporation? In Delaware, that certificate is prima facie evidence of incorporation,[19] but not in all jurisdictions.

If counsel opines that the entity is "duly organized," does that mean the stock which the founders think they own has in fact been legally issued in accordance with the statute? In many start-ups, such is not the case. How about adopting the form of the corporate seal and/or stock certificate? Often that has not been accomplished formally. If counsel opines as to "valid existence," how does the law firm know as a fact that administrative proceedings have not been initiated to revoke the charter because the issuer has "failed to pay any fees, franchise taxes or penalties prescribed by law."[20] Can counsel rely on "good standing" certificates only as to tax matters or does the certificate cover corporate filings as well? The practice varies from state to state. The opinion on "qualification to do business in all states in which the company is required to qualify" is often given by inexperienced counsel but almost never should be, because the inquiry necessary to support the opinion would be prohibitively expensive in almost every case. The compromise caveat in the opinion—qualified "in all jurisdictions in which failure to qualify would have a materially adverse impact" is tied to the notion

[18]*See* Ch. 6 § 6.3.
[19]Del. Code Ann. tit. 8, § 106 (1983 & Supp. 1986).
[20]Tex. Corp. Code Ann. Art. 7.01(B)(1) (Vernon).

that failure to qualify can be cured ex post facto. Such is not, however, universally true.[21]

(g) BUYERS' REPRESENTATIONS

In many Stock Purchase Agreements, the leverage is one-sided, resulting in a litany of representations and warranties by the issuer and only a select few by the investors, limited to the power and authority of each investor to purchase the securities subscribed for. However, there are a host of representations that the seller can legitimately request of the buyer (the term "legitmately" is used in this context to be synonymous with the jargon lawyers use to inquire whether a request they make of the other side is reasonable; does it pass the "smell test" or the "red face test"?).

For example, some types of buyer can be asked for special representations concerning their authority to invest. SBICs are limited to making noncontrolling[22] investments in "small business concerns;" bank loan covenants may inhibit even the largest company's ability, absent approval, to establish subsidiaries.

Given appropriate assurances of authority, the remaining buyers' representations ordinarily have to do with language designed to choke off subsequent allegations that the offering has violated the securities laws. A general reaction against promiscuous abuse of the court system by unscrupulous plaintiffs and their counsel has encouraged lawyers to start building the case against spurious strike suits in the Stock Purchase Agreement and the Investors' Questionnaire. The issues are discussed in general in Ch. 8, § 8.11.

(h) AFFIRMATIVE AND NEGATIVE COVENANTS

Sometimes the agreement becomes confused between the company's *representations* and its *covenants*. Conceptually, the two are quite different. The company "represents" facts, that is, existing statuses. When it "covenants" something, the obligation is promissory; the company is promising to do (or not do) an act in the future. In both cases, the company is liable for breach but the damages are technically different. A misrepresentation entails tort damages while failure to perform a

[21]*See generally* FitzGibbon & Glazer, "Legal Opinions on Incorporation, Good Standing, and Qualification to Do Business," 41 *Bus. Law.* 461 (1986). The applicable standards for corporate counsel in giving opinions generally are set out in two articles in the publication of the American Bar Association's section on Corporation, Banking, and Business Law—i.e. Fuld, "Lawyer's Standards and Responsibilities in Rendering Opinions," 33 *Bus. Law.* 1295 (Mar. 1978); and Fuld, "Legal Opinions in Business Transactions—An Attempt to Bring Some Order out of Some Chaos," 28 *Bus. Law.* 915 (Apr. 1973).
[22]*See* Ch. 20 § 20.23(a).

covenant opens up contract damages.[23] It is not unusual to find promissory statements mistakenly included in the representations and warranties section; viz., "The company's insurance policies are as listed on Exhibit A" (a representation) *and* "the company will maintain those policies in force" (an affirmative covenant). This is a problem principally for the draftsmen of the complaint when and if the agreement is involved in litigation.

The covenants divide into two categories (affirmative and negative) and onto two levels (ministerial and very serious). The ministerial covenants, usually affirmative, have to do with promises the company can keep with relative ease: sending out reports and the like. Breach of the same usually involves only corrective action. (Occasionally, a covenant concerning a control issue will find its way into the Stock Purchase Agreement, i.e., "the company will elect X, Y, and Z, nominees of the investors, to the board of directors." This is usually a rookie mistake. The agreement between the company and the investors is not the place for that type of promise because the company does not elect people to the board, the stockholders do; such provisions belong in the Stockholders Agreement.)

Certain negative covenants are also within the clear power of the company to observe and are, in that sense, ministerial. Thus, typically the company promises it will not engage in certain major activities absent investor consent—for example, payment of dividends, fees to insiders, large borrowings, new issues of stock, mergers, changing management salaries, firing a given officer,[24] redeeming shares; such negative covenants buttress and enlarge the statutory requirements that certain significant proposals—that is, mergers—be put to a shareholder vote. The issues can be important and worthy of spirited debate but the point is that the promisor—the company—can still exercise control over its destiny. It is unlikely the company will violate them if only because the objecting shareholders can restrain any breach.

The covenants that the company cannot control, the more ominous covenants, are those of the loan agreement type, for example, the company will maintain a given net worth and/or specific asset-to-liability

[23]In summary, tort damages entail compensation for the wrong and may include so-called consequential damages (all the forseeable consequences of the wrong, as when a stray spark starts a fire which triggers an explosion); contract damages allow the aggrieved party to obtain the wrongfully denied benefit of his bargain, including lost profits.

[24]A "management" covenant can raise difficult problems if, as so often happens, groups of investors split on the issue of whether a given officer—often the founder—should be fired. The "doves" will recall the founder's major contributions and argue the shabbiness of his dismissal. The "hawks" will be fixedly eyeing the always-dicey bottom line. If the preferred stockholders benefit from a company promise (which cannot be changed absent, say, a ⅔ vote) to retain existing management, a minority of the preferred, *a fortiori* a minority of all the shareholders, can use the clause to block the will of the majority.

coverage. These promises, which can be stated affirmatively or negatively, are dangerous because they are beyond anyone's control; moreover, they usually entail specific remedies. The investors need not start litigation since a well-drafted agreement provides them with practical compensation (in addition to and not in lieu of their other remedies); that is, control of the company "flips"[25] in their favor and/or the founder gives up stock, the equity equivalents of acceleration clauses in a debt instrument.

(i) FORMULA STOCK AND BENCHMARKS

The investors and the founder may not be able to agree on valuation but may nonetheless wish to enter into a relationship. In such cases, the parties will often agree to provisions that specify an initial split of the stock and then specify adjustments in the ratios of stock held depending on future events. In Chapter 9, § 9.6(c), the sample term sheet sets out two versions of a typical "benchmark" arrangement, as it is called. The first method, set out in paragraphs 6 and 7 of the example, entails the granting of incentive stock options to employees if certain conditions are met, the conditions having to do with the successful closing of subsequent rounds of financing at marked up prices; the second, set out in paragraph 11, is to the same effect as a business matter but it entails recapturing stock previously issued to the founders. The use of benchmarks can trigger changes in equity ratios upon the occurrence (or nonoccurrence) of various events; in addition to favorable subsequent rounds of financing, the choices include, as indicated, the failure of the founder to provide a timely exit vehicle (a sale of the entire company or an IPO) or the inability of the company to meet gross and net revenue targets.[26]

§10.2 STOCKHOLDERS AGREEMENT

It would be technically possible to include all the provisions of the Term Sheet in one agreement but it is usually not convenient to do so because of the several parties to the financing documents—the company, the founder, the investors and the key employees; usually none are parties to all the promises entailed in the financing. If counsel were to draft an umbrella agreement, it would be necessary in each subsection to specify not only who was promising what but to whom and with whom, and

[25]*See* Ch. 9, § 9.2.

[26]If the planners use an adjustment in the conversion rate of convertible preferred stock to reallocate equity, there is the danger a taxable event will be created under I.R.C. § 305(c). *See* Ch. 13, § 13.6.

to make sure that no party to the umbrella agreement inadvertently wound up becoming bound to a promise that he lacked the power to perform. Accordingly, the Stock Purchase Agreement is usually accompanied by a Stockholders Agreement, an agreement by and among the founder in his capacity as a stockholder and the investors. The company may, on occasion, be made a party to this agreement for the sake of convenience, but usually only in a supportive role.[27]

A principal reason for a separate Stockholders Agreement, as earlier suggested, is that the company does not control who sits on its managing board, the board of directors; an agreement signed by the company purporting to govern who sits on the board would be circular in the sense that the subordinate would be pretending to exercise power over the supervisor. Therefore, it is advisable to record the understandings, if any, on that important issue in an agreement to which the holders of the majority (or, better, all) of the voting shareholders of the company are parties, since the board is elected by the stockholders. In its simplest form, the stockholders will get together (all or a majority of them) and agree to: (i) maintain a board of X number of people; and, (ii) either to elect specified individuals to the board or, more commonly (and prudently since individuals are mortal and/or they change their minds about serving on boards), to specify how representation on the board is to be allocated among the stockholders. The common stockholders, for example, will be allocated X number of directors and the preferred stockholders Y number; and each class of stock will be given the power to remove their own directors and replace them as they see fit.[28] The agreement may, further, provide for a so-called control "flip," meaning that if the fortunes of the company deteriorate, the preferred stockholders will get more board seats, either vesting control in them for the first time or reinforcing their already existing control.[29]

[27]Voting agreements separate and apart from voting trusts are explicitly authorized in several states, including Delaware. Del. Code Ann. tit. 8, § 218(c) (1983 & Supp. 1986). Depending on the statute, it may be preferable to use a voting trust, but the formalities usually include disclosure, a tiresome requirement. *See* Del. Code Ann. tit. 8, § 218(a) (1983 & Supp. 1986). On the other hand, once stock is deposited in a voting trust, it is a chore for the depositor to get it out and so he is tightly bound. If a signatory falls away from his promises in the Stockholders Agreement, the other parties may need to go to court for specific performance. In most states, *e.g.*, Delaware, voting agreements are limited in duration to the same term afforded voting trusts—10 years. Del. Code Ann. tit. 8, § 218(c) (1983 & Supp. 1986).

[28]The provision that a given class or group of stockholders has the right to elect a director is complicated by the fact that the director so elected, like any director, bears the burden, by statute, of fiduciary duties to *all* the stockholders. *See, e.g., Zahn v. Transamerica Corp.* 162 F.2d 36 (3d Cir. 1947); *see also Gottlieb v. McKee* 34 Del. Ch. 537, 107 A.2d 240 (1954).

[29]Whether the stockholders may all agree in advance on issues which the statute reserves for director action—i.e., selection of officers—is an open issue. *See* Haynsworth, *Organizing a Closely Held Corporation* § 502(g) (1986).

So-called "take me along" provisions are also most appropriately located in the Stockholders Agreement. The issue addressed arises when a third party elects to purchase control of the company. If, say, the preferred shareholders as a class enjoy a controlling position, the purchaser may elect to save money by offering to purchase only that block sufficient to give him a majority of the board. In private companies, this is a harsh result for the shareholders who have not been tapped to participate in the selling syndicate. If they do not enjoy registration rights, for example, they may be locked into a permanent minority position. An old case, *Perlman v. Feldman*[30], has been read to hold that the control element of value in a majority stockholder's position is a corporate asset; when a new shareholder cherry picks, buying only enough stock to give him control, the selling shareholder(s) is required to regurgitate the control element of value to the corporate treasury. While often referred to in negotiations, this holding has not been followed generally[31] and it would be imprudent for minority shareholders to rely on the case as their first line of defense. Accordingly, the Stockholders Agreement customarily contains "take me along" provisions, which provide that, if the majority sell their shares, they are contractually bound to require as a price of the sale that the same offer be extended to the minority shareholders.

As earlier suggested, the corporate charter is often the appropriate place for first-refusal options in favor of the corporation.[32] However, the corporation may not be interested in exercising those rights (or be able to do so) and, consequently, the investors often bargain for first-refusal rights in their favor in the Stockholders Agreement. Such provisions can become quite complicated if a group of buyers and sellers are involved. Assume that the founder wants to sell a specified number of shares to a third party. The investors (assuming that there are several) may have differing appetites for purchasing the founder's shares at the price that has been tendered by the third party. Some may want to buy and some may want to drop. Under those circumstances, the agreement will ordinarily provide that the investors initially have the right to take up their pro rata portion of the offered block, and then, when somebody passes, those investors with the remaining appetite have a second bite

[30]219 F.2d 173 (2d Cir. 1955) *cert. denied.* 349 U.S. 952 (1955). The cases and commentaries on this issue have been collected in Ch. 4 of 1 O'Neal & Thompson, *O'Neal's Oppression of Minority Shareholders* (2d ed.), entitled "Squeeze Out Techniques: Sale of Control and Related Techniques."

[31]Despite some academic support for the contrary position, the cases seem to continue to hold that the sale of a control bloc of shares at a price in excess of current market does not create a liability to minority shareholders or to the corporation. *See* Kaplan, "Fiduciary Responsibility in the Management of the Corporation," 31 *Bus. Law.* 883, 907 (Feb. 1976).

[32]*See* Ch. 4, § 4.9.

of the apple; and, indeed, a third and fourth, until the wishes of all the investors are satisfied. The founder is then free to sell the remainder at the price specified during some reasonable period of time. In that connection, when a stockholder, including the founder or any one of the individual investors, dies, an estate tax problem arises to the extent the shares are illiquid. Taxes must be paid and the shares cannot be sold except at a discount. One method in dealing with the problem is to create a "put" in the estate of the deceased individual shareholder to sell the stock to the corporation or, failing the corporation's ability to purchase, to the remaining principal stockholders. If the company is the party responsible for putting up the cash, the "put" ordinarily would be reflected in the Stock Purchase Agreement. If for any reason, however, the founder has negotiated for his estate to "put" shares to some of the heavyweight investors, the Stockholders Agreement would be the venue for recording that portion of the deal between the parties.

A cautionary note: Requirements that a selling shareholder offer his shares to all the other shareholders may involve an offering which requires registration. As a drafting point, the selling shareholder, if he can sell to a single outside party in a transaction which is exempt under § 4(2)[33] of the '33 Act, should object to being bound to sell to a whole group of shareholders if no exemption for that transaction can be found and the cost of his desire to sell is a public registration.

Rights of first refusal, like registration rights, pose problems when multiple rounds of financing hove into view. Assume the first-round investors bargain for a right—in the nature of a pre-emptive right—to take down their pro rata share of any future financings; when the second round comes along, some of the investors may participate and some pass, but the latter may not agree to extinguish their rights. If the second-round investors also sign an agreement providing "first refusal" rights, the third-round financing can be vexing. Given careless drafting, two sets of investors may own identical, and mutually exclusive, first refusal rights.

(a) TIE BREAKERS

In reviewing the possibility of an indissoluble disagreement—a deadlock among shareholders and/or directors—the potential cost to the business should cast a powerful spell over the organizers of any closely held corporation. Thus, an early-stage financing often involves a very simple corporate structure with no clear allocation of control, that is, two partners (founder and investor), each with 50% of the outstanding stock. Either the charter or the Stockholders Agreement can and should contain planned-in-advance tie-breaking provisions, such as the ap-

[33]*See* Ch. 7, § 7.15.

pointment of provisional directors,[34] a custodial receiver,[35] compulsory arbitration[36], or special rights to petition for dissolution.[37] One of the least complicated is the "shootout" or "Texas auction" arrangement, whereby one shareholder may compel a dissolution of the deadlock by fixing a price on his shares (or a formula for fixing the price) and the other party must elect either to sell or buy at that price.[38]

§10.3 THE EMPLOYMENT AGREEMENT

To attract start-up capital, a firm must demonstrate it has not only the idea but also the people to take the ball and run with it. The founder is a "given," but his skills are often limited to the technical. The embryonic firm has to fill in the entire organization before it can take in any capital—the CEO plus the people under him to carry out instructions—a tall order, particularly since the start-up is recruiting people at the least opportune time, when its future is most uncertain. Entrepreneurial risk taking is laudable but most of us have tuitions to pay and mortgages to meet. Hence, employment agreements are often exquisitely negotiated, with each party entertaining a healthy sense of fear and uncertainty about future events.

(a) SOME GENERAL PRINCIPLES

In the early stages of a company's existence, opposing principles should be balanced in the planner's mind. First, since the unseasoned firm is so dependent on critical people, it is important to tie those employees—the key ones at least—to the company as tightly as possible. It must be kept in mind that the founder and some of the key employees carry the business around in their heads. If they are free to walk out, to set up a new and competing business on the other side of Sand Hill Road in Menlo Park or Route 128 in Lexington, the investors may find that their entire stake has been sacrificed. On the other hand, the savvy planner also realizes that many of those in the first wave will ultimately be fired or passed over. With rare exceptions, the skills required to go from birth to adolescence are not the same as those needed to carry the firm to and through adulthood. The scheme, from the company's point of view,

[34]*E.g.*, Del. Code Ann. tit. 8, § 353 (1983 & Supp. 1986) (court-appointed provisional directors.)
[35]Del. Code Ann. tit. 8, §§ 226, 352 (1983 & Supp. 1986).
[36]Haynsworth, *Organizing a Closely Held Corporation* § 503(b)(3) (1986).
[37]Del. Code Ann. tit. 8, § 355 (1983 & Supp. 1986). (Less than a majority may dissolve in the case of deadlock.)
[38]Haynsworth, *supra* n. 36, at § 5.02(c)(3).

must take into account the real possibility that the very employees who are so critical to early success will be redundant in the later phases.

Against this backdrop is an overlay: the notion of partnership. Courts in important commercial states are increasingly prepared to hold that something like partnership principles govern the relationship of the key players in a closely held company.[39] In the absence of an agreement, this mind-set imports notions of equality and collegiality. If equity sweetens the employment relationship, the board may find a founding employee difficult to shed; partners can be fired only if their original agreement so provides. This possibility is reinforced by another emerging trend—the tendency of the courts to find or imply obligations of continued employment even in the absence of a contract to that effect.[40]

(b) EMPLOYEE MANUALS

Usually it is neither feasible nor cost-effective to write individual agreements for every employee, even in the start-up stage; it would cost more money than it is worth simply to administer and keep track of the terms of each separate agreement. Accordingly, for those employees who are at a level below the key officers, the prudent employer will rely instead on a manual, a written and precise (albeit unilateral)[41] statement by the company of its policies *vis-à-vis* pay, termination, vacations, holidays, sick leave, and the like. If a court is left to its own devices in putting together the terms of the employment relationship, it can be expensive. A start-up firm is particularly vulnerable, as a former employee is quick to realize, since it may not be able to afford the expense

[39] *See, e.g., Donahue v. Rodd Electrotype Company of New England, Inc.* 367 Mass. 578 (1975).

[40] The stated theories vary: (i) an implied covenant of "good faith and fair dealing;" (ii) the idea that is against public policy to fire someone who refuses to follow an illegal or immoral order; to fire "whistle-blowers"; to fire people for performing public service obligations (i.e., jury duty) or for exercising their constitutional rights; (iii) that firings motivated by "bad faith" or "malice" should be redressed; and finally, (iv) that some sort of contract, implied in fact or implied in law, can be teased out of the facts of the particular case. *See generally* Lopatka, "Emerging Law of Wrongful Discharge," 40 *Bus. Law.* 1 (Nov. 1984).

[41] A clear statement in an employment manual, not contradicted by any inconsistent promises, should deter an action based on an allegation entailing the existence of a contract implied in fact. *See Toussaint v. Blue Cross & Blue Shield* 408 Mich. 579, 623, 292 N.W.2d. 880, 896 (1980). Whether even an explicit contract could hold off a court lusting to find for the employee on some sort of public policy ground is a more difficult question. *See* Lopatka, *supra* n. 40, at 31.

of pursuing the case through the various administrative agencies and courts involved in the issue of employer–employee relations.

(c) TERMS OF THE CONTRACT

The contract between the company and its key employees is a highly significant document in venture finance. It specifies salary and other benefits, of course, but the well-drafted version goes far beyond those topics. It deals with control of the company's future and protection of vital assets, including the people who possess the intellectual property which is the backbone of many a start-up firm.

An employment contract reads as if Mr. Smith is being promised a long-term position with Start-up, Inc., for an annual salary plus, perhaps, equity in the firm, in consideration of Smith's promise to perform as, say, CEO for five years. Neither promise, however, is exactly what it seems. Realistically, Start-up's board of directors is saying to Smith, "If we want to fire you, we will pay you X dollars for your equity and Y dollars to buy out the remainder of your contract."[42] Smith is saying to Start-up, "If I decide to quit, you can get some of your stock back for nothing and the rest for Z dollars, plus a restraint to keep me out of your business for, say, one year."

The contract, in other words, is like a prenuptial agreement. As long as the parties are happily married, no one reads the document; the principal issues have to do with the payoff numbers when divorce ensues—what are the partners' remedies in the case of breach? Professor Harold Shepherd at Stanford Law School used to divide his course offerings on the law of contracts into two distinct sections: one having to do with the formulation of the agreement and its administration and the second, which he labeled "Remedies," having to do with the rights of the parties in the event of breach.[43] Employment agreements, because they are not specifically enforceable in the sense of requiring the parties

[42]This view is criticized by some commentators as unduly harsh on the employee because it gives the investors a "valuable option," the right to freeze out the founder/key employee upon the payment of money. Nusbaum & Weltman, "Employment Agreements," in Harroch, *Start-Up Companies: Planning, Financing and Operating the Successful Business* § 11.02[7](1986). Although the holdings are few and far between, a court adopting the partnership view of closely held corporations might restrain the recapture of the employee's equity. *See* the authorities collected in 1 O'Neal & Thompson, *O'Neal's Oppression of Minority Shareholders* Ch. 3 (2d. ed.).

[43]Long-term employment contracts, once viewed by the courts with suspicion, *see*, O'Neal, *Close Corporations* §§ 6.06–08 (1986), are now generally deemed valid, the current exception being a result of the popular attack on "golden parachutes," severance pay agreements in publicly held companies for managers replaced as a result of a hostile takeover. Popular displeasure has been expressed in the Internal Revenue Code, which applies a penalty to "parachutes" in excess of three years' salary. I.R.C. § 280G.

to remain married,[44] become interesting when they fall into Shepherd's latter category: what to do in the case of breach.

(d) SCOPE OF DUTIES

Absent an agreement to the contrary, the law contemplates that the board and/or its delegate—the CEO—tells the employee what to do. Under principles which were developed in an age when this branch of the law was labeled "master and servant," the employee is bound to follow lawful instructions or give up his job. Theoretically, an employment contract could confirm the ancient power relationship. Smith will do whatever Start-up, Inc. wants, wherever it wants the service to be performed, as long as Smith is paid $100,000 a year. In fact, however, such is not the typical case, at least in the case of key employees. Smith, if he is at all in demand, will want to specify in the agreement where he is to work and what duties and responsibilities he is to undertake—for example, chief financial officer and only chief financial officer.

A clever board may in the future attempt to compel Smith to quit by demeaning him in subtle and not so subtle ways (taking away his support, bypassing him on important decisions, moving him to a smaller office, giving him routine, irksome tasks). This gambit involves the doctrine of constructive discharge[45] and raises significant drafting points. How specific should one write the clause denoting the scope of the employee's duties? Is it "petty" for the employee to insist on the use of a car, specific types of medical insurance, precise reporting channels? It should be noted that we are discussing, through symbols, the questions of power and control. In the Stock Purchase Agreement, the investors may believe they had dealt with the control question. The board is legally in charge of the company's affairs and the investors had paid for control of the board. They can become surprised and angry when they learn that, through the introduction of employment agreements, they have to pay for control a second time, buying out overly constraining employment agreements. One further notes the "scope of duties" clause: Many desirable scientists are able (or willing) to work only part time; they may want to retain their university affiliations to the extent possible and it may be in the best interests of the company that they do so. However, when allowing an employee to pursue outside interests, one must be cognizant of the consequences of that election on the employer's claims on inventions. If the individual is a consultant or in-

[44]Williston, *Contracts* § 1423A (3d ed. 1968).
[45]Nusbaum & Weltman, *supra* n. 42, at § 20.02, n. 2 (1986).

dependent contractor, it is harder to enforce a senior claim to the fruits of his inventive efforts.[46]

(e) FRINGE BENEFITS OR "PERKS"

After the employee's salary and duties have been settled, counsel may tend to relax, passing over the sections on fringe benefits as routine. However, some "fringe benefits" can be quite expensive—medical and retirement plans, for example—particularly if the deductibility of the company's payments depends, under the Code, on compliance with a series of quite detailed requirements, including provisions calculated to ensure the benefits are extended in a nondiscriminating manner to most employees.[47] If the employee has the right to certain medical or retirement benefits, the company may find itself with a Hobson's Choice: either fund a special plan for the employee paid in after-tax dollars or increase everyone's benefits.

For mature corporations with resources to devote to the project, administering employee benefits can become an enormously complicated and sophisticated process, with full-time staff concentrating year round on the issues and paid consultants brought in to help make peer group surveys and provide notions on the state of the art. Start-ups ordinarily involve more primitive packages. For example, with the survival of the company in doubt during its early years, it's unlikely that much emphasis will be placed on retirement income and pension benefits. Nor will sophisticated side-benefits—below-market-rate loans, financial-consulting services, health clubs, and the like—be in the typical package. To the extent side-benefits are involved, they will often have to do with the costs of housing and relocation, particularly for executives transferring to high-cost areas, such as Boston and San Francisco. On the other hand, life insurance on the life of key employees is often taken out, but payable to the company in order to give the investors some opportunity to recoup their investment in the event the death of a critical officer, such as the founder, takes the company down with him.[48]

[46] *See* Ch. 16, § 16.7–16.9.

[47] *See generally*, on this issue, I.R.C. § 105(h) (medical plans) and, with respect to pension and profit-sharing programs, I.R.C. §§ 401(a)(3), 401(a)(4), 401(a)(5) and 410(b)(1). The onerous requirements are summarized in Buoymaster & Frank, "Employee Benefit Plans," in Harroch, *supra* n. 2, at § 14.03.

[48] The proceeds of "key man" insurance, as it is called, may either be payable to the company's treasury and consumed in order to carry it over the rough spots caused by the founder's death, or rerouted, through some sort of trust device, to the repayment of investor debt or even the repurchase of stock. Query whether, even though the proceeds are paid to a trust which ostensibly exists outside the company's four walls, the issuer will have the power to redeem stock at a time when the company is shaky or whether the proceeds may nonetheless be viewed as "property of the debtor" under the Bankruptcy Code. *See* Ch. 19, § 19.11(b).

(f) COORDINATED EMPLOYEE ARRANGEMENTS

The board of Start-up, Inc. should make sure that the employment contract dovetails intelligently with the agreements (if any) for the purchase of cheap stock and/or the stock option plan. Whatever the tax results, the fact is that the employee is purchasing equity in the corporation as part of his overall compensation package. To the extent that compensation is being used to motivate the employee, not only to work currently and to perform his duties to the best of his abilities but to remain with the firm as long as the firm wants him, the equity award and the cash should be pointed in the same direction: keep him motivated and on hand. Indeed, agreements respecting the confidentiality of proprietary information should also either be contained in or keyed to the employment relationship and the equity arrangements. If the employee's agreement to keep intellectual property confidential (and, as a necessary complement, not to compete with the firm after termination of the employment relationship) is tied up with the employee's ability to buy equity, the likelihood a court will enforce the obligation is enhanced.[49]

The short of the matter is that a series of agreements—the contract setting compensation and working conditions, the contract setting out the equity arrangements, the contract protecting the firm against unfair competition when the relationship is terminated,[50] the contract governing the ownership of the employee's inventive activities while with the firm[51]—all such agreements should be drafted in a coordinated way, because they all relate to governance of the employer–employee relationship. Accordingly, Chapter 11, "Key Employee Compensation," should be read in conjunction with the remaining sections in this chapter.

(g) PERFORMANCE BONUSES

Since the future of a venture-backed start-up is often highly contingent, it is customary for the employment contract to establish a minimum base salary in a rather modest amount and then to rely on bonuses tied to the performance of the employee and to the performance of the firm. The bonus is not usually "promised" to the employee at the end of each year; the board has discretion in the matter. However, the bargaining usually does not stop at that point. A desired employee will insist on language that removes as much uncertainty (from his point of view) as possible. For example, if the firm is on target in accordance with the projections set forth in the business plan, the CEO may want in writing

[49]*See infra* § 10.3(m).
[50]Ibid.
[51]*See* Ch. 16, § 16.9.

an unconditional promise he is entitled to a bonus of at least X percent of his base salary. Occasionally language will be added specifying the board has discretion but that it "will," unless unusual circumstances dictate otherwise, give "favorable consideration" to a bonus of X percent.

(h) DISCHARGE FOR "CAUSE"

Most employment contracts, including those entered into by start-up firms, retain the concept of discharge for cause, but it is seldom used in practice, because it is believed difficult, to the point of futility, for an employer to prove cause in all but the most grievous cases, for example, conviction of a felony or chronic alcoholism. "Cause" does, of course, include breach by the employee of the employment relationship, which guides this discussion into the issue of termination.

(i) TERMINATION AND EXPIRATION

In discussions of the employment relationship, confusion often crops up, creating troublesome misunderstandings when the agreement is reduced to writing. If the employee demands a "three-year" contract, that means *either* (i) he is promised a salary from, say, Jan. 1, 1986 through Dec. 31, 1988, meaning that the employee is contractually guaranteed a salary over an ever-decreasing amount of time; as of, say, October 1988, the salary protection has shrunk to a matter of months; or (ii) alternatively, a "three-year" contract means that the employee is hired on Jan. 1, 1986 and is entitled to what amounts to three years' severance pay *whenever* he is terminated other than for cause or by his voluntary act. The employer, in effect, has issued an "evergreen" promise to pay him three years' salary regardless of when termination occurs, the day after he is employed or 10 years after. When considering the merits of each scenario, one has to go back to the point that the employment arrangement centers around the cost of buying out the employee's contract. With an evergreen provision, that cost is constant. Employment for a fixed term, on the other hand, makes it easier for the employee to be fired the longer he is with the company and thus fails to give the employee a fixed level of protection. Therefore, a multiyear employment contract usually refers to the evergreen arrangement; strictly speaking, the employee is terminable at will, subject to the severance arrangement. Assuming that the parties' minds have met on the term of the severance, the remaining issues concern price—what events give rise to the obligation of one or the other parties to pay a penalty, and in what amount?

(j) DAMAGES

This discussion started with a proposition that equitable relief is not generally available to compel a firm to continue to employ a given individual (versus paying his salary) for the agreed-upon period or to compel that individual to continue to report for duty at the firm. However, there are indirect ways of achieving that result, by working with the concept of damages. Thus, if an employment contract were to provide that, upon the early termination of a given employee, damages in the millions of dollars would be payable by the firm, that employee, in effect, would enjoy an insured lifetime position because he would be too expensive to fire. Alternatively, if an employee wishing to quit were faced with a provision in his contract that imposed on him an enormous penalty, then he (if able to respond in damages) would be indentured to the firm for the same reason. In fact, except in large public companies (where a multimillion award to a departing CEO may be immaterial to the annual financial results of the firm), huge penalty buyout provisions are uncommon. A start-up cannot afford to be locked into a seven-figure settlement amount for dismissing an individual. A typical provision contemplates that the employee will be paid the balance of his salary, either in a lump sum on a discounted basis or during the balance of the period remaining in the contract. And, from the company's perspective, while the employee's flight may in fact imperil enormous investments, it is questionable whether a court would enforce a huge liquidated damage provision against the employee.[52]

One of the principal reasons for stating the measure of damages is that the parties can, as they should, agree explicitly on the sticky issue of the employee's duty of "mitigation." If the contract is silent, it is not clear whether a given court will (or will not) find the terminated employee has an obligation to mitigate the employer's damages by finding other employment, setting off the employee's new salary against the employer's obligation to pay the old.[53] A duty to mitigate damages, whether express or implicit, includes subsidiary issues: What kind of position is the employee obligated to take? How much effort must he devote to looking for a new job? Where can he be required to take a job? In another city? When the issue is squarely addressed in a contract (as it should be), the possibilities to be covered in the drafting are lengthy. In addition to the ones mentioned, what if the employee elects, after termination, to manage his investments? If mitigation is contem-

[52]Nusbaum & Weltman, *supra* n. 42, at § 11.02[8], n. 69. If no liquidated damage amount is set, most courts will stick to compensating the employer for the cost of hiring a replacement; there is authority for the proposition that damages may include lost profits. *Id.* at n. 67.

[53]For the view that there is a duty to mitigate, see Nusbaum & Weltman, *supra* n. 42, at § 20.02.

plated, should the income from those investments be counted as if it were a salary? What if he is able to resell his vested equity in his old firm at a profit and then finds himself investing the proceeds in a new start-up, serving as chairman of the board of directors? Do director's fees count as salary, particularly if the former employee is devoting most of his time to the new company? The terminated founders of start-up companies are often young men who have interesting business careers in front of them, albeit not of the conventional kind. It is tricky, therefore, to forecast all the kinds of income that should count against the obligation of their former company.

An extended payout to a terminated employee can give rise to another subsidiary issue. The employee is at risk if the start-up seeks some form of relief under the bankruptcy laws; he will bargain, therefore, for security and, failing that, the right to continue to receive financial reports concerning the solvency of his former firm, the former firm in turn being unwilling to give out any information to somebody whose loyalty is no longer reliable.

Another problem on termination, not cosmic but irritating, has to do with the continuation of certain fringe benefits. If the founder has been fired, it is usually agreed that only his base salary continues until the term expires. He no longer accrues any equity emoluments and bonuses are off the horizon. However, the outgoing employee may find it hard to equal the various benefits, such as medical and group life; the expense of obtaining that coverage independently can be quite substantial, particularly since corporations continue to be favored by the tax laws in this regard.[54] The inclination of a firm to continue a fired employee in a group plan must be tempered by examination of the plan's eligibility requirements—is a former employee still an "employee" just because he is still being paid something?[55]

(k) EQUITY RECAPTURE

Often the most potent penalty imposed on a footloose employee is the recapture of nonvested equity, either options or cheap stock. If the draftsman employed by the company has kept the main chance in view, he will recall that the object of an employment agreement is multifaceted: to stimulate the employee's current performance and to keep out of his head visions of sugar plums dangled by competing firms. If valuable equity can be recaptured at a penalty price when the employee

[54] *See* Ch. 3, § 3.7.
[55] The criteria are set out in Treas. Regs. 1.401–1(b)(4).

quits,[56] the term "golden handcuff" becomes apt. It is awkward to provide that the employee who terminates before his promised time has to pay a cash penalty back to the company; he usually does not have the resources to spare and it is more trouble than it is worth to the company to chase him for some sort of cash "cough-up," even though the injury to the investors may be substantial. On the other hand, the vanishing employee may cause the investors to lose their entire investment, perhaps running into millions. The better weapon used to avoid that unhappy result, therefore, is to string out the vesting of equity incentives as long as possible and to provide for forfeiture in the case of the employee's breach. It goes without saying that the employee's power to assign shares subject to forfeiture must be openly and notoriously restricted; otherwise, the possibility of forfeiture could be neutralized by a transfer to a bona fide purchaser whose lack of knowledge cuts off the forfeiture restraint. Further, it is customary to distinguish the level of recapture, depending on the occasion. If, as the earlier discussion assumes, the employee quits voluntarily—in the worst case, to join a competing firm—or is fired for cause, then the most severe recapture is called for. If the employee is fired for reasons other than cause, or dies, then either no provision is made or a modified quantum of nonvested stock is affected. In connection with the company purchasing stock back from employees, one point is often overlooked. The employee may be entitled to the same quantum of disclosure (unless the price is prefixed) as any other seller. To be sure, some senior employees may know all there is to know about the issuer, but others do not. And, the fact that the repurchase is contemplated in a contract does not necessarily mean that the buyer—in this case the company—is relieved of its obligations under Rule 10b–5 of the'34 Act.[57] On another planning point, it may be useful to consider allocating the consideration to be paid to a departing employee among payments which do not generate tax deductions (for example, the repurchase of stock) and those that do, for example, "consulting arrangements" and covenants not to compete. With the employee indifferent to the differences between ordinary income and capital gain, the potential for tax minimization is enhanced.

(l) DEATH AND DISABILITY

The discussion so far has proceeded on the theory that it is relatively clear whether the employee has voluntarily terminated his employment contract or has been involuntarily terminated—fired. There are inter-

[56]Historically, the law has not favored contractual provisions labeled as "penalties." However, the courts have generally upheld provisions recapturing an employee's cheap stock or options at cost, even though value is then well in excess of that figure. *See, e.g., Allen v. Biltmore Tissue Corp.* 2 N.Y.2d 534, 161 N.Y.S.2d 418, 141 N.E.2d 812 (1957).

[57]*See, e.g., Jordan v. Duff and Phelps, Inc.*, 19 *BNA Sec. Reg. and L. Rep.* 469, 471 (Apr. 3, 1987).

stitial issues that should be resolved; for example, if the employee dies or is disabled. Outside of the world of Agatha Christie, death is rarely an ambiguous event; the employee is dead or he is not. "Disability" is a more slippery concept. If the term is left undefined, it is open for the company to attempt to cut loose a given employee by alleging disability when none exists. On the other hand, impaired employees often have the ability to pull themselves together when the question of disability is being considered in a courtroom, particularly alcoholics and (now unfortunately) drug users. The typical provision on disability gives a period of time—three to six months—during which the employee is retained on the theory that the disability is (or may be, at least) temporary. At the conclusion of that period, the contract language often refers to medical advice, a doctor's certificate from the employee (or, if there is a dispute, an examination by a physician employed by the parties) that settles the issue of disability. It is interesting to note that, in the bargaining process, most key employees are concerned at giving the company untrammeled power to claim the employee is disabled if that conclusion enables the company to terminate the employment relationship without paying any of the penalties provided when the relationship is terminated in "breach" of the contract. The obvious contrast is to terminations in the public sector, where the terms of the collective bargaining agreement and civil service regulations are such that many employees compete furiously for a holding that they are "disabled," enabling them to retire on a generous stipend.

If the employment relationship is terminated by death or disability, the norm is to provide that the equity emoluments vest;[58] disability insurance proceeds are paid to the disabled employee;[59] life insurance (to the extent not assigned to the company) is paid to the decedent's estate. There is on occasion a "put" in favor of the estate, entailing an obligation on the part of the company to buy back the equity interest at fair value so as to make the estate liquid. In the case of disability, some sort of salary continuation is often provided, to supplement or replace disability insurance for a period of time.

(m) RESTRICTIONS ON POSTEMPLOYMENT BEHAVIOR: NONCOMPETITION, NONDISCLOSURE, AND "WORK FOR HIRE" CLAUSES

The legal literature on occasion deals with certain promises between an employer and its employees—noncompetition, nondisclosure, and

[58]If the employee owns a large amount of stock, it may be necessary to recapture some portion in the event of his death in order to award the same to his successor.

[59]One planning issue concerns whether to integrate the company's disability payments with Social Security insurance proceeds. The question presents issues well beyond the scope of the Text. The I.R.S.'s founding positions are set forth in Rev. Rul. 69–5, 1969–1 C.B. 125.

ownership of inventions—as if they were entirely separate arrangements, involving discrete legal principles and policy considerations. In fact, in the usual case, all three are closely interrelated, one might even say variations on a single theme. And, at the risk of some confusion for those accustomed to separate presentations, the discussion in the Text will frequently treat them as if they were part of one whole.

The critical issues arise generally after the employment relationship is terminated. That is to say, if an individual is in fact a current employee, there is little controversy about an obligation, either expressly or by implication, not to compete and to maintain his employer's secrets in confidence. (The question of the ownership of inventions is somewhat more complex, as discussed in Chapter 16, §16.7.) Once the employee is out on his own—either fired or by his voluntary act—how far can the employer impose restrictions on his subsequent behavior? Can the employer prevent him from joining or organizing a competitive firm and/or disclosing confidential information? Can a non-compete clause be considered a permissible surrogate for a nondisclosure obligation, on the theory that a ban on competition is the only way effectively to police the confidentiality undertaking? Can the employer assert ownership rights to inventions the employee comes up with, even those invented (at least ostensibly) after the relationship has been severed? Does it make a difference whether the employer is relying on common law principles of unfair competition, a state statute (perhaps a version of the Uniform Trade Secrets Act) or express contractual provisions?

(m)(i) LABELS: "NONCOMPETE" VERSUS "NONDISCLOSURE"?

Depending on the state laws obtaining, it may be a bad idea to style any term of the employment arrangement baldly as a "covenant not to compete" (unless, as discussed below, the covenant is imposed in connection with the sale of a business or a significant stock position). Competition is the American way; labeling a restraint as anticompetitive is simply asking for some court to find a way around it in the clutch. Careful legal work, therefore, should start with the title of the section in the employment agreement, denoting what it is precisely that the company is trying to accomplish—a "covenant not to misappropriate proprietary information," perhaps, in which case the noncompete restriction is structured as a buttress, a way to enforce a nondisclosure obligation which cannot otherwise be realistically patrolled.

Indeed, there are multiple reasons why courts and legislatures are hostile to noncompetition agreements.[60] Strictly enforced, the provi-

[60]The Restatement of Contracts stresses that covenants not to compete are "often the product of unequal bargaining power and . . . the employee is likely to give scant attention to the hardship he may suffer later on." Restatement of Contracts (2d) § 188, *Comment* g (1981).

sions could mean that the former employee cannot make a living in his field. Moreover, many of the most glamorous start-ups were the brain children of free spirits, who left giant oaks to plant little acorns. If IBM had elected to impose, and been allowed to enforce, noncompetive clauses in every possible instance, one wonders what the computer industry in this country would look like today. Prudent counsel should start, therefore, with the presumption that a covenant not to compete may be unenforceable, (pending, of course, a thorough review of state law). Instead of drafting language without substantive impact, the search should be for provisions which will survive, which have a fighting chance of accomplishing some corporate purpose when a valued employee leaves.

The issue, of course, can be serious. The flight of the scientific brains of the company into the arms of a competitor can be a death sentence. If a choice has to be made, the investors are well advised to let the provisions of, say, the registration rights agreement pass without negotiation, directing their counsel to focus in on this area. Given the high level of judicial and legislative hostility,[61] it is sensible to frame each contract individually, tailormade to the particular employee and the threat he poses, once on the loose, to his former employer's prosperity. If he is to serve as the marketing manager, the agreement should zero in on avoiding the harm that an individual in that post can do; perhaps a prohibition on the former employee aiding another firm in contacting customers he cultivated while in the plaintiff's employment. A court is much more likely to enforce a restraint if it is carefully limited to the potential injury facing the employer; this requires that thought be given to each individual case. Off-the-shelf provisions are unlikely to accomplish their stated objective.

It should be noted that emotions run extremely high in these disputes. The work atmosphere in a high tech firm is often intense;[62] the key officers work so feverishly and such killing hours in the development of a new technology that their bond is as close as the marriage sacrament. When one of them decides he owes it to himself to strike out on his own, the emotions can be extremely bitter, the investors and officers of the earlier firm viewing the defection as hideously unfair if the defector is able to parlay his knowledge and experience into the building of a competitor, as is so often the case. Tying employees to a firm for life may be good and accepted practice in Japan but it conflicts with the mobility built into U.S. society. On the other hand, for investors and employees of a given firm to see their hard-earned secrets walk out the door and form the basis for a clone across the street is unfair competition of the most exasperating kind.

[61] *See generally* Nusbaum & Weltman, *supra* n. 42, at § 11.02[6].
[62] *See* Kidder, *The Soul of a New Machine* (1981).

(m)(ii) STATE OF THE LAW—NONCOMPETITION

The precedents are hard to align into a body of black letter rules because the states have adopted quite different approaches to the issues involved, either through the common law of unfair competition and trade secret protection as intepreted by judges and/or because legislation has been enacted. The rights of the two contesting parties—employer and former employee—will often depend on where the action is brought and which state law the court elects to apply. Without attempting to review the authorities,[63] certain general propositions can be extracted, with the caveat that they are just that—general in nature and subject to local exceptions:

First, an obvious point: If the employer, the boss, breaches the employment contract, the employee is released from at least his noncompetition and probably his nondisclosure promises. (In a given context, the obligation to respect trade secrets may exist independent of contract.) The situation dealt with in this section is termination of the relationship because the employ*ee* quits, either in breach of his agreement or because the agreement no longer requires him to stay on.

Secondly, if a postemployment constraint is connected with the sale of a business, courts are more likely to enforce a noncompetition provision.[64] Assume Smith, the sole owner of Widget, Inc., sells all his stock to Jones. Smith agrees to stay on for a period as a consultant and, for two years thereafter, to stay out of the widget business. If Smith attempts to violate his promise, a court will justify intervention by construing the restraint as protection for the goodwill that Jones has just bought.[65] In this instance, the noncompetition covenant need not be tied to the unfair use of proprietary information. The buyer has bargained for certain assets from the seller, including the seller's promise to stay out of the business. (It is not clear why investors purchasing a partial interest in Smith's company are entitled to any less consideration if Smith elects to quit. The goodwill is dissipated in either event.)

Allied to the "sale of the business" concept is the notion that, if the noncompetition restraint is created in connection with the resale of significant equity position back to the company, the liveliness of the restraint is enhanced. As a planning point, therefore, it makes sense

[63]The principles involved as discussed at length in Restatement, Contracts (2d) § 188, *Comment* and *Reporter's Note* (1981). Section 188 would invalidate covenants not to compete if the restraint is "greater than needed" or the employer's need for the restraint is "outweighed" by harm to the employee and "likely injury to the public." Id. at § 188(1).

[64]Restatement, *supra* n. 63, at § 188(2)(a) *Comment* f.

[65]If the sale price is equal to net tangible book value, some courts may be prone to find no purchase of good will and, therefore, no consideration for the promise. For a general discussion, *see Reed Roberts Associates Inc. v. Strauman* 40 N.Y.2d 303,305, 386 N.Y.S.2d 677, 679, 353 N.E.2d 590, 583 (1976).

from the issuer's vantage point to tie the restraint to a buy/sell arrangement respecting the employee's equity. (If the repurchase is at a penalty price—e. g., the employee's cost—or for a *de minimis* amount of stock, common sense would suggest that the stock transaction should lend little help to the restraint's validity.) The two provisions should be expressly tied together, maybe even contained in the same numbered paragraph.[66] The linkage device is not, of course, foolproof. As is the case generally in this area, courts in various states and at various stages approach the issues variously. Some will invent ways to ignore the equity side of the transactions and invalidate the restraint, reasoning that, for example, the price does not reflect a sale of goodwill.

The repurchase-of-equity provisions create a further opportunity for the firm to escape the negative implications of a "covenant not to compete." If the employer is located in a state hostile to postemployment restraints, one possibility is to string out certain benefits for the employee—for example, payment for the stock or deferred salary—and then provide for forfeiture if the employee winds up working for a competitor.[67]

Alternatively, the former employer can sue the *new employer,* not the employee, for tortious interference, coupled with an allegation of wrongful misappropriation of proprietary information; the remedy sought in such a case is damages but the object of the exercise is equitable in nature, to intimidate the competitor and/ or the potential investors so that they refrain from infringing the former employer's domain.[68] To repeat a prior point, the plaintiff's claim is that noncompetition restraints are generally justified as necessary to enforce in the real world the underlying obligation not to misappropriate the employer's rights to its proprietary information.[69] The idea is that, once the employee has been allowed to form a rival firm, the damage has been done, the horse is out of the barn.

The gloss of "reasonableness" colors the discussion and holdings, meaning that the judges are consulting what they perceive to be the

[66]*See* Nusbaum & Weltman, *supra* n. 42, at § 11.02[6](b). The covenant should "clearly state that it relates to the sale of the founder's shares." *Ibid.*

[67]For a case upholding this arrangement, *see Diakoff v. Am. Re-Insurance Co.* 492 F. Supp. 1115 (S.D.N.Y. 1980). Some courts would treat a forfeiture restriction as if it were a covenant not to compete. *Rochester Corp. v. Rochester* 450 F.2d 118 (4th Cir. 1971).

[68]There is some authority for the proposition that the officers and directors of the company which entrances the employee to leave with misappropriated intellectual property under his or her arm may be liable. Coolley, "Personal Liability of Corporate Officers and Directors for Infringement of Intellectual Property," 68 *J. Pat. & Trademark Off. Soc'y* 228 (1986).

[69]There are cases which will enforce the covenant even in the absence of trade secret concerns if the employee's services are "special, unique or extraordinary." *Purchasing Associates v. Weitz* 13 N.Y. F.2d 267, (1963), discussed in Restatement, *supra* n. 64, § 188, *Reporter's Note, Comment* g.

equities and common sense of the situation. Thus, the longer the employee has been employed and/or the higher his station in the company, the more likely a restraint will be enforced. A narrowly focused restraint will be more successful than one which bars the employee from working in any competitive job anywhere in the world.[70] The more sensitive the data to which the employee is privy, the likelier an injunction becomes. Indeed, injunctive relief is possible even if the absence of a contract if the secrets are particularly critical[71] but the failure of the employer to insist on a contract can be highly dangerous; the employer's lassitude cheapens its later assertions that the information is vital and may, in fact, constitute a lack of vigilance which negates the employer's rights under the law of trade secrets.[72]

The discussion to this point is focused on the language the employer should bargain for in the employment contract to protect itself. Venture finance, as indicated, involves the converse view, the flip side so to speak. When a start-up is in the process of organization, it is often the case that its founder and his colleagues are vulnerable to attack from the earlier employer and the planning points have to do with mitigating the chances of that contingency. Thus, if the founder of Start-up, Inc. plans to take with him the members of his entire team at Goliath, Inc., common sense dictates that the departures be staggered, rather than all at once. If the founder plans to leave first, he should wait until he is no longer on the job before soliciting his colleagues. The departing employee should leave all documents behind and take only what can be carried in his own mind—as one noted venture capital attorney likes to advise his clients, employees should walk out the door naked as the day they were born.[73] An offer to pay to the former employer a royalty for a license of disputed technology is ambiguous; it may demonstrate the good faith of those jumping ship (or, of course, may be construed as an admission of liability).

[70]"The extent of the restraint is a critical factor in determining its reasonableness." Restatement, *supra* n. 63, at § 188, *Comment* (d).
[71]The foundation case is *Lumly v. Wagner* 1 De G. M. & G 604, 42 *Eng. Rep.* 687 (Cf. 1852).
[72]*See* Ch. 16, § 16.5.
[73]The vivid phrase was coined by Richard Testa of Testa, Hurwitz & Thibault.

Eleven

Key Employee Compensation

Although venture-backed firms are viewed as technology driven, the fact is that experienced venture investors are accustomed to "bet the jockey, not the horse." The attraction and retention of key people—not only scientists but salesmen, production managers, and financial officers—is a key element in the typical firm's strategy. The "people" problem is often accentuated in the venture universe because many of the traditional corporate perquisites—particularly high salaries—are not available to attract talent. Moreover, in a start-up, people are necessarily hired from the outside; the managers have not had a lengthy "run-up" period while they and the board get to know each other. It is, accordingly, incumbent on all parties involved to think long and hard on compensation issues: how to motivate and retain good people, while not sacrificing the flexibility to make changes when necessary. The chapter should be read in tandem with Chapter 10, § 10.3 et seq., discussing the contracts with key employees.

§11.1 BACKGROUND

In many ways, employee compensation issues are easy to deal with in the start-up universe. The complement of people is usually small, it is rare that the employees are organized into collective bargaining units, health and welfare benefits are primitive and there are ordinarily no pension or profit sharing plans to raise issues under the Employee Retirement and Income Security Act (ERISA).[1] On the other hand, key employees are keenly interested in participating in equity. If the start-up is a howling success, they want to get rich like the investors. The methods used in granting employees "pieces of the action" have grown increasingly more sophisticated since the early days, when stock options more or less exhausted the planner's ingenuity. The overriding principles remain the same, however: keep good people, motivate them and yet be prepared to end the relationship in an affordable manner if things do not work out.

§11.2 GENERAL PRINCIPLES

First, in consonance with the rule that no one has any money to pay the I.R.S. when a start-up is organized, the principal aim of the planners is to put stock or stock equivalents in the hands of employees without occasioning tax liability. As indicated earlier,[2] this is not a simple exercise since, in the final analysis, stock is being awarded for past or future services, a taxable event in classic terms. Second, the equity should be allocated, if possible, in a way that has minimal effect on the start-up's reported earnings. In this connection, a majority of the commentaries on this issue are written by tax practitioners; when a compensation scheme enables the company to take a tax deduction, they view that as an unalloyed "plus." All other things being equal, of course, tax deductions are favorable. But, if the cost of casting a system in a given way is a "hit" to earnings as reported to shareholders, then it is time to revisit the question. Thus, an option should not be weighed exclusively by the after-tax effect on the recipient, the grantee. The fact is that the chief value of a stock option under today's rules may be its effect, or, better its lack of effect, on the grantor. Until the accounting profession changes its mind (which may be soon),[3] the grant of stock options as a form of employee compensation impacts the income statement as of the date of the grant, which is to say not at all, since the value of the option itself as of that date is indeterminate if the grantee's exercise price is equal to "fair value." As the option grows in value,

[1] 29 U.S.C. § 1001 *et seq.*

[2] *See* Ch. 5, §§ 5.1 and 5.2.

[3] GAAP currently provides, APB Opinion No. 25, that the issuer of an option records compensation expense as of the date the option is issued, and then only if the exercise price is less than fair value; options are generally issued at "fair value." The FASB Exposure Draft, when it appears, may recognize compensation expense periodically, as the fair value of the option stock ramps up over the exercise price. *See* XI *Corporate Commentator* 4 (May–June 1986).

culminating on the day it is exercised, the grantor's earnings are unscathed. By way of contrast, a phantom stock plan, which periodically awards to employees "units" ultimately redeemable in cash (the value of the units being tied to stock performance) can have an enormous negative impact on earnings.[4] (To be sure, any issuance of rights to purchase shares has a potential effect on the all-important earnings per share number.)[5]

The issue on this head can be of startling importance. Upon a sale of the company or an IPO, the price paid is usually a very high multiple of earnings. For every dollar in GAAP earnings lost, the existing shareholders, including the employees concerned, may thus sacrifice, say, $30 in value.

A central planning imperative is to tie equity to the performance of the employee. Thus, if shares (or options or stock equivalents) are awarded, it is important that employee "fat cats" are not thereby created, employees who can relax from and after the date of the award and watch their colleagues make them rich. Accordingly, awards, once made, should "vest" over time, meaning that the price is fixed as of the date of the grant but the options or stock can be recaptured for nominal consideration if the employee elects to quit prematurely.

Regardless of how sophisticated the stock or stock option plan may be, it is likely that the employee will have to pay tax at some time on the value he has received. The trick is to match the employee's obligation to pay tax with his receipt of income with which to pay the tax. A nonqualified stock option plan may, for example, entail a substantial tax obligation when the option is exercised even though the stock received on exercise cannot immediately be sold.[6] An employee may find himself paying $5 per share in exercise price for a $10 stock, borrowing to pay the tax (since, under the securities laws, he is locked into the

[4]FASB Interpretation 28 (Dec. 1978); *See also* Miller, *Comprehensive GAAP Guide* at 39.01–39.20 (1987); APB Opinion No. 23, ¶ 32. The distinction lies in the fact that, under the typical stock option plan, the option price and the amount of option shares are fixed as of the date of the grant, APB Opinion No. 25, ¶ 10b, and so any "compensation" is fixed as of that time as well, while, under a phantom stock option plan and other stock bonus and purchase plans, the amount of stock or other compensation varies as circumstances dictate. The fact that the employee must remain in his job for a period to vest the options does not, as of now, mean that the plan has variable terms. ARB Opinion No. 43, attached as Appendix B to APB Opinion No. 25.

[5]Options and warrants are considered "common stock equivalents" and, for purposes of calculating earnings per share, assumed to have been exercised if the market price has exceeded the exercise price for three consecutive months. The calculation includes issuance of the option stock and use by the issuer of the exercise price to purchase its own stock at market. AIN–APB Opinion No. 15 ¶ 51.

[6]*See* Ch. 11, § 11.3(b).

stock for two years),[7] losing the deduction for the interest paid under the Tax Reform Act[8] of 1986, and watching the stock go to $2 when at last he is able to sell it. This is not a result to be savored.

§11.3 STOCK OPTIONS

For many years, the principal method of equity allocation to employees has been stock options or, more specifically, options qualified for particularly favorable tax treatment under the Code.[9] That favorable treatment has beguiled many planners, in considering options as a motivational device, to focus exclusively on the after-tax effects of an option plan on the grantee. As indicated, however, the fact is that the principal benefit has been to the grantor—no impact on reported earnings of the company. To illustrate this point adequately, the mechanics of stock options should be briefly explored.

(a) MECHANICS

A stock option is a right issued to an individual to buy shares of stock in a given issuer at a fixed or formula price (subject to adjustments)[10] over a stated period of time. An option and a warrant are conceptually the same—an option is a warrant exercisable over a longer period. An option is usually issued by the company itself, to be satisfied by newly issued stock, but such is not necessarily the case. Any owner of stock can sell an option—a "call" in trading parlance—on his stock on whatever terms are mutually agreeable; calls are not, however, in the same

[7]Rule 144 omits options from the situations in which the "tacking" of holding periods is permissible. *Compare* Rule 144(d)(1) and (3).

[8]TRA § 511(a) amending I.R.C. § 163(d). Under the statute prior to the Tax Reform Act of 1986, the individual's annual maximum deduction for interest on debt to "purchase or carry property held for investment," I.R.C. § 163(d)(1)(A) and (B), was net investment income plus $10,000; now it is solely net investment income. I.R.C. § 163(d)(1).

[9]I.R.C. § 422A, governs "incentive stock options;" § 422A replaces § 422 with respect to options granted pursuant to plans adopted after May 20, 1976. I.R.C. § 422(c)(7)(A).

[10]The exercise price is routinely adjusted in the case of stock dividends or splits or other forms of nonsubstantive reorganizations. If the issuer is to disappear in a merger, the customary method is to vest all options immediately and allow the employee to exercise them prior to closing, but tax and securities law consequences may dictate alternative strategies—i.e., cash out all options and/or replace them with equity incentives in the acquiring corporation.

family, structurally, as the employee stock options discussed in this chapter.[11]

As the company is issuing the options, there are several events which could be the occasion for a tax of some kind.[12] If the option is to enjoy favorable tax treatment (and perhaps even if it is not), the first step is for the directors to adopt, and the stockholders to ratify,[13] a stock option plan. Adoption of a plan does not, of and by itself, involve the grant of options to any individuals. The plan, first and most importantly, identifies the maximum number of shares which can be issued to all the recipients in the aggregate; this is usually about 5 to 10% of the total stock outstanding, depending on the caliber of the employees and the willingness of the investors to dilute. The plan tells the stockholders the maximum amount of dilution they will suffer if all options are granted and exercised. It also sets out the basic provisions in each option contract, most of which are required under the Code if the options are to be "incentive stock options" under § 422A.

Options are granted to individuals pursuant to individual contracts. The scope of the plan contemplates the issuance of incentive stock options (ISOs) and/or nonqualified options (NSOs) and, perhaps, cash buyouts of the options in lieu of exercise, in the discretion of the issuer or the employee, (Stock Appreciation Rights or SARs).[14]

Assuming the options are to be ISOs, the exercise price in each contract will be fixed at "fair market value" of the stock at the time an

[11]Sometimes, the major or sole shareholder will grant options to key employees on stock he owns; under the Code, this transaction is generally treated as if the issuer granted the options. Treas. Reg. § 1.83–6(d)(1). *See* Kimpel, "Compensation Planning for 'High Tech' Executives" in *Tax Planning for High Tech and New Ventures* 67 (70th Forum Fed. Tax Instit. New Eng. 1984). An incentive stock option is one issued by the "employer corporation" or a parent or subsidiary, I.R.C. § 422A(b), meaning that options granted by a shareholder are nonqualified options or NSOs.

[12]ARB 53, Ch. 13, ¶ 6, reprinted as Appendix B to APB Opinion No. 25, identifies six events in the life of an option: the four mentioned in the Text, plus the date the right to exercise the option vests and the date the option is first exercisable, two dates that are often simultaneous.

[13]Shareholder approval within 12 months before or after the adoption of the plan is required if the options are to be incentive stock options under the Code. I.R.C. § 422A(b)(1). If the options are not designed to qualify under § 422A, shareholder approval is required only if the directors do not have the earlier-delegated authority to issue the necessary shares.

[14]To qualify as an incentive stock option, the option must be approved by the shareholders, expire after 10 years (five years in the case of a 10% stockholder), be granted pursuant to a plan less than 10 years old, carry an exercise price equal to current "fair market value" (110% of such value if the optionee is a 10% stockholder) and be nontransferable. I.R.C. § 422A(b). An incentive stock option may provide that the employee may exercise his option by paying with stock of the issuer and may have a "right" to receive "property" in lieu of stock at option exercise. I.R.C. § 422A (c)(4)(A) & (B).

option is granted.[15] The grantee will have no more than 10 years from the date of the grant in which to elect whether or not to exercise the option, which means, in effect, that the option will not ordinarily be exercised until the tenth year[16] since the prime virtue of an option is that it allows the investment decision maker to postpone his decision until the last instant. Eligible grantees include only employees[17] of the corporation and the options are not assignable.[18] The rule that incentive stock options on no more than $100,000 worth of stock could be granted in any year was redefined by the Tax Reform Act of 1986 so that, effectively, the plan can grant options at the outset on $1 million worth of stock but the amount of options which vest in any year during the 10-year period cannot exceed $100,000.[19] The effect of this provision is to allow the same amount of options per individual as under the old rules but to validate the use of the earliest possible (and presumably lowest possible) exercise price throughout. The oldest options need no longer be exercised first, a significant benefit in any scenario in which the price of the issuer's stock fluctuates both up and down and options are granted sequentially.[20]

Usually, the plan also establishes a committee of the board (not including anyone eligible to participate in the plan)[21] to "administer" the plan—that is, to grant the options—and sets up a system for tying options to performance. Dribbling out grants of options over a period of time can work to tie rewards to performance but such a procedure means, in a rising share value scenario, that the grantee's exercise price will escalate. Hence, the better drafted plans overgrant the number of options in the early stages (a procedure made easier by the Tax Reform

[15]Nonqualified options can be granted at prices below "fair market value" but a taxable event has occurred. I.R.C. § 83(a). For ISO purposes, a "good faith attempt" to set the exercise price at "fair market value" will suffice. I.R.C. § 422A(c)(1). As opposed to the rule under § 83, *see* Ch. 5, § 5.2, value may be discounted for purposes of § 422A if the stock is restricted. *Gresham v. Comm'r* 79 T.C. 20 (1982).

[16]I.R.C. § 422A(b)(3). Of course, the option may be exercised earlier if the employee needs the cash or the stock is public and the employee can sell at what he or she deems to be an advantageous price.

[17]The Regulations define "employees" for this purpose as persons involved in the "legal and bona fide relationship of employer and employee." Treas. Reg. §§ 1.421–6(b)(2) and 1.421–7(h). The definition incorporates the concepts in I.R.C. § 3401(c), which defines an employee for purposes of tax withholding. One of the games often played by planners is attempting to qualify valued directors and consultants as "employees."

[18]I.R.C. § 422A(b)(5).

[19]TRA § 321(a).

[20]TRA § 321(a) eliminated old paragraph (7) and (8) of § 422A(b).

[21]The requirement that the members of the committee be disinterested is found not in the Internal Revenue Code but in the'34 Act rules which exempt certain option transactions from the operation of § 16(b) (recapture of "short swing" profits) of the'34 Act. Rule 16b–3(b).

Act of 1986, as earlier indicated) and then provide for "vesting"; that is, the power of the issuer to recapture granted options lapses in decreasing amounts as the employee's longevity increases. Once an employee terminates or is terminated, he must exercise his options (only those vested, of course) within a short period: usually a month (and not, by law, more than three months)[22] after termination, meaning he loses the ability to postpone his investment decision. (On the other hand, to preserve the ISO status, he must hold the option stock for one year before selling it.)[23] The short fuse on post-termination exercise increases the possibility that a terminated employee's vested options will be allowed by him to lapse (and go back into the pool for someone else) since the exercise price will be (again given a rising stock price scenerio) closer to actual value when he quits than at the tail end of the option period.

The third step, coming after adoption of the plan and the grant of individual options, is the exercise of the option by the grantee. At this point, the risk of ownership shifts to the grantee and the planning points center on how to ameliorate that risk. If the company is planning an IPO, holders may want to exercise so that the shares issued to them are included, subject to the underwriter so agreeing, in the registration statement and sold on the effective date. Otherwise, the holder is locked into the stock for two years after exercising the option, even though the company's shares are publicly traded, since Rule 144 requires a two-year holding period before unregistered stock can be sold publicly and the period during which the option has been held does not count. (Of course, unregistered stock can be sold privately but that involves "haircuts," that is, discounts of up to 50% because of the long-term illiquidity of the security.)

Prior to 1986, an ISO holder planning to exercise on the eve of an IPO and sell in the offering faced a second hurdle. Under the Code, ISO option stock must be held for one year following exercise[24] or else the option is no longer qualified and the gain is, thusly, taxed at ordinary income rates. However, since ordinary income and long-term capital gains are now to be taxed alike, there is renewed appeal in a strategy (discussed below) involving a deliberate disqualification of an ISO.

The final step is the sale of the "property" owned by the option holder—the event which causes him to put his profit in his pocket. In the case of an ISO, there are two exit scenarios: Either the option stock is sold or the option is cashed in by the issuer, with the holder paid in cash the difference between the exercise price and the current value of the

[22]I.R.C. § 422A(a)(2).

[23]I.R.C. § 422A(a)(1). The optionee also cannot sell his shares within two years after the date the option was granted. *Ibid.*

[24]I.R.C. § 422A(a)(1).

stock. An unexercised ISO is not assignable to third parties[25] but, if sold back to the issuer, the holder is being paid for the appreciation in his option shares through the exercise of his "stock appreciation right."[26]

There are, then, four events to focus on if an ISO is planned: plan approval, grant, exercise, and sale. An NSO can entail all four or only the last three; there is no requirement that a plan be adopted for the issuance of NSOs or ratified by the stockholders (as long as the company has enough unissued stock to satisfy the option holders). If the option plan includes SARs—a cash buyout—then the fourth event—sale of option stock—also does not occur as an independent transaction.

(b) ISOs VERSUS NSOs

There are several differences between ISOs and NSOs, differences which continue, with one major exception, after the passage of the Tax Reform Act of 1986. The principal advantage of an ISO is that it postpones tax on the holder's gain (exercise price vs. sales price) until the option stock is *sold;* the tax on an NSO holder occurs upon *exercise,* measured by the difference between exercise price and fair value as of that time.[27] This is a major distinction. The NSO holder has to come up with his tax money earlier in the four-step process, provoking a potentially unacceptable investment risk unless he can sell immediately after exercise. However, as per Rule 144, he cannot sell publicly; that is, he must either hold for two years or sell at a stiff discount, unless he is able to register his stock for sale. Indeed, the interaction of the Code and Rule 144 can produce a script Yossarian could appreciate. On exercise, the NSO holder owes tax on the difference between exercise price and "fair value" calculated *without* regard to the restriction which will lapse,[28] that is, the inability to sell publicly for two years. Let us say the trading price of the stock is $10 and the exercise price is $6. Tax is owed on the $4 of gain. Mr. Yossarian can sell right away in a private transaction but at a gain of, say, only $2. He has to pay tax on $2 of gain that he cannot then realize, forcing him to choose an immediate sale at an economic loss so as to develop a countervailing loss for tax purposes. Alternatively,

[25]I.R.C. § 422A(b)(5). It is possible that an NSO could be made freely transferable, meaning the holder could "exit" by selling the option to third parties; however, such is unlikely since the principal purpose of both ISOs and NSOs is to put equity in the hands of employees as a motivational tool. A company planning to issue rights to acquire stock in order to raise cash usually deals in shorter-term instruments—warrants—and sells the rights at a price somewhat above fair market value.

[26]*See* I.R.C. § 422A(c)(4)(B).

[27]The tax is owed under § 83(a), i.e., the receipt of property, the option stock, in connection with services.

[28]The restriction on the ability to transfer by itself does not, despite the language of § 83, impose a restraint which allows the holder to postpone tax under I.R.C. § 83(b). *See* Ch. 5, § 5.2; cf. *Robinson v. Comm'r* 805 F.2d 38 (1st Cir. 1986).

he can pay his tax and hold the stock for two years and sell without a discount, but—Catch-22—the stock may have gone down in price in the interim. He has paid tax on a gain he has not seen and, two years later, he may have an economic loss in the stock because the price falls. Moreover, the deduction for interest (up to $10,000 per the Tax Reform Act of 1986) on the money he has borrowed is being phased out.[29] He gets a tax loss after two years of agony but, by that time, he may be broke.

There is more, however, to the comparison between ISOs and NSOs. The second major advantage of the ISO over the NSO—that the gain on sale was capital gain if the stock were held for a year after exercise (and the sale succeeded the grant by two years) will be no longer material (with certain exceptions) after the transition rules expire in 1988. More importantly, exercise of an ISO[30] produces tax preference in an amount equal to the difference between the "fair market value" of the stock on exercise and the amount paid—a potential disaster depending on the circumstances.[31] This feature has led some commentators to forecast the death of ISOs.[32]

However, in eliminating the preference for capital gains generally, the Tax Reform Act of 1986 has added luster to what might be called the "wait and see" approach. According to that strategy, the issuer constructs a plan involving ISOs. Then, as some critical date nears—

[29]The limitations on deductibility of investment interest (pre-1987 limited to $10,000 annually) will, after a five-year phase-in period, be limited to matching investment income. TRA § 511(a), amending I.R.C. § 163(d).

[30]The alternative minimum tax puzzle has been well summarized by the author's then-partner (now an officer of Fidelity Corp.) John Kimpel, in these words:

> The employee's exposure to the alternative minimum tax on the exercise of an ISO can create serious problems. Consider the following nightmare: Company X grants an ISO to a key employee to purchase 100,000 shares of its stock at $.60 a share, its then fair market value (total exercise price $60,000). Four years later, after several rounds of venture capital financing and the introduction of a spectacular new product, the company goes public at $10 a share. The employee exercises his option and acquires 100,000 shares of stock for $60,000. The amount of the tax preference item potentially subject to alternative minimum tax is $940,000 ($1 million − $60,000). Since the alternative minimum tax is the excess, if any of (a) 20% [now 21%] of the amount by which taxpayer's adjusted gross income plus items of tax preference less certain itemized deductions exceeds an exemption amount of $30,000 ($40,000, subject post '86 to certain reductions, if a joint return is filed), over (b) the regular income tax paid, the employee in the example above may face a staggering tax bill without having sufficient funds to pay the tax.

Kimpel, *supra* n. 11, at 53.

[31]TRA § 701(a) amended § 57(a)(10) to allow the taxpayer to add the amount of tax preference income to the basis in the stock for purposes of measuring gain on disposition. I.R.C. § 57(a)(3)(B). Capital gain is, of course, no longer an item of tax preference income. I.R.C. § 57(a)(10).

[32]"The Tax Reform Act: What To Do About Stock Options" XI *The Corporate Counsel* 1 (Sept.–Oct. 1986).

an IPO looms, for example—the employee enjoys alternatives. He can exercise the option and hold the shares if alternative minimum tax is not a problem as a practical matter, thereby postponing tax while the Rule 144 period runs; or he can do something to disqualify the option as an ISO—sell before the one-year holding period lapses, for example.[33] Perhaps the issuer will want a tax deduction and would be willing to pay the employee a bonus, accordingly, to make a disqualifying disposition. Moreover, in the event of a disqualifying disposition the gain is the *lesser* of the putative gain on exercise or the actual gain on sale.[34] And, the accounting treatment of NSOs and ISOs is the same; a "hit" to earnings only if the option is *granted* at less than fair value.[35]

[33]A disqualifying disposition may itself raise tax issues. Again to quote John Kimpel:

> The prospect of a disqualifying disposition raises a host of hidden issues, particularly as a result of the proposed regulations recently issued by the I.R.S., which state that the effects of a disqualifying disposition generally will be determined pursuant to I.R.S. § 83. *See* Prop. Regs. § 1.422A–1(b)(1). Three of these are particularly important. *First,* if the stock received upon a disqualifying disposition is subject to a substantial risk of forfeiture, the amount of compensation income will be measured by the difference between the option price and the fair market value of the stock on the date the restrictions lapse. *See* Prop. Regs. § 1.422A–1(b)(3) (Example 3). This treatment raises the question of whether the optionee may make a "protective" election under I.R.C. § 83(b) at the time the ISO is exercised in order to prevent the possibility of additional ordinary income due to appreciation in the value of the stock from the exercise date forward. *Second,* in order for the employer to take the deduction for compensation expense allowed upon a disqualifying disposition, the employer must withhold tax from the income received by the ISO upon the disqualifying disposition. *See* Prop. Regs. § 1.422A–1(b)(3)(Example 4). This requirement raises enormous practical problems and reverses the position taken by the I.R.S. in Rev. Rul. 71–52, 1971–1 C.B. 278, which many employers have relied on as well for ISO's. *Third,* a disqualifying disposition may have a disastrous effect when coupled with the alternative minimum tax. Under Regs. § 1.57–1(f)(5)(i), which was issued prior to ERTA, if the exercise of a *qualified* option and a disqualifying disposition of the stock acquired upon such exercise occurred in the *same year,* no alternative minimum tax would be incurred. But if the disqualifying disposition occurred in a *subsequent year,* the alternative minimum tax payable in the previous year would stand. However, under the TEFRA Conference Report, it appears Congress intended that the disqualifying disposition of *an ISO* would *retroactively* eliminate the tax preference item and thereby the alternative minimum tax regardless of whether such disposition occurred in the same year as exercise or in a subsequent year. *See* H. R. Rep. No. 97–760, 97th Cong., 2d Sess. 475 (1982). Nevertheless, new regulations have not been issued under I.R.C. § 57 to verify that the I.R.S. similarly interprets this legislative intent. Given the contrary intent expressed under Regs. § 1.57–1(f)(5)(i) as applicable to qualified options, this silence leaves some doubt.

Kimpel, *supra* n. 11, at 56–57.

[34]I.R.C. § 422A(c)(2). Exercise and sale within six months may pose problems for directors, officers and 10% stockholders under § 16(b) of the'34 Act. In order to mitigate that result, the plan (ISO or NSO) should be drafted pursuant to the provisions of Rule 16b–3.

[35]Aufmuth, "Selected Tax Accounting Issues in Early and Mezzanine Financings and Venture Capital Partnerships," *Venture Capital After the Tax Reform Act of 1986* 55, 76 (P.L.I. Course Handbook Series No. 422, 1987).

The point is that there is no one "right" answer to the ISO/NSO decision; particularly in view of the uncertainty posed by the FASB proposals, it is impossible to set out any general rules. The ISO vs. NSO question should be examined carefully in light of the facts of each case and the tax, securities and accounting rules in effect at that time.

§11.4 "CHEAP" STOCK

No change is made by the Tax Reform Act of 1986 in the treatment of the issuance of "cheap" or "founders" stock upon organization of a start-up. Usually the best result from any investor's point of view, employee or not, is to obtain founders stock.[36] As discussed in Chapter 5, § 5.1, tax is payable if the employees pay less than "fair value," (and, in such event, the issuer gets a deduction for tax purposes), but the use of "eat'em up" preferred or the "passage of time" approach can negate the bargain element.[37] If vesting is postponed, the § 83(b) election is routinely in order even if the stock is sold at fair market value;[38] cheap stock works best upon organization because low values can best be defended thereat, before trades begin and the issue of value is no longer in the reasonable discretion of the directors. Once an objective value has been established for the common, cheap stock may still be attractive but the tax problem becomes more significant. If the employee pays only a nominal amount for the stock, then he must pay a substantial tax; the free lunch provided by the common/preferred distinction has been lost.

§11.5 "GROSSING UP"

An employee may be issued stock at bargain prices (or for free), plus a cash bonus in an amount sufficient to allow the employee to pay tax on the bargain purchase element. This is a relatively simple transaction, called "grossing up." The result is that the employee gets the stock, after all taxes are paid, at the bargain price he agreed to pay and the employer, since it is paying the employee in cash, has a pot from which to withhold and, accordingly, take the deduction. The problem is that

[36]One of the (rough and tumble) versions of the law of big numbers is that a little number multiplied by a big number is always a big number. An investor in the first venture round who buys stock at $1 per share may make 10 times his money—call it $1 million. The investor who bought in the founders' round at a "few cents" less per share, say 90 cents less, winds up with $10 million.

[37]The problem of issuer withholding, mentioned above, is present in this context as well. Treas. Regs. § 1.83–6(a)(2). Note that "fair value" under § 83 is in excess of economic fair value because of the restricted nature of the security. *See* I.R.C. § 422A(c)(1); § 83(a)(1).

[38]*See* Ch. 5, § 5.2(a).

"grossing up" costs the company money at a time when cash may be scarce and it debits earnings when every drop of reported income may be precious in valuing the company's stock.

§11.6 CONVERTIBLE DEBENTURE PLANS

Some companies have experimented with methods of combining borrowing with stock purchases to achieve the "free upside" result. In its most aggressively planned form, the transaction looks something like the following: Start-up, Inc. issues Mr. Upside a 10-year convertible debenture, interest payable annually at 10%, in the principal amount of $1 million, with the debenture converting at any time prior to maturity into 1 million shares of common stock. The conversion price should be sufficiently in excess of the then market or fair value of the common so that the Service cannot argue that the debenture is worth more than its face amount and, therefore, the employee received a bargain,[39] Mr. Upside borrows the money with which to buy the stock from Start-up, Inc., at, say, 10.5% annually.[40] No cash in fact changes hands. Mr. Upside pays a bit of net interest each year until he elects to make an investment decision. If the stock is now trading at $2 a share (after an IPO), he converts, sells enough stock to pay his loan and his tax and keeps the balance that he owns for "free."[41] If the stock does not move or goes down, he holds the debenture until maturity, cashes it in and unwinds the deal by paying his debt to Start-up, Inc. If Start-up, Inc. should go into bankruptcy in the interim, he "sets off" under the Bankruptcy Code[42] the amounts owed "to and from" and walks away from the transaction unscathed. The interest payable on his loan from Start-up, Inc. is deductible under both current law and the Tax Reform Act because it is set against investment income.[43] The commentators are naturally concerned about this arrangement because it looks too easy and the Service may assert it is a sham, arguing that the taxpayer did not in fact buy the debenture but is paying the net interest amount for an option on the stock.[44] A recent letter ruling[45] appears to validate the

[39]Martin, "Raising Capital for a Closely Held Company," 43 *N.Y.U. Inst. Fed. Tax'n.* § 8.07[3][a](1985).

[40]The interest rate should be equal to at least 110% of the "applicable Federal rate" determined under I.R.C. § 1274(d) in order to avoid the application of I.R.C. § 483.

[41]In the hypothetical; the taxpayer should sell 581,396 shares; the proceeds will be $1,162,792; the tax on the gain is $162,791, leaving $1 million to pay off the loan and 418,604 "free" shares.

[42]11 U.S.C. § 553.

[43]TRA § 511(a), amending I.R.C. § 163(d).

[44]See Martin, "Raising Capital for a Closely Held Company," 43 *N.Y.U. Inst. Fed. Tax'n.* § 8.07[3](a) (1985).

[45]Letter Ruling 8433047, discussed in Martin, *supra* n. 44 at § 8.07[3](a).

underlying theory, even in the absence of a substantial employee down payment, but the accounting treatment is not yet settled.

§11.7 MISCELLANEOUS ITEMS

There are any number of variations on the foregoing themes, including the issuance of junior common stock (no longer favored),[46] so-called "haircut" programs,[47] "book value" stock plans,[48] phantom stock plans, ESOPs, stock bonus plans, and the like, several of which raise tax, accounting, and ERISA issues well beyond the scope of the text.[49]

[46]*See* Ch. 13, § 13.2(a).

[47]A "haircut" or fixed differential plan entails selling stock to an employee at a discount from fair market value, say, $10, subject to the right in the company to repurchase, in the case of a proposed transfer, the stock at the same discount ($10) from then-existing market value. The "accounting and tax considerations are subject to some uncertainty." Aufmuth, *supra* n. 35, at 79.

[48]A "book value" stock plan entails the issuance of a special class of stock whose value is based on book value or some objective formula. To the extent the "book value" stock is convertible upwards into common stock, the arrangement smacks of junior common stock. *See* Buoymaster & Frank, "Employee Benefit Plans," in Harroch, *Start-Up Companies: Planning, Financing and Operating The Successful Small Business* § 14.02[6])(1986).

[49]A useful summary of the array, including qualified retirement plans, deferred compensation plans and incidental benefits, is contained in the article by Messrs. Buoymaster & Frank, *supra* n. 48.

Twelve

Valuation and Pricing

The art of venture capital investment rests, in the first instance, on twin pedestals—selecting the right opportunities and negotiating appropriate values—"Should we make the investment at all and, if so, at what price?". Investment managers of public securities portfolios are, like venture managers, intimately involved with valuation as part of the screening process but the price at which they buy or sell securities is a given; the auction markets generally set prices and the adviser cannot negotiate effectively. He can only wait for the price to move into his target range. This brief chapter highlights the valuation and pricing process in the venture context, with emphasis on the interesting problems involved in valuing early-stage opportunities, before it is possible to pick up cues from comparable sales, historic earnings, or hard assets. Valuation theory is an elegant discipline, demanding intense intellectual effort, well beyond the scope of the text. The simple examples are cited because they represent what ordinarily goes on in the imperfect venture universe, where time and resources are scarce. The instant discussion aims to give entrepreneurs a better grasp of the world they are entering when they begin a price negotiation.

§12.1 CERTAIN TERMS

When a founder determines it is worth his while to attempt to raise money for his concept, the basic issue becomes one of price. If, for example, the business needs $500,000 to get started, how much of the equity in that company should $500,000 in fresh cash command? A brief summary of common terminology will help illuminate the subsequent discussion.

The word capitalization, or its abbreviation "cap," is often used in pricing start-ups, with, on occasion, differing meanings.[1] The "market capitalization" or cap of a company refers to the result obtained by multiplying the number of equity shares outstanding by some assigned per share value. If it has been determined that a share of stock in the company is "worth" $10 and the company has 100,000 shares outstanding,[2] then its market cap is $1 million. The second use of the term has to do with the rate at which future flows are to be valued, a rate sometimes called the discount or cap rate, meaning that that flow of income is to be assigned a one-time value by being "capitalized."[3] Thus, elementary valuation theory teaches that one of the most reliable indicia of value to be assigned to a fledgling (or, indeed, any) enterprise is a number which capitalizes projected income streams. In its simplest form, the question is what an informed investor would pay (i.e., what sum of capital would he put up) in exchange for a promise to pay him annually a certain sum of money? In working out the numbers, it is assumed that the investor wants his capital returned to him plus a competitive rate of interest. The higher the assumed interest rate deemed competitive with other investment opportunities, the higher must be the annual payments, given a fixed amount of capital invested on day one. Alternatively, a fixed amount and number of annual payments can be the given element in the formula; the assumed amount of capital to be invested (i.e., the discounted value of the future payments) is then derived, again as a function of the cap rate selected. As the assumed interest or cap rate goes up, the discounted value of the payment stream goes down; fewer dollars are required on day one to earn the investor, at the higher rate, the forecast income flows.

Another common expression is "before the money" and "after the money." This denotes an ostensibly simple concept, which occasionally trips up even the most sophisticated analysts. If a founder values his

[1]An entirely misleading use of the term "capitalization" rate involves equating it to the price/earnings multiple. Shannon Pratt, *Valuing a Business: The Analysis and Appraisal of Closely-Held Companies* 62 (1981) (Shannon Pratt).

[2]For a variety of purposes in valuation—*e.g.*, earnings per share—it is significant to determine exactly how many shares of a given issuer should be considered as "outstanding." Shares actually in the hands of holders are the easy case; questions arise when dealing with unexercised options, warrants and other rights to purchase shares. *See* Ch. 13, §§ 13.3 and 13.5, for the accounting rules involved in calculating outstanding shares in two formats: primary dilution and full dilution.

[3]The technical difference between a discounting process and a capitalization process is that the former refers generally to a finite series of payments—*e.g.*, ten $1,000 payments over 10 years—and the latter to a hypothetically perpetual stream of payments. *See* Brudney & Chirelstein, *Corporate Finance: Cases and Materials*, 34–35 (3d ed. 1987).

company at $1 million on day one, then 25% of that company is "worth" $250,000—Q.E.D. However, there may be an ambiguity. Suppose the founder and the investors agree on two terms: (i) a $1 million valuation; and, (ii) a $250,000 equity investment. The founder organizes the corporation, pays a nominal consideration for 1,000 shares and, shortly thereafter, offers the investor 250 shares for $250,000. Immediately there can be a disagreement. The investor may have thought that equity in the company was worth $1,000 per percentage point; $250,000 gets 250 out of 1,000, not 1,250, shares. The founder believed that he was contributing to the joint enterprise property *already* worth $1 million. For $250,000, the investor's share of the resultant enterprise should be 22.5%. The uncovered issue was whether the agreed value of $1 million to be assigned to the company by the founder and investor was *prior to* or *after* the investor's contribution of cash.

§12.2 VALUE—TO WHOM?

In whatever language he chooses, each founder takes on the chore of setting a preliminary valuation on the company for purposes of attracting outside capital. The principal point to be kept in mind is obvious but often overlooked. What the *founder* thinks the company is worth is largely irrelevant at this stage.[4] The decision to go forward has been made, and his effort and resources have by now been pledged to the enterprise based on his expectations of risk and reward. When outside financing is being sought, the critical number is what the founder thinks the universe of *investors* will assign as value to the company.[5] The founder's personal valuation comes into play only if the investment community's assigned value is so much lower than his expectation that he is forced to rethink the question whether the game is worth playing at all.

A number of interesting problems arise when the founder attempts to psychoanalyze the investment community, to come up with a number

[4]A number of textbooks are available on the theory and practice of business valuation, *viz.* Hubbard & Hawkins, *Theory of Valuation* (1969); Desmond & Kelley, *Business Valuation Handbook* (1977); *Asset Valuation and Income Determination* (Sterling ed. 1971); Blackman, *The Valuation of Privately-Held Businesses* (1986); Ovens & Beach, *Business and Securities Valuation* (1972); Loscalzo, *Cash Flow Forecasting* (1982); Walker & Petty, *Financial Management of the Small Firm* (1986); Martin & Gustafson, *Valuing Your Business* (1980).

[5]Most conceptions of value in a business context deal with "fair value" or "fair market value." This phrase is usually taken to mean the price at which an interest would change hands between a willing buyer and willing seller, both being adequately informed of the relevant facts and neither being under any compulsion to buy or sell. *See* the articulation of this Rule for estate and gift tax valuation purposes in Treas. Reg. § 20.2031–3.

that will prove attractive. In first-round financings there is often, and indeed ordinarily, no track record on which to base conclusions as to value. Moreover, existing assets—plant, machinery, equipment, accounts receivable[6]—are seldom, if ever, meaningful in a first round.[7]

§12.3 DISCOUNTING THE FUTURE

There are almost as many methods of calculating value as there are world religions, since the questions are metaphysical in part and depend on the appetites of the observer. In one of the most common scenarios, a five-year forecast is prepared, the thought being that in the fifth year (assuming the projections are accurate) an exit strategy will be implemented, that is, investors will sell their securities for cash or the securities will become publicly traded, the equivalent of cash.[8] It is usually assumed that the investors will realize their entire return upon implementation of the exit strategy; there will be no interim returns since all revenues will be retained in the business. The valuation formula most often used in connection with the forecast is relatively simple:

An investor plans to invest X dollars in the enterprise today for some as-yet-to-be-determined percentage of the company's equity. The projections predict the company will enjoy Y dollars of net after-tax earnings as of the day the exit strategy is accomplished, that is, the company

[6]For discussion of various valuation methods based on asset, liquidation and replacement values, *see* Blackman *supra* n. 4, at Ch. 5; Ovens & Beach *supra* n. 4, at Ch. 1; Walker & Petty, *supra* n. 4, at Ch. 10. The Delaware courts have developed a multifaceted approach to value to be used in calculating the awards to be made to shareholders exercising their "dissenters" or "appraisal" rights in the course of a merger. *See* Del. Code Ann. tit. 8, § 262; *see generally*, "Valuations for Dissenting Shareholders" in McCarthy & Healy, *Valuing a Company* 403 (1971). The literature on valuation in insolvency and rate setting proceedings is enormous. *See* Brudney & Chirlestein, *supra* n. 3, at 3; "Valuation in Regulated Industries" in McCarthy & Healy, *supra* at 421. The legal definitions of value used in contested cases have not been noticeably influential to investors in pricing a start-up.

[7]In order to capture the progress of a firm which has no track record of earnings and few tangible assets, imaginative methods are often employed. One such is commonly used by the Gartner Group, a consulting firm (now publicly held) which was itself backed by venture capitalists. Gartner Group uses an indicator entitled the Current Annualized Contract Volume for firms, such as software suppliers, with a large volume of long-term contracts. The indicator assumes (contrary to fact in a given instance, of course) that all existing contracts will remain in force at the current rate for 12 months. The method does not give an accurate snapshot of backlog at any given moment in time but allows the analyst to follow trends in the company's ability to attract business and to interpret potentially misleading movements in the raw data—i.e., gross revenues.

[8]In point of fact, the day of the initial public offering does not automatically make the investors' stock liquid. It is unlikely that their shares will be registered in any significant amount for distribution or indeed be eligible for "dribble out" privileges under Rule 144 until the expiration of a period during which all secondary sales are barred by the underwriters and/or by state securities administrators. *See* Ch. 14, § 14.9

is sold or goes public.[9] The analyst then picks a multiple of earnings per share in order to hypothesize what the stock might sell for in a merger or an IPO. Since there is no way of forecasting that multiple, the next best strategy is to use existing multiples in the given industry. What is the PE (ratio of share price to earnings per share) of companies in comparable fields today?[10] Let's assume that multiple to be 10, meaning that the total market capitalization of the company immediately prior to the IPO will be 10 times the net earnings for such year. The investor then picks that return on his investment which corresponds to the risk he deems himself encountering, taking into account the return on competing investments, again a subjective judgment. He may believe that he is entitled to a 38% compounded rate of return,[11] which means, by rule of thumb in the venture community, that the company's forecast should be holding out the expectation of a "five times"[12]; that is, the investor will get back, before tax, $5 for every $1 invested. If the in-

[9]Some investors work with not one but three forecast scenarios: best, middle, and worst case. They then weight each of the three according to probability of occurrence and come up with a weighted-average result. This is sometimes referred to as the First Chicago method, because it was prominently employed by Stanley Golder when he was managing the portfolio of the venture arm of that bank holding company. *See* Morris, "Pricing of a Venture Capital Investment," Pratt's Guide *supra* Ch. 1, n. 7, at 55. To be sure, attaching probabilities to the occurrence of a given projection is conceptually impure since probability theory requires that no statement whatsoever can be made about the probability of a single event—i.e., there is no probability attached to one flip of a fair coin. Nonetheless, the practice is useful when it is taken for what it is—a way of helping an investor in reaching a decision, rather than purporting to make that decision for him with scientific exactitude. When businessmen measure value using methods such as "First Chicago" they are described as using "personal or subjective probabilities;" Grayson, "The Use of Statistical Techniques in Capital Budgeting" in Brudney & Chirelstein, *supra* n. 3, at 52.

[10]Finding the appropriate PE ratio is often discussed in finance textbooks. *See* Fama, *Foundations of Finance* (1976). As the Text suggests, the most often used criterion is "what other people are willing to pay for comparable streams of earnings." *See* Shannon Pratt, *supra* n. 1, at 61. In addition to matching comparable industries to divine the appropriate PE, one must consider the growth potential and risk of the specific investment in question. In general, the types of firms in which venture capitalists like to invest will have high growth potential (meriting a higher PE ratio) but will be risky (compensated for by a lower PE ratio). The earnings of a highly leveraged company are riskier than those enjoyed by a debt-free firm; one way to compare apples and apples in this environment is to recalculate the earnings of the leveraged company as if it were debt free. *Id.* at 64–66.

[11]The expectations of professionally managed pools is high. Brentwood Associates reportedly targets a "ten times" return in five years. *See* Kozmetsky, Gill, & Smilor, *Financing and Managing Fast Growth Companies*, at xv (1985).

[12]If five years is the time horizon, then compounded rates of return interrelate with multiples of the cash invested as follows:

> To triple one's investment in five years, you need a 25% compounded pretax rate of return;
> To quintuple one's investment in five years, you need a 38% compounded pretax rate of return;
> For seven times one's investment in five years, you need 48%;
> For 10 times one's investment, you need a 58% compounded pretax rate of return.

vestment called for is $250,000, then five times $250,000 is $1.25 million. If the company is forecast to be worth $10 million in year five, then the investor's $250,000 should command 12.5% of the company in year one.[13]

Of course, many of the elements of the formula are highly speculative, particularly the reliability of the company's forecast.[14] The method for taking that subjectivity (risk of error) into account is to adjust the rate-of-return target, or "bogey" or "hurdle rate" as it is sometimes called. If the investor thinks the forecast is suspect, one way of sensitizing the equation to his suspicion is to increase the rate of return target from, say, 38% to as much as, perhaps, a 50% compounded rate of return. If an adjustment has to be made to conjugate a rate of return much higher than 50%, then it's arguable the investor should not make the investment in the first place. Because compounded rates of return in excess of 50% are so unusual, many investors feel it is unrealistic to predicate an investment on that kind of expectation.[15] The power of compounding is enormous. Many neophytes are inhabiting fantasy worlds when they dream of investments continuing to compound at double digit rates over an extended period.

(a) PORTFOLIO MANAGEMENT

In considering the issue of valuation generally, one should understand the environment in which a manager of a venture pool operates; he is investing not in one but in a number of opportunities. One of the foundations of modern portfolio theory is the concept that the return on an asset cannot be viewed by itself; rather it must be judged by its contribution to the portfolio as a whole. Thus, when deciding to invest in a company, the venture capitalist must consider how the expected return on the new investment is correlated with the others he holds,[16]

[13]The model assumes only one round of financing, a highly unlikely contingency. If the investor assumes a subsequent round, he must enlarge the percentage he needs today, using some form of "Kentucky Windage," so that he will end up with 12.5% of the outstanding stock in year five.

[14]For a valuable discussion on how reliable forecasts can be obtained, see Walker & Petty, *supra* n. 4, at 78–87.

[15]Any number of rules of thumb are used by venture capitalists, in part because the universe of possible opportunities is so large that some handy, ready-to-wear criteria are necessary to screen wheat from chaff. Thus, one prestigious fund uses what it calls a "second-round scenario." The manager arbitrarily assumes that, when a second round of financing is called for, no start-up is likely to be given a premoney valuation much in excess of $5 million. Since the manager wants his first-round investment to be "worth" somewhere around 50% more as a result of a second-round mark-up, first round valuation rarely exceeds $2 to $3 million after the money.

[16]*See, e.g.*, Hubbard & Hawkins, *supra* n. 4, at 54–55; for a general exposition of portfolio theory, *see* Hagin, *Modern Portfolio Theory* (1979).

ranking opportunities on both an ordinal and cardinal scale.[17] In a significant sense, a cardinal ranking of sorts is always involved because the portfolio manager does not enjoy an infinite array of opportunities. If he is a venture manager, it is incumbent on him to put his money to work in venture investments, meaning that he has to compare each opportunity with what he has and what he is likely to be offered. If a given deal looks like it is better than anything else in sight, he is likely to take it on the founder's terms, even though his own number (based on his idea of valuation in a perfect universe) would be lower were his alternatives wider.

Again in keeping with the idea that it is the portfolio, not the individual investments, being managed, venture capitalists usually diversify their holdings by categories of risk, investing across varying risk levels: a cohort of start-ups carrying, say, an average (forecast) 40% compounded rate of return coupled with later-round financings which promise lower returns as a tradeoff for better downside protection and the ability to cash out in the near term. Parenthetically, one must recognize that modern portfolio theory cannot be applied uncritically to a venture portfolio because, as one analyst has put it, venture investments "are not available in continuously desirable funding instruments."[18] The new venture manager cannot decide to put 1% of the capital pool in a venture that actually needs 6% of the pool to reach the next development milestone.

(b) NONNUMERICAL FACTORS

Despite the seeming exactitude of a discounted earnings formula, professional venture managers understand that elaborate valuation techniques are not ends in themselves in venture investing because of the enormous uncertainties involved but, rather, tools, inputs which contribute to (but do not determine) a composite judgment based, in the final analysis, on judgment and experience. One can construct elegant models but if, *au fond,* the result depends ultimately on an informed guess as to future earnings which can be shifted from one end of the plausible range to the other by a factor of 100%, mathematical exactitude is trivial, violating the law of significant numbers (multiplying two numbers, one carried out to a single decimal and the other to 10 places). Accordingly, a number of judgmental factors are routinely taken into account in arriving at estimated values. As an obvious example,

[17]To oversimplify, numbers on a cardinal scale indicate only ranking—B is less than A and greater than C. One cannot, for example, add the numbers assigned B and C together and get any meaningful comparison with A. On an ordinal scale, on the other hand, each number has some absolute relation to each other number, a relation going beyond "greater or lesser than."

[18]Costello, *New Venture Analysis; Research, Planning and Finance* 156 (1985)

the investor must consider the outlook for the industry as a whole, the likely competitive position of the issuer, trends in customer tastes, dependence of the business on a few major customers or suppliers, possible product obsolescence, likely capital needs, and the ability to leverage, potential impact of changes in the regulatory climate, and so forth. Much attention will focus on likely market share, in part due to the popularity of the Boston Consulting Group's four-square matrix, which emphasizes market share's influence on a company's ability to become a "cash cow." Valuation based on the discounted value of projected earnings is then adjusted up, down, or sideways depending on the analyst's judgment as to the effect of the nonquantified factors. The outcome is a product only partly of mathematics and principally of judgment and experience.

§12.4 MISCELLANEOUS VALUATION ISSUES

Instead of applying a multiple to projected after-tax earnings in the fifth year, the analyst may elect to work with other revenue streams: gross revenues, net operating earnings, EBIT (net earnings before deducting interest and taxes) or cash flow, perhaps making adjustments to the particular stream based on special factors.[19] Thus, if the company will be carrying a debt burden as of the valuation date, it is the custom to value it debt-free on a pro forma basis, meaning that: (i) Earnings are increased by adding back the amount of interest payable (the pro forma company has no debt); (ii) The appropriate multiple is applied and then; (iii) The principal amount of the debt is subtracted from the resultant number. In such a calculation, if the projection shows excess cash balances as of the valuation date, the debt is reduced by the amount of the cash to reflect a hypothetical pay-down of debt by the company immediately prior to its pro forma debt-free valuation. Similarly, if the firm is likely to require significant capital investment in the future, the cash-flow forecast is fine tuned to account for that expectation.

Another factor for the founder to take into account is the appetite of a given investor for risk. There can be very different standard deviations. Thus, a risk-averse person might rather have an investment which promises a 100% chance of making $40 versus one with a 35% chance of losing $150, a 40% chance of winning $60 and a 25% chance of winning

[19]It is surprising to find in actual practice how often the various methods come out with roughly the same result, meaning that they can be used in tandem, one method checking on the other. Thus, an exit price of 10 times net after tax earnings may otherwise equate (roughly) to one times gross revenue, a six times operating earnings calculation, and/or eight times cash flow. For methods of computing cash flow, earnings and other streams, *see* Desmond & Kelly, *supra* n. 4, at Ch. 5; Hubbard & Hawkins, *supra* n. 4, at 45.

$130.[20] On the other hand, an individual investing a small portion of his or his family's personal fortune may be willing to accept enormous risks for a chance at a home run since the pain of loss is negligible, compared with the pleasure at a celebrated win of the Apple Computer sort. The Hillman family has been in the past a celebrated example of this type of player in venture finance. A corporate manager whose job is on the line if he makes too many mistakes is an entirely different animal.

Special methods of valuation are often applied to firms in specific industries; whether in some abstract sense the method holds water, founders and investors are bound by the customs of the day if they ultimately plan (as they usually do) to sell the firm. Thus, it is often the practice to relate the purchase price of commercial banks to book value and/or total footings.[21] Drilling and exploration companies have traditionally been linked to the estimated value of the company's reserves and financial management firms have been looked upon as acquisition candidates in terms of gross fee income, the thought being that the buyer can impose its own profit margins once it has been able to acquire the desired book of business, market share or (in the case of oil and gas) raw materials. To repeat, the issue of value is in the eye of the beholder. Market share may be a trivial asset to one inquirer and highly significant to another. Cash flow can be all-important or only a supplementary factor.[22]

§12.5 SPECIAL INVESTORS AND SPECIAL SECURITIES

There is a special compartment of the pricing issue that has to do with the identity of the investors and/or the class of security being issued. If the lead potential investor is a business corporation with an interest in the technology, turning the investment into an element in a strategy usually labeled corporate partnership[23] or strategic alliances, the foun-

[20]Some investment advisers, particularly those with volatile histories of performance, cannot understand why clients will prefer their stodgier competitors, managers whose track records suffer by comparison. What the "go go" managers fail to appreciate is that to many (particularly those who have accumulated their capital by their own efforts and wish above all to preserve it), one dollar of loss is twice as painful as one dollar of uncaptured profit.

[21]If a start-up has been able to attract above-average management, one way to "value" that intangible is to figure out the aggregate fees that would be payable to executive search firms to attract people of that caliber, apply a discount and the "value" of that tangible asset results. In seeking out competent managers for start-up firms, some experienced players predict that each $10,000 in starting salary means one month in the search.

[22]The valuation of firms in regulated industries—i.e., railroads, banks, insurance companies, public utilities—are the subject of quite specific rules. *See* McCarthy & Healey, *supra* n. 6, at 421.

[23]*See* Ch. 18, § 18.2, *et seq.*

der is entitled to assume that the investor is looking for benefits that go beyond traditional rates of return. Accordingly, in the appropriate instance, the founder can extort value for what the corporate partner sees as technological potential or other side-benefits from the alliance. To cite a typical case, if a venture capital manager is looking for a discounted rate of return of 40%, a strategic investor may be attracted at 25%. On the other hand, when negotiating with corporate investors in an early round, or indeed in any round, the founder must keep a keen eye on the time value of money. The corporate investment process is longer in many instances than the turnaround time at a professionally managed fund. Founders are often beguiled by the fact that the amount they seek is immaterial to the multinational's overall picture—true but irrelevant since the corporation is only a legal fiction, an abstraction, manipulated by the people in it. And, the investment may be a very significant element of the balance sheet of the decision-maker within the corporation. If he is wrong, the error may not cost the chairman of the board anything but it may cost the decision maker his job. Given the innately convervative tendencies of large corporations, where one mistake can derail a career, the corporate investor can stall a deal to death.

If the instrument being issued is convertible preferred or convertible debt, it is open for the founder to argue that the instrument is worth more than an equivalent amount of common. In the usual case, however, investors are unlikely to pay up for a convertible preferred when, and if, the purpose of the preferred is not to bestow a current return but to solve the founder's tax problems—the "eat'em up" preferred discussed in Chapter 5. On the other hand, an interest-bearing convertible debenture, issued in a later round when the prospects for a current yield are real and the liquidation preference has some significance, is obviously more valuable than naked shares of common stock.

Thirteen

Equity, Debt, and Hybrid Securities

This chapter outlines the types of securities most often encountered in venture finance. The discussion, which heretofore has focused on early-stage financings, expands to include some of the issues encountered in the later rounds, particularly the discussion of debt versus equity in § 13.18.

§13.1 THE "2 PLUS 2 EQUALS 5" FORMULA

As one programs a venture capital financing, the objective, as in corporate finance generally, is to make 2 plus 2 equal 5, that is, to obtain added value for the issuer. Venture capital is, as earlier indicated, a process—the financing of risky enterprises. In the course of a financing, the founder and his allies are, of course, attempting to raise the maximum amount of money for the minimum amount of equity, equity meaning claims on the residual values of the firm after its creditors have been satisfied. A corporation will issue at least one class of common stock because it must; many start-ups stop there; they pursue the simplest capital structure possible in accordance with the KISS principle ("Keep It Simple, Stupid"). However, in so doing, the corporation may close down its chances to pursue the added-value equation—2 plus 2 equals 5—because that equation involves matching a custom-tailored security to the taste of a given investor.

To be sure, the ability of a firm to reward its backers is not unlimited; it depends on the ability of the managers to develop asset values, income, and cash flow,[1] and those numbers are not affected by the makeup of the company's capital accounts. However, different investors have differing appetites for various combinations of risk and reward. If a given investor has a special liking for upside potential leavened with some downside protection, it may "pay up" for a convertible debt instrument. An investor indifferent to current returns prefers common stock. Some preferences are driven by the tax law; corporate investors must pay tax at full rates on interest but almost no tax on dividends.[2] On the other hand, the issuer of the security can deduct interest payments for tax purposes—interest is paid in pretax dollars—but not dividends. The sum of varying preferences, according to the plan, should be such that the issuer will get more for less—more money for less equity—by playing to the varying tastes of the investing population and, in the process, putting together specially crafted instruments, custom made as it were. A potential investor interested in "locking in" a return will want a fixed rate on debt securities instead of a variable rate; the ultimate "lock-in" occurs in a zero coupon bond which pays, albeit not until maturity, not only interest at a fixed rate but interest on interest at a fixed rate.

As the practice of tailoring—hybridizing, if you like—securities has become more familiar and frequent, the traditional categories can become homogenized. Preferred stock may come to look very much like common stock and debt resembles equity. In fact, the draftsmen of the Revised Model Business Corporation Act no longer distinguish between common and preferred stock.[3] Moreover, it may be advantageous (again with a view to making 2 plus 2 equal 5) to work with units or bundles of securities, meaning that an investor will be offered a group of securities, one share of preferred, one debenture, one share of common and a warrant, all in one package.

[1]Cash flow from operations is ordinarily taken to mean the sum of net income computed according to GAAP (generally accepted accounting principles), adjusted for inflows and outflows not taken into account in computing net income. Depreciation expense, for example, is disregarded because it is a noncash expense; amortization of debt is taken into account because it reduces cash even though it is not an expense for GAAP purposes. Cash flow is not, however, a precisely defined term with universal meanings. For example, cash flow is also created from special events, such as tax refunds, proceeds of insurance and, of course, financings—the inflow and outgo of loan proceeds and the net proceeds (or deficit) from trading in capital assets.

[2]Under the Act, corporations now exclude from income 80%, versus 85%, of the dividends received from other corporations. Tax Reform Act of 1986, § 611. Because of the general reduction in corporate taxes, the effective maximum federal rate of tax on dividends received actually goes down, from 6.9% to 6.8%. *Explanation of Tax Reform Act of 1986* (CCH) ¶ 274 (1986).

[3]Revised Model Act § 6.01 (Official Comment).

§13.2 COMMON STOCK

Common stock is the simplest form of equity security. It is not convertible, as a rule, into another type of security; each share enjoys one vote; dividends are payable without limit but only when declared by the board of directors; the common stock holder takes the last turn at the assets, or what is left of them, in liquidation. In a typical corporation, conversion privileges, as if obeying the Second Law of Thermodynamics, run downhill to the common; convertible securities are convertible into common either directly or indirectly, as when Series A preferred is convertible into Series C preferred, which is in turn convertible into common.

As suggested, a security called "common" stock can be complex, as complex as the draftsman wants to provide; there are no hard and fast rules except that there must be *some* class of stock with the residual voting, liquidation, and dividend participation rights. Two complex versions of common stock are frequently encountered: Class A common, which is, in fact, a form of disguised preferred without the special voting rights which some statutes require be inherent in shares labeled "preferred;" and junior common stock, a no-longer-favored security used for a time to get cheap stock into the hands of key employees at minimal tax cost.[4] Class A common, being in fact a form of preferred stock, will be discussed in § 13.4

(a) JUNIOR COMMON STOCK

In contrast to Class B common, junior common owes its existence to a short-lived venture strategy, one no longer deemed viable by most practitioners. The notion arises from the evergreen problem faced by venture-backed start-ups: how to attract superior management talent with little or no money in the treasury. The answer is, of course, to use a different type of currency—equity. The trick, as discussed throughout the Text, is how to get "cheap stock" into the hands of employees without triggering a tax. When the firm is first organized, share values being at their most speculative, it is possible to allocate shares for nominal consideration—so-called "founders' stock;" however, fresh management talent is needed in all phases of the company's march to maturity. As discussed above, the value of a common share becomes difficult to minimize for tax purposes once the shares have been traded in arm's-length

[4]A corporation may issue classes of common stock with differing voting rights and still qualify as an S Corporation, *see* I.R.C. § 1361(b)(1)(D) and (c)(4), as long as the dividend and liquidation rights of the classes are identical.

transactions.[5] Accordingly, counsel for Silicon Valley start-ups came up with the idea of junior common, an inferior class of common stock gradually succeeding to parity with the senior common. The junior common had, when issued, severely limited dividend, voting, and liquidation rights. Thus, it could (in theory at least) be assigned nominal value for tax purposes. The theory is the same as the "eat'em up" preferred approach[6] but has the virtue that it can be used at any time, even after the regular common has established its value by reason of arm's-length trades. The junior stock is "different" from the regular common and, therefore, a low tax valuation is not embarrassed by the trading price of the common. After a period, perhaps tied to the achievement of certain benchmarks, junior common is convertible into regular common. Since conversion from one security to another is not usually deemed to be a taxable event,[7] the idea is that cheap founder's stock could be issuable at any time. There would be no tax on issuance because "value" for tax purposes had been driven down (by the limitation on dividends, voting and liquidation) and conversion was tax-free.

The inevitable assault on junior common was expected from the I.R.S. and, as of this writing, a published position is still under consideration that would tax the spread upon conversion—fair value minus conversion price. The issue was generally mooted, however, when the accounting profession[8] opined (i) that the issuer should recognize as compensation expense the initial difference between the price paid for the junior stock and the fair value of the regular common and (ii) that additional compensation expense be recognized quarterly as the value of the regular common advanced. This effectively nullified the junior common technique since a hit to earnings of that magnitude is unsupportable. There may be a revival if the Fair Accounting Standards Board (F.A.S.B.) reverses its ground,[9] but the I.R.S. remains to be heard from.

[5]*See* Ch. 5, § 5.1(c). A variation on the theme of junior common stock is contemplated by a "haircut" plan, pursuant to which stock is issued to employees at a discount from current value, say, $10, and is only salable by them back to the company at that discount, the thought being that no taxable bargain element is entailed upon issuance. *See* Aufmuth, "Selected Tax and Accounting Issues in Early and Mezzanine Financings and Venture Capital Partnerships," *Venture Capital After the Tax Reform Act of 1986* 55, 79 (P.L.I. Course Handbook Series No. 422, 1987).

[6]*See* Ch. 5, § 5.1(c).

[7]I.R.C. § 1036(a). Section 305(c) appears to be limited to adjustments in the conversion price of *preferred* stock. I.R.C. § 305(d). Several issuers offered junior common stock through incentive or nonqualified stock option plans. Kimpel, "Compensation Planning for 'High Tech' Executives," *Tax Planning for High Tech and New Ventures* (70th Forum, Fed'l Tax Inst. of New Eng., 1984) (Forum).

[8]FASB Interpretation No. 38, interpreting APB Opinion No. 25, applies to all junior common issued after Mar. 14, 1984.

[9]*See* "FASB Accounting for Stock Plans—Update," 10 *Corp. Comm.* 1 (Jan.–Feb. 1985).

§13.3 WARRANTS

*A warrant is, like an option and a conversion privilege, a right to buy a security at a fixed (or formula) price: the "exercise" or "strike" price. A warrant is, in effect, a short-term option and, although often issued in connection with another security—debt with warrants attached—it ordinarily can be, by its terms, traded as an independent security. In contrast, an option, in venture capital usage at least, is usually long-term (up to 10 years) and personal to the holder because the typical recipient is an employee. A conversion right is a right to purchase stock which is inherent in another security—that is, a preferred stock or a debenture—and its characteristics are fixed in part by the security on which it is a parasite. All three labels refer to something which is, itself, a security.[10]

Generally, neither the issuance of warrants nor their exercise (at least by nonemployees) is a taxable event.[11] The I.R.S.'s earlier position that the expiration of a warrant occasioned a tax on the issuer was reversed by Congress in 1984 with the passage of I.R.C. § 1032(a).[12] However, whenever a debt security with warrants attached is issued as a package, original issue discount problems are invited.[13]

For a time, a popular financing device used by emerging companies starved for cash and business contemplated the issuance of contingent warrants, which become exercisable if and when the holder does something for the issuer, buys a given level of product, for example. That device is no longer as attractive, since the S.E.C. has ruled in favor of current and periodic recognition of expense to the issuer.[14]

For accounting purposes, a warrant, like an option, is considered a "common stock equivalent" and, if it has been "in the money" (i.e., exercise price below market price) for three consecutive months, is deemed

[10]The definition of "security" in § 2(1) of the'33 Act includes the right to buy another security. There is a question in some contexts whether a conversion privilege is to be considered a separate security.

[11]Siegel, "Venture Capital Financing: Selected Federal Income Tax Considerations for Venture Capital Investors," in *Forum, supra* n. 7, at 198. The exercise by an employee of a security styled a "warrant" which is actually a nonqualified stock option, (because issued in connection with the performance of services within the meaning of § 83(a)) presumably would occasion a tax on the difference between the strike price and fair value. *See* Ch. 11, § 11.3(b).

[12]The thought was that the issuing corporation had received consideration which, upon expiration of the right, was not an addition to equity and, therefore, had to be taxable income.

[13]*See* Ch. 19, § 19.13(c).

[14]SEC *Staff Accounting Bulletin* 57, (CCH) 6 Fed. Sec. L. Rep. ¶ 74,507 (July 18, 1984). That Bulletin requires that, once it has become likely that the warrants will become exercisable, a "cost" of the warrant be determined equal to the issuer's stock price as of that time minus the exercise price and that cost allocated to the cost of the products sold (i.e., a "hit" to earnings).

to impact earnings per share under the so-called "treasury stock" method—that is, the warrants are deemed exercised, new stock issued at the exercise price and the proceeds to the issuer used to buy in stock at the market price.[15]

§13.4 PREFERRED STOCK[16]

Preferred stock comes in various shapes and sizes, depending on the intent and desires of the planners. Assuming it is so authorized in the charter, the board of directors may fix the rights, preferences and privileges of the preferred—, a practice creating what is known as "blank check" preferred.[17] There are virtually no limits on the board's authority to frame a mosaic of rights and call the same a "preferred" stock.[18] Some of the reasons to prefer (pardon the pun) preferred stock as a financing device have been discussed elsewhere in the Text—that is, the "eat'em up" preferred which makes possible price differentials between prices paid for stock by the investors and the founders.[19] An overriding reason is convenience: Although it is possible to work with other devices, it is particularly handy to use preferred stock as a mechanism to adjust the relationship between the cash and noncash investors; that is, to create specific rights in the cash investors such as special voting rights, antidilution protections, control shifts, "supermajority" veto provisions and the like. A preferred stock can either be voting, nonvoting, or voting only upon certain issues, or upon the happening of certain events. In the case of the convertible preferred customarily issued in a venture

[15]*See* APB Opinion No. 15 and AIN–APB Opinion No. 15 para. 51.

[16]Much of the literature on preferred stock arises in the tax context, the issue being the so-called preferred stock "bail-out" of existing shareholders at capital gains rates by creating and distributing, with respect to the common pro rata and therefore tax-free, a class of redeemable preferred stock which would be held for the requisite period, then be sold by the recipient at a long-term gain to an institutional investor and, finally, redeemed. The result would be to distribute excess earnings at the tax-favored (prior to the Tax Reform Act of 1986) rate. Section 306 of the Code was enacted in 1954 to close the loophole. With the elimination of the distinction between income and gains, it is not likely that tax planners will focus on § 306. However, § 305 remains a problem because it can create a taxable event when stock is distributed to stockholders or a change is effected in the rights of a given class of stock. *See* § 13.6 *infra.*

[17]*See* Ch. 4, § 4.10.

[18]The board resolution is incorporated in a certificate usually called a "certificate of determination," which is filed as an amendment to the charter. Once the board has fixed the rights, however, it may be difficult under state law to provide for subsequent adjustments by the board. *See* Cohen & Shapiro, "Types of Securities" and Harroch, *Start-Up Companies: Planning, Financing and Operating the Successful Business* § 8.02 [4] n. 22 (1986). State securities administrators may object to "blank check" preferred. *See* Ch. 14, § 14.9(a).

[19]*See* Ch. 5, § 5.1(c).

financing, it is the norm to provide that the preferred votes *pari passu* with the common as if it has been converted.

The traditional notion of preferred stock encompasses a share that takes its "par" value in liquidation before the common gets anything (infrequently a meaningful privilege) and has a preferred call on the earnings of the corporation during its life in the form of a regular dividend. A "preferred" dividend implies a *fixed* dividend payable at regular intervals; if the dividend is not declared for any reason (perhaps illegality, if and to the extent sufficient earnings or surplus are not available), it "cumulates," meaning arrearages must be paid in the future before any dividend or liquidating distribution can be paid on inferior classes of stock, such as common. (Unlike interest, cumulative dividends are usually not augumented by an incremental additional payment keyed to the period during which they remain unpaid—interest on interest.) If cumulative dividends are passed for several periods, it is often (but not necessarily) provided that a "default" occurs and something automatically happens, usually in the form of the preferred shareholders getting additional seats on the board. "Participating" preferred is preferred that may or may not enjoy a fixed dividend but in any event participates in excess earnings *pari passu* (or on some other formula) with the common shareholders.

Cumulative dividends expressed in cash terms are not common in start-ups. The idea of paying cash dividends at all makes no sense to some entrepreneurs (e.g., Kenneth Olson at Digital Equipment) because the transaction is ultimately dilutive if and as the issuer, in effect, retrieves the capital paid out in dividends by issuing more stock. More importantly, immature companies often do not have the cash with which to pay dividends.[20] Noncumulative dividends, meaning dividends paid only if, as, and when declared by the board, are the venture capital norm. Indeed, the disclosure document in a preferred stock venture financing often contains a caveat to the effect that the dividends are not only noncumulative, it is "unlikely" the directors will declare them at all. A start-up may, however, distribute future calls on earnings by providing for regular or irregular dividends on the preferred payable in stock, either preferred or common. This is one method of adjusting equity percentages based on performance of the company; if the founders have been missing targets, the board may be able to compensate

[20]To the extent the preferred shares do carry a dividend, corporate shareholders must concern themselves if the dividend is deemed "extraordinary" (generally more than 5%) and the stock is sold within two years. I.R.C. § 1059, amended by the Tax Reform Act of 1986, § 614, in effect provides for a tax to the seller on that portion of the dividend which: (i) escaped tax under the dividend exclusion concept, § 243 of the Code, and, (ii) is deemed "extraordinary." The idea, of course, is to prevent corporate shareholders from disguising gain on the sale of their shares as dividends, the latter being largely tax-free.

the investors by voting the preferred some additional stock.[21] The problem of creating "Section 306 stock" may not be serious since, after 1987, the holder will (with certain exceptions) not care that his or her capital gain has become ordinary income.[22] However, § 305(b) and (c) can create taxable events when a corporation distributes stock to its stockholders in a disproportionate way.[23]

The preferred's liquidation preference is not normally the occasion for much discussion in a start-up financing because none of the interested parties believe that distributions in liquidation of a venture-backed start-up or LBO will extend beyond the secured and unsecured creditors. On occasion, however, venture-backed companies may liquidate with proceeds available beyond the creditors' claims. Indeed, in insolvency proceedings involving substantial assets, something is usually thrown to the stockholders even though the creditors get less than 100 cents on the dollar. (The plan gives lip service to the "rule of absolute priority" in bankruptcy by giving the creditors cash plus securities "valued" at 100 cents, leaving something left over with which to bribe the shareholders not to fight.) In such instances, the preferred liquidation preference may be significant. The preference also becomes significant if the issuer is merged into another company. The founder may argue that the preferred should be required to convert or be automatically converted prior to the merger—the merger is an "exit" vehicle. The investors, on the other hand, will argue that a sale of the company yielding an attractive price to the common stockholders will cause them voluntarily to convert; they are entitled to protection, on the other hand, if the proceeds are so meager that they do not cover the liquidation preference.

Automatic conversion on the eve of an IPO is usually less controversial. Indeed, as indicated earlier, it is often necessary to clean up the balance sheet and cancel various special rights peculiar to separate classes of stock if an IPO is to occur at all; those counsel who have survived a multiparty negotiation, in which the holders (perhaps including former employees who simply detest the company) must be cajoled into converting, can testify to the value of automatic conversion.

§13.5 CONVERSION AND REDEMPTION

A nonconvertible preferred is rarely encountered in the venture universe, where the idea of an unlimited "upside" drives the hopes and

[21] Such dividends are often no more than an irritant to hard working founders and, when a disaster occurs, wind up as the equivalent of additional deck chairs on the *Titanic*.
[22] *See* I.R.C. § 306. One exception is if the shareholder has capital losses in excess of $3,000. Since the distinction between capital gain and ordinary income remains, albeit not the differing levels of tax, capital gains are useful to set against excess capital losses.
[23] *See infra* § 13.6.

designs of the participants. Accordingly, most preferred is convertible into common stock. Conversion means giving up one security—the preferred in the example—and receiving in return another, the so-called "conversion" stock, which is, in the typical case, common. There can be intermediate steps in the process—Class C preferred convertible into Class A preferred, which is convertible in turn into common—if the draftsman have some reason to collect various classes of preferred into a single class prior to conversion into common.[24]

Conversion is in many ways equivalent to the sale of the existing security and the purchase of the conversion stock; a preferred (or, more likely, a debenture) with warrants attached gets the holder to the same place as a convertible preferred—ultimate acquisition of the conversion shares at the price paid for the security initially purchased. The principal distinction between stock with warrants attached and convertible stock is that the conversion privilege is viewed as "inhering" in the security itself, a defensible conclusion in the sense that the privilege cannot independently trade. A warrant, on the other hand, can be (and usually is) detachable from the security it originally accompanied, if indeed it was attached to any security in the first place. A warrant can, accordingly, be bought and sold on its own. One of the consequences of this distinction has to do with holding periods. The holder of a share of convertible preferred or debt is, for purposes of Rule 144, viewed as holding the conversion shares while, and for as long as, he holds the convertible security. Thus, if a holder has owned the convertible security for two years or more, and is not an "affiliate," he can convert and sell immediately within the restrictions of the rule.[25] The holder of debt with warrants attached must wait for two years after he redeems the debt and exercises the warrants to sell the underlying stock.[26]

Since a conversion right is a "heads I win, tails you lose" option in favor of the security holder, one which he will rationally hold until the last possible minute, the issuer naturally likes to mandate conversion as soon as possible. One way to force conversion is to include a right of redemption in favor of the issuer. If the convertible stock is more valuable than the exercise price—or "strike" price as it is called—then

[24]Under the'33 Act, the term "security" includes a "warrant or right to subscribe to or purchase" another security.'33 Act, § 2(1). Conversion stock (the stock to be received on conversion) is not deemed to be "sold" along with the convertible security for purposes of the'33 Act if the conversion privilege is not immediately exercisable,'33 Act, § 2(3). The exchange of the conversion stock for the convertible stock is an exempt *transaction* under § 3(a)(9) of the'33 Act but the conversion stock is restricted stock. The scheme under state law may be quite different, § 401(i)(5) of the Uniform Securities Act providing that the conversion stock is "sold" along with the convertible stock even if conversion is postponed.

[25]*See* Ch. 14, § 14.11.

[26]The holder could sell the debt security and the warrants together, of course, but that unit is usually not the class of stock publicly registered. The issue of the taxation of preferred stock redeemable at a premium under I.R.C. § 305 is discussed at § 13.6.

rational holders will convert in the face of a call. That option is not, however, the most realistic; start-ups lacking the cash may have no credible way to carry through on the threat to redeem. Accordingly, as earlier indicated, the preferred way to get rid of the preferred is to provide that the preferred is converted automatically upon the occurrence of certain events (or the lapse of time). Automatic conversion, however, deprives the preferred stockholder of his choice.

In some financings, the preferred is redeemable at the option of the holder, not the issuer. The purpose of this provision is to allow the investors to exit after the passage of time if no other opportunity (i.e., an IPO) has been presented or if results are disappointing. Whether the redemption option means much in practice is open to question, but it may inadvertently cause problems, as when the preferred is reclassified as debt for various purposes (perhaps invoking penalties under the local usury statute).

For accounting purposes, convertible securities—whether stock or debt—are viewed as "common stock equivalents" and, therefore, deemed converted for both the calculation of "primary" earnings per share and "fully diluted" earnings per share unless the yield—dividends or interest—is more than two-thirds the bank prime rate.[27] Convertible preferred in the venture context rarely satisfies this test and thus impacts earnings per share under both tests, unless the effect of a deemed conversion would be antidilutive.[28]

§13.6 "UNREASONABLE" ANTIDILUTION AND REDEMPTION PROVISIONS UNDER SECTION 305

(a) ANTIDILUTION

A potential surprise for the holders of convertible preferred is suggested by the provisions of I.R.C. § 305(c) concerning taxable "deemed" distributions when changes occur in the conversion ratio or, as covered in the next Section, the redemption price. The statute and Regulations suggest that a taxable event has occurred in the event of a change in the "conversion ratio" of convertible preferred other than (i) a change to take account of stock dividends and splits and (ii) changes pursuant to a "bona-fide, reasonable adjustment formula (including, but not lim-

[27]AIN–APB 15 Opinion No. 26. The yield test, calculated in terms of cost under APB Opinion No. 15, has been modified to an "effective yield" test. FASB Statement No. 85.

[28]A deemed conversion of a convertible security could be antidilutive—i.e., could *increase* earnings per share by dint of the hypothetical event—if either the conversion price is in excess of market price or the yield on the security is greater than the issuer's earnings per share. The rules for avoiding an artificial boost to earnings per share are complex. AIN–APB Opinion No. 15.

ited to, either the so-called market price or conversion price type of formula) . . . which has the effect of preventing dilution."[29] Query what this language means. One example in the Regulations[30] entails the "weighted average" formula and another[31] cites what looks like a "full ratchet" antidilution provision. What formula would *not* be deemed bona fide remains unclear; the statutory language focuses on events which alter the "proportionate" interests of certain shareholders in the corporation's "earnings and profits," presumably meaning provisions which give the preferred holders more stock at the expense of the founders if, for example, the founders miss targets in the business plan. Some practitioners believe this provision can be neutralized; the most obvious method would be explicitly to limit the operation of the adjustments to periods when the corporation has no earnings and profits.[32]

(b) REDEMPTION PREMIUMS

If a redemption premium is deemed an excessive or "unreasonable" redemption premium, then the excess will be considered as the distribution of additional stock constructively received by the shareholders over the period of time during which the preferred cannot be called for redemption;[33] the redemption premium provisions do not state clearly whether the vulnerable preferred stock is stock redeemable at the option of the holder or the issuer, or both; the use of the term "call premium" throughout the Regulations, suggests that, at least, redemption at the option of the issuer is included.[34]

The principal issue under § 305(c) concerns attempts to plan around the Regulations. Assume that the deal between the founders and the cash investors is that the preferred has a "put" to the company and the redemption premium increases if and to the extent the founders fail to meet their goals. If the preferred is made callable immediately, it would appear, for no discernible reason, that § 305(c) does not apply.

[29]Treas. Regs. § 1.305–7(b)(1). It appears that § 305(b)(4) applies only in the event of actual distributions of stock to the holders of preferred stock but, if so, it is unclear why this section mentions changes in conversion ratios. If changes in conversion ratios are contemplated by § 305(b)(4), what is its relation to § 305(c)?

[30]Treas. Regs. § 1.305–3(d)(1)(ii).

[31]Treas. Regs. § 1.305–7(b)(2).

[32]Dreyfus, "Structuring the Venture Capitalist's Investment for Optimum After-Tax Results," 65 *J. of Tax'n* 6, 7 (July 1986).

[33]A "reasonable premium is one "not in excess of 10% of the issue price on stock which is not redeemable for 5 years." Treas. Reg. § 1.305–5(b)(2).

[34]The notion of a redemption premium on stock redeemable at the option of the holder is inconsistent with the traditional reasons for redemption premiums but, were one encountered in practice, it is likely it would be considered, *a fortiori*, a form of bail-out. *E.g.*, Treas. Reg. § 305–5(b)(2). *See* Dreyfus, *supra* n. 32, at 8.

§13.7 DEBT SECURITIES

Start-up founders are not customarily interested in an arrangement for obtaining early stage-capital from investors which requires current interest payments[35] since positive cash flows are not usually forecast in the beginning years. However, in later rounds of financing, a promise to pay a current rate of interest is sufficiently appealing to certain investors so that dilution can be minimized; the tradeoff may favor some form of debt. Moreover, if a start-up requires an emergency infusion of funds, the existing investors are the logical (and sometimes the only) source; in that event, the preferred shareholders may opt for a higher priority status for their fresh money, electing in a dicey period, when the future of the firm is in particular doubt, to advance cash as creditors rather than shareholders. In such event, the investors may demand warrants as well, one typical formula being that an advance in the nature of a "bridge" financing (bridging the company over a difficult period) entitles the lender to "50% warrants." This formula means that one-half the capital loaned divided by the exercise price of a single warrant (which is usually the current fair value of a share of common stock plus, in the case of a long-term warrant, a premium) equals the number of warrants to be issued.

Since a start-up is not yet a solid, credit-worthy performer, the debt securities issued by it are usually hybrids, a cross between equity and debt, meaning at least that the debt is convertible into equity at the option of the holder in order to soup up the expected return to the lender to compensate for the additional risk. Indeed, as part of the risk equation the obligation may be expressly subordinated to the claims of creditors in order to give the struggling company room to put on a better face to its trade creditors and, on occasion, commercial lenders. A subordinated convertible debt security instinctively raises questions whether the security will be recognized as "true debt" when and if the question arises—that is, in an insolvency proceeding[36] or if the I.R.S. elects to challenge the deductibility of interest payments. (A note of caution: Any issuance of debt securities to a wide number of holders requires a review of the Trust Indenture Act;[37] the private offering exemption under that Act is not coextensive with the Regulation D exemption.)[38]

[35]LBOs are in a special compartment of venture finance. *See* Ch. 19.

[36]*See* Ch. 19, § 19.8.

[37]15 U.S.C. § 77(a) *et seq.*

[38]*See, e.g.*, Nussbaum, Hyde, & Christal, "Federal Securities Laws Considerations," in *Acquisitions and Mergers 1986: Tactics, Techniques and Recent Developments* 409 (P.L.I. Course Handbook No. 529, 1986).

§13.8 DEBT VERSUS EQUITY

As long as corporate earnings distributed to stockholders are taxed twice while interest payments to creditors are deductible to the corporate debtor, there will exist a controversy over the nature of a given financial instrument—is it debt or equity?[39] In addition to the question of the deductibility of interest under § 163 of the Code, the issues involve, *inter alia,* nontaxability to the recipient of principal repayments and the dividends-received credit under § 243 of the Code.

Two principal sections of the Code specifically address the issue of debt versus equity—Section 279, dealing with "corporate acquisition indebtedness" in excess of certain amounts, and Section 385, which authorizes the Treasury to issue Regulations on the subject generally. Section 279 has not proven to be particularly influential even in the context of leveraged buyouts because its "bright line" rules are relatively easy to plan around.[40] Section 385 is relevant because it names some of the factors which the Treasury "may include among other factors" in drafting the Regulations. However, no such Regulations, despite extended proposed drafts (indeed, drafts in "final" form), have become effective.[41]

The issue is of great importance in corporate tax planning generally, including but not limited to venture capital financings. The problem is that the learning, absent authoritative Treasury action, must be drawn from a melange of contested cases, and no clear pattern has emerged from the court decisions. The following remarks, accordingly, summarize some of the points to keep in mind without purporting to outline a foolproof guideline for the planner.

Thus, certain fact situations, as is always true in the law, are easy. Some obligations are clearly debt[42] and other clearly equity—no need to go into a lengthy analysis. However, the gray area is wide since there

[39]The potential consequences are gathered in a first-rate review by Bowers, "Debt-Equity Classification: Where Are We Now," in ALI–ABA and ABA Section of Taxation, *Corporate Tax Planning in the 80's* 139–200 (1986).

[40]For example, § 279 does not apply unless the acquisition debt is issued by the acquiring corporation. In an LBO, if the transaction is structured so that the target is the borrower, redeeming its stock with the proceeds of the loan, § 279 is not an issue. Moreover, § 279 by its terms only applies to large deals, transactions with annual interest payments in excess of $5 million.

[41]There is an argument that one version inadvertently was allowed to become effective. *See* Bowers, *supra* n. 39, at 157.

[42]The issue is not only when ostensible debt is to be considered equity but, on occasion, the reverse—when should a "preferred stock," so labeled, be considered a debt instrument, particularly preferred stock which is redeemable at the option of the holder. *See* Siegel, "Venture Capital Financing: Selected Income Tax Considerations for Venture Capital Investors," in *Forum, supra* n. 7, at 189.

are a number of features of a financial instrument which bear on the question.

One approach which judges and influential commentators have used in considering the issue, is subjective: What did the parties intend, with the intention of the parties to be distilled from various objective factors deemed material in shedding light on the question. Another approach, one the Treasury provisionally adopted in its "final" regulations under § 385, is to test all factors which are deemed pertinent and then add them up in a given case, measuring in a supposedly objective way which direction the preponderance of the factors points. Although the "multiplicity of factors" approach is consistent with the language of § 385,[43] the mechanical nature of the test helped it self-destruct when the Treasury realized the weird instruments the fertile minds of tax planners would be able to contrive (e.g., ARCNs[44]) to avoid the thrust of any mechanical test. Another view, popular for a time, focused only on one feature—the debt-to-equity ratio[45]—but that single-minded test, albeit easy to apply, proved too simplistic to cover the varied fact situations arising in practice.

Justice Potter Stewart once said about obscenity that it was difficult to describe but he knew it when he saw it; debt versus equity may be in the same category. Nonetheless, it is incumbent on the organizers of Newco to try to predict how the Service or a court will react to a given set of facts. The threat in the venture capital context remains real. The challenge by the Service to the early rounds of financing in Federal Express resulted in a happy ending, a first-rate opinion which upholds the debt features of a classic venture financing;[46] the alarming point is that the Service saw fit to bring the proceeding in the first place.

[43]The timid suggestion by the drafters of § 385 is that the Treasury "may" want to include references to the following factors:

unconditional promise to pay,
fixed maturity on demand,
fixed principal and interest,
subordination,
debt–equity ratio,
convertibility.

[44]ARCNs are adjustable-rate convertible notes. Interest is keyed to the dividend rate the issuer is paying on its common stock and the call price is set so as to make it almost certain the holder will convert. *See* Bowers, *supra* n. 39, at p. 156. In the Revenue Ruling in which the Service opined that ARCNs are equity, the language suggests the instruments will probably be converted into equity. Rev. Rul. 83–98, 1983–2 C.B. 40 ("under most likely eventualities they will be converted.") That position, although defensible in context—the ARCNs were issued at $1,000 per and paid only $600 at maturity—could be a mischievous invitation for courts to play investment banker. A first-class District Court opinion suggests the courts will not follow that lead. *Federal Express Corp. v. U.S.* 86-2 USTC 9793, 58 AFTR 2d. ¶86-6247 (D. Tenn. 1986).

[45]Caplin, "The Caloric Count of a Thin Incorporation," 17 *N.Y.U. Inst. Fed. Tax* 771 (1959).

[46]*Federal Express Corp. v. U.S., supra* n. 44.

Unfortunately, all that can be said for certain is that the following factors (based on the holdings in the cases, common sense and economic realities) will be taken into account. How much weight is given to each remains an open question:

Is the instrument labeled a debt instrument?

Is there a fixed maturity date?[47]

Does the holder enjoy the typical creditors' remedies?

Is the payment subordinated to other indebtedness?

Is the interest rate competitive?

Is interest fixed or contingent, that is, payable out of earnings?[48]

Does the holder have the right to participate in the venture, that is, a board seat?

Is the putative debt secured?

Is the holder's interest in the issuer's debt proportionate or disproportionate to his stock holdings?

Is the instrument convertible into equity or sold in a package with warrants attached?

Have payments in fact been made on the debt? Has it gone into default without attempts to enforce the rights of the creditors?

What is the ratio of debt to equity, herein of "thin capitalization?"[49]

Are there any sinking fund or serial payment provisions?

Have the creditors and the debtors adopted consistent filing positions?

Is the debtor "bankable," in the conventional sense?[50]

Are any outside creditors loaning on comparable terms?

Are the proceeds used to acquire "capital" assets? (For some reason, this has persuaded some courts that the transaction involves equity capital.)[51]

[47]A demand note has a fixed maturity in a sense if the reviewing court can forecast the likelihood that the creditor will call the note. *See* Bowers, *supra* n. 39, at 166.

[48]Some instruments obviously qualify as debt even without an interest component or a formal note—i.e., trade payables.

[49]At one time, the Service established 5 to 1 as the outer limit for offshore finance subsidiaries. *See* Bowers, *supra* n. 39, at 179.

[50]A loan made when the company is first organized is naturally subject to greater scrutiny. *See Post Corp. v. United States* 640 F.2d 1296 (Ct. Cl. 1981).

[51]*See* Bowers *supra* n. 39, at p. 183.

Is the instrument so structured that there will be a "compulsion to convert?"[52]

The mere recitation of the factors indicates the complexity of the issue. Indeed, the seminal commentary is 271 pages long.[53] In close cases, it may often be impossible to forecast with confidence how a given instrument will be treated and the lesson is, accordingly, to try to avoid creating instruments which will give rise to close questions. (As Justice Holmes said, hard cases make bad law.) When, as and if the Treasury finally acts, it may adopt the approach of creating safe harbors, at least defining what planners can count on as debt. In such event, presumably the government draftsmen will be more liberal than they were in the case of S Corporations, where the safe harbor excludes convertible debt entirely.[54]

[52]Contrast this articulation of the test with the earlier "under most likely eventualities" standard discussed in n. 44 above. *See* Willens, "Debt or Equity? Pronouncements Clarify Status of Convertible Debentures," 16 *Tax Advisor* 707 (1985).
[53]Plumb, "The Federal Income Tax Significance of Corporate Debt: A Critical Analysis and a Proposal" 26 *Tax L. Rev.* 369 (1971). For a recent case listing several of the factors, *see Texas Farm Bureau v. U.S.* 1732 F.2d 437 (5th Cir. 1984).
[54]I.R.C. § 1361(c)(5).

Fourteen

The Initial Public Offering—Herein of "IPOs"

The initial offering of an issuer's securities to the public is usually a watershed event, an achievement of a goal the founders have sought since inception. The transaction is not, however, an unmixed blessing—as the discussion in this chapter will illustrate, a number of considerations should be evaluated before an issuer takes the plunge. Much of the material in this chapter is technical but all parties should review at least § 14.2.

§14.1 BACKGROUND

The initial public offering, routinely abbreviated as the IPO, is a familiar financing device; almost every public company has had an IPO.[1] How-

[1]Some companies become public other than by virtue of a public distribution of their securities. A series of private placements may create enough shareholders—500—so that the corporation must register under § 12(g)(1)(B) of the '34 Act. The ebb and flow of IPOs is charted in a periodical called *Going Public: The IPO Reporter,* published by The Dealer's Digest; founders interested in the ebulliency of the market can get a feel for the current temperature by examining that publication, which tracks, among other things, the price–earnings ratios at which offerings are then being brought to market. One problem for the founder, of course, is that conditions may have changed, sometimes dramatically, by the time his offering is ready to become effective.

ever, the maturity of companies offering securities to the public for the first time started to shrink in the late 1960s as new and unseasoned issuers tested the waters.[2] A new breed of underwriters—Charles Plohn was the 1960s paradigm—grew up to produce for public consumption shares in early-stage companies, on occasion before the issuers had seen their first quarter of black ink. Public finance became a viable option for companies that needed cash to stay in business. "Go bankrupt or go public?" was the jocular question founders would ask themselves in that rising, rambunctious market. IPO in this sense means more than the first public offering. In the venture capital context, it means the culmination of the "exit" plan, the date on which the shares held by the founder, employees, and investors will become liquid and their plan to cash in their chips will approach fruition.[3]

While many of the 1960s underwriters (and more of their clients) are no longer in being, the phenomenon persists. As one might expect, fast-rising markets are fertile ground for IPOs. The volume lessens, but not to zero, in down markets; many of the underwriters which grew up to service the IPO market have not only survived but flourished—Hambrecht & Quist is a prominent example.[4] Moreover, access to the process for first-time issuers has been simplified with the adoption in 1979 of the Form S–18,[5] available for offerings by nonpublic issuers not in excess of $7.5 million. Hence, the IPO option is in front of almost all early-stage companies—not the best option in every case, but one that requires consideration.

§14.2 WHETHER OR NOT TO "GO PUBLIC"

There are two major issues facing a start-up considering an IPO: how to do it most effectively and, secondly, whether to do it at all. The second is the threshold question:[6] Will the issuer be able to raise capital cheaply

[2]One commentary suggests that the SEC's continual bias in favor of public registration, as repeatedly expressed in the Staff's distaste for the private offering exemption (at least until the advent of Regulation D), was an impelling force behind the debut of many start-ups in the public markets. Goldwasser & Halperin, "Introduction to Public Offerings," in *Private and Small Business Offerings* 215 (P.L.I. Course Handbook Series No. 386, 1982).
[3]As Dr. Wang puts it, an IPO is "a rite of passage for entrepreneurial high tech companies." Wang, *Lessons: An Autobiography* 141 (1986).
[4]In a macrosense, the long-term trend is adverse. The number of smaller, regional underwriting firms, traditionally the backbone of the IPO process for issuers below the elite top layer, is shrinking. *See, e.g.*, O'Flaherty, *Going Public: The Entrepreneur's Guide* (1984). In their place, however, are springing up so-called "boutique" underwriters, spinoffs from major investment banking houses, mostly located in New York and exploiting specific niches. *See* Ch. 6, § 6.10, n. 28.
[5]Sec. Act Rel. No. 33–6049 2 (CCH) Fed. Sec. L. Rep ¶ 6038A (1979).
[6]On this issue, *see generally* Prifti, *Securities: Public and Private Offerings* § 1:10–1:13; Lewis, *Taking a Private Company Public* 7 (1984).

and more efficiently on the wings of an IPO than with any other method, taking into account the long-range consequences of becoming a public company?

On the plus side, the culture of venture capital is heavily involved with the proposition that the terms "public company" and "rich entrepreneur" are synonymous. Indeed, the home-run payoffs for celebrated founders are usually identified with a public stock sale. A public market entails (although not for everybody)[7] liquid securities, a classic exit strategy for founders and other shareholders. Moreover, to the extent equity is being raised for corporate purposes, the price of capital obtainable from the public will usually be cheaper because any commodity that can be freely sold is intrinsically more valuable than its illiquid counterpart.

There are collateral benefits as well, beyond price and liquidity. Thus, the company's stock is often purchased by its customers and suppliers and their interest in the company's profits and products is stimulated. A public company can do a broad national public relations job; a well-prepared prospectus projects the company's image favorably from the start. A public market helps stockholders with their estate tax problems,[8] it allows them to diversify, and it simplifies appraisal problems. And, the company now has so-called "Chinese Currency" with which to make additional acquisitions, meaning shares selling at a high multiple of earnings and, therefore, preferable to cash when buying other companies.

There are, however, significant minuses. For example, an IPO takes time; the issuer and underwriter need 60 to 90 days to get ready and the period between filing with the SEC and the effective date takes at least another month or so. Many an issuer undergoes the time-consuming and expensive process,[9] only to see the process abort at the last instant because the IPO "window" has closed; if the issuer has counted on the proceeds of an IPO, the result can be a disaster. Moreover, there are significant transaction costs. Underwriters can receive up to 15% (more or less) of the price of the offering; legal and accounting expenses

[7]*See* Ch. 9, § 9.3(c).

[8]Privately held securities in a decedent's estate may have to be sold at an unfavorable price because the estate needs cash to pay federal and estate taxes. One commentator suggests, however, that the valuation of securities by an auction market restricts the ability of the estate to value stock "creatively" for tax purposes. Lewis, *supra* n. 6, at 10.

[9]One of the most time-consuming chores can be a necessary clean-up of awkward rights in the hands of various categories of shareholders. A private company that has gone through multiple rounds of financing may have created several classes and/or series of stock, all with differing rights (including registration rights). To present an understandable balance sheet to the public, the issuer must often prevail on all shareholders to surrender their unique perquisites unless issuer's counsel has had the prescience to require that all special classes automatically convert into one class of common upon the pendency of an initial public offering.

can bring the total costs up to 25% of the money raised.[10] Fees and expenses involved in private placements, on the other hand, are ordinarily well under 10%. Moreover, once the issuer is public, a number of new legal requirements attach to the conduct of its business.[11] Thus, a public company has to file periodic reports with the SEC (quarterly[12] and annually[13]) plus flash reports when significant events occur.[14] The thrust of these documents is financial, letting the auction markets know how the company is doing on a short-term basis, in itself a potential problem for a management which is unconvinced that the market's avarice for short-term results is a sensible business strategy.[15] The annual meeting becomes a major event—proxies are solicited with an expensive, printed information document complying with the SEC's proxy rules,[16] the disclosure heavily oriented toward exposing managements's compensation package in a manner that suggests key executive compensation is one of the principal clues for analysts to unravel in judging corporate performance[17] (a curiously puritanical view since private analysts' reports seldom mention top management compensation as a principal benchmark of a firm's prospects). Beyond the required reports, the public company[18] must give daily consideration to current

[10]Goldwasser & Halperin, *supra* n. 2, at 220.

[11]Under the Tax Reform Act of 1986, a 50% change in the ownership of a company's stock in a three-year period entails a reduction in the company's ability to carry forward net operating losses unused in prior periods. I.R.C. § 382. The rules are enormously complex and the possibility exists than an IPO could occasion that result inadvertently. Schrotenboer, "How The 1986 Tax Reform Act Changes the Tax Rules for High Technology Companies," 66 *J. Tax'n* 88,91 (Feb. 1987).

[12]Form 10–Q.

[13]Form 10–K.

[14]Form 8–K. There are other statutes which impact on public companies—*e.g.*, Foreign Corrupt Practices Act of 1977, 15 U.S.C. §§ 78(m) *et seq.*, which requires public companies to keep books and records in stated ways. Moreover, a small issuer taking in a lot of cash in an IPO must be on guard that it does not become an "inadvertent investment company." *See* Investment Company Act of 1940, Rule 3a–2.

[15]The bias of the SEC in favor of current disclosure may have, as do most government initiatives, unintended side-effects. According to many economists, since public companies must report short-term earnings, they are often managed with a view to the short term. Stock prices fluctuate on the basis of short-term performance, institutional investors hop in and out of the stock and, in the minds of some critics, the Japanese clean up at our expense by emphasizing the long term. *See* Magaziner & Reich, *The Next American Frontier* 140 (1983).

[16]Regulation 14A and Schedule 14A.

[17]Schedule 14A, Item 8. Compensation arrangements in a private company may be established in accordance with oral understandings, which have to be ferreted out by counsel and reduced to writing, or at least disclosed with particularity, once the company goes public.

[18]Information not called for by one of the prescribed SEC reports (absent insider trading) can probably be withheld without incurring liability. *See SEC v. Texas Gulf Sulphur Co.* 401 F 2d 833 (2d Cir. 1968); Proposed Federal Securities Code § 1304, comment 33. But *see Financial Industrial Fund, Inc. v. McDonnell Douglas Corp.* 474 F.2d 514 (10th Cir. 1973).

disclosure of important events. As yet, the courts have not required instant press releases; absent insider trading, issuers are not, explicitly at least, required to go beyond compliance with the SEC's periodic (monthly on certain issues, otherwise quarterly and annually) disclosure rules,[19] but that position is eroding.[20] Thus, the New York Stock Exchange[21] lectures issuers on the desirability of instant news and special exceptions to the general rule threaten the company's ability to remain silent (e.g., a duty to correct false rumors).[22] Further, a public company is exposed to "strike suits," litigation initiated by underemployed lawyers ostensibly on behalf of a shareholder (usually with an insignificant stake) but in fact designed to corral legal fees. The courts countenance such claims because they are thought to have therapeutic value,[23] restraining management excesses in an era when the public shareholders are otherwise disenfranchised. Finally, a public company can be taken over by a raider in a hostile tender. It is possible to insert so-called "shark repellent" measures in the charter prior to the IPO—supermajority provisions, staggered boards, "blank check" preferred stock—but the underwriters may balk and some state administrators are hostile.[24]

Difficult rules also impact individuals associated with a public company: the directors, officers, and major shareholders. They are, for example, subject to a curious rule which recaptures any profit—called "short swing" profit—they realize on sales and purchases of the company's stock matched within a six-month period.[25] The statute becomes

[19]Form 8–K requires disclosure of certain major events within 10 days after the close of the month in which they occur and states that the registrant "may" report any other developments it "deems of importance." Form 8–K, Item 5.

[20]*See generally* Block, Barton, & Garfield, "Affirmative Duty to Disclose Material Information Concerning Issuer's Financial Condition and Business Plans," 40 *Bus. Law.* 1243 (Aug. 1985). Disclosure of pending merger discussions and tender offers may occupy special status. Wander, "Timely Disclosure: Fall 1986" in *18th Annual Institute on Securities Regulation,* 447 (P.L.I. Course Handbook Series No. 544, 1986).

[21]*New York Stock Exchange Company Manual* Pts. I and II; *American Stock Exchange Company Guide* Part 4, § § 401–405. NASD By-Laws, Sched. D. Pt. II (B)(3)(b), *NASD Manual* (CCH) ¶ 1653A at 1139–40.

[22]The cases are split on the issue whether a public company has a duty to correct false rumors not of its own making. *See* Sheffey, "Securities Law Responsibilities of Issues to Respond to Rumors and Other Publicity," 57 *Notre Dame Law.* 755 (1982).

[23]There has been what some have described as a backlash against "strike suits" in recent years, spurred by Supreme Court decisions restricting the plaintiff's freedom of action in securities litigation. *See, e.g., Blue Chip Stamps v. Manor Drug Stores* 421 U.S. 723 (1975) (limiting standing in 10b–5 actions); *Ernst & Ernst v. Hochfelder* 425 U.S. 185 (1976); ("scienter" required in 10b–5 actions); *Int'l Brotherhood of Teamsters v. Daniel* 439 U.S. 551 (1978) (certain interests not a "security").

[24]*See infra* § 9.9(a). The recent Supreme Court decision upholding the Indiana "control share" statute, *C.T.S. Corp. v. Dynamics Corp. of America,* 55 U.S.L.W. 4478 (April 1987) may make the hostile tender less threatening for companies able to domesticate in a state with a statute of that ilk.

[25]'34 Act, § 16(b).

hard to follow at the margin,[26] and its consequences are severe. Moreover, the threat that an insider will be deemed to have traded on "inside information" means that insiders can safely trade only during specified "window" periods, that is, immediately after the annual or quarterly reports come out; in a curious sense, insiders are no more liquid than they were before the IPO.

Moreover, apart from formal requirements, the onset of a public venue can be embarrassing. The Antar family, when it sold 1 million common shares of Crazy Eddie, Inc.[27] to the public, had to disclose that the family had been virtually using the company as a private bank. Spendthrift Farms, the breeding stable owned by the Combs family, is now in the process of liquidation. When stock was sold to the public, a number of insider dealings between the family and the stable were revealed. Apparently those practices continued after the company became public, litigation ensued, and the result has been a more or less forced liquidation.[28]

(a) PREPARATION FOR THE PUBLIC OFFERING

The planning steps prior to a public offering are outlined in a number of source materials, emphasizing the increase in formality involved in the transition from a private to a public company.[29] Some of the less obvious points which deserve mention have to do with corporate structure. The requirement that the financial statements be audited is well known. However, issuers on occasion forget that the recent acquisition of a significant,[30] unaudited subsidiary may make it impossible to present the requisite audited financials when desired. Moreover, it is often necessary to recapitalize the enterprise. Cross-ownership arrangements must be eliminated and multiple affiliates consolidated so that the public buys an interest in all the eggs, contained in a single basket. Some IPO candidates, veterans of multiple financing rounds, have as many as eight series of preferred stock outstanding. If an IPO does not, by its

[26]For a sampling of commentary and decisions on § 16(b), *see* "SEC Interpretive Release on Rules Applicable for Insider Reporting and Trading," Sec. Act Rel. No. 34–18114, 4 (CCH) Fed. Sec. L. Rep ¶ 26,062 (Sept. 23, 1981); Loss, *Fundamentals of Securities Regulation*, 609-12 (1983 and Supp 1986); *Reliance Electric Co. v. Emerson Electric Co.* 404 U.S. 418 (1972); *Kern County Land Co. v. Occidental Petroleum Corp.* 411 U.S. 582 (1973).

[27]Jacobs, "Taking It To The Street: Going Public Can Mean Debt Free Financing But There Are Other Costs to Consider," *Wall St. J.*, May 19, 1986, at 31d

[28]Crist, "Spendthrift, Once The Pride of Kentucky, Is Humbled" N.Y. *Times*, June 2, 1986, Section C, p. 6, Col. 1

[29]Ernst & Whinney, *Deciding To Go Public* (1984); Goldwasser & Halperin, *supra* n. 2; O'Flaherty, *supra* n. 4.

[30]The term "significant subsidiary" is defined in Regulation S-X, Rule 1-02, to include subsidiaries comprising 10% or more of the issuer's assets or income.

terms, trigger conversion, negotiations are in order to clean up the balance sheet and make it understandable to prospective investors.

§14.3 FORM S–18

The burden of public registration for small issuers was alleviated in 1979,[31] when the Securities and Exchange Commission adopted simplified Form S–18 for the registration of offerings by an issuer, the offering price of which does not exceed $7.5 million.[32] S–18 is superior to the basic form for registering public securities, Form S–1, because it requires only an audited balance sheet as of the end of the company's last fiscal year and statements of changes in financial position and stockholders equity for the last two fiscal years.[33] In contrast, the full blown form used by unseasoned issuers—Form S–1—requires audited balance sheets for the prior *two* fiscal years and income statements for the prior *three* years.[34] Moreover, S–18 financial statements need not comply with Regulation S–X but only with GAAP (generally accepted accounting principles).[35] This can be a significant saving in effort and expense since the office of the SEC's Chief Accountant has enshrined in Regulation S–X over the years idiosyncratic views on accounting with which some members of the accounting profession heatedly differ.

Finally, Form S–18 can be filed and processed in the SEC's local regional offices, a potential advantage when Washington is, as usual,

[31]Sec. Act Rel. No. 33–6049, *supra* n. 5, revised by Sec. Act Rel. No. 33–6489 [Transfer Binder 1983–84] (CCH) Fed. Sec. L. Rep. § 83,430 (Sept. 23, 1983).

[32]Form S–18 may be used for secondary offerings as long as the aggregate price of the secondary issue does not exceed $1.5 million and the entire issue $7.5 million. Form S–18, General Instructions, I(B). As with any rule that puts a maximum cap on the dollar amount of securities to be sold, there are questions concerning integration—i.e., which prior or subsequent sales of securities are to be included for purposes of calculating the $7.5 million cap? *See* Ch. 7, § 7.13.

[33]One interesting problem with the more limited financial reporting under S–18—i.e., not requiring Regulation S–X financials—is that, once the company is "effective" (the registration statement has been cleared by the SEC), it becomes subject to the '34 Act reporting requirements. Accordingly, the annual SEC filing on Form 10–K may require S–X financials for a year in which S–18 does not.

[34]Form S–1 requires "Financial statements meeting the requirements of Regulations S–X," Form S–1, Item 11(e), which means (Rule 301) audited balance sheets as of the end of the two most recent fiscal years and income statements (Rule 302) for the last three years. Forms S–2 and S–3 are available for more seasoned issuers.

[35]Form S–18, Item 21(a)(1). *See* Bloomenthal, *Securities Law Handbook* § 6.10 (1984). S–18 is now available to partnerships, a helpful addition since the Tax Reform Act of 1986 favors the partnership mode. *See generally* Manegold, Arnold, & Diamond, "SEC Form S–18: A Boon to Small Business: Practice Expansion Opportunities in Helping Small Businesses Go Public," 161 *J. Acct.* 102 (May 1986).

overburdened.[36] Regional processing had been unique to Regulation A offerings[37] and the obsolescence of that exemption as a practical matter can be traced, in part, to the redundancy on this point with S–18 filings.

§14.4 SELECTION OF ACCOUNTING PRINCIPLES

If a registrant has consistently used a particular method for reporting its certified results as a private company, it is unlikely that a change will be made on the eve of IPO to a more favorable accepted method since the required disclosure would include a disclosure of the pro forma effects and certain changes (from LIFO to FIFO for example) require that statements for the prior periods be restated—"to alter accounting principles just before going public is short sighted."[38] However, if accountants are being hired in anticipation of an IPO to audit the financials for the first time, the financing may prove to be the occasion for arranging the financial statements (particularly the income statement) to reflect the rosiest picture consistent with GAAP.

The issue ripest for consideration in many instances will be the treatment of software development expenses—should they be capitalized or expensed currently? The question is not trivial. The distinction can make the difference between a profit vs. loss. The rule set out by the Fair Accounting Standards Board is that costs incurred in establishing the technological feasibility of a product are to be expensed and costs incurred thereafter capitalized; the generality of the Rule leaves room, however, for discretion.[39] Other elections in gray areas include the matching of income and expense when payments are received for products (i.e., software programs) which include substantial ongoing service obligations.[40]

For tax purposes, accounting methods have traditionally been elected which minimize current income. For shareholder reporting purposes, on the other hand, immediate recognition has been deemed preferable

[36]Form S–18, General Instructions II. In fact, many issuers do not bother to take advantage of this privilege, preferring the "devil they know" in the Washington office.

[37]*See infra* § 14.12.

[38]Marver, "Planning the Business for a Future Initial Public Offering," in Harroch, *Start-Up Companies: Planning, Financing and Operating the Successful Business* § 21.07 (1986 ed.) A change in accounting principles affects mainly the issues of consistency and comparability—past financials *vis-à-vis* current financials. APB Opinion No. 20, "Accounting Changes" (July 1971) generally governs the issue.

[39]FASB Statement 86, "Accounting for the Costs of Computer Software to be Sold, Leased or Otherwise Marketed." The SEC has imposed a moratorium on the capitalization of certain software costs. Regulation S–X, Rule 3–21.

[40]To match the ongoing expense of customer maintenance and support, a reserve should be established when the income is recognized. Munter & Ratcliffe, *Applying GAAP and GAAS* § 10.12[4][b] (1987).

for obvious reasons. However, the Tax Reform Act of 1986 provisions respecting the difference between tax and book income will now impact this issue significantly.[41] It may be preferable to time book and tax losses, to the extent possible, so they *coincide*—versus diverge—in order to avoid the possibility of an alternative minimum tax.

§14.5 THE PROSPECTUS

The principal disclosure document in a public financing is the prospectus,[42] that portion of the registration statement distributed to offerees and investors. The checklist for describing the company and the offering in the prospectus is Regulation S–K,[43] directly applicable to Form S–1 and S–18 Registration Statements.[44]

The preparation of the prospectus is, in one sense, easy.[45] The first cut at drafting entails selecting a comparable prospectus relating to a security already public and marking it up, using the magic of optical scanning devices and word-processing machinery to take the drudgery out of the chore. Moreover, the preparation of the prospectus is governed by specific SEC advice—Regulation S–K and the instructions on the form used (S–1 or S–18)—which give relatively precise directions as to the topics to be covered in the document and, on occasion, how to cover them: for example, "Describe the general development of the business . . . during the past five years . . . describe the business done and intended to be done by the registrant and its subsidiaries, focusing upon the registrant's dominant industry segment."[46] The road map for prospectus drafting is well defined; even a first-time draftsman should have little concern that something has been totally overlooked if he studies the precedents carefully.

To do the job properly, however, it is useful to ponder what it is the SEC is trying to accomplish. Thus, the intended thrust of Regulation

[41]I.R.C. § 56(f). In light of this provision, private companies may elect to eschew certified statements and keep only one set of books. Will the accountants bless tax statements?

[42]The term "prospectus" occurs in § 5 of the '33 Act, making it unlawful to sell securities unless "accompanied or preceded by a prospectus" which meets the statutory requirements.

[43]Housekeeping details and certain substantive rules (*e.g.*, definitions of terms used in the forms), are contained in Regulation C, promulgated under the '33 Act.

[44]Regulation S–K, Item 10(a)(1).

[45]On prospectus writing, *see generally*, Hellman & Hoffman, "What to Look for in a Stock Prospectus," 72 *Am. Bar Assoc. J.* 96 (Apr. 1986); Jones & Hund, "Filing SEC Registration Statements: A View from the Inside," 157–158 *J. Acct.* 92 (Dec. 1984); Orlanski, "SEC Comments on the Offering Prospectus," 17 *Rev. of Sec. Reg.* 887 (June 1984); Schneider, Manko, & Kant, "Going Public: Practice, Procedure and Consequences," 25 *Corporate Practice Commentator* 89 (Spring 1983); Bloomenthal, Harvey, & Wing, *1985 Going Public Handbook: Going Public, the Integrated Disclosure System and Exempt Financing* (1985).

[46]Regulation S–K, Item 101(2) & (c)(1).

S–K is to reduce the amount of boilerplate which had crept into the document—to make the prospectus informative. For some time, the Commission has been criticized by commentators (including a perennial scold named Homer Kripke[47]) for the fact that disclosure in unregistered placements is ordinarily more meaningful than the ritualistic language in statutory prospectuses, thereby standing the whole thrust of securities regulation on its head and opening the regulators up to their most feared criticism—irrelevance; the markets would function better without them. Tired of rainy weather, the SEC legislated sunshine in Regulation S–K and the instructions to forms S–1 and S–18, attempting to reduce formalistic disclosure and put meat on the bones of the statements made. For example, the Regulation now requires a section entitled, "Management's Discussion and Analysis of Financial Condition and Results of Operations" (MD&A),[48] in which the SEC tries to hold management's feet to the fire, requiring the type of candor one would expect in a Question and Answer session between the issuer's chief financial officer and security analysts. The Regulation calls for mention of such matters as "trends . . . that are reasonably likely to result in the registrant's liquidity increasing or decreasing in any material way . . . [and] unusual or infrequent events . . . that materially affected reported income."[49]

In considering how to phrase the language, one should also keep in mind a canon from which the SEC has never retreated, that public disclosure documents should be decipherable by a nonexpert, a layman.[50] It is true, as critics point out, that more than 75% of the action in the public markets is the result of professionals trading with professionals. Moreover, the Commission has undergone a major reorientation in its attitude toward disclosure by mature public companies, allowing issuers which report periodically to the public to cannibalize those reports for purposes of assembling a registration statement covering newly issued securities.[51] Nonetheless, where new entrants to the public markets are concerned, the SEC has not accepted the thesis that a document which gives up its secrets to sophisticated analysts constitutes adequate disclosure. The prospectus must be drafted with that attitude in mind—

[47]*See generally* Kripke, *The SEC and Corporate Disclosure: Regulation in Search of a Purpose* (1979); Kripke, "The SEC, The Accountants, Some Myths and Some Realities," 45 *N.Y.U. L. Rev.* 1151 (Dec. 1970); Kripke, "Has the SEC Taken All the Dead Wood Out of Its Disclosure System?" 38 *Bus. Law.* 833 (May 1983).

[48]Regulation S–K, Item 303. The SEC has recently issued a "concept release" calling for comments on various revisions to the MD&A sections. Sec. Act Rel. No. 33–6711. [1987 Transfer Binder] (CCH) Fed. Sec. L. Rep. ¶ 84,118 (Apr. 17, 1987).

[49]Regulation S–K, Item 303(a)(1) & (3).

[50]*See* Sec. Act Rel. No. 33–3453 (CCH) 1 Fed. Sec. L. Rep. ¶ 3935.11 (Oct. 1, 1952).

[51]*See* Form S–3; Rule 415, discussed in Prifti, *supra* n. 6, at § 5:13.

coherent information assembled coherently—not only an informative but a "readable" document.[52]

While prospectus writing is an art which does not require years of expertise to master (the plethora of prior examples allowing one to plagiarize shamelessly from the work product of others), that is not to say that experience is immaterial. The behind-the-scenes byplay centers around anticipating the comments likely to be made by the SEC staff (assuming, as is likely to be the case with an IPO, the prospectus is subject to "full review"), thereby shortening the length of the "letter of comment" and, more importantly, the comment period. Counsel's primary obligation in preparing an IPO (after making sure the presentation is accurate) is to get the registration statement effective as quickly as possible; market "windows" for IPOs come along every now and then and it is up to the participants to get the issue out on the street before the window closes. Thus, if the first draft of the prospectus asserts, without more, that the issuer is the "leading manufacturer" of widgets in the country, the SEC staff will routinely respond: "prove it." If the "Use of Proceeds" section is composed of routine language (i.e., "working capital") the staff will try to extort greater specificity. Unfortunately, the staff does not publish its letters of comment. Some source materials have, however, reproduced sample letters[53] and a survey of those materials will give a sense of the staff's favorites.

Some information the staff may zero in on can be confidential—the selling price of the issuer's products to major customers, for example, and the issuer will attempt to persuade the staff such is not necessary for a complete presentation. Formally requesting confidential treatment is open to the registrant[54] but that course of action still leaves sensitive information in a government file, where Freedom of Information requests may uncover it;[55] hence, informal persuasion is the preferred course. No amount of persuasion, however, is likely to eliminate certain sensitive disclosures mandated by Regulation S–K (e.g., the name of any customer representing 10% or more of the issuer's business).[56]

No matter how carefully the prospectus is prepared, an IPO must await the letter of comment and, other than nagging telephone calls, there is nothing the issuer can do but wait for it. Once a registration statement has been filed, within a couple of days (not more than four),

[52]Loss, *supra* Ch. 7, n. 13, at 261–265.

[53]For example, *see* Lovejoy, "SEC Comment Letter," in Halloran, *supra* Ch. 1, n. 16, at 669–676. If the staff's comments are so extensive that a material amendment must be filed under SEC Rule 15c2-8, then revised versions of the preliminary prospectus must be circulated, an expensive process. Lewis, *supra* n. 6, at 64.

[54]Rule 406 sets out the procedure, including the need for a "detailed" explanation why the information is not necessary for the protection of investors.

[55]*See* Rule 406(d).

[56]Regulation S–K, Item 101(c)(1)(vii).

a staff member will adivse whether or not it will be reviewed. Registration statements not to be reviewed can be effective in as short a period as 48 hours; IPOs are routinely subjected to review and a first-time registrant can expect a 25- to 30-day period before receiving staff comments.[57] Once the letter is received and responded to, then the procedure is to ask (two days in advance)[58] for effectiveness at a particular date and time, a practice known for technical reasons as a "request for acceleration."[59] Acceleration is conditioned on a widespread circulation of the preliminary, or "red herring,"[60] prospectus (so-called because there is a legend in red on the preliminary prospectus) among the selling group. Under a new rule, Rule 430A,[61] it will no longer be necessary to file the amendment filling in the price of the security and waiting Commission clearance; the registration statement may now be declared effective and the price (and discounts and syndicate members) filled in within five days.

§14.6 PROJECTIONS

Regulation S–K sets out the SEC policy on projections, which is to "encourage" the use in public reports of "management's projections of future economic performance that have a reasonable basis and are presented in an appropriate format."[62] Rule 175 under the '33 Act and Rule 3(b)–6 under the '34 Act discuss the presentation of "forward looking statements," including projections, in periodic reports and provide a safe harbor from liability unless the statements are shown (the burden of proof is on the plaintiff) to be without "reasonable basis" or not "in good faith."[63]

Despite the SEC's encouragement, issuers have not widely taken advantage of the safe harbor; in part influenced by case law which can be read to say that "good faith" implies a belief that the projections are based on facts that make their achievement highly probable.[64] Moreover, Regulation S–K suggests that projections, once published, must be corrected if they "no longer have a reasonable basis" and[65] registrants

[57]Palm, "Registration Statement Preparation and Related Matters," in *Mechanics of Underwriting* at 130 (P.L.I. Course Handbook Series No. 547, 1987).

[58]Rule 461 requires advice of the effective date not later than "the second business day" before the effective date.

[59]On acceleration, *see generally* Loss, *supra*, n. 26 at 277–283.

[60]For the origins of the "red-herring prospectus" *see id* at 187–189.

[61]Sec. Act Rel. No. 33–6715, [1987 Transfer Binder] (CCH) Fed. Sec. L. Rep. ¶ 84,130 (May 27, 1987).

[62]Regulation S–K, Item 10(b).

[63]In fact, the "Risk Factors" section is composed of "forward looking" statements, albeit of a negative nature. Regulation S–K, Item 503(c).

[64]*Beecher v. Able* 374 F. Supp. 341 (S.D.N.Y. 1974).

are encouraged "not to discontinue . . . projections in Commission filings without a reasonable basis."[66] In other words, once one undertakes the project, it appears there may be a duty to keep the projections up to date and to continue the practice *ad infinitum*, an obligation that most start-ups will cheerfully eschew.[67] Moreover, while (as previously noted) professional venture investors are usually interested in long-range projections, the Commission appears openly skeptical of that time frame. Regulation S–K discusses "some" companies in which projections beyond one year are "unreasonable" and, from the language used, two to three years of projections appear to be about the limit of reasonableness in the SEC's view.[68] In short, the language in Regulation S–K, despite its talk of "encouragement," illustrates throughout an underlying caution on the part of the Commission, a gut feeling that projections are inherently dangerous.

The tension between the SEC's continuing and underlying fear of projections and the professional investor's keen interest[69] is highlighted by the situation in which an IPO rapidly follows a late-round financing. The private placement memorandum for the financing will often be full of material—for example, five-year projections, appraisals—which the prospectus will omit. The question is whether the issuer commits a legal wrong by failing to include such patently material information in the prospectus?[70] The landmark case on the issue of materiality, *TSC Industries Inc. v. Northway, Inc.*,[71] is not dispositive since the materiality is a "facts and circumstances" test. The issue is discussed more fully in § 9.8 above.

§14.7 LIABILITY

Disclosure in an IPO is inextricably bound up with the issue of liability: who, and under what circumstances, repays the investors if there has

[65] Regulation S–K, Item 10(b)(3)(iii).
[66] Id. at Item 10(b)(3)(iv).
[67] Regulation S–K, General Introduction, Item 10(b)(3)(iii) states that the responsibility to correct errors may "extend" to situations when projections (published in reliance on the SEC's policy of "encouraging" their use) are no longer "reasonable"; *See Ross v. A.H. Robins Co., Inc.* 465 F. Supp. 904 (S.D.N.Y.) 1979), *rev'd on other grounds* 607 F.2d 545 (2d Cir. 1979), *cert. denied* 446 U.S. 946 (1980).
[68] Regulation S–K, Item 10(b)(2).
[69] The distinction has at least one substantive explanation. Venture investors view long-range projections, in part, as promissory on the part of management, a standard to be used in judging and compensating management. There is little possibility that the professional investor could be misled into thinking the projections are guaranteed.
[70] *See* Bartlett, "Legal Issues in Late Round Financing," in *Venture Capital After the Tax Reform Act of 1986* (P.L.I. Course Handbook Series No. 422, 1987).
[71] 426 U.S. 439 (1976).

been a material misstatement or omission which impacts the postoffering price of the stock? The issuer is, for all practical purposes, absolutely liable under § 11 of the '33 Act[72] but the issuer may be unable to respond. The directors, as signers of the registration statement, have a heavy burden, which stretches to all those who, under § 12,[73] may be considered "participants" in the sale (i.e., insiders and promoters who participate in the transaction).[74] In fact, counsel may be liable if intimately involved in the preparation of the materials;[75] even major shareholders can be caught.[76] Moreover, underwriters are expressly liable, subject to a so-called "due diligence" defense,[77] under § 11 and experts (e.g., lawyers and accountants) are liable for errors in the "expertised" portions, meaning the legal opinions and certified financial statements. The issues are complicated by the fact that, in dealing with liability, plaintiffs have access to a multiplicity of liability-creating provisions: for example, Sections 11, 12(2) and 17(a)[78] of the '33 Act and § 10b and Rule 10b(5) under the '34 Act.[79]

The threat of liability bites most sharply in an *initial* public offering, when all the information about the issuer is being presented for the first time. Choking off liability if the stock price plunges after the effective date requires counsel and the underwriters to execute a defensive game

[72]Section 11 imposes liability for false registration statements on every person who signed the registration statement, the directors, the accountants, and the underwriters. '33 Act, § 11(a)(1). An interesting question is whether members of an issuer's scientific advisory committee can be held liable as persons "performing similar functions" to directors. § 11(a)(2). The so-called "due diligence" defense, set out in § 11(b), is not available to the issuer.

[73]Section 12(2) extends liability to any person selling a security "by means" of a false prospectus. '33 Act § 12(2). The underwriting agreement will require that an income statement be made public covering the 12 months following the effective date in order to shift the burden of proof from the issuer and the underwriters to the plaintiff. Bloomenthal, Harvey, & Wing, *1985 Going Public Handbook, supra* n. 45, at Appendix p. 18.

[74]*E.g., Klein v. Computer Devices Inc.* 591 F. Supp. 270 (S.D.N.Y. 1984); *SEC v. Nat'l Student Marketing Corp.* 457 F. Supp. 682 (D.D.C. 1978).

[75]*See generally* Cheek, "Professional Responsibility and Self-Regulation of the Securities Lawyer" 32 *Wash. & Lee L. Rev.* 597 (1975).

[76]*See generally,* Ferrara & Sanger, "Derivative Liability in Securities Law: Controlling Person Liability, Respondeat Superior, and Aiding and Abetting," 40 *Wash. & Lee L. Rev.* 1007 (1983).

[77]The leading case on the "due diligence" defense established a very high level of care, *Escott v. BarChris Construction Corp.* 283 F. Supp. 643 (S.D.N.Y. 1968); *see also, Feit v. Leasco Data Processing Equipment Corp.* 332 F. Supp. 544 (E.D.N.Y. 1971); "Remedies for Defrauded Purchases," 12 *Rev. of Sec. Reg.* 953 contains a useful discussion of § 12(2) and the "due diligence" defense.

[78]Currently there is division of authority whether a private right of action lies based on § 17(a).

[79]*See generally* Bloomenthal, *Securities Law Handbook, supra* n. 35, at Chs. 10–17; Prifti, *Securities: Public and Private Offerings supra* Ch. 7, n. 1; Bloomenthal, Harvey & Wing, *1985 Going Public Handbook, supra* n. 45, at Ch. 7.

plan, designed to convince a judge and jury that they had vetted the required disclosures with the requisite care. There is no one source which will outline to the issuer and the underwriters how far the diligence of their management and advisers should proceed. Some law firms prefer to work from a checklist and, indeed, the NASD once composed a 16-item list as a minimum standard,[80] but it was never adopted. A contrary view is held by those who believe that a checklist is a Christmas present to the plaintiff's lawyer, affording him an opportunity to inquire why certain items have been omitted. The most widely cited case, the *BarChris* decision[81] is a learned opinion by a former name partner of a prestigious Wall Street firm, who set up standards which even the most diligent counsel would find hard to meet.

In the abstract, of course, elegant due diligence is a "motherhood" issue. Thus, one commentator suggests "counsel should consider making checks on the reputation and experience of its officers, including ordering Dun and Bradstreet and Proudfoots' reports. . . . The Company's directors should be investigated as well as the management."[82] Practitioners in the field, however, may find academic procedures beyond the practical.

One relatively inexpensive way to limit exposure is to write an expansive and gloomy "risk factors" or "special factors" section.[83] Regulation S–K requires a "risk factors" recitation "if appropriate" and specifies that, if one is included, it should appear immediately following the cover page or summary.[84] In a venture-backed IPO (as in a private placement[85]), such a section is almost always "appropriate." Language calculated to avoid lawsuits is also appropriate in the so-called "MD&A" section, in which Regulation S–K requires "Management's Discussion of and Analysis of Financial Condition and Results of Operations."[86] Since that discussion calls for disclosure of "trends," "forward looking information . . . [such as] future increases in the cost of labor and materials" and oxymorons such as "known uncertainties," the opportunity

[80]NASD Notice to Members 73–17 (Mar. 14, 1973).

[81]*Escott v. BarChris Construction Corp. supra* n. 72. For comment on Judge MacLean's opinion, *see* Folk "Civil Liabilities under the Federal Securities Acts: The BarChris Case," 55 *Va. L. Rev.* 199 (1969).

[82]2 Haft, *Venture Capital and Small Business Financings* § 6.04[8] (1987 ed.).

[83]Some critics feel that a "cold and negative" narrative . . . kills the . . . unreasoning faith so essential in the heart of the investor in new enterprises. Garrett, "Venture Capital Financing Under the Securities Law," Address to National Venture Under the Securities Law," Address to National Venture Capital Association, *SEC News* 12 (June 3, 1975). The analogy is made to the effect on the marriage rate of full disclosure before the ceremony. *Id.* at 13. Other commentators, including the author, believe the effect of generic "risk factors" language is not significant.

[84]Regulation S–K, Item 503(c).

[85]*See* Ch. 8, § 8.3

[86]Regulation S–K, Item 303.

is squarely faced for throwing in cautionary language likely to help contain subsequent litigation by identifying all the possible negative contingencies. The artist will play the "two-handed" game: "on the one hand, competition is increasing while on the other we think our product stands out."

§14.8 SOFT INFORMATION

An issue of interest in the context of an IPO concerns the "soft" information[87] contained in the private placement memorandum and/or the business plan utilized in prior exempt rounds of financing. As indicated, it is customary for the placement memorandum to contain projections, indeed long-term projections, extending over five years. Morever, with an audience of sophisticated investors, management can be extremely candid about the prospects for the business, divulging information which might be viewed as indiscreet if made available to the public. In fact, a number of business plans will contain confidential information—for example, marketing strategies, receptivity of key customers to the product, test results and other proprietary information; such information is protected generally by requiring that each recipient of the placement memorandum execute a confidentiality agreement, obviously an impossibility in an IPO. With that soft information in being, the question arises whether the issuer has an obligation to repeat the gist of it in the prospectus accompaning the IPO.

In analyzing this issue, a number of shifting contexts must be carefully kept in mind. For example, the question of conflict of interest, or *cui bono,* will influence the analysis. The disclosure of soft information is almost always under the control of management. If management elects not to disclose soft information and nondisclosure *benefits* management, then a court will be much more likely to second-guess management's election. Thus, if management is initiating the buyout of a public corporation's shares in a "going private" transaction, any ebullient forecasts about the future of the company will be difficult to withhold; management has an inherent conflict of interest in a "going private" transaction and reticence about the company's glowing future

[87]Soft information has been defined by Carl Schneider as nonfactual items dealing with

> reflections on managerial quality; predictions and forecasts; opinions and beliefs; legal uncertainty; plans, proposals, and negotiations; and motives, purposes, and subjective intentions.

Schneider, "Soft Information—Counseling on Disclosure," *18th Annual Institute on Securities Regulation* Vol. 2 at 351 (P.L.I. Course Handbook Series No. 544, 1986). The distinction between hard and soft information is not exact. Thus, the historical financial statements contain predictions to the extent that estimates of the useful life of assets which form the basis of the depreciation deductions are, in effect, forcasts of future events.

will be viewed, naturally, with a jaundiced eye.[88] Similarly, in an IPO any *negative* soft information should certainly be made a part of the public disclosures.

However, that is not the likely issue. The question involves optimistic information—opinions that the company is on the verge of a breakthrough technologically, projections that show a steep ramp-up in earnings in the years following the IPO, promising results from Beta-tests and indications of interest from customers not yet signed up. The issue before the draftsman is whether the existence of that rosy material in the prior offering documents must worm its way into the prospectus.[89] As earlier indicated, the current state of the law suggests that soft information generally need not be disclosed but the leading cases on point[90] may no longer be reliable. Those cases have generally held that optimistic soft information need not be disclosed but the opinions themselves have noted that the law is in the process of transition.[91] Moreover, the Commission has made it clear that information about a public company is transmitted to the investment community through a variety of different channels and has expressed the view that those channels should be consistent.[92] The Commission has expressed concern about the practice of management's taking one posture about the company's prospects, in, say, the context of labor negotiations and another with the investment community. Understanding that analysts pick up information anywhere they can find it, the Commission has indicated its growing displeasure with public statements to the newspapers that a given company will go bankrupt absent union concessions while increased progress in reducing deficits is cited in the annual report.

[88]Rule 13–(e)(3) Item 9, requires management to furnish any reports, opinions, or appraisals from outside parties to the shareholders considering a "going private" offer.

[89]If the private placement memorandum and/or the business plan was incorporated as an exhibit to the Stock Purchase Agreement covering a private financing and that Agreement was entered into not more than two years before the IPO, it is arguable that Regulation S–K, Item 601(b)(10), requires the documents be filed as part of a "material contract." Once such a filing has been made, then it may be difficult to support the view that the information contained in the documents as filed can be kept from the publicly distributed prospectus.

[90]*E.g., Starkman v. Marathon Oil Co.* 772 F. 2d 231 (6th Cir. 1985); *Flynn v. Bass Brothers Enterprises, Inc.* 744 F.2d 978 (3d Cir. 1984)

[91]In the *Bass Brothers* case, *supra* n. 90, at 986-87, the 3d Circuit said:

> Recently, there have been indications that the law, in response to developing corporate trends, such as the increase in mergers, has begun to favor more disclosure of soft information. In this regard, we note that SEC policy—a primary reason courts in the past have not required the disclosure of soft information—has begun to change. With respect to disclosure of projections of future earnings, the SEC in 1976 deleted future earnings from the list of examples of potentially misleading disclosures in the note which follows Rule 14a–9. More importantly, in 1978 the SEC issued a safe-harbor rule for 'forward-looking' statements such as future earnings, made in good faith. . . .

[92]Sec. Act Rel. No. 33–6504 (Jan. 13, 1984) 2 (CCH) Fed. Sec. L. Rep. ¶ 23, 120B.

Presumably the reason the issue has not yet arisen in a litigated IPO case is that, assuming the omitted information is favorable, the plaintiff will be, by definition, someone who claims he would have bought the security offered had he known of the withheld soft data. A plaintiff of this sort faces substantial standing and reliance problems.

§14.9 BLUE SKYING THE IPO: SUBSTANTIVE REGULATION BY THE "MERIT" STATES

As discussed in Chapter 7, the most significant issue in state securities (or "blue sky") law is "merit regulation," meaning the authority in a given state securities administrator to deny permission to sell securities in the state if he deems the offering to be less than "fair, just and equitable."[93] The "merit" states impose a different standard than the federal disclosure standard, local bureaucrats delving into the substance of the offering's terms on the theory, pioneered in California,[94] that some sales should be intercepted regardless of full disclosure. The system bites heaviest, of course, on IPOs, where the "unseasoned" nature of the security leads regulators to believe that the need for *in loco parentis* protection is the strongest. Massachusetts's puzzling denial of the right of the Apple Computer IPO to go forward in that state is a prime example.[95] To be sure, private placements are theoretically subject to merit screening as well; they are inherently no more nor less "fair" than IPOs. However, counsel for the issuer are usually able to find exemptions in the local version of the federal private offering exemption[96] or avoid the sticky state by eschewing offers or sales therein. IPOs are not generally exempt from scrutiny and it is usually harder to pass over important commercial states if the issue is to be successfully disseminated.[97]

[93]Section 306 of the Uniform Securities Act of 1956 allows for "merit" standards in the area of underwriters' compensation and promoters' "profits or participations." Unif. Sec. Act § 306(a)(F). A majority of states have adopted regulations with merit standards.

[94]*See* Sobieski, "The Uniform Securities Act," 12 *Stan. L. Rev.* 103 (1959).

[95]Perez, *Inside Investment Banking* 35 (1984). There has been a backlash in some states against the administrators attempting to require IPOs to conform with their idiosyncratic views. *See*, Halloran, "Problems of High Tech Offerings," *Blue Sky Laws: State Regulation of Securities 1985* 511, 518 (P.L.I. Course Handbook Series No. 473, 1985).

[96]*See* Ch. 7, § 7.10(b).

[97]Because registration in the merit states is so often painful, a high premium is placed on some kind of exemption if possible—*e.g.*, instantly listing the securities on a national stock exchange in order to take advantage of the exemption in many states for "listed" securities. The American Stock Exchange has in the past instantly listed the securities of a first-time issuer otherwise meeting the requisite standards. The National Associates of State Securities Administrators (NASSA), in the belief that a carte blanche exemption for listed securities is an insufficient safeguard, has suggested that the "listed security" exemption be replaced. Sowards & Hirsch, *Business Organizations–Blue Sky Regulation* 4–128.6 (1982). The effort has not, to date as yet, gotten off the ground.

The process of "blue skying" an issue involves extended discussion—indeed even negotiation—between the issuer and its counsel and the staff in the various states on a variety of issues, discussed below. The regulators are schizophrenic: They want worthy offerings to be available in their states (the Apple Computer ban was an embarrassment in Massachusetts) but deem themselves specially equipped to negotiate fairer terms. The process is a game of continual parry and thrust.[98] To illustrate the foregoing, the Appendix to this chapter sets forth a sample response from a "merit" state, in the nature of a first letter of comment on an IPO, which gives a sense of what issuers and their counsel are in for.

(a) COMMONLY RAISED ISSUES[99]

Of the issues which usually concern "merit" regulators, perhaps the thorniest is regulation of so-called "cheap stock." Cheap stock is usually defined as an equity security issued (i) by a company still in the promotional stage or (ii) within a "recent" period, sometimes as much as three years, prior to the public offering date, (iii) for consideration significantly lower than the proposed public offering price.[100] Under the law of most merit states, cheap stock cannot exceed a given percentage of the shares outstanding after completion of the offering unless the excess cheap stock is placed in escrow. Escrowed securities will be

[98] On merit review, *see generally* Warren, "Reflections on Dual Regulation of Securities: A Case Against Preemption," 25 *B. C. L. Rev.* 495 (1984); Honig, "Massachusetts Securities Regulation: In Search of the Fulcrum," 13 *U. Balt. L. Rev.* 469 (1984); Note, "Compromise Merit Review—A Proposal for Both Sides of the Debate," 60 *Wash. L. Rev.* 141 (1984); Hensley, "The Development of a Revised Uniform Securities Act," 40 *Bus. Law.* 721 (1985); Makens, "Who Speaks for the Investor?: An Evaluation of the Assault on Merit Regulation," 13 *U. Balt. L. Rev.* 435 (1984); Tyler, "More About Blue Sky," 39 *Wash. & Lee L. Rev.* 899 (1982); Goodkind, "Blue Sky Law: Is There Merit in the Merit Requirements?" 1976 *Wisc. L. Rev.* 79; Bartell, "Merit Regulation and Clearing Strategy," in Goldwasser & Maken, *State Regulation of Capital Formation and Securities Transactions* 315 (1983 ed.).

[99] Some of the issues captivating "merit" state regulators are difficult to identify in advance since much of the learning is informal. As one commentary puts it, merit requirements in various states can be set out in published rules or they are promulgated: "informally—i.e., speeches or newsletters . . . are accumulated by Blue Sky attorneys . . . [or by] unwritten policy which manifests itself through tradition, or 'we've always done it this way,' directions of the Administrator, [and the] idiosyncrasy of the examiner." Makens & Halloran, "State Regulation of Public Offerings," in *Private and Small Business Offerings* (P.L.I. Course Handbook Series No. 386, 1982). A recent and useful summary of merit requirements is to be found in Liebolt, "State Securities Registration Requirements: Forms, Procedures, Requirements," in *Blue Sky Laws* 307 (P.L.I. Course Handbook Series No. 534, 1986).

[100] Haft, *supra* n. 82 at § 704[2]. "Cheap Stock" is discussed in detail in a 1955 Policy Statement of the National Association of State Securities Administrators, 38 Proceedings of the NASSA 113 (1955), updated in "NASSA Statement of Policy: Cheap Stock," (CCH) *NASSA Rep.* ¶ 801.

released in time, perhaps early if certain earnings tests are subsequently met; nonetheless,[101] escrowing promotional stock is a stiff penalty for the founders and early investors since it cuts sharply into value. A $10 stock which cannot be sold for, say, one year might suffer a $5 haircut in appraised value in the portfolio of a venture fund. Accordingly, much of the planning for an IPO goes into rebuttal of the state's claim that cheap stock exists or at least persuading the state to accept something less than a formal escrow that is not released until an earnings test is satisfied—i.e. perhaps just a promise to hold the stock off the market for a period of time.[102]

Another popular issue is dilution of the public investors traceable to an offering price well in excess of book value and/or prices charged in the private rounds. In merit states, not only must the rationale behind the offering price be disclosed (a federal requirement)[103] but the promoters must justify a price which appears to be out of line: e.g, if the price earnings "multiple" is higher than, say, 20 or 25 to 1 or if the "dilution" to investors in the public offering is higher than 33.3%.[104] Counsel's job in submitting the prospectus to the agency is usually to make comparisons to offerings recently marketed in the state, a *tu quoque* defense. Also helpful is an independently prepared projection of future earnings, showing why a high price is reasonable.

Beyond cheap stock and excessive dilution, the issues to be raised vary widely from state to state; broad generalities can be misleading. With that caveat, the following rules represent a composite of the regulatory mind set on the objections customarily encountered by fledgling issuers.

Offerings of securities with no voting rights are presumptively unfair.[105] Loans to insiders must be repaid before the IPO is effective and transactions with affiliates will be closely scrutinized.[106] Options for no more than 10% of the shares outstanding after the offering are presumed

[101]Some fiduciaries may be without the power to escrow the shares held in their stewardship.

[102]Parenthetically, cheap stock has not escaped the attention of the SEC's accounting staff, which takes the position that excessively cheap stock issued "in contemplation" of the IPO should be accounted for by increasing the number of shares outstanding in prior periods for earnings per share calculations. *SEC Staff Accounting Bulletin* No. 64, (CCH) 6 Fed. Sec. L. Rep. ¶ 74,131.

[103]Regulation S–K, Item 505(2).

[104]Haft, *supra* n. 82, at § 7.04[5]; Lewis, *supra* n. 6, at 78.

[105]Haft, n. 82, at § 7.04[5]; Lewis, *supra* n. 6, at 82. As of this writing, the SEC's proposal to limit the ability of public companies to take action which cheapens the vote of existing shareholders does not impact on initial public offerings. "The market," in the SEC's words, "may value the assurance of the continuity by management or founding group." Sec. Exch. Act Rel. No. 34–24623 IV A (June 24, 1987).

[106]Haft, supra n. 82, at § 7.04[8]; Lewis supra n. 6, at 81. This is often a harsh problem when an emerging company has attracted key executives by lending them the cash to relocate.

reasonable, excluding options to lenders and options issued in connection with acquisitions.[107] If outstanding options are less than 10% of the outstanding stock but the stock reserved for issuance of options is over that number, a one-year moratorium on the granting of options is required.[108] So-called "supermajority" provisions designed to avoid unwanted takeovers—that is, high class votes required in favor of mergers, "blank check" preferred—are not favored.[109] The preferred shareholders should have a right to director representation during a default in scheduled dividends.[110] Cash paid in by the promotors should represent at least 10% of the aggregate offering price.[111] Selling shareholders must pay their pro rata share of the expenses of the offering unless the issuer had previously entered into an agreement to assume all expenses.[112] And, the amount and nature of underwriters' compensation will be independently reviewed, as discussed in the next section.

§14.10 NASD APPROVAL

"Unreasonable" payments to underwriters for selling an IPO are a source of concern not only to state regulators. The National Association of Securities Dealers (universally referred to as the NASD)—the self-regulatory body established, with SEC blessing, by the investment banking community—formally regulates each issue on a case-by-case basis.[113] The underwriting arrangements must be submitted to the NASD's Committee on Corporate Financing prior to a public offering and the offering cannot become effective[114] absent NASD clearance. The NASD test for "fairness and reasonableness" of the underwriters' compensation is stated in general terms to prevent the maximum fee permissible under the published NASD guidelines (NASD Guide) from becoming the industry standard.[115]

[107]NASSA Statement of Policy, Options and Warrants, (CCH) *NASSA Rep.* ¶ 2801.
[108]*Ibids.*
[109]Lewis supra n. 6, at 82.
[110]NASSA Statement of Policy, Preferred Stock and Debentures, (CCH) *NASSA Rep.* ¶ 3001.
[111]NASSA Proposed Statement of Policy, Promoters' Investment, 1 (CCH) *Blue Sky L. Rep.* ¶ 5341.
[112]*See* Halloran, "Problems of High Tech Offerings," *supra* n. 95, at 581. The obvious lesson is for the investors to insist on such an agreement, perhaps explicitly approved by all shareholders.
[113]The National Association of Securities Dealers, Inc. was organized and registered in 1939 as a "national securities association" under the Maloney Act, § 15A of the '34 Act.
[114]*See* Rule 461(a).
[115]Interpretation of the Board of Governors, Review of Corporate Financing, Article III, § 1 of the Rules of Fair Practice, (CCH) *NASD Manual* ¶ 2151. The factors to be taken into account are the size of the offering, whether it is underwritten on a firm or best efforts basis, the type of securities offered, terms of the underwriters' warrants, the "nature and amount" of overall compensation and conflicts of interest. *See generally* Bloomenthal, Harvey, & Wing, *1985 Going Public Handbook* 3–17 (1986).

In deciding whether compensation is reasonable, the most sensitive issue is not so much the maximum amount, which practitioners speculate is around 16 to 17% of the gross proceeds of the offering, but deciding what comprises "compensation." Typically, an underwriter of an IPO has enjoyed a relationship with the issuer while it was private. It is not uncommon for the investment bankers to have arranged the "mezzanine" round: that is, that round of financing which anticipates the IPO. The investment bankers may have bought stock or received options or warrants in connection with that financing and may receive the same in connection with the IPO as well. The underwriters will bargain for an expense allowance, sometimes nonaccountable,[116] in connection with the offering and require a right of first refusal to underwrite at least the next public financing. All of these items (and others) have value and arguably should be taken into account. Accordingly, in considering how to calculate compensation, the NASD's published guide, officially an "Interpretation" of the Rules of Fair Practice, states that the NASD will "examine closely" any stock purchased by the underwriter within the 12-month period prior to the filing and "normally, but not necessarily," purchases within six months will be considered as part of the "package,"[117] meaning that the difference between the underwriter's purchase price and the IPO price will be factored in. A black letter rule in the Interpretation states that the underwriter should not receive options, warrants or conversion privilege entitling it to purchase more than 10% of the shares offered; such options or rights shall not extend for more than five years nor be exercisable below the public offering price.[118] The Interpretation does not state specifically how the NASD committee will value the noncash elements of the underwriter's compensation but various quasi-authoritative sources provide useful estimates.[119]

The NASD also supervises how stock in an IPO is allocated. Thus, the Interpretation limits the practice of "free riding," that is, allocating "hot" stock (stock in an issue which immediately goes to a premium), as a disguised extra benefit to the underwriter and its special friends.[120] A pattern of the same customers consistently participating in private placements immediately prior to a given underwriter's public offerings will be closely scrutinized. Moreover, the NASD imposes a standard of reasonableness on the amount of stock the issuer reserves for its friends:

[116]The NASD is particularly sensitive to what it construes as unreasonable "nonaccountable" expense allowances.

[117]Interpretation, *supra* n. 115.

[118]*Ibid.*

[119]*See, e.g.,* Bloomenthal, Harvey & Wing, *1985 Going Public Handbook supra* n. 45, at 3–17.

[120]Interpretation of the Board of Governors, "Free-Riding and Withholding," Article III, § 1 of the Rules of Fair Practice (CCH) *NASD Manual,* ¶ 2151 p. 2040.

"issuer-directed securities."[121] Obviously, upon an IPO, it is good business to reserve stock for customers and others who can help the firm in the future. Since the NASD is interested, however, in bona fide public offerings, it insists that the amount of issuer directed securities bear a "reasonable relationship" (interpreted by one commentator as 10%)[122] to the total amount offered and the favored purchasers be "directly related to the conduct of the issuer's business."

A special section of the Interpretation entitled "Venture Capital Restrictions" applies exclusively to IPOs and locks up for 90 days all stock (not just cheap stock) owned by the underwriter unless the offering price was established by an independent comanager which does not own stock (or the question is *de minimis*).[123]

The NASD approval process for a new issue is currently about five to six weeks. The letters of comment fall under four categories: "defer review" means that there is not enough information even to begin review; "defer opinion" means initial information is required on a limited number of pending issues; a "no objection"[124] letter indicates that compensation is reasonable and an "unreasonable letter" means that disciplinary proceedings will be instituted if the offering proceeds.

§14.11 RULE 144

Rule 144 was published by the SEC in 1972[125] to clarify the rules governing the ability of a holder of restricted securities to resell his shares to the public. The problem is as old as the unhappy draftsmanship that went into the original Securities Act of 1933. That statute appears to provide that every sale of stock must be registered under the '33 Act, an absurd proposition; the New York Stock Exchange, where transactions take place in microseconds, would close down. Section 4(1) of the Act comes to the rescue by exempting transactions by persons other than the "issuer" (primary transactions) or an "underwriter."[126] This appears simple enough; all secondary (i.e., nonissuer) transactions are exempt. The draftsman, however, elected to put the substance of the

[121]The rules on "issuer directed securities" are set out both in the context of (i) the fairness and reasonableness of the terms of the underwriting, Interpretation *supra* n. 115, and (ii) free riding, Interpretation *supra* n. 120.

[122]Bloomenthal, Harvey & Wing, *1985 Going Public Handbook supra.* n. 45, at 3-19.

[123]Interpretation, *supra* n. 115.

[124]*See* Rule 461(a) denying acceleration of the effective date until the NASD has issued a "statement expressing no objections to the compensation and other arrangements."

[125]Sec. Act Rel. No. 33–5223, [1971–1972 Transfer Binder] (CCH) Fed. Sec. L. Rep ¶ 78,487 (Jan. 11, 1972)

[126]The precise language in § 4(1) is "transactions by any person other than an issuer, underwriter or dealer."

rule in the definition of the term "underwriter."[127] That term includes the types of entities and people common sense would denote as underwriters—the members of the investment banking syndicate underwriting the placement—plus two additional types, called "statutory" underwriters, namely (i) persons who purchased their stock from an issuer "with a view to . . . the distribution of any security" and (ii) persons "directly or indirectly controlling" the issuer. (The term "distribution" means public distribution.) Using this language, the SEC spread its jurisdiction over secondary transactions in two principal situations: the stock sold had never been registered under the '33 Act, (so-called "investment letter" or "restricted" stock) and/or the seller controlled the issuer (so-called "control" stock). As the SEC reads the section 4(1) and the definition of "underwriter," all secondary transactions should *not* be exempt, rather only those involving trades of stock *other than* "letter" stock or "control" stock.

The fear, of course, was that the registration and disclosure provisions of the '33 Act could otherwise be eroded. If all secondary transactions were exempt, a nonregistered public offering could occur whenever the issuer could find someone to buy the stock, hold it for a little while and then "decide" to sell it publicly; or the owner of a controlling interest in the firm could start to sell off his position, acting as the "alter ego" of the issuer.[128]

To close what it perceived as loopholes, the staff took a long view of the phrase, "with a view to." If Start-up, Inc. sells stock in an exempt private transaction (under, say, § 4(2) of the '33 Act) to Smith, Smith resells in a private transaction to Brown and Brown wants to sell to the public, the sale by Brown is nonexempt because Smith and Brown, *taken collectively,* purchased from the issuer "with a view to" a distribution. This notion involves a tortured reading of the language of the Act (by way of contrast, the definition of "restricted securities" in Rule 144 expressly uses the terms "directly or indirectly from the issuer . . . in a transaction *or chain of* transactions")[129] but was an obvious follow-up step if the SEC did not want unregistered offerings escaping the net.

The awkwardness of the drafting did not, in the final analysis, chill the secondary market. The SEC and the courts worked the language

[127]'33 Act, § 2(11) provides:

> The term "underwriter" means any person who has purchased from an issuer with a view to, or offers or sells for an issuer in connection with, the distribution of any security, or participates or has a direct or indirect participation in any such undertaking, or participates or has a participation in the direct or indirect underwriting of any such undertaking . . . As used in this paragraph the term "issuer" shall include, in addition to an issuer, any person directly or indirectly controlling or controlled by the issuer, or any person under direct or indirect common control with the issuer.

[128]Goldwasser, *The Practitioner's Comprehensive Guide to Rule 144* 26 (2d ed. 1978).

[129]Rule 144(a)(3).

around until it made some modicum of sense. While the statutory language related the registration requirements to the nature of the *transaction,* the real initial inquiry focused on what *kind* of *stock* the holder was trying to sell—was it "letter" stock because it had never been registered and/or was it "control" stock because of who the holder was—a controlling person? If the stock one held was tainted, then the question was not so much *whether* but *when* the stock could be sold under § 4(1) as a nonevasive secondary sale without the necessity either of imposing "investment letter" restrictions on the new buyer (maintaining illiquidity and thereby lowering the price) or registering the stock publicly (thereby incurring expense). It was obvious that at some point the regulators should be able to relax, to allow a secondary sale to progress under § 4(1) regardless of the control status of the holder or the unregistered status of the stock, because the fear of evasion had abated with the passage of time. And that question was frequently addressed, albeit in some of the unhappiest stories in securities regulation.[130] On occasion, the securities bar actually had to work with subjective tests—what was the "intent"[131] (the "view") of Smith when he bought his shares from Start-up, Inc. Did he truly "intend" to hold for "investment purposes." If he later said he was changing his mind, did he do so just because he didn't like the stock any more or because of a valid "change of circumstances," perhaps the loss of his job, a dread disease?[132] Nonsense piled upon nonsense as counsel struggled with a series of "no action" letters issued by the SEC staff, reading the tea leaves to figure out when their clients could sell without registration and without continuing the "investment letter" restrictions.

Finally, the Wheat Report (discussed elsewhere in the Text)[133] engendered Commission action, leading[134] to the promulgation in 1972 of Rule 144, a rule which allows the holders of control or letter stock to sell their shares publicly (no registration and no investment letters) in accordance with the provision of the Rule. The problem of "letter" stock is now more or less at rest, the qualifier required by the fact that staff interpretations[135] now number more than 1,000, dealing with exotic situations the Rule does not decide explicitly.

[130]*See generally* Mandelstam, "How Long Must I Hold?" 25 *U. Miami L. Rev.* 173 (1970); Schneider & Kant, "Uncertainty Under the Securities Act," 26 *Bus. Law.* 1623 (1971).
[131]Note "The Investment–Intent Dilemma in Secondary Transactions," 39 *N.Y.U. L. Rev. 1043* (1964).
[132]A "catastrophic" change was useful. *See* Goldwasser, *supra* n. 128, at 33 n. 21. However, if the stockholder willingly caused the change—i.e., he lost all his or her money at blackjack—it didn't count. *Id.* at 34.
[133]*Disclosure to Investors—The Report and Recommendation to the Securities and Exchange Commission from the Disclosure Policy Study* (1969).
[134]*See generally,* Goldwasser, *supra* n. 128.
[135]*See, e.g.,* Sec. Act Rel. No. 33–6099, 1 (CCH) Fed. Sec. L. Rep ¶ 2705H (Aug. 2, 1979).

(a) PUBLIC INFORMATION

Rule 144 has one important threshold; it is not a left-handed opening through which shareholders can drive an unregistered IPO. Thus, Rule 144 generally applies only to stock in a company[136] that is already publicly held. (That does not mean that the securities of the issuer have been registered and sold under § 5 of the '33 Act; a company can—indeed must—become public over time if and as the number of shareholders exceeds 500.)[137] The emphasis in the Wheat Report is on dissemination of information periodically and currently, shying away from the "Big Bang" theory, which placed so much stock in the contents of a public registration statement. If the information is out in the marketplace, Rule 144 suggests, investors can trade. Indeed, a company with fewer than 500 shareholders may voluntarily supply the requisite information so as to bring Rule 144 into play but the absence of any public float makes it unlikely many would go that route (and Rule 144 is not available to issuers).[138] If the information must be assembled and published to accommodate a secondary seller, why not create a real public offering with an IPO?

(b) HOLDING PERIOD

For the control person, the "manner" and "volume of sale" limitations are never lifted as long as the control relationship continues to exist (and for three months thereafter.)[139] For the holder of unregistered shares

[136]The issuer must either be a reporting company under § 12 of the Exchange '34 Act or make available, roughly, the same information as a reporting company would publish. Rule 144(c)(2).

[137]'34 Act, § 12(g) requires registration if the issuer's total assets exceed $1 million and "a class" of equity security is held "of record" by 500 or more persons. To preserve the benefits of the Rule 144 for its shareholders, the issuer must not only become public but it must be current in its public reporting, hence the promise routinely required by investors in the Stock Purchase Agreement that those reports will be timely filed.

[138]A controlling person is always subject to the "manner of sale" and "volume" limitations (*see* §§ 14.11(d) & (e) *infra*), making it unlikely that enough stock would be sold to make it worthwhile for someone in a position of power to cause the company to skip § 5 of the '33 Act by filing voluntary reports under § 12 of the '34 Act.

[139]Rule 144(k). If a venture partnership which controls an issuer distributes stock in the issuer to a limited partner, the question arises whether the limited partner is tainted and must wait three months before selling. The answer appears to be that the limited partner can, without more, sell immediately. *Compare* Sec. Act Rel. No. 33-6099, *supra* n. 135, *with Hellman, Ferri Investment Associates* no-action letter (avail. No. 16, 1981).

(control or no control), no sales may be made publicly for two years.[140] During the third year, both controlling and noncontrolling persons can sell subject to "volume" and "manner of sale" restrictions, sales which are referred to as "dribbling out" the stock. After three years, noncontrolling persons can sell unregistered stock more or less as they choose.[141] Thus, the table below indicates the impact of the Rule:

	Unregistered Stock		
Holding Period	*2 Years*	*2–3 Years*	*After 3 Years*
Control	no sales	dribble out	dribble out
Noncontrol	no sales	dribble out	free sales
	Registered Stock		
Control	Dribble out		
Noncontrol	Not subject to the Rule at all		

To satisfy the holding period requirements, the holder must have been the "beneficial owner" of the stock for the required period.[142] In the never-ending stand against evasion, however, the SEC draftsman have grafted on a series of complementary rules which enlarge the holding period—lengthen it—if a case can be made the hopeful seller did not truly "own" the securities in the sense he was entirely at risk.[143] The holder cannot count the period during which his position was hedged by a companion short sale, for example.[144] Conversely, in certain circumstances, a holder can expand the period, to "tack" the time he has held the shares in question onto a prior period. For example, stock acquired pursuant to a stock dividend has a holding period which starts when the underlying stock was acquired.[145] For present purposes, one of the most critical of the supplementary rules provides that stock acquired pursuant to a stock option does not start to acquire longevity until the option is exercised but the holding period for stock received upon the conversion of convertible stock is "tacked" back to the ownership of the original security.[146] As elsewhere indicated, this can pose

[140]Rule 144(d)(i).
[141]Rule 144(k).
[142]Rule 144(d)(1).
[143]Rule 144(d)(2).
[144]Rule 144(d)(3).
[145]Rule 144(d)(4)(A). Stock acquired from the estate of a decedent is deemed as having been held from the time the decedent acquired it. Rule 144(d)(4)(G).
[146]Rule 144(d)(4)(B).

a significant problem in the case of nonqualified employee options.[147] Another frequently encountered issue is whether the limited partners of a venture partnership receiving a distribution in kind—usually a distribution of restricted stock in an issuer that has just gone public—can tack holding periods and the answer appears to be that they can, at least if the distribution is pro rata.[148]

(c) DRIBBLING OUT

The bulk of the Rule deals with limits designed to allow secondary trading only in "ordinary" circumstances. What this means is that the SEC, as stated in the release promulgating the Rule,[149] still believes there is a strong public policy supporting registration for significant transactions[150] even when the information is already public. Therefore, the Rule adopts a principle called "dribbling" out, the holders, releasing small (relatively) amounts of stock into the market in routine transactions. Since the owners of restricted securities (not also being "control stock") are released from the dribbling out restraints if they hold their stock for three, versus two, years, the restrictions are a problem mainly for control affiliates. Indeed, control affiliates are impacted more severely as a practical matter because they are usually the holders with a lot of stock to sell. Parenthetically, the question of who is an "affiliate" for purposes of Rule 144 (and any other SEC Rule) can become quite complicated, particularly when stock is attributed to a given holder because of his relationship with another holder.[151]

(d) VOLUME

The volume limitation during any three-month period is the greater of 1% of the shares outstanding or the average weekly trading during the past four calendar weeks.[152] If two or more persons "agree to act in concert" for the purpose of selling, all sales for the account of such persons during any three-month period will be aggregated.[153] This Rule might be deemed to impact in a situation where a venture partnership distributes restricted securities in kind to the limited partners and they

[147] *See* Ch. 11, § 11.3(b).
[148] Sec. Act Rel. No. 33–6099, *supra* n. 135. Compare the issue discussed in n. 139, *supra*, whether the recipient limited partner is tainted for three months by the partnership's control relationship to the issuer.
[149] Sec. Act Rel. No. 33–5223, *supra* n. 125.
[150] *See* Goldwasser, *supra* n. 128, at 119.
[151] Rule 144(a)(1) and (2), defining "affiliate" and "person."
[152] Rule 144(e)(1).
[153] Sec. Act Rel. No. 33–6099, *supra* n. 135, at Question 45.

all sell contemporaneously, but it appears that such sales are not "acting in concert."[154]

(e) MANNER OF SALE

The "manner of sale" limitation requires that all sales be accomplished in "brokers transactions"; that is, the broker does no more than execute the order as an agent and receives no more than the "usual and customary" commission; the broker may not solicit a buy order but the broker may publish bid and ask quotes in an interdealer quotation system[155] and may send out research reports on the stock if the reports are in the ordinary course and satisfy certain other conditions.[156]

§14.12 REGULATION A

Regulation A is a so-called "general exemption" for issuances of securities not to exceed $1.5 million upon the filing of an "offering statement" (comparable to a registration statement) with the local regional office of the SEC and the use of an "offering circular" (comparable to a prospectus) in connection with each sale. The Regulation is not available in the event of certain "bad boy" occurrences—the issuers, its affiliates, or the underwriter is in trouble with the SEC or the Postal Service.[157] Issuers operating at a loss must cut back the amount of stock offered to take into account stock or options previously sold to insiders (unless insiders will lock up for a year).[158] If the issue is below $100,000 and is not advertised, stock can be sold without the offering circular.[159] With the advent of Form S–18, which can also be filed in the SEC's regional offices, and Rule 505 and Rule 506 under Reg. D, allowing issuances substantially in excess of $1.5 million, the occasion for utilizing Regulation A are rare.[160] The one remaining element of substance favoring Regulation A is that disaffected purchasers have no access to Section 11 of the '33 Act, the more or less strict liability section for omissions in a registration statement.[161]

[154]*Ibid.*
[155]Rule 144(g)(2)(iii).
[156]Sec. Act Rel. No. 6099, *supra* n. 135, at Item 62. *See generally* Wolfson, Phillips, & Russo, *Regulation of Brokers, Dealers and Securities Markets* Ch. 19 (1977 & 1985 Supp.).
[157]Regulation A, Rule 252(c).
[158]Regulation A, Rule 253.
[159]Regulation A, Rule 257.
[160]Hicks, 1983 *Limited Offering Exemptions: Regulation D* 11 (1983).
[161]Section 11 applies by its terms to "registration statements;" Regulation A provides for the filing of an "offering statement." Rule 255.

APPENDIX

James Brown, Esq.
Gaston & Snow
14 Wall Street
New York, NY 10005

RE: XYZ Corp. (Examiner Assigned: John Smith)

Dear Mr. Brown:

A preliminary review of the application for registration of the securities of the above-captioned issuer has been completed. As a result of that review, the Securities Division has the following comments. (Note those boxes which have been checked):

____ **1.** The proposed offering does not appear to comply with [State Statute, Sections ____]:
- ____ **a.** It appears the Company may grant options at less than fair market value.
- ____ **b.** It appears the duration of the options may exceed 10 years.
- ____ **c.** It appears the number of options outstanding after the offering is excessive.

____ **2.** The Division requests additional information relating to the offering such as the names of the market makers, volume of transactions, and the underwriter's memorandum.

____ **3.** Please provide the name of your local registered broker-dealer.

____ **4.** Please represent in the prospectus that all future loans to company officials, affiliates, and/or shareholders will be approved by a majority of the disinterested directors.

____ **5.** The issuer appears to be in unsound financial condition.

____ **6.** Please represent in the prospectus that all future transactions with affiliates will be on terms no less favorable than could be obtained from unaffiliated parties.

____ **7.** The Division will require additional disclosure regarding the "blank check" preferred stock. The disclosure must state that the issuance of such stock may not adversely affect the rights of common stockholders.

____ **8.** Regarding the selling shareholders, the Division will require the following:
- ____ **a.** The selling shareholders must pay their pro rata share of the offering expenses.
- ____ **b.** Please represent that no selling shareholders have any outstanding loans, advances, or guarantees from the Company.

___ **c.** Please represent that any loans or advances to selling shareholders will be repaid from the proceeds from the sale of their stock.

___ **d.** Please represent that any guarantees of loans or advances to selling shareholders will be lifted prior to the offering.

___ **9.** The transferability of underwriter warrants does not appear to be in compliance with the NASAA Statement of Policy on Options and Warrants.

All of the preceding comments must be resolved before registration will be permitted. Only responses tendered in writing will be considered as adequately responding to this letter. If you have questions concerning these comments which can be handled expeditiously by telephone, please call; however, we will resume our review which may generate additional comments only after we receive your written response.

Very truly yours,

John Smith
Staff Attorney

Fifteen

Licensing Agreements

Licensing plays a major role on several levels in a typical venture firm's business strategy. A high tech company will both borrow and lend technology, licensing agreements constituting the governing instrument. A distribution, joint marketing, and/or joint venture arrangement with a major corporate partner will usually involve licensing back and forth. Licensing is an integral part of the campaign to protect a firm's intellectual property. While licensing exists outside the venture universe, it is important that venture players understand the structure and dynamics highlighted in this chapter.

§15.1 "LICENSE" DISTINGUISHED FROM OTHER FORMATS

For an early-stage venture in possession of a bright idea, an item of technology based on what the law calls intellectual property,[1] several choices must be made. The novel idea can be developed, and manufactured into a product, and then sold by the firm directly to end users; it can be sold to intermediaries, who will resell it to customers; it can be sold to another manufacturer, who will incorporate it into a new product

[1] *See* Ch. 16. Licensing is not limited to items of intellectual property. Milgrim distinguishes licenses of "industrial property." *1 Milgrim on Trade Secrets,* Ch. 14 (1987). See *infra* § 15.6.

and sell the resultant item as a package; or it can be "licensed" (versus sold) in some form or another to any one of the foregoing in exchange for "royalties" paid over a period of time, or in one lump sum.[2]

(a) LICENSE VERSUS SALE

When considering the question of licensing a product versus selling it, it is useful to keep in mind that the term "owner," as a synonym for licensor, encapsulates a complex agglomeration of concepts. Ownership in a very real sense is the power to control and exclude: to tell others what they can and cannot do with the item "owned."[3] Indeed, ownership is aptly described as a basket of rights respecting an item; that is, the right to manufacture, sell, sublicense, lease, copy, disclose by publication, use internally, incorporate into a product, and so forth. When an owner disposes of his interest, he takes rights out of the basket and deals them off to third parties, who then become "owners" of the item, insofar as the right in question is concerned. The fundamental distinction between a license and a sale, apart from nomenclature, is in the number of rights the existing owner takes from the basket and deals out. If a sale is effected, the owner will empty the basket, or at least almost the entire basket. The new "owner" will succeed to substantially all the rights, will step into the shoes of the transferor. If a license is intended, only specific rights are lifted out of the basket. The rest are retained by the transferee.

Many of the problems in this area arise when nomenclature conflicts with the facts. Thus, when computer software is disposed of at retail, as discussed in § 15.2(c), the transaction looks like a sale. However, the maker of the software does not want the software to be copied so, to reinforce his position, he styles the transaction as a license even though

[2]A franchise agreement is a form of license agreement, usually involving the owner of a trademark—*e.g.*, "McDonalds"—licensing the use of that trademark (and companion items, such as recipes, training manuals, and other items of "knowhow") to individuals and firms interested in cooking and selling hamburgers under a world-recognized label. The Lanham Act, providing federal protection of trademarks, is set out in 15 U.S.C. §§ 1051 et seq.; *See generally* McCarthy, *Trademarks and Unfair Competition* (1984). As earlier indicated, *see* Ch. 1, § 1.3(b), franchising is a separate topic, dealt with only tangentially in the Text. It is important to keep in mind that a license agreement may wind up fitting within the definition of a "franchise agreement" under state or federal law, entailing penalties imposed on the unwitting who fail to recognize the issue. *See*, Fern, "The Overbroad Scope of Franchise Regulations: A Definitional Dilemma," 34 *Bus. Law.* 1387 (Apr. 1979).

[3]One difficulty in grasping what "ownership" means in the law is often traceable to the central, although often ignored, meaning of the word "property"—i.e., the right of the owners "legally [to] refuse to allow their possessions to be used by others." Heilbroner, *The Nature and Logic of Capitalism* 38 (1985).

the "licensee" does not sign an agreement[4] and, indeed, is usually unaware of the licensor's interest and/or characterization of the transaction. Conversely, when the owner of a copyrighted article "sells" the item, he continues to retain the exclusive right to copy the work;[5] the third party "owns" the physical copy—a book, record, disc with a program imprinted on it—but he cannot go out and run off a bunch of copies on his own. Again the basket concept: the owner can, if he so elects, dip into the basket and sell the right to copy, meaning sell the entire copyright, but merely "selling" a copy does not carry the copyright with it. Thus, one commentator has described the "first sale" doctrine in copyright law as meaning that, in the case of a "sale" of a copyrighted work, the new owner has the right "to treat the object as his own."[6] That is misleading of and by itself, as the work in question goes on to point out.[7] "First Sale" means that the customer can resell or rent the object itself without violating the copyright; reselling may violate the agreement between the parties but, as per § 109 of the Copyright Act, it does not violate the statute. However, the new "owner" cannot *copy* the object and resell copies; that right stays in the basket until the new owner takes it out.

Interestingly, if the licensed item is a trade secret, there will be nothing for anyone to "own" unless the creator uses all the resources at his command to keep the information as secret as possible, meaning it can be exploited externally only by licensing, not selling. If trade secrets are disposed of without strings (i.e., "sold") it is likely the *res* itself, the secret, will vanish.[8]

(b) LICENSE VERSUS LEASE

A license agreement is like a lease in that it usually involves an agreement by which the licensor assigns some but not all of his rights in an

[4]Assuming the owner of an item wants to impose restraints after the item has been disposed of for value, it may be imprudent for the owner to describe the transaction as an outright sale or a conditional sale, although the transaction may be just that. In the former case, the legal culture is likely to classify the postdisposition constraints as a "restraint of trade," a bad phrase in the legal lexicon. *See Dr. Miles Medical Co. v. Park & Sons Co.* 220 U.S. 373 (1911). In the latter case, transactions labeled "conditional sales" must comply with formalities established by the Uniform Commercial Code, U.C.C. § 2–106, or, where applicable, the Copyright Act. *See Nimmer on Copyright* § 8.12(B)(1986). In patent law, an "assignment" of the patent is generally deemed to transfer to the assignee the right to sue for infringement while a "license" does not. *See Waterman v. Mackenzie* 138 U.S. 252, (1890), discussed in 1 Eckstrom, *Licensing in Foreign and Domestic Operations* § 1.03 (3d ed. 1984).

[5]17 U.S.C. § 106(1)

[6]17 U.S.C. § 109(a); Miller & Davis, *Intellectual Property: Patents, Trademarks and Copyright* 318 (1983)

[7]*Id.* at 319.

[8]For the belt and suspenders approach, invoking both copyright and trade secret protection, *see* Ch. 16, § 16.5.

item to a licensee and receives in exchange consideration, which is usually paid periodically over a period of time, not in one lump sum. Like a lease, one principal object of the license format is to protect against the licensee's misuse of the licensed property by retaining certain incidents of ownership in the licensor and by binding the licensee to promises to observe and respect the licensor's prior right.[9] There is no overriding legal reason why a license could not be styled as a lease (and vice versa)—both entail retention of ownership in the provider and thus are distinguished from sales—but leases are customarily thought of as applying only to tangible property.[10] (Custom also suggests that a contract which contemplates fixed payments for use is a lease and variable payments based on revenues is a license, but those distinctions can blur. Indeed, as explained below, some license agreements entail only a single payment in consideration of a "perpetual" license, subject to a technical right of reversion if promises in the "license" agreement to respect the intellectual property are violated.) Licenses of certain rights (i.e., patent assignments) are, like long-term leases of real estate, subject to various recordation and other procedural requirements but the general rule is that licensing is a creature of the common law,[11] meaning that there is no bar to the parties calling a contract a "license" even if it displays few of the characteristics conventionally viewed as emblematic of licenses.[12]

[9]The typical subject matter of licenses—intellectual property—is generally grouped under four headings, according to the body of law pursuant to which "ownership" of the property is legally protected: patent, copyright, trademark, and trade secrets. Occasionally, "know how" is treated separately, viewed as something narrower and different than trade secrets; and sometimes trade secrets are viewed as a species of the generic term, "know how." Brunsvold, *1981 Licensing Law Handbook* § 3.02 (1981); LaFuze, "The Uniform Trade Secrets Act And Licensing," in *Recent Developments in Licensing* (ABA Section, Patent, Trademark and Copyright Law) 23 (1981). In a sense, intellectual property is all "know how," information which enables a firm to do something commercially valuable. When "know how" is nonsecret but nevertheless commercially useful, it is sometimes referred to as "show how." Arnold, White & Durkel, *1984 Licensing Law Handbook* § 3.01 (1984).
[10]Davidson & Davidson, *Advanced Legal Strategies for Buying and Selling Computers and Software* § 8.2(b) (1986), make the interesting suggestion that a vendor of computer software consider licensing the abstract program and leasing the physical medium in which it is embodied, the latter agreement designed to reinforce a claim that the diskette be returned or erased when the license is up.
[11]1 Eckstrom, *supra* n. 4, at § 1.03[3][a]. In the motion picture industry, "licenses" are occasionally recharacterized as leases. Davidson & Davidson, *supra* n. 104, at § 8.1(d)(3).
[12]Licenses are usually the product of express agreement. For a discussion of the circumstances which will give rise to a claim an implied licensee has been granted, *see* 1 Eckstrom, *supra* n. 4, at § 1.03[3][c]. As examples of implied—or, if you like, judicially manufactured—licenses, a dispute over ownership of an invention between employer and employee may result in an implied license, perhaps in the nature of "shop rights" (*see* Ch. 16, §§16.7, 16.8, 16.9) or the "sale" of an article may imply a license as to a given use. *Ibid.*

§15.2 COMPUTER SOFTWARE

(a) GENERAL[13]

In recent years, the product most commonly licensed in venture-backed start-ups has been computer software. The computer industry goes through cycles but, in general, the hardware has been ahead of the software, meaning that there are machines capable of performing prodigious tasks of calculation which, nonetheless, sit in the manufacturer's warehouse because programmers have not been able to come up with software to induce potential users to visualize a need the machine can fulfill. Calculation speed is of no commercial value unless an individual can be convinced that he can use the speed to do something important in a business sense. Hence, ever since computers started to sell in bulk, there has been a more or less constant need for new software packages to stimulate hardware sales. Many of the start-ups in the last few years have been, accordingly, software companies—too many in the judgment of some grizzled venture capitalists—but that cynicism has not squelched the parade. And software is an item that is inherently more likely to be licensed than sold, even to the end user.[14] As earlier mentioned, if the owner of the software enters into a transaction which describes itself as a "sale," the new owner has a statutory right under the Copyright Act to resell the item itself to a third party. If that third party who obtains the copy lawfully is ignorant of the existence of the copyright, it may be more difficult to bring an infringement action when and if copying occurs; the common suspicion is that illegal (whether knowing or not) copying will begin to occur at a stage once removed in the chain from the copyright owner unless strings are attached. The handiest way for the owner to minimize exposure to piracy of this sort is to avoid "selling" his product, licensing it instead on protective terms. Indeed,

[13]Some of the other issues raised in licensing computer software—*e.g.*, sales and use taxes—are covered in Chapters 16 and 17.

[14]One of the problems entailed in licensing software is that royalty income had in the past been considered the type of income which would subject a closely held corporation to potential tax penalties as a "personal holding company," I.R.C. § 543, meaning that 60% or more of the income is passive and 50% or more of the voting shares are held by five or fewer individuals, I.R.C. § 541. A "personal holding company" must distribute its income as dividends or pay a penalty tax. Under the Tax Reform Act of 1986, software royalties are not tainted income if received by a corporation: (i) actively engaged in the business of producing, manufacturing or developing computer software; (ii) deriving at least 50% of its gross income from software royalties; (iii) incurring substantial (25% or more of ordinary gross income) trade or business or research and development expenses; and, (iv) distributing most of its passive income (other than software royalties) to its shareholders. Tax Reform Act of 1986, § 645.

once a sale occurs, the "first sale" doctrine provides that the new owner may sell "or otherwise dispose"[15] of the item he has bought; even if no one copies the software, it may be legal for the new owner to make the software generally available on a "service bureau or time share basis, an unwanted result."[16]

(b) SERVICE

One of the features of software programs is that, practically without exception, they contain bugs which must be flushed out after the system is in operation. The agreement should, accordingly, be quite specific on the responsibility of the licensor to supply technical assistance, to come to the rescue when it is impossible for the user, no matter how sophisticated, to figure out what is wrong. (The insufficiency of technical manuals is part of the folklore of computer software.) The customer support problem can be an expensive obligation. If the licensee is a reseller, it must obtain the necessary assurances from the licensor to service customers whose only direct contact is with the licensee and who can be expected to blame the licensee when the system goes down.

(c) ESCROWING THE SOURCE CODE

Software is embodied in two forms: human readable (source code) and machine readable (object code).[17] Since the object code can only be read by a machine, the risk of piracy is largely limited to the manufacture

[15]17 U.S.C. 109(a). *See* Davidson & Davidson, *supra* n. 10, at § 8.1(a)(2).

[16]Bender, "Protection of Computer Programs: The Copyright/Trade Secret Interface," 47 *U. Pitt. L. Rev.* 907, 919 (1986).

[17]The distinction between source and object codes has been aptly summarized in a recent case:

> Normally, a computer program consists of several phases which may be summarized as follows. The first phase is the development of a flow chart which is a schematic representation of the program's logic. It sets forth the logical steps involved in solving a given problem. The second phase is the development of a "source program" which is a translation of the flow chart into computer programming language, such as FORTRAN or COBOL. Source programs may be punched on decks of cards or imprinted on discs, tapes or drums. The third phase is the development of an "assembly program" which is a translation of the programming language into machine language, i.e., mechanically readable computer language. Unlike source programs, which are readable by trained programmers, assembly programs are virtually unintelligible except by the computer itself. Finally the fourth phase is the development of an "object program" which is a conversion of the machine language into a device commanding a series of electrical impulses. Object programs, which enter into the mechanical process itself, cannot be read without the aid of special equipment and cannot be understood by even the most highly trained programmers.

Data Cash Systems Inc. v. JS & A Group, Inc. 480 F. Supp. 1063, 1065 (N.D. Ill. 1979) *aff'd on other grounds* 628 F.2d 1038 (7th Cir. 1980).

(by a machine) of unlicensed copies. Since, however, people can read the instructions in the source code, the licensor is naturally reluctant to give access to it for fear of reverse engineering and/or piracy; one commentary refers to the source code as the "family jewels of a software company."[18] On the other hand, if something goes wrong and the vendor will not or cannot come to the rescue (having gone out of business, for example), the user wants and needs a look at the source code to get to the root of the problem and fix it. A typical solution is to escrow the source code with a third-party professional or an escrow agent under seal, to be broken when the escrow instructions so require.[19] Whether a software escrow agreement will, however, survive the operation of the Bankruptcy Reform Act is open to question; under § 541 of the Act, the source code may be held to be the property of the debtor/licensor's estate and beyond the reach (at least absent further payments) of the licensee, despite the language in the agreement.[20]

(d) "SHRINK WRAP" OR "TEAR OPEN" LICENSES

When copyrighted software is sold at retail, the sale, without more, does not authorize the purchaser to make and resell copies (other than for internal purposes, i.e., "archival" or backup copies) any more than the sale of a book authorizes the purchaser to republish and sell it. However, as indicated above, the seller may want the additional protection afforded by ongoing promissory constraints to prevent the "licensee" from, for example, renting the item on a commercial basis or decompiling or "reverse engineering" the program. Thus, the sale to the end user is usually styled as a perpetual license, subject to forfeiture (legally in the nature of a condition subsequent) in the case of misuse. Since the user picking the package off the shelf does not read and execute a license agreement before buying the item, the license is styled as self-executing, binding the end user as soon as he tears open the plastic wrapper. It remains uncertain whether a court will enforce the terms of such licenses.[21] A recent decision by a federal court in Louisiana[22] held against the licensor on the theory the local Software License Enforcement Act was pre-empted by the Copyright Act and the contractual provisions in the shrink wrap license were somehow contrary to the policies of the federal act. One commentator describes a "shrink wrap" license as the

[18]Davidson & Davidson, *supra* n. 10, at § 8.1(e)

[19]*See generally* Hoffman, *The Software Legal Book* (1985).

[20]Pappons, "The Software Escrow: The Court Favorite and Bankruptcy Law," *1 Santa Clara Comput & High Tech. L.J.* 309 (1985).

[21]Davidson & Davidson, *supra* n. 10, at § 8.1(d)(3).

[22]*Vault Corporation v. Quaid Software, Ltd.* (No. 85-2283, Feb. 12, 1987, U.S.D.C. D. La.). *See* Raysman & Brown, " 'Shrink Wrap' Statute Invalidated," *N.Y. Law J.* pg. 1 (Mar. 10, 1987).

sale of a copy of a program coupled with an "attempted" license of related intellectual property rights.[23] Planning suggestions assembled in a well-known commentary include an attempt to require the retailer to call each customer's attention to the license before selling the item.[24]

(e) SCOPE OF USE

Because of the nature of computers and software, a special set of issues arises in the agreement relating to the permitted uses of the program. If the user owns one computer with one central processing unit (CPU), the issue is relatively simple. But how about a user with a series of remote terminals feeding off a single host computer? What if the user is selling time sharing on one computer to a number of customers? If the license specifies a fee for each of the licensee's CPUs, what about the user who owns a parallel processing machine linking a series of CPUs into one "ultra" computer? How about use of a backup computer? The licensor wants naturally to maximize revenue by assessing a license fee as often as possible (i.e., for each device on which the program is to be run).[25] However, in addition to the foregoing technical problems, software can be easily copied[26] (at least in the absence of built-in codes to prevent copying)[27] and run on all the licensee's machines. Technology, in short, is outdistancing the ability of the software licensor to police a "one fee–one machine" arrangement; new contracts in this area increasingly contemplate licenses based on unlimited use per location or per customer, "site licensing" as it is sometimes called.[28]

[23]Nimmer, *The Law of Computer Technology* § 6.17[1] (1985).
[24]Davidson & Davidson, *supra* n. 10, at § 8.19(d)(5).
[25]Raysman, "Acquisition and Exploitation of Mass-Market Software," in *Computer Software 1984: Protection and Marketing* 561, 564–565 (P.L.I. Course Handbook Series No. 184, 1984).
[26]The Copyright Act allows copying of computer software if the copy is "an essential step in the utilization of the computer program." 17 U.S.C. § 117.
[27]There are a variety of methods being used, with varying degrees of success, to combat unauthorized copying, the bulk involving a built-in protocol which entails the software looking for an authorization instruction before it will operate or unscramble itself. The various systems are outlined in Iscoe "Technical Approaches to Software Protection," *Protection of Computer Systems and Software,* (Hubbard & Shelton ed., 1986). If a package including both software and hardware (for example, a special printed circuit board) is being sold, the licensor will build into the software program an instruction to "look for" the piece of hardware and revert to an "error" mode if it cannot be found. *See* Tracy, "The Search for Copyproof Software," *Fortune* at 83, Sept. 3, 1984.
[28]Raysman, *supra* n. 25, at 564.

§15.3 TRADE SECRET PROTECTION

A principal—indeed *the* principal—objective of many license agreements is the protection of trade secrets. The point of the license is to retain ownership of the secret while commercially exploiting it and to build a fence (sometimes a higher and bigger fence than statutory protections, even if the same are available, can supply)[29] around the property by extorting promises from the end user. A trade secret is no longer legally protected if the owner does not take pains to maintain it, as best he can, in confidence. And, the license agreement is the vehicle to bind the user into cooperating to preserve the secret, or as much secrecy as possible. Indeed the licensor maintains ownership rights by maintaining the status of a trade secret as a *res* (a thing that is capable of being owned).

The chore is difficult because the environment is hostile; in order to exploit the trade secret advantageously, the owner has been compelled to reveal it to outside parties and, as any schoolgirl knows, a secret once revealed is a secret compromised.

To that end, a well-drafted trade secret license should be as emphatic as possible in clamping down on unauthorized disclosure. Suggested provisions include: (i) the intellectual property is the licensor's property and will be used only in confidence; (ii) access will be limited; (iii) the licensee will take all reasonable steps to maintain the information in confidence; (iv) the licensee will maintain confidentiality even if the information is not a secret but simply "know-how;"[30] (v) if appropriate, the licensee will return the material at the end of term; (vi) the licensee is expressly prohibited from decompilation or other attempts to uncover hidden secrets through tactics such as "reverse engineering;" (vii) the licensee will not make or suffer subsequent dispositions without the licensor's consent—that is, sublicensing only to certain customers and/or in certain areas,[31] and so forth; and, (viii) the license will be forfeited in the case of misuse.

[29]There are, as noted in the Text, loopholes in the Copyright Act which justify the explicit protections afforded by trade secret conceptions in the agreement for licensing software. *See* the discussion of decompilation and § 117 of the Copyright Act in Davidson & Davidson, *supra* n. 10, at § 8.1(a)(3) and (4). The authors urge that the input and output formats be the subject of trade secret protection. *Id.* at § 8.2(d)(4)(iii). *See* the discussion of coupling copyright and trade secret protection in Ch. 16, § 16.5.

[30]The entire subject of the license may be nonsecret information. For example, the competition may not recognize what is under their noses (and will not until someone tells them) or it may be expensive, albeit possible, for the competitor to assemble the information. On the question whether nonsecret information is protectable by contract, *see* Ch. 16, § 16.5.

[31]The rights of a computer manufacturer to impose restrictions on the sale of its products by mail order houses was upheld in *O.S.C. Corporation v. Apple Computer Inc.* 792 F.2d 464 (9th Cir. 1986); *See* Todd, "Retail Distribution of Computer Hardware and Software," *Computer Contracts: An In-Depth Study* 98 (MCLE 1985).

§15.4 LICENSING LIVING ORGANISMS

If technology generally is moving at a rapid pace, advances in biotechnology have reached the speed of light.[32] Municipalities have attempted to hold back genetic experiments, (e.g., Cambridge, Mass.) presumably out of a fear that an Andromeda Strain will escape; the federal government is wrestling with profound questions about permissible methods of experimentation with genetic alteration.[33]

The questions involved in figuring out how best to license living organisms are (pardon the pun) in the embryonic stage. Of course, owners of live animals have sold and leased them since the beginning of time. However, the biotechnological products at the heart of today's issues are, albeit tangible personal property like draft animals, caught up with notions of patents, intellectual property and trade secrets. For example, it is a basic principle of patent law that a naturally occurring substance cannot be patented.[34] However, a novel strain of bacteria is an intellectual construct; the owner has a secret process for "making" the product, a process he wants to protect, and the Supreme Court has generally indicated that such may be the subject of patent protection.[35] Potential complications arise from the conclusion that living organisms are unique forms of property because they reproduce themselves.[36] That statement, of course, is true but not necessarily of legal or business significance. Cellular reproduction in the high tech sense, as one commentator has put it, requires more human intervention than the reproduction of a

[32]The confusion is rampant. Thus, on June 26, 1986, the Office of Science and Technology released a guideline document entitled "Coordinated Framework for Regulation of Biotechnology," 51 Fed. Reg. 23302(No.123). On Dec. 9, 1986, three federal agencies significantly involved in the development of the guidelines, the NSF, the FDA, and the USDA, announced they would no longer adhere to them. 51 Fed. Reg. 43397.

[33]The early history is discussed in McGarity & Bayer, "Federal Regulation of Emerging Genetic Technologies," 36 *Vanderbilt L. Rev*. 461 (Apr. 1983). The operative regulations include guidelines developed by the National Institutes of Health, the Federal Insecticide, Fungicide and Rodenticide Act and the Toxic Substances Control Act. *See* Note, "The Rutabaga That Ate Pittsburgh: Federal Regulation of Free Release Biotechnology," 72 *U. Va. L. Rev.* 1529 (Nov. 1986).

[34]*See* Miller & Davis, *supra* n. 6, at 21. Certain types of asexually reproduced plants may be the subject of a "plant patent." 35 U.S.C. § 161.

[35]*Diamond v. Chakrabarty* 447 U.S. 303 (1980).

[36]The general counsel of Genentech, Inc., noting that one cell, properly instructed, can become in one day a billion cells, producing a billion copies of an encoded molecule, analogizes licensing micro-organisms to licensing a "factory." "It is possible to sell a microbial factory, or any other, on an installment basis, pegged to the value the marketplace ultimately sets on its production." Kiley, "Biotechnology: Evolution of a New Venture and its Licensing Strategy," in *Recent Developments in Licensing, supra* n. 9, at 120. Kiley's remarks do not, however, cover the question arising when a licensee of DNA watches the DNA self-mutate into another useful form. Davidson, "Common Law, Uncommon Software," 47 *U. Pitt. L. Rev.* 1037, 1105 (1986).

computer program.[37] As of this writing, a plethora of litigation is under way between major players challenging the validity of one another's patents.[38]

The disputes threaten to widen as patent protection is extended from micro-organisms to animals. Indeed, the United States Board of Patent Appeals recently has taken the issue one step further, reversing a Patent Office decision that refused to grant a patent on a "manufactured" oyster; the Patent Office had agreed to issue a patent on the method but not the oyster itself. The significance of patenting the product as well as the method is that, among other things, protection thereupon issues against the practice of U.S. patented products being manufactured off shore and imported into this country.[39]

§15.5 THRESHOLD CONFIDENTIALITY

At the threshold of the negotiations between the licensor and a potential licensee of secret technology, there exists a serious "chicken versus egg" problem. How does Start-up, Inc. disclose enough of the technology to induce Goliath, Inc. to sign a license agreement without giving away the core secrets? Many large companies will not, as a matter of policy, sign unilateral confidentiality agreements because of the risk that the alleged inventor will later claim that Goliath's entire line of business was derived from the disclosure made; moreover, they return unopened materials which purport to qualify under the heading of what one leading commentator calls "submission of ideas."[40] No entirely satisfactory solution has been found to what is sometimes called the "black box" problem (as in "how can I charge for a peek into the black box?") and is, as one authority put it, "older than recorded history."[41] If no pre-negotiation confidentiality agreement is signed, courts may redress, on

[37] Kirn, "The Use of Common Law Bailments in Connection with The Licensing of Living Organisms," reproduced in *Technology Licensing* 291,294 (P.L.I. Course Handbook Series No. 235, 1987).

[38] The leading case is *Hybritech Inc. v. Monoclonal Antibodies, Inc.* 802 F.2d 1367 (CAFC 1986) in which Hybritech's patents on immunoassays involving monoclonal antibodies were upheld in a decision that one commentator says may make Hybritech and its parent, Eli Lily, into the "Polaroid or Xerox" in the field of diagnostics. 5 *Biotech. L. Rep.* 322, 323 (Oct.–Nov. 1986). The stakes are so high that nearly everyone in the field—e.g., Cetus v. Amgen, Revlon v. Genentech, Johnson & Johnson v. Becton–Dickinson, Hoffman–La Roche v. Genentech—is involved in litigation of one sort or another. *Ibid.*

[39] Pellerin, "Animals Are Patentable, Says Patent Office," 2 *Washington Technology* 1 (Apr. 16, 1987).

[40] *2 Milgrim on Trade Secrets*, § 8.03 (1987).

[41] Finnegan & D'Andrea, "The Black Box Problem: Using Pre-Negotiation Secrecy Agreements to Govern Disclosure of Technology to Potential Licensees," in, *1979 Licensing Law Handbook*, Ch. 7 (Finnegan. ed. 1979).

the basis of implied contract,[42] a theft of Start-up's trade secrets but problems of proof can be difficult. Several large companies have developed a form of written protocol the inventor must sign, sometimes called an "unsolicited suggestion agreement," which waives any claims the submitting person or firm may have except those to which he may become legally entitled under the patent and copyright laws.[43]

§15.6 LICENSING AS AN ALTERNATIVE METHOD OF DISTRIBUTION

Separate and apart from the issue of intellectual property protection is the question whether Start-up, Inc. should attempt to exploit its product on its own or to enter into some sort of an agreement whereby someone else, a bigger firm, joins in that activity in exchange for a split of the profits: a license in the nature of a distribution or marketing agreement, sometimes labeled a joint venture.

The "sell or license" decision is a movable calculation, a series of tradeoffs which must be weighed in each case. On the "license" side of the equation, some of the commonly cited factors are as follows:

- **(i)** If the start-up has no money to create an effective marketing and sales organization, the decision is easy—licensing is the only alternative;
- **(ii)** Cash may be available but there may be other opportunities for its employment (e.g., research and development) which appear more promising;
- **(iii)** Certain markets are not penetrable without the assistance of a muscular licensee;
- **(iv)** The licensee may be able to pollinate the technology with some ideas of its own which will make the product more valuable; this entails so-called VAR (Value Added Reseller) arrangements, the licensee adding value to the product before sending it on its way to the consumer;
- **(v)** Although tying agreements are illegal, the licensee may be able to recommend that the purchasers of the licensee's own products (e.g., a personal computer) use the licensed product (a software program) to get maximum value out of the PC;
- **(vi)** Licensing may enable the start-up to get into a market early, before the competition, and pre-empt a valuable opportunity;

[42] *Id.*

[43] Bender, *supra* n. 16, at § 8.03[2].

(vii) Occasionally, licensing can provide opportunistic income; a field or product the licensor has no interest in exploring thoroughly can yield extra revenue from a licensing arrangement with an interested reseller.[44]

On the other side of the fence, the problems are obvious. Thus, licensing means, by definition, that some of the available profit on the ultimate sale of the product will be shared with an outside firm. More importantly, the licensor surrenders a significant quantum of control over the destiny of its product. No matter how tightly the agreement is drawn, the individuals actually moving the product in the marketplace will not be answerable to the licensor. Further, the licensee, in order to do an adequate job of marketing, will necessarily get to know a lot about the product, opening up the possibility of "piracy." Piracy is a word which suggests a raid by a boarding party on a helpless merchant ship; in fact, various forms of piracy can be a good deal more subtle, some even unintentional, as ideas suggested to the licensee's engineering staff by their growing familiarity with the licensed product somehow seep into "enhanced" or "improved" products which may not be covered by the license at all.

Overall, the notion of licensing as an alternative method of distribution has inherently dangerous overtones, as the licensor loses intimate touch with its customers. A business that does not control its sales force and cannot get firsthand feedback from customers on a minute-by-minute basis may be a business headed for trouble. The licensor, unless the contract insists the product be "signed" with its name, may become invisible, unrecognized by customers or the public at large.[45]

§15.7 NATURE OF LICENSED "PROPERTY"

There are various ways to distinguish between types of license agreements. Legally, the licensed product is either patented, protected by copyright or by the law of trade secrets or is a "hybrid," meaning a combination of two or more of the above. For a variety of reasons, a license agreement should set out as specifically as possible the legal status of the product being licensed. Thus, if the product is the subject of an existing patent, the contract should do something more than merely

[44]There are, of course, other, more technical reasons to license—i.e., to settle a dispute with a competing patent applicant or a former employee concerning rights to the technology. *See* La Paglia, "Basic Considerations in Licensing from the Business Perspective," in *Technology Licensing, supra* n. 37 at 99.

[45]A useful discussion of the considerations involved is contained in Dratler, "Licensing Agreements" in Harroch, *Start-Up Companies: Planning, Financing and Operating the Successful Business* Ch. 16 (1986).

incorporate the issued patent as an exhibit; the license of a patented device often includes related nonpatented (and perhaps nonpatentable) technology, which may or may not be secret. And, when both patented and nonpatented items are bundled into a single license, interesting questions arise about the licensee's obligation to pay when and if the patent is declared invalid or expires.[46] The way to avoid a dispute is to describe each item covered by reference to its mode of protection—that is, patented and nonpatentable-but-secret—and then cover expressly all possible contingencies. Thus, if certain technology is not patented when the license is granted, the agreement should specifically address what happens if the patent does, or does not, issue. Does the patented product command a higher price simply because it has been patented?[47] It is risky, in short, to describe the licensed product solely in business terms, without reference to legal status, because the argument then remains open that the quantum of protection for the licensed product drives, in part, the royalty and other terms of the license agreement. Another reason to describe each item separately stems from the notion that "mandatory package licensing" constitutes patent misuse. If possible, the agreement should separate each item of intellectual property and, despite the fact that no business imperative may require the practice, specify a separate element of the royalty for each.[48]

§15.8 FIELD OF USE

However the product is classified as a legal matter, agreements also fall into categories depending on what it is the licensee plans to do—that is, to use the product internally, to copy[49] and/or manufacture the prod-

[46]*See infra* § 15.17.

[47]As indicated *infra,* § 15.17, the patent monopoly cannot be used to exact a royalty for use of a patented product after the patent expires. *Aronson v. Quick Point Pencil Co.,* 440 U.S. 236,265 (1979). But the license of a trade secret entails royalties for the one-time disclosure of the secret; the issue arises whether royalties can continue even after the secret descends into the public domain. *Compare 2 Milgrim on Trade Secrets,* § 10.01[2][a][iii] n. 74 (1987) (trade secret rights "normally expire[s] upon matters becoming generally known within an industry") *with 2 Milgrim on Trade Secrets* § 6.05[4] (1987) ("there is authority indicating that the courts . . . will enforce the promise to pay royalties after secrecy is lost").

[48]*See infra* § 15.17.

[49]The purchaser of a software program will naturally want to copy it for internal purposes so as to have a back-up in case the program is accidentally erased. This right is protected to an extent by the 1980 amendments to § 117 of the Copyright Act, 17 U.S.C. § 117, meaning a copyright is not infringed by archival copying. It is not clear whether, despite the language in the Act, a licensor can restrict *by agreement* the right to copy for internal purposes.

uct, to modify it, to distribute it, to incorporate it into another product and sell the result. The point is that, as earlier indicated, the verb "license" covers a variety of possible commercial arrangements. A well-drafted agreement will start with a statement of exactly what it is the licensee is authorized to do, which of the entire bundle of ownership rights is being transferred.

Indeed, within each category of activity, there are subsidiary questions. If the license is engaged to "distribute" the product, that term means at least the right to sell products to third parties. The question arises whether the licensee has the right to sublicense or to subdistribute and, if so, on what terms.[50] This right has substantial practical consequences. If the licensee can sublicense, a number of terms are up for negotiation: Does the sublicensed product continue to carry the original licensor's name? Will the trade secrets be protected by a chain of covenants?[51] The right to "modify" may only contemplate the correction of errors—debugging software, for example—or it may entail substantive improvements to the product, technology which may be the subject of a "back license" from the licensee to the licensor.[52]

The right to incorporate the licensed product into another product and sell the result is known, for some obscure reason, as an "OEM License," the acronym OEM standing for original equipment manufacturer. Why the licensee, rather than the licensor, is nicknamed the "original" manufacturer is a mystery. Indeed, it is not quite clear what the word original is supposed to mean in this context. Nonetheless, the term is solidly in place. When Start-up, Inc. licenses its widgets to Goliath, Inc. for insertion in the megamachine Goliath sells to the public, the deal is described as an OEM[53] arrangement.

[50]Generally, a license is not considered assignable by the licensee absent agreement to the contrary and, in keeping with that notion, specific permission from the licensor is required to sublicense. 1 Eckstrom *supra* n. 4 at 1.03[3][i].

[51]The so-called multilevel issues are collected in Dratler, *supra* n. 45, at § 16.06[2].

[52]The issue of modifications in the area of computer software poses a number of difficult questions if the agreement is not specific, starting with the basics—who owns the modifications? Davidson & Davidson, *supra* n. 10, at § 8.2(c). The authors suggest the agreement provide that the user must assign all rights in modifications back to the licensor. *Id.* at § 8.2(c)(a). If the licensor of a patented item requires a "grant back," a promise by the licensee to license or convey back to the licensor any patents granted on improvements to the licensed product, this does not per se constitute an illegal extension of the patent monopoly. *Transparent-Wrap Machine Corp. v. Stokes & Smith Co.* 329 U.S. 637 (1947). *See infra* § 17.17.

[53]As one commentary points out, the OEM does *not* manufacture; it *assembles* components made by others. Davidson & Davidson, *supra* n. 10, at § 1.3. The phrase "Value Added Reseller" or VAR is sometimes used indiscriminately with OEM. In a VAR arrangement, ordinarily the licensed product does not disappear.

§15.9 "MOST FAVORED NATION" CLAUSES

Technology moves fast in today's world and a licensee (who may have paid a giant up-front fee to enable the licensor to finish product development) will feel justifiably aggrieved if the product is subsequently licensed to the licensee's competitors on more favorable terms. Consequently, many agreements contain so-called "most favored nation" clauses, provisions which ratchet down the existing license terms to whatever better terms are enjoyed by the newcomer. This clause is particularly hard to draft since the possibility of ambiguity is unusually large—what is "more favorable," versus simply different. Each license will contain some distinct language (assuming any negotiation occurs at all) and there is the question of comparability. What if the first license entails periodic payments out of net profits and the second involves a lump sum payment?[54] If the licensor settles a dispute with an alleged infringer and that settlement involves some sort of license, does the compromise agreement consist of a "license" within the meaning of a most favored nation clause in an earlier agreement?[55]

§15.10 OTHER LIMITATIONS ON LICENSEE EXPLOITATION

A license agreement may also be limited by its geographical or type-of-customer extension. Thus, a licensor may want to split its product between two licensees: one operating on the East Coast and one on the West. Alternatively, a medical software start-up may feel that Corporation X would be a good partner in merchandising to the non-for-profit hospital market while Corporation Y has better connections with health maintenance organizations. "Vertical" restraints—those imposed by a licensor upon a licensee—are generally legal in the face of state and federal antitrust legislation, but any restraint requires consideration of whether competition is being "unreasonably" restrained.[56]

§15.11 EXCLUSIVITY

In its most extreme form, a licensor could license, for a fee, anyone and everyone to promote the licensed product anywhere each licensee wants to: "come one, come all." However, if the license arrangement entails investment by the licensee, then some form of exclusivity is mandatory as a *quid pro quo*. For many years, well-meaning legislation naïvely

[54]*See* cases collected at Cascio, "Key Provisions for Technology Licensing Agreements" 160 in *Technology Licensing* (P.L.I. Course Handbook No. 235, 1987).
[55]*Id.*, at 163
[56]*See infra* § 15.17.

prohibited the U.S. government from granting exclusive licenses on its technology, which meant by and large that the technology, since it could be exploited by anyone, was exploited by no one.[57]

Until the advent of the Tax Reform Act of 1986, there was a major tax advantage to exclusive licensing of a patent because an assignment of "all substantial rights" therein, albeit by way of a license versus an outright sale, produced capital gain rather than ordinary income.[58] An exclusive license to exploit the licensed product anywhere in the U.S. for an unlimited period of time was deemed such an all-encompassing assignment. The issue remains significant because the "all substantial rights" test also determines whether intellectual property is property for purposes of § 351 of the Code, the section postponing tax on the gain in an exchange of stock for appreciated property.[59] A large body of law has grown up around the question of when an "exclusive" license is exclusive for purposes of conveying "all substantial rights" of the licensor in the product.[60] It has become clear in the course of the cases interpreting the phrase, even the term exclusive can be ambiguous.[61] Thus, if the licensor is preserving for itself, (and not another licensee) the right to sell alongside with the licensee, it would not appear that exclusivity has been achieved for tax purposes even though the licensee enjoys the only outside license; these arrangements are sometimes called dual distribution arrangements. Further, a licensee which purports to be exclusive may expire after a limited period of time; a licensee may be content with a short-term exclusive because it gives the licensee the necessary head start on the pack; it is, in fact, exclusive. Nonetheless, a license limited in time—for less than the life of the patent—is also not deemed an assignment of *all* substantial rights of the licensor for tax purposes.[62] The provisions relating to exclusivity are inexorably tied to the issue of termination, particularly, as discussed in the next section, termination by the licensor by reason of the licensee's failure to exploit the product with sufficient vigor.

[57]*See* Ch. 18, § 18.6(b), n. 37.

[58]I.R.C. § 1235, which provides that the transfer is a sale or exchange whether or not the payments are made periodically and/or are contingent on use.

[59]*See* Ch. 5, § 5.1(b).

[60]*Hooker Chemicals and Plastics Corp. v. U.S.* 591 F.2d 652 (Ct. Cir. 1979). *See* Treas. Reg. 1.1235–2(b)(1), defining "all substantial rights." *See also* the extended discussion in 2 Eckstrom, *supra* n. 4 at § 14.03[1][a].

[61]*Bell Intercontinental Corp., Inc. v. U.S.* 381 F.2d 1004 (Ct. Cl. 1967).

[62]*PPG Industries, Inc. v. Comm'r* 55 T.C. 928 (1970). The issue whether the grant of an exclusive license in a patent, trademark or copyright amounts to an "assignment" which should be recorded in the appropriate federal office is explored in Dratler, *supra* n. 45, at § 16.03[2].

§15.12 DUTY OF LICENSEE TO EXPLOIT

One of the most difficult issues in licensing, a subset of the overall desire of the licensor to control the activities of the licensee, is the obligation of the licensee to "exploit" the licensed product. (The imposition of a duty to exploit arises, naturally, most often when the license is exclusive but may be significant if the license is less than totally exclusive; i.e., exclusive for a specific period.)

At first glance, one would think a licensee would have a natural affinity for maximum exploitation since the licensee sought out the license in the first place.[63] However, there is room for wide differences of opinion as to what constitutes an acceptable level of effort to get the product into the most appropriate markets. License agreements commonly hold the licensee to a requirement that it use its "best efforts" to exploit the licensed product. The application of that standard to the facts of particular case, however, may be a good deal less than satisfactory. Some courts have suggested that best efforts do not mean "heroic" efforts;[64] and, as the parties fall out, litigation will ensue because "best efforts" is a phrase susceptible of any number of meanings.[65] It is possible, and therefore usually preferable, to objectify the notion of "best efforts."[66] Thus, it is common to find a minimum level of financial performance as the obligation of the licensee. The specific benchmark can be minimum royalties, (the licensor's principal interest), but that number may be hard to estimate in any equitable way before the program starts. Hence, the minimum may be something more within the licensee's control—that is, invest so many dollars in promotion by a certain date, establish so many dealerships. "Front ending" the royalty payments—requiring a substantial advance or down payment against future royalties—is a customary method for gaining the licensee's interest and attention.[67] Whether a minimum royalty provision negates the implied obligation on the licensee to use its best efforts to exploit above and beyond the royalty is an open question.[68]

[63] On occasion, a firm may license a given technology solely for the purpose of keeping it out of the hands of a competitor.
[64] *Bloor v. Falstaff Brewing Corp.* 601 F.2d 609 (2d Cir. 1979).
[65] *See* Becker, "Licensing in the Chemical Industry," 55 *J. Pat. Off. Soc'y* 759, 774 (1973).
[66] There are cases holding that, even if the agreement is silent, the licensee has an obligation (stemming from the implied obligation of good faith and fair dealing between contracting parties) to use best efforts to exploit. *See Perma Research & Development v. Singer Co.* 402 F. Supp. 881 (S.D.N.Y. 1975), *aff'd* 542 F.2d 111 (2d Cir. 1976) and other cases cited in Cascio, *supra* n. 54, at 170.
[67] In view of the difficulty of equitable relief and/or estimating damages, the licensor's remedy for failure to perform on the licensee's part is usually cancellation of the license or cancellation of the exclusivity. *See supra* § 15.15.
[68] *See Vacuum Concrete Corp. of America v. American Machine & Foundry Corp.* 169 U.S.P.Q. 287 (1971).

§15.13 ENHANCEMENTS AND IMPROVEMENTS

One of the haziest and most difficult areas has to do with "enhancements," "improvements," and/or "derivative works" relating to the licensed product.[69] A number of issues need definition. What is an improvement, versus a wholly new idea outside the scope of the license agreement entirely?[70] The licensor usually wants all such improvements to inhere, ipso facto, in the definition of the licensed product. A licensee with good bargaining position may argue that improvements, if the product solely of its own efforts, should be its property or, at worst, the joint property of the licensor and the licensee with, perhaps, a royalty adjustment to take into account the effort put in by the licensee. The licensor may counter with a demand for the right to use and exploit any improved products for its own purposes, and, indeed, the right to license the same out to somebody else. The process pursuant to which the licensor is granted rights to improvements contrived by the licensee is known as "back licensing" or "grant backs."[71] Back licensing and cross-licensing are becoming more common, as, for example, major U.S. and Japanese firms are joining together to pool their technology, each sharing in the fruits of that pooling arrangement. The question of improvements can operate in the reverse direction. The licensee, either directly or through a most favored nation clause (*see* § 15.9, above) may insist that the licensor include all improvements occurring in its laboratories during the term—"updates" as they are sometimes called—within the scope of the license.

§15.14 CALCULATION OF ROYALTIES

Royalty income is a function of the base selected; that is, the number of units sold by the licensee and the net or gross revenues of the licensee from the sale of the units. This can be expressed as a percentage, fixed or variable (e.g., 3% of annual sales up to $1 million, 2% of all sales over that number) or an absolute amount: X dollars per unit sold. When a start-up is getting going, it is often financed by a prepayment of royalty

[69]Improvements to a licensed computer software often arise when the program is "modified" by the user. *See* the discussion, *supra* n. 52.

[70]Section 101 of the Patent Act adds "improvements" to the previously mentioned items ("process, machine, manufacture, or composition of matter") as a separate class of patentable items, 35 U.S.C. § 101. *See supra* § 15.4 concerning biogenetic products—what happens when a licensed microorganism self-mutates?.

[71]*See 2 Milgrim on Trade Secrets* § 10.01[2](f)(1987). Despite the holding in the *Transparent-Wrap* case that grant backs are legal, *supra* n. 52, antitrust law views them with "repugnance" because, arguably, the grant backs extend the patent monopoly and diminish the licensee's motivation to improve. *2 Milgrim, supra,* at § 10.01[2](f).

income, raising potential accounting issues as to when and how much of the prepaid amount should be taken into income in subsequent periods.[72] The art of setting the royalty base, the measuring stick, derives from an analysis of the risks and rewards the parties wish to share. A "net profit" royalty (versus gross revenues) obviously gives the licensor an interest in the licensee's ability to control costs; "profits" may be defined in this context as the savings which the licensed product engenders. Indeed, a royalty can be the result of a combined calculation: $1 per unit sold plus 3% of all sales.[73]

The amount of a royalty will usually be a function of the contribution the parties bring to the relationship. Thus, if the licensee is buying an "accommodation" license—one taken only to avoid arguments concerning potential infringement—the royalties will be at the lower end of the scale. Care must be taken not to get too elaborate in defining royalties if the licensor and licensee are competitors since any well-drafted agreement will include verification procedures. Thus, a "net profit" (or even a gross sales) license may not be advisable because the licensee may not want to expose to the licensor the prices it is charging and/or its cost of manufacture.

A final, and important, point on royalty negotiations. Many inexperienced founders tend to view the royalties their start-ups are asked to pay for a necessary piece of technology as an ordinary expense of doing business, perhaps not terribly significant. Thus, the seller of a bundled hardware/software package may readily agree to pay the software author "5% of gross revenues" on the theory that 5% is not a big number. The problem is that 5% *is* a big number once competition looms, as it almost always does. If a unit sells for $100 and the actual cost to make it is $20, then a $5 royalty adds 20% to the manufacturing cost. Put another way, the party burdened with a royalty of that dimension must be able to make the product much more cheaply than the competition if the maker is to compete effectively. A 5% royalty may be cheap if it enables the licensee to save an equivalent or greater amount but it is not a trivial number, particularly if it pays for something the competition does not have to buy.

[72]While there is no conceptual limit under the antitrust laws on how high a royalty may be charged, *2 Milgrim on Trade Secrets* § 10.01[2](a) (1987), patent misuse can arise if the patentee charges discriminitory rates or conditions a given rate on the licensor's agreement to license other products. *Ibid.*

[73]There are additional variations on the theme mentioned in the Text—i.e., $1 per unit manufactured or installed, a fee measured by weight or volume, a fee measured by value added, a fee measured by use—i.e., oscillations of a machine. A fee measured by units sold (vs. sales) gives the licensee more leeway in pricing.

§15.15 NOTICES TO AND ACTIONS AGAINST THIRD PARTIES

To facilitate actions against infringers or unauthorized converters of intellectual property, the agreement will usually require the licensee to affix "patent," "patent pending," and "copyright" notices[74] in the places suggested by the relevant statute sufficient to provide the basis for infringement actions or other equitable remedies.[75]

Whatever the form of notice, protection is not self-executing; somebody has to undertake the burden of bringing an action against an unlawful infringer, copier, or converter of the intellectual property in question. The agreement should allocate the obligation to undertake a defense or prosecution on that party—licensor or licensee—with the greater economic interest in maintaining the confidentiality or exclusivity of the material. The expense, of course, can be shared, but the responsibility for enforcement (and defense) should be focused so that at least one of the parties is forever alert to possible violations.

§15.16 WARRANTIES

Licensees are naturally interested in obtaining warranties by the licensor that there is no prior or competitive claim to the information, that it does not infringe somebody else's patent, offend a copyright or unlawfully derive from someone else's trade secrets.[76] In a case of copyrighted material or trade secrets, the warranty which relates to title should not be a major problem for the licensor since the warranty is, in effect, an undertaking that the licensor did not acquire the information by its own illegal activities (copying in the case of a copyright or obtaining unauthorized disclosure in the case of trade secrets.) A warranty against apparent patent infringements is a more difficult prob-

[74]There is no statutory requirement that the owner of a trade secret legend the written materials memoralizing the secret but, as discussed in Ch. 16, that practice "enhances" protection. *See* Davidson & Davidson, *supra* n. 10, at § 8.4(c), for useful examples of the form of legends to use.

[75]Use of the term "patent pending" gives no protection until the patent is issued. *See* Miller & Davis, *supra* n. 6, at 127–128. Notice of the patent, by marking the product, is a condition for the recovery of money damages. *Id.* at 128. On the more important issue of notice of a claim of copyright protection, *see id.* at 390.

[76]The party with the most significant economic interest in challenging the licensor's monopoly may be the licensee itself. The doctrine of "license estoppel"—that the licensee could not contest the licensor's patent—is now repealed. *Lear, Inc. v. Adkins* 395 U.S. 653 (1969).

lem since a patent prohibits anyone from exploiting the idea even though they independently arrived at the notion in ignorance of the prior patent or claim. It is possible for the licensor to conduct a patent search; in fact, if the licensed product is patented, such a search necessarily has been conducted, if only by the Patent Office. However, if no patent is pending, a search is expensive and there is no guarantee, even when a patent has been issued, that the search covered all the bases. A foreign patent may be filed in this country for up to one year after its filing in a foreign country and be granted a priority in the United States.[77] Moreover, patents, once issued, can easily be challenged.[78] Consequently, the licensor is at risk for events beyond its control when a warranty against infringement claims is demanded. In such a case, it is in the licensor's interest at least to limit damages to the amount of the royalties paid by the licensee under the agreement.

The negotiation of warranties in license agreements (indeed, in contracts of sale as well) include other important promises—that is, that the product or process works the way it is supposed to and that there are no unforeseen or undisclosed hazards associated with its use; these are sometimes labeled "performance warranties."[79] The entire area of product liability lawsuits has become a nightmare for manufacturers in this country as awards have gone completely out of sight, at least in the view of the defense bar and their clients. Accordingly, license agreements (not governed explicitly by, but nonetheless de facto subject to, the Uniform Commercial Code)[80] should be drafted with extreme care on the warranty issue.[81] This is an involved story about which, for present purposes, a few notes must suffice. The consumer movement has collided with what sellers and licensors believe to be the limits of a manufacturer's ability to respond and the result is a proliferation of consumer-oriented statutes, massive litigation and much learned dis-

[77]35 U.S.C. § 119.

[78]"In many United States Courts of Appeal, litigated patents have been found invalid more often than valid." *See* Miller & Davis, *supra* n. 6, at § 1.2.

[79]Dratler, *supra* n. 45, at § 16.03[9].

[80]Davidson & Davidson, *supra* n. 10, at § 2.2(a)(1). *See* Ch. 17, § 17.2(2).

[81]The principal federal statute, the Magnuson Moss Warranty and Improvement Act, 15 U.S.C. §§ 2301–2312, imposes restrictions on disclaimers of warranties and limitations of liability for consequential damages; it applies to "any tangible personal property which is distributed in commerce . . . which is normally used for personal, family, or household purposes." 15 U.S.C. § 2301(1). The Act requires, for example, that disclaimers be positioned notoriously on the item, or near it at the point of sale. State laws, for example, in California the Song–Beverly Consumer Warranty Act, Calif. Civ. Code §§ 1790–1797, also govern the proper mode for disclaiming implied warranties. The federal and state statutes generally apply to consumer products and not to items licensed between commercial concerns, but the thrust of the statutory language has a powerful influence over the courts and should, therefore, be observed whenever possible.

cussion.[82] It is critical, therefore, for a prudent licensor to deny in the agreement (to the extent allowable by law) responsibility for any implied warranties of any sort, including particularly the warranties of "merchantability" and "fitness" under the Uniform Commercial Code, except to the extent the parties otherwise expressly agree.[83] The licensor should very explicitly set out what it is that is warranted and for what period of time, defining carefully not only the warranty period but also when the statute of limitations on the warranty begins to run—that is, when the defect is first discovered or when it first could have been discovered in the exercise of due diligence by the licensee. The licensor is ordinarily taking major risks if all responsibilities for "indirect," "consequential," "incidental" or "special" damages are not specifically denied. The terms entail differing nuances, but they each involve damages which result in a chain reaction from the failure of the goods to perform as required. Thus, if a software program breaks down, the "direct" damages are the loss of what was paid for the program in the first place and the costs directly incurred in fixing it. Indirect, incidental, special or consequential damages, (whatever adjective is applied by the court considering the case) have to do with such matters as the loss of business during the period of time that the computers were down; such damages can amount to several orders of magnitude in excess of direct or out-of-pocket costs. The licensor's best result, of course, is to limit damages to costs of repair, after a grace period in which the licensor is given the opportunity to repair.

From the licensee's standpoint, the above principles operate in reverse. Since the licensee may find itself liable to some third party for consequential damages, it will fight hard for an unrestricted right to go against the licensor in any such case, making itself merely a conduit to the extent possible.

§15.17 ANTITRUST CONSIDERATIONS

The discussion in the Text will refer only summarily to a fertile field of legal dispute in the law of licensing, the question whether a given licensing practice offends the antitrust laws. A full-scale treatment of this important subject is well beyond the scope of the Text.

While antitrust issues may seem at first blush out of place in the microworld of venture capital, such is far from the case. Thus, start-ups are often involved in antitrust litigation, as when a company, needing a particular item of technology to stay in business, defends Goliath,

[82]Uniform Commercial Code §§ 2–314 (merchantability) and 2–315 (fitness). The Code requires that disclaimers be "conspicuous." U.C.C. § 2–316.
[83]*See* Ch. 17, § 17.2(c).

Inc.'s claim of license violation with a countercharge that Goliath, Inc. is attempting to drive competition from the marketplace.[84] Moreover, a given licensing practice may suggest a whole range of possible antitrust violations. These include a tie-in or tying arrangement (when the availability of a desired product is conditioned on purchase of an undesired product);[85] refusals to license;[86] extending royalty payments beyond the life of the patent;[87] and establishment of patent "pools," with no licensing allowed to nonmembers of the pool.[88] Generally, license restrictions confining the licensee to a particular territory are lawful,[89] as are restrictions to a particular field of use[90] and on the quantity of articles the licensee may make and sell. License restrictions respecting sale price are, as one might imagine, more sensitive.[91]

[84]*See, e.g., Lektro–Vend Corp. v. Vendo Co.* 660 F.2d 255 (1981), *cert. denied* 455 U.S. 921 (1982).

[85]*E.g., Morton Salt Co. v. G.S. Suppiger Co.* 314 U.S. 488 (1942) "Tie-in" arrangements are usually held violative of law; if a patented product is involved, the illegal tie constitutes "misuse" of patent. *Ibid.* Proof of an illegal tie-in requires evidence that the licensor had the power to "force" the purchaser to accept the undesired product. *Jefferson Parish Hosp. Dist. No. 2 v. Hyde* 466 U.S. 2 (1984). The many possibilities for creating sophisticated tying arrangements were dealt a heavy blow by the Ninth Circuit in the now-celebrated *Data General* case. *Digidyne Corp. v. Data General Corp* 734 F.2d 1336 (9th Cir. 1984) *cert. denied* 105 S. Ct. 3534 (1985). Data General was trying to restrict the use of its operating system software to central processing units which it manufactured. The classic antitrust issues—Was software a "product? What was the appropriate market to use in measuring Data General's monopoly power?—all went against Data General. The fact that Data General was trying to "lock in" principally its own customer base did not persuade the court of appeals that the market influence was trivial. *Id.* at 1340, 1341.

[86]Unilateral refusals to license (versus agreements among firms) are generally legal. *SCM Corp. v. Xerox Corp.* 463 F. Supp. 983 (D. Conn. 1978), *aff'd in part* 645 F.2d 1195 (2d Cir. 1981), *cert. den.* 455 U.S. 1016 (1982).

[87]Generally, an attempt to charge royalties after the 17-year period has expired is deemed an illegal "extension" of the patent monopoly. *Brulotte v. Thys Co.* 379 U.S. 29 (1964). The issues become complicated if the technology is patentable but a patent never issues. Can the licensor claim perpetual royalties? According to *Aronson v. Quick Point Pencil Co.* 440 U.S. 257 (1979), the answer apparently is that it can. A related issue is whether the licensor of a trade secret can collect royalties after the "secret" has lawfully passed into the public domain. Based on the famous "Listerine" case, the answer appears to be "Yes." *Warner-Lambert Pharmaceutical Co. Inc. v. John J. Reynolds, Inc.* 178 F. Supp. 655 (S.D.N.Y. 1959) *aff'd per curiam* 280 F.2d 197 (2d Cir. 1960).

[88]A concerted (versus unilateral) refusal to deal is per se illegal. *United States v. Besser Manufacturing Co.* 96 F. Supp. 304 (E.D. Mich. 1951) *aff'd,* 343 U.S. 444 (1952). However, cross-licensing arrangements or assignments to a particular agent may be upheld depending on, *inter alia,* whether the purpose is to exclude competitors. *See* Simon, "Basic Antitrust Considerations in Patent and Know-How Licensing" in *1980 Licensing Law Handbook* § 2.12 (1980). Patent pooling may be justified if it is, for example, the only way to resolve disputes over the validity of a patent.

[89]35 U.S.C. §261 specifically legitimizes territorial restrictions in patent licenses.

[90]A licensor may dictate the customers to which a licensee may sell and/or the type of article. *General Talking Pictures Corp. v. Western Electric Co.* 304 U.S. 175, *aff'd on rehearing,* 305 U.S. 124 (1938).

[91]The issue is whether the holding in *United States v. General Electric Co.* 272 U.S. 476 (1926) (upholding price restrictions) is valid today.

An important issue deserves special mention at this point. "Package licensing" involves an economic imperative: the necessity in a technologically complex world of including several patents, plus nonpatentable or nonpatented material, such as trade secrets, in a single license. The problem arises because "mandatory package licensing"—the practice of charging the same royalty for a single patent as for a bundle of patents—is generally deemed, based on the current state of the law, to constitute patent misuse.[92] Licensors faced with the business necessity of licensing a potpourri of intellectual property are compelled to craft their agreements in such a way that each item appears to be licensed separately.[93]

[92]*American Security Co. v. Shatterproof Glass Corp.* 268 F.2d 769 (3d Cir. 1959).
[93]*See* 1 Eckstrom, *supra* n. 4, at § 6.01[3][c].

Sixteen

Intellectual Property

As indicated in the discussion of licensing in the preceding chapter, intellectual property is often the lifeblood of venture-backed firms. The exposition in this chapter touches only the high spots, a summary of applicable law. Although cast in legal terms, nonlawyers should find the materials useful in guiding them in some of their critical evaluations—for example, some of the considerations applicable in deciding whether to apply for patent protection.

§16.1 BACKGROUND

Intellectual property is a legal construct of particular importance to start-ups and early-stage companies because that type of property often forms the only asset on the balance sheet when the company is organized. High tech start-ups, in particular, are often founded on ideas. Since early-stage companies are fragile animals, it is critical that they be in a position to protect the core asset: information which is important to them commercially. It is their power to deal with such information as the "owner," which gives them a lease on life. Accordingly, much of the legal work involved in start-up companies has to do with exploring the vitality and limits of the company's protection of its "property"[1] against misappropriation.

The protection of intellectual property goes back to the beginnings of commercial society. Because such property is transportable across state lines virtually with the speed of light, some form of coordinated national (and international) treatment is required. For each state to employ its own patent protection policies, for example, could lead to chaos, the right to use exclusively the xeroxography process being the property of the inventor in one state but, because he was beaten to the local patent office, the right of another nimble applicant 50 yards away across the state line. Moreover, clumsy and competitive doctrinal differences and disputes might stifle the development and disclosure of useful inventions.[2] The interaction of the threads which cause information and ideas to become property someone can own, therefore, is an important theme in venture capital.

The label "intellectual *property*" should be used with some caution. Patents, copyrights, and trade secrets are property in that they can be conveyed and hypothecated.[3] But the underlying themes of the law are not tied to precepts inherited from the ancient doctrines surrounding the law of real and tangible personal property. Protection of intellectual property involves twin currents—the promotion of innovation ("promoting the progress of science and useful arts," in the language of the patent and copyright clause of the Constitution) and protecting fairness and honesty in business competition.[4] Thus, a trade secret question, on the other hand, may revolve not so much on whether A "owns" a particular item of information but on how he acquired it—fairly or unfairly. The validity of a patent may depend on whether the applicant has disclosed enough about his invention to educate others.

The care and maintenance of intellectual property as a commercial asset is generally subsumed under four primary categories: patents;

[1] "Intellectual property is, in effect, a property right in discovered knowledge." *Microbiological Research Corp. v. Muna* 625 P. 2d 690, 696 (Utah 1981). *See generally* Epstein, *Modern Intellectual Property* 151 (1986); Calvey, "Proprietary Protection of Product or Service", Harroch, *Start-Up Companies: Planning, Financing and Operating the Successful Business* (1986); *Milgrim on Trade Secrets* (1987); Davidson & Davidson, *Advanced Legal Strategies for Buying and Selling Computer Software* (1986).

[2] Countries with undeveloped and unsophisticated patent systems appear less successful in producing interesting and useful inventions than the United States. *See* Miller & Davis, *Intellectual Property: Patents, Trademarks and Copyright* § 1.1 (1983).

[3] The question of how one perfects a security interest in intellectual property is complex, involving the interplay of the Uniform Commercial Code procedures and the federal provisions for recording documents affecting patents, trademarks, and copyrights in central "registers." *See generally* Bramson, "Intellectual Property as Collateral—Patents, Trade Secrets, Trademarks and Copyrights," 36 *Bus. Law.* 1567 (July 1981).

[4] *See generally* Klitzke, "Trade Secrets: Important Quasi-Property Rights," 41 *Bus. Law.* 555 (Feb. 1986).

copyrights; trademarks (each protected by statute); and trade secrets, protected by the common law of unfair competition, contractual provisions, state statutes, and trade practices.

§16.2 PATENTS

Article 1, § 8, Clause 8 of the Constitution provides:

> The Congress shall have the Power . . . To promote the Progress of Science and useful Arts, by securing for limited Times to Authors and Inventors the exclusive Right to their respective Writings and Discoveries. . . ."[5]

Under federal law a patent grants to the holder the exclusive use of the patented invention for a relatively extensive—17 years—period of time, thereby creating a legally sanctioned and enforceable monopoly.[6] Indeed some of the first patent issues were addressed in the Statute of Monopolies, adopted in England in 1623, which was "a reaction" *against* the unrestricted grant of patent monopolies.[7]

(a) CONDITIONS TO PATENTABILITY

The operative conditions for gaining patent protection are set out in the statute: "[w]hoever *invents* or *discovers* any *new* and *useful process, machine, manufacture,* or *composition of matter,* or any new and useful *improvement* thereof"[8] may obtain a patent. Subject to conditions mentioned below, in the United States the first to invent (versus the first to file) is the owner; the date of filing is presumed (a rebuttable presumption) to be the date of invention.

To qualify under the statutory language, the subject must, first, be both novel[9] and useful. Novelty means at least that the invention not

[5]This language does not explicitly provide that regulation of patents and copyrights by the states is pre-empted. However, the specific grant of a power to Congress, as opposed to the more general language of the Interstate Commerce Clause, creates a strong presumption that federal regulation is paramount. On the other hand, trademark protection (which will not be dealt with other than summarily in the Text) is not specifically mentioned in the Constitution and, therefore, federal regulation is founded on the commerce clause. *See* Miller & Davis, *supra* n. 2, at 8.

[6]35 U.S.C. § 154, creating in the patentee "the right to exclude others from making, using or selling the invention throughout the United States." The term of the monopoly is a maximum of 14 years in the case of design patents. 35 U.S.C. § 173.

[7]Miller & Davis, *supra* n. 2, at 6 (Emphasis in original).

[8]35 U.S.C. § 101. (Emphasis added.).

[9]35 U.S.C. § 102. The notion of novelty overlaps with the constitutional suggestion that patents protect "inventors." Thus, a finder of a naturally occurring composition of matter is not protected.

have been previously "known or used by others in this country, or patented or described in a printed publication in this or a foreign country before the invention thereof."[10] The idea is that inventors should not be allowed to patent material in the public's possession; the concept also encourages inventors to patent inventions quickly,[11] since, as discussed below, an invention described in printed material or in public use or on sale for more than one year cannot be patented, even by the inventor.[12]

"Useful" means that there be some utility to the invention, capable of some "beneficial use."[13] Further, the invention or discovery must be nonobvious.[14] A stand-alone algorithm is not patentable,[15] nor is a formula, of and by itself.[16] Thus, Einstein could not have patented (although he developed the idea while working in a patent office) the formula $E = MC^2$.

The tests of novelty and nonobviousness overlap. The novelty test means that something substantially identical to the invention had not been previously disclosed; the nonobvious test means that the prior art is surveyed and the question is asked whether an ordinarily skilled practitioner would have found the invention obvious.[17]

[10]*Ibid.*

[11]35 U.S.C. § 102(b). If two inventors claim that each "made" the invention first, the trier of fact will consider the "respective dates of conception and reduction to practice" and the "reasonable diligence of the one who was first to conceive and last to reduce to practice." 35 U.S.C. § 102(g). The concept of "reduction to practice" entails either actual or constructive reduction, the latter consisting of filing the application. Calvey, *supra* n. 1, at § 15.03[2]. The planning point is that start-up firms should memorialize all inventions in a contemporaneous written record by, for example, signing, dating, and countersigning notebooks.

[12]35 U.S.C. § 102. § 102 actually entails two concepts—"anticipation," meaning events occurring prior to invention (therefore destroying the notion of novelty) and "statutory bar"—i.e., 12 months elapsing between certain events (*e.g.*, public use) and the date the application is filed. Compare clauses (a) and (b) of § 102.

[13]35 U.S.C. § 103.

[14]35 U.S.C. § 103; ("obvious . . . to a person having ordinary skill in the art to which said subject matter pertains.")

[15]*Gottschalk v. Benson* 409 U.S. 63 (1972). The term "algorithm" must be approached with some care. As used in the *Benson* case, it means a mathematical formula and is not patentable unless applied (as *Benson* has been interpreted) to the physical elements of an "apparatus" claim or the process steps of a "method" claim. *South Corp. v. United States* 690 F.2d 1368 (C.A.F.C. 1982). To the extent the term "algorithm" means "a methodology to effectuate a highly efficient business system," it may be patentable. *Paine Webber, Inc. v. Merrill Lynch, Inc.* 564 F. Supp. 1358 (D. Del. 1983). For the view that the law, post *Benson,* remains in a state of disarray, *see* Chisum, "The Patentability of Algorithms," 47 *U. Pitt. L. Rev.* 959 (1986).

[16]*Parker v. Flook* 437 U.S. 584 (1978).

[17]There are "secondary" tests for nonobviousness: *e.g.*, do experts express disbelief at the discovery? *Graham v. John Deere Co.* 383 U.S. 1 (1966); is the product an immediate commercial success? *See* Miller & Davis, *supra* n. 2, at 79.

The novelty issue also overlaps with a doctrine entitled "statutory bar." Lack of novelty itself is a bar of sorts—the bar to a successful application if something has occurred prior to the invention which renders it no longer novel. Statutory bar has to do with events which occur more than 12 months prior to the date the inventor *files* his application. If Smith invents something novel and does not file his application within 12 months from the date of any one of the following events, Smith is barred:

Issuance of a prior foreign or domestic patent;

Printed publication, foreign or domestic;

Public domestic use;

Domestic sale;

Foreign patent application (if the foreign patent is granted before Smith's domestic application.)[18]

Note that several of the events described above are liable to be acts by the inventor himself—public domestic use of the invention by the inventor followed by 12 months of inactivity is a bar; he is hoist by his own petard. The thrust of the doctrine is to impel people to apply for the patent and thus educate the public as soon as possible. The senior inventor cannot beat a later inventor who, say, publishes in a foreign country if the senior inventor lets 12 months slip away. A lackadaisical inventor also risks being tagged with having "abandoned" the invention.[19] Without such motivations, inventors might be encouraged, at least so the theory goes, to enlarge the 17-year monopoly.

(b) CLAIMS INTERPRETATION

In interpreting patent claims, certain presumptions are used, similar in concept to the principles of statutory construction. Thus, the doctrine of "equivalence" deals with inventions which do not literally fall within a written claim. If the patent claimed does not precisely overlap the allegedly new invention but, nonetheless, the two are "practically interchangeable," an infringement action may lie. The issue on whether or not to file for a patent (see § 16.6) has to do in part with the question of whether a wily infringer can read the filed patent and design an invention which is in effect the same but just different enough on paper

[18] 35 U.S.C. § § 102(b) and (d).

[19] 35 U.S.C. § 102(c) bars a patent to one who has "abandoned the invention."

to survive attack. The doctrine of equivalence is supposed to be a practical rule, allowing a court to apply common sense in such instances.

The "equivalence" doctrine has, however, a counterpart—that of "literal overlap"—which works in the opposite direction, meaning that even a precise overlap between the patented claim and the description of a new device or process will not per se prove infringement if the two items do not do "the same work in substantially the same way and accomplish the same result."[20]

§16.3 COPYRIGHT

Copyright protection was designed for works of literary and artistic merit, to protect authors against piracy of the expression of their ideas. Copyright protection has become increasingly important in venture capital due to the growth of early-stage companies selling computer software. It is generally thought that protection is most readily found under the Copyright Act,[21] rather than the patent laws, since the time and expense of patent application and enforcement make it cost-efficient to patent only the most creative, important, and long-lived programs.[22] The advantage of patent protection is the breadth of the claims. The patent protects concepts and ideas, not just the manner of expression used by the programmer. Indeed, the notion that the Copyright Act protects only the expression of an idea or a concept, versus the idea itself, is central to the entire protective schemata. Ideas are in the public domain. For example, the author of the play, *Death of a Salesman,* Arthur Miller, has the exclusive right to exploit the expression of that plot he wrote, not the idea, itself.[23] (If someone copies both Miller's plot and

[20]*Autogiro Co. of America v. United States* 384 F.2d 391, 399 (Ct. Cl. 1967).

[21]The 1976 Copyright Act was amended in 1980 to make it clear that computer programs are copyrightable. 17 U.S.C. § 117. Special copyright protection for computer chips is provided by the Semiconductor Chip Protection Act of 1984, 17 U.S.C. §§ 901–914, geared to particular problems of chip manufacturers. A semiconductor chip is manufactured by means of a "mask," a screen through which light passes in a particular configuration and imprints an image on a template—the chip. The design of a mask—like the plans for a building—can be copyrighted but, prior to 1984, there was no statutory protection against someone using another's mask to make chips, just as the copyright law does not protect against the misuse of building plans. In an enormously complex act, that result has been altered. 17 U.S.C. §§ 901–914. *See generally* Stern "Determining Liability for Infringement of Mask Works Rights under the Semiconductor Chip Protection Act," 70 *Minn. L. Rev.* 271 (1985).

[22]*See generally,* Anthony & Colwell, "Litigating the Validity and Infringement of Software Patents," 41 *Wash. & Lee L. Rev.* 1307 (1984). One of the early problems had been a Patent Office fear that the bureaucrats would choke on the volume of applications. *See generally* Chandler, "Proprietary Protection of Computer Software," 11 *U. Balt. L. Rev.* 195 (1982).

[23]17 U.S.C. § 102.

his characters, but not his exact language, the question would be analogous to the "look and feel" issues discussed in § 16.4(a).)

§16.4 SUMMARY OF THE STATUTE

The present Copyright Act was passed in 1976.[24] Protection starts when the work is "fixed in any tangible medium of expression,"[25] and endures until 50 years after the death of the author.[26] The owner of the copyright has the exclusive right to make copies of the work[27] and he controls adaptations.[28] "In dealing with copyrights, it is important to distinguish between the copyright itself and the tangible property which in which the expression is embedded—"the right to reproduce a painting is distinct from the ownership of the painting and the purchaser . . . can only obtain the right to make reproductions of it if those rights are expressly transferred by the original creator."[29] Violation of the Act can be a crime.[30]

The fundamental notion in copyright law is that of originality. The alleged owner's rights depend on the work having originated within him; he cannot have copied it from someone else. To repeat, the protected work is not the idea in and of itself; it is the *expression* of the idea that is protected.[31] The essence of originality is not novelty[32] but rather that the author made up the work by himself—the common example is that an author could copyright *Romeo and Juliet* by proving that he did not copy it from Shakespeare.[33]

"Fair use" is a defense against an infringement action; the statute, § 107, defines fair use not in words but by giving examples: "use by

[24]17 U.S.C. § 101 *et seq.* Federal law pre-empts state laws that protect rights equivalent to those protected under the Copyright Act, but not those that function in the interstices. 17 U.S.C. § 301(b). *Sears, Roebuck & Co. v. Stiffel Co.* 376 U.S. 225 (1964). *See generally* Bender, "Protection of Computer Programs: The Copyright/Trade Secret Interface," 47 *U. Pitt. L. Rev.* 907 (1986).
[25]17 U.S.C. § 102(a).
[26]17 U.S.C. § 302(a). The term of protection for works made for hire is 75 years. 17 U.S.C. § 302(c).
[27]17 U.S.C. § 106(2). The specific rights of the owners are to make and/or distribute copies, to prepare derivation works, to perform the work and to display it publicly.
[28]17 U.S.C. § 106.
[29]Bramson, "Intellectual Property as Collateral—Patents, Trade Secrets, Trademarks and Copyrights," 36 *Bus. Law.* 1567, 1595 (1981).
[30]17 U.S.C. § 506.
[31]17 U.S.C. § 102(a) ("tangible medium of expression").
[32]Thus the telephone book can be copyrighted. *Hutchinson Telephone Co. v. Fronteer Directory Co. of Minnesota, Inc.* 770 F.2d 128 (8th Cir. 1985).
[33]Miller & Davis, *supra* n. 2, at 289.

reproduction in copies . . . or by any other means . . . for purposes such as criticism, comment, news reporting, teaching . . . scholarship or research."[34] Controversy engendered by the fair use doctrine in recent years has been cloaked with First Amendment overtones,[35] involving the issue how far an author can go in quoting excerpts from another's work.[36]

The aggrieved owner of a copyright has several remedies: injunctive relief,[37] impoundment of the offending copies,[38] actual damages[39] and "statutory damages" of up to $50,000[40] (useful when actual damages are difficult to prove). Copyright protection is basically self-executing,[41] the protection ensuing from the time the expression is fixed in a tangible medium. There is no overriding need for the government to impel an author to register his work, since the Act does not protect against independent creation, only copying. There are, however, reasons for the author to register, the principal (but not the only) one being that an owner cannot sue for infringement until he has registered.[42] In any event, it is important that the copyright owner give the requisite notice that the work is protected and has not become part of the public domain.[43] The acceptable copyright indicia (i.e., the letter "c" in a circle, the word "copyright" or the abbreviation "Copr."[44]) should appear along with the date of publication and the name of the copyright owner.[45] (The Copyright Office has indicated where and how notices respecting machine-readable systems should appear.)[46]

[34] 17 U.S.C. § 107.

[35] The "fair use" doctrine recently was narrowly construed by the Supreme Court in *Harper & Row v. The Nation Enterprises* 105 S. Ct. 2218 (1985), in which the unauthorized reproduction of selected material from President Ford's memoirs was held to be an infringement. Certain works are deemed so important—the Zapruder films of President Kennedy's assassination, for example—that they cannot be copyrighted. *Time Inc v. Bernard Geis Associates* 293 F. Supp. 130 (S.D.N.Y. 1968).

[36] 17 U.S.C. § 107.

[37] 17 U.S.C. § 502.

[38] 17 U.S.C. § 503.

[39] 17 U.S.C. § 504(b).

[40] 17 U.S.C. § 504(c)(2).

[41] *See* Miller & Davis, n. 2, at 385.

[42] The owner may wait to register until the infringement has been discovered and he has decided to sue. 17 U.S.C. § 411(a). However, failure to register can forfeit some rights permanently, such as the right to recover preregistration damages in certain instances. 17 U.S.C. § 412.

[43] *See, e.g., Data Cash Systems Inc. v. JS & A Group, Inc.* 628 F.2d 1038 (7th Cir. 1980) (construing the 1909 Act). The new Act is more forgiving in favor of authors on this point. *See* 17 U.S.C. § 405 (a)(2); Miller & Davis, *supra* n. 2 at 386.

[44] 17 U.S.C. § 401(b)(1).

[45] 17 U.S.C. § 401(b)(2)(3).

[46] 37 C.F.R. § 201.20(g).

(a) SPECIAL PROBLEMS WITH COMPUTER SOFTWARE[47]

As stated, the 1976 version of the Copyright Act, as amended in 1980, makes it plain that computer software is protected;[48] (Software is also patentable and, of course, open to trade secret protection.) The issues involved are properly the subject of a separate text. Only a few will be summarized here. The point to be kept firmly in mind is that enormous consequences may ensue from the success or failure of a given firm in preserving its exclusive right to exploit its assets; that is, its software.[49]

As an example of some of the issues one must confront, if a given software program[50] is construed as entailing only an idea, and only a limited number of expressions of that idea are possible, then a court may deny copyright protection on the theory the owner of the copyright might otherwise own the idea itself by copyrighting the few possible means of expression.[51] Moreover, a functional, utilitarian creation is not, in and of itself, copyrightable—indeed, it has been argued (albeit without much success) that certain ROM (Read Only Memory) programs are not copyrightable because the logic has been incorporated into the circuitry of the machine—a "useful article."[52]

There are, in addition, open issues created by the language of the statute itself having to do with the rights of the *users* of software programs to adapt the program for a special use, to "enhance" (a different issue from "adapt"), to debug, and to make backup copies.[53]

[47]The definition of computer "software" is eminently subject to the remark:

> [E]xperts in the computer field, while using exactly the same words, uniformly disagree as to precisely what they mean.

Honeywell, Inc. v. Lithonia Lighting, Inc. 317 F. Supp. 406, 408 (N.D.Ga. 1970).

[48]17 U.S.C. § 117. The 1980 revision affirmed and clarified what is generally taken to be the resolution of the issue in the 1976 Act, which added to the definition of "copies" the language "communicated . . . *with the aid of a machine or device.*" *See* Chandler, *supra* n. 22, at 215. The leading case, *Apple Computer, Inc v. Franklin Computer Corp.* 714 F.2d 1240 (3d Cir. 1983) rejected, *inter alia,* the argument that one could not copyright an item which couldn't be seen.

[49]*See generally* a useful discussion of the array in Ch. 3, "Protecting Technology," Davidson & Davidson, *supra* n. 2. Stern "Section 117 of the Copyright Act: Charter of the Software Users' Rights or an Illusory Promise?," 7 *W. New Eng. L. Rev.* 459 (1985).

[50]Generally, there are two principal software components which are eligible for protection—the program (the operating instructions to the computer) and the data base (the information stored in the computer). *1 Bender Computer Law: Evidence and Procedure* § 2.06[1] (1987). *See* Chandler, *supra* n. 22, at 196.

[51]Davidson & Davidson, *supra* n. 1, at § 3.39(b)(1). Since there are only a few ways to write basic input and output programs, a copyright which protects more than verbatim copying is probably not available. *Ibid.*

[52]*Id.* at § 3.3(b)(2).

[53]Stern, *supra* n. 49, at 465–466.

Currently, the most-discussed problem is referred to by the colorful label "look and feel." The issue has to do with a software program which is not an exact copy of an earlier, copyrighted program (indeed, it may be written in a different computer language) but "looks and feels" much like it—the structure and sequencing, the logic and/or the formats the program uses on the screen are similar. As one commentator has analogized the issue, a novel is organized into a number of chapters with a plot and characters;[54] the problem is whether a second work which borrows the characters and plot but uses different language is an infringement. Several recent cases[55] have opted to find infringement, given in most instances proof that the copying was not accidental. The technical question under the Copyright Act, again, has to do with the contrast between noncopyrightable "ideas" and copyrighted "expressions" of those ideas. The ultimate result will, it can be expected, be determined by the twin policies underlying the protection of intellectual property—sufficient protection to encourage original work but not so much that the area of inquiry becomes out of bounds to the creatively minded, who want to stand on the shoulders of genius in order to advance science and technology.

It can be expected that some time will pass before the application of the Copyright Act to software has been entirely thrashed out into a coherent body of rules. The technology itself creates a bewildering, to the noncomputer literate lawyer, array of problems—for example, when source code (human-readable) is translated into object code (machine-readable) by means of a compiler, does the object code become a derivative work, co-authored by the owners of the code and the compiler?[56] Nonetheless, the creators of software programs do rely heavily on the Copyright Act and lenders and investors are prone to credit the owner

[54]Haynes & Durant, "Patents and Copyrights in Computer Software Based Technology: Why Bother With Patents?"; 4 *Computer Lawyer* 1, 4 (Feb 1987)

[55]One of the earliest cases on this issue, tried by the author's firm, is *SAS Institute, Inc. v. S & H Computer Systems Inc.* 605 F. Supp. 816 (M.D. Tenn. 1985), in which the court found infringement. The *SAS* result was also obtained in *Whelen Associates Inc. v. Taslow Dental Laboratory* 609 F. Supp. 1307 (E.D. Pa. 1985), *aff'd,* 797 F. 2d 1222 (3d Cir. 1986) and *Broderbund Software Inc. v. Unison World Inc.* 231 U.S. P.Q. 700 (N.D. Cal. 1986). *See generally* Franklin, "Missapropriated Law, Copyright Law and Product Compatibility," 4 *Computer Lawyer* 8 (1987).

[56]The answer is "no," but for highly technical reasons. Davidson & Davidson, *supra* n. 1, at § 3.3(c)(4).

as having created valuable property rights; § 117 may not be perfect but it is "better than nothing."[57]

§16.5 TRADE SECRETS

Trade secrets are protected, if at all, under state law, the actual doctrine applied going under a variety of labels (*e.g.*, "trade secrets," "unfair competition," "unfair trade practices," and/or the tort of "misappropriation"). The most widely accepted definition of a trade secret occurs in the 1939 edition of the Restatement of Torts.[58] The Uniform Trade Secrets Act definition is generally similar to the Restatement version.[59]

In thinking about trade secrets conceptually, it is useful to keep in mind that a trade secret is a form of property, not as formally defined as a patented or copyrighted item but property nonetheless. Trade secrets can be bought and sold, licensed and hypothecated; they are assets in a bankruptcy proceeding and can support a criminal proceeding if stolen.[60] The critical element of a trade secret is implied by the name itself, that it be a secret.[61]

[57]*See* Stern, *supra* n. 49, at 483. Unhappy with copyright and/or trade secret protection, some software owners have protected at least the distinctive mark carried by their software under the federal trademark statute. *See* Chandler,*supra* n. 22, at 213.

[58]Restatement of Torts, § 757, *Comment* b, (1939 ed.) (Restatement). The Restatement of Torts (Second) deleted the language concerning trade secrets on the ground that the law of unfair competition was no longer a subsection of tort law. Restatement of Torts (Second), Introductory Note. Modern trade secret law had its genesis in the English case of *Morrison v. Moat* 68 *Eng. Rep.* 492, 9 Hare 241 (1851) (protecting a secret recipe for a patent medicine).

[59]Uniform Trade Secrets Act (Supp. 1987). The Uniform Act covers secrets which the owner has not yet had an opportunity to put to use. Russo, Derwin, & Hale, "The Impact of the Uniform Trade Secrets Act on California Trade Secret Law," 1 *Trade Secret Law Rep.* 4 (May 1985); *See generally 1 Milgrim on Trade Secrets, supra* n. 1, at §§ 1.01 through 1.10.

[60]*See* Milgrim, "Developing, Using and Protecting Trade Secrets in Employment Contracts," in *Computer Contracts: An In-Depth Study* 401 (MCLE 1985).

[61]Restatement § 757, Comment "The subject matter of a trade secret must be secret;" 1 *Milgrim on Trade Secrets, supra* n. 1, at §§ 2.03, 2.07. This statement, however, should be understood in context. The majority view is, as the text suggests, that "The contract cannot make a secret out of a situation when none exists." *State Farm Mutual v. Dempster* 174 Cal. App. 2d 418 344 P.2d 821 (1959). However, there are cases which focus on the wrongful act of misappropriation of otherwise public information. *Goldberg v. Medtronic Inc.* 686 F.2d 1219 (7th Cir. 1982). Perhaps the most eloquent statement of the rationale based on breach of confidence is that of Justice Holmes in *E.I. DuPont de Nemours Powder Co. v. Masland* 244 U.S. 100, 102 (1917):

The Restatement requirement that the secret be "used in one's business," (language reminiscent of the requirement that a patented invention or discovery be "useful") is in fact relatively easy to satisfy (except possibly in cases where the business has not yet begun).[62] The very fact that a firm is trying to protect the information implies utility. The requirements for patentability—novelty, nonobviousness, involvement of the inventive mind in developing a "process, machine, manufacture, or composition of matter"—are not required, at least in so many words.[63] A customer list, for example, cannot be patented but it is an example of a trade secret, at least in some jurisdictions, if it is maintained in confidence.[64]

The principal chore of the owner of a trade secret is to exercise the necessary quantum of diligence in protecting the secret as he uses it commercially.[65] The burden requires a coherent effort to impose as high

---

> The word "property" as applied to trademarks and trade secrets is an unanalyzed expression of certain secondary consequences of the primary fact that the law makes some rudimentary requirements of good faith. Whether the plaintiffs have any valuable secret or not the defendant [a former employee] knows the facts, whatever they are, through a special confidence that he accepted. The property may be denied but the confidence cannot be. Therefore the starting point for the present matter is not property or due process of law, but that the defendant stood in confidential relations with the plaintiffs, or one of them. These have given place to hostility, and the first thing to be made sure of is that the defendant shall not fraudulently abuse the trust reposed in him. It is the usual incident of confidential relations. If there is any disadvantage in the fact that he knew the plaintiff's secrets he must take the burden with the good.

[62]*See* the more liberal provision of the Uniform Act, cited *supra* n. 59.

[63]"Novelty" in the sense that term is used in patent law is not necessary, 1 *Milgrim on Trade Secrets, supra* n. 1, at § 2.08[2], but novelty in the sense of secrecy—not heretofore in the public domain—is a requirement. *See* Klitzke, *supra* n. 4, at 559.

[64]Restatement § 757, *Comment* b. Despite the Restatement definition, the law is uncertain, some jurisdictions dividing between retail and wholesale customer lists. 1 *Milgrim on Trade Secrets, supra* n. 1, at § 2.09[7]. In the computer related trade secret cases, it would appear that some courts are insisting that the subject matter be to some degree original or novel. *See, e.g., Com-Share Inc. v. Computer Complex Inc.* 338 F. Supp. 1229 (E.D. Mich. 1971).

[65]"Obviously, if the owner of a trade secret wants to exploit it, he cannot keep it entirely secret—i.e., from his own employees." *Fleming Sales Co. Inc. v. Bailey* 611 F. Supp. 507 (N.D. Ill. 1985). "Trade Secret: means information . . . that . . . is the subject of efforts that are reasonable under the circumstances to maintain its secrecy." Uniform Trade Secrets Act § 1. For an example of a typical provision to be inserted in an employment contract to enhance secrecy, *see Structural Dynamics Research Corp. v. Engineering Mechanics Research Corp.* 401 F. Supp. 1102, 1112 (E.D. Mich. 1975). *See also* Marcellino & Kenfield, "Due Diligence As A Two Edged Sword: The Potential Liability of Venture Capitalists Funding High Tech Start Ups," 2 *Computer & High Technology L. J.* 41, 49 (1986)

a degree of confidentiality as possible under the circumstances,[66] the circumstances being that the secret is of no use commercially[67] unless it can be employed in the production process and, thus, has to be communicated to people. The measures demanded fall into two categories: contractual and practical. The principal contract procedures have been outlined in Chapter 15, § 15.3; they involve perserverance, a devotion to ensuring that each exposed employee, including employees of licensees and other third parties, actually signs and returns a confidentiality agreement. On the practical level, a prudent employer will also employ various common sense devices to enhance secrecy: that is, stamping documents confidential, maintaining locked files, requiring "password" access to software programs, sign in/sign out regulations in restricted areas and strict controls over any publications by employees in technical journals.[68]

Required filings with government agencies may pose special problems to the extent that they require disclosure of proprietary information. However, various federal agencies accept and grant requests to treat filed information as confidential and the Freedom of Information Act contains an exemption for "trade secrets and commercial or financial information obtained from a person and privileged or confidential."[69]

Prior to the enactment of the 1976 Act, publication was a prerequisite for copyright protection. Since that requirement is no longer necessary,[70] program owners are apt to affix the copyright notice and contemporaneously attempt to enforce the type of constraints which typify a trade secret protection program—a belt and suspenders approach. In this scenario, copyrighted material is not registered but, as earlier indicated, registration is not a condition to protection in the broad sense,

[66]The Comment to the Restatement definition includes the following language:

> Substantially, a trade secret is known only in the particular business in which it is used. It is not requisite that only the proprietor of the business know it. He may, without losing his protection, communicate it to employees involved in its use.

[67]A trade secret must have some economic value, either actual or potential. Uniform Trade Secrets Act, *supra* n. § 1(4)(i).

[68]*See Jostens Inc. v. National Computer Systems Inc.* 318 N.W. 2d 691 (Minn. 1982) (article published by employees in a journal resulted in loss of trade secret protection.) *Compare Sperry Rand Corp. v. Pentronix Inc.* 311 F. Supp. 910 (E.D. Pa. 1970) (legends on documents, doors locked, and visitors screened). A trade secret can be disclosed (indeed, sometimes must be disclosed) outside the circle of the owner's employees and licensees and still remain a secret. *RTE Corp. v. Coatings Inc.* 267 N. W. 2d. 226 (Wis. 1978) (subcontractor).

[69]5 U.S.C. § 552(b)(4).

[70]17 U.S.C. § 302(a); 1 *Milgrim on Trade Secrets, supra* n. 1, at § 2.06(a)[1] & [2].

although certain rights are foregone absent registration;[71] morever, the Copyright Act pre-empts state copyright law, but not trade secret laws.[72] There are advantages and disadvantages to copyright versus trade secret protection—that is, trade secret law only impacts on persons privy to the secret through unauthorized disclosure. On the other hand, copyright protection extends to the expression of the idea and not the idea itself; trade secret law protects both. The planning point is that, in contrast with the issue discussed in the next section, the owner can have his cake and eat it too.

§16.6 PATENT VERSUS TRADE SECRET PROTECTION—IS A "PADLOCK BETTER THAN A PATENT?"[73]

The issue before a start-up company in possession of valuable technology is whether to press forward with a patent claim or attempt to shroud the invention in secrecy, relying on the law of trade secrets to preserve sovereignty over the intellectual property.[74]

The threshold inquiry is whether the item is patentable in the first instance. Is it an invention,[75] which is not obvious,[76] novel,[77] useful,[78] the patentability of which is not barred by earlier disclosure?[79] Is the item invented a "process, machine, manufacture, or composition of matter?"—that is, is it something other than a law of nature, a mathematical equation, an abstract idea, a fundamental truth or a naturally occurring substance, all of which are viewed as nonpatentable?

If the invention is patentable, *should it* be patented? The choice must be made, of course; a patent is a public disclosure, destructive of the

[71]17 U.S.C. § 411–12. It is customary to assert in the license agreement covering computer software that the accompanying documentation is a trade secret since some of the information useful in pirating the program is contained therein. Davidson & Davidson, *Advanced Legal Strategies for Buying and Selling Computers and Software* § 8.2(d)(4)(ii) (1986).

[72]1 *Milgrim on Trade Secrets, supra* n. 1, at § 2.06[a][3].

[73]*Globe Ticket Co. v. Int'l Ticket Co.* 90 N.J. Eq. 605, 104 A. 92 (1919).

[74]In the leading case of *Kewanee Oil Co. v. Bicron Corp.* 416 U.S. 470 (1974), the Court decided that states may provide trade secret protection for secrets which could have been patented but were not.

[75]Nonobviousness, appearing for the first time in the Patent Act of 1952, is an articulation of the earlier standard that something must have been *invented. See* Miller & Davis, *supra* n. 2, at 73.

[76]35 U.S.C. § 103 Nonobviousness does not import the pre-1952 notion that the invention result from a "flash of creative genius." *See* discussion in *Graham v. John Deere Co., supra* n. 17, at 15. *Cuno Engineering Corp. v. Automatic Devices Corp.* 314 U.S. 84, 91 (1941).

[77]35 U.S.C. § 102.

[78]35 U.S.C. § 101.

[79]35 U.S.C. § 102.

very notion of a trade secret. Indeed, in view of the bias in the Patent Act in favor of the diligent inventor, the choice cannot be long postponed.[80]

Patent protection extends for 17 years and no more.[81] Efforts to extend the patent beyond that period may constitute "misuse,"[82] while trade secret protection goes on (theoretically) forever.[83] A patent application, once granted, can be challenged and the challenger wins, in some courts at least, more often than not.[84]

The patent applicant, moreover, is subject to a "duty of candor"—he must include in his claim all the material information of which he is aware, at the risk of invalidity. One of the features of the patent process is that, once the patent claim issues, it is available for inspection by one and all. Indeed, the foundation for a patent monopoly (the tradeoff, as it were) is to "promote the Progress of Science and useful Arts" and the patent process is, accordingly, viewed as educational in nature.[85] The possibility, therefore, exists that a competitor can inspect the claim and design around it by twisting a few knobs. (The issue in such a case is how broadly the claims will be interpreted, a question which will be influenced, in turn, by the fact that the inventor is—or is not—pressing a pioneer patent versus a much later improvement which "sits on the shoulders of earlier pioneer inventors."[86]) Further, the patent process entails time and expense; trade secret protection is cheap and immediate.

On the other hand, during the 17-year period, the protection afforded the patentee to make, use, and sell the invention is absolute.[87] If someone else independently and innocently comes up with the same invention, the owner of the patent is protected;[88] if, on the other hand, someone legally figures out the trade secret and patents the invention first, the

[80]*See supra* § 16.2(a).

[81]35 U.S.C. § 154.

[82]*Rohm and Haas Co. v. Dawson Chemical Co.* 599 F.2d. 685, 688 (5th Cir. 1979), *aff'd,* 448 U.S. 176 (1980).

[83]*See* Ch. 15, § 15.7.

[84]*See* Miller & Davis, *supra* n. 2, at 13.

[85]Patents form a "great library of technical information." Navin, *Patents* 3 (Rev. ed. 1966) *See Digital Equipment Corp. v. Diamond* 653 F.2d 701 (1st Cir. 1981). Patent applications are maintained in confidence until the application is granted so that secrecy is not lost by *filing* for patent protection.

[86]*See* Miller & Davis, *supra* n. 2, at 126.

[87]35 U.S.C. § 154.

[88]The senior inventor—i.e., the one who conceives first—who reduces an invention to practice and pursues his or her claim with diligence will take priority over the junior inventor even if the latter files first, 35 U.S.C. § 102, unless the doctrine of "statutory bar," *see supra* n. 12, disqualifies the senior inventor. If three or more competing inventors are involved, there arises an interesting paradox (often encountered in formal logic) where A can be prior to B, B prior to C and C prior to A. *See* Miller & Davis, *supra* n. 2, at 62.

senior inventor may not only lose protection, he may not be able to exploit his own technology.[89] The enigma facing the owner of a trade secret—if he wants to exploit, he must disclose, which means he may lose his protection—does not face the patentee. As one court has suggested, outsiders may use "all proper means" (sometimes labeled "reverse engineering") to discover a trade secret.[90] Moreover, even though challengers often win, the task of objecting to a filed patent can be expensive and, by statute, patents are presumed valid.[91] And, in the appropriate instance, courts can award treble damages (triple the amount of a "reasonable royalty").[92] Indeed, some recent decisions have been awarding monumental damages, leading one commentator to opine that the risk of potentially massive corporate and personal liability far exceeds the anticipated profit from the potentially infringing activity."[93]

The ultimate answer to this question is beyond the scope of the Text. As a general rule, however, founders should be encouraged to seek patent protection because (if for no other reason) potential investors tend to feel more secure in the presence of a presumptively valid patent. Moreover, if the item is to be sold rather than licensed, it may be that patent protection is the only available option.[94] Finally, the fact that a patent has been applied for and/or granted does not mean that trade secret or copyright is irrelevant. There is no inconsistency between protecting an invention under the patent laws and legally protecting collateral information under state doctrines governing trade secrets or the Copyright Act.[95]

§16.7 WHO OWNS INTELLECTUAL PROPERTY?—EMPLOYER VERSUS EMPLOYEE (VERSUS CONSULTANT, VERSUS CUSTOMER)

The facts are familiar. Start-up is in the business of programming and selling customized software products (or is it services?) to public ac-

[89] The complicated issues engendered by such a case involve questions concerning "concealment" by the senior inventor and "prior art considerations" in the path of the junior inventor, discussed at some length in 2 *Milgrim on Trade Secrets* § 8.02[2] (1987).

[90] Reverse engineering is simply the independent discovery of trade secret or confidential information achieved through the dissection and inspection of a product lawfully acquired and not subject to an express or implied obligation to maintain confidence.

Unif. Trade Secrets Act, Commissioner's Comment. *See generally* Raskind "Reverse Engineering, Unfair Competition and Fair Use" 70 *Minn. L. Rev.* 385 (1985).

[91] 35 U.S.C. § 282.

[92] 35 U.S.C. § 284.

[93] *See* Cook, "Massive Damages and Other Tough Remedies for Patent Infringement: The Dawn of a New Era" 3 *Computer Lawyer* 22 (1986).

[94] 2 *Milgrim On Trade Secrets, supra* n. 89, at § 8.02[1].

[95] *See supra,* §§ 16.3 and 16.5.

counting firms. Barkis is a long-time employee, working as a low-level programmer on anything that comes along. Boylan is a hot-shot programmer with experience in high-level programming at one of Start-up, Inc.'s competitors. Start-up has just hired Boylan away to work on an exciting new generation of software. Bovary is an independent consultant hired by Start-up to assist Boylan and Barkis in developing the project. *There are no written contractual understandings.* Each party works on the software both in Start-up, Inc.'s facilities and at home on nights and weekends. The result is truly revolutionary and in great demand. Start-up starts marketing the software, only to see Boylan quit and organize his own company to compete in the market. Barkis thinks that is a good idea, so he does too. And, to Start-up's surprise, Bovary is seeking protection for his ownership rights under the copyright and/or patent laws. To top it all off, one of Start-up's customers—Macbeth and MacDuff, CPA—has introduced into the market its own line of software, which bears some similarity to Start-up's product but is much "enhanced." Start-up suspects, but cannot prove, that the foundation of the program Boylan and Barkis came up with may have originated in technology already owned and maintained as a trade secret by Start-up.

The foregoing is a typical exam question, which will take a first-class student about two hours of fast writing just to cover the basics. The issues are summarized in the following sections; a detailed examination is well beyond the scope of the text.[96]

§16.8(a) "WORK-FOR-HIRE," "HIRED TO INVENT," AND RELATED DOCTRINES

The easy case, or at least the easiest, is Boylan, involving the so-called "work-for-hire" doctrine as the concept has been articulated in Copyright Law and its counterparts in patent and trade secret law.[97] "If one is employed to devise or perfect an instrument . . . [that] which he has been employed and paid to accomplish becomes . . . the property of his employer. Whatever rights as an individual he may have had . . . he has sold in advance to his employer."[98] Section 102(b) of the Copyright Act incorporates this doctrine explicitly into the statute.[99] The work-for-hire doctrine applies to works either "created by an employee within

[96]For an authoritative discussion, see 2 Callman *Unfair Competition, Trademarks and Monopolies,* Ch. 14 (4th ed. 1982).
[97]17 U.S.C. § 201(b).
[98]*Solomons v. United States* 137 U.S. 342, 346 (1890).
[99]17 U.S.C. § 201(b).

the scope of [his] employment, or . . . specially commissioned or ordered."[100]

Once that safe ground is left behind for an ocean of fact situations, the law—indeed, the principles behind the law—become fuzzier. Of course, it appears unfair for an employee to accept pay and use his boss's facilities, then claim personal ownership of the device he dreams up on the theory that he was not explicitly hired to invent the device. But, let us assume the employee is a truck driver and he uses the long trips to think up the intellectual foundations for a piece of software designed to tell McDonald's where to locate its hamburger stands. If he uses the PC at the office to noodle the idea around, does the trucking company own the rights? What about the notion that we want to encourage people to invent new items of technology (and, so far at least, only people create inventions)?

Absent a contract, it is probably true that the truck driver owns the software. The fact of the employment relationship and the use of facilities are likely to be considered incidental,[101] the judicial rhetoric being that the employee does not "mortgage" his entire brainpower to the employer when he is hired.[102] Where a court will come out if the facts are somewhere in between the two boundary cases is not clear. Typically, the judge will attempt to divine the expectations of the parties and look to a host of relevant facts: Did the employer encourage or discourage R&D by employees? Has the employee assigned inventions to the employer in the past? Was the employee, if not hired for a particular piece of research, at least working generally as a researcher? How close is the invention to the main line of the employer's business? Was the invention the result of skills that the employee was taught while in the employ of the employer or due to the "general level" of skills he brought with him? (cf. Boylan's situation). The test, in the absence of a contract, is one of the "totality of the circumstances" and the evidence supporting the employer's case for an implied contract must be

[100]*See* Miller & Davis, *supra* n. 2, at 368. If the idea is patentable, only the original inventor can file for the patent. 35 U.S.C. § 111. If the employer is entitled to the patent, it must be by virtue of the fact that the inventor has assigned the patent once granted or assigned the right to obtain the patent in the name of the inventor. 35 U.S. §§ 102(f), 111, 116. In the patent area, the counterpart of the "work for hire" doctrine operates so as to imply such an assignment. *See* Mislow, "Necessity May Be the Mother of Invention, But Who Gets Custody? The Ownership of Intellectual Property Created By An Employed Inventor," 1 *Santa Clara Computer and High Technology L. J.* 59, 62 (1985).

[101]*See Nimmer on Copyright, supra* Ch. 15, n. 4, at § 5.03(B); 1 *Milgrim on Trade Secrets* § 5.02[4] (1987). The issue often turns on the question whether the employee took pieces of paper when he left. *see, e.g., Analogic Corp. v. Data Translation Inc.* 371 Mass. 643, 646–47, 358 N.E.2d 804, 806–07 (1976).

[102]*Public Affairs Associates Inc. v. Rickover* 177 F. Supp. 601, 604 (D.D.C. 1959), *rev'd on other grounds* 284 F.2d 262 (D.C. Cir. 1960), *vacated per curiam* 369 U.S. 111 (1967).

"clear and satisfactory."[103] Thus, again in the absence of a contract, discoveries made by an employee after termination of his employment or otherwise on his own time are probably his property, provided that he did not misappropriate the employer's trade secrets in arriving at his discovery.[104]

When faced with a particularly difficult case, courts have often attempted a middle ground by vesting ownership in one party but allowing the other party "shop rights" in the invention, a form of co-ownership.[105] The possessor of a shop right has a nonexclusive right to use the invention for its own purposes without paying for it but not the right to resell it to others. The normative case is when the employee owns the invention and the employer owns the shop rights, but a "reverse shop rights" circumstance is possible.[106] The shop rights doctrine is most commonly found in patent law,[107] seldom applied explicitly in trade secret cases[108] and rejected in copyright law. The utility of "shop rights" in a venture context is questionable; if the venture-backed startup is founded on the idea that it will have the exclusive right to sell certain technology, an award of shop rights is a distant second prize.[109]

The case of Bovary, the independent contractor, raises a new set of problems. Since Bovary was never an "employee," the above-cited principles establish no ownership rights in the client. Therefore, absent a contractual provision to the contrary, Bovary can argue that he owns the product if he can prove that it was his creative input that made it possible.[110] However, that result seems unfair if Bovary, albeit employ-

[103]1 *Milgrim on Trade Secrets* § § 5.02[4](d),(e) 1987). The legal theories exploitable by the employer include implied contract, breach of the employee's duty of loyalty and misappropriation of a corporate opportunity. Marcellino & Kenfield, "Due Diligence Is A Two Edged Sword: Potential Liability of Venture Capitalists Funding High-Tech Start-Ups," 2 *Computer & High Tech. L.J.* 41 (1986).

[104]*See, e.g., Automated Systems, Inc. v. Service Bureau Corp.* 401 F.2d 619 (10th Cir. 1968) (no wrongful use of trade secrets held).

[105]The law is "fairly clear" that employers have "shop rights" in any invention developed by an employee during working hours even though the employee was hired in a noninventive capacity. *See* 1 Eckstrom, *Licensing in Foreign and Domestic Operations* § 6.02[4] (3d ed. 1984).

[106]For an example, *see Mainland Industries Inc. v. Timberland Machines* 649 P.2d 613 (Or. Ct. App. 1982).

[107]4 *Deller's Walker on Patents* 507 (1965 ed. & Supp. 1985). Although it had earlier appeared in other writings, the phrase is commonly attributed to the Court's opinion in *United States v. Dubilier Condenser Corp.* 289 U.S. 178 (1933), a landmark case holding for the employee.

[108]One case apparently applying the doctrine is *Kinkade v. N.Y. Shipbuilding Corp.*, 122 F. 2d 360 (1956).

[109]*See* Nimmer, *supra* n. 101, at § 4.02[2].

[110]"In the absence of express contract provisions, the independent contractor retains control of distribution and reproduction of the software delivered to the employer. This is true even if the employer expressly assigns and commissions the work." *Id.* at § 4.05. 17 U.S.C. § 201(b) applies the "work for hire" doctrine to employees; it is not clear that it applies to independent contractors. Davidson & Davidson, *supra* n. 1, at § 4.4(d)(2).

ing his own creative efforts, was acting under the "control" of Start-up, picked the brains of Barkis and Boylan, and it was understood that Start-up wanted to develop the software to sell it to others—indeed, was in that business.[111]

The MacDuff and MacBeth situation turns on different considerations. If the software was "sold" or licensed but the copyright retained, then the purchaser does not have the right to make and sell copies. If, however, the item sold was not copyrighted but protected as a trade secret, the "supplier of a product embodying a trade secret risks its loss on sale."[112]

The Bovary example also calls up issues involving various classes of joint ownership and the rights of the various parties as "joint owners," which are generally beyond the scope of the text. The problems in this area, including but not limited to those resulting from joint creative efforts, are sufficiently difficult[113] that the lesson is clear—the rights to intellectual property should be addressed in a written agreement whenever possible.

§16.9 OWNERSHIP OF TECHNOLOGY ALLOCATED BY CONTRACTS

As discussed more fully in Chapter 17, the prudent course for any firm, depending on technological development for its success or survival is to induce key employees—at least those engaged in research—to execute agreements assigning any ideas developed by them to the company.[114] The employer's object is to confirm and make certain the result in instances where the employer would probably be deemed to own the invention anyway and to produce a different result whenever possible if patent, copyright, or trade secret law would otherwise vest ownership in the employee or consultant.[115] In this connection, the patent law is quite specific. Only the original inventor can file for the patent.[116] The employer needs an assignment of the patent or, if the assignment is of

[111] *See* Nimmer, *supra* n. 101, at § 4.05.
[112] 1 *Milgrim on Trade Secrets* § 5.03[4] (1987).
[113] *See generally* Soma, *Computer Technology and The Law* § 2.18 at 67–70 (1983).
[114] There are technical distinctions, which go beyond the scope of the Text, between agreements which assign intellectual property, which specify who is the original owner of the property and/or which disregard ownership in favor of obligations to hold information in confidence and not exploit it. Since a principal incident of ownership is the right to exclude others, an agreement not to exploit an item is equivalent, as between the contracting parties, to an agreement allocating ownership.
[115] It is not necessary that trade secrets be protected by contract. *Q-Co Industries Inc. v. Hoffman* 625 F. Supp. 608 (S.D.N.Y. 1985). However, the lack of a contract may be equated by a court with a fatal lack of concern on the owner's part. *Motorola, Inc. v. Fairchild Camera and Instrument Corp.* 366 F. Supp. 1173, 1185 (D. Ariz. 1973).
[116] 35 U.S.C. § 111.

the right to file the claim, it must be an assignment of the right to file in the inventor's name.[117]

Given the suspicion that contracts of this nature can be crammed down an employee's throat,[118] the provisions should be drafted carefully and creatively.[119] Some of the notions the draftsman should consider are as follows:

One interesting possibility is to use a carrot as well as a stick, providing in the agreement that the company owns all inventions in the fuzzy area (i.e., outside the strict work-for-hire scope), but that it will pay extra for the employee's assignment of a given item—a cash bonus, for example, or, if technological advance is critical, the creation of an in-house venture fund or like vehicle to exploit the invention and cut the employee in on the profits. According to the weight of authority, the employer's willingness to continue the employment relationship creates sufficient consideration, as a technical matter,[120] to support an existing employee's agreements respecting intellectual property, but a fresh payment may induce a court more readily to find the agreement "reasonable," a standard imposed to prevent unfairness.[121]

In terms of the "stick"—that is, the penalties imposed on the employee for breach—the agreement should be as specific as possible to prevent a court from cutting back on the employer's rights in the guise of "construing ambiguous language." The audience for the penalty provision is not only the employee in question but any competitor[122] to whom he seeks to migrate or venture fund financing the new entity, since vicarious liability is expressly recognized in the appropriate instance.[123]

If the assignment extends to inventions the employee dreams up in his spare time, the contract should say so. Moreover, if the employer is

[117]*See* Miller & Davis, *supra* n. 2, at 98.

[118]Cal. Lab. Code § 2870 restricts the right of employers to cause employees to assign inventions made without use of the employer's resources or secrets.

[119]Recently, the sensitivity of the courts toward the need to protect against the theft of technology has been rising. *See* Weiss, "Trade Secret Litigation and the Presentation of the Trade Secret Owner Case," 1 *Trade Secret L. Rep.* 273 (1986).

[120]*See* the cases collected in Mislow, *supra,* n. 100. There are significant cases to the contrary. *Ibid.*

[121]*See Nimmer On Copyright, supra* n. 101, at § 5.03(B).

[122]The theories of liability include the claim that the competitor was a joint or contributing tortfeasor, an aider and abettor, a principal responsible for the acts of its agent (the faithless employee) or a participant in a civil conspiracy. *See generally* Marcellino & Kenfield, "Due Diligence As A Two Edged Sword: Potential Liability of Venture Capitalists Funding High-Tech Start-Ups," 2 *Comput. & High Tech. L.J.* 41 (1986).

[123]*See* the checklist for investors considering a start-up founded by an employee who has spun off from another firm in Davidson, "Venture Capital and Trade Secrets: A Tale of Two Situations," 1 *Trade Secret L. Rep.* 50 (July 1985). As the author puts it, ". . . before the spin off, the venture investors want the benefit of a weak trade secret law . . . after the spin off, they want the benefit of a strong trade secret law." *Ibid.*

to enjoy shop rights, the contract should be specific on the issue. Of course, even with the greatest of specificity, there are limits to what a court will enforce; an assignment purportedly supported only by the employer's willingness to keep an existing employee on the payroll and which covers inventions clearly outside the scope of the employment will probably not be upheld.

A clever employee who stumbles over a blockbuster invention will terminate the employment relationship before he surfaces the idea. Accordingly, the contract may affirmatively require the employee to disclose currently to the employer everything he is working on, to hold his creative efforts in confidence, to keep records of the same, to disclose all follow-on activities for a year or so after the employment is terminated and to notify the employer of all postemployment applications filed for copyright or patent protection so that the employer has a chance to assert ownership claims.[124]

There are some statutory wrinkles. California, as usual, has enacted a statute limiting the circumstances under which the employer can require inventions to be assigned.[125] Moreover, the Copyright Act requires that the assignment of a copyright from one owner to another (vs. a provision that confirms who is the initial owner) should be registered.[126]

In describing the information to be kept confidential, there is the question of specificity. One approach is to draft a promise that the employee will keep all "confidential information confidential."[127] The more specific alternative (and the one most likely to be enforced) is to focus the agreement on documents the employer marks as confidential and/or to attach exhibits listing the items of concern. A clause specifically calling for the return of documents is advisable, not because it cannot be avoided in the age of copying machines but because the unauthorized misappropriation of papers is often an influential factor in cases involving ex-employees and trade secrets.[128] Similarly, a post-termination affirmation in writing by a departing employee acknowledging his obligations can be influential in the outcome of a subsequent proceeding.

[124]An open-ended agreement to assign any invention "hereafter conceived" has been held to be too broad. *Guth v. Minnesota Mining & Mfg. Co.* 72 F.2d 385 (7th Cir. 1934). Milgrim recommends an "invention 'maturation' period of one year." 1 *Milgrim on Trade Secrets* § 5.02[4] (1987).

[125]Three similar statutes—those of California, Minnesota, and Washington—are reproduced and discussed in 1 Eckstrom, *supra* n. 105, at § 6.02 [6A].

[126]17 U.S.C. § 205.

[127]The court in *Motorola Inc. v. Fairchild Camera and Instrument Corp.* 336 F. Supp. 1173 (D. Ariz. 1973) found language of this type too vague to enforce. *See also* Webb, "A Practitioner's Guide to Confidentiality Agreements," 1 *Trade Secret L. Rep.* 61 (July 1985).

[128]*See supra.* n. 100. It should be noted that the theft of trade secrets can be a crime, Cal. Pen. Code § 499c, as can be the receipt of stolen trade secrets, Cal. Pen. Code § 496.

A noncompetition clause is, in a significant sense, a complement to a clause dealing with the ownership of inventions; while it may be hard to prove the employee misappropriated an invention, especially after he leaves, competition is open and notorious, and, if the ex-employees cannot work for a competing firm, why should he bother to keep the information for himself? The problem is, as discussed more fully in Chapter 10, that noncompete clauses are often narrowly construed.

Seventeen

Some Special Problems of Computers

The burst of energy in venture capital in the past two decades has been, in part, a function of the computer revolution, as venture-backed hardware and software companies have come of age. The introduction of computers has caused various institutions and disciplines—including the law—to react in interesting ways. This chapter summarizes briefly some of the new learning on computers and the law, a legal discipline in the process of germination.

§17.1 BACKGROUND[1]

Computer law is a mosaic, made up of some novel and specially created doctrines interwined with the traditional legal disciplines applied to

[1]For the history of computers, running from Pascal's computing machine through Sperry Rand's Univac I to IBM's series of models, *see* 1 Bender, *Computer Law: Evidence and Procedure,* § 1.02 (1987). Computers of commercial importance in today's market are entirely digital (versus analog) computers, meaning that the computer works with discrete numbers, versus solving problems by analogy. A digital computer is usually thought of in five segments: input, storage (or memory), control, logic, and output. Control and logic are often referred to as the central processing unit, or CPU.

the new technology. Thus, there are certain statutes and rules which specifically address computer-related issues. For example, "mask works,"[2] the design of silicon chips, were not deemed adequately protected under the Copyright Act[3] and a special statute was passed,[4] tailored to the needs of the semiconductor chip industry. Theft and other criminal acts involving the use of computers is the subject of specific criminal statues, the thought being that existing laws did not adequately define or deal with some of the new kinds of "property" created by computers.[5]

However, as of today, computer-specific statutes and rules have not occupied the field. The bulk of transactions in hardware and software are subject to the general provisions of law—the Internal Revenue Code and the Uniform Commercial Code, for example. As always, when old law is applied to govern novel and unforeseen issues, it is fascinating to watch (and often perilous to predict) how judges and juries go about fitting suits of clothes onto shapes for which they were not cut. When a court wrestles with the fact that, for example, software does not fit into neat cubbyholes—it is both a set of ideas (instructions in an artificial language) *and* a machine which drives other machines—the results are often eccentric.

The problems of reconciling old law with new science are exacerbated by the variant rates of change. The law does not move or adapt very rapidly. On the other hand, the state of the art moves extremely rapidly in computer architecture and software. New products provide spectacular breakthroughs in computational capacity and artificial intelligence,[6] but, because they are new, they often need extensive debugging after they have been ostensibly "sold."[7] Long periods of adjustment raise difficult questions about when the item in question has in fact been transferred—when it is "accepted," no longer subject to the buyer's

[2]A mask is "[a] pattern of characters that is used to control the retention or elimination of portions of another pattern of characters." Gordon, *Computer Software: Contracting For Development and Distribution* 504 (1986). *See* Moore & Susman, "The Semiconductor Chip Protection Act," 1 *Computer Lawyer* 11 (Dec. 1984). Registration under the Act is a mandatory step for protection, which is limited to 10 years. Protection commences on the earliest of the date on which the mask mark is first "commercially exploited" anywhere in the world and the date on which the mask mark is registered.

[3]*See* Scott, *Computer Law,* § 12.1, 3 (1985).

[4]The Semi-Conductor Chip Protection Act, 17 U.S.C. §§ 901–914.

[5]See *infra* § 17.4.

[6]Artificial intelligence, or AI, refers to complicated computer programs which manipulate powerful expert systems. An interesting, perhaps ominous, question involves the ownership for copyright purposes of a computer-generated work—who is the "author?" Possibilities include the user, the author of the generator program or, *mirabile dictu,* the computer itself. *See* Samuelson, "Allocating Ownership Rights in Computer Generated Works," 47 *U. Pitt. L. Rev.* 1184, 1190 (1986).

[7]*See* 1 Bender, *supra* n. 1, at § 2.06[3](e); see also Conley & Bryan, "A Unifying Theory for the Litigation of Computer Software Copyright Cases," 6 *Computer Law J.* 55, 59 (1985).

right to reject. How long, on the other hand, can the seller fuss with the item, once installed, before the buyer can elect to cancel the order because it was never filled—the gizmo never worked properly?

Rapidly advancing technology is intimidating, creating additional problems. As the unusual properties of computers create apprehension in many, that fear becomes coupled with a naïve belief that the computer is never wrong. If the answer comes out of the computer, it must be correct. When the computer told Ford Motor Credit that Mr. Swarens had not paid for his car, Ford employees ignored canceled checks (plus a shotgun) and repossessed the car, resulting in punitive damages. As the court said, "Trust in the infallibility of a computer is hardly a defense."[8] Supineness in the face of superior technical knowledge (viewed as a black art) often results in contracts that should not have been signed.

Much of the relevant material is referred to elsewhere in the text. The purpose of this chapter is to give a summary of some of the more important issues specific to computers which have occasioned notice and controversy in recent years. The discussion is not systematic, concentrating on selected rules and issues which separate computer law from the law governing oscilloscopes or cows or oranges.

§17.2 CONTRACTS

(a) WHAT LAW APPLIES?

As a threshold inquiry, the parties to a contract involving computers are bound to inquire what body of law will be applied in the event of a dispute. The Uniform Commercial Code (U.C.C.), in effect in some form in all states except Louisiana, applies to "transactions in goods;"[9] transactions in services are governed generally by the common law. Under the U.C.C., computer hardware is indisputably a "good;"[10] whether software is a "good" or a service is not yet settled, because the nature of the agreement between the parties can vary from pole to pole. Thus, if A hires B to consult on A's data-processing problems and, in the process, B develops a piece of customized software, one would expect the rule to be that B provided a service because that was the predominant theme, or gravamen, to use a favorite legal expression, of the parties' understanding. One of the author's former colleagues would characterize such an agreement as a "warm-body" contract.[11] On the

[8] *Ford Motor Credit Co. v. Swarens* 447 S.W.2d 53, 57 (Ky. Ct. App. 1969).
[9] U.C.C. § 2–102.
[10] *See* Davidson & Davidson, *Advanced Legal Strategies for Buying and Selling Computers and Software,* § 2.1(a) (1986).
[11] *See* Bigelow & Nycum, *Your Computer and the Law* 118 (1976).

other hand, if a retail computer store sells you a canned software package to run on your PC, even though the sale may be styled as a "license,"[12] common sense would indicate that a standardized product—or "good"—had been sold and the law generally applicable to such transactions brought to bear on any dispute.[13]

If the Uniform Commercial Code applies to a transaction or circumstance, then a substantial element of predictability is introduced into the planning process since the U.C.C. has been carefully drafted by skilled practitioners and has been adopted (albeit with variations) in all states other than Louisiana. Moreover, a body of commentary (official and otherwise) has grown up around the individual provisions.[14]

(b) BUNDLED HARDWARE AND SOFTWARE

Certain issues can become complicated when hardware and software are purchased from the same vendor, the hardware being, for example, off the shelf and the software customized. If a court tries, for analytical purposes, to separate physically different but functionally inseparable items, confusion can reign. If the software does not perform, for example, has the vendor of a bundled package delivered anything?[15] In this connection, the agreement licensing the use of software may specify the

[12]Expensive computers—main frames—are often leased rather than sold. If the transaction is styled as a lease, there remains the further issue whether it shall be considered for tax purposes a true lease or a sale accompanied by a financing. The Internal Revenue Service, *see* Rev. Rul. 55–540, 1955–2 C.B. 39, suggests the question whether a lease is a true lease or a sales contract be answered by examining all the facts existing at the time of the transaction. A lease is treated as a sale if the "rental" payments will earn equity for the lessee, the lessee will acquire title after a stated amount of "rentals," the "rental" payments materially exceed the current fair rental value, a purchase option can be acquired by the lessee at a nominal price, some portion of the payments are specifically designated as interest and/or the amount of "rental" payments in the short term is an inordinately large percentage of the sum necessary to secure title. *Id. See also* Rev. Proc. 76–30, 1976–2 C.B. 847 (in which the I.R.S. provides guidelines for advanced rulings on leveraged lease transactions). A brief summary of these guidelines can be found in Nimmer, *The Law of Computer Technology*, § 6.14[2] (1985).

[13]Note "Computer Programs as Goods Under the U.C.C.," 77 *Mich. L. Rev.* 1149 (1979). Most software licenses are drafted with the presumption that the U.C.C. will apply *See* Davidson, "Common Law, Uncommon Software," 47 *U. Pitt. L. Rev.* 1037, 1051 (1986).

[14]The U.C.C. is based, in large part, on a compilation of state law but the law of any given state may be at variance with the U.C.C. on a given point. Moreover, the U.C.C. introduces some novel concepts. U.C.C. § 2–104, Comment 2, for example, creates higher obligations for merchant vendors than for nonmerchant vendors, a distinction otherwise rare in state law.

[15]*See Burroughs Corp. v. Century Steel Inc.* 99 Nev. 464, 664 P.2d 354 (1983). (Vendor's failure to deliver a "workable" software system on time breached the hardware lease agreement); *Carl Beasley Ford Inc. v. Burroughs Corp.* 361 F. Supp. 325 (E.D. Pa. 1973) (despite separate agreements for the physical equipment and the programming, the two were virtually inseparable).

type of hardware on which it may be run to ensure the software functions properly,[16] a provision which can raise antitrust issues if the license is viewed as entailing a "tying" or "tie-in" arrangement.[17]

(c) LIMITING EXPOSURE

A computer failure, more often than not, is a major business catastrophe.[18] If the computer is down or the software does not work properly, the entire firm may be at stake. For example, a multibillion-dollar bank processing the records of mutual fund clients can find itself faced with enormous potential losses if the computer misplaces the shareholder records, sales are not recorded properly, and dividend checks go out to the wrong parties. Business reliance on computers has proceeded to the point that they are literally the lifeblood of the organization. The question as to who is at fault when a major glitch occurs—buyer or seller (licensor/licensee or lessor/lessee)—can involve a disaster, in commercial terms. The vendor is interested in providing the item (hardware and software) as close to "as is" as possible, limiting the seller's obligation to a duty for a limited period of time to fix problems as they occur—that is, replacement and repair. Boilerplate clauses limiting the vendor's liability are often executed uncritically by an unwitting buyer.[19] In such event, contemporaneous promises concerning performance can be excluded by "integration" or "merger" clauses[20] (the agreements of the parties are integrated or merged into one document, including all exogenous promises) or the parol evidence rule (extraneous evidence cannot be used to contradict unambiguous terms of a written agreement intended to be the entire agreement);[21] the time in which a disgruntled

[16]*See* Todd, "Retail Distribution of Computer Hardware and Software," *Computer Contracts: An In-Depth Study* 73 (MCLE 1985).

[17]*See* Ch. 15, § 15.17. The issues involved in the practice of "bundling" are addressed specifically in Bender, "Single Pricing for Hardware and Software," 1968 *Law of Software Procedures* D–1 (1968).

[18]Within a year of switching to a computer system that never worked, a 40-year-old company went bankrupt. *Triangle Underwriters Inc. v. Honeywell Inc.* 457 F. Supp. 765 (E.D.N.Y.) *aff'd in part,* 604 F.2d 737 (2d Cir. 1979).

[19]A further issue arises when the immediate vendor is, as is often the case, a reseller, as opposed to the manufacturer. *See* Wisterich, *Computer Contracts: An In-Depth Study* 15 (MCLE 1985); *See* Bigelow & Nycum, *supra* n. 11, at 111. For an example of a standard form contract, *see id.,* Appendix F, at 207.

[20]Davidson & Davidson, *supra* n. 10, § 2.2(d)(1). The authors make the interesting suggestion that the buyer take advantage of the seller's "integration" clause in the course of the negotiation by insisting that all sales literature be expressly incorporated into the contract. *Id.*

[21]U.C.C. § 2–202 (1978). An agreement

> May be explained or supplemented (a) by course of dealing or usage of trade . . . or by course of performance . . . ; and (b) or by evidence of consistent additional terms unless the court finds the writing to have been intended also as a complete and exclusive statement of the terms of the agreement.

buyer may sue may be limited;[22] "consequential" damages[23] may be excluded, and implied warranties (the U.C.C. warranties of "merchantability"[24] and "fitness")[25] disclaimed.[26]

The buyer, having signed such a contract, is not entirely helpless. Contract provisions that are "unconscionable" will not be enforced[27] and clauses limiting the buyer to an "exclusive" (i.e., very narrow) remedy in the event of breach will not be enforced if that remedy fails in its "essential purpose."[28]

For the vendor of computer hardware and software, selection of the appropriate exculpatory provisions may be critical. The courts are mindful of the typical buyer's lack of technological sophistication and are willing to strike down contractual miniaturization of the otherwise applicable warranties and remedies even though the buyer is an experienced businessman.[29] The vendor faces two chores: First, he and his counsel must understand the legal climate in the state in which the transaction occurs in order to evaluate risks; although the U.C.C. is a "uniform" law, terms such as "unconscionable" admit of many meanings. Secondly, the litigated cases routinely show a failure of the parties' minds to meet. As discussed in the next section, it is worthwhile to ensure the customer understands in advance the limits on what is being sold.[30]

[22]U.C.C. § 2–725(1) allows the parties to agree to a minimum of a one-year limitation period.

[23]Sometimes called indirect or special damages, the term refers to claims for, *e.g.*, lost profits and consequential economic loss—as when the shareholders' entire investment is lost when the firm is put out of business by the equipment failure. *See* U.C.C. § 2–715.

[24]U.C.C. § 2–314 states that "a warranty that the goods shall be merchantable is implied in a contract for their sale if the seller is a merchant with respect to goods of that kind," and "unless excluded or modified other implied warranties may arise from course of dealing or usage of trade."

[25]If the seller had "reason to know any particular purpose for which the goods are required and the buyer is relying on the seller's skill or judgment", a warranty of fitness is implied unless excluded or modified in the agreement. U.C.C. § 2–315 (1978). Since software is usually designed for a specific function, the question arises whether it falls automatically within the implied warranty. *See* Davidson, *supra* n. 13, at 1052.

[26]Such disclaimers are prohibited under the law in certain States. *See, e.g.*, Cal. Civ. Code §§ 1790–1795. 7 (West 1983). (Song–Beverly Consumer Warranty Act.)

[27] If the court as a matter of law finds the contract or any clause of the contract to have been unconscionable at the time it was made, the court may refuse to enforce the contract, or it may enforce the remainder of the contract without the unconscionable clause, or it may so limit the application of any unconscionable clause as to avoid any unconscionable result.

U.C.C. § 2–302(1).

[28]U.C.C. § 2–719(2).

[29]*See, e.g., A & M Produce Co. v. F M C Corp.* 135 Cal. App. 3d 473 (1982)

[30]Cases evidencing the sorry products of misunderstandings are collected in 2 Bender, *Computer Law: Evidence and Procedure* § 4 B.11 (1987).

(d) DESCRIBING THE ITEM SOLD

Frequently, the task in front of the planner drafting and negotiating agreements for the supply of computer hardware and software is to understand a cardinal fact of commercial life. The buyer has no interest in buying a computer, any more than a traveler from New York to Chicago wants to buy an airplane. What he wants is a result—high speed, accurate calculations which accomplish a business objective. And it is open for the buyer to go into the market to order that result—a customized, labor-intensive computer consulting and service agreement may contemplate just that arrangement.[31] The obstacle, of course, is price. If the vendor understands that it is to be a guarantor, assuring each buyer it will obtain the result specially desired, most computer packages are going to become expensive. The risk the vendor takes must be paid for.

Accordingly, intelligent planning suggests that, given time and a contract price that makes negotiation worthwhile, the parties become as specific as possible as to their intentions and objectives. If the buyer elects to assume the risk the system will not work, then it is incumbent on the buyer to put the system to a rigorous test *before* it "accepts" (and pays for) the items. Acceptance is a term of art with legal consequences; the buyer has a right to reject[32] goods until it has had a reasonable time to inspect[33] and that inspection should go well beyond attending a demonstration in the seller's plant and giving the machinery the "smoke" test ("turn it on and see if it smokes"). Precisely defining when the product has been finally accepted can protect the vendor as well. A court may hold, in the absence of a specifically negotiated clause, that the buyer can reject the goods after a period of use if it is somehow "unfair" (in hindsight) to bind the buyer to accept a system which would not become operational until after a lengthy debugging period.[34]

Further, since every vendor is required (regardless of limitations of

[31]One of the author's partners makes the point that, in contracts involving computer software, the vendor is often selling a service while the user is buying a product. *See* Sherry, in *Computer Contracts: An In-Depth Study* 2 (MCLE 1985).

[32] Rejection of the goods must be within a reasonable time after their delivery or tender and the buyer must reasonably notify the seller of its rejection . . .

U.C.C. § 2–602.

[33] [T]he buyer has a right before payment or acceptance of the goods to inspect them at any reasonable place and time and in any reasonable manner.

U.C.C. § 2–513(i).

[34]In the often-cited case of *Carl Beasley Ford Inc. v. Burroughs Corp.* 361 F. Supp. 325 (E.D. Pa. 1973), the equipment was delivered 14 months before its rejection.

warranties) to deliver precisely what the buyer ordered[35] (herein the doctrine of "perfect tender"), the buyer may wish to publish precise technical specifications, putting the seller on notice as to what is desired. To be sure, it may be unfeasible to pursue the RFP route—that is, to hire a consultant to prepare "request for proposals"—since, among other things, the vendor's input is reduced. However, a buyer with a specific piece of architecture in mind should usually be precise in annotating what it has in mind. An obvious caution in this approach is that the buyers (or their consultants) should know their onions; a court is unlikely to look behind the product's performance if technical "specs" were met as drafted.

Added issues for draftsmen and planners to consider are raised by consumer protection statutes, principally the federal Magnuson Moss Warranty Act and Improvement Act[36] and, in California, the Song–Beverly Consumer Warranty Act,[37] each of which impinges on limitations of warranties in consumer transactions. The statutes apply certainly to PCs and probably to mass-produced software.[38] Song–Beverly goes to the extent of requiring California makers of consumer goods sold under express warranty to establish service and repair facilities within the state,[39] a nod in the direction of the fact that many computer transactions require extensive maintenance and support if the buyer is to get the benefit of its bargain.

[35] If the goods or the tender of delivery fail in any respect to conform to the contract, the buyer may (a) reject the whole; or (b) accept the whole; or (c) accept any commercial unit or units and reject the rest.

U.C.C. § 2–601.

[36] 15 U.S.C. §§ 2301–2312 (1982).

[37] Cal. Civ. Code §§ 1790–1795.7 (West 1985).

[38] The definition of consumer product in the Magnuson Moss Warranty Act includes,

> any tangible personal property which is distributed in commerce and which is normally used for personal, family or household purposes . . .

15 U.S.C. § 2301(1). The California Act contemplates:

> any new product or part thereof that is used, bought, or leased for use primarily for personal, family, or household purposes, except for clothing and consumables.

Cal. Civ. Code § 1791 (West 1985).

[39] (a) Every manufacturer of consumer goods sold in this state and for which the manufacturer has made an express warranty shall: (1) Maintain in this State sufficient service and repair facilities reasonably close to all areas where its consumer goods are sold to carry out the terms of such warranties or designate and authorize in this State as service and repair facilities independent repair or service facilities reasonably close to all areas where its consumer goods are sold to carry out the terms of such warranties . . .

Cal. Civ. Code § 1793.2 (West 1985).

§17.3 TORTS

The limitations on liability in computer vendor contracts suggest that an aggrieved buyer should consider seeking compensation in an action based on tort principles—principles which involve legal "wrongs" arising out of the tortfeasor's intentional or negligent conduct. A suit "sounding" in tort, as lawyers like to say, is not brought "on the contract" and the contractual limitations, therefore, do not apply (or so the theory goes). Thus, a plaintiff with a defective piece of hardware or software will often try to find a culpable act—a misrepresentation by the seller of a fact, made intentionally or knowingly, on which the plaintiff relied in entering into the transaction.[40] Further, when a computer system causes an accident—a computer turns off the gas for failure of payment, according to the mistaken information input into the computer, the checking account shows overdraft just as the happy couple is closing on their coveted apartment—the owner will go against the vendor and others in the chain of title on traditional product liability theories.

The "accident" cases impose liability on the manufacturer and/or vendor for negligence, which in turn calls up issues involving the standard of care the defendant's conduct is to be measured against. Except in strict liability instances,[41] the theory of liability depends on a successful allegation that the defendant did less or more than a hypothetical person—the "reasonable man"—would have done under the circumstances. What makes the computer tort cases especially interesting is that computers are a labor-saving device of the highest order, employed as a substitute for human actions—indeed, human decision making. In a leading case[42] a computer cut off electrical service to an unoccupied house during the winter. The issue was whether the utility was bound to check the computer results by hand. There was no error in inputting nor glitch in the machine; however, a hard copy file, had it been examined manually, would have prevented the harmful instruction. The court held the utility could not rely on the computer to shield itself from liability for negligent performance.[43]

[40]Because of the operation of the so-called "economic loss rule," which limits damages for negligence in the buyer/seller relationship, the most common tort theory essayed by frustrated contracting parties is based on fraud. 2 Bender, *supra* n. 1, at § 11.04[2].

[41]According to a leading authority, there are as yet no cases explicitly imposing strict liability for computer malfunctions. 2 Bender, *supra* n. 1 at § 11.03[4] (1987).

[42]*Pompeii Estates Inc. v. Consolidated Edison Co. of New York Inc.* 91 Misc.2d 233, 397 N.Y.S.2d 577 (Queens County Civ. Ct. 1977).

[43]*Id.* at 237, 397 N.Y.S.2d at 580. There is at least academic authority for the suggestion that, as computer use becomes ubiquitous, the *failure* to employ a computer may constitute negligence. 2 Bender, *supra* n. 41, at § 11.02[8].

Of course, public utilities are not likely to check computer decisions by hand. If that were the mandated proper "standard of care," few would buy computers in the first place, particularly since the computer will correct more errors than it "causes," using cause in the sense of lulling people into a false sense of security. The utility will either eat the occasional damage award or, better, buy a superior software package which contains various additional checks designed to screen errors.

The development of fault-free software, however, may not progress, even asymptotically, toward the ideal; the rise in complexity is increasing, rather than decreasing, the chance of errors that can harm people. A recent survey uncovered some alarming instances: A patient undergoing radioactive therapy was killed when the machine gave him 80 times the prescribed dose; an air defense system failed in the Falkland Islands war at a cost of 20 sailors; the Bank of New York was forced to borrow $23.6 billion overnight from the Federal Reserve to cover a software-induced failure to deliver government securities to customers on time. "An error as tiny as a misplaced semi-colon can cause a system to malfunction."[44] In all such cases, except perhaps the Falkland Islands incident, redress is likely to be sought in litigation based on principles drawn from the law of torts.

§17.4 COMPUTER CRIME

A rising concern is shared by commentators and state legislatures that the modern computer has become a happy hunting ground for the adept, wily criminal[45] An occasional spectacular embezzlement raises spectres of a failure of the banking system as billions are wired, computer to computer, to Swiss bank accounts. Industrial sabotage possibilities are scary, as a competitor inputs a rival factory's computer secretly and instructs the robots to rise up and destroy each other. Moreover, computer-processing and storage capacity are increasingly valuable assets in and of themselves, assets that can be stolen over the telephone.

Several state legislatures have reacted,[46] redefining the criminal statutes on theft to take into account theft of information, defining unauthorized access to a computer as a criminal offense and penalizing unauthorized modification or destruction of data stored in computer. In jurisdictions which have not specifically addressed the issue, the problem is that the generic statutes penalizing larceny may not stretch to

[44]*See* Davis, "Costly Bugs: As Complexity Rises, Tiny Flaws in Software Pose a Growing Threat," *Wall St. J.* Jan. 28, 1987, at 1, col. 6.

[45]*See* materials collected in Nimmer, *supra* n. 12, at § 9.07.

[46]The states that have redefined theft statutes are listed in Nimmer, *supra* n. 12, § 9.05[2] n. 35. *See also* Hubbard & Shelton, *Protection of Computer Systems and Software* 148 (1986).

cover "computer property" and/or deem the same to have been "taken" or "carried away" within the meaning of the statute.[47]

A federal crime results from the misuse of an electronic funds transfer system.[48] And, the 1984 Counterfeit Access Device and Computer Fraud and Abuse Act[49] deals with computer abuse in the area of national security, tampering with information in U.S. government computers or pirating financial information maintained by financial institutions defined in the Right to Financial Privacy Act of 1978[50] and the Fair Credit Reporting Act.[51]

§17.5 SALES AND USE TAXATION

Sales taxes are excise taxes—that is, transaction taxes—assessed in all states on goods sold in the state. Only a few states explicitly attempt to assess taxes on service transactions. The sales tax is assessed against the seller (because collection would otherwise be too difficult). Multistate sellers have engendered endless litigation on the issue whether an out-of-state vendor can be held liable for the tax by the destination state, given constitutional limitations on the extraterritorial effect of state laws and the prohibition on states imposing unreasonable burdens on inter- (vs. intra) state commerce. To avoid some of the constitutional problems, most states impose a complementary tax called a use tax, ostensibly levied upon the use of the goods in the destination state (goods sold in the state and not being held for resale) which are not subject to sales tax.

As usual, computer software poses special problems. First, is it a good or a service? The statutes are all over the lot, making distinctions between packaged vs. customized software, and application vs. operating programs; accordingly, each statute must be examined individually.[52] In cases where the state statute is not specific, the courts have approached the issue metaphysically—whether software is "tangible" or

[47]*Hancock v. State* 402 S.W.2d 906 (Tex. Crim. App. 1966) (the court concluded the statute did cover copying).

[48]*See* Electronic Fund Transfer Act, 15 U.S.C. § 1693 (1982). There are other federal criminal statutes potentially applicable—*e.g.*, the Copyright Act. *See* Nycum, "Torts and Crime," *Computers & The Law* 226 (3d ed. 1981).

[49]Act of Oct. 12, 1984, P.L. No. 98–473, 98 Stat. 2190 *codified as amended at* 18 U.S.C. § 1030 (Supp. 1987).

[50]Act of Nov. 10, 1978, P.L. 95–630, 92 Stat. 3697, *codified as amended at* 12 U.S.C. §§ 3401–3422.

[51]Act of Oct. 26, 1970, P.L. No. 91–508, 84 Stat. 1128, *codified as amended at* 15 U.S.C. §§ 1681–1681(t).

[52]State-by-state analyses are provided in several source materials. *See, e.g.*, the listings in Davidson & Davidson, *supra* n. 10, § 6.7(a) n. 44.

"intangible;" could the software "exist" outside the physical medium in which it was expressed, (cf. Bishop Berkeley's question whether the tree falls if no one is around to see or hear it). The trend, as one might imagine, is in favor of taxing software, particularly that of the off-the-shelf, packaged variety.[53] Similarly, to the extent software is viewed as tangible property, property taxes are assessed in certain states, for example, California.[54]

[53]*See generally* Davidson & Davidson, *supra* n. 10, at § 6.7(a). *See also* White & Vanecek, "Taxpayer Beware! The Current State of Computer Software Taxation," 60 *Taxes* 373 (1982).

[54]Davidson & Davidson, *supra* n. 10, at § 6.7(b). The taxation of software in California is sufficiently complex as to justify detailed legal commentary. *E.g.*, Schnotenboer, "California Sales Taxation of Computer Software," 1 *Santa Clara Computer and High Tech L.J.* 107 (1985).

Eighteen

Strategic Alliances—Corporate and Nonprofit

Corporate investors have become increasingly important in venture finance, hunger for technology driving the arrangements. However, special issues—tax and business—arise when a match is made between a corporate giant and an immature concern. The same hunger for technology has made it possible for not-for-profit research generators—teaching hospitals, universities—to get their feet wet as partners in new ventures, not just as licensors. The prospect of megareturns has captured the attention of academics and, again, special issues are encountered. It is important for all interested parties to appreciate the behavior dynamics of corporate and university partners—what constraints they face, what drives their decision making. Unpleasant surprises are avoidable if there is an adequate understanding of the system standards of the institutional players.

§18.1 INTRODUCTION

Since venture capital is importantly identified with the high tech phenomena, it depends on research, experimentation, and development.

The traditional sources of those activities in the United States have been agencies of the federal government; major corporations; universities and other not-for-profit, research-generating institutions (e.g., teaching hospitals and think tanks); and, lastly, venture-sponsored entities. In the 1950s and 1960s, the federal research effort was enormous. In the author's tour as Undersecretary of the Department of Commerce in the late 1960s, the Assistant Secretary for Science and Technology plotted for his own amusement the rising curve of federal expenditures for civilian and military research and development on a graph. Had the trend not been halted, the line would have intersected the GNP before the year 2000.

That scenario has drastically changed. While the federal government continues to fund billions of dollars in research, an increasing share is going for defense purposes. There are, surely, civilian spinoffs from military research, but it is not an economical way to get from point A to point B, to depend on exhalations from research into Stealth bombers and amphibious tanks to create new civilian industries and products. The federal effort is decreasing at a time when one of the most influential books on the coffee tables in board rooms and executive offices in the United States is entitled *Innovations: The Attacker's Advantage.*[1] The curtailment of government research and development programs has put pressure on the other two legs of the table—the universities and technologically oriented start-ups—to provide the research industry needs to remain competitive. Consequently, the universities are looking to replace the federal dollar by maximizing the returns available from the commercialization of their in-house research.

The links between not-for-profit research generators and the venture capital industry are discussed in the latter half of this chapter. The alliance between high tech ventures and major, research-hungry corporations is the subject of the following discussion.

§18.2 STRATEGIC ALLIANCES WITH CORPORATIONS: CORPORATE PARTNERING

To a major corporation, a marriage between it and a small, high tech company holds enormous potential appeal. First, it is the usual myth

[1]Foster, *Innovations: The Attacker's Advantage* (1986). The author, a McKinsey & Co. partner, has tracked the life and death of American corporations and extruded a regression analysis, which shows that the survivors have been those firms which engage in what Schumpeter called the driving element of capitalism—"creative destruction." Schumpeter, *Capitalism, Socialism and Democracy* 81 (3d ed. 1980). At well-managed firms, innovation is a way of life. Thus, at 3M Corporation, according to the chairman, "we like to see 25 percent of each year's sales generated from products and services that were new in the previous five years." Costello, *New Venture Analysis: Research, Planning and Finance* viii (1985) (remarks of Lewis Lehr).

(and the more than occasional fact) in the R&D area that great oaks from little acorns grow, meaning that some of the most innovative "breakthrough" ideas of the twentieth century have been germinated in the classical inventor's garage, not the research laboratories of a major company. The management of Goliath, Inc. has come to understand that, as often as not, outstanding researchers and investigators cannot be enticed to join their research staff as salaried employees. Accordingly, "if you can't beat'em, join'em," meaning that Goliath will seek to enter into some form of contractual arrangement under the broad label of "corporate partnering" as the answer—the best of all possible worlds, whereby the megacorporation gets the benefit of the technology at a relatively manageable cost and the researchers retain their independence. (Before one goes off the deep end, however, the phenomenon should be put in perspective. High tech start-ups account for an enormous amount of innovation but their resources are limited. In any one year, IBM standing alone spends more on R&D than the aggregate amount of venture capital financings. Indeed, many research projects are well beyond the resources of a start-up, often, beyond the resources of any one corporation, thus requiring federal government assistance or a consortium effort.

§18.3 BUSINESS ASPECTS

Certain background observations should be made before the details of the corporate partnering relationship are examined. First, the idea is here to stay. There have been, to be sure, some spectacular failures—Exxon's adventures in venture capital come immediately to mind. But there have been enough conspicuous successes to continue to attract the attention of the Fortune "500".[2]

Secondly, it is clear that, once a marriage is made, there are cultural differences between the entreprenuerial mind-set and the corporate mentality, having largely to do not so much with perverse people but with the *structure* of large institutions. James Buchanan won the 1986 Nobel Prize in economics for elaborating elegantly on a more or less obvious proposition—that people within a political system behave so as to maximize their personal outcomes. Such is also the case in a large

[2]For some of the noteworthy companies which currently enjoy (or have enjoyed) corporate investment relationships, *see* Rind, "Dealing With The Corporate Venture Capitalist," in *Pratt's Guide To Venture Capital Sources,* 108 (11th ed. 1987). One of the most fortunate successes is the Warner & Swasey purchase, for $50,000, of 25% of Wang Laboratories, a relationship Dr. Wang immediately regretted because, in his words, ". . . the alliance never made sense strategically. Although I was given an inside look at a larger company, what I saw was bureaucracy and internal strife." Wang, *Lessons: An Autobiography* 117 (1986).

industrial organization, and it is critical that the founder understand the point so that he can appreciate what is motivating his corporate partners. He must understand that the corporation itself is an abstraction. It represents a basket of a number of interests, sometimes synchronized and sometimes competing. It acts, as only it can act, through people—a large number of people processing decisions vertically up and down the corporate hierarchy and horizontally from division to division. Theoretically, people in a large company are working together for the good of the institution; in fact, of course, they are often competitors. For some, their near-term, and perhaps long-term, interest is focused first on figuring out ways for each of them to succeed within the corporate structure and, often as a complement to that strategy, figuring out ways that their competitors for desirable job opportunities fail; finally, often in distant third place, the players attempt to maximize the outcome of the corporation itself. This phenomenon was colorfully brought home to the author when his firm represented a major Midwestern corporation engaged, as a defendant, in product liability litigation. The product in dispute had been initiated by manager A, who had since gone to other responsibilities within the corporation; direction to the litigation team was being provided by manager B. It became difficult to figure out the instructions being given by manager B; they seemed to be self-defeating, until the key to the Rosetta Stone made itself apparent. Manager B actually wanted his corporation to lose the lawsuit, thereby embarrassing manager A and maximizing manager B's chances to beat A to the finish line—the job for which they were both competing. This lesson needs endless repetition when dealing with a major company. The people at the table have their own agendas, which do not necessarily coincide with the interests of the company for which they work.[3]

§18.4 LEGAL ASPECTS

There is some question whether there exists any profound and distinct body of learning, at least in the legal sense, that fits under the heading of "corporate partnering" or "strategic alliances." Public corporations may invest in start-up companies but, with special exceptions,[4] the character of the investor entails no particular legal consequences. When a big company enters into research, production, and marketing arrange-

[3]Several technology-hungry corporations have established internal free-standing venture funds to make venture investments—*e.g.*, "Raytheon Ventures," *Corporate Venturing News* (Mar. 25, 1987) 5.

[4]For example, a corporate equity investor, public or private, disqualifies the issuer from electing S Corporation status. *See* Ch. 3, § 3.2.

ments with smaller partners, the question remains: "What . . . if anything, distinguishes a strategic partnership from an everyday distribution or joint marketing arrangement between participants at different levels in a product distribution chain . . .?"[5]

The seminars and source materials do not readily provide a response to the question.[6] The discussions generally have to do with issues involving investment relationships and licensing/joint venture agreements, subjects which are part and parcel of the venture capital culture and treated elsewhere in the text.[7]

Accordingly, the thrust of this discussion has to do principally with questions at the margin, issues that arise in connection with, or because of, an overlap between the legal rules and business conventions respecting the governance of large, publicly held companies on the one hand and small, privately held entities on the other.[8]

(a) TAX AND ACCOUNTING ASPECTS

Assume that a major publicly held company, Goliath, Inc, wishes to join forces with Start-up, Inc. to pursue an opportunity. The transaction may pose significant tax and accounting issues. In general, Goliath is schizophrenic *vis-à-vis* the cash it expends. For tax purposes, current deductibility is the preferred outcome. For shareholder reporting purposes, on the other hand, capitalization and gradual amortization are preferred to an immediate impact on the income statement.

(b) R&D OR R&E EXPENSES

As stated, Goliath is naturally interested in enjoying any tax benefits which result from the expenditure of its funds, meaning instant deductibility. To achieve that result, the relationship must, first, be structured in noncorporate form—as a joint venture or a partnership—so that Goliath's funding is not sterilized, in terms of ability to produce tax losses, as an equity investment. Since, in the typical case, Goliath's money is contributed for the purposes of research, the planners of the

[5]Gilburne, "Strategic Alliances: The Emerging Relationship Between Innovation and Consolidation in the Computer Industry," 3 *Computer Lawyer* 1, 2 (May 1986)

[6]*See, e.g.*, the discussion in *Corporate Partnering: Advantages for Emerging and Established Companies* (P.L.I. Course Handbook Series No. 220, 1986).

[7]*See* Ch. 15, § 16.6

[8]Much of the experience in corporate partnering as it exists in the venture capital world arises, not surprisingly, in the computer business, particularly since computer technology involves, in the final analysis, a systems approach to problems. There are usually several vendors—small and large—involved in the creation of a given system, entailing commercial symbiosis as a necessary element of the ultimate product. One obvious example is the relationship between Lotus, the supplier of the Lotus 1–2–3 program for computer software, and the IBM personal computer on which it runs.

relationship must focus on § 174 of the Code, which governs the current deductibility of research or experimental expenditures "paid or incurred by [the taxpayer] . . . in connection with his trade or business."[9] Absent § 174, most research and development expenses are of a type which must be capitalized (rather than deducted under § 162 of the Code) and amortized over the life of the asset to the creation of which they contribute.[10]

As discussed in Chapter 5, § 5.3(b), in order to qualify for § 174 treatment, the expense must comprise research in the "experimental or laboratory sense," (versus ordinary testing and inspection, tool design, trial production runs, and the like).[11] If expenses for R&E are accelerating, Goliath will also be sensitive to the possibility of a credit against tax for the incremental increase under § 41 (formerly § 44(f)) of the Code.[12]

When research is conducted in a corporate partnership, there is a risk that the Service will argue Goliath is passively buying the technology or the right to exercise it, instead of incurring the costs on its own behalf. The question whether Goliath is in fact spending the money so as to qualify for § 174 (and § 41) treatment has to do with the extent to which Goliath shares control and risk in the venture: A guaranty ("whether express, implied or imposed by local law")[13] by Start-up that the technology will work can be fatal to Goliath's claim.

(c) CONSOLIDATED RETURNS

The foregoing discussion assumes that Goliath and Start-up are each partners in a partnership (or a joint venture which is expressly, or is deemed, a partnership for tax purposes) to engage in research. If Goliath contributes capital by buying securities in Start-up, then the expenses belong to Start-up for tax purposes (since Goliath is a corporation, Start-up cannot elect S Corporation status) unless Goliath buys enough stock that, under § 1501 of the Code, the two corporations may elect to file a consolidated tax return. The privilege of filing consolidated returns is extended to members of an "affiliated group," meaning a parent and its subsidiaries connected through 80% stock ownership, measured in terms of both value and voting power.[14] The effect of the election is to

[9] I.R.C. § 174(a).

[10] Treas. Reg. 1.174–1. "Research or experimental expenses which are in turn treated as expenses not deferred and amortized under § 174 must be charged to capital account." The rules for shareholder reporting purposes start from the opposite premise. Under FASB Statement 2 (Oct. 1974), R&D expenses must be expensed until such time as it is clear there is an asset with a useful life to which an amortization schedule can attach.

[11] Treas. Regs. 1.174–2(a)(1).

[12] See Ch. 5, § 5.5.

[13] Treas. Regs. 1.174–2(b)(3).

[14] I.R.C. § 1504(a).

consolidate income and loss on a single return and to wash out intercorporate transactions. The thrust of the consolidated return provisions are to: (i) prevent the taxation of the same income or loss to more than one member of the group; (ii) minimize the tax consequences of intercompany transactions; and (iii) restore to income the losses of a subsidiary which exceed the group's investment as soon as it becomes clear that the losses will not be offset by future earnings or additional investment.

The regulations fleshing out the consolidated return sections are complex, dealing in large part with basis adjustments to the stock held by a parent in a subsidiary designed to reflect the subsidiary's prior income or loss, the object being to prevent double counting of such income or loss when and if the parent disposes of its stock in the subsidiary.[15]

(d) "DIVIDENDS RECEIVED" DEDUCTION

If Goliath invests in Start-up at some percentage lower than 80% of its voting power, then Goliath, as a corporation, is entitled to capture its share of Start-up's earnings at a tax cost only slightly in excess of a single tax as and if the same are distributed as dividends because of the "dividends received" deduction in § 243(a) of the Code.[16] The "dividends received" deduction has been reduced by the Tax Reform Act of 1986 from 85% to 80% of the dividend paid, but the decrease in overall corporate rates means that the rate of federal tax to Goliath remains about the same.[17]

The existence of the credit introduces an element of potential discord into the relationship to the extent that other shareholders of Start-up are individuals, unincorporated entities and/or organizations exempt from federal tax. Unlike interest, dividends are not deductible to the issuer and, therefore, to the extent earnings are repatriated to the shareholders in the form of dividends, they are doubly taxed to the noncorporate shareholders.

(e) HYBRID RELATIONSHIPS

If Goliath enters into a contract with Start-up whereby it will purchase widgets from Start-up, incorporate those widgets into its products and sell the combination at retail, the expense of buying the widgets is deductible (presumably) as a trade or business expense under § 162 of the Code. If Goliath is contemporaneously buying an equity interest—say a long-term warrant—in Start-up, the possibility arises of tradeoffs

[15] Treas. Regs. § 1–1502.
[16] I.R.C. § 243(a).
[17] I.R.C. § 11.

(within limits) in the purchase of the widgets versus the warrants, in order to minimize Goliath's tax liabilities. By boosting the price paid for the widgets and diminishing the amount paid for the warrants *pro tanto,* Goliath will enjoy an immediate tax advantage. If Start-up is relatively tax-indifferent at that stage, then Start-up will not object. Similarly, if Goliath is making payments to a joint venture it expects to deduct currently under § 174, as well as some form of equity in Start-up, the attraction of adding to one price and subtracting from the other is obvious. The risk that the Service will attack arrangements which do not pass the "red face" test is apparent.

§18.5 EQUITY BASIS OF ACCOUNTING

Whatever effect the results at the operating level have on Goliath's tax returns, the question arises—what consequences the investment entails for Goliath's earnings as reported to its shareholders. Under APB Opinion 18[18] the accounting profession is of the view that Goliath should take into its financial results its pro rata share of Start-up's results if Goliath "controls" Start-up. Control is presumed at ownership of 20% of Start-up's voting power. Otherwise, Goliath treats its investment as an investment, reporting gain or loss when the same is disposed of. The influence on Goliath's overall earnings per share may be immaterial but, in a large corporation, the managers of each profit center are usually compensated based on the performance of the unit they supervise. An investment in Start-up may reflect initial losses or may simply sit there for a while, not doing its part in meeting the current rate of return target (or "bogey") established for the manager on whose books the investment is carried. A creative corporate partnering relationship requires, in short, that the management of Goliath do some internal reshuffling of ROA (return on asset) and ROI (return on investment) targets so that long-term investments do not unfairly penalize someone's performance ratings.

§18.6 JOINT VENTURE

It is quite common for Goliath and Start-up to enter into an arrangement styled as a "joint venture."[19] As has been earlier noted, a joint venture is ordinarily deemed a general partnership under state law, albeit for

[18]*See* AICPA Interpretations of APB Opinion No. 18; FASB Interpretation 35; FASB Technical Bulletin 79–19.

[19]Several of the principal elements in the Goliath/Start-up joint venture relationship have been covered elsewhere in the Text; *see* Ch. 15 on Licensing Agreements, Ch. 9 on the Term Sheet; Ch. 10 on the Stock Purchase Agreement, and Ch. 5, § 5.4 on R&D Partnerships.

a defined purpose, limited in time. Thus, joint venturers owe the same reciprocal duties to each other as partners in a partnership.[20] The assumption is that Goliath and Start-up wish to develop for their joint benefit an item or field of technology and to share in the benefits if the development efforts are successful. Current deductibility of the expenses of the enterprise is important to Goliath, and often a matter of indifference to Start-up. The joint venture agreement must deal with certain critical business issues—for example, control of the venture, funding, division of profits and termination.[21]

(a) CONTROL OF THE JOINT VENTURE

Control of a joint venture is usually vested in a committee composed of representatives of each side, the people most involved in the process and invested with the power of decision. "The kiss of death for any joint venture is for its board to be a play board when the real power is back at corporate headquarters."[22]

When, as is often the case, the parties have discrete areas of responsibility—Start-up doing the research and Goliath providing the resources for sales, marketing, and distribution—Start-up's management may not realize how important it is that they have a voice in the management of Goliath's sales force. If Start-up's management does not have a say in the decisions whether to discharge unproductive salesmen and replace them, to direct salesmen in the field to concentrate on high profit lines of business and to target particular customers, then its products can be at the mercy of distracted, uninterested salespeople concentrating on other items in Goliath's line and the venture can fail—an annoyance to Goliath but a disaster to Start-up.

(b) MISCELLANEOUS JOINT VENTURE ISSUES

Funding provided by Goliath is ordinarily controlled by "milestones," achievement benchmarks which can be monitored by the controlling committee with respect to technical qualifications, on-time performance and market penetration. Consultants are often employed to break ties if the parties disagree on progress payments against ambiguous mile-

[20]*See* Ch. 3, § 3.5. *See* Taubman, "What Constitutes a Joint Venture," 41 *Cornell L. Q.* 640, 641 (1956); Williston, *Contracts* § 318, at 555–556, § 318A, at 563–565, 574, 579 (3d ed 1959); Crane & Bromberg, *Partnership* § 35 (1986); Reuschlein & Gregory, *Agency and Partnership* § 266 (1979).

[21]Carrying out an R&D joint venture has been made less offensive to antitrust objections by the passage of the National Cooperative Research Act of 1984, (Pub. L. No. 98–462,98 Stat. 1815), enacting 15 U.S.C. 4301. The law applies a rule of reason and limits treble damage liability.

[22]Remarks of E. Martin Gibson, president of Corning Glass Works Health and Science Group, reprinted in 19 *In Vivo* 15 (Nov./Dec. 1986).

stones, an ambiguity that is often inherent because the "product," if truly the end result of experimentation, is shrouded in some mystery when the drafting occurs. The issue of cost overruns is often neglected in the initial drafting, usually to the detriment of Start-up, which must bargain for needed completion monies without a shred of leverage in the absence of contractual provisions.

As a practical matter, a system of reporting is critical to smooth sailing. Frequent reporting is needed to alert Goliath to a pending milestone and generally to maintain interest in the project among easily diverted managers in the Goliath organization.

Title to the technology[23] is a matter which should absolutely be dealt with in the agreement; it is remarkable how often this simple precept is overlooked. If the agreement does not deal with the issue, it is probable that Goliath will be deemed the owner, having advanced the money and endured the risk of loss.[24] The ownership of collateral products, developed during the joint venture but not expressly within the specifications in the agreement, is a cloudier issue unless the agreement adequately addresses it. Any provisions allocating the ownership of technology should, of course, be endorsed by all the scientific personnel employed on the project; dividing ownership rights between Start-up and Goliath may be an empty exercise if it turns out that a given employee or consultant actually owns the technology.[25]

The issue whether the joint venture should be incorporated or operated as a partnership is dealt with elsewhere in the text[26] but the point deserves another mention here. If Start-up is contributing technology to an incorporated joint venture in exchange for stock, the technology will not qualify as "property" for purposes of § 351 (no tax on transfers of appreciated property) unless Start-up is transferring substantially all its rights to the technology.[27] In the typical joint venture, Start-up may wish to retain rights, resulting in a taxable transfer unless other devices—that is, multiple levels of stock—are employed.[28]

Whenever the products are to be manufactured by Start-up (and distributed by Goliath or incorporated into Goliath's products), there may be a question whether Start-up will be functionally capable of producing the necessary quantities. A promise to fulfill Goliath's "requirements," a time-honored phrase in contract law,[29] may look like good news but

[23]*See* Ch. 16.

[24]For an interesting system developed by Professor Sohlman at the Harvard Business School for allocating rights in accordance with a "three box" protocol, see 19 *In Vivo, supra* n. 22, at 19.

[25]*See* Ch. 16, § 16.7.

[26]*See* Ch. 3, § 3.6.

[27]*See* Ch. 5, § 5.1(b).

[28]*See* Ch. 5, § 5.1(c), Note that the use of preferred stock spoils the S Corporation election. Ch. 3, § 3.2.

[29]*See* Williston, *Contracts* 104 (1957 & Supp. 1986).

the damages for failure to perform can be severe, encompassing Goliath's lost profits, and Start-up would be well advised to negotiate "out" clauses which go beyond *force majeure*[30]—that is, events beyond Start-up's power to influence.

Often overlooked is the fact that a joint venture involving Goliath and Start-up calls for analysis of the Hart–Scott–Rodino amendments to the Clayton Act.[31] If Start-up has assets or sales of $10 million and Goliath is investing more than $15 million or acquiring more than 50% of the venture, the Federal Trade Commission (and Justice Department) must be notified (and fail to object) before the transaction closes.[32]

§18.7 ALLIANCES WITH NOT-FOR-PROFIT ENTITIES

(a) BACKGROUND

Alliances between institutions of higher learning and the business community have a long history. For example, the land grant universities have been responsible over the years for miraculous advances in agricultural science, providing the foundation for a multibillion dollar industry.

As business hunger for innovation and technology increases, the instances of industry–academic cooperation are multiplying. Massachusetts Institute of Technology set a pattern in 1948 by establishing a program giving companies access to the university's resources in exchange for an annual fee. MIT currently has 300 affiliates, including a third of the *Fortune* "500," who pay between $10,000 and $100,000 a year and, in exchange, are able to interface with professors, obtain advance word of scientific discoveries and visit the campus.[33] The Stanford Research Park, established in 1951, was a key ingredient in the development of Silicon Valley in Northern California. The rentals alone have yielded Stanford more than $2 million annually over the past 30 years—indeed, a number of universities are following the Stanford example (giving rise to an organization entitled the Association of University Research Parks).[34] There are celebrated examples of joint ar-

[30]*Force majeure* is usually confined to acts of God and other uncontrollable contingencies—i.e., a transportation strike.

[31]Hart–Scott–Rodino expressly applies to joint ventures. 15 U.S.C. § 18(a).

[32]The waiting period for Hart–Scott–Rodino clearance is 30 days, which can be shortened. 15 U.S.C. § 18(b)(2).

[33]*See* Main, "Business Goes to College for A Brain Gain," *Fortune* (Mar. 16, 1987) at 80.

[34]*Id.* at 84. The Research Triangle Park, operated in North Carolina on behalf of Duke, the University of North Carolina, and North Carolina State, is now larger than its chief competitors—the Stanford Research Park and the Princeton Forrestal Center in New Jersey. Hayes "Triangle Park: North Carolina's High-Tech Pay Off" N.Y. *Times*, Sun. Apr. 26, 1987, § 3, at 12.

rangements between major universities and major corporations—e.g. Monsanto, in 1982, agreed to pay Washington University $62 million over an eight-year period; some 30 projects are under way, jointly pursued. Hoechst, a German chemical company, supports the molecular biology department at Massachusetts General Hospital.[35]

(b) PATENT LICENSING

Most major universities maintain a patent office, which licenses university-developed technology.[36] However, the income from that source has not been robust. For example, Harvard's patent office, opened in 1977, took in only $200,000 in 1986. Stanford, in the middle of Silicon Valley, may be an exception (the director of Stanford's office of technology licensing expects $6 million in revenue this year) but, by and large, a passive patent-licensing policy has not proven to be a bonanza for universities. As the author and a colleague have pointed out in another paper:

> [l]icensing university owned patents (usually derived from federally funded research) for a royalty, avoids the risks of university entanglement with industry, but confronts certain characteristics of American business which limit the chances for success. By its nature, university research rarely produces results which are ready for the market. Further research and development, building on the basic findings of the university, is in all but the rarest case necessary to determine if the perceived commercial potential is even there. This can be costly, and much of American industry seems adverse to taking such risks, concentrating instead on short term profits. American industry also has an evident bias towards the products of its own "in-house" research. When industry can be attracted to invest in university research products, the return to the university is discounted by the additional expenditures which industry must undertake.[37]

[35]According to the National Science Foundation:

> Discussions about university-industry research coupling began to intensify around 1978 . . . There is . . . strong anecdotal evidence of increased activity. Several large and visible agreements for long term research collaboration between companies and universities have been signed within the past few years, for example, Harvard-Monsanto; Washington University-Mallinckrodt Inc.,; Harvard Medical School-Seagrams; MIT-Exxon; Carnegie Mellon-Westinghouse; Massachusetts General Hospital (Harvard)-Hoechst A.G.; and most recently, Washington University-Monsanto.

"University–Industry Research Relationships: Myths, Realities and Potentials," *Fourteenth Ann. Rep. of the Nat'l Sci. Board* 11 (Oct. 1, 1982).

[36]Some universities contract out the function to an independent patent management firm, *e.g.*, Research Corporation or University Patents, Inc.

[37]Bartlett & Siena, "Research and Development Limited Partnerships As A Device To Exploit University Owned Technology," 10 *J. of College & U.L.* 435 (1983–84). *See also* Culliton, "Biomedical Research Enters the Marketplace," 304 *New Eng. J. Med.* 1195 (May 1981).

Parenthetically, the paucity of patent licensing activity on the university level has been historically paralleled by the lack of commercial productivity from patents generated by the federal government, the root cause in this instance being the unwillingness until 1980 of the government generally to grant exclusive licenses. Since Congress acted in that year,[38] the government now grants exclusive rights, (no more than eight years, unless the licensee is a small business) subject to a right in the government (in the nature of a "shop right") to use the invention and so-called "march-in" rights to grant licenses if the original licensee is not exploiting the patent. University licensing practices frequently include shop and march-in rights in favor of the licensor.

(c) EXIT VEHICLES

Because the returns from straight licensing have been modest, the recent thrust has been toward the university attempting to participate in the so-called "exit vehicle" itself, the bonanza company organized around a given item of technology. The University of Florida, for example, saw Gatorade develop on its campus and has never gotten over the shock that it didn't bother to acquire an equity interest in the exit vehicle. So far, however, there has been a good deal more discussion than action in this area, despite recommendations from various sources that universities become involved in organizing what might be called "private label" venture capital funds.[39] As far as the author is aware, only one organized, structured entity with substantial dedicated resources has been created to date—Commtech International, a limited partnership[40] affiliated with SRI International (formerly the Stanford Research Institute). Commtech has raised several million dollars in order to investigate, screen, and exploit the available technology generated at SRI, with a view to creating entities around the most promising items, the equity to be shared in each case among SRI, Commtech, and the investors putting up the capital for exploitation of the specific item of tech-

[38]Patent and Trademark Acts, *Pub. L. No.* 96–517, § 8(b), 94 Stat. 3024 (1)80), codified at 35 U.S.C. § 200–211.

[39]*See, e.g.*, Cremmins & Keil, *Enterprise In The Non-Profit Sector,* (1983). The authors of the study (sponsored by the Rockefeller Brothers Fund) recommended that a pool of venture capital be created for nonprofit enterprises called, in their words, "the non-profit enterprise development corporation," the object of which would be to provide the "working capital and expertise necessary to raise the level of enterprise in the non-profit sector." *Id.* at 117.

[40]Commtech was organized by the author's firm. Some of the reasons for nonprofit timidity have to do with the trustees' concern that a high-visibility commercial enterprise might focus unwanted attention from the I.R.S. and/or curtail the appetite of traditional funding sources. *See* Cremmins & Keil, *supra* n. 39, at 68–69. Moreover, issues of prudence are magnified in a nonprofit environment.

nology. Whether the Commtech mode of operation will prove to be the pattern remains to be seen.

(d) AUTHORITY

The authority of a university or other tax-exempt institution to enter into commercial relationships has to be examined on a case-by-case basis. Many a university, particularly one publicly sponsored, has formed a "research institute" governed by a board of trustees appointed by the chairman of the university's governing board. Among the several reasons for organizing such a vehicle not the least is to avoid issues concerning legal authority and independence—that is, to vest power over activities such as joint industry/university ventures in an entity which is not a creature of statute nor ancient grantor documents and is not subject to the oversight and governance of the public members of the board of regents. If no such entity exists, the issue of *ultra vires* should be taken seriously by any potential partner. A challenge to the legal authority of a tax-exempt institution to pursue commercial ventures is likely to be brought by its statutory guardian, usually the State Attorney General, a more formidable opponent than an aggrieved shareholder.[41]

(e) UNRELATED BUSINESS ACTIVITIES

Most nonprofit institutions—"§ 501(c)(3) entities" as they are usually called, pursuant to the section of the Internal Revenue Code that governs the tax-exempt status of most of them[42]—routinely engage in a variety of unrelated or marginally related business activities, albeit not necessarily of the venture capital variety. For example, most museums maintain a cafeteria, sell postcards and prints of their *objets d'art* to the public, and rent out physical space for parties and commercial functions. The typical university runs a bookstore, and its football and basketball teams are business operations unto themselves. The university employs its real estate for profit (as in the case of the Stanford Research Park), may sponsor summer European tours in connection with the symphony orchestra, runs summer camps using university facilities and licenses the university name discretely. Hospitals (the border line between not-for-profit and profit is breaking down with the advent of such organizations as Hospital Corporation of America and Humana) are

[41] *See* Gilliland, "Joint Venturing University Research: Negotiating Cooperative Agreements," 40 *Bus. Law.* 971 (May 1985). The University of Virginia's contractual arrangements with the University of Virginia Alumni Patents Foundation are typical. *See* 2 Eckstrom, *Licensing in Foreign and Domestic Operations* Ch. 17A (3d ed. 1984).

[42] Sections 501(c), 501(d), 501(e), 521, 527, and 528 of the Internal Revenue Code describe the types of non-profit organizations qualifying for tax-exempt status, the majority being classified under § 501(c).

branching out into the operation of nursing homes, extended-care facilities and similar revenue-generating projects designed to develop alternative income streams for the hospital and, in the bargain, to increase patient flow.

The entry of not-for-profits into entirely unrelated business ventures was highlighted in the postwar period, when rich alumni began donating stock in their companies to their favorite institutions to obtain deductions and to avoid tax on the sale. In fact, the Internal Revenue Code amendments dealing with the unrelated income of tax-exempt enterprises was prompted by a transaction in 1950, when a group of wealthy graduates donated the Mueller Macaroni Company to New York University. Mueller's competitor, Ronzoni, objected on the basis that it was faced with unfair competition because, under the law in effect at that time, Mueller's profits were tax-exempt.[43]

(f) TAX-EXEMPT STATUS

Not-for-profit organizations are not automatically exempt from federal income taxation; a determination letter or Revenue Ruling is required. The critical issue for purposes of the present discussion is whether a 501(c)(3) entity may have its exemption revoked if a trade or business in which it is involved exceeds the permissible limits. The general statement in the Treasury Regulations[44] suggests that a charitable organization risks the loss of its exempt status either (i) if it "operates a trade or business as a *substantial part* of its activities,"[44] unless the operation of that trade or business "is in furtherance of the organization's exempt purpose or purposes," or (ii) if the organization is "organized or operated for the *primary purpose* of carrying on an unrelated trade or business."[44] The issue of entire loss of exempt status comes up principally in connection with quasi-religious organizations. It is unlikely that the venture capital activities in which a 501(c)(3) entity engages would take that activity outside the entire scope of the Code; it would be imprudent to devote such a high percentage of the nonprofit's resources to venture investing as to constitute that activity as the "primary purpose." Indeed, the principal purpose of participating in exit vehicles is, presumably, to capitalize on marginal opportunities which would otherwise be lost or surrendered to outside sources, not to turn the exempt entity's entire resources over to owning and controlling for-profit enterprises.[45]

[43] *See* Cremmins & Keil, *supra* n. 39, at 19.

[44] Treas. Reg. § 1.501(c)(3)–1(e)(1) (Emphasis Supplied.)

[45] I.R.C. § 170(e)(4)(B) provides a deduction for corporate taxpayers making "qualified research contributions" of new scientific equipment to not-for-profit educational and research organizations if used for "research and experimentation purposes."

(g) UNRELATED BUSINESS TAXABLE INCOME

Assuming that tax-exempt status is not itself threatened, a 501(c)(3) entity is nonetheless interested in reducing, perhaps to zero, the amount of income subject to tax under §§ 512 and 513 of the Code, imposing tax on "unrelated business taxable income" or UBTI. Unrelated business taxable income is defined in § 513 as

> income from a trade or business, the conduct of which is not substantially related, aside from the need of the charitable organization for income or funds or the use it makes from the profits derived, to the exercise or performance by such organization of its charitable, educational, or other purpose or function constituting the basis for its exemption.

Obviously, charities are authorized to raise endowment funds and to invest the same to support the activity. Thus, returns from investments in a corporation not "controlled"[46] by the exempt organization qualify as investment income under § 512(b)(1) (dividends and interest) or § 512(b)(5) (gains from the sale or exchange of property) and escape categorization as UBTI. Moreover, income from royalties of technology licensed to business ventures is generally exempt under § 512(b)(2). Further, if the exempt organization is engaged in some form of joint venture or partnership with a business enterprise, the enterprise produces "income derived from research,"[47] *and* the entity is a "college, university or hospital," § 512(b)(8) exempts such income from tax. If the entity is not "a college, university or hospital"—that is, is an unaffiliated research institute—income from research generally is exempt as long as it is "primarily" for purposes of carrying on "fundamental research," the results of which are freely available to the general public. (This distinction should be compared with the tests established under the Code and Regulations to measure whether an entity is organized and operated exclusively for "scientific"[48] purposes and thus qualifies as a public charity in the first place.) If the not-for-profit entity is a limited partner in a partnership (or joint venture), the income in the hands of the tax-exempt entity has the same character as it did in the hands of

[46] I.R.C. § 512(b)(13). *See* Treas. Regs § 1.512(b)–1 (1)(4) defining "control" as stock ownership of at least 80% of all classes of stock—i.e., the definition in I.R.C. § 368(a).

[47] "Research," in this context, is not limited to basic or "fundamental research." I.R.C. § 512(b)(9). *See generally* Kertz, "Tax Exempt Organizations and Commercially Sponsored Scientific Research," 9 *J. Coll. & U.L.* 69 (1982–83)

[48] "Scientific," according to Treas. Regs. § 1.512(1)-1(f)(3) means scientific research "in the public interest"—i.e., freely available to the public or for certain specified purposes (educating students or curing diseases or published for the benefit of the "interested" public). Such research may include applied research but not such pedestrian activities as testing products. *See generally Midwest Research Institute v. United States* 744 F.2d 635 (8th Cir. 1984).

the partnership; thus if a partnership or joint venture in which the tax-exempt entity invests is engaged in a "trade or business" other than the business of investing in securities, UBTI is the likely result. Accordingly, tax-exempt investors look for an incorporated entity somewhere between themselves and the business being conducted. Income may also be considered taxable if it results from leveraged investments, a concept discussed *infra* in Chapter 20, § 20.24.

Some tax-exempt entities are unfazed by taxable income; the tax is simply one, and only one, element to factor into the rate of return calculation. Others become paranoid at the mere thought of filing tax returns.

(h) ACADEMIC INTEGRITY AND OTHER ISSUES

Beyond the question of taxes, there has been a noisy debate on whether universities and other exempt institutions compromise their basic purposes—to educate and disseminate information—when entering into arrangements with businesses naturally concerned with maintaining technology in the strictest secrecy so as to protect the business firm's proprietary interest. As discussed elsewhere, the definition[49] builds into the very structure of a "trade secret" an obligation on the part of the owner to use reasonable methods to protect the same from coming into the public domain. A number of university- and industry-sponsored conferences have discussed that issue.[50] Allied with the tension between secrecy and education is the question of whether university researchers are being corrupted by their pursuit of solutions to industry's specific problems, their efforts turned away from both teaching and the development of nonspecified pure research.

A series of compromise solutions have been arranged to sanitize university–business alliances. Thus, it is generally provided in university–industry agreements that the results of the joint technological efforts be maintained in secrecy for a reasonable period of time, at least long enough to allow the industrial firm to file for patent protection. Then if the patent issues, (since the applicant is under a duty of candor[51] to disclose how the gizmo works in the patent claim) there is no necessary tension between town and gown. However, if the technology is not patentable, the venture must maintain enough confidentiality to allow the industrial firm to exploit it as a trade secret. Otherwise, there's no competitive advantage to the arrangement whatsoever. One of the

[49]For the most widely accepted expression, as set forth in, *Restatement of Torts* (1939 ed.), *see* Ch. 16, § 16.5.

[50]The Conference at Pajaro Dunes, Calif., in 1982 is perhaps the most significant; that conference's final statement is reproduced in 9 *J.Coll. & U.L.* 533 (1982–83).

[51]*See* Ch. 16, § 16.2(a).

problems with trade secret protection for technology developed on a university campus is that the usual method of preserving confidentiality in industry—requiring the execution of confidentiality agreements by all technical employees—may be impossible in the case of tenured faculty. They simply won't sign. Similarly, if a company providing funding, in order to preserve trade secret protection, asks for the right to review publications, the faculty is often ready to find overtones of censorship.

In this connection, arrangements between university researchers and a given university vary widely. It is probable that the university, without more, owns the technology developed in the course of the faculty member's employment.[52] If so, a typical arrangement will give the researcher some portion of the profits or equity (if equity is involved) for his efforts, with another portion to be directed toward the ongoing efforts in the researcher's laboratory, and the rest belonging to the university. Some Cassandras forecast that those universities which are ready, willing and able to make the most lucrative deals for researchers will find all the best researchers working for them.

[52]*See* Ch. 16, § 16.8; *see generally United States v. Dubilier Condenser Corp.* 289 U.S. 178 (1933).

Nineteen

Leveraged Buyouts—Venture Capital Version

Acquisitions of existing, profitable companies using leverage are as old as corporate finance. The current interest rate and tax environment have given such transactions high visibility; the abbreviation LBO is used to describe transactions, including both public and private firms. Venture capitalists have invested in LBOs for many years, the expected returns equaling the targets on their portfolios generally because of the leverage factor. The discussion in this chapter attempts to demystify the principal business and legal aspects of LBOs.

§19.1 STRUCTURE

The term "leveraged buyout" (LBO) is applied to the purchase of a firm, or the operating division of a firm, from its owners by an investment group, the price paid being funded in large part by borrowings secured by the assets transferred to the new group in the transaction. An LBO is a financing that involves an acquisition versus an investment; the structure of the deal ordinarily requires use of the assets of the target entity as collateral, the new group acquiring them "free and clear" and hypothecating them in the course of raising the purchase price. It is awkward to pledge a company's assets in aid of the purchaser's acquisition price unless all existing shareholders have relinquished their claims—hence the notion of a buyout. While some of the previous owners may participate in the investment group—rolling over their investment—they do so as new players. They first sell their existing interests and, based on an independent decision, join the purchasing group as and when invited to do so. The nexus between the assets and the prior owners is entirely broken as a legal matter.

An LBO is, in a sense, a bootstrap operation. The firm in question is acquired with funds provided (in large part) from its own sources—that is, the collateral value of its assets or cash flow. Nonetheless, there is nothing, at least intrinsically, morally wrong or economically inefficient in the form of the transaction. Were the prior owners to liquidate and then sell the assets distributed in liquidation at auction, the successful purchasers would, in all likelihood, finance the price in part by borrowing against the assets purchased, much in the same way a home buyer takes out a mortgage to finance his purchase or construction of a home. An LBO entails a high degree of leverage—up to 10 parts debt to 1 part equity in some cases, more in others—but so does a home mortgage.

The principal distinction—and often the advantage—of an LBO is that the assets may be leveraged without paying off the existing unsecured creditors of the target firm. With the transaction properly structured, those creditors remain in place—unconsulted and, indeed, unnotified in most instances—as the ownership changes and the assets are pledged to secure acquisition indebtedness.

The legal issue in LBOs, then, principally involves the existing unsecured creditors. Will they be able, in a subsequent processing, to raise an objection, usually under the label "fraudulent conveyance," that the acquired firm was leveraged to the point that its unpledged asset values were not sufficient to satisfy its unsecured indebtedness, or that it transferred and or pledged assets without receiving adequate consideration therefor? Were the law to require that existing creditors be dealt with to their satisfaction, compensated in some way for the fact that much of the firm's prior equity has been changed into debt, many LBOs would become unattractive. The legal issues raised by LBOs are largely caught up with methods to minimize the chance a court will rearrange the transaction and/or impose penalties because of the unsecured creditor bypass.

The business opportunities in an LBO can be beguiling, driven in large part by the fact that interest is tax-deductible. The trick is to find assets either unencumbered or pledged for substantially less than their actual collateral value and/or a stable cash flow from operations. The assets are, in effect, written up to fair value in the course of the LBO, discarding the anemic balance sheet values assigned by the conventions of cost accounting, unadjusted for inflation. The asset base and/or cash flow stream supports a high degree of leverage, maximizing return on equity if debt service can be earned.[1] Indeed, some of the debt takes the form of a purchase money note, the seller taking back a subordinated note, which lessens the burden of finding outside financing and, in the bargain, gives comfort to the senior lenders that there is a "cushion" beneath their loan. Cash flow is, to be sure, debited by the increased interest and principal requirements but the interest component is subsidized; federal and state governments in effect pay part of the interest cost by allowing those costs to be deducted from taxable income. In many instances, interest costs are further ameliorated by sweetening the lender's projected returns with equity "strips," usually in the form of warrants entitling the lender to participate in some portion of the equity "upside." To create management equity incentives, management is given a significant stock position in the new firm at a time when it is most feasible without occasioning tax—that is, when equity values are ostensibly low since the debt (and perhaps preferred stock to the cash investors) "eats up" so large a portion of the asset side of the balance sheet.[2] In an LBO, management can receive, in effect, "founders' stock" in a mature company.

On the "sell" side, there are advantages as well. Corporate sellers of unloved divisions are often attracted to LBOs because of the possibility that the purchase price can be so structured that the seller will not incur a "loss;" the interest rate on the purchase money debt can be adjusted downward, and therefore the ostensible price upward, so that the transaction appears to be at par on the seller's books.

The possibility of extraordinary profits are based on a combination of factors. High leverage creates the possibility of a venture-type return on equity: 30 to 40% compounded annually. If interest rates fall (and real interest rates are high as of this writing), that return gets an artificial boost. Most importantly, management motivation is enhanced—a key point.[3] In a traditional start-up investment, one of the biggest risks is the ability of untested management to run the company. That downside risk is moderated to the point of elimination in an LBO—

[1] A simple example illustrates the effect of leverage. If Company A, leveraged with $80 million in debt and $20 million in equity, is able to pay off $10 million in the principal amount of its debt, the equity, *ceteris paribis*, has increased 50% even though the return on assets has been only 10% ($10 million on $100 million). *See* Donnelly, "Partnerships Open Leveraged Buyouts to Individuals Willing to Take The Risk," *Wall St. J.* Mar. 3, 1987, at 35.

[2] *See* Ch. 5, § 5.1(c) respecting "eat 'em up" preferred stock. Since the lenders require a high degree of certainty in the projections of future cash flow, it is not customary for a leveraged buyout to include a contingent form of payment—i.e., an "earn-out."

[3] If management is replaced or redirected, the focus is often on squeezing out excess expense. Some managers, caught up in the culture of public megainstitutions, are found to be confused between fixed and marginal expense, believing certain overhead expenses to be fixed when they are in fact marginal.

existing management has already been earning close to the projected returns. Moreover, historians of LBOs are highly impressed by the way that management improves—the same people get better—with a heavy personal stake in the business. One of the first things the managers do, once their new hats are in place, is take a hard look at all the lines of business; they are psychologically free at last to sell much beloved but underperforming assets, accelerating debt paydown.

Finally, a firm eligible for LBO treatment holds out the possibility of not two[4] but three exit strategies—a sale of the firm, an IPO (cf. the fabled Gibson greeting cards transaction)[5] *or* another LBO. In this sense, LBOs are like perpetual motion machines. The new purchasing group finally pays off the debt to the point that there is room for a refinancing—enter purchasing group number two. The author recalls that a client firm bought in an LBO in the early 1960s for $1 per share was sold in the early 1980s for $80 per share to younger members of management succeeding to the reins of power; the sellers were invited into the new group at $2.50 a share.

LBOs are not, of course, the exclusive province of venture finance. Indeed, measured by volume, the most significant LBOs involve the purchase and restructuring of major public companies—the purchase, for example, of Beatrice Foods by the leading firm specializing in gigantic LBOs, Kohlberg, Kravis, Roberts, Inc. In the public arena, the transactions are often driven by giant egos, self-styled Titans battling in the media for control of huge public companies. The debt financing for such high-visibility transactions has been, more often than not, arranged by Drexel Burnham Lambert, one of whose senior officers, Michael Milken, happened upon the realization that cash flow and management could constitute more credit-worthy assets than the traditional collateral: plant and equipment, accounts receivable, and inventory. Venture managers eschew the public arena, however. A venture-backed LBO may, on infrequent occasion, involve a public company but rarely one put "into play" through a threatened or actual hostile tender. The principal problem in public LBOs, apart from the legal issues, is the overbid, the scenario in which one purchasing group goes to great time and expense to arrange a publicized purchase and the attendant fi-

[4]Redemption or repurchase of the investors' shares is not commonly considered an exit strategy; public companies often repurchase shares when market values are depressed but, by definition, that strategy does not apply when the stock does not trade. For a discussion of the restructuring strategy in a management buyout (MBO), *see* § 19.14.

[5]Gibson Greeting Cards was acquired in an LBO by an investor group including the former Treasury Secretary, William Simon; it shortly thereafter went public at an enormous profit. *See* Waters, "Banking on the Entrepreneur: The Leveraged Buyout Boom," *Inc.* 46 (Sept. 1983).

nancing, only to be countered by an overbid on the eve of the closing.[6] Venture firms are too thinly staffed to pursue potential blind alleys or to man the barricades in a hostile tender environment; moreover, the investors are private and pacific, anxious to avoid litigation or the public eye. Hence, they tend to work with sellers who are willing and able to bind themselves to the transaction at an early date.

The legal structure of an LBO is often discussed in the literature but usually in terms opaque even to practitioners—"upstream dividends, reverse triangular mergers."[7] The instant discussion will attempt to illuminate the essence of the transaction by exploring the principles that drive the maneuverings of the parties to package structures which minimize risk of a subsequent legal or tax challenge.

§19.2 CREDITORS' RIGHTS

The "equality" notion is one of the fundamental doctrines in bankruptcy, one which contributes to the equitable nature of the bankruptcy process. Outside bankruptcy, the rights of creditors and the relationship between them and their debtors are determined by their contractual arrangements. If a debtor is in trouble, the first creditor to get in line takes the prize, a practice described as "snatch and grab" or "jostling."[8] In an insolvency proceeding, equality of treatment within classes of debt[9] becomes, in essence, the substitute for the pre-existing negotiated

[6]The aspiring purchaser of a public target usually attempts to secure an exclusive option (a "lock-up") or at least a promise from the target's board of directors not to auction the division or company (a "no shop" agreement). The directors are well advised to protect themselves against subsequent litigation by providing an "out" in the lock-up agreement if compelled to deal with an overbidder; reference in the agreement to the target board's power to disregard a lock-up if called upon to do so by their "fiduciary" duty primarily means the lock-up option fails if the new bid is significantly higher. *See* Bryer & DeRose, "Representing a Public Company in a Leveraged Buyout Transaction: An Update," in *Leveraged Acquisitions and Buyouts* 188–89 (P.L.I. Course Handbook Series No. 510, 1986). Another device to protect purchasers is the "break-up" fee, a fee payable by the target in the case of an overbid to cover the purchaser's expenses.

[7]As LBOs grow in popularity, the labels attached to various items of technical apparatus are growing in complexity and vividness—i.e., "alphabet stock," "declining redemption value participating preferred." The labels refer to exotic securities designed, in the main, to "eat up" balance sheet value so that management can obtain the equivalent of "founders' stock" without paying tax. *See* Ch. 5, § 5.1(c). Thus, "declining redemption value preferred" is a class of preferred, the redemption value and conversion price of which start out in a posture weighted heavily against the common shareholders (thereby depreciating the value of the common); those rights "decline" if and as the managers hit their targets, in effect reallocating stock to management tax-free. In the opinion of some practitioners, the language of I.R.C. § 3.05, *see* Ch. 13, § 13.6, does not pose a problem in this instance because it does not literally apply.

[8]Aaron, *Bankruptcy Law Fundamentals* § 10.01 (1986).

[9]11 U.S.C. § 726(b).

relationships. The trustee in bankruptcy is given extraordinary powers to review and avoid prebankruptcy creditor actions that threaten to upset the fairness of the proceeding.[10] Since creditors in an LBO must assume the worst case—that is, subsequent bankruptcy—their eyes must be keenly fastened on what a subsequent trustee might be able to do to their interests in the name of "fairness" and "equality of treatment."

Whether LBOs are "fair" and/or in the public interest is the subject of increasing comment, much of the controversy surrounding transactions which entail taking a public company "private."[11] The concerns revolve around the issue whether public shareholders are adequately represented in the negotiations for their stock, particularly when the management of the firm is an integral part of the acquisition group. However, as indicated, venture-backed LBOs do not customarily involve the acquisition of public companies, most venture capitalists preferring the more tranquil atmosphere of private deals. The "fairness" question in private LBOs does not concern so much the selling shareholders (although they can be harmed if they are passive and the management insiders are on both sides of the deal) but the existing creditors if and to the extent that, after the transaction, the surviving entity, universally labeled "Newco" in LBO parlance, is unable to pay its bills.[12]

Any creditor, of course, is at risk; debtors are rendered insolvent for a variety of reasons and the creditor must take his lumps along with other interested parties. However, an unsecured creditor of a target firm has a special handicap to the extent substantial assets are distributed or pledged without countervailing consideration in a transaction that bypasses the interests of general creditors.

§19.3 UNSECURED CREDITORS' BYPASS

To restate an earlier point, the assets or cash flow of the "target" are being hypothecated to raise cash to distribute to the target's shareholders—the previous owners. The liens against the targets' assets are substantially increased in the process; there is, thus, less "equity" in those assets for the benefit of general unsecured creditors. The entire process involves a corporate recasting, which has the feel and smell of

[10] 11 U.S.C. § 544 (the so-called "strong arm" clause); *see generally* Teofan & Creel, "The Trustee's Avoiding Powers Under the Bankruptcy Act and the New Code: A Comparative Analysis" 85 *Com. L. J.* 542 (Dec. 1980).

[11] Sommer, *Going Private: A Lesson in Corporate Responsibility,* [1974–1975 Transfer Binder] (CCH) Fed. Sec. L. Rep. ¶ 800,010 (1974); Lowenstein, "Management Buyouts" 85 *Colum. L. Rev.* 730 (1985).

[12] A hard core of academics argue vehemently that leveraged buyouts, at least those arranged with the participation of existing management, are fraught with unfairness. *See* Lowenstein, *supra* n. 11, at 740 n. 34 (1985). But *see* Booth, "Management Buyouts, Shareholder Welfare, and the Limits of Fiduciary Duty," 60 *N.Y.U.L. Rev.* 630 (1985).

a liquidation. If a traditional liquidation were to occur, however, the assets would be monetized and the proceeds distributed in strict order of priority: secured creditors first until they are entirely satisfied, unsecured creditors next, and then (and only then) the equity owners. The equity owners would ultimately get their price but only after each unsecured creditor was paid in full. In an LBO, the equity owners get the value of their equity but the unsecured creditors remain as they were. If the ensuing company is, or likely to become, insolvent, the "bypass" appears to have been unfair, violating the priority which the creditors bargained for when they extended credit.

The legislature and the courts have not yet developed a coherent doctrine for dealing with LBOs, particularly the issue of fairness to existing general creditors of the target in the event of subsequent insolvency. As is almost always the case when the law is in transition, wrestling with novel transactions, judges paste together a pastiche of existing rules in an attempt to reach equitable results in particular cases. The problem for the planner is that he must deal with uncertainty: When rules developed for one purpose migrate into a new arena, drafted into service as regulating principles in a new venue, odd results can occur.

The mosaic of rule which must concern the parties to an LBO is made up of several parts. First, because "transfers" occur in the course of the transaction, there is the possibility such transfers can and will be set aside in a subsequent proceeding, meaning that (i) the values transferred will be recaptured (i.e., the selling shareholders have to return the price and/or secured creditors regurgitate prior payments) or (ii) that the results of the transfers themselves will be invalidated, meaning that the security interests claimed by the new lenders will be disregarded in calculating priorities. Setting aside transfers is usually based on doctrines labeled "fraudulent conveyence"[13] and "preference,"[14] ancient insolvency rules now memoralized in the federal Bankruptcy Code and in various state statutes.[15]

Secondly, when a creditor participating in an LBO comes to present a claim in a subsequent insolvency proceeding, a judge may use the doctrine of equitable subordination, also enshrined in the Bankruptcy Code,[16] to place the claimant further down or at the end of the line, subordinating its interest to those asserted by other parties in the assets being liquidated.

Thirdly, the courts may find a reason, usually resulting from a control relationship, for alleging that an insider of Newco has responsibility to

[13] 11 U.S.C. § 548. *See infra* § 19.4.

[14] 11 U.S.C. § 547. *See infra* § 19.6.

[15] N.Y. Debtor & Creditor Law § 273 (McKinney) (fraudulent conveyance) and § 15(6–a) (McKinney) (preference)

[16] 11 U.S.C. § 510(c). *See infra* § 19.8.

pay compensation for the losses that Newco's insolvency engenders. The labels attached to this legal doctrine are various—that the controlling shareholders or creditors of Newco are its "alter ego"; that they have "fiduciary" duties to Newco general creditors and minority stockholders; that Newco is simply an "instrumentality" of the controlling group. When liability is founded on this rationale, the results can be quite alarming, because the damages, at least in theory, are not limited to amounts advanced by the controlling persons; whatever damages/losses their breach of duty has proximately caused will be compensable.[17]

§19.4 FRAUDULENT CONVEYENCE

Of primary concern to lenders in an LBO is a doctrine which dates back to 1571,[18] prohibiting debtors from making transfers that "hinder, delay or defraud" their creditors, a doctrine historically labeled "fraudulent conveyance." This doctrine, now enshrined in the Uniform Fraudulent Conveyance Act[19] and in the Bankruptcy Code,[20] holds that a debtor cannot "manipulate his affairs in order to shortchange his creditors and pocket the difference."[21] The classic fraudulent conveyance—the debtor transfers his property on the eve of insolvency for little or no consideration with intent to frustrate his creditors—is the easy case. The more difficult problem, which typically confronts the planners of an LBO, is the notion that a transfer that was never intended to defraud creditors can be a *constructive* fraudulent conveyance if certain aspects of the transaction, particularly the consideration deemed to have been received, are properly viewed as unfair or harmful to creditors generally.

The fraudulent conveyence doctrine is now set out in § 548 of the Bankruptcy Code, and the language of that statute deserves close attention by counsel putting together an LBO. Section 548 concerns transfers made and obligations incurred within one year before the date a bankruptcy petition is filed.[22] (Transfer means the payment of money or the granting of a security interest; "obligation" in this context is an obligation of the debtor in guaranteeing the payment of another's debt.)

[17]An extremely valuable discussion on the entire issue of lenders' liabilities is contained in Davis, *Emerging Theories of Lender Liability* (Chairman, ABA Div. of Prof. Educ. 1985) (Theories of Lender Liability).

[18]Statute of 13 Elizabeth, Ch. 5 (1570).

[19]7A Uniform Laws Ann. 427.

[20]11 U.S.C. § 548 (1982); *see generally* Macey, "Preferences and Fraudulent Transfers under the Bankruptcy Reform Act of 1978," 28 *Emory L. J.* 685 (1979).

[21]Baird & Jackson, "Fraudulent Conveyance Law and Its Proper Domain" 38 *Vand. L. Rev.* 829 (May 1985).

[22]Under state fraudulent conveyance statutes, the conveyance may be vulnerable for longer periods of time, six years in New York for example. N.Y. Debtor & Creditor Law § 273 (McKinney).

A transfer is voidable at the option of the trustee in bankruptcy[23] under 548(a)(1) if it is made with *actual* intent to hinder, delay, or defraud a present or future creditor—the easy case. The more troublesome provisions are the constructive fraudulent conveyence rules set out in § 548(a)(2) of the Act.[24] The tests involve four concepts: (i) Did the debtor *receive*[25] less than "reasonably equivalent value" for the transfer or obligation? *and* (ii) was the debtor either "insolvent" on the date the transfer was made or became insolvent as a result of the transaction?[26] *or* (iii) as of the date of the transaction, was the debtor about to engage in business with "unreasonably small capital?"[27] *or* (iv) did debtor intend to incur, or believe it would incur, debts beyond its ability to pay?[28]

The question of the debtor's receipt of "reasonably equivalent value" is a difficult one and practitioners are loath to rely on that test to insulate LBO transfers and guarantees from subsequent attack under § 548. The problem is that, at least arguably, Newco itself (the debtor) is receiving *no* value because the existing creditors are being bypassed and the ultimate proceeds being paid out to the shareholders.[29] Consequently, as outlined below, the protective actions taken by counsel focus heavily on the question of solvency and adequate capitalization for Newco after the transaction.

There is a safe harbor set up under the Bankruptcy Code for lenders who take a security interest and/or accept a guaranty for "value" and "in good faith."[30] The "for value" issue appears to raise the same concerns as the term "reasonably equivalent value." Good faith means at

[23]The trustee in bankruptcy has the power—called the "strong arm" power—under § 544 of the Bankruptcy Code to assert the rights of a hypothetical creditor at the time of the filing with a judicial lien or an unsatisfied execution or a hypothetical bona fide purchaser of real estate.

[24]There has not been a plethora of cases as yet on fraudulent conveyances in an LBO context. Torres, "Minority Shareholder Protection in Leveraged Buyouts," 13 *Sec. L. J.* 356 (1986) (less than 20 cases in which the term is used). The leading case is *United States v. Gleneagles Investment Co. Inc.* 565 F. Supp. 556 (M.D. Pa. 1983), involving the issue of the lender's "good faith" under the Pennsylvania fraudulent conveyance statute. About one-half the proceeds of the secured debt went to the selling shareholders and the lender "knew or strongly suspected" the conveyance would render the debtor insolvent.

[25]Note that, under the statutory language, the "reasonably equivalent" notion depends on what the debtor *received* versus what the creditor advanced. 11 U.S.C. § 548(a)(2)(A).

[26]11 U.S.C. § 548(a)(2)(B)(i)

[27]11 U.S.C. § 548(a)(2)(B)(ii)

[28]11 U.S.C. § 548(a)(2)(B)(iii)

[29]Professors Baird and Jackson, *supra* n. 21, at 831, set out a free market theory which argues that creditors should be free to bargain or not to bargain for much of what is now driven by "off the rack" (as they put it) provisions in the federal statute and the Uniform Act. They argue the LBO transaction is not conceptually different from a borrowing by an existing firm coupled with a dividend to shareholders, a practice they feel should be governed by contract and not by a per se rule. *Id.* at 853. *See* the discussion of corporate "restructurings" *infra* § 19.14.

[30]11 U.S.C. § 548(c)

least that the transaction should be an arm's length transaction; it probably circles back again to the issue of solvency, this time calling into question the knowledge (or constructive knowledge) of the transferee concerning the debtor's solvency and imposing some obligation on the transferee to investigate solvency.[31]

§19.5 GUARANTEES

A fraudulent conveyence attack can be made not only on the security interests of the senior lenders to Newco but on their attempts to enforce guarantees against one of the family of corporations that make up Newco in a multilevel, complex LBO. The making of the guarantee is "an obligation incurred" within the meaning of § 548 of the Bankruptcy Code and, thus, voidable in a subsequent insolvency proceeding involving the guarantor. It is possible, of course, to structure an LBO without the use of parent and subsidiary corporations. Indeed, that result is preferable from the point of view of the lenders, the operating assets being owned by the debtor alone. Not only do lenders prefer a simplified transaction so as to eliminate the necessity of guarantees; to the extent there are intercorporate transfers in the course of an LBO, additional avenues of attack are opened up in subsequent insolvency proceedings on state law grounds, as outlined below.

While the lenders prefer as few moving parts possible, because each subsidiary transaction is itself an opening to attack, nevertheless complex multilevel corporate structures have desirable aspects. Thus, in structuring an LBO, the purchasing group is driving for the best-looking balance sheet possible for the company, Newco, which will be responsible for repayment of the debt.[32] A handsome balance sheet gives comfort to trade creditors and other parties doing business with Newco in the future. If the deal involves purchase money debt (deferred payments of the purchase price) subordinated to senior secured debt, the trick is to cause the secured debt, and only that debt, to be a direct obligation of the company holding the collateral; the purchase money debt is, if possible, to be the primary obligation of the parent of the operating company. The operating company must guarantee its parent's debt but that guaranty will be in the footnotes to, and not an integral part of, the operating company's balance sheet, meaning that the "Shareholders Equity" line on the operating company's financial statements will be that much larger. To achieve this result, it is necessary to engage in complicated structuring and the maneuvers ordinarily require that cash

[31] *See United States v. Gleneagles, supra* n. 24.

[32] *See* the discussion, including an analysis of comparative balance sheets, by Benjamin, "Leveraged Acquisitions," in *Leveraged Acquisitions and Buyouts, supra* n. 6.

be "upstreamed"—that is, be transferred as a dividend from the subsidiary to the parent at some point in the transaction.

Loans involving guarantees are not often litigated.[33] For the question to arise in court, both the primary obligor and the guarantor must first be insolvent and then a fight must break out between the guaranteed party and the creditors of the guarantor over whether the unsatisfied portion of the former's debt is a valid claim in the guarantor's proceeding (and whether any security interest collateralizing the same is valid). Complex, multiparty issues of this sort tend to be settled by negotiation.

Parenthetically, the question of an "upstream" guaranty involves different issues than those presented by a "downstream" or "cross-stream" guarantees.[34] That is, if a parent guarantees a creditor in consideration of the creditor advancing funds to a subsidiary, it is not hard to track the benefit accruing to the parent from the transaction. However, if the subsidiary (as in the typical LBO) is guaranteeing the parent's debt (or one company under common control with another issuing a cross-stream guaranty), the benefit to the guarantor is harder to find. One argument (not convincing in the LBO context) is that a loan that enables the parent to pay its debts makes it more likely that the affiliate, the subsidiary, can stave off bankruptcy if circumstances might otherwise dictate.[35]

§19.6 PREFERENCES

A long-standing doctrine in bankruptcy empowers the trustee to avoid statutory "preferences."[36] The underlying notion is based, again, on the principle of equality. No creditor should be unfairly "preferred" over another. In contrast to the fraudulent conveyance sections, the test in § 547 of the Bankruptcy Code is relatively objective: A preference is a transfer to a creditor for or on account of an "antecedent debt" made while the debtor was insolvent, which enables the creditor to obtain more than he would have, had the preference not been made. Transfers within 90 days of the filing are tested as preferences[37] (and insolvency

[33]Rosenberg, "Intercorporate Guaranties And The Law of Fraudulent Conveyances: Lender Beware," 125 *U. Pa. L. Rev.* 235, 239 (Dec. 1976)

[34]The "solvency" issue is complicated if the question involves the balance sheet of the maker of a guaranty—i.e., can a debtor be rendered "insolvent" by an obligation which appears only in the footnotes to the balance sheet? Some commentators believe such should be the result. Rosenberg, *supra* n. 33, at 256.

[35]*Id.* at 245.

[36]11 U.S.C. § 547. *See generally* 4 *Collier on Bankruptcy* Ch. 547 (15th ed. 1979); McCoid, "Bankruptcy, Preferences and Efficiency: An Expression of Doubt," 67 *Va. L. Rev.* 249 (1981)

[37]11 U.S.C. § 547(b)(4)

of the debtor is presumed during that 90-day period)[38] unless the transferee was an "insider," in which case the testing period is lengthened to one year before the filing. (If a preferential transfer to a noninsider is made more than 90 days preceding the filing, the trustee can be expected to look to the fraudulent conveyance section of the Act as a second line of attack.)

Most of the troublesome issues in this area have to do with the timing of the financing. If the debtor incurs a debt by ordering and receiving goods from vendors and pays 60 days later, is that payment a transfer "on account of an antecedent debt?"[39] The timing issue is most acute, conceptually at least, for lenders against fungible assets—inventory and accounts receivable—who assert a security interest in the nature of a "floating lien," a lien which will necessarily attach in the future to collateral not even in existence when the loan was made. The obvious argument is that a security interest in such collateral ("after acquired" collateral) was *necessarily* granted on account of an antecedent debt. The new Bankruptcy Code addresses this issue by formulating an inquiry into whether the lender has "improved its position" in the 90 days (one year in the case of an insider) prior to the date of the filing; only the incremental security is attackable.[40]

§19.7 BULK SALES

If the LBO involves a sale of all the assets of the target to Newco (versus a merger or a sale of stock), then the organizers must take into account Article 6 of the Uniform Commercial Code as in effect in the state the law of which is applicable to the transfer, the "bulk sale" law.[41] In all but the most unusual LBOs, § 6–103 will be consulted. That section provides that the elaborate advance notice-to-creditors provisions required in the case of a bulk sale do not apply if Newco assumes the

[38]11 U.S.C. § 547(f)

[39]Transfers involving a "contemporaneous exchange for new value" or as payment of a debt incurred and payment made "in the ordinary course of business" are not preferences if payment is made "'according to ordinary business terms." 11 U.S.C. § 547(c)(1) and (2); *see* 2 *Collier Bankruptcy Manual* § 547.10 (1987). The problem is that debtors in trouble routinely slow down in paying their bills. A creditor who begins howling for payment in "the ordinary course" but doesn't get paid until later can be diligent but unlucky.

[40]11 U.S.C. § 547(c)(5). When a debtor transfers a security interest to a creditor—i.e., executes a pledge—a curious concept in the Uniform Fraudulent Conveyance Act § 3, insists that the security be in an amount "not disproportionately small as compared with" the amount of the debt. Of course, a creditor only obtains an interest in collateral up to the amount of its debt; the fact that a $1 million asset secures a $10,000 debt does not mean that the creditor can collect more than $10,000. However, a prudent creditor will stipulate that the debt is only secured by that amount of the collateral which equals the amount of the debt. *See* Rosenberg, *supra* n. 33, at 247.

[41]Uniform Commercial Code (U.C.C.), Art. 6 (Official Text 1978).

target's obligations, gives notice by publication of its obligation to pay, and is "solvent after becoming so bound."[42] The joker in the deck is, as usual, the question of solvency. A leavening factor is that the Article has a short statute of limitations; actions must be brought within six months after the transfer unless the transfer has been "concealed."[43] Notice by publication would seem to negate an allegation of concealment.[44] Informing the appropriate credit agencies (for example, Dun & Bradstreet) is also recommended by careful practitioners. Caution should be observed, however, since several states have enlarged the boundaries of the statute.[45]

§19.8 EQUITABLE SUBORDINATION

Equitable subordination is a doctrine originating in the ancient idea that a court sitting in "equity" (insolvency courts are traditionally considered courts of equity) has inherent powers to avoid unfairness. The doctrine, articulated specifically in § 510(c) of the Bankruptcy Code, is quite drastic on its face.[46] A putatively "secured" creditor can find its claim not only unsecured but in fact subordinated to the claims of general unsecured creditors;[47] a court may treat the loan as a contribution to capital.

The Code refers to, but does not define, the principles of "equitable subordination," which allow a Bankruptcy Court to set aside a security interest or subordinate a creditor's claim if the amorphous principles have been offended. Some type of misconduct[48] on the part of the cred-

[42]U.C.C. § 6–103(6). Article 6 does not apply to service businesses. *See* U.C.C. § 6–102, Official Comment.

[43]U.C.C. § 6–111.

[44]*See Columbian Rope Co. v. Rinek Cordage Co.* 461A.2d 312 (Pa. Sup. Ct. 1983).

[45]*See Quinn's Uniform Commercial Code Commentary and Law Digest* § 6–102[A][6] (Supp. 1986, No. 2)

[46]11 U.S.C. § 510(c). The leading case standing for the initiation of equitable relief in bankruptcy to correct "unfairness" is *Pepper v. Litton* 308 U.S.295 (1939); also influential is the Supreme Court's opinion in *Taylor v. Standard Gas & Electric Co.* 306 U.S.307 (1939). One of the most alarming (from the lender's standpoint) modern cases is *Connor v. Great Western Savings & Loan Association* 69 Cal.2d 850, 447 P.2d 609 (1968), where the lender was held liable for defects in the construction it had financed. One of the better discussions on the general issue is contained in Bernstein, "Leveraged Buy Outs: Legal Problems and Practical Solutions," in *Leveraged Buy Outs,* at 119 (Diamond Ed. 1985). *See also* De Natale & Abram, "The Doctrine of Equitable Subordination as Applied to Nonmanagement Creditors," 40 *Bus. Law.* 417 (1985).

[47]*See In re Process–Manz Press Inc.* 236 F. Supp. 333 (N.D. Ill. 1964), *rev'd on other grounds,* 369 F.2d 513 (7th Cir. 1966), *cert. denied* 386 U.S. 957 (1967), discussed in Chaitman, "Equitable Subordination of Bank Claims," 39 *Bus. Law.* 1561, 1569 (1984).

[48]Ash, "The Lender" in *Leveraged Buyouts and Acquisitions supra* n. 6 at 192. The other two requirements are injury to creditors (or an unfair advantage for the claimant) and consistency with the other provisions of the Bankruptcy Code. Ash, *supra,* at 194.

itor is required, but that term can be broadly interpreted in accordance with the traditionally flexible powers of a court "sitting in equity."[49] The cases have generally involved a control relationship, which the lender has abused as, for example, managing the corporation for its own benefit.[50]

In this connection, it would be the rare lender that would style itself as being in "control" of a debtor, but the danger of a "strip" equity position is obvious;[51] it may give a court the only excuse it needs to punish lenders the judge thinks have stepped beyond their classic role. When lenders hold shares that entitle them to vote for directors, intellectual gymnastics are not required to justify a court finding some element of "control;" thereupon, it is a short leap to postulate a "fiduciary duty" imposed on the lender. And, as has often been remarked, the appearance of the term fiduciary duty in a judicial opinion means bad news for the alleged fiduciary.[52]

§19.9 CONTROLLING PERSON LIABILITY

Given a finding of control, equitable subordination does not, unhappily, complete the parade of horribles. If the lender is deemed in control of the debtor at the conclusion of a leveraged buyout,[53] other liabilities can be imposed,[54] on occasion entailing an affirmative recovery against the lender.[55] The lender is a deep pocket; when things go wrong, an equity interest or other indication of control can be an attractive nuisance for plaintiff's counsel, whether the plaintiff be a disappointed

[49]If the creditor is also a shareholder in a "thinly" capitalized firm, the shareholder may be deemed to have breached his duty adequately to capitalize the corporation. Chaitman, *supra* n. 47, at 1561, n. 2.

[50]The doctrine can be used as a handy way to apply the fraudulent conveyance notion without finding a conveyance that fits precisely within the statutory framework.

[51]*See supra* Text accompanying note 2.

[52]Bartlett, *The Law Business: A Tired Monopoly* 138 (1982).

[53]The possibility that a dominant lender will incur liability by reason of its dominance is not peculiar to LBOs; the heavy leverage, however, induces lenders in LBOs to insist on protective provisions which, ironically, may increase exposure because they erase the lines between conventional lender status and that category of persons to whom the law assigns fiduciary responsibility. *See* Clarke, "The Fiduciary Obligations of Lenders in Leveraged Buyouts," 54 *Miss. L. J.* 423 (1984).

[54]The *Farah Manufacturing* case, discussed in Ch. 9, § 9.2(a) n. 9, illustrates circumstances in which a punitive recovery exceeds the amount of the creditor's debt. *Compare* the result in *Farah with* the holding of the Second Circuit in *In re W.T. Grant Co.* 699 F.2d 599 (2d. Cir. 1983), where the court held that a bank's imposition of conditions on its advancement of funds did not constitute a breach of duty. Perhaps the most significant discussion of this issue appears in a 1975 article by one of the author's former colleagues. Douglas–Hamilton "Creditor Liabilities Resulting From Improper Interference with the Management of a Financially Troubled Debtor," 31 *Bus. Law.* 343 (Nov. 1975).

[55]Note that a lender with knowledge can be held liable for the borrower's failure to withhold from the employee's wages. I.R.C. § 3505(b).

creditor, an illegally terminated employee or even the victim of a toxic waste release.

The spectre of controlling person liability perforce introduces an element of sobriety into negotiations between counsel for the promoters of what might be called extreme LBOs and counsel for the major institutional lenders, many of whom (in the author's experience at least) entertain grave doubts on the advisability of LBOs where the leverage gets into double numbers. If a lender is so insecure that it bargains for the right to open the debtor's mail each morning, the lender may be biting off more than it can chew.

§19.10 INSIDERS

The Bankruptcy Code defines the term "insider" as including any director or officer of the debtor and/or any person "in control" of the debtor.[56] A lender deemed to be an insider loses various advantages under the Code. For example, as earlier indicated, the relevant time frame for challenging statutory preferences is extended from 90 days to one year prior to the filing if the beneficiary of the alleged preference is an insider.[57] The insider notion, moreover, has implications which extend beyond bankruptcy. Intrinsic to the concept of most leveraged buyouts is the feature that management will continue in place and enjoy an enlarged equity position in Newco. The problem is that management, in such a case, stands on both sides of the transaction. No one knows more about the affairs of the firm for sale than its management, yet management is an integral part of the team acquiring the assets. A minority, nonmanagement shareholder, therefore, has a head start on a complaint that the price is not fair. Protections are required in such cases—that is, negotiations should be carried out by disinterested third parties on both sides and an expert's opinion should be procured to validate the purchase price—a so-called "fairness" opinion.[58] Whether

[56] 11 U.S.C. § 101(30)(B)(i)–(iii).

[57] 11 U.S.C. § 547(b)(4)(B)(i); *see generally* Lundgren, "Liability of a Creditor in a Control Relationship with Its Debtor," 67 *Marq. L. Rev.* 523 (1984).

[58] The question of the weight to be accorded a "fairness" opinion is surrounded with some uncertainty. Fairness opinions prepared and delivered overnight are inherently suspect. *See Weinberger v. UOP, Inc.* 457 A.2d 701 (Del. 1983); *Joseph v. Shell Oil Co.* 482 A.2d 335 (Del. ch. 1984). Certainly if the last trade in the shares of an LBO candidate (public or private) was $10 and an offer comes in for $15, anyone can see that 15 is a larger number than 10. One of the issues, however, is whether the investment bankers, in the hypothetical stated, should be charged with responsibility of seeing whether someone else would pay $20. Questions may also be raised when the investment banker is entitled to a larger fee (a success fee) if the transaction under scrutiny closes. *Id.* at 192. Nonetheless, in light of *Smith v. Van Gorkom* 488 A.2d 858 (Del. 1985), it would be the rare director of a public company who will act without a fairness opinion of some kind; that case held the directors liable for acting precipitously in accepting merger terms and the opinion appears to say that a "fairness" opinion would have protected the board.

there is some obligation, in a management buyout, on the directors of the target in effect to auction the assets by holding open the bidding process and actively soliciting alternative bids is a question that has not yet been settled in the courts.[59] Parenthetically, the conflict problems are exacerbated if an ESOP is utilized as a source of acquisition financing because of the possibility that the pension assets of the rank-and-file employees (an ESOP is a defined contribution employee benefit plan subject to ERISA) are being used to support a program in which the top-level management obtains a disporportionately high—or "carried"—interest in the stock of Newco.[60] If the management has influence with the "plan fiduciary," the chance of overreaching is significant.

§19.11 STATE LAW ISSUES

(a) USURY

In several states, the legislature has imposed a maximum limit on the legal rate of interest. Citibank's credit card operations are headquartered in South Dakota, for example, because, among other things, of the absence of an applicable usury statute. Many such statutes govern only "consumer" transactions. However, other statutes are not so limited (or may be interpreted to apply to LBOs); a usurious agreement may not only be void under state law[61] but even may involve penalties.[62] Avoiding the impact of usury statutes involves a comparison of the stated rate on the loan with the statutorily permissible rate and analysis of any additional elements the state may count in computing interest (commitment fees, for example, or, if the debt is accompanied by warrants, the value of the warrants). If usury is a problem, an inquiry must be made whether the statute can be avoided by limiting the contacts with the difficult state to below that level which will give the state jurisdiction over the debt.

(b) VOIDABLE DISTRIBUTIONS

LBO counsel must consider state corporate laws that proceed on the basis of the same family of principles as the fraudulent conveyance

[59]If management stands significantly on both sides of the transaction, the protection of the so-called "business judgment" rule may not shield the organizers from a minority shareholder lawsuit challenging the fairness of the price paid and the procedures used—i.e., the quantum of disclosure—in dealing with the minority. *See* McCune & Kirk, "Leveraged Buyouts by Management," 16 *Rev. of Sec. Reg.* 769 (1983).

[60]On the use of ESOPs in an LBO, *see infra* n. 89.

[61]N.Y. General Obligation Law § 5–511 (McKinney).

[62]*N. C. Gen. Stat.* § 24–2 (borrower recovers twice the interest).

doctrine—that is, that the declaration of a dividend or redemption of stock is beyond the power of a corporation if the creditors are thereby disadvantaged. Thus, Delaware provides that a corporation may not redeem its shares if capital is "impaired" at the time or the transaction would impair capital.[63] A separate but related state law doctrine disfavors off balance sheet transactions—that is, the guaranty by one corporation of the debt of another—because of underlying suspicion that guarantees by their nature are unduly generous to the guaranteed party.[64] A cautionary note: many state laws impose liability for violations of the statute explicitly on the officers and directors of the corporation committing the offense and the new Delaware statute does not contemplate indemnification of directors for actions in violation of law.[65]

(c) STATE TAXES

The usual thrust of tax counsel in an LBO is to concentrate on federal taxes. State taxes, particularly transfer taxes, may prove embarrassing if counsel in a multimillion dollar transaction forgets that State A levies a tax on the issuance and transfer of securities in an instance where, had the closing physically been moved across the river to State B, no tax would have been levied. Similarly, intercorporate transactions, nontaxable under federal law, may not be tax-free in a given state. The simplest state tax issue has to do with the places of residence of the selling shareholder(s), if individuals. For several millions of dollars in state tax savings, it may worth it for the seller to dispose of his Manhattan apartment and move to New Jersey or Florida in order to claim he has effectively and legally moved his taxable presence by the time of the closing.[66]

§19.12 DAMAGE CONTROL

The statutory precepts constitute the principal red and amber lights for those structuring LBOs. As suggested earlier, the single most important precaution is to establish "solvency" before and after the transaction, usually through an expert's opinion,[67] that the debtor (i) has enough

[63]Del. Code Ann. tit. 8, § 160(a) (1983 & Supp. 1986).

[64]The issue under state law is whether a domestic corporation has the power to guarantee the debts of another. Kreidmann, "The Corporate Guaranty," 13 *Vand. L. Rev.* 229 (1959).

[65]*See* Ch. 4, § 4.12.

[66]Obviously the state from which one emigrates may contest the move for state tax purposes.

[67]One author suggests, *inter alia,* that the seller's accountants should give an opinion as to solvency; the investment bankers should opine as to solvency; the assets should be appraised; and pro forma financial statements prepared which show a "fair salable value" balance sheet. Poscover, "Avoidance Techniques Through Case Analysis," in *Emerging Theories of Lender Liability, supra* n. 17, at 400. As of this writing, acountants are writing

capital, (ii) will be able to pay its bills and (iii) has assets fairly valued in excess of liabilities. This process can be expensive if each parcel of real estate and each major item of equipment must be separately considered by an independent appraiser. Independent accountants, at a price, will review cash flow projections and offer comments short of an audit but more than simply a validation that 2 + 2 = 4. If it can be established beyond peradventure that the debtor was not rendered insolvent by reason of the transaction, much of the legal ammunition available for attacking the transaction falls away. The law does not insist that the debtor enjoy the same quantum of creditworthiness that existed prior to the transaction—otherwise LBOs would be impossible without creditor consent. It does, however, require that the unconsulted creditors not find an insolvent borrower substituted for a previously solvent credit.

If solvency can be established, then the issues are fewer; they have to do largely with structuring so as to avoid accidental imperfections. Thus, lenders desire to loan directly to the corporate entity to which the pledged assets will belong because they then avoid the argument that it is beyond the power of one corporation (be it the parent or the subsidiary) to respond for the debts of another;[68] if the assets are in corporation A (which may have creditors of its own) and the LBO loan is technically to corporation A's parent, the LBO lender has one extra hurdle. Similarly, the LBO lender is anxious to perfect its security interest exactly at or prior to the time (literally the minute and hour) that the funds are advanced.[69] Further, lenders are wary of transactions that require the declaration of dividends or the redemption of stock. Again, a chain is only as strong as its weakest link—a dividend or redemption can be attacked under state law.[70] Often, because of tax or other considerations, the foregoing fears cannot be satisfied—loan proceeds must be "upstreamed" or "downstreamed" by way of dividends or redemptions, coupled with guarantees, but the lenders' distaste remains constant and those incidents are avoided whenever possible.

---

solvency opinions but this first big plaintiff's recovery could cancel the practice. See "Legal Time Bomb: Big Accounting Firms Risk Costly Lawsuits by Reassuring Lenders," *Wall St. J.*, Jan. 14, 1988, p. 1.

[68]*See supra* § 19.11(b). Depending on the form of the transaction, it may be important to avoid the implication the loans are being advanced for the purpose of acquiring stock in violation of the federal margin requirements. *See* "The Impact of the Federal Reserve Margin Regulations on Acquisition Financing," 35 *Bus. Law.* 517 (Jan. 1980).

[69]The lender on occasion will search for a structure which entails a loan to the target *prior to* the LBO closing, securing a lien on the target's assets at a time—before any payout to target shareholders—when the target is at its most solvent. The target then distributes the proceeds of the loan in liquidation or in redemption of the shares of the selling shareholders.

[70]*See supra* § 19.11(b).

§19.13 FEDERAL TAX CONSIDERATIONS

(a) "NOLs" AND GENERAL UTILITIES

The following remarks are not designed as a primer on the enormously complicated tax issues that arise in the course of corporate reorganizations. Volumes are required to deal with the tax complexities of taxable versus nontaxable mergers, "poolings" versus "purchases," installment sales, and the like. The summary set forth below concerns only a few highlights, representative of problems frequently encountered in the course of an LBO.

The desired tax result is, of course, no tax paid on the LBO transaction and minimum taxes to be paid in the future. The deductibility of interest payments will continue to dampen Newco's tax liability dollar for dollar; the Tax Reform Act of 1986 makes no change in that rule. However, the accelerated cost recovery system and investment tax credits are subject to transition rules, modified (in the case of ARCS[71]) or on the way out (the investment tax credit[72]) after Dec. 31, 1986, meaning that future tax liabilities will be enlarged. The opportunity to shelter against future taxes will be further reduced in that net operating loss carry forwards will be cut back more severely than in the past, the governing principle being that it is unfair to "traffic" in NOLs, as they are called. A change in ownership of the loss corporation such as the change entailed by an LBO is an appropriate occasion, at least in the government's view, to reduce the ongoing value of the NOLs.[73] (NOLs are, however, not usually a driving force in LBOs because the underlying thesis is the refinancing of a positive and consistent flow of cash.) The repeal of the so-called *General Utilities*[74] doctrine means that the shareholders of Newco, unless prepared to suffer a double tax, will not be able to step up the depreciable base of Newco's assets to parallel the write-up on its general

[71]The new rules are found generally in I.R.C. § 168(e).

[72]Tax Reform Act of 1986 § 211(a).

[73]The new tests under I.R.C. § 382 are extremely complicated. They are bottomed on the notion that, if more than 50% of the shares of the loss corporation change hands in a relatively short period of time (three years), the annual deduction attributed to the NOL should not exceed the tax benefits the loss corporation would have achieved had it sold all its assets and invested the proceeds in long-term, tax-exempt securities. Moreover, NOL carry forwards are entirely disallowed unless the loss corporation passes the "continuity of business" test for two years after the event. *See* § 621 of the Tax Reform Act of 1986. *See also* General Explanation of the Tax Reform Act of 1986 (CCH) pg. 2288–327.

[74]Tax Reform Act of 1986, §§ 631, 632, and 633.

books of account triggered by the new purchase price.[75] The effect will not be to stop the game; Newco's organizers can still tender cash to the old shareholder(s) for their stock and only one tax is entailed—on the selling shareholders' gain. If it is necessary to "squeeze" out minority shareholders, a tax-postponed merger,[76] in which the majority of the old shareholders get stock, will entail no tax except that paid by those shareholders receiving cash or "boot" in the transaction. Moreover, the purchase of assets or a division from Goliath, Inc. is largely unaffected by the Tax Reform Act since no liquidation subsequently results. Finally, Newco's inability to write up its newly acquired assets and depreciate from the higher base (without paying tax) will not necessarily be fatal. Even under the old law, many purchasers elected to pass on the privilege afforded by *General Utilities* since the cost involved paying immediate tax occasioned by the recapture of accelerated depreciation and the investment tax credit.

(b) DEDUCTIBILITY OF INTEREST

There is omnipresent concern that interest deductions will be disallowed in an LBO on the theory the debt is not "true debt" but equity. The question whether debt is debt for tax purposes, involving principally §§ 279[77] and 385 of the Code, is not limited to LBOs, of course, and is discussed in some detail elsewhere in the text.[78]

[75]The Tax Reform Act of 1986, § 633(a)(1) and § 633(d)(1)–(7) provides transitional (prior to Jan. 1, 1989) relief from the effect of the repeal of *General Utilities* for qualified corporations—i.e., more than 50% of the stock (measured by value) is held by 10 or fewer individuals (or trusts or estates) and on liquidation, the fair market value of the stock is less than $5 million. There may remain, after the Tax Reform Act of 1986, one way in which the purchaser may achieve a step-up, in a limited sense, of the purchase price without tax penalty. The so-called "mirror" approach involves Newco segregating the assets bought into separate subsidiaries with a view to subsequent resale, allocating the purchase price among the stock in the subsidiaries. When the time comes (perhaps immediately) to dispose of an asset, Newco sells the stock of the subsidiary without tax except on postacquisition gain. Neither Newco nor the purchaser is able to write up the depreciable assets of the target using this technique. There is some question whether the "mirror" approach is viable after the Tax Reform Act. *See* Weinberg, "Selected Tax Considerations in Leveraged Buyouts," in *Leveraged Acquisitions and Buyouts* 131 (P.L.I. Course Handbook Series No. 549, 1987). The complexities of LBOs can be appreciated when one reflects that the "mirror" approach has already given rise to a "son of mirror" approach. *Id.* at 134.

[76]The enormously complicated rules for postponing tax in the course of a corporate reorganization are set out principally in I.R.C. § 368.

[77]The tests under § 279 are as follows: (i) annual interest exceeds $5 million; (ii) the obligation is issued for stock or two-thirds of the assets of another corporation; (iii) is subordinated to trade creditors or other debt; (iv) is convertible into equity or carries warrants; and, (v) the debt–equity ratio is higher than 2 to 1 or interest coverage is less than "3 times." Various ways to avoid the impact of § 279 are set out in Weinberg, *supra* n. 75, at 118–120.

[78]*See* Ch. 13, § 13.8.

The principal issue in an LBO, as suggested by the term leveraged, is the "thinness" of the capitalization—the debt-to-equity ratio. Some practitioners will not rule on the deductibility of interest in a leveraged buyout if the ratio of debt to equity exceeds, say, 10 to 1.[79] Moreover, that ratio will decrease to the extent investors hold debt securities in the same proportion as they hold equity—for example, "strip" financing—and/or the debt takes on other equity features, such as convertibility.

There are other tax issues arising whenever interest payments are made. For example, if Newco issues debt securities to the public with a maturity of more than one year, the Internal Revenue Code requires they be in registered form or interest is nondeductible.[80] If the holder of an interest (or dividend) paying instrument fails to furnish its taxpayer identification number, the payor must withhold 20% of the payment.[81]

(c) ORIGINAL ISSUE DISCOUNT

The strip form of financing creates a potential original issue discount problem.[82] The question arises when debt is sold in a package, that is, a note or debenture bundled with a warrant, option, or a share of stock. To illustrate, assume a debenture carries a $1,000 par value (meaning that, on maturity, the principal amount due is $1,000) and a $100 per year interest coupon. If the purchaser pays $1,000 in exchange for the debenture plus a warrant, the economic fact is that the debenture has been purchased at a discount, the discount equal to the value of the warrant. If that warrant were, for example, worth $50, then the debenture has been bought for $950. Consequently, the stated interest rate on the debenture (10%) is not, in economic terms, the real interest rate. The real interest rate is $100, divided by $950, or approximately 10.52%. Put another way, when the issuer of the debt pays $1,000 on maturity, the holder is receiving $950 in principal and $50 in additional interest. The Code requires that the extra $50 in interest should be recognized for tax purposes by the holder (and deductible by the issuer) over the life of the debenture.[83] Original issue discount poses problems for the debenture holder because it will be paying tax on money it is not currently receiving. The seemingly simple calculation to indicate the existence of OID—the "stated redemption price at maturity"[84] of a debt

[79]The first version of the § 385 Regulations, ultimately withdrawn along with all other versions, would have focused on the debt-to-equity ratio as the key test.

[80]I.R.C. § 163(f).

[81]I.R.C. § 3406.

[82]*See generally* I.R.C. § 1271–1275.

[83]I.R.C. § 1272

[84]I.R.C. § 1273(a)(1)(A)

instrument exceeds its "issue price"[85]—can become complicated when the consideration paid is nonpublicly traded property and the issue price must be calculated based on estimated values. Indeed, calculating the "redemption price" can be tricky if, for example, contingent interest payments are involved, as in an "earn-out" transaction.[86] The simple point to be made at this juncture is that OID should be dealt with expressly by the parties. Since OID accelerates tax to the holder and deductions to the issuer, it is not a neutral event. The agreement should take that contingency expressly into account, at least providing for consistent filing positions.[87]

§19.14 RESTRUCTURINGS

A recently popularized transaction—best referred to as a quasi-LBO or, more properly, a quasi-MBO—is exemplified by a corporate restructuring in which the assets do not change hands absolutely. The form of the transaction includes, like a customary LBO, piling a substantial debt burden on an existing firm and increasing the leverage factor significantly. Instead of using the proceeds to buy out the existing shareholders, however, the firm pays an extraordinary dividend to its shareholders, thereby driving down the price of the outstanding shares. Management (and any allied investors) purchase new equity and obtain options at the reduced price, usually a generous percentage of the equity. The shareholders, happy with their newly found wealth (the dividend can be a significant portion of the previous market price), are unlikely to object. By virtue of the fact that (as in an LBO) the market is being forced to recognize unappreciated values, the package that the shareholders receive adds up to more than the pretransaction market price of their shares. The advantage of this transaction over the traditional LBO is twofold: First, by encumbering the assets up to the limits of prudence, management intercepts a hostile raid. Two parties cannot hypothecate the same collateral and realize on hidden values—once management has done it, the raider has no bargain to shoot at. Secondly, since there is no formal sale of the assets or the company, there is no "overbid" problem. Many management buyouts in recent years have served only to trigger an auction ultimately won by someone other than management. If those in control do not propose to buy or sell the firm, no auction can start. Restructurings are so new that it cannot be forecast as yet whether they will become a venture capital favorite.

[85]I.R.C. § 1273(a)(1)(B)

[86]An "earn-out" is entailed when the consideration paid to selling sharholders in a corporate acquisition includes future contingent payments, depending on the acquired corporation's postacquisition earnings.

[87]*See* Weinberg, *supra* n. 75, at 120–128.

§19.15 BUSINESS TERMS OF THE BUYOUT

Many of the business terms of an LBO are the same as in the case of a start-up. The character labeled the "founder" in the text is, however, not a familiar player in an LBO since the basic asset of an LBO is not usually some living individual's novel idea. The closest analogy is the management of the successor firm; he or they, perhaps together with the individual who acted as the catalyst in putting the deal together (i.e., the promoter), are the holders of the "cheap" or "free" stock in the purchasing vehicle. Their shares are the equivalent of "founder's stock," acquired with sweat equity. The investors own, as in a start-up, an equity position that is technically prior, in terms of preference on liquidation, to that of the managers/promoters. Contrary to the start-up circumstance, however, cash flow exists and is used to service debt, often multiple levels of debt. At the top, insurance companies and banks make conventional secured loans, such term debt collateralized by plant and equipment, plus a so-called "revolver," meaning debt in varying amounts secured by inventory and receivables. The interest cost of the secured debt is usually keyed off the prime rate or LIBOR (the London-Interbank Offered Rate). Below that layer is the "mezzanine" debt: subordinated, high-yield securities (usually called "junk bonds"), the yield provided by a combination of high interest rate coupled with an equity "kicker" or "strip" in the form of warrants or stock, the two elements combining to produce a projected rate of return that is commensurate with the risk. (To obtain a target rate of return for high-yield debt, many lenders will use the yield on the lowest rated corporate securities—straight B—and shoot for a total return equal to some multiple, say 150%, of that rate.)

The secured debt is often written with an interest cost involving a mixture of fixed and variable interest rates. Sometimes the senior debt is split among various lenders. The "revolver" is usually made by an asset based lender—that is, a finance company or factor. The long maturities of the term loan are taken by long-term lenders, such as insurance companies, and the shorter maturities by commercial banks, where the lending horizon is traditionally five years or less. An important element of subordinated debt is the purchase money debt, taken back by the seller. The interest rate on that debt is often a function of the purchase price that the seller wishes to report to its shareholders. If the seller wants to inflate the price, it agrees to a favorable rate and other terms in the purchase money debt.[88]

[88]In economic terms, the worth of a fixed-income security is a function of the principal amount *and* the interest rate. Monkeying with the rate to influence the ostensible principal amount is described as the "$500 cat" device: "I'll swap you my $500 cat for your $500 dog."

Equity is provided by venture investors, management, those selling shareholders who elect and are invited to roll over their investment and, on occasion, an Employee Stock Ownership Plan (ESOP).[89] The equity stock held by the investors and/or mezzanine lenders will bring out all the issues so familiar in the venture context—for example, board seats, registration rights, antidilution, mandatory redemption, pre-emptive rights, control "flips," and the like. New points will, however, surface. Thus, if the seller is a big company spinning out a subsidiary or division, the "representations" and "warranties" section in the purchase agreement takes on a new meaning since there will in fact be a solvent party to respond in the case of a breach. With debt being a significant element in the capital structure, the terms of the debt instrument(s) are subject to protracted negotiation; for example, affirmative and negative covenants can become a battleground, since the price of failure will be acceleration of the debt from term to demand status. In fact, since debt instruments usually contain cross-default provisions, an uncured default in an agreement in one loan covenant may accelerate all the loans. The tension usually arises over control, management attempting to preserve its flexibility to manage Newco in the face of the strait jacket, which the creditors are attempting to put in place around Newco. Thus, if Newco wants to sell a major asset, to change accounting firms, to award executive bonuses or to finance a new plant, the term loan agreement presented by the creditors' counsel will seek to impose an obligation on Newco to seek a waiver from the creditor(s) in each case. In such instances, debtor's counsel can be counted on to wave the threat of equitable subordination under the nose of the lender, but that doctrine is infrequently occasioned and, as earlier discussed, usually requires an

[89]ESOPs are a tax-favored device for increasing, at least theoretically, the equity share of employees in a business firm. The notion was introduced by a San Francisco lawyer, Louis Kelso, and championed for years by Senator Russell Long. The attraction of ESOP financing is driven by tax considerations. Newco obtains tax deductions on the payments made to the ESOP, and the interest cost on acquisition debt incurred by the ESOP is tax subsidized in that 50% is tax-exempt. *See* Stoney & Zonana, "Tax Considerations in Leveraged Acquisitions," in *Leveraged Buyouts* 41 (P.L.I. Course Handbook Series No. 393, 1983); Lederman, Citron, & Macris, "Leveraged Buyouts: An Update," in 2 *Fifteenth Annual Institute on Securities Regulation* 281 (P.L.I. Course Handbook Series No. 393, 1983). Economically, the ESOP substitutes the firm's own stock, in whole or in part, for the assets which would otherwise generate the income necessary to fund employee retirement benefits. The employees' long-term risk is, accordingly, tied to the fortunes of the employer. The principal conceptual difficulty with an ESOP-financed management buyout arises when the ESOP (representing the rank-and-file employees) buys its shares at a price higher than that paid by the management insiders, the sole justification being that the ESOP owns convertible preferred and the insiders common. *See* the discussion of the Dan River management buyout ($22.50 per share for the ESOP, $2.06 for management) in Lowenstein, *supra* n. 11, at 761–762. Excesses in this regard can and will be restrained. See "Correspondence on Proposed Leveraged Buy-out of Scott & Fetzer Co.," 12 *BNA Pension Reporter* 1182 (Aug. 29, 1985).

act of misconduct. Lenders are also sensitive to "controlling person" liability but the rubric is that "traditional" lenders' covenants will not create that exposure.[90]

(a) SELECTING THE RIGHT OPPORTUNITY

The LBO purchaser's strategy is, first, to obtain some form of preferred (preferably exclusive) position as a potential purchaser of the target company, subsidiary, or division so that it does not do a lot of work only to see the prize go to someone else, the so-called "overbid" problem. The methods range from a "no shop" promise coupled with, or integrated into, a letter of intent; a "break-up" or "topping" fee, being a cash payment by the target to cover expenses in case of an overbid; and a "lock-up," meaning an option on enough in the way of stock or assets to tie up the transaction.[91] (In that connection, some sellers will reject out of hand the entire concept of an option but will sign something called a purchase agreement, which gives the purchaser a liberal set of escape options in the form of closing conditions and confines damages for nonperformance to forfeiture of a modest down payment. Despite the nomenclature, such a purchase agreement is the equivalent of an option.)

Next, the purchaser prepares, or causes to be prepared, a "book," a summary of the transaction that functions as a private placement memorandum. This document, which harbors the all important forecasts, is prepared with an eye on what potential lenders and investors use as rules of thumb in appraising the opportunity. Thus, asset-based lenders will use "loan to value" ratios varying in accordance with the nature of the collateral—for example, 80% of "good" (90 days old or less) receivables, 50% of inventory[92] and varying percentages, normally between 50% and 80%, of the appraised value of real estate and machinery and equipment, the percentage, depending on what the lender believes

[90]*See supra* § 19.9.

[91]*See supra* n. 6.

[92]Although tangible assets are often called "hard assets," there is much room for judgment when looking at values. Thus, depending on the method of accounting (LIFO or FIFO), there may be hidden value in the inventory. On the other hand, in liquidation both accounts receivable and inventory are often worth less than their stated values because account debtors stop paying and the auction sales of inventory realize only scavenger's prices. Other adjustments are also in order, namely: Elimination of charges imposed on a subsidiary to the extent such charges for general and administrative support are noncompetitive; and elimination of salaries and the elaborate perquisites of "no show" family members.

the asset will go for in some kind of a liquidation sale.[93] Lenders will also calculate loan values as a function of historical cash flow; the usual figure they work with is EBIT—that is, net earnings before interest and taxes. (Interest is ignored because the lender is starting the calculation afresh, on the assumption that all debt will be replaced, and figuring out what Newco can afford by way of interest. Taxes have been excluded on the theory that, with a substantial increase in interest deductions after the financing, taxes will not in fact be paid, an assumption subject to change after 1986 as corporate tax burdens have been increased.) A particular pension fund might consider a figure of five or six times EBIT as the conventional loan amount, meaning the credit available from a lender without the necessity of an equity kicker. Another way of looking at that calculation is to look at "coverages." Thus, if EBIT is $100,000 and the lender loans six times EBIT, or $600,000, at 12% interest, the annual interest is $72,000 a year and interest coverage is 1.38 to 1.

In pricing an LBO, the purchasing group makes a series of calculations. First, with a sense of the market for senior secured and unsecured debt, how much can be borrowed from conventional sources: banks and insurance companies? Next, is there enough asset or cash flow coverage to support mezzanine debt—subordinated debt with an equity strip (cheap stock) or "kickers" (long-term warrants) entailing a handsome projected rate of return on a composite basis. Third, how much, if anything, will the seller take back in the form of deferred payments? Fourth, how much equity does the lenders' free stock (see above) amount to? Fifth, how much equity will management require in the form of cheap stock. Lastly, how much cash can be raised for the rest of the equity?[94] The total of these numbers kicks out a tentative purchase price. Whether the seller is attracted depends on a comparison of alternatives. If the seller has determined to dispose of the assets, what is the liquidation value, including severance costs for employees, compared with the purchaser's offer?

The preferred nominees for an LBO are mature businesses in non-volatile industry sectors, without an immediate need for large capital expenditures. In negotiating the terms of the debt, it is obviously in the buyer's best interests to minimize principal payments in the early years.

[93]The question of the "value" of assets depends on the factual situation in which such value will become significant. Thus, the ladder of possible scenarios starts with the scrap value of the assets; value of the same as at forced liquidation, orderly liquidation and in current use; replacement cost of fixed assets; replacement cost plus intangible assets and, lastly, replacement cost, intangible assets, and goodwill. Golz, "Valuation and LBOs: Value of Target at Time of Transaction a Key Factor," 11 *Valuation Journal* 4 (1987).

[94]As earlier indicated, one of the major risks in start-up financing—that management will not cut the mustard—is not usually presented in an LBO. Accordingly, acceptable (forecasted) rates of return on the equity may be lower than in early stage ventures. *See* Donneley, "Valuing LBOs Takes Analysis of A Distinct Kind," *Wall St. J.*, Apr. 2, 1987, p. 31.

Some form of balloon payment is preferable; indeed, a so-called zero coupon security may be highly desirable because the issuer can enjoy current tax deductions for interest accrued and not paid while the holder, if a tax-exempt institution, will be indifferent to its tax treatment. On the other hand, tax considerations aside, the lenders' comfort often requires that some targeted portion of the debt—say 50%—will be scheduled for repayment in some near-term period, say, five to seven years.

Twenty

Organizing the Venture Capital Pool

The venture capital process starts with investors, the sources of capital. Much of that capital, although no means all, is aggregated in limited partnerships run by professional managers. Since those partnerships play such a prominent role in the business—set the tone as it were—it is important for all interested parties to have a general understanding of how they work from a legal, financial, and accounting point of view. Much of the material in this chapter is technical and should be skimmed by readers other than lawyers and accountants. However, the hopeful founder of a venture partnership should not shrink entirely from the technical material—especially §§ 20.7 and 20.8—because substantial economic effects ensue from the way what is mistakenly called the boilerplate is arranged.

§20.1 BACKGROUND

The first venture capital pool of significance accepting capital from outside investors (versus family investment vehicles centered around the fortunes of a given rich family) was American Research & Development Corporation (AR&D), organized in corporate form and operated as a closed-end investment company registered under the Investment Company Act of 1940, with shares listed on the New York Stock Exchange. Subsequent models, however, have not generally followed AR&D in its selection of the legal vehicle through which to conduct operations. With rare exceptions,[1] the venture capital pool has been structured as a limited partnership. The professional managers of the pool have participated as general partners in the investor partnership (as it is often called) and the capital has been raised from investors purchasing limited partnership interests. The following discussion highlights certain recurring issues in the organization of venture partnerships[2] but does not attempt to cover each issue presented to the draftsman; a number of form books list the points in great detail.[3]

§20.2 PARTNERSHIP VERSUS CORPORATION

The issue of partnership versus corporation has been discussed in the context of organizing the start-up corporation.[4] With the Tax Reform Act of 1986, it is also timely to inquire whether a significant number of venture pools will elect to organize as corporations. It is unlikely that such will be the case. To be sure, the melt-down of the distinction between income and gains relaxes much of the significance of passing through gains to individual partners without the loss of their characterization for tax purposes.[5] Nonetheless, elimination of double taxation

[1]Venture pools organized exclusively for the account of non-U.S. residents and domiciled offshore are routinely organized as corporations since the "tax haven" jurisdictions favored for such domiciles generally do not recognize limited partnerships as a legal entity (with the prominent exception of Bermuda).

[2]Tax consequences of operating in partnership form are set out in loose-leaf notebook form by the CCH Tax Transaction Library entitled *Organizing the Partnership Venture* (Millman & Oswald ed. 1987)

[3]For a checklist of the questions involved in drafting partnership agreements *see generally* Volz & Berger, *The Drafting of Partnership Agreements* 5 (1976). An admirable discussion of the venture partnership is contained in an essay authored by Messrs. Halloran, Morrow, & Currie, "Agreement of Limited Partnership," reproduced in Halloran, Benton, & Lovejoy, *Venture Capital and Public Offering Negotiation* 1–132 (1984) (Halloran). Each provision in the agreement is analyzed and commented upon extensively. A useful commentary on new developments, containing forms, is found in *Fourth Annual Structuring Partnership Agreements* (Halloran & Nathan chairmen 1987); the thrust is towards real estate and oil and gas partnerships.

[4]*See* Ch. 3, § 3.6.

[5]The Tax Reform Act of 1986 has eliminated the distinction in *rates of tax* between ordinary income and capital gain but the distinction in *the character of the tax* remains significant for certain purposes, including the limitation on the deductibility of capital losses. I.R.S. § 1211.

will continue to attract investors to the partnership format. Moreover, some practitioners openly expect that favorable tax treatment for gains will be restored by Congress and the corporate form, once elected, cannot be discarded tax-free.[6] Concededly, if there is to be only one limited partner, it is arguable that the relationship between the manager and the sole investor might well be structured in a form that eliminates the partnership format entirely—that is, the managers become employees of the limited partner which invests directly or through wholly owned subsidiaries in the portfolio opportunities. Even in the face of the favored treatment of capital gains pre-1987, a fully taxable corporate investor could engage managers, at little after-tax cost to itself and with the same after-tax results for the managers, by structuring the relationship either (i) as a partnership, with gains passed through to the managers as partners, or (ii) by eliminating the partnership, the managers being employees of the investor, their allocable shares of gains paid to them in the form of bonuses with the tax "grossed up"[7] and the employer taking advantage of the deduction. However, there has always been a cultural attachment on the part of managers toward receiving their income in the form of gains, which in turn has driven the election to adopt the partnership format even when only one investor has been involved. That notional bias can be expected to continue to tilt in favor of the partnership format.

§20.3 CERTAIN TERMINOLOGY

Assuming election of the limited partnership form, the general partner is usually itself a partnership, sometimes general and sometimes limited, the general partners of which are the managers of the enterprise. The reason to interpose an additional entity is convenience.[8] Under the Uniform Limited Partnership Act (U.L.P.A.), if a general partner of a limited partnership dies or retires, the partnership technically dissolves; the remaining general partners can continue the business (if the agreement so states) but the admission of a new general partner may require

[6]With the demise of the *General Utilities* doctrine, *see* Ch. 19, § 19.13(a), the possibility arises that a corporate liquidation will occasion not only one but two taxes—at the corporate and at the shareholder level. *See* Tax Reform Act of 1986 §§ 631 and 634, amending I.R.C. § 336.

[7]"Grossing" up the tax means paying the employee a bonus of, say, $1,000 and then paying him enough in addition so that he nets $1,000 after paying his tax (or nets what he would have netted had the tax been calculated at the favorable rate heretofore applicable to long-term capital gains.

[8]Some tax practitioners are concerned about the practice of using a vehicle as the general partner; they believe that it strengthens the managers' position on the so-called *Sol Diamond* issue, *see infra* § 20.10, if each individual is a partner directly in the investor partnership.

the specific consent of all the limited partners, a potentially difficult chore.[9] Accordingly, the individual general partners participate through an intermediate entity which continues in being even if one of its members dies or retires and to whom new members may be appointed without consulting the limited partners. Because the terminology overlaps—the general partner of a general partnership, which in turn is the general partner of a limited partnership—experienced practitioners have invented discrete nomenclature to describe each entity. In the author's firm, the limited partnership which holds the assets is the investor partnership. The general partner of the investor partnership is the GPGP or GPLP, depending on whether it is a general or a limited partnership. The individual partners of the GPGP or GPLP are the managers. The limited partners of the investor partnership are the investors.

§20.4 INSTALLMENT PAYMENTS

A venture partnership typically does not invest its capital all at once; the process of screening and selecting investments may take several years before the partnership is substantially invested. (The partnership is seldom fully invested since significant cash must be held in reserve for follow-on investments in portfolio companies needing extra cash.) Accordingly, it is customary to take the investors' contributions down in installments, or tranches, to use a popular term on Wall Street. The agreement will typically provide that one-third of the committed capital is due on organization and the GPGP will call for the remainder in, say, two installments "estimated to occur" in the second and third year of the partnership's life.[10] The problem arises when a given partner fails to honor his obligations. The norm is to provide for a stiff penalty if the investor defaults—that is, to "haircut" the interest by providing that the defaulter's interest in either profits and/or capital will be reduced to some fraction of what the contribution already made would entitle the investor to. Whether such a penalty will stand up in litigation is not settled since conventional wisdom in the law dictates that the courts are not inclined to enforce penalties. The 1985 amendments to the Delaware version of the Uniform Act make it clear that a defaulting partner

[9]Depending on state law, the admission of a new general partner to a limited partnership may require the specific consent of all the partners. *See* Halloran, *supra* n. 3, at 86. U.L.P.A. (1916) § 9(1)(e). The Revised U.L.P.A., (adopted in 1976) expressly allows the agreement to authorize advance consent. 6 Del. Code Ann. tit 6, § 17–401 (1985); R.U.L.P.A. § 401.

[10]The Federal Reserve Board has taken the view that installment payments in a *publicly* offered partnership syndication are an extension of credit subject to the proscriptions of Regulation T, but that staged payments in a private offering are not subject to regulation. Federal Reserve Board Release (Mar. 1972) § 5–470 (interpreting § 220.13 of Regulation T). *See generally* Hensley & Rothwell, "Regulation T & Public Offerings of Limited Partnerships: Time For A Change," 39 *Bus. Law.* 543 (Feb. 1984).

can be subjected to various penalties, including subordination of the partner's interest, forced sale, reduction or forfeiture of that interest, redemption at an appraised value, and other grievous consequences.[11]

§20.5 CAPITAL ACCOUNT

The mechanics of partnership accounting involve the creation of an animal called the "capital account," a bookkeeping entry established for each partner and maintained in accordance with very precise rules established by Treasury Regulation.[12] In this case, the tax treatment and sound economic and accounting principles are generally in agreement.[13] The initial credit to the capital account is the amount of money (or the fair market value of property) contributed by the partner to the capital of the partnership. Realized profits and losses are run through the partner's capital account, meaning that, as of the end of each accounting period, the partnership's books are closed and profits or losses realized since the last closing are allocated to the capital accounts of the partners in accordance with the allocation formula then in effect. Distributions decrease the capital account of the partner to whom the distribution is made in the amount of the distribution: If the distribution is "in kind"—that is, if property other than cash is distributed—the property is deemed sold as of the date of the distribution and the fair market value of the property is the measuring stick for the deduction from the distributee's capital account. A capital account is a book entry, a "parking" vehicle where profits and losses are parked and then held[14] pending distribution. One might compare it with a checking account at a bank. It is the vehicle for all deposits and withdrawals. Upon final liquidation, proceeds are distributed in accordance with a hierarchy of instructions that entails distributing through each partner's capital account.[15]

(a) QUALIFICATION AS A PARTNERSHIP

Pursuant to the applicable Regulations, a partnership will not be treated as an "association taxable as a corporation" under §§ 7701(a)(2) and

[11]Del. Code Ann. tit 6, § 17–502(c) (1985). *See* Basile, "The 1985 Delaware Revised Uniform Limited Partnership Act," 41 *Bus. Law.* 571, 589 (Feb., 1986).

[12]Treas. Regs. § 1.704–1(b)(2)(iv). *See generally* McKee, Nelson, & Whitmire, *Drafting, Amending, and Analyzing Partnership Agreements Under The New Partnership Allocation Regulations* § 3.02[1] (1986).

[13]*Id.* at § 3.01[1].

[14]Ordinarily, a venture partnership will expressly provide that partners are not entitled to interest on their capital.

[15]If profits and losses are religiously run through capital accounts as they should be, then at the end of the day the final distribution should zero all balances. Unfortunately, mistakes not worth tracing may leave something over at the end of this process, requiring a provision in the agreement for distributing leftovers.

761(a) of the Code if it meets two out of the four tests specified in the Regulations.[16] The most critical is unlimited liability. In a true partnership, some individual entity (other than the partnership itself) must be liable for the debts of the partnership. In a limited partnership, this means, of course, that the general partners must be liable and, in the view of the Service, not only technically but in fact—that is, there must be resources at stake.[17] A corporation without assets or an insolvent individual will not do as the sole general partner of a limited partnership, according to the most authoritative source: the celebrated Rev. Proc. 72–13.[18] Law firms advising clients are not bound to the strict letter of Rev. Proc. 72–13, since it adumbrates only the facts on which the Treasury will grant advance rulings, but it provides the basic framework. Thus, it is generally the view that a sole corporate general partner must maintain a net worth (exclusive of its interest in the partnership) of approximately 10% or more of the partnership's contributed capital (15% if total contributions are less than $2.5 million), different law firms varying in how far they will depart from the 10% standard.

Most practitioners, reluctant to sterilize cash in a corporate general partner, have blessed a device whereby the corporate general partner owns as an asset a note drawn on the sponsor of the partnership in the necessary amount. Further, the addition of an individual general partner of some personal substance (or a general partnership made up of such individuals) will make the issue much more manageable.[19] For partnerships considering the use of a C corporation as a corporate general partner (and which do not have any corporations as limited partners), attention should be paid to § 448 of the Code,[20] which now provides that partnerships with a C corporation as a partner may no longer use the cash method of accounting.

§20.6 INTEREST IN PROFITS AND LOSSES

To be considered a true "partner," versus an employee, the general partner (or general partners taken together) should enjoy at least a 1% interest in profits and losses of the investor partnership.[21] The GPGP's interest in profits is easy—a "carried" interest (i.e., not paid for) ranging

[16]Treas. Regs. § 301.7701–2(a).

[17]"Substantial assets (other than [the GPGP's] interest in the [investor] partnership)." Treas. Regs. § 305.7701–2(d)(1).

[18]1972–1 C.B. 735.

[19]Counsel's opinion on partnership qualification will deal with additional requirements—*e.g.*, that the partnership will be conducted in accordance with the local version of the Uniform Act, Treas. Regs. § 301–7701–2(d), and that the limited partners not own over 20% of the stock in a sole corporate general partner. Rev. Proc. 72–13, 1972–1 C.B. 735.

[20]Added by § 801 of the Tax Reform Act of 1986.

[21]*See* Rev. Proc. 74–17, 1974–1 C.B. 438.

in the area of 20% is the norm. Merely allocating losses to the GPGP (versus allocating profits) has, however, no economic effect if the GPGP has nothing to lose (i.e., puts up no capital). To be sure, the GPGP could be required to invest 1% of the entire investor partnership's capital but, given a $100 million investor partnership, a $1 million requirement could be beyond the GPGP's means. Hence, the recommended practice is to create a liability but postpone its potential effect.[22] Thus, the partnership instrument may require the GPGP to endure at all times 1% of the losses and to restore, upon dissolution and winding up, the deficiency, if any, in the GPGP's capital account. Such a provision clearly means that the GPGP is at risk to the tune of 1% and is blessed by an early Revenue Procedure.[23]

However, that provision may be deemed overly harsh by the GPGP because it is unlimited, at least potentially, in amount. Accordingly, based on a later IRS pronouncement,[24] many practitioners are willing to support arrangements that provide that the GPGP's capital account will not go into a negative position[25] as long as the limited partners have positive capital balances and that the GPGP's exposure is limited, in the nature of an obligation to restore on termination the *lesser* of the deficit balance in its capital account (presumably none) or 1.01% of the difference between the limited partners' capital contributions and the amount (presumably nominal) the GPGP has contributed. Since most venture partnerships do not borrow, the two versions of the GPGP's exposure wind up in about the same place.

In many partnerships, the entire issue is moot—the "free ride" system is unacceptable as a business matter and the investors insist that the GPGP put up cash. If the partnership is a clone of an earlier successful partnership, for example, it is the norm that the managers expose some of the assets acquired in prior iterations to risk in the new partnership.

[22]Most practitioners insist that all parties purporting to act as general partners put up *some* cash, if only to avoid treatment of the carried interest allocation as a transaction between the partnership and a partner acting "other than in his capacity as a member of such partnership." I.R.C. § 707(a)(1) and (2).

[23]Rev. Proc. 74–17, 1974–1 C.B. 438. The "responsibility for losses" issue is different from the question of unlimited liability discussed in the previous section. Arguably, any solvent general partner is a true partner in the liability sense, even though the allocation sections do not state that any losses are chargeable to its capital account, since the general partner is ultimately responsible for all losses in excess of the partnership's capital. The 1% issue has to do with whether the general partner is a true partner in the sense of sharing losses with the other partners, even though there is plenty of capital to pay creditors.

[24]Rev. Proc. 84–67, 1984–2 C.B. 631.

[25]Some practitioners insist that the GPGP actually contribute 1% "in situations where the general partners are not required to make up deficit balances in their capital accounts on liquidation," Halloran, Morrow & Currie, *supra* n. 3, at 28. Based on one of the most authoritative commentaries, it does not appear that the 1% interest must be maintained at all times. McKee, Nelson, & Whitmire, *Federal Taxation of Partnerships and Partners* 3–66 (1977).

§20.7 COMMON DRAFTING MISCUES

If the GPGP is, for one reason or another, contributing real cash, there is a chance that its "carried interest" and its interest on account of its cash investment will become confused. Thus, assume the limited partners are putting up $99 million and the GPGP $1 million and the profits are split 80% to the limited partners and 20% to the GPGP. In such a case, the carried—that is, free—interest to the GPGP is 19%, rather than 20%. That is fair enough, perhaps, but often not what the organizers had in mind. If the instrument states that the GPGP has a carried 20% interest in profits and 80% is allocated among the *partners* (not only the limited partners) in accordance with respective capital contributions or capital accounts,[26] then the GPGP enjoys a pure 20% carry.

Another frequently encountered drafting error arises when the instrument purports to subordinate the GPGP's carried interest to some form of preferential payment to the cash investors.[27] Assume a scheme, for example, whereby the investors are allocated 99% of the profits until they have recouped their investment and then an 80/20 split obtains. The way this provision is usually meant to operate is that: (i) almost all the profits are allocated to the investors until the recoupment date; then, (ii) almost all the profits are allocated to the GPGP until its allocation equals 20% of the investors' allocation; then, (iii) the allocation is 80/20. The idea is that, at the end of the day, when all hits, runs, and errors have been totaled, the aggregate allocation should be 80% for the limiteds and 20% for the general(s).[28] In fact, well-drafted agreements so provide; they contain an adjustment provision operative as of the date of dissolution and winding up, which provides that the distributions in liquidation will be so skewed as to achieve the 80/20 outcome overall.[29] If, however, the agreement says, as some do, 99/1 until re-

[26]The norm is to peg the allocation formula to capital contributions versus capital accounts. While the results are likely to be the same in most instances, the proportion arising out of the fixed nature of capital contribution is more representative of what the investors believe they are buying—i.e., a specific percentage interest in profits, versus one that may change.

[27]The subordination notion, which is tied to priority allocations and/or distributions pending recoupment, should be contrasted to the rate of return "bogey" concept, discussed in § 20.11, *infra*, wherein the measuring stick is a targeted current or cumulative return on investment. The underlying principle is conceptually the same, i.e., only superior performance rewarded.

[28]A preferential return, in the eyes of some practitioners, can introduce biases—i.e., an incentive to concentrate on near-term payoffs or to postpone distributing in kind especially promising portfolio positions until all the value has been squeezed out. Dauchy & Harmon, "Structuring Venture Capital Limited Partnerships," 3 *Computer Law.* 1 (1986).

[29]The preferential distribution to the investors may include an interest component—all their money back plus a compounded X% return. Variations in this area revolve around the time value of money and whether the interest component is calculated on committed capital or capital actually contributed to the partnership.

coupment and then 80/20, at the end of the day the GPGP will have a lot less than 20% of accumulated profits.

Yet another problem is encountered when the draftsmen confuse distributions versus allocations and/or capital contributions versus capital accounts. Thus, as a variation on the foregoing theme, some agreements require that distributions to the GPGP be postponed until the limited partners have achieved some targeted amount of distributions, usually equal to their contributed capital. Indeed, holding the GPGP's share of allocated profits within the partnership is a handy way of assuring that there is cash available in case the GPGP is called on to "cough up" prior allocations of profits (see below) in order to make the entire process come out right. However, if profits are allocated in part to the *partners* (not just the limited partners) in accordance with the balances in their *capital accounts* (versus their capital contributions), a disproportionate retention of profits in the GPGP's account can result in an unwitting increase in the GPGP's share of profits.

A third drafting error occurs when the agreement simply provides a 80/20 split of profits and a 99/1 split of losses, allocated annually. The point is relatively obvious. If the GPGP is allocated 20% of a huge profit in year one and there then ensues nine years of losses followed by liquidation, the GPGP will have more in its pocket at the end of the day than was intended. A provision called a "cough-up" or a "look-back" requires a corrective recall from the GPGP of prior distributions in the year of liquidation to correct unintended results.

Alternatively, the agreement may provide that profits and losses are allocated at the end of each period so that they cancel out prior opposing allocations and then, starting from zero as it were, profits and losses are allocated in the agreed-upon percentages. Thus, if a large gain is experienced in year one, followed by a large loss in year two, the loss is so allocated as to neutralize the gain and, when and as the correction has been applied, the process goes on its way as originally intended. The result is to create a netting effect with respect to interim gains and losses so that, on liquidation, the timing of gains and losses is immaterial and only the cumulative effect counts.[30] To make this system work properly, either the partnership must hold back some or all of the GPGP's allocated profits in its capital account or the agreement make provision for a cough-up upon liquidation.

There is a moral to the story. The organizers of a venture fund should take the first draft of the allocation and distribution sections and sit down with their counsel and accountants. Various profit and loss scenarios should then be run over the hypothetical life of the partnership

[30]Another way to accomplish this result is to provide that gains and losses are to be allocated in each period so that the cumulative net effect is 20% of gains to the GPGP and 80% to the limited partners.

and the results compared. The question is whether the allocation and distribution sections consistently deliver the intended result—so much to the general partners and so much to the limited partners at the end of the day. This is a *very important* recommendation. In the author's experience, there are significant hidden differences between a number of partnerships that look alike, differences that may ensue to everyone's surprise when the partnership is liquidated.

§20.8 FEES AND EXPENSES

Another controversial issue, where again careless drafting is often encountered, has to do with the allocation of expenses. The notion of a standard norm is prevalent—that is, that industry standards contemplate a management fee of between 2% and 3% of the assets of the investor partnership, perhaps subject to "break points" in a large partnership—for example, 3% of the first $10 million, 2% of the next $20 million, and so forth. The provision appears to be uncomplicated but matters are not that simple. Thus, a commonly encountered confusion arises in computing the measuring base for the fee calculation; the choices include a given percentage (say, 2.5%) of: (i) the actual cash contributed by the investors; or, (ii) the amount they have committed to contribute (a much larger figure than actual cash in the early going, since investor contributions are usually made in installments); or, (iii) the aggregate capital accounts of the partnership (a figure subject to diminution as losses are incurred or distributions in excess of profits are made); or, (iv) the appraised value of the assets of the investor partnership. If there is one most frequent pick, it is to select committed capital, the aggregate amount the investors have agreed to put in. The problem with actual cash (versus committed cash) is that, if contributions are made in installments, the measuring base of the management fee is quite small in the early years and yet the expenses remain constant. Measuring the management fee against the appraised value of the assets of the investor partnership might make abstract sense in that it rewards the managers if the assets go up and penalizes them if shrinkage occurs, but it puts a good deal of pressure on the subjective process of appraising assets. Moreover, such a system may artificially spur the managers to invest assets prematurely.[31]

A somewhat subtler issue has to do with the relationship between the management fee and the expense allowance. It was at one time generally understood that the purpose of a management fee was not to provide a profit to the GPGP but to compensate it for the ordinary and

[31]Some agreements provide for a Consumer Price Index inflator, annually amending the management fee upward.

necessary expenses of running the partnership; that understanding may be changing as the size of some of the recently organized partnerships[32] inflates, but there remains the central underlying notion that the management fee is in the nature, primarily, of a reimbursement. Indeed, the size of many recently organized partnerships has been driven by the necessity for a denominator large enough to throw off fees adequate to pay bills. Since the cost of two professional managers, secretarial service, rent, reports to investors, and unallocated travel is in the neighborhood of $500,000 annually in today's market, the minimum size of a typical pool, at a 2.5% annual fee, is not much less than $20 million.

The often overlooked question is: Which expenses are included within the management fee and which are chargeable to the investor partnership? Obviously, a $500,000 annual allotment will not cover a number of the investor partnership's expenses, assuming the managers are to take any salaries at all. Legal fees for making investments, for example, can amount to $20,000–$25,000 per investment. If the investment is successfully closed, that amount can be capitalized and added to the cost basis of the investment but the fees incurred in structuring deals that turn out to be dry holes have to be charged to someone. So also with the legal and accounting costs of maintaining the investor partnership, preparation of tax returns, brokerage commissions, litigation costs, expenses of investor relations (limited partners meetings are often held in exotic venues), and travel expenses associated with successful and/or unsuccessful portfolio investments. In each case there are three sources for the payment: (i) capitalize the expense and charge it to the basis of the investment (another way of saying that the investor partnership pays in the end); (ii) charge it to the investor partnership as an annual expense; or, (iii) lay off the expense on the GPGP, against the management fee.

The current custom is to construe the expenses included within the management fee—that is, the GPGP's problem—quite sparingly. Typically, the management fee covers only salaries of the full-time professionals and administrative personnel and the ordinary and necessary G&A expenses involved in routine operations of the investor partnership. Legal and accounting fees, and, in fact, all the other costs mentioned, are charged to the investor partnership as a current or capital expense. Consulting fees, for example, can be a major burden; many managers routinely elect to obtain a consultant's report when considering an investment. Typically, consulting fees are added to basis or

[32]The Warburg Pincus partnership recently closed with assets in excess of $1 billion. The new dynamic includes the fact that leveraged buyouts are now a popular venture strategy. Moreover, some funds argue that the better deals require enormous capital commitments to get to maturity, particularly in the health care/biotechnology segments. If a fund is unable to support its fledgling companies in the later rounds, it may find its profits diluted by rivals with a surplus of resources.

charged to the investor partnership—the GPGP usually cannot afford to pay them. (A well-drafted agreement will contain restrictions on the payment of consulting fees to affiliates of the GPGP so that the consulting fee is not a disguised addition to the GPGP's compensation. Similarly, when and if managers serve on the boards of portfolio companies and are paid directors' fees, it is the usual rule that such fees are either remitted to the investor partnership or credited against the management fee, to avoid double counting.)[33]

If a placement agent is retained, its fee could be paid by the GPGP (on the theory that it is the promoter's responsibility to raise the money); however, such is not the practice.[34] Placement fees are generally paid by the investor partnership, in which case there is a choice: Either the capital accounts of all the partners will be debited, or the fees will be charged to the capital accounts of only those partners who are introduced by the placement agent.

It is customary for the managers to form a service corporation and assign the management fees to it in consideration of its providing the general and administrative services for which the GPGP is responsible. This entitles the employees of the corporation to certain fringe benefits (group life and health insurance), which remain more favorable on an after-tax basis than if they were partners in, or employees of, the partnership.

§20.9 SUBSTANTIAL ECONOMIC EFFECT

A complicated set of Regulations under § 704 of the Code requires that any allocation of profits and losses, to be recognized for tax purposes, have "substantial economic effect." Since venture partnerships are not tax-driven nor leveraged significantly, the bite of the § 704(b) Regulations is not usually dangerous; they are designed to impact on situations where profits and losses are allocated in one direction as an economic matter and in another direction for tax purposes. Since there is often

[33]*See* Halloran, *supra* n. 3, at 70.

[34]If the GPGP is not responsible for raising the funds—i.e., the partnership is sponsored by a limited partner or its affiliate—the usual adjustment is to reduce the "carry" from 20% to some lesser number—say, 15% or 10%—and/or for the sponsoring investor to share in the "carry" to that extent. Further, organizational expenses of the investor partnership—principally legal and accounting fees—are often subject to a cap, with the GPGP (or, more probably, the lawyers and accountants) shouldering the excess.

confusion on the "substantial economic effect" test,[35] it is worth repeating that the fact a partner is allocated an interest in profits and losses that does not correspond with the capital he has contributed is not dispositive for purposes of measuring "substantial economic effect;" such allocations are the province of the partners in the course of their negotiations. What interests the Treasury in this context is an allocation system that is keyed to some form of tax minimization scheme, as when a high-income partner is getting 50% of the economic distributions but 80% of the losses. To repeat, allocating losses and profits specially in order to save taxes is not typical of venture partnerships, where the emphasis is on achieving high rates of return in an economic sense.

§20.10 CARRIED INTEREST

The award of a carried interest in profits to the general partners of a venture partnership is not deemed by most practitioners to be a taxable event, despite the fact that the holding in a celebrated early case, *Sol Diamond*,[36] can be read to the contrary. (The award of a free interest in *capital* would clearly be taxable.) Writing in 1979, eight years after *Sol Diamond*, a leading commentator referred to the "mystery" surrounding the Tax Court decision and mused:

> Perhaps one reason why the *Sol Diamond* decision has not bothered taxpayers more is that there may have been a non-deliberate conspiracy to disregard it in cases not involving the same tax abusive characteristics that were present in that decision.[37]

[35]The "substantial economic effect" test against which special allocations are measured is in fact a multipart test. The phrase "economic effect" is satisfied if: Profits and losses are reflected in the partners' capital accounts; upon liquidation, the proceeds (after allocation of profits or losses in the last year and payment of bills) are distributed in accordance with capital accounts; and, finally, as indicated in the Text, deficit capital balances are restored. Treas. Regs. § 1.704–1(b)(2)(ii). The qualifier "substantial" refers to a murky test that, in essence, has overtones of the famous "Pareto Optimality" condition in economics. A distributive share status is not Pareto Optimal if it is possible to transfer $1 in wealth from one player to another and produce a net gain (or loss) in the results of both the players as a group—transferor's loss is less than transferee's gain. When the loss and gain are in equilibrium, the status is Pareto Optimal. Under Treas. Regs. 1.704–1(b)(2)(ii), the requirement that the allocation be "substantial" is lost if special allocations are made which improve the after-tax effect on one partner and do not diminish the after-tax effect of the other or others.

[36]56 T. C. 530 (1971), *aff'd* 492 F. 2d 286 (7th Cir. 1974)

[37]Willis, *Partnership Taxation* 49 (1981 Supp.). The facts of *Sol Diamond* indicate that, had the partnership been liquidated on the day the "carried" interest was awarded, the beneficiary of the "carry" would have realized value based on the built-in value of the assets transferred to the partnership. If, as is the case in the typical venture partnership, only cash is contributed on organization, a test which looks at liquidation value of the GPGP's interest on "day one" would result in no tax.

The plethora of venture and other funds employing the "carried interest" formula makes it likely as a political matter (in the author's judgment at least) that the "conspiracy" to disregard *Sol Diamond* will continue indefinitely. The issue becomes sticky, however, if the individual acquiring the "carry" is also an employee of one of the limited partners, as when a bank or bank holding company organizes a venture partnership in which it is the sole limited partner and attempts to install one of its officers (who may wish to remain a bank officer to protect valuable fringe benefits) as a partner with a "free" interest in profits. The risk exists that the partnership will be disregarded and the partner/employee charged with a tax on the assignment of the carried interest.[38] Some practitioners recommend that the recipients of a carried interest make the election under § 83(b) of the Code to limit their exposure to the date of the initial transfer; it is the author's experience that most recepients do not do so because they do not want to admit to the possibility that they have "perform[ed] services in connection with" the transfer.[39]

§20.11 TEMPORARY INVESTMENTS AND RATE OF RETURN "BOGIES"

In the course of events, the investor partnership will draw down cash from the investors in anticipation of investments being made. Such funds are invested for a return in liquid fixed-income instruments, creating income to the partnership.[40] Investors often demand that such income not be included in the profits in which the GPGP enjoys a carried interest on the theory that the GPGP is not being paid 20% of profits to run a money market fund. That thinking—that venture investors are paid to do something special—occasionally manifests itself in an allocation scheme which ties the GPGP's share of profits to profits in excess of some target, or "bogey." The notion is that anyone can earn a return on capital that does no more than equal some index: the composite yield

[38]In G.C.M. 36346 (July 25, 1977), a proposed Revenue Ruling disavowing *Sol Diamond* was discussed but the ruling was never published. The dispute over whether the "carried interest" produces ordinary income (versus capital gain) to the GPGP is, of course, somewhat mooted since the Tax Reform Act of 1986 but the question remains whether a taxable event occurs *when* the interest is awarded. One reason for the Service's apparent reluctance to enter the lists on this issue may stem from the difficulty in valuing such an interest at inception.

[39]*See* Ch. 5, § 5.2 discussing I.R.C. § 83(b)(1). *See also,* I.R.C. § 707(a), discussed *supra* n. 22.

[40]If entities subject to ERISA own more than 25% of the aggregate profits interests, idle funds should be invested in commercial paper so as to ensure compliance with Department of Labor Interpretative Bulletins governing the status of venture funds in which ERISA entities are substantial players. See *infra* § 20.24, n. 91.

on Treasury securities, for example. The venture managers should be compensated if and only if the profits from the fund exceed that index. The thought is conceptually sound, but experience teaches that one should be cautioned that the drafting issues are difficult. Presumably the share of profits allocable to the GPGP will increase as the record of performance exceeds the index. Since performance is tracked in accordance with unrealized appreciation, questions arise not only as to valuation of the illiquid securities in the fund but also on the appropriate periods during which such appreciation should be deemed to have occurred for purposes of comparing indexes. The problems are exacerbated if phantom capital accounts are being maintained to account for partners admitted and withdrawing in midstream; the draftsman of the allocation provisions has to juggle at least three moving targets—realized profits and losses, unrealized appreciation or depreciation, and the target return or "hurdle rate." One way to cut through some drafting formalities is to eschew the carried interest in whole or in part and cause the investor partnership (or the investors directly) to lend the managers, nonrecourse, the sums necessary for them to buy directly 20% of the stock offered for sale in each portfolio opportunity. The interest rate on the loaned funds becomes, in effect, a form of hurdle rate, albeit on an investment-by-investment basis.

§20.12 DISTRIBUTIONS

Since partners are taxed on their allocable shares of partnership profits, whether distributed or not, the possibility arises that a partner may incur state and federal tax liability without receiving the cash with which to pay the same. Accordingly, most agreements provide that the GPGP must distribute each year a given percentage, say 35%, of realized profits, in order to yield to the partners approximately what they will owe in taxes. The GPGP almost always has discretion to make additional distributions even if it is not required to do so. If the management fee is tied to partnership assets (not the recommended practice),[41] the GPGP has an obvious conflict of interest.

A well-run GPGP is usually proud to distribute securities in companies which have become liquid because the practice is appealing to the limited partners who, under Rule 144, can "tack" the holding period during which the partnership owned the security to their own holding period and, absent other constraints, sell immediately.[42] An increasing

[41]*See infra* § 20.8.

[42]*See* Ch. 14, § 14.11, for a discussion of SEC Rule 144. Tacking is allowable if the distribution in kind is pro rata; if a distribution is made in liquidation of a single limited partner's interest—i.e., on withdrawal—a no-action position may be obtainable if the withdrawal was involuntary. *See* Halloran n. 3, at 83. It is unclear whether a directorship held by a general partner of the partnership taints the limited partner so that no sale can be made under Rule 144 for three months after the distribution. *Ibid.*

percentage of limited partners are wary of lodging discretion in the GPGP with respect to distributions. Indeed, it is fashionable for the investors to *insist* that the GPGP distribute shares of each portfolio company once it has gone public, even though the profits have not been technically realized prior to the distribution. The theory is that the investors are perfectly capable of managing public securities. Moreover, the fear is that the GPGP will be unwilling to distribute out to the partners' "hot" stock since the GPGP will forfeit its share of subsequent appreciation in so much of the holding as represents the capital portion. (To illustrate, if the partnership bought 100 shares of Hot Stock, Inc. for $10 per share and the entire holding is now worth $5,000, the GPGP will receive on distribution its 20% share of the $4,000 gain, meaning shares worth $800 or 16 shares. If the GPGP were to hold the shares in the partnership, the "engine" that can produce further gains for the GPGP will be 20 shares, not 16.[43])

§20.13 VESTING THE MANAGER'S INTEREST

The question of vesting is often a difficult negotiation point. Assume A and B are the nominated managers of an investor partnership with a life of 10 years; each enjoys a 10% carried interest in profits. If A elects to quit after four years, he may argue that the partnership's funds are substantially invested and he should continue his profits interest to maturity, albeit as a limited partner, or be bought out at that interest's fair value. The investors, on the other hand, may contend that, as Yogi Berra said, "It ain't over until it's over." The job of monitoring portfolio investments is just as critical as the initial investment process and A is bailing out prematurely. This conflict can be resolved in part by postponing vesting—by cashing a footloose partner's interest out at bargain prices if he quits the enterprise prematurely. The process involves establishing a valuation formula, which gradually increases the generosity of A's severance over time; if he elects to withdraw in year one, he receives his cost, which is virtually nothing; in each succeeding year, he will receive on termination an increasing fraction of the fair value of his interest.

§20.14 THE PARTNERSHIP PRIVATE PLACEMENT MEMORANDUM

One of the curiosities of the venture business is that venture capital managers, hypercritical of ambiguities in the business plans presented

[43]Some commentators recommend in such instances that the GPGP distribute to itself 20 shares and pay in cash the cost of the extra four shares to the cash investors. Dauchy & Harmon, "Structuring Venture Capital Limited Partnerships," 3 *Computer Law.* 1 (1986).

to them by hopeful founders, are often quite reticent in outlining in a private placement memorandum what it is they plan to do with the money they are soliciting from investors. It is only the occasional partnership memorandum, for example, which includes projections against which performance can be measured. More frequently, the organizers of the investor partnership will refer to historical compounded rates of return as reported in the trade press or to a so-called track record. (Some practitioners require that track records be assembled in such a way as to pass muster under the SEC Rule[44] imposed upon registered investment advisers, even though it is not directly applicable to most venture managers.)

Moreover, the focus of the investment strategy is usually outlined in generalities. There may be a tilt to the program—biomedical and health sciences, leveraged buyouts, turnarounds—but, in the interests of "flexibility," escape language in the document gives the managers the opportunity to take advantage of a broad range of opportunities.

The generality of the partnership selling document reflects some history. When the first venture partnerships were organized, it was generally conceded that the managers enjoyed unique expertise. The investors, as experienced in business and finance as they might be, had little to contribute to the process since venture capital was perceived as an esoteric art, a mystery shared by only a few initiates. That balance of intellectual power and experience has shifted somewhat over the years as the controllers of the sources of capital have become initiated. Nonetheless, opportunities crop up at unexpected points of the compass and the fashion is not to require a concentrated focus by the investing partners.

§20.15 CONTROL ISSUES

The typical venture limited partnership is managed by the GPGP but some investors are not content with a passive role. With increasing frequency, investors want some voice in the partnership's affairs. In the past, a stiff arm has been applied by managers to investors seeking a stronger voice, a play on the lurking fear—a legitimate fear, to be sure—that the investors can be exposed to liability as general partners if they insist on powers which might encroach on the U.L.P.A. prohibitions against their taking part in the "control or management" of the partnership.[45] Thus, the conventional wisdom has been that limited partners enjoyed limited liability as a tradeoff, in consideration of their agreement to eschew a role in control and management.

As the pioneering partnerships were being organized in the 1960s and

[44]Investment Advisors Act, Rule 206(4)–1. The gist of the Rule is that an adviser who refers to its track record must print the entire record, warts and all.
[45]U.L.P.A. § 7 (1916).

early 1970s, counsel were sensitive to the danger of losing limited liability as the powers of the limited partners were enlarged. However, they were on occasion pressed to find ways to allow the investors to express their views without peril. Advisory committees provided a forum for structured discussions between the managers and representatives of the investors, but genuine power was not shared. The investors, unable to pull their chips from the pot until winding up, were left only with the right to call the game off—to compel early liquidation of the partnership if terminally unhappy with the managers' performance. This is sometimes called the "nuclear bomb" approach and is rarely exercised.

The investors' impotence has not been a critical problem in venture finance; almost all funds managed by experienced professionals have produced satisfactory returns. Moreover, results are not expected to crystallize in a venture fund until the later stages, at which point the unhappy investors might just as well await the term of the partnership (10 to 12 years) to expire in accordance with its terms. The issue became significant, however, in recent years when some of the ill-considered and inadequately managed tax shelter limited partnerships carelessly invested in real estate and oil and gas. When those partnerships encountered problems, the investors were often presented with a Hobson's Choice. If they formed a committee to oust the managers, they were risking being tagged as general partners, and in an insolvent partnership to boot. If they sat back and took their lumps, their investment remained in the hands of proven incompetents. For this and other reasons, augmented limited partner suffrage came about through the Revised U.L.P.A. (R.U.L.P.A.) adopted in 1976.[46] That statute, wherever adopted, allows limiteds to participate without peril in a series of activities *vis-à-vis* the partnership: advising, consulting, acting as surety and, significantly, voting to fire specific general partners.[47] Moreover, crossing the line (if,

[46]Revised Uniform Limited Partnership Act, 6 U.L.P.A. § 101 *et seq.* (1976), as amended in 1985 (R.U.L.P.A.).

[47]Section 303(b) of the R.U.L.P.A. provides in part that:

> A limited partner does not participate in the control of the business within the meaning of subsection (a) solely by . . . voting on one or more of the following matters: (i) the dissolution and winding up of the limited partnership; (ii) the sale, exchange, lease, mortgage, pledge, or other transfer of all or substantially all of the assets of the limited partnership other than in the ordinary course of its business; (iii) the incurrence of indebtedness by the limited partnership other than in the ordinary course of its business; (iv) a change in the nature of the business; or (v) the removal of a general partner.

It is not entirely clear from the language whether the limited partners are allowed to *initiate* a vote to dismiss a particular general partner or are only authorized to vote on a motion made by other general partners. It can also be argued that, if the action arises in a state which has not adopted the R.U.L.P.A., liability can be imposed by a local court. The conflict of laws provisions of the R.U.L.P.A. (§ 901) provide that the law of the domiciliary state's law controls. However, if the domicile is entirely one of convenience—i.e., no substantial contacts—a different result might occur. *See* Note, "Foreign Limited Partnerships: A Proposed Amendment to the Uniform Limited Partnership Act" 47 *S. Calif. L. Rev.* 1174 (1974).

for example, the limited partners could veto specific investment decisions) will expose the limited partners only to a small slice in the universe of potential complainants, those who actually were fooled by the limited partners' contrary-to-fact status.[48]

§20.16 MEETINGS AND COMMITTEES

Regardless of the allocation of technical legal power, well-drafted partnerships contemplate investor input as a matter of good investor relations. An annual meeting between the investors as a group and the managers has never been deemed to cross the forbidden boundary under any version of the U.L.P.A. Such meetings tend to be reporting sessions, rarely the occasion for discussion of substantive issues, but they are *de rigueur*. Frequent written reports to the investors are a traditional obligation of the managers, bringing the limited partners up to date on the performance of the portfolio companies, new investments, and valuation changes. And, some agreements require the generals to hold special meetings on the call of a specified percentage of the limited partners. Whether or not the agreement so requires, more aggressive limited partners take the occasion for frequent private meetings (Japanese investors are famous for this practice) with the managers. The most active limited partners are usually those corporate investors to whom the deal stream is significant (including those investment opportunities not favored by the managers) for purposes of possible direct investment or co-investment. (To the extent the GPGP is required to show investment opportunities to the investors with a view to their becoming co-investors with the partnership, the investors are said to enjoy "window rights.")[49] Finally, two standing committees are typically contemplated in the organizational documents: the Advisory Committee and the Valuation Committee.

[48] [i]f the limited partner's participation in the control of the business is not substantially the same as the exercise of the powers of a general partner, he is liable only to persons who transact business with the limited partnership with actual knowledge of his participation in control . . .

R.U.L.P.A. § 303(a). It is an open question whether a limited partner with the power to approve all investments over a certain dollar figure is participating "substantially the same" as a general partner.

[49] The existence of co-investment or "window" rights in favor of the limited partners as a group can cause the GPGP thorny problems. Thus, how does the GPGP chose among limited partners competing for the same investment? What if the business plan contains information the investors are not authorized to see? Note that a critical exemption from the Investment Advisors Act of 1940 may depend on the GPGP *not* rendering investment advice directly to the limited partners. *See infra* § 20.25.

§20.17(a) ADVISORY COMMITTEE

The Advisory Committee, whose members are often compensated by the partnership, is composed of individuals selected for their technical and/or special expertise and not affiliated (ordinarily) with any of the limited partners. The job of the Advisory Committee members is to do just what the name implies: to provide advice and counsel on screening and making portfolio investments. The Committee's formal meetings are usually episodic; members are called on individually when a matter crops up in their area of expertise. They are usually featured speakers at annual meetings of the limited partners, exploring new and interesting areas of science. On occasion, members are given a percentage of the carried interest, usually by becoming limited partners in the GPGP (thereby turning it into a GPLP).

(b) VALUATION COMMITTEE

The Valuation Committee has more specific functions. First, the committee sits on the issue of valuation, a particularly sensitive question in those partnerships in which the management fee is measured by appraised asset value. The issue of valuation is also significant when assets are distributed in kind, when a partner is being admitted or is withdrawing after the commencement of operations and, perhaps most importantly from the manager's standpoint, when management's performance is being rated. Since limited partners are (either de facto or de jure) locked into the partnership for its 10- to 12-year life, one might conjecture that the rating of portfolio performance on an interim basis is not significant. However, most venture managers harbor the ambition to commence a second fund as soon as the fund they are currently managing is "substantially invested."[50] The track record of investments in the fund currently under management, therefore, is significant in enticing both current and new investors to participate in the new fund.

§20.18 CONFLICTS OF INTEREST

The second function of the Valuation Committee is to resolve conflicts of interest, a significant issue. Some partnerships lay down rigid laws prohibiting conflicts; thus, the managers are bound to bring to the investor partnership's attention all investments that might be of interest to

[50]A fund may be substantially invested even though only half, more or less, of its cash has been actually used to purchase portfolio securities; if the remainder is, as it usually should be, earmarked for follow-on investments in the portfolio companies in which the fund currently has a position, then the fund is deemed to be substantially invested.

the investor partnership. Indeed, teeth can be added to this section by insisting that the managers' personal investments be limited to their interest in the investor partnership and to minority positions in publicly traded securities. (In corporate law, this area of concern is generally described under the heading of "corporate opportunity").[51] Partnerships with strict limitations on corporate opportunity also clamp down hard on self-dealing and co-investment, requiring that the partnership neither buy nor sell securities from any manager or affiliate thereof (an almost universal provision) and that the managers refrain from investing in portfolio opportunities either prior to, coincident with, or subsequent to the partnership's purchase of shares. Finally, the stricter versions of this section require the managers to devote all their time to the activities of the partnership (no outside business activities[52]).

Other schematics are much looser, on the theory that the partnership may be deprived of significant opportunities and the managers' motivation diminished. Should a titan of the business elect to manage other people's money in addition to his own, it would be curious for the investors not to want the opportunity to invest in companies in which the titan plans or already holds a position. Moreover, some of the most successful venture managers are running two or more venture partnerships, all of which may have investable funds.[53] In cases in which there is some elasticity in the arrangements, the conflicts are usually sanitized by running them past the Valuation Committee for consideration and approval (or, in the odd case, disapproval). In a given case, the committee will prick up its ears if the managers are investing at one price and the partnership is coming in, albeit in a later round, at a higher price.[54]

§20.19 METHODS OF VALUATION

The appropriate methods for valuing illiquid securities in a venture portfolio can be troublesome. In the Release setting forth the SEC's views on how values should be calculated for restricted securities held

[51]Henn & Alexander, *Law of Corporations* 625–62 (1983).

[52]If the management of the investor partnership is an affiliate of a commercial or investment bank, other conflicts may arise; thus, one has to worry about inside information and "Chinese Walls" and/or the partnership's investments being used to bail out bad loans made by the bank.

[53]Michael Halloran shrewdly remarks that the severity of the conflicts section varies "inversely with the . . . general partner's track record." Halloran, *supra* n. 3, at 48.2.

[54]It can be predicted that investors will become more sensitive to conflicts as a result of litigation arising out of the publicized troubles of A. David Silver, the quondam general partner of two funds which are in liquidation as of this writing. The allegations include the charge that the assets of fund No. 2 were used to attempt to bail out fund No. 1's investments. Ely, "Dr. Silver's Tarnished Prescription," *Venture* 54 (July 1987).

in the portfolio of registered investment companies,[55] the Commission requires fiduciaries in charge of the valuation function to treat each case on its own merits and to avoid standard formulas, such as the commonly quoted 15% discount, or haircut, for securities not publicly salable. Whatever the situation in publicly traded funds owning restricted securities, the Commission's suggestions are utopian in the context of a venture partnership—the time and money are not available to do much more than approximate values on the basis of informal rules of thumb.

The first principle is, of course, cost. In keeping with the fundamentals of cost accounting, assets are carried at cost until something happens to compel a change in that judgment. The first such change is usually a subsequent-round financing at a price higher or lower than the initial round. If the subsequent financing is at a lower price, it would be unusual for the Valuation Committee not to adjust the carrying value downward. The higher price requires a somewhat more sophisticated analysis. If there are no new investors in the subsequent round—to put the simplest case, if the investor partnership is the only outside investor in the first and second round—then an increase in the price paid per share should not be, of and by itself, conclusive. When new investors are brought into the syndicate (and assuming that price is not fixed by corporate partners who are willing to pay extra for access to technology), the custom is to mark values to the price at which the last trade was executed. This can create an anomaly on occasion, arising out of the fact that, when a company goes public, the investors' ability to sell is usually restricted by either the underwriters' holdback (to allow the market to stabilize without the selling pressure of secondary offerings) or the handcuffs of a Blue Sky administrator.[56] Going public, accordingly, may require the investor partnership actually to write *down* its investment. If, for example, the last-round price was $5 a share, stock is issued to the public at $6 but the investor partnership's shares are tied up for a year or more, rules of thumb might require a haircut of as much as, say, 30% to account for the illiquidity of the position the investor partnership holds, albeit in a public security.

Another anomaly resulting from the propensity to use the price of private financings as a benchmark (absent any superior alternative) can occur in the rare instance where a start-up is so successful it never requires a second, third, or fourth round of financing. Such a company may be carried at its initial cost indefinitely while an inferior company, requiring additional rounds, finds its valuation boosted by the prices obtained in the subsequent rounds.

[55]Inv. Co. Act Rel. No. 40–5847 [Accounting Services Release Transfer Binder] (CCH) Fed. Sec. L. Rep. ¶ 72,135 (Oct. 21, 1969).
[56]*See* Ch. 9, § 9.3(c).

Nonetheless, it is common to use private-round prices as an appropriate and, barring unusual circumstances, conclusive indicia of valuation and to employ a formula for haircuts when the investor partnership holds an illiquid position in a public security. If the sale is restrained only by Rule 144, the haircut normally hovers around 15%. If the security cannot be traded for a year or more, the haircut is as high as 33.33%; intermediate lock-ups occasion haircuts in between those points.

§20.20 LIQUIDITY

Investors in a venture partnership understand, when they subscribe, that their interests are illiquid. However, as circumstances change, investors may want to get out before the partnership liquidates.[57] The question is whether and how they can do so.[58]

If a limited partner can find a private buyer, then the unit can be sold, absent some curious and unusual contractual restriction that limits alienability absolutely, or a legal restriction based on the possibility that the transfer would subject the remaining partners to a loss of benefits or status.[59] To be sure, in order to qualify technically as a partnership, the investment units are supposed to lack the element of "free transferability," the theory being that free transferability is a corporate, not a partnership, attribute.[60] To satisfy this requirement, partnership agreements routinely provides that the GPGP must,[61] as a technical

[57]One way for a partner to get out, rarely exercised, is to round up enough votes to dissolve the partnership. *See supra* § 20.15.

[58]The admission of new limited partners at the beginning of the partnership can be controversial if the sponsors pursue a multiple closing strategy. The "first-in" limiteds may object if subsequent investors take a ride on their money and ordinarily want to close the offering down on a fixed and early date.

[59]If the partners wish to restrict assignments (versus a technical restraint on admission of the assignee to the partnership), a first refusal option would be the normal device. Note that such a provision does not restrict transferability for purposes of I.R.C. § 7701. *See* Treas. Regs. § 301.7701–2(e)(2). An absolute restriction on alienation would be of dubious legality in some states except if a legal rule would be broken by reason of the transfer or some other harm caused. In that category are the ban on unregistered public offerings in the'33 Act, the loss of an exemption (100 or more beneficial holders) from the Investment Company Act of 1940 or the provision in § 708 of the I.R.C. providing that a partnership terminates for tax purposes if 50% or more of the capital or profits interest are sold in any 12-month period. R.U.L.P.A. § 702, suggests that the agreement may restrict assignments but the Comment says "there was no intention to affect in any way usual rules regarding restraints on alienation of personal property." *See* Halloran, *supra* n. 3, at 77–80.

[60]I.R.C. § 7701. *See supra* § 20.5(a) for the "4 attribute" test.

[61]Under the R.U.L.P.A. § 704(a), the assignor may give the assignee the right of admission "in accordance with authority" in the certificate; that authority is routinely conditioned in the certificate on GPGP approval.

matter, approve the admission of any transferee as a substituted limited partner.[62] This convention is, however, artificial because a transfer by assignment of the economic substance involved is not restrained. Without threatening the fiction that the interests are not "freely transferable," limited partner A can transfer all the economic value he owns to Assignee B at will. The technical constraint—that, absent the permission of the GPGP, Assignee B cannot become a limited partner and, therefore, cannot vote on matters appropriate for limited partner action—is largely trivial since limited partners are ordinarily indifferent to the existence of that right in the first instance.[63] In short, partnership shares are freely transferable unless subject to a specific limitation in the agreement. Indeed, "master limited partnership" interests (a scheme by which certificates of participation are sold in a single interest held by a sole limited partner) are traded on the New York Stock Exchange.

However, it may be that a limited partner cannot find an assignee and wants the partnership to cash him out. The problem is that the very nature of a venture capital partnership makes it awkward to allow partners to withdraw prior to liquidation. The valuation problems have been alluded to; moreover, the partners as a group have invested on the assumption that a critical mass of assets would exist. Although partnership funds may be held in liquid form, once the cash and liquid securities shrink to around the 50% mark, the partnership is viewed as fully invested because of the necessity of allocating funds for follow-on investments in existing portfolio companies. Accordingly, it is the rare instrument that allows limited partners the unilateral right to withdraw their stake.

Nonetheless, involuntary withdrawal issues cannot be avoided in some

[62]The substitution of one partner for another as of a date other than the close of the fiscal year (which is almost always the calendar year) occasions tax issues as to the ownership of losses and profits incurred up to the date of substitution. Technically, a partnership does not realize a profit or loss until the end of the accounting period. However, the admission of partners on the 364th day of a tax shelter partnership's year, such partner purporting to buy an entire year of losses, was offensive to the tax collector's sensibilities. Therefore § 706(d)(3) of the Code provides for pro-ration.

[63]It appears clear that an assignee, not admitted as a limited partner, is nonetheless a partner for tax purposes. There are some dissenters from that position, *see* Halloran, *supra* n. 3, at 81, but the issuance of millions of dollars in master limited partner units has gone forward without challenge (as yet) to counsel's opinion that holders of the economic interest, though not formally admitted as partners, are "partners" for tax purposes. However, in light of the fact that such units actively trade, counsel to the MLPs are unwilling to advise that the partnership lacks the corporate characteristic of "free transferability" even though the master partnership interest never moves. New § 7704 of the I.R.C. treats publicly traded partnerships as corporations for tax purposes unless invested principally in real estate or oil and gas. Existing MLPs are not affected until 1997.

instances: for example, an individual partner dies or a general partner elects to quit.[64] It could prove to be a severe hardship to insist that a partner's estate sit on an illiquid, hard-to-value investment for several years. Hence, there are circumstances in which the managers will wish to consent, albeit on an ad hoc basis, to withdrawals.

Complications arise, however, in the course of an interim liquidation of a partner's interest because the book value of the partners' capital account does not, except by virtue of the rarest of coincidences, effectively reflect fair value. The securities in any active portfolio almost certainly entail unrealized appreciation or depreciation. A public mutual fund "marks to market" every day; shares are traded on the basis of current net asset values and transactions in mutual fund shares do not entail individual capital adjustments. In the case of an interim withdrawal by a partner, however, not only must the valuation hurdle be resolved but distributions in excess of the partner's capital account (by reason of his interest in unrealized appreciation) must also be made. The method commonly employed to accomplish this result is to hypothesize a sale at fair value of all the partnership's assets as of the effective date of the withdrawal, to allocate the resulting profits (or losses) to the capital accounts of all the partners pro rata and to distribute the withdrawing partner's capital account, as adjusted, to him or his estate. Distributions in redemption may, of course, be made in kind and no tax is due at the partnership level (because the partnership is not a tax-paying entity)[65] on the distribution of appreciated securities or other property.

[64]The agreement will routinely provide that no general partner may withdraw unless the limited partners consent since, among other things, the withdrawal of the last general partner terminates the partnership. In fact, if the individual who is the driving force behind the partnership should die or retire, the agreement may give the limited partners a right to liquidate the partnership, even though technically nothing has happened because the key individual was a partner in an entity—the GPGP—which continues as the general partner of the investor partnership. If the last remaining general partner nonetheless disappears despite a ban on withdrawal—i.e., he dies—the agreement usually provides that a majority of the remaining limited partners can elect to continue as long as a new general partner can be found in a timely fashion with adequate net worth to continue "pass through" tax status—i.e., to satisfy the unlimited liability criterion of § 7701. *See supra* § 20.5(a). In such event, the agreement can compel the minority limited partners to remain as partners but not beyond, of course, the remaining stated term of the partnership; although the Regulations provide apodictically that a limited partnership under the U.L.P.A. lacks continuity of life, Treas. Regs. § 301.7701–2(b)(3), query the result if a majority of partners have the right to continue the business indefinitely.

[65]Under the 1984 amendments to the I.R.C., distributions in kind by a corporation became a taxable event at the corporate level, the tax measured by the fair value of the property less the corporation's adjusted basis. I.R.C. § 311(d)(1), now I.R.C. § 311(b)(1). A tax may also be assessed on the recipient shareholders. A partner may realize gain upon any distribution by the partnership but only to the extent "any money" distributed exceeds the adjusted basis of its interest. I.R.C. § 731(a)(1).

Finally, there is the problem of payment; the partnership may not be liquid enough to pay out a sizable sum and it may be awkward to break up the partnership's stockholdings. The better drafted agreements, accordingly, provide for staged payments over time. In the case of a general partner who dies or who simply wants to quit, no payment may be necessary—the parties may agree that the general partner's interest is converted to that of a special limited partner and the business carried on to liquidation without any payout of partnership assets. However, each general partner's interest in profits is in reality awarded, albeit not for tax purposes, as compensation for past and future services. Thus, the withdrawing general partner's share of the "carried" profit interest may have to be recaptured to compensate a new general partner.

Admission of a new partner, general or limited, poses problems which are mirror images of the foregoing. If a new partner is admitted somewhere down the road, the assets will have appreciated (or in some cases, depreciated). The question arises whether it is fair to allow the newly admitted partner to share in profits from appreciation antedating his arrival. One preferred provision is to adjust all capital accounts as if there were a withdrawal, assigning the appreciated profits or losses[66] to the existing partners, and starting the newly admitted partner on a "level playing field," entitled to share only in profits and losses as they occur from and after the date of its admission.[67]

It is easier to describe in principle the theories that underly partnership provisions governing withdrawals and admissions than to draft the actual language. The task of setting out in precise detail what happens to profits interests and capital accounts is formidable, particularly when it is necessary to run two sets of partnership books. The virtue of the partnership form—its enormous flexibility—creates such a wide range of possibilities that drafting becomes enormously complicated. Just as the draftsman thinks he's covered all contingencies another interesting hypothetical comes to his attention.

[66]One way to accomplish the procedure is to run a system of phantom capital accounts to which unrealized appreciation and depreciation are posted as of each appraisal period. *See* Halloran, *supra* n. 3, at 91–96.

[67]A partnership technically terminates under § 708(b)(1)(B) of the Code if, within a 12-month period, there is a sale of "50 percent or more of the total interest in partnership capital and profits." The effect of such a technical termination is to treat the partnership as having distributed all its assets to the partners, who contribute them to a new partnership. Gain is recognized to the extent that "money" distributed to a partner exceeds the partner's adjusted basis. I.R.C. § 731(a)(1). The termination may also result in an adjustment in the basis of the partnership's assets and other random consequences can result from, *e.g.*, the partnership's taxable year closing. *See* Nad, "Dispositions of Partnership Interests and Partnership Property," 43 *N.Y.U. Ann. Inst. on Federal Taxation* § 29[12] (1985).

§20.21 RESTRICTIONS ON THE GPGP's POWERS

The GPGP is usually granted plenary powers to deal with the partnership assets so that, as an attractive opportunity looms, the partnership is not faced with an officious lawyer on the other side questioning a manager's power to sign documents. However, certain powers are sensitive, particularly the power to borrow for purposes of leveraging partnership investments or to organize an SBIC, the latter implying the power and purpose to leverage due to the nature of SBICs. So-called 501(c)(3) entities, for example, educational institutions and foundations, may wind up with taxable income if their investments are leveraged, giving rise to "unrelated debt-financed income;"[68] hence, a prohibition on borrowing is ordinarily the price of admission for such nonprofit investors. Similarly, the use of certain trading strategies (e.g., short sales and commodities futures) are usually frowned on by nonprofit limited partners, since income from such activities may not qualify as income from "investments" and, thus, not be excluded[69] from the definition of "unrelated business taxable income."[70]

§20.22 STANDARD OF CARE—INDEMNIFICATION

Indemnification of the GPGP entails generally the same principles as are raised by the indemnification of corporate directors—that is, indemnification is a function, in large part, of the duties owed by the managers to the members, and vice versa.[71] (Massachusetts offers an unusual distinction, by denying meaningful indemnification provisions in any limited partnership offering interests to noninstitutional investors.)[72] A question arises whether, given the recent change in the Del-

[68]I.R.C. § 514. For a general discussion of "unrelated debt–financed income," *see* 2 Phelan, *Non-Profit Enterprises: Law and Taxation* § 11:19 (1985). *See* Ch. 18, § 18.7(e). Authorizing the partnership to invest in an SBIC, or indeed any managed entity (another venture partnership for example), raises the spectre of dual management fees. In such event, the fee at the senior partnership level, including the "carried" interest, is usually limited—1% of the assets under double management is typical.

[69]I.R.C. § 512(b).

[70]*See* Treas. Regs. 1.512(b)–1(d)(2).

> [I]f an organization is engaged in the trade or business of writing options . . . the exclusion will not be available.

Typically, the agreement will also bar the purchase by the partnership of securities on margin because the same give rise to debt-financed income. *Elliot Knitwear Profit Sharing Plan v. Comm'r* 71 T.C. 765 (1979), *aff'd* 614 F.2d 347 (3d Cir. 1980).

[71]*See* Ch. 4, § 4.13. A manager's right to indemnification cannot be precisely co-extensive with his legal obligations as a manager or else there would be little point to the indemnification provisions, at least *vis-à-vis* the shareholders or partners.

[72]Mass. Blue Sky Regulations, § 13.305(2)(E)(iv), IA (CCH) *Blue Sky Rep.* ¶ 31,465.

aware general corporation laws authorizing a limitation on the scope of director liability,[73] partnership agreements should not limit the exposure of the GPGP to the same extent—that is, no liability except in cases of personal profit or statutory violations. Several blue sky statutes insist that the indemnification provisions of real estate partnerships indemnify the GPGP only in cases of liability based on allegations of simple negligence[74] but Massachusetts is the only state so far to apply that rule to all investment partnerships.[75]

§20.23 CREATURES OF STATUTE—SBICs AND BDCs

Some venture capital pools are creatures of statute, organized as Business Development Companies (BDCs) or Small Business Investment Companies (SBICs).[76] As such, they are subject to a number of special rules, certain of which are highlighted in the following discussion.

(a) SBICs

The genesis of the SBIC has been outlined in Chapter 6, § 6.6. The advantage of the format for venture pools is, of course, the ability to borrow federal funds for investment at advantageous rates. Thus, some venture funds are organized as SBICs and some elect to operate SBICs as subsidiaries of the main partnership. This section summarizes some of the rules which a venture pool organized as an SBIC must follow in its investment policies.

Subject to exceptions, an SBIC is not permitted to own or control more than 50% of the voting power of the issuer,[77] rarely a concern in a traditional venture financing and relatively easily managed. For example, if the SBIC wants control to reside in the investors (versus the founder), it usually brings in a sympathetic partner and the two of them may own a majority of the stock in the aggregate as long as there is no

[73] *See* Ch. 4, § 4.13.

[74] *E.g.*, Calif. Blue Sky Regulations, Admin. Code tit. 10, Ch. 3, Rule 260.140.111.4, 1 (CCH) *Blue Sky L. Rep.* ¶ 11,964.

[75] Some promoters are attempting to obtain informed waivers by the investors of the protections afforded by the Massachusetts requirements. It remains to be seen whether that strategy will be effective in a pinch.

[76] Regulation E under the'33 Act provides a simplified format—registration by notification—for public offerings ($5 million or less) of the securities of an SBIC or a BDC.

[77] Under the rule, an SBIC may own rights to purchase more than 50% of a firm on a fully diluted basis, but that privilege should be exercised with "caution." Chase, *supra* Ch. 6, n. 1, at 142. The SBIC's permissible quantum of the vote shrinks to 20% if the portfolio company has 50 or more shareholders and no other stockholder owns a larger percentage. An SBIC can control a portfolio company temporarily if necessary to protect its investment. Miller, *supra* Ch. 6, n. 16 at 1684.

express agreement between them *vis-à-vis* control. The Regulations contain broad prohibitions on conflicts of interest,[78] covering quite remote relationships. For example, any partner of a director of an SBIC is an "associate"[79] of the SBIC and, as such, may not "indirectly" borrow money from a director of a firm which the SBIC in question is financing. Simply outlining the reach of that rule illustrates how unwitting violations could occur: Smith, a law partner of an SBIC director, buys a house from Jones, a director of one of the SBIC's portfolio investments, and gives back a purchase money mortgage. The entire notion of co-investment—the SBIC and one of its shareholders investing in the same opportunity—is less popular than in the venture world generally because of the conflicts rules.[80]

A number of relatively harmless but annoying rules further constrain an SBIC's business activities. Thus, debt financings must be for a minimum of five years and only a "reasonable" prepayment penalty may be involved.[81] The aggregate amount of funds loaned and/or invested in any one firm cannot exceed 20% of the licensee's "private capital," a number calculated according to quite detailed SBA rules.[82] An SBIC cannot become a general partner in any unincorporated concern or become jointly or severally liable for the obligations of the concern;[83] it may purchase options or warrants expiring no later than six years from the termination of the financing.[84] For some curious reason, an SBIC can invest in preferred stock redeemable at the option of the holder but no such redemption privilege can be exercised for five years and the redemption price must be determined by a "legal and reasonable" formula based on "book value or earnings" of the concern.[85] In short, the price of government assistance is overregulation, often harmless but always a nuisance.

(b) BDCs

BDCs are Business Development Companies organized under the 1980 amendments to the Investment Company Act of 1940.[86] The amendment was designed to release venture funds electing to be treated as BDCs

[78] 13 C.F.R. § 107.903 (1987).

[79] 13 C.F.R. § 107.3 (1987).

[80] The terms of the transaction for the SBIC must be at least as favorable as for its affiliate. *See* Miller, *supra* Ch. 6, n. 16, at 1686.

[81] 13 C.F.R. § 107.301(a) (1987). The term can be less if reasonably necessary as part of an "overall sound financing," whatever that means. 13 C.F.R. §§ 107.301 and 107.504(b)(1).

[82] 13 C.F.R. § 107.303 (1987).

[83] 13 C.F.R. § 107.320(a) (1987).

[84] 13 C.F.R. § 107.320(b) (1987).

[85] 13 C.F.R. § 107.321(b) (1987).

[86] 15 U.S.C. § § 80a–53–64 (Supp. 1981). For a full discussion of the statutory scheme, *see* Halloran, n. 3, at 159.

from some of the strictures of the '40 Act, which had theretofore prevented most of them from offering their shares to the public. The new animal is defined in the statute as a closed-end fund which invests 70% or more of its assets in "Eligible Portfolio Companies," meaning, generally, privately held companies as to which to the BDC renders "significant management assistance." The amendment was designed to lure venture funds into the public markets but the scheme has not as yet worked. The '40 Act still poses significant problems for BDCs[87] and only a handful of new entrants[88] have registered.

§20.24 SPECIAL INVESTORS

In organizing a venture partnership, the sponsors are compelled to take into account the identity of certain types of investors, principally pension funds and offshore entities. A dramatic, at least in relative terms, rise in venture partnership investing is largely traceable to the infusion of pension assets, as the managers of tax-exempt funds have discovered the attractiveness of venture capital returns. However, that growth has not been facilitated by the erratic performance of the Department of Labor in wrestling with the issue of whether the managers of the venture capital pools—the general partner or partners—should be deemed managers of "plan assets" under the Employee Retirement Income Security Act of 1974 (ERISA).[89] If the manager of the pool were deemed to be managing "plan assets" in a fiduciary capacity under ERISA, then the statute and the Department of Labor regulations would impose various constraints drafted with the Central States Teamsters Fund in mind, requiring in turn largely unacceptable changes in how venture managers traditionally go about their business. The fiduciaries overseeing the investment of pension assets are barred from participating, for example, in the profits of the partnerships within their stewardship. Indeed, newspaper headlines reflect with monotony the indictment of yet another corrupt union official for taking a surreptitious "piece of the action" in the investments made by on behalf of the union members. The very nature of the relationship between a venture capital manager and the investors, however, is one of profit sharing. Moreover, again

[87]The most difficult section in the'40 Act is § 17, the "transactions with affiliates" section, which retains significant fangs, particularly in the co-investment area. Halloran, *supra* n. 3, at 191. On § 17 generally, *see* Bartlett & Dowd, "Section 17 of the Investment Company Act—An Example of Regulation by Exemption," 8 *Del. J. Corp. Law.* 449 (1983).

[88]For an up to date discussion, *see* Testa, "Federal Regulation of Venture Capital Companies," in *Venture Capital After The Tax Reform Act of 1986* 123, 131 (P.L.I. Course Handbook Series No. 422, 1987).

[89]Employee Retirement Income Security Act of 1974, 29 U.S.C. § § 1001 *et seq.* The person who exercises control over plan assets is a "fiduciary" under ERISA according to § 3(21), and a fiduciary is held to a high standard of care, § 404, and loyalty, § 406.

because the legislative language was drafted in a different context and culture, ERISA contains stern prohibitions on conflicts of interest. In many venture partnerships, on the other hand, the investors are content, indeed enthusiastic, about co-investment in portfolio opportunities with the managers, who are often leading figures in venture investment in their own right.

The narrow technical issue facing the Labor Department is whether only the *limited partnership interests* constitute "plan assets" or whether the *investments the partnership makes* are also "plan assets." In the former case, the strict fiduciary obligations imposed by ERISA would extend only to that manager making the decision to invest in the partnership in the first instance—that is, the bank, insurance company, or investment adviser administering the pension fund's portfolio. The managers making the partnership's portfolio investments, the individual general partners, would be one step removed from the process, akin to the officers of an industrial company, (e.g., General Motors), in which pension funds and the funds of millions of other investors are commingled. If, on the other hand, impelled by the omnipresent "thin edge of the wedge" or Pandora's Box syndrome, the Labor Department were to disregard the venture partnerships as pass through entities—again with the Central States Teamsters in mind—fiduciary responsibilities would land on the shoulders of the general partners, an ill-fitting suit. The Department has wrestled with this problem from 1979 to 1986,[90] when it published its final position.[91]

The Regulation first provides a general *de minimis* test. If ERISA entities hold less than 25% of the interests in a venture partnership, then the partnership is unaffected;[92] its assets are not "plan assets." However, many venture partnerships, given the current activity of pension funds, handily exceed the 25% threshold. With respect to such funds, the Regulation defines an entity called a Venture Capital Operating Company (VCOC); as long as a venture partnership qualifies as a VCOC, the managers of the Partnership are not ERISA fiduciaries. Like the Investment Company Act scheme, the test is an asset test—50% of the VCOC partnership's portfolio, measured at cost, must be invested in "venture capital investments" or "derivative investments" (investments which grow out of venture capital investments).[93] Temporary

[90]What the Department of Labor refers to as the "Final Regulation" is officially a series of Interpretive Bulletins amending 29 C.F.R. Parts 2509, 2510, 2520, and 2550. The text of the Final Regulation (the "Regulation") appears in 51 Fed. Reg. 41262 (Nov. 13, 1986). The Regulation became, with certain exceptions, effective on Mar. 13, 1987. § 2510.3–101(k).

[91]The Regulation does not apply to entities "in existence on March 13, 1987" *Id.*

[92]The test is whether, immediately after the most recent acquisition of an interest, 25% or more of the *value* of any class of equity interests in that entity is held by benefit plan investors. § 2510.3–101(f)(1). Accordingly, the Regulation creates an ongoing responsibility to patrol values whenever the interests of the partners shift *inter sese*. If the venture fund is publicly held, its assets will not be plan assets. § 2510.3–101(a)(2).

[93]§ 2510.3–101(d)(1)(i).

liquid investments do not count against the partnership.[94] A "venture capital investment" is an operating company in which the partnership enjoys "management rights," that is, "contractual rights directly between the investor and an operating company" to "substantially participate in" or "substantially influence" the management of the portfolio investment.[95] The rights must be specific to the fund in question; a fund cannot take advantage of the fact that the lead investor in a group has management rights.[96] This means that *each* venture fund will need a contractually provided board seat, or other equivalent rights, in each investment.[97]

A "fund of funds" (a venture fund that invests in other venture funds) cannot be a VCOC, since a venture partnership's investment as a limited partner in another venture partnership will not be a qualified investment for purposes of the 50% test.[98] Venture partnerships will be able to hold the stock in companies which have implemented their exit strategy (i.e., have merged or completed an IPO) and thereby extinguished the contractual board seat or other rights for 30 months after the exit strategy was implemented (or 10 years after initial investment, whichever is later).[99]

The practical effect of the Regulation will, it is forecast, be manageable; initially, funds with pension investors owing 25% or more of the interests will demand a board seat in every Stock Purchase Agreement, since that is the only specific example cited to date by the Labor Department as constituting "management rights."[100] Boards may grow too large as a consequence, in which case the company will be run by the executive committee. As this procedure proves awkward, either the Department of Labor will mention some additional specifics as constituting "management rights" (e.g., frequent inspections and reporting, plus observer rights at board meetings) and/or the law firms most active

[94]"Short term investments pending long-term commitment" or "distributions to investors" are excluded. § 2510.3–101(d)(i). Note 29 to the Regulation suggests "short term investments" include "commercial paper and similar investments" but that a portfolio of the same cannot be held indefinitely. Compare the definition in § 3(a)(3) of the Investment Company Act of 1940 ("government securities and cash items").

[95]§ 2510.3–101(d)(3)(ii).

[96]*The Final Regulation* § VI,B(2)(a).

[97]The only example cited in the preamble to the Regulation defining "management rights" mentions "a contractual right to appoint a member of the portfolio company's board." *Final Regulation* VI,B(1)(c). In such a situation, it is incumbent on the partnership actually to exercise the right, of these on one occasion or "not on a sporadic basis"—the Regulation is not clear. *Id.*

[98]*Ibid.* The "fund of funds" phenomenon will continue, it can be predicted, the managers eschewing the notion of a partnership and seizing the option of registering as investment advisers, qualifying under the recent loosening of the Investment Advisers Act of 1940. *See infra* § 20.25.

[99]§ 2510.3–101(d)(4).

[100]*See supra* n. 95.

in this area will begin, collectively, to opine favorably and the Department will stand by in silence.

The second class of investors deserving of special treatment are offshore entities. If the entity is not engaged in a "trade or business" in the United States, it is not subject to tax like a domestic entity;[101] moreover, there is no withholding on distributions of capital gains at the water's edge.[102] Glossing over a number of complexities, the Code provides that, for example, an Italian industrial company electing to invest in U.S. equities or fixed-income securities does not suffer a tax within the United States on gains from the sale or exchange of the securities it holds as long as the Italians are not engaged in a trade or business inside the United States. (Again, it must be kept in mind that the Code distinction between ordinary income and capital gains continues to operate post-1986 despite the elimination of the distinction in *levels* of U.S. tax.) And the rule is that passive investing in securities is not, of and by itself, tantamount to conducting a trade or business.[103]

Some tax practitioners are alarmed that an investment in a venture partnership might be deemed "engaging in a trade or business" even though it is clear that limited partnership interests are "securities" under U.S. law. The hitch is that the members of the venture partnership are deemed to be engaged in the business in which the partnership is engaged[104] and the managers of a venture partnership do not ordinarily describe themselves as passive investment advisers. Rather they trumpet their expertise in going beyond the selection of investments. Thus, the general partners are often on the boards of the portfolio companies and "add value," if all goes according to plan, by participating actively in decisions made by the management. (In fact, to avoid classification as a fiduciary under ERISA, the general partners of a venture fund with substantial pension investors must make sure the fund enjoys so-called "management rights" *vis-à-vis* one-half of its portfolio.)[105]

The concern that venture investing is significantly different from routine portfolio investing has prompted the establishment of so-called "clone funds"—that is, corporations established in tax-haven jurisdictions such as Bermuda or the Netherlands Antilles which make investments side by side with the onshore venture partnership. The notion is that the managers of the onshore fund, albeit the same individuals sharing in the profits interest of the clone fund, wear their active man-

[101]I.R.C. § 882 provides that foreign corporations engaged in a U.S. trade or business shall pay tax on income and gains effectively connected with that trade or business like U.S. corporations.

[102]*See* I.R.C. §§ 881(a), 1442(a).

[103]*See infra* n. 106.

[104]A limited partner which is a foreign corporation or a nonresident alien individual will be considered to be engaged in trade or business within the U.S. if the partnership is so engaged. I.R.C. § 875(1); Rev. Rul. 75–23, 1975–1 C.B. 290; *Donroy, Ltd. v. United States* 301 F.2d 200 (9th Cir. 1962).

[105]*See supra* n. 95.

agement hats only as partners in the onshore fund. That fashion has waned recently, however. Several prestigious law firms in the U.S. are now issuing opinions that investing in a venture partnership is not tantamount to establishment of a "trade or business" in the U.S.,[106] although other firms continue to entertain doubts. Serious problems can be expected to arise when and if offshore investors and ERISA entities invest in the same funds if the ERISA entities go over 25%; the "management rights" the fund must obtain in order to square itself with the Department of Labor may be anathema in the context of the "trade or business" analysis. The problem facing offshore entities is analogous to the issue confronting tax-exempt entities, discussed earlier;[107] under § 512(c) of the Code, a charity is also engaged in the business in which the partnership engages, meaning that activities of the partnership going beyond investing could in fact saddle the charity with taxable income.[108]

A final point on the trade or business subject: If counsel takes the position that the partnership is not engaged in a "trade or business," then losses of the partnership are deductible under § 212, rather than § 162 of the Code; the attractiveness of § 212 losses for individuals has been substantially lessened since § 67 of the Code imposes a 2% "floor." Itemized deductions, including deductions under § 212, are only deductible to the extent they exceed 2% of adjusted gross income.[109]

A second problem with offshore investors can arise if the venture partnership is deemed to have invested in a "United States real property holding corporation" under the Foreign Investment in Real Property Tax Act (FIRPTA)[110] The definition of "United States real property holding corporation" is any domestic corporation if the fair market value of its real estate in the United States exceeds 50% of the fair market

[106]The decision most often relied on is *Higgins v. Comm'r of Internal Revenue* 312 U.S. 212 (1941); in that case, the taxpayer had extensive investments in corporate stocks and securities. He devoted a considerable portion of his time to the management of his interests, hired a staff to assist him and used an office located in the U.S. for these management activities. His investments were of a long-term nature, although changes, redemptions, and maturities caused limited shifting in his portfolio. He did not participate directly or indirectly in the management of the corporations in which he invested. The Supreme Court concluded that, no matter how large an estate or how continuous or extensive the activities required to manage it, the management of securities investments, including keeping records, collecting income, and making investment decisions, does not constitute a trade or business as a matter of law. *See also Chang Hsiao Liang v. Comm'r of Internal Revenue* 23 T.C. 1040 (1955), *acq.*, 1955–1 C.B. 4.

[107]*See* § 20.21 *supra* and Ch. 18 § 18.7(e).

[108]*See Service Bolt & Nut Co. Profit Sharing Trust v. Comm'r* 53 AF TR 2d 84-526 (6th Cir. 1983). *See also* Ch. 18, § 18.7(e). The penalty for incurring "unrelated business taxable income" is the payment of a tax but some tax-exempt institutions are particularly hostile to the entire idea of filing income tax returns.

[109]"Trade or business" expenses are deducted as part of the calculation of adjusted gross income. I.R.C. § 62(a)(1).

[110]I.R.C. § 897 *et seq.*

value of its assets.[111] A nonresident limited partner is deemed to hold a proportionate share of the partnership assets, meaning that the offshore entity will be treated as a shareholder in the portfolio company and thus potentially hold a "United States real property interest." Pursuant to FIRPTA, gain or loss derived by a foreign corporation or a nonresident alien individual from the sale or other disposition of a U.S. real property interest is subject to tax as though effectively connected with the conduct of a trade or business within the U.S. even if, as a factual matter, the activities of such foreign corporation or alien individual do not amount to the conduct of a U.S. trade or business. The planning point is apparent: Venture funds with offshore partners should eschew investing in real estate or in entities which largely invest in real estate. The hidden difficulty is equally apparent: The 50% test can include many corporations inadvertently, firms which believe themselves to be in the widget business but which are over the line because, for example, of extensive investments in a plant.[112]

§20.25 AVOIDING REGISTRATION UNDER THE'40 ACTS

There are, as always in the law, traps for the unwary in organizing the venture pool. Most importantly, the organizers should seek to avoid the necessity of registering the fund under either of the 1940 Acts (the Investment Company Act or the Investment Advisers Act). Despite amendments to those acts in 1980 designed to alleviate the problems faced by venture capital partnerships,[113] it is clearly desirable not to have to register at all.

The exemption from the Investment Company Act most commonly availed of provides that an entity which would otherwise qualify as an investment company—and venture capital pools naturally qualify by reason of their activities—need not register if its securities are held by 100 or fewer persons (and the issuer "is not making and does not presently propose to make a public offering").[114] In most instances, the

[111]I.R.C. § 897(c)(2).

[112]Even if a U.S. corporation satisfies the 50% test, its stock is not considered to be a "U.S. real property interest" if (i) shares of that class of stock are regularly traded on an established securities market, and (ii) the selling shareholder owns 5% or less of that stock at all times during the five-year period before the date of sale or disposition. I.R.C. § 897(c)(3).

[113]For a discussion of the 1980 "business development company" amendments to the Investment Company and Investment Advisory Acts of 1940, *see* Halloran, *supra* n. 3, at 159 *et seq.; see supra* § 20.23(b).

[114]Investment Company Act of 1940, § 3(c)(1). It should be noted that the 100 "beneficial owner" test applies to all outstanding securities (other than short-term paper); thus, long-term promissory notes might be included, another reason to avoid leverage in a venture fund.

definition is relatively simple to apply: Count the number of limited and general partners, and, if the count comes up fewer than 100, the partnership is exempt. As the number creeps up toward 100, there are, to be sure, complicated attribution and aggregation questions revolving around the proper definition of the term "person." The Investment Company Act[115] now provides that one must look through the entity and count the number of partners or shareholders if and only if the entity purchases 10% or more of the "voting securities" in the investment entity *and* the investment represents more than 10% of the total assets of the purchasing entity. Since the rule purports to be objective—a "black letter" rule—it should be relatively easy to deal with. However, as legal philosophers like to testify, no exact rule is exact.[116]

For example, as a technical matter a limited partnership interest is not usually considered a "voting security" and, therefore, the "rule of 10" should not count limited partners. Not so fast! The SEC Staff has published no-action positions that make it imprudent to rely on the language of the Rule in this respect. If a limited partner otherwise qualifies under the 10/10 rule for "look through" treatment, the staff reserves the right to claim that the technicalities of the Uniform Limited Partnership Act will not preclude the possibility of a "look through" to the limited partner's members.[117]

Moreover, the more successful funds are now operating in a multiple mode—Smith Brown Associates I, Smith Brown Associates II, and so forth—and those managers must face the possibility that, in applying the "100 or fewer persons" test under the § 3(c)(1) exemption, the staff may (in defining who is the issuer) "integrate" legal entities; that is, the staff may treat separate limited partnerships as one "organized group of persons so that the members of all the partnerships will be counted together."[118]

The second issue, registration under the Investment Advisers Act, is conceptually much like the Investment Company Act problem. For years,

[115]Investment Company Act § 3(c)(1)(A).

[116]The classic example is a seemingly precise rule which states that no "vehicles" are allowed in Central Park. Does this mean bicycles, tricycles, pogo sticks, a little red wagon towed by a three-year-old child? It is important to keep in mind that the "rule of 100" in § 3(c)(1) applies by its terms to the holder of any security, voting or not.

[117]*See, e.g., C & S Investment Fund* (avail. July 18, 1977).

[118]*PBT Covered Option Fund* (avail. Feb. 17, 1979) ("an important question is whether [interests in the two partnerships] would be considered materially different by a reasonable investor qualified to purchase both.") *See also Oppenheimer Arbitrage Partners* (avail. Dec. 26, 1985). In *Oppenheimer* although both partnerships were engaged in risk arbitrage transactions, one was designed for tax-exempt ERISA plans; it used no leverage and engaged in no short sales, uncovered options or "classic" arbitrage. The other was designed for individuals; it used the maximum leverage possible, and engaged in short sales, uncovered options, classic arbitrage, futures contracts and repurchase agreements. The staff agreed that the two need not be integrated.

practitioners were concerned that venture partnerships constituted unregistered investment advisers because of the quite expansive definition in the Investment Advisers Act as to what activities so qualify.[119] The crutch on which counsel were accustomed to lean was, again, a "numbers" exemption, the exemption in the Act for investment advisers whose clients number 15 or fewer in any year.[120] When the first partnerships were organized, this language did not pose a problem in most cases, since the investing families were generally quite limited in number, generally fewer than 10. However, as the activity became more popular, the number of limited partners crowded the "14 or fewer" threshold. In some cases a single fund would take in more than 14 partners and in others the success of the first fund would give rise to others; fund number 2, fund number 3, and so forth, the first fund not entirely wound up at the time when the second, and perhaps the third, were commencing operations. Recognizing this problem, counsel took the view that the investment advisory "client" to be counted for purposes of the 14 or fewer limitation was the fund itself and not the limited partners in the fund. This gave the SEC staff problems because of the Commission's cultural imperative to the effect that entities organized for the purpose of doing something are to be disregarded as mere artifices.

The problem culminated in a celebrated opinion in the Court of Appeals for the Second Circuit in the *Abrahamson* case, the first version of which contained language supporting the SEC's view.[121] Since that position would effectively have strangled many of the big players in the venture capital industry in their cribs, the bar was able to prevail on the judges to withdraw their opinion on the point and substitute a footnote which expressly acknowledged the Court did not need to rule, and therefore was not ruling, on that specific issue. The Court of Appeals's reversal of its field was construed as a reprieve by the industry and business continued on the basis of that seemingly innocent language. Since that time, the Commission has readdressed an essentially absurd situation and issued a rule to the effect that the fund constitutes one advisee for purposes of the Investment Advisers Act.[122]

[119]An investment adviser is anyone who, for compensation, advises others "either directly or through publications or writings, as to the value of securities or as to the advisability of investing in . . . securities." Investment Advisers Act, § 202(a)(11). Some law firms have taken the view that the general partners are not advising "others" when they invest the partnership's funds since they themselves are a part of the partnership.

[120]Investment Advisers Act § 203(b)(3).

[121]*Abrahamson v. Fleschner* 568 F.2d 862 (2d. Cir. 1977), *cert. denied* 436 U.S. 913 (1978).

[122]Inv. Adv. Act Rule 275.203(b)(3)–1(a)(2). However, if the general partner advises the limited partners directly on their investments or counsels them on transferring their assets from one fund to another, such limited partners may be individually counted as clients. If the limited partners of a fund enjoy co-investment rights—"window" rights as they are called—the GPGP should be careful not to render independent investment advice to the investors on a particular security.

The Commission has, as well, lightened up by rule on the most troublesome problem for those venture funds thinking about registering under the Investment Advisers Act—the historic ban on performance-based compensation.[123] If a venture fund takes in investors in units of $500,000 or more (or the investor's net worth exceeds $1 million), the carried interest takes into account losses as well as gains (and/or unrealized depreciation if unrealized appreciation drives compensation) and certain disclosures are made, performance compensation is allowable.[124]

§20.26 RUMINATIONS ON A NEW MODEL

It is remarkable that the structure of a venture partnership has not changed remarkably since at least 1965, when the author worked on the first Greylock partnership. During that period, the world has seen all sorts of permutations and improvements in financial instruments—junior common stock, junk bonds, zero coupon bonds, variable-rate mortgages—all designed to make securities more palatable to potential purchasers. However, few have given any thought to anything but incremental drafting improvements in the organization of a venture partnership. Thus, we continue to see the time-honored limited partnership format, with investors represented at an evaluation committee meeting episodically, a 20% carried interest for the managers, a 2.5% management fee, a limited number of general partners, etc.

Many of the professionals in charge of capital pools have by now been in the game long enough, both as limited partners and direct investors, to feel themselves qualified to contribute to the screening process. Accordingly, the future may hold out changes in the traditional format. The author anticipates, for example, that, with confidence in their own abilities, the investors in future venture funds will insist on a limited right to "play or drop" on an investment-by-investment basis. The obvious objections will be dealt with in the instrument to avoid the uncertainties and delay currently inherent in one-shot financings—for example, the limiteds may be given a short fuse, "put up or shut up" in, say, 15 business days; any limited who drops on more than X number of occasions will be signaling its intention to drop out of the entire syndicate. Today's general partners may feel that is an onerous imposition, but the market is changing and sophisticated limiteds may no longer be content to invest passively; several of the large LBO funds are so organized today.

[123]Inv. Adv. Act, Rule 205(1).
[124]Inv. Adv. Act, Rule 205–3.

Further to this point, most of today's funds, either expressly in the instrument or by informal arrangement among the partners, are limited to investing in a particular mode; that is, one fund will be a seed or preseed fund, another a conventional venture fund, a third specializing in mezzanine financings, a fourth in LBOs, and so forth. The author expects new funds will be devised, borrowing some of the attractive wrinkles currently being marketed in the investment community—that is, the grouping under one umbrella of a variety of different investment universes—equities, fixed income, tax-free bonds, mortgage-backed securities, and so forth, each subpool being managed by a professional or professionals particularly experienced in that mode of investment. The investor can shift money around among the various subpools on a periodic basis, depending on its views of overall market conditions.[125] Measured against this standard, current venture partnerships are overly rigid. If someone wants an array of investment opportunities in the early-stage arena, under current conditions he has to invest in a gaggle of unrelated funds. Venture partnership organized on the new principles might offer several separate subpools or pockets of investments—seed, conventional, mezzanine, LBOs, turnarounds and public securities, with a limited right to transfer from one pocket to another prior to the time commitments are made. (The privilege of reallocation in midstream will be, to be sure, only sparingly granted.) If a particularly attractive prospect, (say, an LBO) were to crop up in one pocket, the pension manager in charge will hear about it and have the chance to play, the whole system emphasizing flexibility, within limitations, to move money around, depending on where the most attractive opportunities are occurring at the time—to fish where the fish are biting, in other words.

Further, a venture fund may elect to pursue the "managing the managers" approach, a relatively recent phenomenon on the investment landscape. Under that system, the investor partnership is split into pools; the senior professionals in charge of the partnership have the right and obligation to change managers in a given subpool in the event performance is substandard. This could be facilitated in the venture environment by tying the upside potential for individual managers to the portfolio opportunities they select, making them actual employees as well as directors of the portfolio companies and rewarding them with equity partnerships at that level. They might all have a small piece of the "carry" enjoyed by the umbrella partnership but the vesting and recapture provisions surrounding their rights could be so structured that termination is a realistic possibility. They would sink or swim, in other words, largely on their own performance. If their investments turned sour, they could follow the investment out the door. The investors would, thus, have a way to change horses without having to go through the clumsy process of attempting to withdraw their capital from the fund as a whole.

[125]*But see* the impact of Rule 203(b)(3), discussed *supra* n. 122.

Table of References

Title	Section
Aaron, *Bankruptcy Law Fundamentals* § 10.01 (1986).	19.2
Acquisitions and Mergers 1986: Tactics, Techniques and Recent Developments (P.L.I. Course Handbook, Series No. 529, 1986)	13.7
"Adding Pounds," *Inc.* (Mar. 1985), 140	6.15
AICPA Interpretations of APB Opinion 18	18.5
AIN–APB Opinion No. 15 ¶ 26	13.5
AIN–APB Opinion No. 15	13.3, 13.5
AIN–APB Opinion No. 15 ¶ 51	11.2, 13.3
ALI–ABA *Corporate Tax Planning in the '80's*, 26, 33 (1986)	5.1(b)
Alma Securities Corporation, SEC No-action Letter (Aug. 2, 1982) (Fed. Sec. Library, No-act file)	7.4(b)
American Stock Exchange Company Guide Part 4, §§ 401–405	14.2
Anderson "Pushing Ivory-Tower Scientists into the High-Tech Race," *N.Y. Times* Feb. 15, 1987, F–6	6.3
Andrews, *Creative Product Development: A Marketing Approach to New Product Innovation and Revitalisation* (1975)	2.2(b)
Andrews, "How Much for a Security Blanket?" *Venture* (Feb. 1986) 49	6.4
Andrews, "The Siren Song of Vancouver," *Venture* (July 1987) 35.	6.15

Financing and Operating the Successful Business (1986 ed.)

Reference	Section
Baird & Jackson, "Fraudulent Conveyance Law and Its Proper Domain" 38 *Vand. L. Rev.* 829 (May 1985)	19.4
1 Balotti & Finkelstein, *The Delaware Law of Corporations and Business Organizations* § 6.10 (1986)	4.9, 4.17
Banoff, "Conversions of Services Into Property Interests: Choice of Form of Business," 61 *Taxes* 844 (Dec. 1983)	5.1(b), 5.1(c), 5.2
Bartell, "Merit Regulation and Clearing Strategy," Goldwasser & Maken, *State Regulation of Capital Formation and Securities Transactions* 315 (1983 ed.)	14.9
Bartlett, *The Law Business: A Tired Monopoly* 138 (1982)	9.2(a), 19.8
Bartlett, "Legal Issues in Late Round Financing," *Venture Capital After the Tax Reform Act of 1986* (P.L.I. Course Handbook Series No. 422, 1987)	14.6
Bartlett & Dowd, "Section 17 of the Investment Company Act—An Example of Regulation by Exemption," 8 *Del. J. Corp. Law.* 449 (1983)	20.23(B)
Bartlett & Lapatin, "The Status of a Creditor as a Controlling Person" 28 *Mercer L. Rev.* 639 (1977)	9.2(a)
Bartlett & Siena, "Research and Development Limited Partnerships As a Device To Exploit University Owned Technology," 10 *J. of College & U.L.* 435 (1983–84)	18.7(b)
Basile, "The 1985 Delaware Revised Uniform Limited Partnership Act," 41 *Bus. Law.* 571, 573 (Feb. 1986)	3.6, 3.6(d), 20.4
"Basis Rules of General Application," I.R.C. §§ 1011–1 24	5.1

Wealth," 12 *J. of Fin. Economics* 289, 295 (1983)	
Bigelow & Nycum, *Your Computer and the Law,* 118 (1976)	17.2(a), 17.2(c)
Bigler, *Venture Capital: A Perspective* (1983)	1.1, 1.2
5 *Biotech. L. Rep.* 322, 323 (Oct.–Nov. 1986)	15.4
Bishop, *The Law of Corporate Officers and Directors—Indemnification and Insurance* (1981)	4.13
Bittker & Eustice, *Federal Income Taxation of Corporations and Shareholders,* ¶ 3.17 (4th ed. 1979)	5.1(b)
Black, "R & D Credit Revised by '86 Act But in Restricted Fashion," 66 *J. of Tax'n* 1, 12 (Jan. 1987)	5.5
Blackman, *The Valuation of Privately-Held Businesses* (1986)	12.2
Block & Barton, "Securities Litigation: Contribution and Indemnification Under the Federal Securities Laws," 11 *Sec. Reg. L. J.* 351 (Winter 1984)	4.13
Block, Barton & Garfield, "Affirmative Duty to Disclose Material Information Concerning Issuer's Financial Condition and Business Plans," 40 *Bus. Law.* 1243 (1985)	14.2
Block, Barton, & Radin, "Indemnification And Insurance of Corporate Officials," 13 *Sec. Reg. L. J.* 239 (Fall 1985)	4.13
Block, Barton, & Radin, "The Business Judgment Rule: Application, Limitations and the Burden of Proof," *Directors and Officers Liability 1986: A Review of The Business Judgment Rule* (P.L.I. Course Handbook Series No. 525, 1986)	4.13
Bloomenthal, *Securities Law Handbook* § 6.10 (1986–87 ed.)	14.3, 14.7
Bloomenthal, Harvey & Wing, *1985 Going Public Handbook: Going*	6.16, 8.6, 14.5, 14.7, 14.10

Public, the Integrated Disclosure System and Exempt Financing § 313; 3–17 (1985)	
Blue Sky Laws: State Regulation of Securities (P.L.I. Course Handbook Series No. 534, 1986)	14.9(a)
The Bond Buyer, (Mar. 26, 1987), 279	6.14
Booth, "Management Buyouts, Shareholder Welfare, and the Limits of Fiduciary Duty," 60 *N.Y.U.L. Rev.* 630 (1985)	19.2
Bowers, "Debt-Equity Classification: Where Are We Now," ALI–ABA and ABA Section of Taxation, *Corporate Tax Planning in the 80's* 139–200 (1986)	13.8
Bramson, "Intellectual Property as Collateral—Patents, Trade Secrets, Trademarks and Copyrights," 36 *Bus. Law.* 1566, 1567, 1595 (1981)	16.1, 16.4
Brandt, *Entrepreneuring: The 10 Commandments for Building A Growth Company* (1982)	2.3
Brock & Evans, *The Economics of Small Businesses: Their Role and Regulation in the U.S. Economy,* (1986)	1.5
Brown, *Franchising: Realities and Remedies* (rev. ed. 1982)	1.3(b)
Brown & Davis, "Indemnification of Directors and Officers and Limitations on Director Liability," 18 *Annual Inst. on Sec. Reg.* Vol. 2, 117, 139 (P.L.I. Course Handbook Series No. 544, 1986)	4.13
Brudney & Chirelstein, *Corporate Finance: Cases and Materials,* (3d ed. 1987)	12.1, 12.2, 12.3
Brunsvold, *1981 Licensing Law Handbook* § 3.02 (1981)	15.1(b)
Bryer & DeRose, "Representing a Public Company in a Leveraged Buyout Transaction: An Update," *Leveraged Acquisitions and Buyouts* 188-89 (P.L.I. Course Handbook Series No. 510, 1986)	19.1

Reference	Section
Capital," 25 *Bus. Law.* 1001 (Apr. 1970)	
Chandler, "Proprietary Protection for Computer Software, 11 *U. Balt. L. Rev.* 195 (1982)	16.3, 16.4, 16.4(a)
Chapot, "Limitations on Sources of Passive Income Against Which Passive Losses Will Be Deductible," 6 *Tax Management Weekly Report* 574, 578 (1987)	3.7
Chase, Shields, Lambert, Baker & Shillito, *Small Business Financing: Federal Assistance & Contracts* (1983)	6.1, 6.5, 20.23(a)
Cheek, "Professional Responsibility and Self-Regulation of the Securities Lawyer" 2 *Wash. & Lee L. Rev.* 597 (1975)	14.7
Chisum, "The Patentability of Algorithms," 47 *U. Pa. L. Rev.* 959 (1986)	16.2(a)
Clarke, "The Fiduciary Obligations of Lenders in Leveraged Buyouts," 54 *Miss. L. J.* 423 (1984)	19.9
Cloven Financial Corp. [1977 Transfer Binder], (CCH) *Fed. Sec. L. Rep.* ¶ 82,091 (Apr. 5, 1979)	7.12
"Clubs With Capital Ideas: They're Good Places to Meet People Who Might Invest in Your Business," *Changing Times* (Jan. 1986) 77	6.13
Cohen & Reddick, *Successful Marketing for Small Business* (1981)	2.2(b)
Cohen & Shapiro, "Types of Securities," Harroch, *Start-Up Companies: Planning, Financing and Operating the Successful Business* § 8.02 [4] n. 22 (1986)	13.4
2 *Collier Bankruptcy Manual* § 547.10 (1987)	19.6
4 *Collier on Bankruptcy* Ch. 547 (15th ed. 1979).	19.6
Colorado Life Ins. Co. SEC No-action Letter (Feb. 2, 1977), [1977] (CCH) Fed. Sec. Microfiche 14, frame J14	7.1
Comment, "Golden Parachutes: A Perk That Boards Should Scrutinize	8.8

and Terminating Subchapter S Corporations Ch. 2 (rev. ed. 1980)	
C & S Investment Fund, SEC No-action Letter (avail. July 18, 1977)	20.25
Culliton, "Biomedical Research Enters the Marketplace," 304 *New Eng. J. Med.* 119 (May 1981)	15.11, 18.7(b)
Dauchy & Harmon, "Structuring Venture Capital Limited Partnerships," 3 *Computer Lawyer* 1 (1986)	20.7, 20.12
Davidson, "Venture Capital and Trade Secrets: A Tale of Two Situations," 1 *Trade Secret L. Rep.* 50 (July 1985)	16.9
Davidson & Davidson, *Advanced Legal Strategies for Buying and Selling Computers and Software* § 1.3 § 2.1(a), § 2.2(a)(1); § 2.2(d)(1); § 3.3(b)(2); § 3.3(c)(4); § 3.39(b)(1); § 6.7(a); § 8.1(a)(2); § 8.1(d)(3); § 8.1(d)(5); § 8.1(e); § 8.2(b); § 8.2(c); § 8.2(d)(4)(ii); § 8.2(d)(4)(iii); § 8.4(c) (1986)	15.1(b), 15.2(c), 15.2(d), 15.3, 15.8, 15.15, 15.16, 16.1, 16.4(a), 16.5, 16.8(a), 17.2(a), 17.2(c), 17.5
Davis, "Costly Bugs: As Complexity Rises, Tiny Flaws in Software Pose a Growing Threat," *Wall St. J.* Jan. 28, 1987, 1, col. 6	17.3
Davis, *Emerging Theories of Lender Liability* (Chairman, ABA Div. of Prof. Educ. 1985)	9.2a, 19.3
Deaktor, "Integration of Securities Offerings," 31 *U. Fla. L. Rev.* 465 (1979)	7.12
4 *Deller's Walker on Patents* 507 (1965 ed. & Supp. 1985)	16.8(a)
Deloitte, Haskins & Sells *Tax Aspects of High Technology Operations* 100 (1985)	3.7, 5.4
DeNatale & Abram "The Doctrine of Equitable Subordination as Applied to Nonmanagement Creditors," 40 *Bus. Law.* 417 (1985)	19.8
Desmond & Kelley, *Business Valuation Handbook* (1977)	12.2, 12.4

Reference	Section
American Bar Association, "Section 4(2) and Statutory Law," 31 *Bus. Law.* 485 (Nov. 1975)	
Federal Reserve Board Release § 5–740 (Mar. 1972) (interpreting § 220.13 of Regulation T)	7.9, 20.4
Fern, "The Overbroad Scope of Franchise Regulations: A Definitional Dilemma," 34 *Bus. Law.* 1387 (1979)	1.3(b), 15.1(a)
Ferrara & Sanger, "Derivative Liability in Securities Law: Controlling Person Liability, Respondeat Superior, and Aiding and Abetting," 40 *Wash. & Lee L. Rev.* 1007 (1983)	14.7
15th Annual Institute on Securities Regulation (P.L.I. Course Handbook Series No. 428, 1983)	7.2
2 *Fifteenth Ann. Institute on Securities Regulation* (P.L.I. Course Handbook Series No. 343, 1983)	19.15
The Final Regulation § VI, B(1)(c), B(2)(a) (Dept. of Labor Interp. Bull., 51 Fed. Reg. 41262, Nov. 13, 1986)	20.24
Financial Independence Investment Corporation, SEC No-action Letter (Oct. 30, 1985)	7.12
"Financing a Franchise," *Inc.* 89, 92 (April 1987)	6.5
Finnegan & D'Andrea, "The Black Box Problem: Using Pre-Negotiation Secrecy Agreements to Govern Disclosure of Technology to Potential Licensees," Finnegan (ed.), *1979 Licensing Law Handbook* Ch. 7 (1979)	15.5
Fisher & Ury, *Getting to Yes: Negotiating Agreements Without Giving In* (1981)	9.3(a)
FitzGibbon & Glazer "Legal Opinions on Incorporation, Good Standing, and Qualification To Do Business," 41 *Bus. Law.* 461 (1986)	10.1(f)
Folk, "Civil Liabilities under the Federal Securities Acts: The BarChris Case," 55 *Va. L. Rev.* 199 (1969)	14.7

Fourth Annual Structuring Partnership Agreements (Halloran & Nathan Chm 1987) 20.1

Foster, *Innovations: The Attacker's Advantage* (1986) 18.1

Franklin, "Missappropriated Law, Copyright Law and Product Compatibility," 4 *Computer Lawyer* 8 (1987) 16.4(a)

Freidrich, "The Unincorporation of America?", 64 *J. Tax'n* 3, 4 (1987) 3.7

Frome & Max, *Raising Capital: Private Placement Forms and Techniques* 673 (1981) 9.3

Fuld, "Lawyers' Standards and Responsibilities in Rendering Opinions," 33 *Bus. Law.* 1295 (1978) 10.1(f)

Fuld, "Legal Opinions in Business Transactions—An Attempt to Bring Some Order out of Some Chaos," 28 *Bus. Law.* 915 (1973) 10.1(f)

Future Of Small Business in America, Part 1, "Hearings Before the Subcommittee on Antitrust, Consumers and Employment of the Committee on Small Business, House of Representatives," Washington 1978 1.5

Gadsby, "The Securities and Exchange Commission and the Financing of Small Businesses," 14 *Bus. Law.* 144 (Nov. 1958) 7.14

Garn, *The Role of Small Business Enterprise in Economic Development* (1981) 1.5

Garrett, "Venture Capital Financing Under the Securities Law," address to National Venture Capital Association, *SEC News* 12 (June 3, 1975) 14.7

General Explanation of the Tax Reform Act of 1986 (CCH) at 2288–327 19.13(a)

Gerald Gerstenfeld, No-action Letter from SEC (Dec. 3, 1985), Wash. Serv. Bur. Microfiche, fiche 976, frame F11 7.4(b), 7.4(c), 8.2

Factor," 11 *Valuation Journal* 4 (1987)	
Goodkind, "Blue Sky Law: Is There Merit in the Merit Requirements?" 1976 *Wisc. L. Rev.* 79	14.9
Gordon, *Computer Software: Contracting for Development and Distribution* 504 (1986)	17.1
Grayson, "The Use of Statistical Techniques in Capital Budgeting," Brudney & Chirelstein, *Corporate Finance: Cases and Materials,* at 52 (3d ed. 1987)	12.3
"Growing Companies: Tax and Business Planning for the '80s, *"ALI–ABA Course of Study* (cosponsored by Mass. CLE, 1984)	3.7
Gumpert, *Growing Concerns: Building and Managing the Smaller Business* 3 (1984)	1.5
Haft, *Venture Capital and Small Business Financings* § 6.04[8]; § 704[2]; § 704[5]; § 704[8] (1987 ed.)	6.1, 6.6, 14.7, 14.9(a)
Hagin, *Modern Portfolio Theory* (1979)	12.3(a)
Halloran, "Investment Company Act and Investment Advisors Act: Considerations for Private and Public Venture Capital Funds—The Small Business Investment Incentive Act of 1980," Halloran, Benton & Lovejoy, *Venture Capital and Public Offering Negotiation* 159 (1984)	1.2, 1.4
Halloran, "Problems of High Tech Offerings," *Blue Sky Laws: State Regulation of Securities 1986* 511, 518 (P.L.I. Course Handbook Series No. 473, 1985)	14.9, 14.9(a)
Halloran, Benton & Lovejoy, *Venture Capital and Public Offering Negotiation* (1984)	1.2, 6.10, 7.9, 10,1, 10.1(e), 10.3(e), 14.5, 20.1, 20.3, 20.6, 20.12, 20.18, 20.20, 20.23(b), 20.25

Reference	Section
Halperin, *Private Placement of Securities* 67 (1984)	7.1, 8.1(a), 8.2, 8.3, 8.6, 8.7, 8.8
Hansen, *Marketing: Text and Cases* (4th ed. 1977)	2.2(b)
Harroch, *Start-Up Companies: Planning, Financing and Operating the Successful Business* (1986)	1.4, 3.2, 7.9, 7.10(b), 7.10(c), 7.12, 8.1(a), 8.2, 8.3, 8.5, 8.6, 8.7, 8.8, 10.1, 10.1(e), 11.7, 13.4, 15.6, 15.8, 15.11, 15.15, 15.16, 16.1, 16.2(a),
Haslett & Smollen, "Preparing A Business Plan," *Pratt's Guide to Venture Capital Sources* (11th ed. 1986)	2.1, Appendix Ch.2
Haudek, "The Settlement and Dismissal of Stockholders' Action—Part II: The Settlement," 23 *SW L. J.* 765 (1969)	4.13
Haynes & Durant, "Patents and Copyrights in Computer Software Based Technology: Why Bother With Patents?" 4 *Computer Lawyer* 14 (Feb. 1987)	16.4(a)
Haynsworth, *Organizing a Small Business Entity* § 3.02(d); § 5.04(b)(2); § 5.05(d)(7); § 5.05(d)(4); (1986)	3.2, 4.4, 4.8, 4.9
Haynsworth, *Organizing a Closely Held Corporation* § 5.02(c)(3); § 5.02(g), § 5.03(b)(3) (1986)	10.2, 10.2(a)
Haynsworth, *Selecting the Form of a Small Business Entity* § 1.05(b) (1985)	3.5
Heilbroner, *The Nature and Logic of Capitalism* 38 (1985)	15.1(a)
Hellerstein, *State and Local Taxation* (4th ed. 1978)	4.17
Hellman, Ferri Investment Associates, SEC No-action Letter (avail. Nov. 16, 1981)	14.11
Hellman & Hoffman, "What to Look for in a Stock Prospectus," 72 *Am. Bar Assoc. J.* 96 (April 1986)	14.5

Henn & Alexander, *Law of Corporations* § 49, § 130; 625–62 (3d ed. 1983)	3.5, 3.6, 4.8, 20.18
Hensley, "The Development of a Revised Uniform Securities Act." 40 *Bus. Law.* 721 (1985)	14.9
Hensley & Rothwell, "Regulation T and Public Offerings of Limited Partnerships: Time for a Change," 39 *Bus. Law.* 543 (Feb. 1984)	20.4
Heskoff, *Marketing* (1976)	2.2(b)
Hicks, *Exempted Transactions Under The Securities Act* §§ 11.02(1), 11.06(3) (1983)	7.1
Hicks, *Limited Offering Exemptions: Regulation D,* (1983 and 1985 ed.)	7.2, 7.6, 7.8, 8.6, 14.12
Hoffman, *The Software Legal Book* (1985)	15.2(c)
Holbrist, *Pension Reform Handbook* ¶ 181 (1984)	7.11
Holtz, *2001 Sources of Financing for Small Business* (1983)	6.1
Honig, "Massachusetts Securities Regulation: An Evolving Matrix," 27 *Boston Bar J.* 10 (Nov. 1983)	7.10(c)
Honig, "Massachusetts Securities Regulation: In Search of the Fulcrum," 13 *U. Balt. L. Rev.* 469 (1984)	7.10(c), 14.9
H. Rep. 97–760, 97th Cong., 2d Sess. 475 (1982)	11.3(b)
H.R. Conf. Rep. No. 99–841, 99th Cong., 2d Sess. (1986)	5.5
H.R. Rep. No. 152, 73d. Cong., 1st Sess. (1933)	7.1
Hubbard & Hawkins, *Theory of Valuation* at 54–44 (1969)	12.2, 12.3(a), 12.4
Hubbard & Shelton, *Protection of Computer Systems and Software* 148 (1986)	17.4
"The Impact of Federal Reserve Margin Regulations on Acquisition Financing," 35 *Bus. Law.* 517 (1980)	19.12
Innovation Revisited, "Hearing Before the Committee on Small Business House of Representatives," Washington (1982)	1.5

Aggregate or an Entity?", 16 *Vand. L. Rev.* 377 (1963)
"The Job Generation Process," Cambridge, MA:MIT program on Neighborhood and Regional Change, 1979 — 1.5
Johnston, "Corporate Indemnification and Liability Insurance For Directors and Officers," 33 *Bus. Law.* 1973, 1998–99 (Apr. 1978) — 4.13
Joint Economic Committee, Congress of the U.S. "The Role of Small Business Enterprise in Economic Development," May 14, 1981 — 1.5
Jones & Hund, "Filing SEC Registration Statements: A View from the Inside," 157–158 *J. Acct.* 92 (Dec. 1984) — 14.5
Jordan, "The Close Corporation Provisions of the New California General Corporation Law," 23 *U.C.L.A. L. Rev.* 1094 (1976) — 4.7

Kaplan, "Fiduciary Responsibility in the Management of the Corporation," 31 *Bus. Law.* 883, 907 (Feb. 1976) — 10.2
Kertz, "Tax Exempt Organizations and Commercially Sponsored Scientific Research," 9 *J. Coll. & U.L.* 69 (1982–83) — 18.7(g)
Kidder, *The Soul of a New Machine* (1981) — 10.3(m)
Kiley, "Biotechnology: Evolution of a New Venture and its Licensing Strategy," *Recent Developments Licensing* at 120 — 15.4
Kimpel, "Compensation Planning for 'High Tech' Executives," *Tax Planning for High Tech and New Ventures* 67 (70th Forum Fed. Tax Instit. of New Eng., 1984) — 11.3(a), 11.3(b), 13.2(a)
Kirn, "The Use of Common Law Bailments in Connection with The Licensing of Living Organisms," *Technology Licensing* 291, 294 (P.L.I. — 15.4

LaPaglia, "Basic Considerations in Licensing from the Business Perspective," *Technology Licensing* 99 (P.L.I. Course Handbook Series No. 235, 1987)	15.6
Larson, "The Best Laid Plans," *Inc.* (Feb. 1987) 27, 60, 64	2.9
Laser Fax Inc., SEC No-action Letter (Sept. 16, 1985)	7.12, 7.13
Lederman, Citron & Macris, "Leveraged Buyouts: An Update," 2 *Fifteenth Annual Institute on Securities Regulation* 281 (P.L.I. Course Handbook Series No. 393, 1983)	19.15
Leegstra & McArthur, "State Tax Considerations in Structuring a Business Venture as a Joint Venture/Partnership, C Corporation or S Corporation," 2 *N.Y.U. Inst. on St. & Loc. Tax'n. & Conf. on Prop. Tax'n.* Ch. 13 (1984)	3.2
Legler, Frank & Hoy, *Building a Comprehensive Data Base on the Role of Small Business in the U.S. Economy, and Its Policy Implication Questions*	1.5
Leveraged Acquisitions and Buyouts (P.L.I. Course Handbook Series No. 549, 1987)	19.13(a), 19.13(b), 19.13(c)
Leveraged Buyouts (P.L.I. Course Handbook Series No. 393, 1983).	19.5
Levine, "A Challenge to Massachusetts Merit Regulation of Securities: An Empirical Analysis," 31 *Bost. B. J.* 26 (Jan./Feb. 1987)	7.9
Lewis, *Taking a Private Company Public* 7; 10; 64; 78; 81; 82 (1984)	14.2, 14.5, 14.9(a)
Liebolt, "State Securities Registration Requirements: Forms, Procedures, Requirements," *Blue Sky Laws* 307 (P.L.I. Course Handbook Series No. 534, 1986)	14.9(a)
"Life After Industrial Revenue Bonds," *Venture* (Feb. 1987) 71	6.14
Lindsey, *The Entrepreneur's Guide to*	6.1, 6.16

Lundgren, "Liability of a Creditor in a Control Relationship with Its Debtor," 67 *Marq. L. Rev.* 523 (1984)	19.10
McCarthy, *Trademarks and Unfair Competition* (1985)	15.5
McCarthy & Healy, "Valuation for Dissenting Shareholders" in *Valuing a Company* 403 (1971)	12.2
McCarthy & Healy, "Valuation in Regulated Industries," in *Valuing a Company* 421 (1971)	12.2, 12.4
McCoid, "Bankruptcy, Preferences and Efficiency: An Expression of Doubt," 67 *Va. L. Rev.* 249 (1981)	19.6
McCune & Kirk, "Leveraged Buyouts by Management," 16 *Rev. of Sec. Reg.* 769 (1983)	19.10
McDermott, "The Private Offering Exemption," 59 *Iowa L. Rev.* 525 (1974)	7.15
MacEwan, "Blue Sky Offerings of Reg. D Offerings," 18 *Sec. & Commodity Reg.* 103 (1985)	7.9, 7.10(c)
Macey, "Preferences and Fraudulent Transfers under the Bankruptcy Reform Act of 1978," 28 *Emory L. J.* 685 (1979)	19.4
McGarity & Bayer, "Federal Regulation of Emerging Genetic Technologies," 36 *Vanderbilt L. Rev.* 461 (Apr. 1983)	15.4
McKee, Nelson, & Whitmire, *Drafting, Amending, and Analyzing Partnership Agreements Under the New Partnership Allocation Regulations* § 3.02[1] (1986)	20.5
McKee, Nelson, & Whitmire, *Federal Taxation of Partnerships and Partners* 3–66 (1977)	20.6
McKeever, *Start Up Money: How to Finance Your New Small Business* (1984)	6.1
Magaziner & Reich, *The Next American Frontier* 140 (1983)	14.2
Main, "Business Goes to College for a	18.7

Brain Gain," *Fortune* 80 (Mar. 16, 1987)

Makens, "Who Speaks for the Investor?: An Evaluation of the Assault on Merit Regulation," 13 *U. Balt. L. Rev.* 435 (1984) — 14.9

Makens & Halloran, "State Regulation of Public Offerings," *Private and Small Business Offerings* (P.L.I. Course Handbook Series No. 386, 1982) — 14.9(a)

Mancuso, *How to Prepare and Present a Business Plan* (1983) — 2.1

Mancuso, *How to Write a Winning Business Plan* (1985) — 2.1, 2.9

Mandelstam, "How Long Must I Hold?", 25 *U. Miami L. Rev.* 173 (1970) — 14.11

Manegold, Arnold, & Diamond, "SEC Form S–18: A Boon to Small Business: Practice Expansion Opportunities in Helping Small Businesses Go Public," 161 *J. Acct.* 102 (May 1986) — 14.3

Manning, *Legal Capital* 16–22 (1981) — 4.4

Manning, "Reflections and Practical Tips on Life in the Boardroom After Van Gorkom," 41 *Bus. Law.* 1 (Nov. 1985) — 4.13

Marcellino & Kenfield, "Due Diligence as a Two-Edged Sword: Potential Liability of Venture Capitalists Funding High-Tech Start-Ups," 2 *Computer & High Technology L.J.* 41, 49 (1986) — 16.5, 16.8(a), 16.9

Martin, "Raising Capital for a Closely Held Company," 43 *N.Y.U. Inst. Fed. Tax'n* § 8.06 [2](b); § 807[3](a) (1985) — 5.1(d), 5.2, 11.6

Martin, *Financing the Growing Business* (1980) — 6.1

Martin & Gustafson, *Valuing Your Business* (1980) — 12.2

Martin & Sylvester, "Key Issues in Negotiating the Venture Capital Contract," *Private Placements, 1986: Current Development in Private Financings* 199,205 (P.L.I. Course Handbook Series No. 522, 1986) — 10.1, 10.1(e)

Reference	Section
Miller, *Comprehensive GAAP Guide* 39.01–.20 (1987)	11.2
Miller, "Small Business Investment Companies: Licensing, Tax and Securities Considerations," 36 *Bus. Law.* 1684, 1979 (1981)	6.6, 20.23(a)
Miller & Davis, *Intellectual Property: Patents, Trademarks and Copyright* § 1.1; § 1.2; § 13; § 62; § 73; § 98; § 126; § 127–128; § 143; § 289; § 318; § 368; § 385; § 386; § 390 (1983)	4.3, 15.1(a), 15.4, 5.15, 15.16, 16.1, 16.2, 16.2(a), 16.4, 16.6, 16.8(a), 16.9
Mills, "Mathematics of Cumulative Voting," 1968 *Duke L.J.* 28	4.11
Mislow, "Necessity May Be the Mother of Invention, But Who Gets Custody? The Ownership of Intellectual Property Created By An Employed Inventor," 1 *Santa Clara Computer & High Technology L. J.* 59, 62 (1985)	16.8(a), 16.9
Monroe, "Master Limited Partnerships Are Defying Death Notices," *Wall St. J.*, Mar. 30, 1987, 6	3.6(a)
Moore & Susman, "The Semiconductor Chip Protection Act," 1 *Computer Lawyer* 11 (Dec. 1984)	17.1
Morris, "The Pricing of a Venture Capital Investment," in *Pratt's Guide to Venture Capital Sources* 55 (11th ed. 1986)	2.10(a), 12.3
Mullaney & Blau, "An Analytic Comparison of Partnerships and S Corporations as Vehicles for Leveraged Investments," 59 *J. of Tax'n* 142 (1983)	3.2
Munter & Ratcliffe, *Applying GAAP and GAAS* § 10.12[4][b] (1987)	14.4
Murray & Langley, "Taxing Matters: Relatively New Form of Business Structure Is Causing Controversy," *Wall St. J.*, June 30, 1987, 1, col. 6	3.6(a), 3.6(d)
Nad, "Dispositions of Partnership Interests and Partnership Property," 43 *N.Y.U. Ann. Inst. on Federal Taxation* § 29[12] (1985)	20.20

Reference	Sections
Nusbaum & Weltman, "Employment Agreements," Harroch, *Start-Up Companies: Planning, Financing and Operating the Successful Business* § 11.02[7]; § 11.02[8]; § 20.02 (1986)	10.3(c), 10.3(d), 10.3(j), 10.3(m)(i), 10.3(m)(ii)
Nussbaum, Hyde, & Chrystal, "Federal Security Law Considerations," *Acquisitions and Mergers 1986: Tactics, Techniques and Recent Developments* 409 (P.L.I. Course Handbook No. 529, 1986)	13.7
Nycum, "Torts and Crime," *Computers & The Law* 226 (3d ed. 1981)	17.4
Office of Science and Technology, "Coordinated Framework for Regulation and Biotechnology," 51 Fed. Reg. 23302 (No.123)	
O'Flaherty, *Going Public: The Entrepreneur's Guide* (1984)	14.1, 14.2(a)
Olson "Learning the Dangers of Success: The Education, of an Entrepreneur," *N.Y. Times*, July 19, 1987, 2	2.10(a)
O'Neal, "Close Corporation Legislation: A Survey and an Evaluation," 1972 *Duke L.J.* 867	4.7
O'Neal, *Close Corporations* § 3.60; §§ 6.06–08, (1986)	4.1, 4.8, 10.3(c)
O'Neal, "Restrictions on Transfer of Stock in Closely Held Corporations: Planning and Drafting," 65 *Harv. L. Rev.* 773, 778 (1952)	9.6(c)
O'Neal's Oppression of Minority Shareholders (2d. ed.), § 7.14 (1975)	3.7, 10.2, 10.3(c)
101-4th T.M. Corporations—Pre-Organization Planning (1984)	5.1(b), 5.3(a)
Oppenheimer Arbitrage Partners, SEC No-action Letter (avail. Dec. 26, 1985)	20.25
Organizing the Partnership Venture, (Mellman & Oswald ed.) 1978	20.1
Orlanski, "SEC Comments on the Offering Prospectus," 17 *Rev. of Sec. Reg.* 887 (June 1984)	14.5
Osgood, "The Law of Pensions and Profit-Sharing," § 2.25 (1984)	7.11

Ovens & Beach, *Business and Securities Valuation* (1972) 12.2

Pacific Physician Services, Inc. SEC No-action Letter (Aug. 20, 1985) 7.12

Painter, *Business Planning: Cases and Materials* 122 (2d ed. 1984) 5.1(b)

Painter, *Corporate and Tax Aspects of Closely Held Corporations* §§ 1–1.5 (2d ed. 1981) 3.6

Palm, "Registration Statement Preparation and Related Matters," *Mechanics of Underwriting* 85, 130 (P.L.I. Course Handbook Series No. 547, 1987) 9.3, 14.5

Pappons, "The Software Escrow: The Court Favorite and Bankruptcy Law," *1 Santa Clara Comput. & High Tech. L.J.* 309 (1985) 15.2(c)

Patton, "The Private Offering: A Simplified Analysis of the Initial Placement," 27 *Bus. Law.* 1089 (1972) 7.15

PBT Covered Option Fund (avail. Nov. 2, 1979) 20.25

Peat Marwick & Mitchell, *Small Business Innovation Research Grants: How to Obtain Them to Finance Your Ideas*

Pellerin, "Animals Are Patentable, Says Patent Office," 2 *Washington Technology* 1 (Apr. 16, 1987) 15.4

Perez, *Inside Investment Banking* 33, 35 (1984) 6.15, 14.9

Perez, *Inside Venture Capital: Past, Present, and Future* 109–110 (1986) 2.2(a), 6.13

2 Phelan, *Non-Profit Enterprises: Law and Taxation* § 11:19 (1985) 20.21

Plumb, "The Federal Income Tax Significance of Corporate Debt: A Critical Analysis and a Proposal" 26 *Tax L. Rev.* 369 (1971) 13.8

Poscover, "Avoidance Techniques Through Case Analysis," *Emerging Theories of Lender Liability* 400 (Davis ed. ABA Div. of Prof. Educ. 1985) 19.12

Pratt, *Valuing a Business: The Analysis and Appraisal of Closely-Held Companies* 62 (1981)	12.1, 12.3
Pratt's Guide to Venture Capital Sources (11th ed. 1986)	1.1, 6.1, 7.4(c), 10.1, 10.1(e), 12.3, 18.3
Prifti, *Securities: Public and Private Offerings* § 4:01; § 5:13, § 1A:12 (1983)	7.1, 8.6, 14.2, 14.5, 14.7
Printing Enterprises Management Science Inc. SEC No-action Letter [1982–83 Transfer Binder] (CCH) *Fed. Sec. L. Rep.* ¶ 77,415 at 78,517 (Mar. 23,1983)	7.4(b)
Private Placements 1986: Current Developments in Private Placement Financings (P.L.I. Course Handbook Series No. 522, 1986)	7.3, 7.9, 7.10(c), 10.1, 10.1(c)
Prosser & Keeton, *Torts* § 108 (1984)	10.1(d)
Quinn's Uniform Commercial Code Commentary and Law Digest § 6–102[A][6] (1986 Supp. No. 2)	19.7
Raskind "Reverse Engineering, Unfair Competition and Fair Use" 70 *Minn. L. Rev.* 385 (1985)	16.6
Raysman, "Acquisition and Exploitation of Mass-Market Software," *Computer Software 1984: Protection and Marketing* 561, 564–565 (P.L.I. Course Handbook Series No. 184, 1984)	15.(e)
Raysman & Brown, "'Shrink Wrap' Statute Invalidated," *N.Y. Law J.* at 1 (Mar. 10, 1987)	15.2(d)
"Raytheon Ventures," *Corporate Venture News,* Mar. 25, 1987, 5	18.3
Recent Developments in Licensing (ABA Section, Patent, Trademark and Copyright Law, 1981)	15.1(b)
"Redefining 'Public Offering or Distribution' for Today," address of Linda C. Quinn, director, Division of Corporation Finance to Fed'l Regulation of Securities Committee," Nov. 22, 1986, 5	7.13

California Trade Secret Law," 1 *Trade Secret Law Rep.* 4 (May 1985)

Sage Systems Corp. Preliminary Prospectus, Mar. 27, 1969 — 6.16
Samuelson, "Allocating Ownership Rights in Computer Generated Works," 47 *U. PA. L. Rev.* 1184,1190 (1986) — 17.1
Sanders, "SBA Financing Sources," in "Financing Growth Oriented Ventures: Where The Money Is," 39 *Bus. Law.* 647 (1984) — 6.6
Schaeftler, *The Liabilities of Office: Indemnification and Insurance of Officers and Directors* (1976) — 4.13
Schneider, "Soft Information—Counseling on Disclosure," *18th Annual Institute on Securities Regulation* Vol. 2 at 351 (P.L.I. Course Handbook Series No. 544, 1986) — 14.8
Schneider & Kant, "Uncertainty Under the Securities Act," 26 *Bus. Law.* 1623 (1971) — 14.11
Schneider, Manko, & Kant, "Going Public: Practice, Procedure and Consequences," 25 *Corporate Practice Commentator* 89 (Spring 1983) — 14.5
Schrotenboer, "California Sales Taxation of Computer Software," 1 *Santa Clara Computer & High Tech L.J.* 107 (1985) — 17.5
Schrotenboer, "How The 1986 Tax Reform Act Changes the Tax Rules for High Technology Companies," 66 *J. Tax'n* 88,91 (Feb. 1987) — 14.2
Schumpeter, *Capitalism, Socialism and Democracy* 81,132 (3d ed. 1980) — 1.2, 18.1
Scott, *Computer Law,* § 12.1 (1985) — 17.1
Sebring, "Recent Legislative Changes in the Law of Indemnification of Directors, Officers and Others," 23 *Bus. Law.* 95, 105 (Nov. 1967) — 4.13
Sec. Act Rel. 33–1285, (CCH) 1 *Fed. Sec. L. Rep.* ¶ 2740 — 7.15

Sec. Act Rel. No. 33–6504 (CCH) 2 *Fed. Sec. L. Rep.* ¶ 23,120B (Jan. 13, 1984)	14.8
Sec. Act Rel. No. 33–6683 [Transfer Binder 1986–87] (CCH) *Fed. Sec. L. Rep.* ¶ 84,054 (Jan. 16, 1987)	7.2, 7.5, 7.6, 7.11, 8.1(a)
Sec. Act Rel. No. 33–6711 [1987 Transfer Binder] (CCH) *Fed. Sec. L. Rep.* ¶ 84,118 (Apr. 17, 1987)	14.5
Sec. Act Rel. No. 33–6715, [1987 Transfer Binder] (CCH) *Fed. Sec. L. Rep.* ¶ 84,130 (May 27, 1987)	14.5
Sec. Act Rel. No. 5560 [1974–75 Transfer Binder] (CCH) *Fed. Sec. L. Rep.* ¶ 80,066. (Jan. 24, 1975)	7.1
Sec. Act Rel. No. 34–2463–S (July 29, 1987)	3.5
Sec. Exch. Act Rel. No. 34–11532, [1975–76 Transfer Binder] (CCH) *Fed. Sec. L. Rep.* ¶ 22,730 (July 11, 1975)	8.2
Sec. Exch. Act Rel. No. 34–23763 [1986–1987 Transfer Binder] (CCH) *Fed. Sec. L. Rep.* ¶ 84,048 (Oct. 31, 1986)	8.2
Sec. Exch. Act Rel. No. 34–24623. IVA (June 24, 1987)	14.9(a)
"SEC Interpretive Release on Rules Applicable for Insider Reporting and Trading," Sec. Act Rel. No. 34-18114, 4 (CCH) *Fed. Sec. L. Rep.* ¶ 26,062 (Sept. 23, 1981)	14.2
SEC *Staff Accounting Bulletin* 57, (CCH) 6 *Fed. Sec. L. Rep.* ¶ 74,507 (July 18, 1984)	13.3
SEC Staff Accounting Bulletin No. 64, (CCH) 6 *Fed. Sec. L. Rep.* ¶ 74,131	14.9(a)
"The Section '4(1½)' Phenomenon: Private Resales of 'Restricted' Securities," 34 *Bus. Law.* 1961 (1979)	7.1
The SEC Today, July 2, 1987 (Vol. 87–124)	3.7
Sheffey, "Securities Law Responsibilities of Issues to Respond to Rumors and Other Publicity," 57 *Notre Dame L. Rev.* 755 (1982)	14.2
Sherman & Williams, "State Securities Laws Considerations of Raising	8.8

Reference	Section
Testa, "The Legal Process of Venture Capital Investment," *Pratt's Guide to Venture Capital Sources* 66 (11th ed. 1987)	10.1
Thackray, "Investment Banking's One-Man Shops," *N.Y. Times*, Jan. 12, 1986, § 3, at 1	6.10
Throop, "Federal Regulation of Securities Committee Comments on the Wheat Report," 25 *Bus. Law.* 39 (Nov. 1969)	7.1
T.M. 384 Restricted Property Section 83 (1982) (T.M. 384)	5.2, 5.2(a)
Todd, "Retail Distribution of Computer Hardware and Software," *Computer Contracts: An In-Depth Study* 98 (MCLE 1985)	15.3, 17.2(b)
Torres, "Minority Shareholder Protection in Leveraged Buyouts," 13 *Sec. L. J.* 356 (1986)	19.4
Tracy, "The Search for Copyproof Software," *Fortune* (Sept. 3, 1984), 83	15.2(e)
"Triangle Park: North Carolina's High-Tech Pay Off" *N.Y. Times*, Apr. 26, 1987, § 3, p. 12	18.7
Tyler, "More About Blue Sky," 39 *Wash. & Lee L. Rev.* 899 (1982)	14.9
"University City Science Center: Whaley Probes the New Role of Education for Future Managers," *Focus* (Aug 15, 1985), 64, 65	6.4
"University-Industry Research Relationships: Myths, Realities and Potentials," *Fourteenth Ann. Rep. of the Nat'l Sci. Board* 11 (Oct. 1, 1982)	18.7
Van Dorn, "Deductions for Start Up Expenditures," in *Tax Planning for High Tech and New Ventures* 27 (70th Forum, Fed. Tax Instit. New England 1984)	5.3(a)
Vaughn, *Franchising: Its Nature, Scope, Advantages and Development* (1974)	1.3(b)

Reference	Section
Vent. Cap. J. (May 1987)	9.2(a)
Venture (Aug. 1986), 90	6.8
Venture (May 1987), 88	5.4, 7.12
"Venture Capital Consulting Firm Partnerships: A Team Approach to Venture Investing," *Venture Capital Journal* 6 (Nov. 1986)	6.17(e)
Verticom Inc., SEC No-action Letter (Feb. 12, 1986)	7.13
Volz & Berger, *The Drafting of Partnership Agreements* 5 (1976)	20.1
Vulture Petroleum Corporation, SEC No-action Letter (Feb. 2, 1987)	7.13
Walker & Petty, *Financial Management of the Small Firm* (1986)	12.2, 12.3
Wander, "Timely Disclosure: Fall 1986," *18th Annual Institute on Securities Regulation,* 447 (P.L.I. Course Handbook Series No. 544, 1986)	14.2
Wang, *Lessons: An Autobiography* 117; 141 (1986)	14.1, 18.3
Warren, "Reflections on Dual Regulation of Securities: A Case Against Preemption," 25 *B. C. L. Rev.* 495 (1984)	14.9
Warren, "A Review of Regulation D: The Present Exemption Regimen for Limited Offerings Under the Securities Act of 1933," 33 *Am. U. L. Rev.* 355 (1984)	7.2
Waters, "Banking on the Entrepreneur: The Leveraged Buyout Boom," *Inc.* (Sept. 1983), 46	19.1
Webb, "A Practitioner's Guide to Confidentiality Agreements," 1 *Trade Secret L. Rep.* 61 (July 1985)	16.9
Weinberg, "Selected Tax Considerations in Leveraged Buyouts," *Leveraged Acquisitions and Buyouts* 131, 134 (P.L.I. Course Handbook Series No. 549, 1987)	19.13(a), 19.13(b), 19.13(c)
Weiss, "Trade Secret Litigation and the Presentation of the Trade Secret Owner Case," 1 *Trade Secret L. Rep.* 273 (1986)	16.9

Brokers, Dealers and Securities Markets, (1977 & 1985 Supp.)

Woodtrails Seattle Ltd., No-action Letter from the SEC [1982–83 Transfer Binder] (CCH) *Fed. Sec. L. Rep.* § 77,342 (Aug. 9, 1982) — 7.4(c)

Yeager, "Getting in on the Self-Insurance Trend," *Am. Lawyer* 14 (May 1987) — 4.13

Table of Cases

Name	Section
Abrahamson v. Fleschner 568 F.2d 862 (2d. Cir. 1977), *cert. den.* 436 U.S. 913 (1978).	20.25
Allen v. Biltmore Tissue Corp. 2 N.Y.2d 534, 161 N.Y.S. 2d 418, 141 N.E.2d 812 (1957).	10.3(k)
Alves v. Comm'r 79 T.C. 864 (1982) *aff'd* 734 F. 2d 478 (9th Cir., 1984).	5.2
A & M Produce Co. v. F.M.C. Corp. 135 Cal. App. 3d 473 (1982).	17.2(c)
American Bantam Car Co. v. Comm'r 11 T.C. 397 (1948). *aff'd per curiam* 177 F.2d 513 (3d Cir. 1949), *cert. den.* 339 U.S. 920 (1950).	5.1(b)
American Security Co. v. Shatterproof Glass Corp. 268 F.2d 769 (3d Cir., 1959).	15.17
Analogic Corp. v. Data Translation Inc. 371 Mass. 643, 646–47, 358 N.E.2d 804, 806–07 (1976).	16.8(a)
Apple Computer, Inc v. Franklin Computer Group. 714 F.2d 1240 (3d Cir. 1983).	16.4(a)
Armstrong, Jones & Co. v. SEC 421 F.2d 359 (6th Cir.), *cert den.,* 398 U.S. 958 (1970).	7.14
Aronson v. Quick Point Pencil Co. 440 U.S. 257 (1979).	15.7, 15.17

Table of Statutes and Regulations

Index